Alan Rogers

the best
campsites

2010 EDITION

in **Britain** & **Ireland**

INSPECTED & SELECTED SINCE 1968

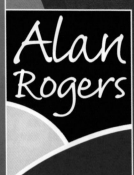

Compiled by: Alan Rogers Guides Ltd

Designed by: Paul Effenberg, Vine Design Ltd

Additional photography: T Lambelin, www.lambelin.com
Maps created by Customised Mapping (01769 540044)
contain background data provided by GisDATA Ltd
Maps are © Alan Rogers Guides and GisDATA Ltd 2009

Published by: Alan Rogers Guides Ltd,
Spelmonden Old Oast, Goudhurst, Kent TN17 1HE
www.alanrogers.com Tel: 01580 214000

British Library Cataloguing-in-Publication Data:
A catalogue record for this book is available
from the British Library.

ISBN 978-1-906215-23-1

Print managed in Great Britain by DPI Print & Production Ltd
and printed by Stephens & George Print Group

Mixed Sources
Product group from well-managed
forests and other controlled sources
www.fsc.org Cert no. SGS-COC-003625
© 1996 Forest Stewardship Council

INSPECTED
SINCE 1968
& SELECTED

Contents

Alan Rogers – in search of 'the best'

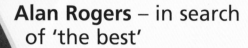

Alan Rogers Guides were first published over 40 years ago. Since Alan Rogers published the first campsite guide that bore his name, the range has expanded and now covers 27 countries in five separate guides. No fewer than 20 of the campsites selected by Alan for the first guide are still featured in our 2010 editions.

There are well over 5,000 camping and caravanning parks in Britain and Ireland of varying quality: this guide contains impartially written reports on almost 600, including many of the very finest, each being individually inspected and selected. We aim to provide you with a selection of the best, rather than information on all – in short, a more selective, qualitative approach. New, improved maps and indexes are also included, designed to help you find the choice of campsite that's right for you.

We hope you enjoy some happy and safe travels – and some pleasurable 'armchair touring' in the meantime!

How do we find the best?

The criteria we use when inspecting and selecting campsites are numerous, but the most important by far is the question of good quality. People want different things from their choice of site so we try to include a range of campsite 'styles' to cater for a wide variety of preferences: from those seeking a small peaceful park in the heart of the countryside, to visitors looking for an 'all singing, all dancing' park in a popular seaside resort. Those with more specific interests, such as sporting facilities, cultural events or historical attractions, are also catered for.

The size of the park, whether it's part of a chain or privately owned, makes no difference in terms of it being required to meet our exacting standards in respect of its quality and it being 'fit for purpose'. In other words, irrespective of the size of the park, or the number of facilities it offers, we consider and evaluate the welcome, the pitches, the sanitary facilities, the cleanliness, the general maintenance and even the location.

" ...the campsites included in this book have been chosen entirely on merit, and no payment of any sort is made by them for their inclusion."

Alan Rogers, 1968

INSPECTED SINCE 1968 & SELECTED

Expert opinions

We rely on our dedicated team of Site Assessors, all of whom are experienced campers, caravanners or motorcaravanners, to visit and recommend campsites. Each year they travel some 100,000 miles around Europe inspecting new campsites for the guide and re-inspecting the existing ones. Our thanks are due to them for their enthusiastic efforts, their diligence and integrity.

We also appreciate the feedback we receive from many of our readers and we always make a point of following up complaints, suggestions or recommendations for possible new campsites. Of course we get a few grumbles too – but it really is a few, and those we do receive usually relate to overcrowding or to poor maintenance during the peak school holiday period. Please bear in mind that, although we are interested to hear about any complaints, we have no contractual relationship with the campsites featured in our guides and are therefore not in a position to intervene in any dispute between a reader and a campsite.

Independent and honest

Whilst the content and scope of the Alan Rogers guides have expanded considerably since the early editions, our selection of campsites still employs exactly the same philosophy and criteria as defined by Alan Rogers in 1968.

'telling it how it is'

Firstly, and most importantly, our selection is based entirely on our own rigorous and independent inspection and selection process. Campsites cannot buy their way into our guides – indeed the extensive Site Report which is written by us, not by the site owner, is provided free of charge so we are free to say what we think and to provide an honest, 'warts and all' description. This is written in plain English and without the use of confusing icons or symbols.

Looking for the best?

HIGHLY RESPECTED BY SITE OWNERS AND READERS ALIKE, THERE IS NO BETTER GUIDE WHEN IT COMES TO FORMING AN INDEPENDENT VIEW OF A CAMPSITE'S QUALITY. WHEN YOU NEED TO BE CONFIDENT IN YOUR CHOICE OF CAMPSITE, YOU NEED THE ALAN ROGERS GUIDE.

- PARKS ONLY INCLUDED ON MERIT
- PARKS CANNOT PAY TO BE INCLUDED
- INDEPENDENTLY INSPECTED, RIGOROUSLY ASSESSED
- IMPARTIAL REVIEWS
- OVER 40 YEARS OF EXPERTISE

Written in plain English, our guides are exceptionally easy to use, but a few words of explanation regarding the layout and content may be helpful. For England we have used official tourist board regions and the counties within them. For Wales, Scotland and Ireland (North and South) we use the counties.

The Reports – *Example of an entry*

Index town
Park name
Postal address (including county) T: **telephone number.** E: email address
alanrogers.com web address (including Alan Rogers reference number)

A description of the park in which we try to give an idea of its general features – its size, its situation, its strengths and its weaknesses. This section should provide a picture of the park itself with reference to the facilities that are provided and if they impact on its appearance or character. We include details on pitch numbers, electricity (with amperage), hardstandings etc. in this section as pitch design, planning and terracing affects the park's overall appearance. Similarly we include reference to pitches used for caravan holiday homes, chalets, and the like. Importantly at the end of this column we indicate if there are any restrictions, e.g. no tents, no children, naturist sites.

Facilities
Lists more specific information on the park's facilities and amenities and, where available, the dates when these facilities are open (if not for the whole season). Off site: here we give distances to various local amenities, for example, local shops, the nearest beach, plus our featured activities (bicycle hire, fishing, horse riding, boat launching). Where we have space we list suggestions for activities and local tourist attractions.

Open: Park opening dates.

Directions
Separated from the main text in order that they may be read and assimilated more easily by a navigator en-route. Bear in mind that road improvement schemes can result in road numbers being altered.

O.S.GR: Ordnance Survey grid references are included for those using OS maps.

GPS: references are provided as we obtain them for satellite navigation systems (in degrees and minutes).

Charges 2010 (or a general guide)

Maps, campsite listings and indexes

For this 2010 guide we have changed the way in which we list our featured campsites and also the way in which we help you locate the parks within each region.

We now include a map immediately after our Introduction to that region. These maps show the towns near which one or more of our featured parks are located.

Within each regional section of the guide, we list these towns and the park(s) in that vicinity in alphabetical order.

You will certainly need more detailed maps for navigation, for example the Ordnance Survey road atlas. We provide O.S. references and G.P.S. coordinates for each park to assist you. Our three indexes will also help you to find a park by its reference number and name, by region and park name, or by the town where the park is situated.

Facilities

Toilet blocks

We assume that toilet blocks will be equipped with WCs, washbasins with hot and cold water and hot showers with dividers or curtains, and will have all necessary shelves, hooks, plugs and mirrors. We also assume that there will be an identified chemical toilet disposal point, and that the campsite will provide water and waste water drainage points and bin areas. If not the case, we comment. We do mention certain features that some readers find important: washbasins in cubicles, facilities for babies, facilities for those with disabilities and motorcaravan service points. Readers with disabilities are advised to contact the site of their choice to ensure that facilities are appropriate to their needs.

Shop

Basic or fully supplied, and opening dates.

Bars, restaurants, takeaway facilities and entertainment

We try hard to supply opening and closing dates (if other than the campsite opening dates) and to identify if there are discos or other entertainment.

Children's play areas

Fenced and with safety surface (e.g. sand, bark or pea-gravel).

Swimming pools

If particularly special, we cover in detail in our main campsite description but reference is always included under our Facilities listings. We will also indicate the existence of water slides, sunbathing areas and other features. Opening dates, charges and levels of supervision are provided where we have been notified.

Leisure facilities

For example, playing fields, bicycle hire, organised activities and entertainment.

Dogs

If dogs are not accepted or restrictions apply, we state it here. Check the quick reference list at the back of the guide.

Off site

This briefly covers leisure facilities, tourist attractions, restaurants etc. nearby.

Charges

These are the latest provided to us by the parks. In those cases where 2010 prices have not been provided to us by the parks, we try to give a general guide.

Opening dates

These are advised to us during the early autumn of the previous year – parks can, and sometimes do, alter these dates before the start of the following season, often for good reasons. If you intend to visit shortly after a published opening date, or shortly before the closing date, it is wise to check that it will actually be open at the time required. Similarly some parks operate a restricted service during the low season, only opening some of their facilities (e.g. swimming pools) during the main season; where we know about this, and have the relevant dates, we indicate it – again if you are at all doubtful it is wise to check.

Sometimes, campsite amenities may be dependant on there being enough customers on site to justify their opening and, for this reason, actual opening dates may vary from those indicated.

Special pitches

We note an ever increasing number of 'special' pitches under a variety of fancy names (for example, Executive, Panorama, Super). These provide a range of extra facilities such as waste water disposal, TV and phone connections, hardstanding, patios, etc. and they are often booked up well in advance. Readers interested in such pitches should contact the park concerned to check exactly what is provided. People with disabilities are also advised to telephone before turning up to ensure that facilities are appropriate to their particular needs.

Whether you're an 'old hand' in terms of camping and caravanning or are contemplating your first trip, a regular reader of our Guides or a new 'convert', we wish you well in your travels and hope we have been able to help in some way.

We are, of course, also out and about ourselves, visiting parks, talking to owners and readers, and generally checking on standards and new developments.

F330 Our NEW Holiday Home section

Over recent years, more and more parks in Britain and Ireland have added high quality holiday home accommodation in the form of caravan holiday homes, chalets and lodges. In response to feedback from many of our readers, and to reflect this evolution in campsites, we have decided to introduce a separate section on caravan holiday homes and chalets (see page 330). If a park has decided to contribute to this section, it is indicated above our site report in the main body of the guide with a page reference where the full details are given. We feature parks offering some of the best accommodation available and have included full details of one or two accommodation types at these parks. Please note however that many other campsites listed in this guide may also have a selection of accommodation for rent.

We wish all our readers thoroughly enjoyable Camping and Caravanning in 2010 – favoured by good weather of course!

THE ALAN ROGERS TEAM

Scotland
page 262

Northern
Ireland
page 294

Northumbria
page 226

Cumbria
page 215

North West
England
page 207

Yorkshire
page 188

Republic of Ireland
page 302

Heart of England
page 162

Wales
page 233

East of England
page 144

Southern
England
page 102

South West England
page 12

South East
England
page 127

London
page 140

Channel Islands
page 325

The Alan Rogers Awards

The Alan Rogers Campsite Awards were launched in 2004 and have proved a great success.

Our awards have a broad scope and before committing to our winners, we carefully consider more than 2,000 campsites featured in our guides, taking into account comments from our site assessors, our head office team and, of course, our readers.

Our award winners come from the four corners of Europe, from southern Portugal to Slovenia, and this year we are making awards to campsites in 13 different countries.

Needless to say, it's an extremely difficult task to choose our eventual winners, but we believe that we have identified a number of campsites with truly outstanding characteristics.

In each case, we have selected an outright winner, along with two highly commended runners-up.

Listed below are full details of each of our award categories and our winners for 2009.

Our warmest congratulations to all our award winners and our commiserations to all those not having won an award on this occasion.

THE ALAN ROGERS TEAM

Alan Rogers Progress Award 2009

This award reflects the hard work and commitment undertaken by particular site owners to improve and upgrade their site.

WINNER

FR40180	Le Vieux Port, France

RUNNERS-UP

FR29050	L'Orangerie de Lanniron, France
AU0265	Park Grubhof, Austria

Alan Rogers Welcome Award 2009

This award takes account of sites offering a particularly friendly welcome and maintaining a friendly ambience throughout reader's holidays.

WINNER

FR71070	Domaine de l'Eperviere, France

RUNNERS-UP

NL6970	t'Weergors, Netherlands
UK0805	Woodovis, England

Alan Rogers Active Holiday Award 2009

This award reflects sites in outstanding locations which are ideally suited for active holidays, notably walking or cycling, but which could extend to include such activities as winter sports or water sports

WINNER

SV4200	Bled, Slovenia

RUNNERS-UP

FR29010	Ty Nadan, France
CZ4720	Frymburk, Czech Republic

Alan Rogers Motorhome Award 2009

Motorhome sales are increasing and this award acknowledges sites which, in our opinion, have made outstanding efforts to welcome motorhome clients.

WINNER

DE3003	Wulfener Hals, Germany

RUNNERS-UP

NL5675	Vliegenbos, Netherlands
DE3833	LuxOase, Germany

Alan Rogers 4 Seasons Award 2009

This award is made to outstanding sites with extended opening dates and which welcome clients to a uniformly high standard throughout the year.

WINNER

ES87420	La Marina, Spain

RUNNERS-UP

FR74230	Le Giffre, France
ES89650	Picos de Europa, Spain

Alan Rogers Seaside Award 2009

This award is made for sites which we feel are outstandingly suitable for a really excellent seaside holiday.

WINNER

IT68200	Baia Domizia, Italy

RUNNERS-UP

CR6765	Kovacine, Croatia
NL6870	De Lakens, Netherlands

Alan Rogers Country Award 2009

This award contrasts with our former award and acknowledges sites which are attractively located in delightful, rural locations.

WINNER

NL6285	Wildhoeve, Netherlands

RUNNERS-UP

FR85260	La Guyonniere, France
UK2030	Wareham Forest, England

Alan Rogers Rented Accommodation Award 2009

Given the increasing importance of rented accommodation on many campsites, we feel that it is important to acknowledge sites which have made a particular effort in creating a high quality 'rented accommodation' park.

WINNER

FR34110	Yelloh! Village Le Club Farret, France

RUNNERS-UP

SV4210	Sobec, Slovenia
DK2010	Hvidbjerg Strand, Denmark

Alan Rogers Unique Site Award 2009

This award acknowledges sites with unique, outstanding features – something which simply cannot be found elsewhere and which is an important attraction of the site.

WINNER

IT60370	International Jesolo, Italy

RUNNERS-UP

AU0525	Fisching 50+, Austria
PO8030	Rio Alto, Portugal

Alan Rogers Family Site Award 2009

Many sites claim to be child friendly but this award acknowledges the sites we feel to be the very best in this respect.

WINNER

IT60200	Union Lido, Italy

RUNNERS-UP

FR83020	Esterel Caravaning, France
HU5370	Napfeny, Hungary

Alan Rogers Readers' Award 2009

We believe our Readers' Award to be the most important. We simply invite our readers (by means of an on-line poll at www.alanrogers.com) to nominate the site they enjoyed most.

The outright winner for 2009 is:

WINNER

ES83900	Vilanova Park, Spain

The West Country is a diverse region of beautiful sandy beach steep craggy cliffs, desolate moors and rolling green hills. Home of clotted cream teas, it also boasts a range of historical and modern attractions, including th celebrated Eden Project.

Alan Rogers

THE SOUTH WEST COMPRISES: CORNWALL, DEVON, SOMERSET, BATH, BRISTOL, SOUTH GLOUCESTERSHIRE, WILTSHIRE AND WEST DORSET.

With its dramatic cliffs, pounded by the Atlantic ocean, and beautiful coastline boasting warm waters, soft sandy beaches and small seaside towns, Cornwall is one of England's most popular holiday destinations. The coast is also a surfers' paradise, while inland the wild and rugged Bodmin Moors dominate the landscape. In Devon, the Dartmoor National Park has sweeping moorland and granite tors where wild ponies roam freely. Much of the countryside is gentle rolling green fields, dotted with pretty thatched cottages. The coastline around Torbay is known as the English Riviera which, due to its temperate climate, allows palm trees to grow. Stretching across East Devon and West Dorset is the fossil-ridden Jurassic Coast, a World Heritage Site. West Dorset is also home to Lyme Regis and Weymouth, which comes alive in summer when regular entertainment, including a carnival and fireworks, is held along the seafront. Famous for its cider and cheese, Somerset is good walking country, with the Exmoor National Park, which also straddles Devon. Wiltshire's natural attractions include the Marlborough Downs, Savernake Forest and the River Avon. It also boasts one of the most famous prehistoric sites in the world, the ancient stone circles of Stonehenge.

Places of interest

Bath: World Heritage Site full of Roman an Georgian architecture, elegant streets such the Circle and Royal Crescent, Roman bath

Bristol: steeped in maritime history with t world's first great Ocean Liner; Brunel's Clifton Suspension bridge; range of museums and art galleries.

Cornwall: seaside town of St Ives; Land's End; Eden Project; Penzance and St Michael's Mount.

Devon: popular seaside resorts of Torquay Paignton and Brixham; cities of Exeter and Plymouth.

Somerset: Weston-Super-Mare; Wells Cathedral; Cheddar Gorge and Wookey Hole caves.

West Dorset: Dorchester, home of Thoma Hardy; Isle of Portland; Abbotsbury village with swannery.

Wiltshire: Salisbury; Glastonbury; Longlea manor house and safari park.

Did you know?

Chesil Beach is an 18 mile stretch of fortress-like walls of pebbles, formed 12,000 years ago.

There are numerous white horses carved into the landscape across the South West

The Jurassic Coast is a Natural World Heritage Site stretching for 95 miles.

The Black Death entered England throug the port in Weymouth in 1348.

Britain's oldest complete skeleton, Cheddar Man, was buried in Gough's Ca 9,000 years ago.

At 404 feet Salisbury Cathedral has the tallest medieval spire in the world.

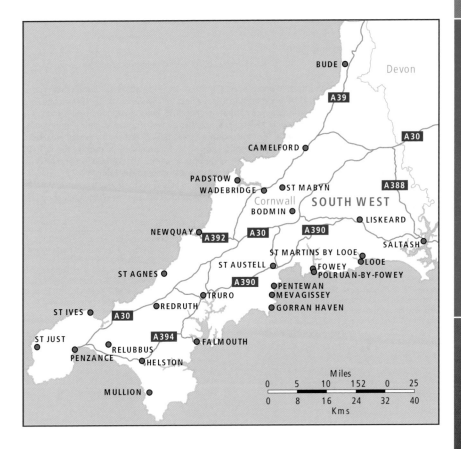

Maps and campsite listings

For this 2010 guide we have changed the way in which we list our parks and also the way in which we help you locate the parks within each region.

We now include a map immediately after our Introduction to that region. These maps show the towns near which one (or more) of our featured parks is located. Within each regional section of the guide, we list these towns and the park(s) in that vicinity in alphabetical order.

Because of the large number of parks that we feature in the West Country we have further split this region into three areas: **Cornwall** (starting on this page), **Devon** (page 47) and the counties of **Somerset, Wiltshire** and **West Dorset** (page 79), each with a separate map.

You will certainly need more detailed maps for navigation, for example the Ordnance Survey road atlas. We provide O.S. references and G.P.S. coordinates for each park to assist you. Our three indexes will also help you to find a park by its reference number and name, by region and park name, or by the town where the park is situated.

Bodmin
Mena Caravan & Camping Park
Lanivet, Bodmin PL30 5HW (Cornwall) T: **01208 831845**. E: mena@campsitesincornwall.co.uk
alanrogers.com/UK0270

A peaceful, simple park, Mena is tucked away in the Cornish countryside, yet close to the main routes, and a warm welcome await visitors. A few years ago it was a field for cows and with hard work and care it has been developed into a comfortable, yet natural site. Set in 15 acres of secluded countryside, it is spacious and never crowded offering only 25 level grass pitches on well drained, slightly sloping grass. There are 12 electricity connections (10A). The land includes a small fishing lake and a wooded area. Now open all year, developments include a new reception and shop. Mena means 'hilltop' in the Cornish language and the site is actually situated at the geographical centre of Cornwall, overlooked by Helman's Tor, one of the highest points on Bodmin Moor. It is also close to the Saints' Way, the pilgrim route from Ireland where they crossed by land from Padstow to Fowey on their way to France. With its position, visitors can choose between beaches on the north or south coast. Lanivet village has a shop and a pub serving meals.

Facilities
Four toilet and washbasin cabins are in an older wooden building. Two new showers and two toilets are behind the veranda building. On the opposite side of the site is a new en-suite facility for disabled visitors, part of a building housing a large games room with three quarter size snooker table, TV and darts. Shop (with gas). Swings, etc. for children in the central grass area. Fishing lake (licence required). Two mobile homes for hire. Off site: Lanivet village with shop and pub 2 miles. Riding 1 mile. Golf 2 miles. Bicycle hire 3 or 5 miles. Nearest beach 8 miles. Eden Project 4 miles.

Open: All year.

Directions
From the A30 Bodmin bypass, exit at the A30/A391 Innis Downs roundabout. Take the A389 north signed Lanivet and Bodmin. After 0.5 miles take first right (filter lane) and pass under the A30. Turn first left (Lostwithiel, Fowey) and in 0.25 miles turn right at top of hill (Celtic Cross on the left). Continue for 0.5 miles and take first right into lane and site in 100 yds. O.S.GR: SX041625. GPS: 50.430267, -4.757167

Charges guide
Per unit incl. 2 persons	£ 9.00 - £ 19.00
incl. electricity	£ 14.00 - £ 23.50
extra person	£ 4.00 - £ 5.00
child (3-16 yrs)	£ 1.50 - £ 2.50
dog	£ 1.00 - £ 2.00

No credit or debit cards.

Bodmin
Eden Valley Holiday Park
Lanlivery, Lostwithiel, Bodmin PL30 5BU (Cornwall) T: **01208 872277**.
E:enquiries@edenvalleyholidaypark.co.uk **alanrogers.com/UK0280**

A pleasant, peaceful touring park, Eden Valley Holiday Park has plenty of sheltered green space and a natural, uncommercialised atmosphere. This has been enhanced by careful planting of trees and shrubs to form a series of linked paddocks with an unfenced stream running through. With 56 numbered touring pitches in total, each paddock contains 10-15 pitches spread around the perimeter. There are 20 hardstandings and 40 pitches have electricity connections (5/10A). Awning groundsheets must be lifted on alternate days. A separate field contains 35 private caravan holiday homes. A large, well equipped activity play area with adventure type equipment on grass is in one of the hedged paddocks. The park is now owned by Darren and Ginny Hopkins and their young family and they welcome families and couples to enjoy their park with its colourful trees and grassy paddocks. They plan to add some log cabins for rent. The village pub is within walking distance and there are several good local restaurants. Indoor tennis courts (Bodmin) and a swimming pool are nearby. The Eden Project is very close. The nearest beach at Par is some 4 miles.

Facilities
There are two well-equipped toilet blocks, one with individual cubicles. En-suite family washroom and unit for disabled visitors. Fully equipped laundry room. Motorcaravan service point. Gas supplies. Play area. TV room. Games room. Putting green. Torch useful. Off site: Fresh water fishing 1.5 miles or sea fishing 3 miles. Beach 4 miles. Bicycle hire 4 miles. Riding 2 miles. Golf 1.5 miles.

Open: Easter/1 April - 31 October.

Directions
Park approach road leads off A390 road 1.5 miles southwest of Lostwithiel. Follow white or brown camping signs. No other approach is advised. O.S.GR: SX083592. GPS: 50.40191, -4.69805

Charges guide
Per unit incl. 2 persons and electricity	£ 11.00 - £ 15.00
extra person	£ 1.50 - £ 2.00
child (4-15 yrs)	£ 1.00 - £ 1.50
dog	£ 1.00 - £ 2.00

No single sex groups (excl. bona fide organisations).

Bodmin
South Penquite Farm
South Penquite, Blisland, Bodmin PL30 4LH (Cornwall) T: 01208 850491. E: thefarm@bodminmoor.co.uk
alanrogers.com/UK0302

South Penquite offers real camping with no frills, set on a 200-hectare hill farm high on Bodmin Moor between the villages of Blisland and St Breward. The farm achieved organic status in 2001 and runs a flock of 300 ewes, a herd of 40 cattle and horses. The camping is small scale and intended to have a low impact on the surrounding environment. Tents or simple motorcaravans (no caravans) can pitch around the edge of three walled fields, roughly cut in the midst of the moor. You can find shelter or a view. Four yurts – round Mongolian tents – are available to rent in one field, complete with wood-burning stoves. It is also possible to have your own camp fire. You can buy bags of wood from the farmhouse. You will also find horses, ponies, chickens, geese, ducks and turkeys who show their approval or not by the skin around their necks changing colour! A farm walk of some two miles takes you over most of the farm and some of the moor taking in a Bronze Age hut settlement, the river and a standing stone. It is also possible to fish for brown trout on the farm's stretch of the De Lank river – a tributary of the Camel. The farm's website offers a fascinating insight into life and work at South Penquite.

Facilities
Smart new pine-clad toilet block (hot and cold), with a separate provision of four family-sized showers operated with solar-heated rainwater. Two undercover washing up sinks (hot and cold), plus two outside Belfast sinks. Washing machine and dryer. Small fridge and freezer. home produced lamb, burgers and sausages available. LPG gas. Facilities for field studies and opportunities for educational groups and schools to learn about the local environment. Bush craft days. Fishing (requires an EA rod licence and tokens available from the Westcountry Rivers Trust). Dogs are not accepted. Off site: Walking, riding and cycling. Sustrans Route 3 passes close by. North and south coasts within easy reach. Horse riding 1 mile. cycle hire 1 mile. Local inns 1.5 miles and 2.5 miles.

Open: 14 May - mid October.

Directions
On the A30 over Bodmin Moor pass Jamaica Inn and sign for Colliford Lake and watch for St Breward sign (to right) immediately at end of dual-carriageway. Follow this narrow road over open moor for 2 miles ignoring any turns to left or right. Also ignore right turn to St Breward just before the South Penquite sign. Follow track over stone bridge beside ford through farm gate and then bear to left to camping fields. Walk back to book in at Farm House. O.S.GR: SX104752. GPS: 50.5445, -4.671833

Charges 2010
Per person	£ 6.00
child (5-16 yrs)	£ 3.00

50% deposit of total cost.
No credit cards.

Bodmin
Ruthern Valley Holidays
Ruthernbridge, Bodmin PL30 5LU (Cornwall) T: 01208 831395. E: camping@ruthernvalley.com
alanrogers.com/UK0306

This is a little gem of a site set in 7.5 acres of woodland, tucked away in a peaceful little valley not far from Bodmin. The park was landscaped over 30 years ago with an amazing range of trees and shrubs. It is now owned by Andrew and Nicola Johnson who will bring their talents and expertise to this tranquil small park. There are 16 touring pitches informally spaced but numbered in the main, tree-lined field, six with electricity, and a further 13 in smaller fields and alcove areas amongst the woods with a small stream meandering through and alive with bluebells when we visited. The landscaping lends itself to the informal layout of the level touring pitches and the self catering accommodation. Twelve wooden chalet/bungalows and six caravan holiday homes blend into the natural wooded environment. A very good adventure-type play area is set away from the pitches, and a small, basic toilet block and a little shop complete the provision. This is a site for relaxing with time to enjoy the simpler pastimes of walking or birdwatching. Over 40 different species of bird have been recorded.

Facilities
The small toilet block provides everything necessary including a shower each per sex plus washing machines, dryer. Newly built shower and solar hot water heating system. Shop with basic provisions shares with reception (reduced hours in low season). Barbecue hire. Play area with excellent equipment including five-a-side goal posts. Dogs are not accepted in touring areas during July/Aug. Bicycle hire (delivered to site). Off site: Nearest pub 3-4 miles. Riding 4 miles.

Open: April - October.

Directions
Approaching Bodmin from A30 or A38 turn right at first mini roundabout and proceed anti-clockwise on the inner ring road. Go straight over double mini-roundabout, leaving Bodmin on A389/A391 towards St Austell. Ignore first Nanstallon - Ruthernbridge sign, after 1.5 miles, at top of hill, turn right. At Nanstallon village sign (0.75 miles), turn left then filter left. Continue for 1 mile dropping down into Ruthernbridge. Turn left immediately before bridge. Site is on left in 300 yards. O.S.GR: SX012668. GPS: 50.46455, -4.8019

Charges guide
Per unit incl. 2 persons	£ 11.00 - £ 13.00
incl. electricity	£ 13.00 - £ 15.50
extra person over 4 yrs	£ 2.50

Bude
Wooda Farm Holiday Park

Poughill, Bude EX23 9HJ (Cornwall) T: 01288 352069. E: enquiries@wooda.co.uk

alanrogers.com/UK0380

Wooda Farm is spacious and well organised, with some nice touches. A quality, family run park, it is part of a working farm, under two miles from the sandy, surfing beaches of Bude. In peaceful farmland with plenty of open spaces (and some up and down walking), there are marvellous views of sea and countryside. The 220 large pitches are spread over four meadows on level or gently sloping grass. There are 142 with electricity (10A), 73 hardstanding hedged 'premier' pitches (electricity, water, waste water) and five premier pitches with Sky TV, linked by tarmac roads. A late arrivals area has electricity. Beside the shop and reception at the entrance are 55 caravan holiday homes for let. A few friendly farm animals welcome assistance at feeding time! Tractor and trailer rides, archery and clay pigeon shooting with tuition are provided according to season and demand, plus woodland (to find the pixies) and orchard walks and excellent coarse fishing. There is much to do in the area – sandy beaches with coastal walks, and Tintagel with King Arthur's Castle and Clovelly nearby. A member of the Best of British group.

Facilities

Three well maintained toilet blocks, one heated, include a unit suitable for disabled people, two baby rooms and five en-suite family bathrooms for hire (small charge). Two laundry rooms. Motorcaravan service point. Self-service shop with off-licence. Attractive courtyard bar with bar meals and pleasant restaurant with home cooking. Play area in separate field. 9 hole 'fun' golf course (clubs provided). Games room with TV. Badminton. Tennis. Gym. Coarse fishing in 1.5 acre lake (permits £1.50 per half day, £2.50 per day). Certain breeds of dogs not accepted. Caravan storage. Internet access. WiFi. Off site: Local village inn is five minutes walk. Leisure Centre and Splash Pool in Bude.

Open: 1 April - 31 October.

Directions

Park is north of Bude at Poughill; turn off A39 on north side of Stratton on minor road for Coombe Valley, following camp signs at junctions. O.S.GR: SS225080. GPS: 50.84331, -4.51857

Charges guide

Per unit incl. 2 persons	£ 12.00 - £ 19.00
incl. electricity	£ 14.00 - £ 21.00
incl. water and drainage	£ 16.00 - £ 26.00
extra person	£ 3.50 - £ 5.00
child (3-15 yrs)	£ 2.00 - £ 3.50

Camping Cheques accepted.

Bude
Sandymouth Holiday Park

You might also like to consider...

Camelford

Lakefield Caravan Park

Lower Pendavey Farm, Camelford PL32 9TX (Cornwall) T: 01840 213279. E: lakefield@pendavey.fsnet.co.uk

alanrogers.com/UK0360

Lakefield is a small, simple touring park on what was a working farm. Now the main focus is on the BHS-approved equestrian centre. With only 40 pitches, it is no surprise that the owners, Maureen and Dennis Perring, know all the campers. The well-spaced pitches backing onto hedges and with 24 electric hook-ups (16A) are in view of the small, fenced lake watched over by one of Cornwall's first wind farms. The white-washed café/reception, converted from one of the old barns is open all day offering traditional Cornish fare. A dozen colourful picnic tables are dotted about the site.

Facilities

Simple but adequate toilet block. Washing machine and dryer in the ladies' and a dishwashing sink and a laundry sink outside but under cover. Toilet for disabled visitors at Riding Centre. Shop and tea room. Gas supplies. Torches may be useful. Off site: Fishing (sea 4 miles, coarse 5 miles). Golf 2 miles.

Open: 1 April - 30 September.

Directions

Follow B3266 north from Camelford. Park access is directly from this road on the left just before the turning for Tintagel, clearly signed.
O.S.GR: SX097852. GPS: 50.635058, -4.687648

Charges guide

Per unit incl. 2 persons	£ 6.00 - £ 10.00
extra person (5 yrs and over)	£ 1.00
electricity	£ 2.50

Falmouth

Pennance Mill Farm Chalet & Camping Park

Maenporth, Falmouth TR11 5HJ (Cornwall) T: 01326 317431.

alanrogers.com/UK0450

Pennance Mill Farm has been in the hands of the Jewell family for three generations and is listed as a typical Cornish farmstead in an Area of Outstanding Natural Beauty (AONB) and you can enjoy the woodland walk with 200-year-old beech trees. The camping area is situated in four sheltered south-facing and fairly level fields with views over the countryside and providing for 75 pitches, all of which have 16A electricity and eight hardstanding. Caravans are accepted however this is not a site for those who like neat manicured lawns and flower beds.

Facilities

The two toilet blocks are fully equipped. The first near the entrance is the original one but it is well kept with good hot water, washing machine, dryer, laundry and dishwashing sinks. The block in the top meadow is more modern, heated and includes dishwashing sinks. Small farm shop including some basic provisions (open 09.00-10.30 and 17.30-18.30). Gas supplies. Small play meadow with new play equipment. Table tennis. Off site: New Maritime Museum. Tennis, golf course and pitch and putt within walking distance. Coastal footpath to the Helford River.

Open: Easter - November.

Directions

From Truro, follow signs for Falmouth on the A39. At the first roundabout pass Asda then turn right at next roundabout signed Maenporth and industrial estates (on Bickland Water Road). Follow brown international camping sigps for 1.5 miles and continue down the hill to site on your left as the road bends to the right. O.S.GR: SW789307. GPS: 50.134983, -5.092667

Charges guide

Per person	£ 5.00 - £ 6.00
child (over 3 yrs)	£ 1.75 - £ 2.50
pitch incl. electricity	£ 6.50 - £ 7.50

Fowey

Penmarlam Caravan & Camping Park

Bodinnick-by-Fowey, Fowey PL23 1LZ (Cornwall) T: 01726 870088. E: info@penmarlampark.co.uk

alanrogers.com/UK0195

Penmarlam is situated high above the estuary opposite Fowey, close to the village of Bodinnick which is famous for being the home of Daphne du Maurier. The original field is level and sheltered with 30 pitches which are semi-divided by bushes. The newer field with 35 pitches has a slight slope, is divided with wild banks and enjoys good countryside views. Both fields have circular concrete access roads. All pitches have 16A electricity and six also have water and drainage. The modern reception, shop and the toilet facilities are well situated between the two fields.

Facilities

The modern, colourful and heated toilet block is fully equipped including a baby and toddler room in the ladies' and a separate en-suite unit for disabled visitors which can double as a family room. Laundry facilities. Licensed shop with fresh fruit and vegetables. Coffee machine (reduced hours in low season). Video, DVD and book library. Off site: Fishing and boat launching 500 m. Beach 1 mile. Riding 3 miles. Golf 6 miles. Car or passenger ferry for Fowey.

Open: 1 April - 31 October.

Directions

From main A390 road at East Taphouse take B3359 towards Looe. After 5 miles fork right (Bodinnick and ferry). Site is signed on the right 1 mile past village of Lanteglos Highway, just before Bodinnick village. O.S.GR: SK130527. GPS: 50.34434, -4.62289

Charges guide

Per unit incl. 2 persons and electricity	£ 13.00 - £ 22.50
extra person	£ 3.50 - £ 7.00
child (3-15 yrs)	£ 1.50 - £ 3.00

17

Fowey
Penhale Caravan & Camping Park
Fowey PL23 1JU (Cornwall) T: 01726 833425. E: info@penhale-fowey.co.uk
alanrogers.com/UK0285

Penhale is a traditional campsite on four and half acres of rolling farmland with magnificent views across the countryside to St Austell Bay. The Berryman family run an arable and beef farm alongside the campsite. The atmosphere here is relaxed and there is plenty of room in the touring fields. The fields do slope but a number of pitches have been levelled. In total, there are 56 pitches for all types of units, 34 with 16A electricity hook-ups. Ten holiday caravans occupy a separate field. It is possible to walk to Polkerris beach a mile away and Fowey is just a mile and a half. The attractive, busy town of Fowey with its narrow streets is on the river of the same name and is a sailor's paradise (Regatta week is late August). Daphne du Maurier's association with the town is celebrated at the Literary Centre and with an annual Arts Festival in May. This is the landscape of wooded valleys, hidden coves and sandy beaches that inspired her books. There are many lovely walks and the site has produced directions. There are no public footpaths direct from the site but permission has been given to access those across private property.

Facilities	Directions
One fully equipped toilet block at the bottom of the touring fields. Laundry room. Reception at the farmhouse stocks basic necessities. Off site: Sandy beach, pub and watersports centre at Polkerris beach 1 mile (windsurfing, sailing, paddle surf, kayak). Fishing and boat launching 1.5 miles. Three golf courses within 7 mile3. Shops and restaurants Fowey 1.5 miles. Garage with shop 600 yds. Bicycle hire 5 miles.	From the A390 take B3269 for Fowey and 1 mile before town turn right at roundabout by petrol station on the A3082 St Austell road. Site is about 600 yds on the left. O.S.GR: SK105526. GPS: 50.34309, -4.66848

Open: Easter/1 April - 8 October.

Charges guide

Per unit incl. 2 persons and electricity	£ 11.00 - £ 17.00
extra person	£ 4.00 - £ 5.00
child (4-15 yrs)	£ 2.00
dog	£ 1.00 - £ 2.00

Gorran Haven
Sea View International
Boswinger, Gorran Haven, Saint Austell PL26 6LL (Cornwall) T: 01726 843425.
E: holidays@seaviewinternational.com alanrogers.com/UK0150

Sea View is an impressive, well-cared-for park, its quality reflected in the awards it has won. The enthusiastic owners Mr and Mrs Royden and their team are continually improving the park with the aim of providing quality camping. The new area at the top of the park with uninterrupted views is very smart, with 31 large, hedged, fully serviced grass pitches and a new toilet block providing excellent, en-suite family shower rooms. The remaining, established pitches (163, also with views) all have 16A electricity and 43 are fully serviced, including 12 hardstandings suitable for large motorhomes. There are 38 caravan holiday homes for hire in a separate area. Although somewhat exposed, the park is colourful with flower beds and flowering shrubs and has well manicured grass of exceptional quality. The area around the swimming pool is particularly attractive with sunbathing areas with free sunbeds on tiled terraces surrounded by flowers creating private little areas, all with magnificent views of the sea and the distant headland. Adjacent is a barbecue area with tables set out to take advantage of the view. A large recreation field provides plenty of play equipment as well as tennis, football and crazy golf. There is plenty to do and see in this area, from the gardens of Heligan and Trelissick, to Lanhydroc House and the seal sanctuary, not forgetting the safe beaches, one of which is only a half mile walk away.

Facilities	Directions
Excellent toilet facilities are well maintained and heated providing for all needs, including en-suite facilities, bathrooms (on payment), baby baths and facilities for disabled visitors. Campers' kitchen. Well equipped laundry. Motorcaravan service point. Shop and off-licence with gas (June - end Sept). Takeaway (Whit - mid Oct). Swimming pool (heated end May - mid Sept). Large recreation field. Fenced play area for under 7s. Adventure playground. Games room. WiFi. Certain breeds of dog are not accepted. Off site: Fishing and boat launching 2 miles. Riding 2 mile. Bicycle hire 5 miles. Golf 9 miles. Community bus picks up at the park.	From St Austell take B3273 towards Mevagissey; 1 mile before Mevagissey village turn right at Gorran and campsite sign and continue towards Gorran for 5 miles. Fork right at sign and follow signs to park. O.S.GR: SW991412. GPS: 50.2369, -4.820033

Open: 1 April - 31 October.

Charges guide

Per unit incl. 2 persons and electricity	£ 6.00 - £ 32.50
serviced pitch	£ 8.00 - £ 35.00
super pitch (fully incl.)	£ 10.00 - £ 56.00
extra person (over 5 yrs)	£ 3.00 - £ 5.00
dog (limited breeds and numbers)	£ 3.00
Special off-peak offers.	

Helston

Silver Sands Holiday Park

Gwendreath, Ruan Minor, Helston TR12 7LZ (Cornwall) T: **01326 290631**.
E: **enquiries@silversandsholidaypark.co.uk** **alanrogers.com/UK0070**

Silver Sands is a small, peaceful 'away-from-it-all' park in a remote part of the Lizard peninsula, the most southerly part of mainland Britain and an 'area of outstanding natural beauty'. It is tucked away behind two other holiday home parks (possible noise in season). The park itself has 16 caravan holiday homes, along with 36 touring pitches of which 20 have 10A electrical hook-ups. The pitches are large, attractively situated and divided into individual bays by flowering shrubs and bushes. The adjoining tent field has similar pitches (seven with electricity) where the shrubs are growing (some pitches are slightly sloping). The park is only reached after passing Culdrose Naval Base and the Goonhilly Earth Station down a single track road. A half mile footpath leads down through a small valley to the twin beaches of Kennack Sands (one is dog-free). A member of the Countryside Discovery group.

Facilities

The fully equipped toilet block includes an en-suite room for disabled visitors, doubling as a family room. Some play equipment. An undeveloped three-acre field can be used for walking, kite flying, etc. Off site: Restaurant nearby, pub within walking distance. Fishing 1 mile. Bicycle hire 5 miles. Boat launching 2 or 7 miles. Riding 5 miles. Golf 6 miles.

Open: Easter - mid September.

Directions

From Helston take A3038 Lizard road. After Culdrose turn left on B3293 passing Goonhilly after 4 miles. At next crossroads turn right (Kennack Sands), continue for 1.5 miles then left to Gwendreath on single track road - site is 1 mile. O.S.GR: SW732170. GPS: 50.00900, -5.16900

Charges guide

Per unit incl. 2 persons, 2 children and electricity	£ 14.00 - £ 19.50
extra person	£ 3.20 - £ 4.10
child (under 16 yrs)	£ 1.80 - £ 2.50
dog, boat or extra car	£ 1.80 - £ 2.50
Reductions for some bookings.	

Helston

Boscrege Caravan Park

Ashton, Helston TR13 9TG (Cornwall) T: **01736 762231**. E: **enquiries@caravanparkcornwall.com**
alanrogers.com/UK0480

A pretty little site covering 12 acres and hidden deep in the countryside in an area of outstanding natural beauty (AONB), Boscrege will suit those who want a quiet peaceful base for their Cornish holiday. The main large touring field nestles at the foot of Tregonning Hill with its striking hill top cross, and has neatly cut grass with a gentle slope from the top. The pitches are generously spaced around the edge, backing on to hedging and leaving plenty of room in the centre for ball games. Three small, attractive paddock areas, two with caravan holiday homes (26 in total), the other for touring units, complete the total provision of 51 pitches, 40 with 10A electricity. A nature trail has been developed which will help you identify the birds which can be seen around the park. This park is a welcome retreat for couples and families with young children.

Facilities

The traditional style toilet block is showing its age somewhat but is fully equipped including a smaller basin for children (M/F). Washing machine, dryer and microwave. Reception keeps emergency supplies. Two play areas for smaller children and central ball area. Amusement machines, pool table and TV room. New nature trail and dog-walking area. Mobile shop call daily 09.00. Off site: Godolphin House and garden. Whole of the tip of Cornwall easily accessible – the Lizard, Lands End. Nearest beach (Praa Sands) 2 miles. Fishing 1 mile. Golf and riding 2 miles. Bicycle hire and boat launching 5 miles.

Open: Easter/1 April - 31 October.

Directions

From Helston take A394 for Penzance. At top of Sithney Common Hill turn right just before Jet garage onto B3302 (Hayle) road. Pass Sithney General Stores on left and take next left for Carleen and Godolphin Cross. Continue to Godolphin Cross village and turn left at side of Godolphin Arms signed Ashton. Proceed up hill bearing left at top until you see camp signs where road turns sharply left and go straight over into lane leading to Boscrege. O.S.GR: SW593305. GPS: 50.12501, -5.36751

Charges guide

Per unit with 4 persons and electricity	£ 11.70 - £ 20.70
extra person	£ 2.00
No charge for dogs (max. 3).	

Helston

Mullion Holiday Park

Helston TR12 7LJ (Cornwall) T: 0870 4447774. E: touring@weststarholidays.co.uk

alanrogers.com/UK0490

For those who enjoy plenty of entertainment, both social and active in a holiday environment, Mullion would be a good choice. This holiday park is situated on the Lizard peninsula with its sandy beaches and coves. It has all the trimmings – indoor and outdoor pools, super play areas, clubs, bars and a wide range of nightly entertainment. Recent developments include a new look 'Stargate Club' and a 'village square' with a bandstand. These amenities form the core of the park and are well organised and managed. The touring area past the holiday homes has a more relaxed atmosphere. It is set on natural heathland with clumps of bramble and gorse which provide breaks and recesses making for a more informal layout. Linked by a circular gravel road, all 160 pitches are numbered, 10 with hardstanding and 105 with electricity connections (16A). Land drainage could be a problem if there is heavy continuous rain. A resident warden is now based at the entrance to the touring section. Eurotents for hire.

Facilities

A central modern toilet block is fully equipped and includes a baby unit and bath. It is supplemented with additional 'portacabin' style facilities for high season. Two washing machines. Large launderette in main complex. Freezer pack service. Large supermarket with off licence. Pub with family room, restaurant and takeaway (half board or breakfast options). Stargate Club with live shows and cabarets, satellite TV. Excellent play areas (fenced). Toddlers' soft play area. Amusement arcade, bowling alley. Heated outdoor pool (26/5-8/9), heated indoor fun pool, both supervised. Sauna and solarium. Crazy golf, pitch and putt. Barbecue.

Open: 20 May - 9 September.

Directions

From Helston take A3083 for The Lizard and continue for 7 miles. Site on left immediately after the right turning for Mullion. O.S.GR: SW698185.
GPS: 50.021117, -5.214717

Charges guide

Per pitch	£ 12.75 - £ 27.50
incl. electricity	£ 15.75 - £ 30.50
full services	£ 17.25 - £ 32.00
awning	free - £ 5.00
dog (max 2)	£ 5.00

Half-board or breakfast options available.

Helston

Lower Polladras Touring Park

You might also like to consider...

Lower Polladras Camping
Quiet rural and very friendly

Winners of a Gold David Bellamy Conservation Award 2008. Escape to this peaceful and rural family run park which is ideally situated for exploring South West Cornwall. We have sheltered and level touring pitches, some of which are hard-standings. All our shower and toilet blocks have unlimited free hot water. There is also a play area and nearby nature and dog walk.

We can store caravans in a secure compound if desired; we will then site and level it, ready for you. We have a small fleet of luxury caravans for hire, all with double glazing and full central heating. Our site is open from April to January. Low Season Specials Deals.

Carleen, Helston, Cornwall, TR13 9NX
Tel. / Fax. 01736 762220 • Email: lowerpolladras@btinternet.com • www.lower-polladras.co.uk

Liskeard

The Colliford Tavern Campsite

Colliford Lake, Saint Neot, Liskeard PL14 6PZ (Cornwall) T: 01208 821335. E: info@colliford.com

alanrogers.com/UK0300

Colliford Tavern must be unique, quietly situated high on Bodmin Moor near Colliford Lake but hidden and protected by tall pines with a camping area and a tavern. The camping area is quiet and simple and has been kept very natural with short grass (helped by the rabbits) and sheltered from the moor by tall pines. The main field provides 40 fairly level pitches with 19 electric hook-ups (16A) and six hardstandings. Reception is in the tavern building. The tavern is run as a free house with a bar, dining room, a family room with outside terrace, garden, water wheel and a good, fenced play area with a Wendy House. It is open to campers and caravanners and the general public. Ideally situated for Colliford Lake and the Moor, be it for walking, fly fishing (permits available) or birdwatching, the park is also suitable for excursions to both the north and south coasts. Discounted entrance is available to the adjacent Colliford Adventure Park.

Facilities

The pine-fitted, heated toilet block is fully equipped and includes a baby room and unit for disabled people (no shower). Service wash and tumble dry (Monday to Friday). Restaurant and bar. Play area. Some occasional family entertainment. Tickets for the Eden Project (20-30 minutes by car). Barbecues permitted with prior permission.

Open: All year.

Directions

Approaching on the A30 travelling south, pass the Jamaica Inn and site is signed a further 1-1.5 miles on the left. Follow for 0.5 miles and site is signed beside Colliford Lake Park. O.S.GR: SX168730.
GPS: 50.536933, -4.582267

Charges guide

Per unit incl. 2 persons and electricity	£ 18.00
extra person (over 12 yrs)	£ 4.00
child (5-12 yrs)	£ 2.00

Looe
Trelay Farmpark
Pelynt, Looe PL13 2JX (Cornwall) T: 01503 220900. E: stay@trelay.co.uk
alanrogers.com/UK0400

Situated a little back from the coast, just over three miles from Looe and Polperro in a rural situation, this is a real gem of a park. Neat, tidy and quiet, despite the name, there is no farm. On your right as you drive in, and quite attractively arranged amongst herbaceous shrubs, are caravan holiday homes (15 privately owned, some let by the park). The touring area is behind and slightly above, on level to gently sloping, neatly cut grass. An oval hardcore road connects the good sized, numbered pitches that border the site and back onto hedges, the majority with rural views. There are 43 pitches with electricity hook-ups, with a further 12 pitches for tents, etc. Outside the main season the central area is kept free for ball games. You will receive a good welcome from the enthusiastic owners, Heather and Graham Veale and their family, who live in the chalet bungalow near the entrance where the small reception is located.

Facilities	Directions
Excellent, spacious chalet-type toilet block, purpose built, heated, well equipped and maintained, with large cubicles. Some semi-private washbasins. En-suite unit with ramp for disabled visitors (key from reception); it includes a baby bath. Washing machine and dryer. Gas supplies. Free use of fridge/freezer and ice pack service. Tourist information including map sales and loan. Off site: Village with pub, shops and bus service 0.5 miles. Looe and Polperro within 3 miles. Bus service from the village.	From A390 Lostwithiel road take B3359 south at Middle or East Taphouse towards Looe and Polperro. Site is signed 0.5 miles past Pelynt on the left. From Looe take A387 towards Polperro and after 2 miles turn right onto B3359 towards Pelynt. Site is signed 1 mile on right. O.S.GR: SX210545. GPS: 50.36225, -4.518883

Open: 30 March - end October.

Charges guide

Per unit incl. 2 persons	£ 7.50 - £ 12.00
extra person	£ 3.50
electricity	£ 2.00
dog	£ 1.00
No credit cards.	

Mevagissey
Tregarton Park
Gorran, Mevagissey, Saint Austell PL26 6NF (Cornwall) T: 01726 843666. E: reception@tregarton.co.uk
alanrogers.com/UK0155

Run by the welcoming Hicks family, Tregarton Park itself dates back to the 16th century. It is little wonder that the listed buildings have created some problems in providing modern facilities, although the Hicks have done well with their conversions to create a pleasing environment. The 12 acre caravan park is made up of four meadows, with wonderful rural views. The 125 pitches, all with electric hook ups (10A), some with hardstanding, are of generous size with most separated by either hedges or fencing. All have been terraced, as the park itself is quite hilly. Reception provides a well stocked shop, tourist information and a takeaway service offering freshly cooked food including a daily delivery of Cornish pasties. The large heated outdoor pool is surrounded by decked terraces, with tables and chairs where one can relax and watch the children – in fact, it is the focal point of the park. An adventure playground is in one of the meadows where there is also an impressive all-weather tennis court (free). Close to the small harbour town of Gorran and about 2.5 miles from Mevagissey, with several beaches close by, this is an ideal site for those who do not want lots of entertainment, but would enjoy the option of various activities available nearby.

Facilities	Directions
The fully equipped toilet block has been completely revamped and includes some excellent features. Facilities for disabled visitors. Laundry room. Well stocked shop with groceries and camping supplies (Whit-2/10). Takeaway (Whit - mid Sept). Gas supplies. Heated swimming pool (Mid May - Mid Sept). Tourist information. Dog exercise meadow. Adventure playground. All weather tennis. WiFi. Off site: Bus stop at entrance. Bicycle hire 3 miles. Golf 5 miles. Heligan Gardens 2 miles. Mevagissey 2 miles. Beaches 2 miles. Eden project 9 miles. Fishing trips available from Mevagissey and Gorran Haven.	Leave St Austell travelling south on the B3273 and pass through London Apprentice and Pentewen. Follow Tregarton Park's brown tourist signs by turning right at the crossroads at the top of the hill towards Heligan and Gorran Haven. Do not go into Mevagissey. O.S.GR: SW989435. GPS: 50.2588, -4.829417

Open: 4 April - 31 October.

Charges guide

Per unit incl. 2 persons, electricity and awning	£ 8.00 - £ 25.00
extra person (over 4 yrs)	£ 3.00 - £ 6.00
dog (max. 2)	free - £ 3.00

21

Mullion

Franchis Holidays

Cury Cross Lanes, Mullion TR12 7AZ (Cornwall) T: **01326 240301**. E: **enquiries@franchis.co.uk**

alanrogers.com/UK0485

A small rural site, Franchis is ideally situated for exploring the Lizard peninsula in an 'Area of Outstanding Natural Beauty'. Mature trees edge the site's two fields (a total of 4 acres) that slope slightly, with 70 pitches arranged around the perimeters. There are 33 with 10A electricity. Natural woodland areas and a stream will keep children occupied. Continuing past the fields into a wooded area are six small bungalows and six mobile homes, some privately owned and some to rent. There is a small toilet block for each field and a small shop that opens morning and evening. Phil and Kate, who have owned the site for the last three years, will be pleased to welcome you and advise you in exploring the area. The Lizard is a unique area with unspoilt coves and the Helford river. Goonhilly Earth station is just up the road and you pass by the extensive Culdrose Naval base on your way to the site.

Facilities

Two traditional small toilet blocks. Two washing machines and two driers. Freezer for ice blocks. Small shop (18/7-30/9). Tourist Information. Small library. Play area. Dog exercise field. Tourist information. Mobile homes and chalets for rent. Off site: Helston 5 miles. Beach 2 miles. Fishing and boat launching 2 miles. Sailing 4 miles. Riding and golf 2 miles.

Open: Easter - 31 October.

Directions

From Helston take the A3038 road for the Lizard. After passing Culdrose take the A3083 signed Mullion and after about 2 miles watch for site directly on the right. O.S.GR: SW696204. GPS: 50.039, -5.21843

Charges guide

Per unit incl. 2 persons and electricity	£ 12.00 - £ 16.00
extra person	£ 1.00 - £ 1.50

Newquay

Trevornick Holiday Park

Holywell Bay, Newquay TR8 5PW (Cornwall) T: **01637 830531**. E: **bookings@trevornick.co.uk**

alanrogers.com/UK0220

Trevornick, once a working farm, is a modern, busy and well run family touring park providing a very wide range of amenities close to one of Cornwall's finest beaches. A modern reception with welcoming staff sets the tone for your holiday. The park is well managed with facilities and standards constantly monitored. It has grown to provide caravanners and campers (no holiday caravans but 68 very well equipped 'Eurotents') with 440 large grass pitches (350 with 10A electricity and 55 fully serviced with electricity, water, drain and TV connection with DVD channel) on five level fields and two terraced areas. There are few trees, but some good views. Providing 'all singing, all dancing' facilities for fun packed family holidays, the farm buildings now provide the setting for the Farm Club. Recently refurbished, it provides much entertainment from bingo and quizzes to shows, discos and cabaret. The Stables Grill also opens for breakfast and the Hungry Horse provides takeaway food. The rest of the development provides a pool complex, an 18 hole golf course, with a small, quiet club house offering bar meals and lovely views out to sea and three fishing lakes. Next door is the Holywell Bay 'fun' park (reduced rates) and the sandy beach is five minutes by car or a downhill walk from the park. An innovative idea is the 'Hire shop' where it is possible rent anything you might have forgotten from sheets, a fridge, travel cot, etc. to a camera or a wet suit to catch the famous Cornish surf!

Facilities

Five modern toilet blocks provide showers (20p), two family bathrooms, baby bath, laundry facilities and provision for disabled visitors. Well stocked supermarket (from late May). Hire shop. Bars (with TV), restaurant, cafe and takeaway. Entertainment (every night in season). Pool complex with heated outdoor pool, paddling pool, sunbathing decks, solarium, sauna and massage chair. Health and beauty salon. Super Fort Knox style adventure playground. Crazy golf, Kiddies Club and indoor play area (supervised for 2-8 yr olds, small charge). Amusement arcade and bowling alley. Teenagers' room. 18-hole pitch and putt with golf pro shop. Bicycle hire. Coarse fishing with three lakes. Only limited facilities at Easter and from 8 Sept. Off site: Riding within 1 mile. Bicycle hire and boat launching 4 miles.

Open: Easter - mid September.

Directions

From A3075 approach to Newquay - Perranporth road, turn towards Cubert and Holywell Bay. Continue through Cubert to park on the right. O.S.GR: SW776586. GPS: 50.384983, -5.128933

Charges guide

Per person	£ 4.95 - £ 9.30
child (4-14 yrs)	£ 1.30 - £ 6.55
electricity	£ 4.75
'super premium' or 'jumbo' pitch incl. electricity	£ 8.95
dog	£ 3.45 - £ 3.75
Families and couples only.	
Many special discounts.	

See advertisement on page 26

Newquay
Newperran Holiday Park
Rejerrah, Newquay TR8 5QJ (Cornwall) T: 01872 572407. E: holidays@newperran.co.uk
alanrogers.com/UK0160

Newperran is a large, level park in rural Cornish countryside. Being on high ground, it is quite open but this also gives excellent views of the coast and surrounding countryside. The owners, Keith and Christine Brewer, have rebuilt the reception, shop and pub to a very high standard. The traditional layout of the park provides a number of flat, well drained meadows divided into over 370 individual pitches with 10/16A electricity. Some fields have larger and reservable spaces with more free space in the centre. There are now 77 fully serviced pitches, some with hardstanding and a TV point. Newperran is only 2.5 miles from Perranporth beach, but there is a free heated swimming pool with sunbathing area and paddling pool on the park. A state of the art entrance barrier is now in place operating on recognition of your number plate. The Pub or Cottage Inn as it is called, is a very comfortable area with a log burner for low season warmth and family entertainment such as quiz nights in high season. A separate café operates on a franchise basis. This is a well run park with plenty of space and activities for families with a few caravan holiday homes to rent. There are plans to provide a specialist naturist area but advanced booking will be required.

Facilities
Toilet facilities comprise four clean blocks, two heated, all refurbished to a very high standard. Facilities include washbasins in cabins, family rooms, baby room, hairdressing room and a unit for disabled visitors. Laundry room. Well stocked self-service licensed shop. Licensed bar (mid May - Oct). Café (all season). New outdoor heated swimming pool with paddling pool (Whitsun - Sept). Adventure playground and separate toddlers' play area. Games room with TV. TV room. Off site: Riding or golf 2 miles. Fishing 1 mile. Goonhavern village within walking distance with pubs and post office. Beach 2.5 miles.

Open: Easter - October.

Directions
Turn off A3075 to west at camping sign 7 miles south of Newquay and just north of Goonhavern village. O.S.GR: SW794546. GPS: 50.350433, -5.101817

Charges guide
Per unit incl. 2 persons and electricity	£ 13.90 - £ 20.60
extra person	£ 4.50 - £ 7.85
child (3-15 yrs)	£ 2.35 - £ 6.10

See advertisement on page 26

Newquay
Trevella Caravan Park
Crantock, Newquay TR8 5EW (Cornwall) T: 01637 830308. E: holidays@trevella.co.uk
alanrogers.com/UK0170

One of the best known and respected of Cornish parks with its colourful flowerbeds (a regular winner of a 'Newquay in Bloom' award), Trevella is also one of the first to fill up and has a longer season than most. Well organised, the pitches are in a number of adjoining meadows, most of which are on a slight slope. Of the 250 pitches for touring units (any type), some 200 can be reserved and these are marked, individual ones. Over 200 pitches have electricity (10A), with 59 serviced pitches (with hardstanding, electricity and TV hook-ups, water, waste water), some extra large with sewage drain as well. Trevella is essentially a quiet family touring park. The accent is on orderliness and cleanliness with on-site evening activities limited, although Andy's Kitchen offers good home-cooked food. Access is free to two fishing lakes, (permits from reception); with some fishing instruction and wildlife talks for youngsters in season. There is a pleasant walk around the lakes, which are a haven for wildlife and a protected nature reserve. It is possible to walk to Crantock beach but check the tides first. A member of the Best of British group.

Facilities
Kept very clean, three blocks provide good coverage with individual washbasins in private cabins for ladies, hairdressing room and baby room. Laundry. Freezer pack service. Well stocked supermarket (Easter - Oct). Café (including breakfast) and takeaway. Heated outdoor pool. Games room. Separate TV room. Crazy golf. Large adventure playground. Play and sports area. Pets corner. Fishing. Off site: Shuttle bus service to Newquay in high season. Nearest beach is 0.5 miles on foot, 1 mile by car and Newquay is 2 miles. Pubs and restaurants at Crantock, 1 mile. Riding 1 mile, golf 3 miles

Open: Easter - 31 October.

Directions
To avoid Newquay leave A30 or A392 at Indian Queens, straight over crossroads with A39 and A3058, left at A3075 junction and first right at campsite sign. O.S.GR: SW802598. GPS: 50.3973, -5.096133

Charges guide
Per person	£ 4.20 - £ 7.30
child (3-16 yrs)	£ 2.30 - £ 5.20
pitch incl. electricity	£ 4.00
incl. services	£ 8.00 - £ 11.00
Families and couples only.	

See advertisement on page 27

23

Newquay
Treloy Touring Park
Newquay TR8 4JN (Cornwall) T: 01637 872063. E: treloy-tp@btconnect.com
alanrogers.com/UK0205

Just three miles from the wonderful beaches around Newquay, yet peacefully located away from the crowds, Treloy is a pretty park. Family owned and run, there are 197 pitches, many level, some slightly sloping, all with 16A electricity (new system) and 20 fully serviced. All are used for touring units and perhaps this contributes towards the relaxed family atmosphere. There are concrete hardstandings for caravans which are attractively interspersed with shrubs and form a pleasant landscape feature. Elsewhere hydrangea edge the roads around the more open pitches and more trees are being planted. St Mawgan, the RAF air sea rescue base and Newquay's airport are nearby but there is little disturbance. There is an hourly bus service to Newquay from the park entrance which means the coast and beaches can be enjoyed without taking the car. On return to Treloy there is the Park Chef and the Surfrider's Bar for meals and drinks. If you do not fancy the beach there is a pool on the park. This is a real family park providing for all ages.

Facilities
Two new toilet blocks, one with showers, the other with toilets and washbasins only. Baby room with two large sinks. En-suite facilities for disabled visitors (key). Laundry. Gas. Shop with all necessities. Bar (20/5-1/9). Pleasant café with a good reputation and including breakfast (20/5-1/9). Swimming pool (walled and gated). Play areas and field with goal posts. Nature trail. Family entertainment such as magic shows, bingo, folk and rock music. Off site: Fishing 1 mile. Golf 0.5 miles. Riding and boat launching 3 miles. Other beaches such as Watergate Bay, Mawgan Porth and Porth beach are a short car journey.

Open: 20 May - 15 September.

Directions
From A39 St Columb Major take the B3059 for Newquay. Park is signed after about 4 miles. O.S.GR: SW858625. GPS: 50.432867, -5.0125

Charges guide
Per unit incl. 2 persons	
and electricity	£ 13.75 - £ 21.45
extra person	£ 5.00 - £ 7.35
child (3-14 yrs)	£ 3.00 - £ 4.45
dog	£ 1.00 - £ 2.50

See advertisement on page 27

Newquay
Hendra Holiday Park
Newquay TR8 4NY (Cornwall) T: 01637 875778. E: jn@hendra.co.uk
alanrogers.com/UK0210

Hendra is a long-established holiday park for all the family with a wide range of facilities and a comprehensive entertainment programme. There are comedians, show bands, cabaret, dancing, bingo, discos, plus a super pool complex. The 548 touring pitches are on well mown, mostly terraced grass fields with country views and mature trees, some more sheltered than others. There are 280 caravan holiday homes in separate fields to rent. With tarmac roads and lighting, 311 pitches have electricity (16A) and 28 pitches are fully serviced including water, electricity, light, sewer drainage, satellite TV connections and some innovative awning pads (dogs are not accepted on these pitches). The entrance and reception are very attractive with a mass of well tended flower beds which, along with the other facilities, form an attractive, village-like centre to the park. The 'star of the show' at Hendra is the Oasis complex consisting of an indoor fun pool with flumes, river rapids and beach. It is open to the public – really a mini water-park. The outdoor heated pool with grass sunbathing area is free to campers and activities are well catered for with a range of amenities. The park is only 1.5 miles from Newquay and its surfing beaches and a bus to the town passes the gate. Hendra welcomes families and couples.

Facilities
Three modern fully equipped toilet blocks including facilities for babies and disabled visitors. Large launderette. Motorcaravan services. Gas supplies. Well stocked shop. Various bars and restaurants, open all season (limited hours in early season). Pizzeria (main season only). Takeaway. Outdoor swimming pool. Indoor pool complex (cost £2.60 per person or, if pre-booked, £13.20 for 7 tickets). Various play areas including one for soft play. Minigolf. Bowling. Off site: Fishing or riding 1 mile. Bicycle hire or golf 2 miles. Beach 1.5 miles.

Open: 23 March - 31 October.

Directions
Park is on left side of A392 Indian Queens - Newquay road at Newquay side of Quintrell Downs. O.S.GR: SW833601. GPS: 50.402433, -5.04915

Charges guide
Per unit incl. 2 persons	
and electricity	£ 16.00 - £ 25.20
extra person	£ 4.70 - £ 8.50
child (3-14 yrs)	£ 1.40 - £ 5.60
vehicle	£ 1.35 - £ 1.90

Minimum charges apply at peak times.

See advertisement opposite

ndependent, top star graded parks, offering fabulous facilities,
perb locations and superior service - especially for families and couples

cornwall's finest parks

Mawgan Porth's best kept secret!

Relaxing 5 star holidays in peaceful Cornish countryside,
just a 15 minute woodland walk from a large, sandy beach.
For families and couples only who prefer a no club/bar site.

0800 634 6744
www.SunHavenValley.com

Dolbeare Park
Caravan and Camping

An exceptional five star gold oasis hidden
in the Cornish countryside near to Plymouth
and the beautiful Rame Peninsula

Open all year

- 60 large gravel and grass pitches, all with electric
- Shop selling fresh bread, Takeaway & Off License
- Children's adventure play area & area for ball games
- Laundry, WiFi, Dog friendly, Easy access

www.dolbeare.co.uk

PL12 5AF

Visit our website to read our reviews and special offers
Including weekend specials & over 55's one week from £49

01752 851332

- Heated swimming pool
- Licensed family bar
- Free entertainment
- Café / takeaway
- On site shop
- Electric hook-up
- Free showers
- Recreation Area
- Laundry / baby baths
- Adventure playground
- TV and games room
- Treloy golf course nearby
- Driving range nearby
- Coarse fishing nearby

Treloy
Touring Park

Telephone:

01637 872063

Or visit us at:

www.treloy.co.uk

Newquay, Cornwall TR8 4JN

Everything you need for an
unforgettable Cornish holiday

CARAVAN AND CAMPING PARK
Trevella Park
CRANTOCK NEWQUAY CORNWALL

★ Tenth year David Bellamy Gold Award
★ Modern facilities including heated swimming & paddling pools
★ Set in beautiful parkland surroundings
★ Nature reserve and two fishing lakes
★ Luxury Rose Award caravans
★ Online booking available at www.trevella.co.uk

One of Cornwall's Finest Parks

01637 830308

holidays@trevella.co.uk   www.trevella.co.uk

Newquay
Trethiggey Touring Park

Quintrell Downs, Newquay TR8 4LG (Cornwall) T: 01637 877672. E: enquiries@trethiggey.co.uk
alanrogers.com/UK0530

Trethiggey is a garden-like park with a ten-month season, set three miles back from the busy Newquay beaches and night life, with an enjoyable, informal style. With natural areas including a small wildlife pond and fishing lakes to enjoy, conservation is high on the agenda. There are 157 pitches, 110 with 16A electricity, some with hardstanding and a few also serviced with water and sewerage connections. Some level pitches are formally arranged, with others more informal on gently sloping grass amidst 12 caravan holiday homes. A tent field is opened for the main season.

Facilities	Directions
Two fully equipped, heated shower blocks, one in traditional style. En-suite facilities for families and disabled visitors. Baby bathroom. Motorcaravan service point. Laundry facilities and wetsuit wash. Games room at each toilet block with TV and amusement machines. Shop. Café and takeaway. Adventure play area and recreation field. Coarse fishing. WiFi. Off site: Riding 2 miles. Golf and bicycle hire 3 miles. Newquay within 3 miles with nightly minibus service (book in shop). Pub within walking distance.	Site is a few hundred yards south of roundabout where A393 crosses the A3058 at Quintrell Downs (beside the A3058). O.S. GR:SW846596. GPS: 50.396833, -5.0283

Open: 2 March - 2 January.

Charges guide

Per person	£ 4.25 - £ 6.85
child (4-15 yrs)	£ 1.85 - £ 4.25
pitch incl. electricity	£ 3.20 - £ 6.00
dog	£ 1.80 - £ 2.50

See advertisement on page 25

Newquay
Newquay Holiday Park

Newquay TR8 4HS (Cornwall) T: 01637 871111. E: enquiries@parkdean.com
alanrogers.com/UK0200

Part of the Parkdean Group, Newquay Holiday Park lies peacefully on a terraced hillside only just outside the town, two miles from the beaches and town centre. Its main feature is an attractively laid out group of three heated swimming pools with a giant water slide (with lifeguards) and 'green' sunbathing areas overlooked by a terrace. With a large proportion of caravan holiday homes (for let), there are still two fields used for touring units. These provide 187 marked pitches in hedged fields, some sloping, marked out by lines on ground but with nothing between them. Electricity (16A) is available.

Facilities	Directions
Two good sized, modern toilet blocks include a unit for disabled visitors and baby bath. An extra block is opened for the main season when facilities may be under pressure. Launderette. Well stocked self-service shop (gas from reception). Bar/lounge with Sky TV. New café/restaurant with all day food also 'pub grub' in evenings. Outdoor pool complex with slide (and lifeguards). Pitch and putt and crazy golf. Playground. Adventure play area for older children. Children's club. Recreation field. Amusement arcade. Dogs or other pets are only permitted on certain pitches.	Park is east of Newquay on A3059 road 1 mile east of junction with A3058. O.S.GR: SW853626. GPS: 50.4225, -5.0245

Open: Easter - October.

Charges guide

Per unit incl. 4 persons	£ 7.00 - £ 27.00
incl. services	£ 10.00 - £ 30.00
extra person (over 3 yrs; up to 4 people)	£ 2.00 - £ 4.00
dog	£ 2.50

Newquay
Trekenning Tourist Park

Saint Columb Major, Newquay TR8 4JF (Cornwall) T: 01637 880462. E: holidays@trekenning.co.uk
alanrogers.com/UK0310

Trekenning is a very useful park with easy access just off the A39 roundabout at St Columb Major. It comprises a large sloping field with neatly cut grass and all the facilities tucked into the top corner. There are 75 pitches, 68 with 10A electricity and semi-terraced. The A39 runs parallel to one side of the site, so there may be road noise. The star of the show is undoubtedly the kidney shaped pool and paddling pool which are in a garden-like setting with gazebos and sun loungers surrounded by lawn and overlooked by a patio bar at the top – lovely for summer evenings.

Facilities	Directions
Two toilet blocks, one with showers and washbasins, the other with two en-suite bathrooms (50p) and six large family showers, well refurbished. Laundry room. Free freezer service. Shop for basics (July/Aug). Bar (all season) with food on demand. Takeaway including breakfasts (B.H.s and July/Aug). Play area. Outdoor pool with poolside bar (Whitsun - end Aug). Games room. Off site: Fishing 1 mile. Riding and golf 2 miles. Bicycle hire 6 miles.	Take A3059 turning to Newquay from St Columb Major then turn immediately left; park is signed (this was the old road). O.S.GR: SW907625. GPS: 50.42182, -4.94265

Open: All year.

Charges guide

Per unit incl. 2 persons and electricity	£ 15.00 - £ 20.00
extra person	£ 4.75 - £ 7.00
child (3-15 yrs)	£ 2.00 - £ 4.50

Newquay
Monkey Tree Holiday Park
Rejerrah, Newquay TR8 5QR (Cornwall) T: **01872 572032**. E: **enquiries@monkeytreeholidaypark.co.uk**
alanrogers.com/UK0165

Monkey Tree covers 56 acres and boasts an impressive entrance and smart reception. There are 500 pitches with 450 for touring units and 50 caravan holiday homes to rent in their own area. The pitches in the original part of the park benefit from mature hedging which offers a degree of privacy which the newer ones lack, but all have been planted with individual hedges. The pitches are of a good size and most have electricity (13/16A). Serviced pitches with hardstanding are being developed including some extra large pitches which include the use of private facilities in the toilet block. All the family should find something to keep them happy. For the little ones there is a morning Kid's Club, for older children there are adventure playgrounds, well fenced for safety, trampolines, bouncy castles and an amusement arcade and pool tables. There is an outdoor heated pool, paddling pool and a sauna. The restaurant and club are popular, with children's entertainment for children early evenings, and bingo, karaoke, disco and cabaret acts to follow. Themed weekends are organised early and late in the season, with Halloween being especially popular.

Facilities

The original block (refurbished) supplements two new modern timber blocks with heating, providing for all needs including facilities for babies and disabled visitors. Private en-suite facilities for use with the super pitches. Laundry. Motorcaravan services. Gas supplies. Shop (mornings only in low season). Club with entertainment, bar and restaurant (main season and B.Hs). Takeaway (high season). Outdoor pool and paddling pool (Whitsun - end Sept). Trampolines (supervised, with charge). Bouncy castles. Three adventure play areas. Amusement arcade. Fishing lakes. Caravan storage. Off site: Golf, riding, boat launching and sailing 5 miles.

Open: All year.

Directions

Follow the A30 ignoring all signs for Newquay. At Carland Cross with windmills on the right, carry straight over following signs for Perranporth. After 1 mile turn right at Boxheater Junction on the B3285 signed Perranporth and Goonhavern. Follow for 0.5 miles then turn right into Scotland Road for 1 mile to park on the left. O.S.GR: SW801546. GPS: 50.352218, -5.091659

Charges guide

Per person	£ 3.75 - £ 6.20
child (3-14 yrs)	free - £ 3.75
pitch incl. electricity	£ 3.50
incl. services	£ 7.50 - £ 10.50

AWARD WINNING TOURING FAMILY HOLIDAY PARK
Just minutes away from Perranporth and Newquay

FREE Heated Pool
FREE Family Entertainment
FREE Kiddies Club
Luxury Caravans available
Tel: 01872 572032
www.monkeytreeholidaypark.co.uk
Monkey Tree Holiday Park. Rejerrah, Newquay, Cornwall TR8 5QR. Ref: ARG1

Newquay
Sun Haven Valley Holiday Park
Mawgan Porth, Newquay TR8 4BQ (Cornwall) T: **01637 860373**. E: **sunhaven@sunhavenvalley.com**
alanrogers.com/UK0215

An attractive, well maintained holiday park, Sun Haven Valley is on the edge of a small valley with views of the opposite hills. Owned and thoughtfully run by the Tavener family, it caters mainly for couples and families with children. On a gently sloping hillside, around 30 caravan holiday homes for rent border the top field with a central area of neatly cut grass left free for play. The lower field is edged by a small trout stream (unfenced) and provides over 100 level, grass touring pitches (standard and large sizes), marked by tram lines and accessed by a circular road. In peak season extra pitches are provided on the other side of the road. The facilities and play area are situated between the two fields with some walking required. A footpath leads to the beach (15-20 minutes' walk) and the small village of Mawgan Porth. There are eating places within walking distance and an organic farm with a shop next door - apparently Tesco and Asda will deliver to the site! An unusual recycling activity whereby any left behind body boards, chairs, tables and toys can be borrowed by other campers seems to be much appreciated.

Facilities

A large, centrally situated toilet block is fully equipped, with a smaller one in the far corner. Two en-suite family rooms double as facilities for disabled visitors. Laundry. Fridge and freezer. Microwave. Toaster. Basic foodstuffs available in reception. Play area. TV room. Games room with computers and amusement machines. WiFi (around reception). Mobile phone reception difficult. Mobile homes and chalets for rent. Off site: Fishing 100 yds. Golf 1 mile. Riding 5 miles. Bicycle hire and boat launching 7 miles.

Open: Easter - 31 October.

Directions

From B3276 at Mawgan Porth take narrow unclassed road up the Vale of Lanhorne for 1 mile. Site is on the left. O.S.GR: SW861667. GPS: 50.46203, -5.01385

Charges guide

Per unit incl. 2 persons, electricity	£ 15.00 - £ 27.00
extra person	£ 3.00 - £ 5.00
child (under 14 yrs)	free - £ 3.50
dog	£ 1.00 - £ 4.00

See advertisement on page 27

Padstow

Padstow Touring Park

Padstow PL28 8LE (Cornwall) T: **01841 532061**. E: **mail@padstowtouringpark.co.uk**
alanrogers.com/UK0430

Padstow Touring Park has wonderful views over the surrounding countryside. Originally open fields, bushes and shrubs have grown to break up the gently sloping fields. There are 150 pitches, most with 10A electricity and some with hardstanding. 'Kernow' pitches have access to private, en-suite facilities. The site can accommodate up to 34 ft. motorhomes. Padstow itself is a mile away, either by public footpath through the fields (20-30 minutes) or by bicycles on the road. A bus service passes (the site is a request stop) and reception holds timetables. Rick Stein's restaurant or bistro may tempt you – and there are many others in Padstow.

Facilities	Directions
Three toilet blocks, including one new with under-floor heating, en-suite shower rooms, facilities for disabled visitors and a family room. Exclusive washrooms for use with the 'Kernow' pitches. Full laundry facilities. Reception/shop for gas, camping equipment and provisions. Bread to order. Play area. WiFi access. Off site: Nearest beach is at Padstow, others are within 2 miles. Access to the Camel Trail cycle route. Riding or fishing 2 miles. Golf 5 miles.	Park is situated on the main A389 road into Padstow, on the right about 1 mile before the town. If towing or in a motorhome avoid A389 between Wadebridge and St Issey; instead take B3274 which can take large units. O.S.GR: SW912739. GPS: 50.52705, -4.949183

Open: All year.

Charges guide

Per unit incl. 2 persons and electricity	£ 13.50 - £ 18.50
'Kernow' pitch	£ 17.50 - £ 26.50
extra person	£ 3.50 - £ 4.50
child (3-15 yrs)	£ 2.00 - £ 3.00

Pentewan

Pentewan Sands Holiday Park

Pentewan, Saint Austell PL26 6BT (Cornwall) T: **01726 843485**. E: **info@pentewan.co.uk**
alanrogers.com/UK0250

Pentewan Sands is a popular, well-managed family park with an ideal position right beside a wide sandy private beach. A busy, 32-acre holiday park with lots going on, there are 501 touring pitches, 401 with electricity, and 120 caravan holiday homes for hire. The good sized pitches are on level grass with nothing between them. They are marked and numbered by frontage stones, mostly in rows adjoining access roads. A good heated pool with a paddling pool is beside the Beach Club. For 2010 this area is due to be rebuilt providing new indoor pools, both a lap pool and a fun pool, a gym, kids' zone and new bar and restaurant. The bar and restaurant will be open all day and serving good value food in season. A full entertainment programme, beach activities, scuba diving, windsurfing courses and a club for children are organised, and a small watersports centre is on the beach. Jet-skis are not permitted and 4WD vehicles are not allowed on the beach. The Pentewan Valley Trail, a six mile route for cycling or walking follows the old carriageway to Mevagissey with its throngs of tourists (two miles by the main road). The park and the beach have been owned by the Tremayne family for over 60 years.

Facilities	Directions
Four main toilet blocks receive heavy use in peak season but are maintained by individual cleaners. Two bathrooms, a baby room and facilities for disabled people. Well equipped laundry room. Motorcaravan service point. Large, self-service shop with off-licence, bistro and fast food (Easter - mid Sept). Bars, bar meals (Easter - mid Sept, limited hours early and late season). Entertainment programme. Swimming pools (supervised and open Whitsun - mid Sept). Playground. Games room. Tennis. Bicycle hire. Slipway and boat launching (Whitsun - mid Sept). Freezer service, battery charging service. Gas. Caravan and boat storage. Dogs are not accepted. WiFi around reception and bar. Bus stop 400 yds. from site. One per hour. Off site: Riding or golf 2 miles. Bicycle hire in village 0.5 miles.	From St Austell ring road take B3273 for Mevagissey. Park is 3.5 miles, where the road meets the sea. O.S.GR: SX018468. GPS: 50.288283, -4.78575

Charges guide

Per unit incl. 2 persons and electricity	£ 13.55 - £ 29.50
extra person	£ 2.99 - £ 5.00
child (3-15 yrs)	£ 1.20 - £ 3.75
extra small tent, boat or car	£ 1.70 - £ 2.40
Sea front pitch plus 10-20%.	

Open: 1 April - 31 October.

Penzance
Bone Valley Caravan & Camping Park
Heamoor, Penzance TR20 8UJ (Cornwall) T: **01736 360313**. E: enquiries@bonevalleycandcpark.co.uk
alanrogers.com/UK0018

A small garden-like park tucked away at the back of Penzance, Bone Valley has five caravan holiday homes to let and 17 touring pitches. There is also room for a few few tents tucked behind hedges and all is accessed by a circular roadway. The park is surrounded by tall trees with the fresh water in the small stream coming straight off the moors (good for keeping bottles cold). The philosophy of its owner can be summed up by his words, 'use your common sense and there is no need for rules and regulations'. A bus leaves from the village every half hour to Penzance but it only takes about 25 minutes to walk.

Facilities	Directions
The small toilet block is traditional in style, bright and cheerful. Washing machine, dryer with large sink. Reception carries some emergencies supplies. Simple meals served in a pleasant room with TV/radio and small library. Kettle, tea ,coffee and sugar provided with welcome drink on arrival. Off site: Village has shops, pub etc. Beach, boat launching, bicycle hire and fishing 1.5 miles.	Take the A30 from Penzance. At second roundabout take fourth exit signed Madron. Take fourth turn right into Joseph's Lane signed Gulval, then next left signed Bone Valley. Park is 600 yards on the left. O.S.GR: SW461318. GPS: 50.13414, -5.5526

Open: All year.

Charges guide

Per person	£ 3.00
pitch	£ 4.00 - £ 6.00
electricity	£ 3.00

Penzance
Wayfarers Camping & Caravan Park
Relubbus Lane, St Hilary, Penzance TR20 9EF (Cornwall) T: **01736 763326**. E: elaine@wayfarerspark.co.uk
alanrogers.com/UK0065

Wayfarers is a neat and tidy garden-like park reserved for adults only in rural Cornwall. Sheltered by perimeter trees and consisting of two finely mown fields interspersed by shrubs and palm-like trees, 42 places are available for caravans (up to 23 ft. single axle), motorcaravans (up to 22 ft) and tents, plus four holiday caravans to rent. There are 36 pitches with 16A electricity with hardstanding available on 24. Should you enjoy walking you can follow the River Hayle down to St Erth. There are many more suggestions with maps and a good display of leaflets in the information room, including a star chart.

Facilities	Directions
The modern toilet block is fully equipped. Ladies have a wash cubicle and there are two smart en-suite shower rooms (key system). Fully equipped laundry. Dishwashing sinks in the house. Shop stocks basics. No twin axle caravans. Dogs are not accepted. Off site: Two pubs with food in Goldsithney 1 mile. Fishing 1 mile. Golf 1.5 miles. Riding 1 mile. Bicycle hire 2 miles. Boat launching 5 miles. Beach 2 miles. Sailing 5 miles.	Following the A30 Penzance road take the A394 Helston road after the St Ives turning. Follow for 1 mile then turn left on the B3280 and pass through Goldsithney village and site is 1 mile further on left. O.S.GR: SW559314. GPS: 50.133167, -5.416833

Open: April - September.

Charges guide

Per unit incl. 2 persons and electricity	£ 11.00 - £ 19.00
extra person	£ 5.00

Polruan-by-Fowey
Polruan Holidays Camping & Caravanning
Polruan-by-Fowey PL23 1QH (Cornwall) T: **01726 870263**. E: polholiday@aol.com
alanrogers.com/UK0190

Polruan is a rural site in an elevated position on the opposite side of the river to Fowey, 200 metres from the Coastal path. With 47 touring pitches and 10 holiday caravans to let, this is a very pleasant little site. The holiday homes are arranged in a neat circle, with a central area for some touring units, including seven pitches with gravel hardstanding and electricity, one fully serviced. The remaining touring pitches are in an adjacent field with eight electricity hook-ups, which is part level for motorcaravans and part on a gentle slope for tents. There are lovely sea views, but it could be a little exposed to the wind.

Facilities	Directions
The fully equipped sanitary block has modern, controllable showers, large enough for an adult and child. Laundry room and dishwashing sinks. Motorcaravan service facilities. Range of recycling bins. Reception (with a small terrace) doubles as a shop for everyday needs. Gas. Drinks machine and freezer for ice packs. Tourist information and bus timetables (for Looe, etc). Sloping field area with swings for children. Off site: Coastal path 200 m. Fishing 0.5 miles. Riding or bicycle hire 3 miles. Golf 10 miles.	From main A390 at East Taphouse take B3359 towards Looe. After 5 miles fork right signed Bodinnick and ferry. Watch for signs for Polruan and site to left. Follow these carefully along narrow Cornish lanes to site on right just before village. O.S.GR: SX133509. GPS: 50.32759, -4.62515

Open: Easter - 1 October.

Charges guide

Per unit incl. 1 or 2 persons and electricity	£ 11.00 - £ 17.00
extra person	£ 1.50 - £ 3.00
No credit cards.	

Redruth

Lanyon Holiday Park

Loscombe Lane, Four Lanes, Redruth TR16 6LP (Cornwall) T: **01209 313474**
E:**info@lanyonholidaypark.co.uk** **alanrogers.com/UK0016**

Lanyon's location is a pleasant surprise after the somewhat grey landscape found in parts of the tip of Cornwall. Tucked away down a lane, the holiday caravans are attractively situated with hedged touring fields beyond. A neat tarmac road curves around to reception, the pub and an indoor swimming pool. There are 25 large hedged touring pitches around the edge of two level fields and room for around 40 tents in high season in a separate field. A large play area for children is overlooked by the roof top terrace of the bar. This is a pleasant, nice relaxed destination for a family holiday with something for everyone and splendid views across the surrounding countryside to the sea. Lanyon is well positioned for travel to the north and south coasts. The nearest beach is at Porthreath, although the park itself offers a small heated pool and meals are available in the pub. The holiday homes include 26 that are privately owned and 18 available to rent.

Facilities

Three fully equipped toilet blocks, the one attached to reception with heating. The other two are of 'portacabin' type but well maintained. Showers may be in short supply at peak times. Laundry room. Bar serving meals (22/5-5/9). Heated indoor pool (10 x 4 m. Apr - Oct). Games room. Play area and trampoline. Off site: Riding, fishing and bicycle hire 2 miles. Golf 5 miles. Beach 5 miles. Watersports at St Stithian's reservoir 1 mile.

Open: Easter - 31 October.

Directions

From southwest side of Redruth take B3297 Helston road. After 1 mile enter Four Lanes village. Pass two shops then take second right into Loscombe Lane. Follow to park on right. O.S.GR: SW683387. GPS: 50.20292, -5.24554

Charges guide

Per unit incl. 2 persons and electricity	£ 14.00 - £ 22.00
extra person	£ 2.00 - £ 8.00

Minimum stay 5 nights in high season.

LANYON HOLIDAY PARK

Here at Lanyon Holiday Park, Cornwall we offer one of the best quality campsites in Cornwall. Camping pitches are large with short grass, Motor Homes, RVS and Touring Caravans are welcome. Self Catering modern Lodges and Holiday Static Caravans are available to hire

explore south cornwall

Tel No: 01209 313474 || info@lanyonholidaypark.co.uk
Loscombe Lane, Four Lanes, Nr. Redruth, Cornwall, TR16 6LP
www.lanyonholidaypark.co.uk

Redruth

Tehidy Holiday Park

Harris Mill, Illogan, Redruth TR16 4JQ (Cornwall) T: **01209 216489**. E: **holiday@tehidy.co.uk**
alanrogers.com/UK0115

A traditional family park, Tehidy offers 30 touring pitches, 24 mobile homes to rent and six bungalows. Set on a wooded hillside with a stream at the bottom, there is direct access to a woodland walk alive with primroses and bluebells in springtime. The pitches are terraced where necessary and some are hedged, with others part fenced and with views across the countryside. All have 10A electricity and there are a few with hardstanding. The nearest beach is at Portreath which has a deep rock pool for swimming at low tide. The owners live on site and are constantly looking for ways to improve the site and to provide a peaceful and relaxing environment. Whilst the grass is neatly cut, the banks are left for nature to develop. There is a request bus stop outside the entrance for Truro, St Ives and Newquay. This is surfing country but you can also windsurf at St Stithian's reservoir. Tehidy Country Park (250 acres of woodland) is nearby, together with Tehidy Golf Club.

Facilities

Modern fully equipped toilet block. Laundry facilities. Reception with shop area. Games room and tourist information. Play area with small trampoline. Picnic tables. Woodland walk. Local takeaway delivery. Pub and restaurant within walking distance. WiFi. Dogs are not accepted. Off site: Beach 2.5 miles. Golf 1 mile. Bicycle hire 1 mile. Riding 2.5 miles. Sailing 4 miles.

Open: March - November.

Directions

Leave A30 at exit for Redruth, Porthtowan and Portreath. Follow further signs for Porthreath and pick up signs to site. O.S.GR: SW681433. GPS: 50.244939, -5.252935

Charges guide

Per unit incl. 2 persons and electricity	£ 12.00 - £ 18.00
extra person	£ 2.00

See advertisement on page 25

Relubbus
River Valley Country Park
Relubbus, Penzance TR20 9ER (Cornwall) T: **01736 763398**. E: rivervalley@surfbay.dircon.co.uk

alanrogers.com/UK0060

River Valley is a quiet park set in the 18 acres of a partly wooded, peaceful river valley. It offers a mix of 106 timber lodges, caravan holiday homes and 40 touring pitches. The large, well spaced touring pitches are in small meadows or natural clearings. Most are clearly defined with shrubs, hedges or trees and 15A electrical connections are available. The caravan holiday homes and lodges, some privately owned, are in more or less separate areas, beside the river at the far end of the park or on the hillside at the back. A fence separates the park from the river and there is a pleasant walk for 2.5 miles alongside it. Much of the valley is a protected nature reserve and the park encourages wildlife by not using weed killers and by leaving parts uncut – badgers, foxes, herons, kingfishers and glow-worms are regular visitors. St Michael's Mount is only three miles and can be reached by footpath. This is a very special park, very well run by Brian and Eileen Milsom. A member of the Surf Bay Leisure Group.

Facilities

Three well maintained toilet blocks include family shower rooms. Some private cabins for ladies and make-up room with hair dryers. Separate laundry facilities and baby bath. Motorcaravan service point. Shop and takeaway (Easter - September). Off site: Bicycle hire 5 miles. Riding, fishing and golf 3 miles. Beach 3 miles.

Open: 31 March - 27 October.

Directions

From A30 at St Michaels Mount roundabout, take A394 towards Helston. At next roundabout take B3280 to Relubbus. In about 3 miles in village turn left just over a small bridge. O.S.GR: SW566320. GPS: 50.142906, -5.412685

Charges 2010

Per unit incl. 4 persons and electricity	£ 15.00 - £ 32.00

Min. charge 2 adults per vehicle.

Saint Agnes
Beacon Cottage Farm Holidays
Beacon Drive, Saint Agnes TR5 0NU (Cornwall) T: **01872 552347**. E: beaconcottagefarm@lineone.net

alanrogers.com/UK0125

Amazing views greet you as you arrive at Beacon Farm. The stark remains of Wheal Coates tin mine stand out against the cliffs and views over the sea stretch for 25 miles – as far as St Ives. A mixed beef and arable farm, Beacon has its own home bred herd of beef cows and calves. The buildings and the impressive stone walls are extremely well maintained. One large, sloping field and a smaller one enjoy sea views but can be less sheltered than the pitches in smaller paddocks which are sheltered by walls and trees. In all there are 70 pitches of varying size, 42 with 10A electricity. This is a truly popular area with walkers and birdwatchers. A 10 minute walk takes you to Chapel Porth beach an unspoilt sandy cove offering excellent swimming and surfing, with caves and rock pools to explore. St Agnes with good shops and restaurants is 1.5 miles away by car or you can walk through fields past the foot of St Agnes' Beacon. Beacon Farm has been in the same hands for many generations and has been welcoming visitors to stay since 1927. Two stone holiday cottages are available to rent.

Facilities

Good stone built toilet blocks are fully equipped and include a family room. Baby bath and changing mat. Laundry room. Fresh supplies are kept in reception (papers, milk, bread and eggs). Fish and chip van calls once a week. Play area with adventure type equipment. Off site: Fishing and beach 0.5 miles. Riding 1.5 miles. Bicycle hire 2 miles. Golf 3 miles.

Open: Easter/1 April - 30 September.

Directions

From the A30 travelling west take the B3277 (signed St Agnes) at the Chiverton roundabout. At the mini-roundabout approaching St Agnes, turn left for Chapel Porth and follow brown Beacon Cottage Farm signs. O.S.GR: SW705503. GPS: 50.30567, -5.2249

Charges guide

Per unit incl. 2 persons and electricity	£ 18.50 - £ 24.50
extra person	£ 4.50
child (2-12 yrs)	£ 3.00
dog	£ 2.00

33

Saint Austell
Heligan Park
Saint Ewe, Saint Austell PL26 6EL (Cornwall) T: 01726 843485. E: info@heliganpark.co.uk
alanrogers.com/UK0410

A peaceful, attractive park in a mature garden setting, Heligan Park complements its sister site, Pentewan Sands with its busy beach life and many activities. One can enjoy the mature trees and flowering shrubs here which have been further landscaped to provide an attractive situation for a number of holiday homes (some 17 to rent). These face out over a part of the 'Lost Valley' of Heligan fame with the touring pitches below on sloping grass, some terraced and others in a more level situation (some with hardstanding) amongst trees and shrubs. In all, there are 100 good sized touring pitches, 80 with electricity (16A). Part of the park's boundary actually edges The Lost Gardens of Heligan (although nothing can be seen), and at some time the land must have been part of the Gardens. The many facilities of Pentewan Sands are open to Heligan Park visitors. There is access to the Pentewan Trail to walk or cycle into Mevagissey or Pentewan. You can take a bus for the trip back up the hill.

Facilities
Fully equipped and well kept, the modern, heated toilet block includes a unisex room with bath and small size bath. Extra showers in separate block. Fully equipped laundry room. Small shop (Easter - 14/09). Adventure playground. Off site: Beach/sailing 1.5 miles. Riding 2 miles. Golf 3.5 miles. Bicycle hire/boat launching. Lost Gardens of Heligan next door.

Open: Mid January - end November.

Directions
From St Austell ring road take B3273 for Mevagissey. After 3.5 miles, pass Pentewan Sands, continue up the hill and turn right following site signs. Park is on the left just before reaching Heligan Gardens.
O.S.GR: SW999464. GPS: 50.288833, -4.812083

Charges guide
Per unit incl. 2 persons and electricity	£ 10.70 - £ 24.95
extra person	£ 1.95 - £ 4.20
child (3-15 yrs)	£ 1.05 - £ 3.10
extra tent, car or boat	£ 1.55 - £ 2.00

Saint Austell
Trencreek Farm Country Holiday Park
Hewas Water, Saint Austell PL26 7JG (Cornwall) T: 01726 882540. E: reception@trencreek.co.uk
alanrogers.com/UK0415

Trencreek Farm is a friendly, well equipped park set in 56 acres of rolling Cornish countryside of woodland and lakes and is a wonderful place for a family holiday. Although no longer a working farm, there are some animals to see, including pot bellied pigs and pigmy goats, carefully kept in pens. The grassy pitches are of a good size, most with electrical connections and arranged around the edges of sloping fields. The camping fields surround the former, central farm buildings which have been converted to house all the amenities, including a heated swimming pool. Also very popular are four small course fishing lakes, each of which is stocked with a different range of fish. The park managers, Bev and Gary Cox, have worked hard to bring the park up to standard and encourage a happy and friendly atmosphere. In peak season they organise a club for children (15.00-17.00, Monday to Friday), along with quiz nights in the bar. The animals are an obvious attraction for children and the fishing lakes for fathers, but there is always the pool for the rest of the family. Mobile homes and chalets are available for rent. A member of the Surf Bay Leisure group.

Facilities
Two traditional style toilet blocks are supplemented by a chalet block containing five en-suite units per sex (charged). Launderette. Shop. Bar, restaurant. Takeaway food. Heated swimming pool. Tennis court. Sports field. Fishing (small charge). Adventure play area. TV and games room. Children's farm. Off site: Nearest beach 4 miles. Golf (18-hole) 3 miles. Riding and bicycle hire 4 miles. Shipwreck rescue and heritage centre 5 miles. The Lost Gardens of Heligan 3 miles. Eden Project 3 miles.

Open: 7 April - 29 October.

Directions
Site is four miles west of St Austell. Take the A390 and then fork left to join the B3287 and the site is 1 mile further on the left. O.S.GR: SW965484.
GPS: 50.30075, -4.85708

Charges guide
Per unit incl. 2 persons	£ 8.50 - £ 16.00
incl. electricity	£ 10.45 - £ 18.00
extra person (over 3 yrs)	£ 1.50
dog	£ 1.00

Saint Austell

Carlyon Bay Caravan & Camping Park

Bethesda, Carlyon Bay, Saint Austell PL25 3RE (Cornwall) T: 01726 812735. E: holidays@carlyonbay.net
alanrogers.com/UK0290

Tranquil open meadows edged by mature woodland, well cared for by the Taylor family who live on site, provide a beautiful holiday setting with the nearest beach five minutes walk from the top gate. The original farm buildings have been converted and added to, providing an attractive covered, central area with a certain individuality of design which is very pleasing. Pitches are in five spacious areas and allow for a family meadow and a dog free meadow (high season only). There are 115 marked pitches with electricity (10/16A), some with hardstanding and 8 have full services. All are on flat, terraced or gently sloping grass with flowers and flowering shrubs or edged with trees. In addition to the attractive kidney shaped pool and paddling pool there is now a large rectangular pool (also heated) within a walled and paved area which is excellent for sunbathing. This forms part of the central area at the heart of the site and complete with tables and chairs it is the place to enjoy family entertainment in high season. There is also a pleasant family pub and Kidsworld for children within walking distance.

Facilities

Three individually designed, modern toilet blocks (one heated) provide a full range of comfortable facilities for all your needs. Fully equipped laundry. Modern reception with little shop. Takeaway (May - mid Sept). Heated swimming and paddling pools (Whitsun - Sept). TV lounge. Crazy golf. Play areas. Eden Project tickets. Dogs are accepted but max. 2. Off site: Pub 1 mile. Bus on main road. Golf. Riding 3 miles. Bicycle hire 4 miles. Sailing 2 miles. Boat launching 5 miles. Coastal footpath nearby. Eden Project 2 miles.

Open: Easter/1 April - end September.

Directions

From Plymouth on A390, pass Lostwithiel and 1 mile after village of St Blazey, turn left at roundabout beside Britannia Inn. After 400 yds turn right on a concrete road and right again at site sign. O.S.GR: SX053526. GPS: 50.34085, -4.737217

Charges guide

Per unit incl. 2 persons, electricity	£ 13.00 - £ 28.00
extra person	£ 5.00
child (3-15 yrs)	£ 4.00

Camping Cheques accepted.

- Award winning family park 2 miles from Eden Project
- Up to 180 touring pitches (no statics) • Footpath to large sandy beach
- Close to championship golf course • Heated swimming & paddling pool
- Set in over 30 acres of meadows and mature woodlands
- Ben's Play World for kids nearby • Pool, table-tennis and crazy-golf

For colour brochure call: **01726 812735**
www.carlyonbay.net e-mail:holidays@carlyonbay.net

Saint Ives

Ayr Holiday Park

Higher Ayr, Saint Ives TR26 1EJ (Cornwall) T: 01736 795855. E: recept@ayrholidaypark.co.uk
alanrogers.com/UK0030

Ayr Holiday Park has an unparalleled position overlooking St Ives Bay and Porthmeor beach and is a popular well cared for site. On first arrival it may seem to be all caravan holiday homes, but behind them is a series of naturally sloping fields with marvellous views providing a total of 90 pitches, of which 40 are for touring caravans and motorcaravans. These pitches are on grass, all with 16A electricity and several fully serviced. An extra field for tents is open in July and August. A 'state of the art' toilet block provides excellent facilities in a colourful and modern design.

Facilities

The excellent toilet block includes two family shower rooms and facilities for baby changing and disabled people. Wetsuit showers. Fully equipped laundry room. Motorcaravan point. Games room with TV, hot drinks and snack machines. Adventure play area. Contact park if you wish to take a dog. Off site: Spa shop nearby. Tate Gallery and beaches within walking distance. Leisure centre with indoor pool nearby. Golf 1 mile. Riding 2 miles. Sea and coarse fishing 2-3 miles.

Open: All year.

Directions

Follow signs for St Ives for heavy vehicles (not town centre). After 2 miles join the B3311 and then the B3306 1 mile from St Ives. Still heading for St Ives turn left at mini-roundabout following signs through residential areas. Park is 600 yds at Ayr Terrace. O.S.GR: SW515388. GPS: 50.21261, -5.48928

Charges guide

Per unit incl. 2 persons, electricity	£ 12.75 - £ 30.50
extra person	£ 3.50 - £ 6.00
child (5-16 yrs)	£ 1.75 - £ 3.00

Saint Ives

Little Trevarrack Holiday Park

Laity Lane, Carbis Bay, Saint Ives TR26 3HW (Cornwall) T: 01736 797580. E: info@littletrevarrack.co.uk
alanrogers.com/UK0035

Little Trevarrack is a traditional Cornish park covering 20 acres, with wonderful views from the top of the site across St Ives bay towards Hayle and the surrounding countryside. It is owned by Neil, son of the owners of Polmanter Park, and Annette Osborne and has a smart, large reception and entrance. There are 234 pitches, in five open fields (the top ones with gentle slopes), 153 with 10A electricity and 15 with water and drain as well. Bushes and hedging have grown to provide individual pitches and give a continental appearance to the park. A smart heated outdoor pool also provides a paddling pool and sunbathing area. Landscaped and fenced, a new play area is alongside. Carbis Bay with its safe sandy beach is ideal for families with young children and is less than a mile away. In high season a bus runs hourly into St Ives. This is a developing park which will provide a quiet, peaceful base from which to explore St Ives and the southern tip of Cornwall.

Facilities

The large, central toilet block is modern and well equipped. Baby room and facilities for disabled visitors in the reception building. Laundry. Heated swimming and paddling pools (27/5-12/9). Games room. Internet access and WiFi. Play area and play field. Wild flower field with paths for dog walking. No kites allowed. Early and late arrivals area. Off site: Golf and riding 2 miles. Bicycle hire 4 miles. Beach and fishing 1 mile. Dogs are banned from the St Ives beaches in high season.

Open: 1 April - 30 September.

Directions

Follow signs for St Ives and take A3074 to Carbis Bay. Site is signed on left opposite junction to Carbis Bay beach. Follow road for 150 yds, cross small crossroads and site is the second turn on the right.
O.S.GR: SW52737. GPS: 50.187233, -5.470833

Charges guide

Per unit incl. 2 persons and electricity	£ 15.50 - £ 26.00
extra person	£ 3.50 - £ 6.50
child (3-15 yrs)	£ 2.00 - £ 4.50
dog (max. 2)	£ 1.00 - £ 2.50

Saint Ives

Polmanter Tourist Park

Halsetown, Saint Ives TR26 3LX (Cornwall) T: 01736 795640. E: reception@polmanter.com
alanrogers.com/UK0050

A popular and attractively developed park, Polmanter is located high up at the back of St Ives, with wonderful sea and country views. The Osborne family has worked hard to develop Polmanter as a complete family base. Converted farm buildings provide a cosy bar lounge with a conservatory overlooking the heated swimming pool. The 250 touring pitches (no caravan holiday homes) are well spaced in several fields divided by established shrubs and hedges giving large, level, individual pitches with connecting tarmac roads. There are 87 serviced pitches with electricity, water, waste water and TV point, ten with hardstanding. Another 113 pitches have 16A electricity. It is a busy park with a happy atmosphere within 1.5 miles of St Ives. A footpath leads from the park (20 minutes downhill) or there is a bus service from the park in high season (hourly, 10.00 - midnight). A member of the Best of British group.

Facilities

Three fully equipped toilet blocks can be heated and include en-suite family rooms. Facilities for disabled visitors. Baby room. Fully equipped laundry. Motorcaravan service point. Well stocked shop. Bar with food and family area (Whitsun - mid Sept). Takeaway. Heated swimming pool (Whitsun - mid Sept). Some entertainment (peak season). Tennis. Putting. Play area. Sports field. Games room. Off site: Golf 1 mile. Fishing, riding, bicycle hire and boat launching within 2 miles. Indoor pool and leisure centre at St Ives. Note: dogs are banned from the St Ives beaches in high season.

Open: 1 April - 31 October.

Directions

Take A3074 to St Ives from the A30 and then first left at a mini-roundabout taking 'Holiday Route' (B3311) to St Ives (Halsetown). At T-junction turn right for Halsetown, right again at the Halsetown Inn then first left. O.S.GR: SW509392. GPS: 50.196183, -5.491017

Charges guide

Per unit incl. 2 persons and electricity	£ 15.00 - £ 28.00
extra person	£ 3.00 - £ 7.00
child (3-15 yrs)	£ 2.50 - £ 5.50
dog (max. 2)	free - £ 3.00

Camping Cheques accepted.

Saint Ives
Trevalgan Touring Park

Saint Ives TR26 3BJ (Cornwall) T: 01736 792048. E: recept@trevalgantouringpark.co.uk
alanrogers.com/UK0040

Trevalgan is owned by the same family that owns Ayr Holiday Park. It is a quiet, traditional style of park, located on the cliffs 1.5 miles west of bustling St Ives. It is a truly rural location where you can enjoy spectacular views and an abundance of flora and fauna. There are 120 clearly marked pitches (88 with 16A electricity and some with water as well) in two level fields edged by Cornish stone walls – it could be a little exposed on a windy day. The park is very popular with walkers with direct access to the coastal path. A member of the Countryside Discovery group.

Facilities

A fully equipped toilet block includes a baby room and facilities for disabled visitors. Motorcaravan service point. Campers' kitchen. Small shop (in reception). Mobile shop calls daily. Gas supplies. Games field, adventure play area and crazy golf. Giant draughts and chess. Purpose built games room with TV and coffee machine. Off site: Fishing 3 miles, bicycle hire 8 miles, riding and golf within 2 miles. Regular bus service to St Ives and back June - mid Sept. As well as the coastal path, a path leads to St Ives across the fields (30-40 minutes).

Open: 1 May - 30 September.

Directions

Approach site down a narrow Cornish lane from the B3306 St Ives - Lands End road, following sign. O.S.GR: SW490400. GPS: 50.20769, -5.51882

Charges guide

Per unit incl. 2 persons	
and electricity	£ 12.75 - £ 30.50
extra person	£ 3.50 - £ 6.00
child (5-16 yrs)	£ 1.75 - £ 3.00
dog	£ 1.50 - £ 3.00

RAC AA

For a more rural experience

'A touring park just 2 miles from St.Ives town centre. Beautiful scenery, new facilities, serviced pitches, summer bus service to town. Ideal for families, walkers, cyclists - explore St.Ives and West Cornwall.'

www.trevalgantouringpark.co.uk   Telephone: 01736 792048

Saint Just
Roselands Caravan & Camping Park

Dowran, Saint Just, Penzance TR19 7RS (Cornwall) T: 01736 788571. E: info@roselands.co.uk
alanrogers.com/UK0025

Roselands is a small, family owned park situated on the Cornish moors overlooking the village of St Just and with marvellous views of the sea and countryside around Lands End. In all there are 14 holiday homes to let, 17 level grassy touring pitches (all with 16A electricity) and some provision for tents. The owner's home provides a bar and conservatory, along with reception and a small shop, sit in the centre of the park. The conservatory acts as a community family room with games, internet facility and tourist information with a play area outside and a games room nearby. This area is very popular with walkers and birdwatchers. The park itself originated in 1972 in old clay pits – the area where most of the holiday homes are located was one of the pits and is consequently very sheltered. Subsequent owners have added to the house and the current owners, Craig and Kerry with their young family do everything themselves. This includes running the little bar which also serves food and making suggestions for walks and what to see and do. Craig is very knowledgeable and will also organise fishing trips.

Facilities

Small traditional toilet block, fully equipped and can be heated. Laundry facilities. Small shop mainly for basics and gas. Bar with bar food served in conservatory (all year). TV and internet access. Play area. Games room. Bicycle hire. Off site: Fishing and Golf 1 mile. Riding 2 miles. Beach and surfing 2 miles at Sennen Cove. Boat launching 5 miles. Nearby Lands End and Cape Cornwall. Minack Outdoor Theatre.

Open: 1 January - 31 October.

Directions

Take the A3071 from Penzance for St Just. Follow for 5.5 miles and 0.5 miles before St Just turn left at sign for site. O.S.GR: SW386302. GPS: 50.11323, -5.658

Charges guide

Per unit incl. 2 persons	
Per unit incl. 2 persons	£ 8.00 - £ 10.00
incl. electricity	£ 10.00 - £ 12.50
extra person	£ 2.00
child (under 5 yrs)	£ 1.00

Saint Mabyn
Glenmorris Park
Longstone Road, Saint Mabyn PL30 3BY (Cornwall) T: 01208 841677. E: info@glenmorris.co.uk
alanrogers.com/UK0230

The beaches of north Cornwall and the wilds of Bodmin Moor are all an easy drive from Glenmorris Park. The park is being gradually improved and carefully maintained by the Hayman family and it provides a spacious and relaxed atmosphere. There are 80 level pitches, 60 with 16A electricity, on well drained and well mown grass with 20 hardstandings. There are some caravan holiday homes to let. A nice, sheltered outdoor pool is an added attraction. The local village inn has a good reputation for food. The Camel Trail is only two miles, providing a means to cycle or walk to Bodmin, Wadebridge or Padstow.

Facilities

The fully equipped modern toilet block includes an en-suite unit per sex. Laundry. Heated outdoor swimming pool and paddling pool (late May - early Sept), surrounded by a sheltered, paved and grass sunbathing areas. Good, fenced adventure play area with bark safety base. Play area for small children. Games room. Caravan storage. Off site: Fishing, riding or golf 3 miles, bicycle hire 5 miles.

Open: 1 April - mid October.

Directions

From Bodmin or Wadebridge on A389, take B3266 north signed Camelford. At village of Longstone turn left signed St Mabyn and brown camping sign. Site is 400 yds. on right. Ignore all other signs to St Mabyn. O.S.GR: SX053732. GPS: 50.5278, -4.745183

Charges guide

Per person	£ 4.00 - £ 5.50
child (3-15 yrs)	£ 1.25 - £ 1.50
electricity (16A)	£ 3.30

Saint Martins by Looe
Polborder House Caravan & Camping Park
Bucklawren Road, Saint Martins by Looe PL13 1NZ (Cornwall) T: 01503 240265.
E: reception@peaceful-polborder.co.uk alanrogers.com/UK0320

Polborder House is a lovely site which may appeal to those who prefer a quiet, well kept little family site to the larger ones with many on-site activities. With good countryside views, up to 36 touring units can be accommodated on well tended grass. Pitches are marked with some hedging between pairs of pitches to give privacy and most have electrical connections (16A). There are several hardstandings and 17 serviced pitches. The new owners, Amanda and Dale Byers, live on the park and are most helpful. The nearest beach a 20-25 minutes walk from a gate in the corner of the park.

Facilities

The fully equipped sanitary block (key entry) includes a baby room, laundry room, and three covered sinks outside for dishwashing. En-suite toilet unit for disabled visitors has a ramped approach. Rubbish is recycled. Shop for gas and basics, and some camping accessories. Toddler's play area. Hut with tourist information. Off site: Fishing, golf and boat launching within 2 miles. Riding 6 miles. Restaurant 500 m. Diving school at Seaton, scuba centre and fishing trips at Looe. Seaton 2 miles, Looe 2.5 miles.

Open: All year.

Directions

Park is less than half a mile south of the B3253. Turn off 2 miles east of Looe and follow signs to park and Monkey Sanctuary at junctions; care is needed with narrow road. O.S.GR: SX283555. GPS: 50.377217, -4.4185

Charges guide

Per unit incl. 2 persons and electricity	£ 12.50 - £ 21.00
extra person	£ 4.00 - £ 5.50
child (5-16 yrs)	£ 2.00 - £ 3.00

Saltash
Dolbeare Caravan & Camping Park
Saint Ive Road, Landrake, Saltash PL12 5AF (Cornwall) T: 01752 851332. E: reception@dolbeare.co.uk
alanrogers.com/UK0440

Ian and Chris are now the proud owners of this small, but well-kept park. Dolbeare is in a rural setting (but very easily accessible from the main A38) and consists of a large rectangular field of neat grass edged with trees and sloping slightly at the top, connected by a gravel road, and a camping paddock. All 66 pitches are on hardstanding and have 16A electricity connections. An extra field provides the camping paddock and can also be used for rallies. Part of it is set aside for a games field with a dog walk being developed at the top of the park.

Facilities

The fully equipped heated toilet block to one side of the field. Indoor dishwashing sinks. Laundry next to reception. Fridge and freezer in camping field. Motorcaravan services. Reception doubles as a small shop for basics including gas (limited hours out of main season). Site barrier (card system with £5 deposit). Low level adventure playground. Giant chess. Off site: Fishing and riding 3 miles. Golf 5.5 miles. Nearest beach 8 miles.

Open: All year.

See advertisement on page 27

Directions

Crossing the Tamar Bridge into Cornwall, continue on A38 for a further 4 miles. In Landrake village turn right following signs and site is 0.75 miles on the right. O.S.GR: SX366616. GPS: 50.43064, -4.30551

Charges guide

Per unit incl. 2 persons and electricity	£ 13.20 - £ 18.60
extra person	£ 3.50
child (5-16 yrs)	£ 2.25

Truro

Porthtowan Tourist Park

Mile Hill, Porthtowan, Truro TR4 8TY (Cornwall) T: **01209 890256**. E: **Admin@PorthtowanTouristPark.co.uk**

alanrogers.com/UK0014

This delightful, sheltered park is set a mile back from the pretty seaside village of Porthtowan, a haven for surfers but enjoyed by families who can explore the rock pools and coves. The beach has Blue Flag status. In an Area of Outstanding Natural Beauty, tall chimney stacks are a reminder of the tin mining for which this area of Cornwall was once renowned. This is now a peaceful spot with plenty of space on the park and tall trees surrounding the three camping fields. There are 80 pitches around the edges of the fields, on level grass and half with 10A electricity. There are a few hardstandings. The park is attractively laid out with tarmac roads and flowering shrubs. The facilities were spotless when we visited in high season. There is a recycling box for odds and ends left behind by holidaymakers but of potential use to future visitors. A large adventure-type play area in the centre of the large top field is popular. There is a waiting list for seasonal pitches and caravan storage. The Coast-to-Coast Tramway trail passes within half a mile of the site. The Newquay - St Ives bus stops in the village.

Facilities	Directions
Modern fully equipped toilet block with two en-suite family rooms also suitable for disabled visitors. Shop in reception. Games room with tourist information. Adventure type play area. Fish and chip van calls Wednesday teatimes. Bicycle hire by arrangement. Off site: Nearest beach 1 mile. Riding 200 yds. Fishing and golf 8 miles.	From the A30 take exit for Redruth, Porthtowan and Portreath and follow signs for Porthtown for 2 miles. At T-junction turn right up hill to park on the left just past a restaurant. O.S.GR: SW694463. GPS: 50.27374, -5.23768

Open: 1 April - 30 September.

Charges guide

Per unit incl. 2 persons and electricity	£ 11.50 - £ 19.00
extra person	£ 2,50 - £ 4.00

A quiet family site with large level pitches on the outskirts of the village. Close to Blue Flag beach, Coastal Path and Cycle Trail, and central for touring Cornwall.

Mile Hill, Porthtowan, Truro, Cornwall. TR4 8TY
01209 890256
admin@porthtowantouristpark.co.uk
www.porthtowantouristpark.co.uk

Truro
Chacewater Park

Cox Hill, Chacewater, Truro TR4 8LY (Cornwall) T: 01209 820762. E: enquiries@chacewaterpark.co.uk

alanrogers.com/UK0010

For those who want to be away from the hectic coastal resorts and to take advantage of the peace and quiet of an 'adults only' park, this will be an excellent value-for-money choice. Chacewater has a pleasant rural situation and the site is run with care and attention by Richard Peterken and his daughters Debbie and Mandy. It provides 100 level touring pitches, all with electricity (10A) and 80 with hardstanding, in two large field areas (slight slope) edged with trees or in small bays formed by hedges. There are 29 serviced pitches (electricity, water, and drainage connections) and an area for dog owners. The modern reception is not at the entrance but through the park to one side in a pleasant courtyard area. Truro is only 5 miles and there is a good choice of beaches north or south within 5-10 miles. A bus stop is only 100 yards from the park entrance.

Facilities

The main toilet block provides well equipped showers and two en-suite units. Laundry room. Second fully equipped block near reception providing roomy showers open direct to outside. Gas supplies. Icepack service. Library in reception. Only adults are accepted (over 30 yrs). One dog (certain breeds) only by arrangement. Off site: Golf, riding and bicycle hire, all within 3 miles. Bus stop 100 yds. Cornish tramways/railway coast-to-coast trail to walk or cycle nearby.

Open: 1 May - 30 September.

Directions

From the A30 about 28 miles west of Bodmin take A3047 signed Scorrier and continue under bridge to roundabout and take left towards St Day. Continue for 500 yards turning right at the crossroads onto the B3298 signed St Day and continue for 1 mile. Turn left at the crossroads and continue for 0.75 miles, then turn left at the crossroad with blue camping sign (by Truro Tractors). Chacewater Park is the next right. O.S.GR: SW742439. GPS: 50.250802, -5.172557

Charges guide

Per unit incl. 2 persons	£ 13.00 - £ 16.00
dog (one only)	£ 1.00

Weekly rates for pre-booked pitches.
Discounts for senior citizens.

Truro
Killiwerris Camping & Caravan Park

Penstraze, Chacewater, Truro TR4 8PF (Cornwall) T: 01872 561356. E: killiwerris @aol.com

alanrogers.com/UK0012

Tucked down a Cornish lane, Killiwerris is a rare find. It has been developed from a large garden and the field surrounding the house into a small and delightful touring park which provides 20 good sized pitches for caravans and motorcaravans. Of these, 17 are semi-separated either by low fencing or hedging, all with hardstanding in the front field with flowering shrubs sheltered by Monteray pines and other indigenous trees. The birds love it, as do adult humans – the park is 'adult only' so it is very peaceful. Three further pitches are found in the back field. Electricity (10/16A) is available for all the pitches with water points between two. The park is now owned by the Ashurst family and being centrally situated five miles from the city of Truro and four from the coastal village of St Agnes, this is an ideal base to explore the Cornish countryside.

Facilities

A small heated toilet block provides for all needs with one shower each for men and women, and ladies having one toilet/washbasin cubicle. Grab rails for disabled visitors. Separate laundry room. Off site: Bus stop 8 minutes level walk. Chacewater village (shop, pub, etc.) 1 mile. Beach 4.5 miles. Fishing 2 miles. Golf 2 miles. Riding 1.5 miles. Bicycle hire 2-3 miles.

Open: Easter - end October.

Directions

Using the A30 in the direction of Penzance, exit at Chiverton Cross roundabout (this is large roundabout 28 miles west of Bodmin signed for Truro and St Agnes). Take third exit for Blackwater and in 500 yards turn left into Kea Down Road. park is 1 mile on right. O.S.GR: SW753455. GPS: 50.2655, -5.155

Charges guide

Per unit incl. 2 persons, electricity and awning	£ 12.00 - £ 16.00
extra person	£ 3.50
dog (max. 2)	£ 0.50

No credit cards.

Truro
Trethem Mill Touring Park
Saint Just-in-Roseland, Saint Mawes, Truro TR2 5JF (Cornwall) T: 01872 580504. E: reception@trethem.com
alanrogers.com/UK0090

The Akeroyd family are proud of their park and work hard to keep it really well maintained. They aim to attract couples and families who seek peace and tranquillity, and can manage without a bar and on-site entertainment. Trethem is a 'strictly touring' park with 84 pitches all with electricity, 15 with water and waste water. Over 60 are on hardstanding with TV connections. The pitches are large, most on slightly sloping ground, some terraced, with the lower field more level and sheltered. All are individual or in bays, divided by hedging (some still growing) giving your own area. Generally there is a good spacious feel. There is a circular tarmac access road and careful landscaping (the park is a mass of colour in season). The area around reception is particularly pretty where a small watermill has been built amongst the flowers – the sound of gently flowing water is very relaxing. St Mawes is a very popular, pretty village on the Roseland peninsula, which is itself an 'area of outstanding natural beauty'. Only three miles away, Trethem Mill is well placed for either sailing, walking the coastal path around the peninsula, visiting the gardens of Trelissick or Heligan, or simply lazing on the nearby beaches.

Facilities	Directions
The well equipped central toilet block is kept spotlessly clean and is heated in cooler weather. En-suite facilities for disabled visitors which can double as a family room. Baby room (under 4s). Reception/shop, only small but well stocked and licensed. Freezer for ice packs (free). Motorcaravan services. Well equipped, fenced adventure playground (closed at 21.00). Extra field for dog walking. WiFi throughout park. Off site: Fishing 1.5 miles. Bicycle hire 2 miles. Golf 6 miles. Riding 8 miles.	From Tregony follow A3078 to St Mawes. About 2 miles after passing through Trewithian, watch for caravan and camping sign. O.S.GR: SW863264. GPS: 50.19003, -5.00096

Open: 1 April - 3 October.

Charges guide

Per unit incl. 2 persons and electricity	£ 15.00 - £ 22.00
extra person	£ 5.00
child (3-14 yrs)	£ 4.00
dog	£ 1.00

trethem mill
TOURING PARK
★★★★★

...not everything
is black and white...

www.trethem.com

St Just In Roseland Truro Cornwall TR2 5JF   Tel: 01872 580504

Truro
Summer Valley Touring Park
Shortlanesend, Truro TR4 9DW (Cornwall) T: 01872 277878. E: res@summervalley.co.uk
alanrogers.com/UK0510

Summer Valley is a quiet and mature, but very pleasant, small rural park suitable for visiting both the north and south coasts of Cornwall. South facing, the park consists of a large well kept grass area with reception and facilities to one side. A tarmac road circles this and mature trees edge the whole site providing shelter but still allowing rural views. Caravans go on the central area which slopes gently and is divided down the centre with more mature trees and shrubs. The pitches around the perimeter area are semi-divided by shrubs and used more for tents. There is provision for 60 units of all types, but only 50 are used, 45 with electricity connections (10/16A). A Countryside Discovery site.

Facilities	Directions
A good quality toilet block is well maintained. Unisex showers. Washbasins in cabins and one shower/toilet en-suite per sex. Laundry facilities. Campers' rest room with library. Reception/licensed shop for basics. Gas supplies. Small play area.Off site: Village of Shortlanesend within walking distance with post office and pub. Fishing 2.5 miles. Golf 3 miles. Riding 5 miles. Bicycle hire 2.5 miles.	From Truro take the B3284 north, signed Perranporth. Follow for 2.5 miles and site is signed on left just through the village of Shortlanesend. O.S.GR: SW 800479. GPS: 50.29098, -5.08823

Open: 31 March - 31 October.

Charges guide

Per unit incl. 2 persons	£ 11.50 - £ 15.00
extra person	£ 1.00 - £ 1.50
electricity	£ 2.00

41

Truro

Silverbow Park

Goonhavern, Truro TR4 9NX (Cornwall) T: 01872 572347.
alanrogers.com/UK0120

Silverbow has been developed by the Taylor family over many years and they are justifiably proud of their efforts. They believe Silverbow is a way of life and staying is an experience – they have certainly created a relaxed and tranquil atmosphere seeking to encourage couples and young families (teenagers are not accepted). Hard work, planting and landscaping has provided a beautiful environment set in 21 acres. There are 90 tourist pitches which are all of good size and include 69 'super' pitches in a newly developed area, with electricity, water and drainage, which are even larger. Many are on a slight slope with some attractive views. There are also 15 park-owned, high quality leisure homes. Much free space is not used for camping, including an excellent sports area with two grass and two all-weather tennis courts, as well as wild meadow and wooded areas ideal for walks. A natural area with ponds has been created to encourage wildlife (Silverbow was the first in Cornwall to gain the coveted '5-year Bellamy Gold' award for conservation). The park is 2.5 miles from the long sandy beach at Perranporth (30 minutes' walk away from traffic) and six miles from Newquay.

Facilities

Two good toilet blocks include private cabins, four family shower/toilet rooms, two accessible for wheelchairs, and a bath on payment. Laundry room. Motorcaravan services. Free freezer service. Shop for basics (mid May-mid Sept). Covered, heated swimming pool and small paddling pool (mid May - mid Sept) gated and sheltered by high surrounding garden walls. Games room. Adventure playground. Play field. Tennis. Off site: Gliding, riding and fishing nearby. Concessionary green fees are available at Perranporth golf club. Pub within walking distance.

Open: Early May - end September.

Directions

Entrance is directly off the main A3075 road 0.5 miles south of Goonhavern. O.S.GR: SW781531.
GPS: 50.336567, -5.120633

Charges guide

Per unit incl. 2 persons	£ 10.00 - £ 20.00
extra person under 50 yrs	£ 3.00 - £ 6.00
extra child (2-12 yrs) or	
adult over 50 yrs	£ 2.50 - £ 4.50
full service pitch incl. electricity	£ 6.00
dog	free - £ 1.50

Children over 12 yrs with or without parents not accepted. Discounts available.

Truro

Penrose Farm Touring Park

Goonhavern, Truro TR4 9QF (Cornwall) T: 01872 573185. E: penroseholidays@hotmail.co.uk
alanrogers.com/UK0140

Penrose Farm, owned and run by the Welch family, has a quiet and comfortable atmosphere on the edge of the village of Goonhavern. The park is level and sheltered, with the pitches spread over five fields with flower beds and bushes set amongst them. These colourful flowers and those at the entrance give the park a neat and well cared for feel. There are over 100 pitches, many with hardstanding, water and drainage, plus a few seasonal places and some privately owned caravan holiday homes. A play area will amuse children and the family are now offering a simple café menu, including breakfast. It is only a short walk to the village and its popular pub, and buses to Newquay stop in the village. The superb beach at Perranporth is only 2.5 miles. To retain the quiet family image, there are no plans for bars or entertainment and only couples and families are welcome.

Facilities

The fully equipped and refurbished toilet block is well maintained and includes two en-suite family rooms. Facilities for disabled visitors. Well equipped laundry. Small shop. Gas supplies. Takeaway incl. breakfast. Playground. Caravan storage. Off site: Fishing or riding 0.5 miles, golf 1 mile.

Open: 1 April - 31 October.

Directions

Take A30 from Exeter past Bodmin and Indian Queens. Just after wind farm take B3285 to Perranporth. Park is on the left as you enter Goonhavern village.
O.S.GR: SW790535. GPS: 50.340133, -5.106567

Charges guide

Per unit incl. 2 persons	
and 10A electricity	£ 12.00 - £ 21.00
incl. services	£ 14.00 - £ 25.00
extra person (5 yrs and over)	£ 3.00 - £ 3.50
dog	free - £ 2.00

Families and couples only.
Less 50p for over 60s if booked.

Truro

Cosawes Park

Perranarworthal, Truro TR3 7QS (Cornwall) T: 01872 863724. E: info@cosawes.com

alanrogers.com/UK0185

Cosawes is set in a beautiful wooded valley where there are woodland and river walks and the park offers a quiet and relaxing holiday. The Fraser family have owned the site for many years and the recent upgrading of the facilities is excellent, particularly for a site that is open all year. Cosawes now offers 25 large, serviced pitches on gravel hardstandings, each on its own fenced space. These are particularly popular with motorcaravan owners and very useful for twin-axle vans. This still leaves around 35 grass pitches which are slightly sloping, some with electricity. A separate large residential area is private and away from the touring section. The situation of the park makes it good for visiting both the north and south coasts. Falmouth with its maritime museum is well worth visiting, whilst the north coast is popular for its surfing beaches. St Ives, Lands End and the unique Lizard peninsula are all within easy reach.

Facilities

Modern new block beside the new serviced pitches provides 2 en-suite family rooms also good for disabled visitor. Toilets, laundry and dishwashing facilities are downstairs, upstairs are showers and washbasins in cubicles. Another older block is near reception. Dog walking field. WiFi (charged). Walks from site. Off site: Golf and bicycle hire 5 miles. Sailing and boat launching 3-5 miles. Beach at Falmouth 7 miles. Two pubs within walking distance. Supermarket 3 miles.

Open: All year.

Directions

Site is midway between Truro and Falmouth. Approaching from Truro via A39, after village of Perranarworthal, site is signed to the left and is 300 yds up the lane on the left. Use the second entrance. O.S.GR: SW768375.
GPS: 50.197026, -5.128319

Charges guide

Per unit incl. 2 persons	
and electricity	£ 13.00 - £ 15.00
hardstanding, serviced pitch	£ 16.00 - £ 18.50
extra person	£ 1.00 - £ 2.00

Truro

Carnon Downs Caravan & Camping Park

Carnon Downs, Truro TR3 6JJ (Cornwall) T: **01872 862283**. E: info@carnon-downs-caravanpark.co.uk
alanrogers.com/UK0180

Carnon Downs is an excellent all-year park run personally and enthusiastically by Simon Vallance, a very forward-thinking owner. It has been thoughtfully laid out in a series of fields covering 20 acres so that all pitches back onto hedging or areas of flowering shrubs and are arranged to provide some pleasant bays or other, more open grass areas. Gravel roads connect the 150 pitches, most with electricity and over 70 with hardstanding. Of these 55 are serviced, with the newer ones being exceptionally large and surrounded by young shrubs. On arrival you will receive a warm welcome, a neatly presented layout plan of the park and a touring information pack.

Facilities

Two excellent modern, light and airy, heated blocks include en-suite units and dishwashing and facilities for disabled people. Another well maintained block, also heated, includes some washbasins in cubicles and showers (unisex). Three good family bath/shower rooms, one suitable for use by disabled people or families. Mother and toddler room, two baby sinks and full sized bath. Two laundries with freezers. Motorcaravan service point (ask at reception). Good adventure-type play area. Football field. General room with TV. Caravan storage. Off site: Pub/restaurant 100 yds across the road. Fishing 5 miles. Riding or bicycle hire 2 miles. Golf 1 mile. Bus outside site Truro/Falmouth.

Open: All year.

Directions

From Truro take A39 Falmouth road. After 3 miles, park entrance is directly off the Carnon Downs roundabout. O.S.GR: SW805406.
GPS: 50.22529, -5.08012

Charges guide

Per unit incl. 2 persons and electricity (10/16A)	£ 17.70 - £ 25.50
extra person	£ 3.00
child (5-16 yrs)	£ 2.50
all-service hardstanding	£ 2.00

Wadebridge

Trewince Farm Holiday Park

Saint Issey, Wadebridge PL27 7RL (Cornwall) T: **01208 812830**.
alanrogers.com/UK0500

A well-established and popular park, Trewince Farm is four miles from Padstow has been developed around a dairy farm with magnificent countryside views. Careful landscaping with flowering shrubs and bushes makes this an attractive setting. There are 35 caravan holiday homes discreetly terraced, some privately owned, some to let. Two touring areas on higher ground provide both hardstanding and level grass pitches with a sheltered tent area. Over half of the 120 touring pitches have electricity (10A) and 34 have water and drainage. The park's main feature is an excellent sheltered, walled and heated swimming pool with paddling pool, and paved sunbathing area. Farm rides and Cornish pasty suppers in the barn are organised in the high season.

Facilities

Two fully equipped, well-maintained toilet blocks include washbasins in cabins, hair care rooms, dishwashing under cover and laundry rooms. Also children's room with bath (20p) and facilities for disabled visitors. Well stocked shop (all season) by reception. Fish and chip van calls twice weekly, a butcher once a week. Swimming pool. Play area. Games room. Crazy golf. New fishing lake. Off site: Riding 3 miles. Golf and bicycle hire 3.5 miles. Beach 4.5 miles. Pubs and restaurants in nearby village of St Issey. Camel Trail nearby for walking or cycling (goes to Padstow).

Open: 23 March - 31 October.

Directions

From Wadebridge follow A39 towards St Columb and pick up the A389 for Padstow. Site signed on left in 2 miles. Follow for a short distance to the park entrance on the right. O.S.GR: SW937715.
GPS: 50.571937, -4.913213

Charges guide

Per unit incl. 2 persons	£ 9.00 - £ 14.00
incl. electricity	£ 10.00 - £ 15.50
plus hardstanding, drainage	£ 11.00 - £ 16.00
extra person	£ 3.50
child (3-15 yrs)	£ 1.85 - £ 2.90

Wadebridge
The Laurels Holiday Park

Padstow Road, Whitecross, Wadebridge PL27 7JQ (Cornwall) T: **01209 313474**.
E: **info@thelaurelsholidaypark.co.uk   alanrogers.com/UK0505**

This is a small park in a garden-like setting of which the managers Edna and Ray are very proud. It is very well maintained and provides 32 level pitches with 16A electricity. Some have hardstanding and some are extra large. Neat hedging marks the pitches and the central area with shrubs and plants is kept clear for enjoyment. A good play area for children is well fenced from the A39 which could be the cause of some road noise. The Camel Trail for walking or cycling is close and follows the estuary from Wadebridge to Padstow. A bus stops outside the site.

Facilities

Well kept fully equipped toilet block. Laundry. Facilities for drying wetsuits. Freezer and communal fridge. Play area with trampoline. Off site: Shops 1 mile. Beach 4 miles. Riding, bicycle hire, boat launching 3 miles. Fishing 5 miles. Camel Trail (walking/cycling).

Open: Easter - 31 October.

Directions

The Park is 0.5 miles from the Royal Cornwall Showground, at the junction between the A39 and A389 Padstow Road, at Whitecross, 2 miles from Wadebridge. O.S.GR: SW958716.
GPS: 50.50827, -4.88192

Charges guide

Per unit incl. 2 persons and electricity	£ 14.00 - £ 22.00
extra person	£ 4.00 - £ 8.00
child (2-15 yrs)	£ 2.00 - £ 4.00
dog	£ 1.00 - £ 2.00

Cornwall & Devon
John Fowler Holidays
You might also like to consider...

45

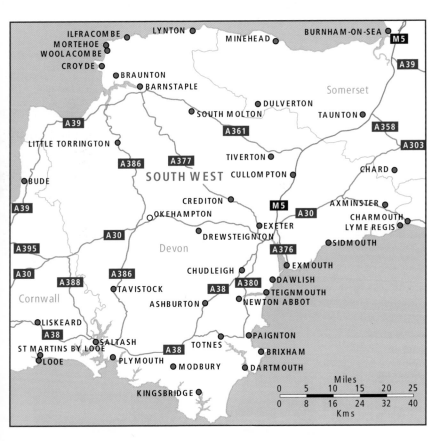

Ashburton
River Dart Country Park

Holne Park, Ashburton TQ13 7NP (Devon) T: **01364 652511**. E: **info@riverdart.co.uk**

alanrogers.com/UK0950

The park is marketed as 'River Dart Adventures', where campsite and adventure experiences are enjoyed by old and young from all over Europe. It does become busy at weekends and school holidays with supervised activities for seven year olds and upwards, such as climbing and canoeing. The camping and caravanning area is in the more open parkland overlooking the woods and is mainly on a slight slope with some shade from mature trees. There are 185 individual pitches of very reasonable size, marked by lines on the grass, some slightly sloping, with 105 electrical connections (10/16A) and 12 hardstandings. Once part of a Victorian estate with mature woodland on the edge of Dartmoor in the beautiful Dart valley, the park and its activities are now open to the general public on payment. It features a variety of unusual adventure play equipment (e.g. a giant spider's web) arranged amongst and below the trees, 'Lilliput Land' for toddlers, Jungle Fun, and woodland streams and a lake with a 'pirate ship' for swimming and inflatables, fly fishing and marked nature and forest trails – all free to campers except fishing. There is a new Commando assault course and falconry displays in high season (Thursdays).

Facilities

Two wooden toilet blocks, one quite smart, the older a little tired, can both be heated. Washbasins in cubicles, baby facilities, laundry, freezer, en-suite unit for disabled visitors (access by key), family bathroom and drying room. Motorcaravan service point. Shop. Restaurant, bar. Sunday carvery. Takeaway (20/7-31/8). Large TV and games room. Indoor climbing room (some of these open all year for the activities on offer). Small, heated swimming pool (all season). Tennis. Max. two dogs per pitch. Off site: Bicycle hire or riding 4 miles. Golf 6 miles.

Open: 1 April - 30 September.

Directions

Signed from the A38 at Peartree junction, park is about 1 mile west of Ashburton, on the road to Two Bridges. Disregard advisory signs stating 'no caravans' as access to the park is prior to narrow bridge. O.S.GR: SX734701. GPS: 50.51698, -3.78869

Charges guide

Per unit incl. 2 persons and electricity	£ 18.00 - £ 25.00
extra person (over 3 yrs)	£ 6.00 - £ 7.00
dog (max. 2)	£ 3.00

Camping Cheques accepted.

Axminster

Hawkchurch Country Park

Hawkchurch, Axminster EX13 5UL (Devon) T: 01297 678402. E: enquiries@hawkchurchpark.co.uk
alanrogers.com/UK1725

Although just four miles from the historic seaside town of Lyme Regis and two miles from Axminster itself, Hawkchurch Park enjoys a peaceful, rural situation with wonderful views over the Axe Valley. The park is set on a sloping hillside with a number of camping areas and is edged at the back with tall mature trees. In total there are just over 390 pitches with around 100 occupied by seasonal units in their own area and another section of 33 privately owned mobile homes. A further five are available to let. Most of the touring pitches have been levelled and have either concrete or gravel hardstanding, 208 have 16A electricity. Tent pitches are on grass and mostly in their own fields. A pleasant bar/restaurant is a nice addition but has limited hours out of the main season. The village of Hawkchurch is around a mile away with narrow roads and is best avoided when towing.

Facilities

Two traditional toilet blocks which have been modernised, and one newer block near the tenting area. All are fully equipped and one is heated. Family washroom and baby changing unit. Washing machines. Shop for basics in reception. Bar/restaurant open weekends and on demand out of main season. Dog walking area. Possible to arrange bicycle hire on site. Off site: Beach at Lyme Regis and Charmouth both 4 miles. Golf at Seaton (15 mins drive).

Open: 15 February - 4 January.

See advertisement on page 345

Directions

The best route to avoid narrow roads is to leave the A35 between Charmouth and Axminster at the Hunters Lodge pub and travel north on the B3165 for 1.5 miles. At Wareham Cross signpost follow sign to left for Hawkchuch and site almost immediately on left. O.S.GR: SY344985. GPS: 50.7824, -2.930506

Charges guide

Per unit incl. 2 persons, electricity	£ 12.00 - £ 18.00
extra person	£ 2.50 - £ 3.00
child (0-16 yrs)	free - £ 2.00

Axminster

Andrewshayes Caravan Park

You might also like to consider...

Barnstaple

Greenacres Touring Caravan Park

Bratton Fleming, Barnstaple EX31 4SG (Devon) T: 01598 763334
alanrogers.com/UK0700

A neat, compact, rural park on the edge of Exmoor, Greenacres is managed and run alongside, but separately from, the farm owned by the family. Drive through the farm access to the park (clearly signed) – you will need to go back and call at the house to book in. No tents are taken. The site has 30 very large, well drained pitches (all with 16A electric hook-ups) with connecting gravel paths to the road – in theory you can get to your unit without stepping on the grass. The top area is level, the lower part next to the beech woods is semi-terraced to provide six hardstandings and some hedged places. There are marvellous views outside the beech hedge that shelters the site. The family has opened up a woodland walk through newly planted trees and across the fields to a secluded valley picnic area beside a stream to take advantage of the marvellous views and surroundings.

Facilities

The neat, clean toilet block with showers (1 male, 1 female) on payment (20p). Units for disabled visitors (and general use in peak times). Laundry room, with sink, spin dryer, iron and ironing board, dishwashing room. Washing lines provided. Gas supplies. Tourist information kiosk. Area for children with football and volleyball nets and swings, separated from the 2-acre dog exercise field. Off site: Fishing 3 miles. Riding 6 miles. Golf 12 miles. Pubs, restaurants and takeaways within 3 mile radius.

Open: Easter/1 April - 19 October.

Directions

From North Devon link road (M5, exit 27) turn north at South Molton onto A399. Continue for 9 miles, past turning for Exmoor Steam Centre and on to Stowford Cross. Turn left towards Exmoor Zoological Park and Greenacres Farm is on the left. O.S.GR: SS660404. GPS: 51.147633, -3.917517

Charges guide

Per unit incl. 2 persons and electricity	£ 8.25 - £ 12.50
extra person (over 7 yrs)	£ 1.50 - £ 2.25
dog	free
No credit cards.	

Braunton
Lobb Fields Caravan & Camping Park
Saunton Road, Braunton EX33 1EB (Devon) T: 01271 812090. E: info@lobbfields.com
alanrogers.com/UK1140

Lobb Fields has two camping areas providing 180 pitches on sloping grass, with a few hardstandings. 12 pitches are reserved for seasonal caravans, and 61 have 16A electricity hook-ups. A third field is open for campers for 28 days only in high season. The pitches are marked and grass roads lead to the amenities. As the two toilet blocks are at the very bottom or very top of the fields, some up and down walking is inevitable. Lobbs Fields may be close to many holiday activities, but it is also a peaceful retreat for those wanting a quiet holiday. Braunton village, Saunton Sands, the famous Tarka Trail for cycling, Baggy Point for walking, the biosphere at Braunton Burrows (one of only 13 similar special reserves in the country), Marwood Gardens, and windsurfing and water skiing on the Taw estuary are just some of the many attractions within a short distance of Lobb Fields. If you just want to sit and relax, then the pitches at the park offer views of the Taw estuary and Saunton, as well as magnificent sunsets.

Facilities

Two elderly toilet blocks (one in each field) have all the usual facilities. Two family/baby rooms. Laundry. Cleaning and maintenance can be variable. The lower block can be heated and has good facilities for disabled visitors. Hair dryers and irons available from reception (£5 returnable deposit). Play area. Surf shop. Off site: Nearest shops less than a mile. Fishing, golf, riding and bicycle hire 1 mile. Boat launching 1.5 miles.

Open: 29 March - 29 October.

Directions

Take A361 Barnstaple to Braunton road, then the B3231 (signed Croyde) to Braunton. Park is 1 mile from Braunton on the right – take care through Braunton as roads are quite narrow and busy. O.S.GR: SS474370. GPS: 51.11165, -4.181233

Charges guide

Per unit incl. 2 persons	£ 6.00 - £ 18.00
'prime' pitch	£ 9.00 - £ 23.00
extra person	£ 3.00 - £ 5.00
dog	£ 1.00 - £ 2.00

Brixham
Galmpton Park
Greenway Road, Galmpton, Brixham TQ5 0EP (Devon) T: 01803 842066
E: galmptontouringpark@hotmail.com **alanrogers.com/UK0850**

Within a few miles of the lively amenities of Torbay, Galmpton Park lies peacefully just outside the village of Galmpton, overlooking the beautiful Dart estuary just upstream of Dartmouth and Kingswear. A family park, some 120 pitches (60 marked for caravans) are arranged on a wide sweep of grassy, terraced meadow, each pitch with its own wonderful view of the river. Situated on the hillside, some parts have quite a slope, but there are flatter areas (the owners will advise and assist). There are 90 electrical connections (10A) and 23 pitches have water and drainage. There is a separate tent field. Galmpton is a quiet and simple park (with the gates closed 23.15 - 07.30) in a most picturesque setting, within easy reach of all the attractions of South Devon. A member of the Countryside Discovery group.

Facilities

A central, substantial looking toilet block provides clean facilities including three washbasins in cabins, a very attractive under 5's bathroom (key), baby unit and hair care areas. Dishwashing room also with washing machine, dryer, iron and ironing board. Reception/shop sells a wide range of basics including gas. Bread to order. Good adventure play equipment. Dogs (max. 2 per unit) are accepted at the owner's discretion and not mid July and Aug. Motorhomes over 21 ft. are not accepted. Off site: Local pub is 5 minutes walk.

Open: Easter - 30 September.

Directions

Take A380 Paignton ring road towards Brixham until junction with the Paignton - Brixham coast road. Turn right towards Brixham, then second right into Manor Vale Road. Continue through the village, past the school and site is 500 yds. on the right. O.S.GR: SX885558. GPS: 50.391650, -3.568070

Charges guide

Per unit incl. 2 persons and electricity	£ 14.00 - £ 18.10
extra person	£ 3.50
child (5-15 yrs)	£ 2.50
dog (off peak only)	£ 0.50
Various discounts available.	

Galmpton Touring Park, Greenway Road, BRIXHAM, Devon, TQ5 0EP. Tel: +44 (0)1803 842066
www.galmptontouringpark.co.uk

49

Brixham

Hillhead Caravan Club Holiday Park

Hillhead, Brixham TQ5 0HH (Devon) T: 01803 853204. E: enquiries@caravanclub.co.uk

alanrogers.com/UK0845

Hillhead is a fully refurbished Caravan Club park set in 22 acres of beautiful Devon countryside. Originally developed in the 1960s within what is now a coastal protection area two miles from Brixham, the park has benefited from a £3 million redevelopment. Unusually for a Caravan Club site, it offers a full entertainment programme in peak season. Hillhead comprises 239 pitches, all with electrical hook-ups and many with fine views. Amenities are to a uniformly high standard, notably the main complex, based around an attractive courtyard and housing a shop, bar, games room and restaurant. The children's play area is outstanding with a range of imaginative items including a large wooden fort. Hillhead is rightly proud of its strong commitment to sound environmental practice, with a plan to promote species diversity and the encouragement of good practice by site workers and visitors alike.

Facilities

The two sanitary blocks are new and maintained to a high standard. Each block includes 3 private family bathrooms (key from reception) and facilities for disabled visitors. Laundry facilities. Motorcaravan service point. Shop. Bar and restaurant. Swimming pool (heated May - Sept). Play area. Skateboard ramp. Games room. TV. Entertainment in season. Games field. WiFi. Off site: Nearest beach and coastal path 2 miles. Bus stop at site entrance. River Dart boat trips. Paignton, Torquay and Brixham. Golf (18-hole) and riding 2 miles. Bicycle hire 2.5 miles.

Open: 14 March - 5 January.

Directions

Site is well signed from the A379 Paignton - Dartmouth road and is located on the B3205 (Slappers Hill Road). Entrance is on the left after 400 yards. O.S.GR: SX904534. GPS: 50.369621, -3.544816

Charges guide

Per person	£ 4.90 - £ 8.80
child (5-16 yrs)	£ 1.80 - £ 4.40
pitch incl. electricity (non-member)	£ 11.80 - £ 16.80

Brixham

Landscove Holiday Park

You might also like to consider...

333

Chudleigh

Holmans Wood Holiday Park

Harcombe Cross, Chudleigh TQ13 0DZ (Devon) T: 01626 853785. E: enquiries@holmanswood.co.uk

alanrogers.com/UK0940

Close to the main A38 Exeter - Plymouth road, with easy access, this attractive, neat park makes a sheltered base for touring south Devon and Dartmoor. The hedged park is arranged on well kept grass surrounding a shallow depression, the floor of which makes a safe, grassy play area for children. Many attractive trees are growing and the park is decorated with flowers. In two main areas and accessed by tarmac roads, there are 116 level pitches (including a number of seasonal pitches) and 25 smart mobile homes in a private area. There are 100 pitches with electrical hook-ups (10A) and 70 with hardstanding, electricity, water and drainage. A picturesque eight-acre meadow is provided for tents. There may be some traffic noise on pitches to the west of the park. This is a pleasant, well run park.

Facilities

The single, good quality toilet block includes facilities for babies and disabled visitors. Laundry room. Children's play area. Caravan storage. Dogs are not accepted. Off site: Pub/restaurant nearby in Chudleigh village. The beach or Dartmoor are 7 miles and Haldon Forest for walks is 2 miles. Sunday market at Exeter Racecourse (2 miles). Fishing 1 mile. Golf or riding 4 miles.

Open: Mid March - end October.

Directions

From Exeter on the A38 Plymouth road, 0.5 miles after the racecourse and just after a garage, take Chudleigh exit (signed). Park is immediately on the left. From Plymouth turn off A38 for Chudleigh/Teign Valley, then right for Chudleigh. Continue through the town and park is 1 mile. O.S.GR: SX882811. GPS: 50.61985, -3.582833

Charges guide

Per unit incl. 2 persons and electricity	£ 12.00 - £ 18.00
extra person	£ 2.20 - £ 3.00
child (4-14 yrs)	£ 1.90 - £ 2.00

Crediton
Yeatheridge Farm Caravan Park

East Worlington, Crediton EX17 4TN (Devon) T: 01884 860330. E: yeatheridge@talk21.com

alanrogers.com/UK1060

Yeatheridge is a friendly, family park with riding, fishing lakes, and indoor pools. Based on a 200-acre farm, nine acres have been developed over many years into an attractive touring park. Around the site there are views of the local hills and Dartmoor away to the south, and Exmoor lies to the north. The touring area is very neat and tidy with a spacious feel as units are sited around the perimeter or back onto hedges, leaving open central areas. The 85 numbered pitches are flat, gently sloping or on terraces and are sufficiently large, 80 with electricity. Seasonal units take 25 pitches and there are four caravan holiday homes. You can explore three woodland walks ranging from 1 to 2.5 miles and the banks of the River Dalch. There are two deep coarse fishing lakes (bring your own rod), the top one offering family fishing and the lower one for serious fishing (age 14 or over and free of charge). Horse riding is available on site (best to bring your own hat) with hour-long and park rides available. The ponies and goats are also popular. The owners, Geoff and Liz, are constantly upgrading the park (recently opening a new reception and amenity building) and they try very hard to make everyone feel at home.

Facilities

Two toilet blocks provide family rooms, washbasins in cubicles, showers and facilities for babies. En-suite room for disabled visitors. Laundry. Motorcaravan service point. Shop. Bar, restaurant and snack bar (hours vary acc. to season). Unsupervised indoor swimming pools, toddlers' pool and water slide (10.00-20.00 hrs). Fenced play area with fort for under 10s (parental supervision). Football field. TV room. Games room. Fishing. Riding.

Open: 22 March - 29 September.

Directions

Park is off the B3042 Witheridge - Chawleigh (not in East Worlington). From M5 exit 27 onto A361 to Tiverton. Turn left onto A396 for 0.5 miles then right on B3137 almost to Witheridge, then left on B3042 for 3 miles to site, well signed down concrete roadway on left. O.S.GR: SS770114. GPS: 50.8887, -3.7501

Charges guide

Per unit incl. 2 persons	£ 7.50 - £ 13.50
extra person over 4 yrs	£ 2.20
electricity	£ 1.30
awning or pup tent	£ 1.00 - £ 2.00
dog (first two)	£ 0.50 - £ 1.00

Yeatheridge Farm *Caravan & Camping Park*
01884 860330
www.yeatheridge.co.uk
If you are a country lover, there is everything to interest you here.
2 ½ miles of wood & riverside walks. If you wish to explore beautiful Devon,
then there could not be a better location.

NEW ON-SITE RESTAURANT

Croyde
Ruda Holiday Park

Parkdean Holidays, Croyde Bay, Croyde EX33 1NY (Devon) T: 01271 890477. E: enquires@ruda.co.uk

alanrogers.com/UK1150

Ruda Holiday Park is a recent addition to Parkdean Holidays, now comprising 12 parks in Scotland, Wales and southwest England. Ruda is right beside a Blue Flag beach and provides 313 camping and touring pitches in two distinct areas. A large camping area divided into four sections is reserved for tent campers and motorcaravans (there are some electricity hook-ups around the perimeter and it is served by two toilet blocks). Touring caravan and motorcaravan pitches, all with 13A connections, are in a separate field across the road and have direct access to the beach. Here, the toilet facilities are modern with coded entry to stop day visitors using them. A central complex (away from the camping fields) houses a supermarket, laundry, food outlets and all of the entertainment clubs and bars.

Facilities

Two blocks in the camping fields provide toilets, showers with preset controls, and communal washbasins; these are aging but were clean at the time of visit. A separate bathroom with toilet can be accessed by wheelchairs (key from reception), however there are no aids for visitors with disabilities. A third, modern building provides all facilities in the touring field. Laundry facilities. Bar, restaurant, snack bar and takeaway. Amusement arcade. Cascade Tropical pool. Adventure playground. Tennis court. Sports field. Fishing lake. Supermarket, boutique and hire centre. Surfing equipment for hire. Direct access to sheltered beach. Caravan holiday homes and lodges for hire. Dogs are not accepted. Off site: Surfing. Lundy Island excursion.

Open: March - November.

Directions

From Barnstaple, take A361 signed Braunton and Ilfracombe. At Braunton, take sharp left (narrow road) towards Croyde (signed) and follow the road all the way to the beach. Entrance to Ruda is on the right. O.S.GR: SS561331. GPS: 51.135183, -4.2352

Charges guide

Per unit incl. 4 persons	£ 9.00 - £ 30.00
pitch with services	£ 12.00 - £ 38.00

Prices are for pitch and up to four persons; maximum of eight persons per pitch.

Cullompton

Forest Glade Holiday Park

Cullompton EX15 2DT (Devon) T: **01404 841381**. E: **enquiries@forest-glade.co.uk**

alanrogers.com/UK1000

Forest Glade, owned and run by the Wellard family, is set in the Blackdown Hills (designated an Area of Outstanding Natural Beauty) deep in mid-Devon away from the hectic life on the coast. A sheltered site set amongst woodland with extensive walking without using your car, there are 80 level touring pitches, 68 of which have electricity connections, 4 have full services and 42 have hardstanding. Touring caravans must book in advance and the easiest route for them will be explained then (phone bookings accepted). Although set in the country, the beaches of East Devon are a fairly easy drive away. There is a small heated, covered pool with a paddling pool and patio area outside, and a large games room (up a flight of steps, so not suitable for disabled visitors). The surrounding forest makes this a dog lover's paradise.

Facilities

There is one main toilet block, heated in cold weather, with some washbasins in cubicles. Separate suite for visitors with disabilities. Laundry with washing machines and dryers. Baby room. Extra facilities of 'portacabin' style with toilets, washbasins and showers are at the swimming pool. Drain for motorcaravan tanks. Shop is quite well stocked including gas, bread and pastries with a takeaway (open evenings except Sunday). Microwave in kitchenette. Adventure playground. Games room. Swimming pool (free). Sauna. All weather tennis court. Separate area for ball games. WiFi internet access. Caravan storage. New wildlife information room. Off site: Fishing or riding 1.5 miles. Golf 6 miles. Beach 17 miles.

Open: Mid March - end October.

Directions

Park (at the top of a steep hill) is 5.5 miles from M5 exit 28. Take A373 for 3 miles, turning left at camp sign, just past thatched pub on right, towards Sheldon. Park is on left after 2.5 miles. This access is not suitable for touring caravans owing to a steep hill - phone the park for alternative route details. O.S.GR: ST101073. GPS: 50.857833, -3.277517

Charges 2010

Per unit incl. 2 persons and electricity (10/16A)	£ 13.50 - £ 18.00
extra person	£ 5.20
child (10-18 yrs)	£ 3.00
child (4-9 yrs)	£ 1.50

Dartmouth

Little Cotton Caravan Park

Dartmouth TQ6 0LB (Devon) T: **01803 832558**. E: **enquiries@littlecotton.co.uk**

alanrogers.com/UK0835

This lovely, family run park on the outskirts of Dartmouth is ideally situated for exploring this attractive area of South Devon. Well tended and immaculate, the 7.5 acre park is open and grassy. On level and gently sloping ground, it is situated on a hilltop and has views across the other fields. There are 95 pitches, all with electricity (16A) and mostly level with some hardstanding available. The park is divided into four areas with one dedicated to rallies. A dog walking area is to one side. Barbecues are allowed if supported off the ground.

Facilities

The modern, heated toilet block is centrally situated. It is very clean, light, airy and warm. Some washbasins are in cubicles. Free showers are preset. Excellent facilities for disabled visitors. Laundry facilities. Unisex baby room. Well stocked shop in reception. Bread and sandwiches to order. Freezer. Off site: Dartmouth Castle and the steam railway can be easily accessed by ferry. Beach, fishing and boat launching 2 miles. Golf 3 miles.

Open: 15 March - 31 October.

Directions

Park is on the outskirts of Dartmouth on the A3122 next to Dartmouth 'park and ride'. From Totnes take A381 (Kingsbridge) and turn left at Halwell on A3122. Site is on right just before entering Dartmouth. O.S.GR: SX857508. GPS: 50.345106, -3.607606

Charges guide

Per unit incl. 2 persons and electricity	£ 14.25 - £ 19.00
extra person	£ 3.00
child (3-14 yrs)	£ 2.00

Dawlish

Leadstone Camping

Warren Road, Dawlish Warren, Dawlish EX7 0NG (Devon) T: **01626 864411**. E: info@leadstonecamping.co.uk

alanrogers.com/UK1095

Leadstone provides traditional camping at its best in a series of hedged grass fields, sloping in parts, in a natural, secluded bowl. In an area of designated outstanding natural beauty, the beach and sand dunes of Dawlish Warren are only a half mile walk. The area can get somewhat frenzied in peak holiday times but Leadstone provides a haven of peace and tranquillity. Owned by the same family since 1974, the Leadstone welcome is personal and the site totally relaxed. In all, there are 137 pitches, 102 with 16A electricity. A regular bus service passes the gate every 15 minutes. The toilet facilities are centrally situated but of the Portacabin variety. This is due to the site's situation on the seaward side of the Warren road where it is subject to Coastal Preservation regulations (it must be possible to move buildings within 24 hours). However, the provision is good under the circumstances, if somewhat short on toilets. Extra toilet pods are brought in for peak times. The site is only open for a short season but is popular and well run. Dawlish Warren is renowned for its good weather and average temperatures of over 70 degrees are not uncommon.

Facilities

Fully equipped, centrally located Portacabin-style provision is well kept. Unisex showers (20p for 5-6 minutes). Washing machines. Basic supplies and gas from reception. Play area with real tractor. Off site: Beach with shops, cafés, etc. at Dawlish Warren 0.5 miles. Golf 0.5 miles. Bicycle hire 2 miles. Riding 5 miles. Boat launching 7 miles.

Open: 13 June - 7 September.

Directions

From Exeter follow the A379 Teignmouth road (M5 exit 30). After Starcross watch for left turn to Dawlish Warren and site is on right after 0.5 miles. O.S.GR: SX973780. GPS: 50.59396, -3.45162

Charges guide

Per person	£ 6.25 - £ 7.75
child (3-14 yrs)	£ 2.40 - £ 2.75
pitch	£ 4.00 - £ 4.50
electricity	£ 3.00

53

Dawlish
Lady's Mile Holiday Park

Exeter Road, Dawlish EX7 0LX (Devon) T: **01626 863411**. E: **info@ladysmile.co.uk**
alanrogers.com/UK1010

Lady's Mile is a popular, large family touring park that caters well for children. It has extensive grassy fields (with some trees for shade), in addition to the main landscaped camping area, which is arranged in broad terraces. There are **486** pitches, mostly marked by lines but with nothing between them, and most with electricity. It is a 20 minute walk to a good sandy beach at Dawlish Warren and ten minutes to Dawlish beach, but the park also has a good sized, outdoor swimming pool with 200 ft.-plus slide, paddling pool and a paved surround plus a super heated indoor pool (20 x 10 m) with 100 ft. flume and separate paddling pool (with lifeguards). A large bar complex has a family area overlooking the indoor pool and an entertainment programme. Below is a spacious games room and a new separate disco and bar. A sloping recreation field is ideal for kite flying and the large fenced adventure playground has a safe, sand surface. The park is popular over a long season, with reservation necessary for high season.

Facilities

Four toilet blocks of various ages and styles, but of a good standard, are well spaced around the main areas of the park with an additional shower block. Facilities for disabled visitors. Four family bathrooms (50p). Two launderettes. Shop. Fish and chip takeaway. Bars and entertainment programme. Restaurant and carvery (half-board option available). All Easter - mid Sept. Indoor (Easter - Oct) and outdoor (May - Sept) pools. Adventure play area. Games room. Ball area with nets. Tarmac area at reception for late arrivals. Winter caravan storage. Off site: Golf, riding and bicycle hire 1 mile. Fishing 3 miles.

Open: 13 March - 31 October.

Directions

Park is 1 mile north of Dawlish with access off the A379 (Exeter - Teignmouth) road. O.S.GR: SX969778. GPS: 50.59525, -3.459467

Charges guide

Per unit incl. 2 persons and electricity (10A)	£ 12.75 - £ 27.50
extra person over 2 yrs	£ 1.00 - £ 3.50
dog	£ 1.50 - £ 3.50

Low season special offers.
Low season discount for OAPs.

Dawlish
Golden Sands Holiday Park
You might also like to consider...

333

Dawlish

Cofton Country Holidays

Starcross, Dawlish EX6 8RP (Devon) T: **01626 890111**. E: info@coftonholidays.co.uk
alanrogers.com/UK0970

A popular, family-run park, Cofton is 1.5 miles from a sandy beach at Dawlish Warren. It has space for 450 touring units on a variety of fields and meadows with beautiful country views. Although not individually marked, there is never a feeling of overcrowding. The smaller, more mature fields, including a pleasant old orchard for tents only, are well terraced. While there are terraces on most of the slopes of the larger, more open fields, there are still some quite steep gradients to climb. There are some 450 electrical connections (10A), 16 hardstandings and 14 'super' pitches. One area has 66 park-owned holiday homes for let. A well-designed, central complex overlooking the pool and decorated with flowers and hanging baskets houses reception, a shop and off-licence and a bar lounge, the 'Cofton Swan', where bar meals are available. A family room and bar are on the first floor of this building and there is an outdoor terrace and some light entertainment in season. The adjacent supervised heated kidney-shaped pool with a paddling pool, has lots of grassy space for sunbathing. Coarse fishing is available in five lakes on the park. The adjoining unspoilt woodland of 50 acres provides wonderful views across the Exe estuary and a woodland trail of two miles to Dawlish Warren.

Facilities

Toilet facilities comprise six blocks, well placed for all areas, one of very high standard. Facilities for disabled visitors and babies. Hair dryers. Two launderettes. Gas available. Ice pack hire service. Bar lounge with meals (Easter - late Oct). TV. Shop. Fish and chip shop also serving breakfast. Swimming pool (overall length 100 ft. open Spr. B.H - mid Sept). Games room. Adventure playground in the woods overlooking the pools and two other well equipped play areas. Coarse fishing (from £25 per rod for 7 days, discount for senior citizens outside July and August. Caravan storage. Seasonal pitches.) Off site: Beach 1.5 miles. Woodland walks/pub 0.5 miles. Golf 3 miles.

Open: All year.

Directions

Access to the park is off the A379 road 3 miles north of Dawlish, just after Cockwood harbour village. O.S.GR: SX965797. GPS: 50.6126, -3.460467

Charges guide

Per unit incl. 2 persons and electricity	£ 13.00 - £ 26.00
hardstanding pitch	£ 16.50 - £ 28.00
serviced pitch	£ 19.50 - £ 32.00
extra person (over 2 yrs)	£ 2.50 - £ 4.50

Small discount for Senior Citizens outside peak season. Camping Cheques accepted.

See advertisement on the back cover.

Dawlish

Peppermint Park

Warren Road, Dawlish Warren, Dawlish EX7 0PQ (Devon) T: **01626 863436**. E: info@peppermintpark.co.uk
alanrogers.com/UK1090

Now part of the Park Holidays group, Peppermint Park is a green oasis in a popular holiday area. Extensive, green, sloping fields edged with mature trees have been partly terraced to give level pitches for caravans and some more informal areas that cater for tents. There are 60 holiday homes (many privately owned but some to rent) along with timber lodges to rent close to a small fishing lake. There are 250 touring pitches, 200 with electricity, which are marked and numbered. Tarmac roads allow easy access to all areas. Nightly entertainment is staged in the Peppermint Club in high season. This park's main advantage is the large, safe Blue Flag beaches of Dawlish Warren and its associated pleasure complex that are within walking distance (700 yds) making it ideal for families. A passenger ferry operates from Starcross (two miles) across the estuary to Exmouth during high season. Dawlish Warren nature reserve is adjacent and includes an 18-hole links golf course.

Facilities

The two well kept sanitary blocks can be heated. Two units (WC, washbasin and shower) for disabled visitors. Fully equipped baby room. Laundry (washing machines, dryers and free irons). Shop with gas. Coffee shop. Bar with entertainment. Restaurant and takeaway (28/5-10/9). Swimming pools (28/5 - early Sept). Adventure playground. Small coarse fishing lake (£5 day ticket). Off site: Golf at Dawlish Warren (links course), 9-hole course at Starcross.

Open: 15 March - 28 October.

Directions

Leave the M5 at exit 30 and take A379 Dawlish road. Pass through Starcross (7 miles) then turn left to Dawlish Warren just before Dawlish. Continue for 1.5 miles down hill and park is on left in 300 yards. O.S.GR: SX978788. GPS: 50.599367, -3.446967

Charges guide

Per unit incl. 2 persons	£ 15.00 - £ 20.00
incl. electricity (16A)	£ 15.00 - £ 28.00
extra person (2 yrs and over)	£ 2.00 - £ 4.00

Drewsteignton

Woodland Springs Touring Park

Venton, Drewsteignton EX6 6PG (Devon) T: **01647 231695**. E: enquiries@woodlandsprings.co.uk

alanrogers.com/UK1250

Hidden away in a corner of the Dartmoor National Park, Woodlands Springs is a haven of peace and tranquillity. Set in a dip, it is sheltered by woodland with some views across the rural countryside. It provides 85 fairly level, grass pitches (39 with hardstanding) and 53 with electricity, with a circular gravel access road and a central toilet block. Small Shop and off licence; bread is baked daily. A large field provides good dog walking. The resident owners provide a warm welcome on this quiet park that only accepts adults. With 600 miles of public right-of-way on Dartmoor, there is plenty to keep walkers busy.

Facilities

New toilet block including full facilities for disabled people. Chemical disposal. Dog kennels for rent. Off site: Fishing 3 miles. Riding 5 miles. Golf 9 miles. Castle Drogo and the Mythic Gardens nearby.

Open: All year.

Directions

From M5 exit 31 take A30 towards Okehampton. At Whiddon Down turn on A382 (Moretonhampstead). After 0.5 miles left at roundabout. After 1 mile turn left at caravan sign, then left and park is 150 yds. O.S.GR: SX694911. GPS: 50.706417, -3.850667

Charges guide

Per unit incl. 2 persons, electricity	£ 15.00 - £ 20.00
extra person	£ 2.00

Exeter

Webbers Caravan & Camping Park

Castle Lane, Woodbury, Exeter EX5 1EA (Devon) T: **01395 232276**. E: reception@webberspark.co.uk

alanrogers.com/UK1100

Set in a lovely location in East Devon, with rural views, this family run park has developed over 20 years to one that can boast spacious, modern facilities, yet still retain its relaxed, rural atmosphere. The 115 marked, grass pitches are large, with the majority level and a few gently sloping. Some of the higher pitches have marvellous views across the Exe river valley. There are 100 electricity connections (10/16A). The park is surrounded by fields and visitors can watch the wildlife and grazing sheep from a fenced walk around the park perimeter.

Facilities

There are three modern toilet blocks, one is a light and airy building with 4 family shower rooms, a bathroom (£1) and a unit for disabled visitors (WC, shower and washbasin). Laundry facilities. Motorcaravan service point. Small shop at reception for essentials. Ice pack service. Gas supplies. Play area and games field. All year caravan storage. Off site: Woodbury village within walking distance with excellent pub/restaurant, post office, etc. Exeter 6 miles. Fishing or golf (Woodbury Park Golf Club) 1 mile. Riding 4 miles. Bicycle hire or boat launching 5 miles.

Open: April - October.

Directions

From M5 exit 30 take A3052 (Sidmouth) for 5 miles and turn right at Halfway Inn. From A30, Daisymount exit, take B3180 for 3 miles to Halfway Inn and go straight across at crossroads. All routes then follow B3180. After 2 miles turn right into lane (signed Woodbury and caravan parks). Follow downhill for 1 mile to park on left just before Woodbury village. O.S.GR: SY017874. GPS: 50.678083, -3.392017

Charges guide

Per unit incl. 2 persons, electricity	£ 12.00 - £ 18.00
extra person (over 3 yrs)	£ 3.00

Exmouth

Devon Cliffs Holiday Park

Haven Holidays, Sandy Bay, Exmouth EX8 5BT (Devon) T: **01395 226226**

alanrogers.com/UK1260

Haven Holiday's flagship park, Devon Cliffs at Exmouth, is a very large, vibrant holiday resort, complete with its own almost private sandy beach. There are over 1,600 caravan holiday homes here (400 for hire). They are arranged in avenues on the attractively landscaped, hilly site around a central complex full of top class amenities. Overlooking this complex is a small, modern touring area providing 43 very neat pitches for caravans and motorcaravans, a good toilet block and its own warden. Fully serviced (electricity, aerial point, water and drain), each pitch has areas of gravel, concrete and grass.

Facilities

Very neat and clean toilet facilities. Excellent room for visitors with disabilities. Launderette. Shopping arcade. Variety of eating options. Two indoor 'show bars'. Indoor and outdoor pool complex (outdoor 22/5-31/8). Spa centre. Sports facilities. Amusements hall. Evening entertainment and clubs for children. Adventure play areas. Beach. Tents accepted 24/7-4/9. Off site: Exmouth centre 2.5 miles with hourly bus. Bicycle hire 2.5 miles. Golf and riding 6 miles.

Open: 20 March - 2 November.

Directions

From the M5 exit 30, take the A376 signed Exmouth. On the outskirts of the town (just after a garage), turn left at traffic lights following signs for Budleigh Salterton, Littleham, Sandy Bay and the park. O.S.GR: SY033805. GPS: 50.615645, -3.366387

Charges 2010

Per unit incl. up to 4 persons and services	£ 17.00 - £ 46.50
extra person	£ 2.00 - £ 3.00

See advertisement on page 349

Ilfracombe
Napps Touring Holiday Park
Old Coast Road, Berrynarbor, Ilfracombe EX34 9SW (Devon) T: 01271 882557. E: info@napps.fsnet.co.uk
alanrogers.com/UK1120

Set in an idyllic location in North Devon, this popular, family-run site offers peace and quiet on site, with plenty to see and do off site. A path just outside the gates leads down to a private beach with safe bathing; although it is only 200 yards to the gate, there are 200 steps down to the beach so it is not suitable for wheelchair users. Combe Martin and Ilfracombe beaches are also close by. The 200 touring pitches, most with views of Watermouth Bay, are terraced and spacious, 87 are serviced with electricity, water tap and waste point, and another 78 have a 10A hook-up.

Facilities

Two modern toilet blocks include open plan washbasins, showers and family wash cubicles. Laundry. Licensed shop. Gas supplies. Bar with terrace and light entertainment during high season. Takeaway. Heated outdoor pool with paddling pool and toddlers' slide. Tennis. Ceramic studio for children. Games room. Adventure play area. Caravan storage. Off site: Beach and fishing 200 yds. Golf and boat launching 1.5 miles. Bicycle hire and riding 5 miles.

Open: 1 March - 15 November.

Directions

Leave M5 at exit 27, take A361 to South Molton and then A399 to Combe Martin. Site is 1.5 miles west of Combe Martin on the A399 (signed). O.S.GR: SS559475. GPS: 51.208517, -4.064083

Charges guide

Per unit incl. 2 persons, electricity	£ 10.00 - £ 25.00
extra person over 10 yrs	£ 1.00 - £ 4.00
child (5-10 yrs)	£ 1.00 - £ 3.00

Ilfracombe
Hele Valley Holiday Park
Hele Bay, Ilfracombe EX34 9RD (Devon) T: 01271 862460. E: holidays@helevalley.co.uk
alanrogers.com/UK1145

Hele Valley is a well-established park which has been in the same family for over 30 years. Located a mile from Ilfracombe in a wooded valley, it is only a few minutes walk from Hele Bay beach. Here, quaint coves and coastal paths reveal a genuine smuggler's cave. Apart from the 80 attractively laid out caravan holiday homes (20 for rent), the park caters for tents and motorcaravans only because of the difficult access. Some 50 pitches are set in two fields surrounded by trees and hedges. Some of the pitches are terraced. Eight grass pitches for motorcaravans have electricity and 50 for tents have hook-ups.

Facilities

The bright, airy and modern toilet block (access by key with deposit required) provides a mixture of open and enclosed washbasins. Separately, a deluxe baby room, complete with pretty frieze and chiming mobiles and a well-fitted unit for disabled visitors. Two good adventure play areas and a play field. Parents must keep children away from the steep-sided stream running the length of the park. Off site: shops, pubs and cafés 5 minutes walk. Ilfracombe 1 mile. Beach and golf 400 yards. Riding 4 miles. Bus service in main road.

Open: 24 May - 7 September.

Directions

From Ilfracombe take A399 towards Combe Martin. With Ilfracombe pool on the left, proceed down the hill for a further 400 m. and, at brown sign, take sharp right turn (easier from Combe Martin). Go down steep road and continue to T-junction (right-angled and narrow). Turn right to park. O.S. GR: SS533474. GPS: 51.205404, -4.101202

Charges 2010

Per unit incl. 2 persons, electricity	£ 18.00 - £ 31.00
extra person	£ 4.00 - £ 6.00

Ilfracombe
Watermouth Cove Holiday Park
Ilfracombe EX34 9SJ (Devon) T: 01271 862504. E: info@watermouthcoveholidays.co.uk
alanrogers.com/UK1257

This park is set in a lovely position, being at the side of a stream as it flows into the harbour and sea at Watermouth Cove. It has its own private beach from where there are lovely views across the sea to Hangman's Hill. Part of the park is arranged on the fairly level valley floor, whilst the tent area is on the side of the private headland with beautiful views of the coast from the higher ground. Electricity hook-ups (10A) are available. Children will enjoy fishing from the rocks, and there is an adventure play area with organised activities during high season.

Facilities

New heated facilities are provided in good quality 'portacabin' style units arranged in a U-shape with decking and seating joining them together. Showers are preset, have non-slip bases and a glass partition. The camping field has its own toilets. Laundry. Shop. Bar, restaurant and takeaway (weekends only in low season). Play area and activities for children (high season). Entertainment. Off site: Ilfracombe is nearby. Coastal roads and paths are numerous.

Open: 16 March - 28 October.

Directions

From M5 exit 27 follow signs for Barnstaple A361. At South Molton roundabout turn right on A399 for 16 miles (signs to Combe Martin). Go through Combe Martin on A399. After 2 miles Watermouth Cove is clearly signed on the right. O.S.GR: SS557482. GPS: 51.212484, -4.071298

Charges guide

Per unit incl. 2 persons	£ 7.50 - £ 26.00
extra person	£ 2.00

57

Ilfracombe
Stowford Farm Meadows

Berry Down, Combe Martin, Ilfracombe EX34 0PW (Devon) T: **01271 882476**. E: **enquiries@stowford.co.uk**
alanrogers.com/UK0690

Stowford Farm is a friendly, family park set in 500 acres of the rolling North Devon countryside, available for recreation and walking, yet within easy reach of five local beaches. The touring park and its facilities have been developed in the fields and farm buildings surrounding the attractive old farmhouse and provide a village like centre with a comfortable spacious feel. There are 710 pitches on five slightly sloping meadows separated by Devon hedges of beech and ash. The numbered and marked pitches, some with hardstanding, are accessed by hard roads; most have electricity (10/16A) and there are well-placed water points. The Old Stable Bar offers entertainment in high season including barn dances, discos, karaoke and other musical evenings. There is also much for children to do, from the indoor heated pool and under cover mini-zoo (Petorama) where they can handle many kinds of animal (on payment), to the wide range of organised activities on offer. In low season some facilities may only open for limited hours. Stowford also provides plenty to keep the whole family occupied without leaving the park, including woodland walks and horse riding from the park's own stables. However, it is also a good base for exploring the North Devon coast and Exmoor. A new development of 40 very smart holiday lodges with wonderful views has been added to the park.

Facilities
Five identical toilet blocks, each looked after by resident wardens, are fully equipped and provide good, functional facilities, each block with laundry facilities and dishwashing. The newest block (in field 5) has under-floor heating and includes facilities for disabled visitors. Extra good facilities for disabled visitors and private family washrooms are beside reception. Well stocked shop (with holiday goods and gas). Good value takeaway with restaurant area. Bars and entertainment in season. Indoor pool (22 x 10 m; heated Easter - Oct) at a small charge. Riding. 18-hole pitch and putt. Crazy golf. Bicycle hire. 'Kiddies kar' track (all charged). Games room. Large play area. Games and activities organised in high season. ATM. Woodland walks. Dogs welcome in three sections (max. 2 per pitch). Summer parking and winter caravan storage. Caravan centre with caravan sales, workshop, accessories and repair centre. Off site: Fishing and boat launching 4 miles.

Open: All year.

Directions
From Barnstaple take A39 towards Lynton. After 1 mile turn left on B3230. Turn right at garage on A3123 and park is 1.5 miles on the right. O.S.GR: SS565438. GPS: 51.174983, -4.05475

Charges guide
Per unit incl. 2 persons and electricity	£ 8.20 - £ 28.00
extra person	free - £ 4.50
child (5-12 yrs)	free - £ 2.50
dog	£ 1.60 - £ 2.60

Low and mid season discounts for over 50s.

Ilfracombe
Hidden Valley Touring & Camping Park

West Down, Ilfracombe EX34 8NU (Devon) T: **01271 813837**. E: **relax@hiddenvalleypark.com**
alanrogers.com/UK0710

The owners, Martin and Dawn Fletcher, run this aptly named family park to high standards. In a sheltered valley setting between Barnstaple and Ilfracombe beside a small stream and lake (with ducks), it is most attractive and is also convenient for several resorts, beaches and the surrounding countryside. The original part of the park offers some 67 level pitches (standard, large, 'super' and 'premium' pitch options) on three sheltered terraces. On hardstanding, all have electricity (16A) and TV connections (leads for hire), with a water point between each pitch. Kingfisher Meadow, a little way from the main facilities and reached by a tarmac road, provides a further 58 pitches.

Facilities
Two modern toilet blocks (one for each area, one heated) are tiled and have non-slip floors. Some washbasins in cubicles, some en-suite with toilets in the Kingfisher Meadow block. Bathroom (tokens). Baby room. Complete facilities for people with disabilities. Laundry facilities. Supplementary clean 'portacabin' style facilities in the original area. Motorcaravan service facilities. Gas supplies. Shop. Coffee shop (breakfast and lunch). Therapy suite. Play areas. Up to 2 dogs are accepted (otherwise by prior arrangement). Caravan storage. Off site: Fishing or golf 2 miles. Bicycle hire 4 miles. Riding 5 miles. Beach 5 miles.

Open: All year.

Directions
Park is on the A361 Barnstaple - Ilfracombe road, 3.5 miles after Braunton. O.S.GR: SS499408. GPS: 51.146533, -4.14555

Charges guide
Per unit incl. 2 persons	£ 15.00 - £ 38.00
extra person	£ 3.00 - £ 5.00
child (3-15 yrs)	£ 2.00 - £ 4.00
dog	£ 0.50 - £ 2.00

Discounts for over 50s.

escape to the

Stowford Life

Stowford Farm Meadows is a family owned, award winning touring **caravan and camping site** close to Combe Martin in the beautiful surroundings of the **North Devon** countryside.

Open all year round so come and enjoy the Stowford life.

To book call us on

01271 882476

Combe Martin Devon EX34 0PW

Visit our website to request a free colour brochure

www.**stowford**.co.uk

Kingsbridge
Higher Rew Caravan & Camping Park

Malborough, Kingsbridge TQ7 3BW (Devon) T: **01548 842681**. E: enquiries@higherrew.co.uk

alanrogers.com/UK0826

The Squire family have developed this rural park on their farm which is located about a mile up a single track lane from South Sands, near Salcombe. South Sands is ideal for boating, sailing and windsurfing as well as providing safe bathing. A ferry runs to Salcombe town. The five miles of estuary which stretches between Salcombe and Kingsbridge is a local nature reserve famed for its unique marine habitats and bird watching opportunities. You can travel the length of it by the 'Rivermaid' ferry. The rural views from the park are amazing but you have to climb a little higher to see the sea. The coastal path can be reached by footpaths from the park. There used to be a dairy herd on the farm but the buildings are now used to provide camping facilities which include a covered play area for children under 11 years. For older children there is a play barn with table tennis, a skittle alley and a pool table. A tennis court is available to hire. A large, sloping, open field has been terraced to provide 90 grass pitches, 60 with 16A electricity.

Facilities

Toilet facilities have been completely refurbished to a high standard. Unisex showers are in a separate, light and airy part with the laundry and dishwashing sinks. Showers are metered (20p for 4 minutes). Freezer for ice packs. Tourist information. Reception with shop for basics and some camping bits (open main season). Play area. Tennis court. Skittle alley. Caravan storage. Off site: Beach, fishing and sailing 1 mile. Boat launching 3 miles. Riding 5 miles. Golf 4-5 miles.

Open: Easter - October half term.

Directions

Park is clearly signed from Malborough. Follow signs to Soar for 1 mile. Turn left at Rew Cross, then first right for Higher Rew. Take care with single track roads, although there are always plenty of passing places. O.S.GR: SX73381. GPS: 50.230174, -3.805647

Charges guide

Per unit incl. 2 persons	£ 5.00 - £ 14.00
extra person	£ 2.00 - £ 3.00
child (2-17 yrs)	free - £ 1.00
electricity	£ 2.00

No credit cards.

HIGHER REW
Higher Rew Camping and Touring Caravan Park
Malborough, Kingsbridge, Devon, TQ7 3BW
Email: enquiries@higherrew.co.uk Tel: 01548 842681
Higher Rew is a family run park in an area of outstanding natural beauty close to the beautiful Salcombe Estuary. We have, over many years, created a relaxed caravan and camping park for your enjoyment.

Kingsbridge
Karrageen Caravan & Camping Park

Bolberry, Malborough, Kingsbridge TQ7 3EN (Devon) T: **01548 561230**. E: phil@karrageen.co.uk

alanrogers.com/UK0825

Karrageen is to be found in a wonderful area of Devon, near Kingsbridge and Salcombe, with a mixture of rolling countryside, hidden coves, cliff tops and sandy beaches. You can walk, sail, surf or just relax and enjoy the wonderful scenery. This is a small family park run personally by the Higgin family, and situated in the hamlet of Bolberry, one mile up the lane from Hope Cove. The main camping field slopes gently with either sea or rural views. It has been terraced with hedging to provide 70 grassy pitches with 54 electricity connections (10A). There are some 20 places specifically designed for touring caravans.

Facilities

The attractively decorated toilet block includes two curtained washbasins for privacy. En-suite provision for disabled visitors doubles as a family shower room. Parent and baby room. Laundry room. Separate dishwashing (metered as it is spring water, 20p). Freezer for ice packs. Shop including some basic camping equipment. Fresh baguettes and croissants daily. Calor and camping gas. Takeaway (evenings only, last orders 19.00). No play area as such but two open areas for ball games. Off site: Fishing, boat launching and beach 1 mile. Golf 3 miles. Riding 6 miles. Salcombe, sailing Mecca and fishing port with sandy beaches 3.5 miles. Kingsbridge, ancient market town 6 miles.

Open: Easter - 29 September.

Directions

Travelling south from Exeter on the A38, take the A3121 (signed Ermington and Modbury). Follow signs to Kingsbridge and Salcombe. At Malborough, turn sharp right through the village, following signs for Bolberry for 0.6 mile. Turn right to Bolberry, then after 0.9 miles the park is on the right. On the left is a concrete drive to Karrageen House and reception. Take care with single track lanes, although there are plenty of passing places. O.S.GR: SX692391. GPS: 50.23929, -3.84004

Charges guide

Per unit incl. 2 adults, 2 children	£ 11.00 - £ 19.00
extra person	£ 3.00 - £ 5.00
child (under 17 yrs)	£ 1.00
electricity	£ 2.00 - £ 3.00

No credit cards.

Kingsbridge

Slapton Sands Camping & Caravanning Club Site

Middle Grounds, Slapton, Kingsbridge TQ7 2QW (Devon) T: 01548 580538

alanrogers.com/UK0830

Slapton is a charming village with tiny lanes and cottages, a shop and two historic pubs, one dominated by the ruined tower of an old monastery. The Club site is situated on a well kept meadow overlooking the bay – the sea views are panoramic from some areas of the site, with shelter provided by some large bushes and the surrounding hedge. There are 115 grass pitches, some with a slight slope, and electricity (16A) is available for 46 (including 10 hardstandings). Motorcaravans and tents are accepted but the planners will only permit eight caravan pitches which are kept for club members.

Facilities	Directions
The modern toilet block is central, can be heated and is kept very clean, with washbasins in private cabins. Useful parent and child room and separate unit for disabled visitors (with key). Washing machine and dryer (and outside lines). Motorcaravan service point. Reception has a small library, gas and freezer for ice blocks. Small play area. Off site: Riding 0.5 miles. The Field Studies Centre arranges guided walks and short study courses on a wide variety of interests and can issue fishing permits for the Ley. Beach fishing is also popular.	From A38 Exeter - Plymouth road, take the A384 to Totnes. Just before town, turn right on the A381 to Kingsbridge, then A379 through Stokenham and Torcross to Slapton Sands. Half way along the beach road turn left to Slapton village and site is 200 yds on right. Note: Avoid very narrow Five Mile Lane from the A381 signed Slapton 6 miles from Kingsbridge. O.S.GR: SX825450. GPS: 50.29065, -3.65059

Open: March - October.

Charges guide

Per person	£ 4.90 - £ 8.25
pitch (non-member)	£ 5.65

Little Torrington

Smytham Manor Leisure

Smytham Manor, Little Torrington EX38 8PU (Devon) T: 01805 622110. E: info@smytham.co.uk

alanrogers.com/UK1065

A family owned, rural retreat of 25 acres, Smytham Manor is hidden away in its own valley some 10 miles south of Bideford and 18 miles north of Okehampton. Part landscaped with neat grass and magnificent trees, the house is to one side of the valley with some privately owned mobile homes and more to the other side with pretty gardens. Tents have space in the walled garden where the swimming pool is situated and caravans go on terraced grass opposite. There is room for 45 units, of which 44 can have 16A electricity connections. Some pitches have gravel hardstanding.

Facilities	Directions
Very smart, heated toilet block with every modern facility, including provision for disabled visitors which double as a baby room. Bar with terrace overlooking the valley (open evenings, weekends only low season). Milk, bread and daily essentials at reception. Swimming pool (May - Sept). Adventure playground. Games room. Off site: Fishing, golf and bicycle hire 2 miles. Riding 4 miles. Beach 8 miles. Great Torrington 2 miles or along the Tarka Trail.	From Bideford follow A386 Okehampton road through Great Torrington. Turn right to park after 2 miles. From A30 pick up A386 south of Okehampton and go north for 18 miles towards Great Torrington. O.S.GR: SS484163. GPS: 50.925141, -4.157663

Open: March - October.

Charges guide

Per unit incl. 2 persons and electricity	£ 13.50 - £ 23.00
extra person (over 5 yrs)	£ 1.50 - £ 2.50

Lynton

Channel View Caravan & Camping Park

Manor Farm, Barbrook, Lynton EX35 6LD (Devon) T: 01598 753349. E: relax@channel-view.co.uk

alanrogers.com/UK0680

Channel View is a quiet, family-run park set in a sunny, south-facing position overlooking Lynton and Lynmouth. The gently sloping ground provides fairly level pitches which are mostly on hardstandings. The park is divided into two areas, an open area that is sheltered by bushes and trees and one that is more exposed but has views. There are 15 serviced pitches with electricity, water and drainage, and 60 with electricity (16A). The grass is well cared for and there is site lighting, although a torch would be useful. There is a café on the site that also offers takeaways.

Facilities	Directions
The modern and very clean toilet and shower block is partly tiled. Showers are free (here are three steps down to the ladies showers from the toilets). Baby changing/family washroom. Facilities for disabled visitors (Radar key). Laundry. Café. Small shop. Play area. Off site: Lynton and Lynmouth, Exmoor and the Doone Valley are nearby. Many walks can be started from the site. Riding 1 mile. Fishing 1 mile. Golf 15 miles. Beach 2 miles.	On the A399 from Ilfracombe, turn left on A39 and continue past the turn for Lynton to site on the left after 2 miles. Do not approach from Lynton/Lynmouth. O.S.GR: SS724482. GPS: 51.21800, -3.82930

Open: 15 March - 15 November.

Charges guide

Per unit incl. 2 persons	£ 10.00 - £ 15.00
incl. electricity	£ 12.00 - £ 14.00
extra person	£ 3.00 - £ 4.00
child (6-16 yrs)	£ 1.00 - £ 3.00

61

Modbury
Moor View Touring Park
California Cross, Modbury PL21 0SG (Devon) T: **01548 821485**. E: info@moorviewtouringpark.co.uk
alanrogers.com/UK0820

Moor View has a gently sloping position with terraced, individual, fairly level grass pitches with marvellous views across to the Dartmoor Tors. This is a park in a lovely corner of Devon, run personally by the enthusiastic owners, Edward and Liz Corwood. A member of the Countryside Discovery group and an 'adults only' park. It provides 68 pitches of varying size, connected by hardcore roads. All are on hardstanding with 10A electricity, water and drainage. Bushes and shrubs planted between the pitches are growing well giving the park a more mature feel. A two acre field provides space for the odd rally.

Facilities

Traditional style, heated toilet facilities have access from a courtyard area and are kept clean, providing all necessary facilities including a laundry room and sink, and covered dishwashing sinks. Shop. Takeaway in season (to order, 18.30-20.30). TV room. WiFi. Off site: Golf 5 miles, riding and fishing 6 miles. A local country pub is within walking distance, the small town of Modbury is 3 miles.

Open: All year.

Directions

Leave the A38 at Wrangaton Cross, signed Ermington, Modbury and Yealmpton. Turn left and straight on at crossroads signed Modbury, Kingsbridge for 3 miles to California Cross. Leave garage on left and follow towards Modbury (B3207). Park is 0.5 miles on left. O.S.GR: SX705533. GPS: 50.363691, -3.817444

Charges guide

Per unit incl. 2 persons	
and electricity	£ 7.95 - £ 20.95
tent pitch	£ 8.95 - £ 14.95

Mortehoe
Warcombe Farm Camping Park
Station Road, Mortehoe EX34 7EJ (Devon) T: **01271 870690**. E: info@warcombefarm.co.uk
alanrogers.com/UK0725

This park is set in a quiet position on a hill above Woolacombe. It is a large, fairly open site on gently sloping land. There are 250 level or fairly level pitches, some secluded and some extra large with hardstanding and electricity, and others fully serviced. Shrubs and trees help to divide some of the pitches. Two hardstanding pitches are designed to provide facilities and access for disabled campers. In total, 160 pitches have electricity hook ups (16A). The site has panoramic views across to the sea and at its centre has a fully fenced, lovely, well kept lake that is a haven for wildlife.

Facilities

Two modern toilet blocks are spotlessly clean, with free preset showers. En-suite facilities in one block. Family bathrooms and facilities for disabled visitors (coded locks). Laundry with washing machines, dryers and iron. Motorcaravan services. Shop. Takeaway (w/ends only in low season). Play area. Fishing. Torches useful. Off site: Woolacombe beach is 1.5 miles. Public footpaths and cycle trails (the Tarka Trail is on the doorstep). Riding and golf 1 miles. Bicycle hire 4 miles.

Open: 15 March - 31 October.

Directions

From Barnstaple on A361 follow signs for Ilfracombe. At Mullacott Cross (10 miles from Barnstaple) turn left and follow B3343 for Woolacombe. After 1.8 miles turn right for Mortehoe. Park is first right in 500 yards. O.S.GR: SS477457. GPS: 51.190441, -4.180639

Charges guide

Per unit incl. 2 persons	
and electricity	£ 12.50 - £ 28.00
serviced pitch	£ 15.00 - £ 30.00
extra person	£ 2.00 - £ 4.00

Newton Abbot
Woodville Caravan Park
Totnes Road, Ipplepen, Newton Abbot TQ12 5TN (Devon) T: **01803 812240**. E: info@woodvillepark.co.uk
alanrogers.com/UK0915

A lovely little site for 'adults only', Woodville is in a sheltered situation, attractively laid out with a wide variety of shrubs and trees. There are 26 pitches all with hardstanding and 16A electricity. They are accessed by a circular roadway which provides a central lawned area. A caravan storage area is to one side. This is a quiet site with few services, although the park is adjacent to a garden centre which also sells food and drinks. Dainton Park golf course is directly opposite and Ipplepen village is within walking distance and has three pubs. The owners live on the site and take a pride in their park.

Facilities

A fully equipped toilet block also provides a separate unit for visitors with disabilities. Washing machine and freezer. Vans selling fish and chips and eggs call weekly. Wooden chalet with tourist information doubles as reception open for an hour or two each morning. Off site: Shop and golf course adjacent. Three pubs within walking distance. Bus service on main road. Fishing 5 miles. Beach 7 miles.

Open: 1 March - 1 January.

Directions

From Newton Abbot follow A381 Totnes road for about 3 miles. Site is on the right just after Fermoys Garden Centre. The site gate is kept closed. O.S.GR: SY296913. GPS: 50.49505, -3.62965

Charges guide

Per unit incl. 2 persons	
	£ 13.50 - £ 14.50
extra person	£ 3.00 - £ 3.50
pet	£ 0.50

Newton Abbot

Dornafield

Two Mile Oak, Newton Abbot TQ12 6DD (Devon) T: 01803 812732. E: enquiries@dornafield.com

alanrogers.com/UK0880

The entrance to Dornafield leads into the charming old courtyard of a 14th-Century farmhouse giving a mellow feeling that is complemented by the warm welcome from the Dewhirst family. Having booked in, continue down the lane (with a tree covered bank alive with wild flowers) to the Buttermeadow, a tranquil valley providing 75 individual pitches on flat grass, separated by grassy ridges and in some places, wild rose hedges. You pass the walled Orchard, secluded and cosy for tents. Or take the road up the hill to Blackrock Copse with large luxury pitches with all facilities including a chemical disposal point and cleverly concealed TV connections. Electricity points are 10A. Whilst having been carefully designed, the environment remains natural. Dornafield is a member of the Caravan Club's 'Affiliated site' scheme, with both members and non-members made welcome. Member of the Best of British Group.

Facilities

Both modern toilet blocks are excellent and heated, with some washbasins in cubicles and comfortable roomy showers, but the new block up the hill could be said to be 'state of the art' with under-floor heating and a heat recovery system. Both blocks have facilities for disabled visitors and babies. Laundry rooms. Shop. Gas supplies. All-weather tennis court. Games room. Play areas. All-year caravan storage. Off site: Local inn 0.5 miles. Fishing 2.5 miles. Golf 1 mile.

Open: 13 March - 1 January.

Directions

Park is northwest of A381 Newton Abbot - Totnes road. Leave A381 at Two Mile Oak Inn, opposite garage, and turn left at crossroads after about half a mile. Entrance is on the right. O.S.GR: SX848683. GPS: 50.50032, -3.63717

Charges guide

Per unit incl. 2 persons and electricity	£ 13.00 - £ 24.00

Dornafield

For Caravans & Camping

Reservations • Dornafield, Two Mile Oak, Newton Abbot, Devon, TQ12 6DD• Tel: 01803 812732 • Fax: 01803 812032 • www.dornafield.com • enquiries@dornafield.com

Beautiful 14th century farmhouse location in 30 acres of glorious South Devon. So quiet & peaceful yet so convenient for Torbay & Dartmoor. Superb facilities to suit the discerning caravanner. Including 60 all service pitches. Shop, games room, adventure play area, tennis & golf. Our brochure is only a phone call away.

Newton Abbot

Parkers Farm Holiday Park

Higher Mead Farm, Ashburton, Newton Abbot TQ13 7LJ (Devon) T: 01364 654869

E: parkersfarm@btconnect.com alanrogers.com/UK0960

Well situated with fine views towards Dartmoor, Parker's Farm is a modern touring site on a working farm. Close inspection reveals a unique chance to experience Devon country life at first hand, with pigs, sheep, goats, calves and rabbits to feed and touch. The 100 touring pitches are set directly above the farm buildings on broad terraces giving groups of flat pitches, all with good views across the valley (over the A38 which may give some road noise). Electricity (12A) is provided throughout and hardstandings are available. Trees and hedges have matured nicely on the terraces, with many more planted. Caravan holiday homes are available to hire. In addition the Parker family has added a family bar which provides entertainment in the main season (live singers, family bingo, children's entertainers) and a restaurant using locally sourced ingredients. Farm walks are tremendously popular.

Facilities

Two modern and clean shower and toilet blocks provide good facilities with two family shower rooms. Baby bathroom. En-suite room for disabled visitors. Laundry. Shop (Easter - mid Oct). Restaurant, comfortable bar with family room (Easter, then Whitsun - mid Sept) and entertainment. Games room. Indoor play and TV area. Large outdoor play area. Trampolines. Caravan storage. Caravan holiday homes to hire. Rallies welcome. American motorhomes accepted by prior arrangement. Off site: Bicycle hire 5 miles. Golf 4 miles. Riding 5 miles.

Open: Easter - 31 October.

Directions

From Exeter on A38, 26 miles from Plymouth, turn left at Alston Cross signed Woodland Denbury. Site is 400 yards. O.S.GR: SX757702. GPS: 50.525093, -3.724482

Charges guide

Per unit incl. 2 persons	£ 7.00 - £ 16.00
incl. electricity	£ 9.00 - £ 23.00
extra person	£ 3.00
child (3-15 yrs)	£ 2.00
dog	£ 1.50

63

Newton Abbot
Ross Park

Park Hill Farm, Ipplepen, Newton Abbot TQ12 5TT (Devon) T: **01803 812983**
E: **enquiries@rossparkcaravanpark.co.uk alanrogers.com/UK0910**

Ross Park has to be seen to appreciate the amazing floral displays with their dramatic colours, that are a feature of the park. These are complemented by the use of a wide variety of shrubs which form hedging for most of the 110 pitches to provide your own special plot, very much as on the continent. Many pitches have wonderful views over the surrounding countryside and for those who prefer the more open style, one small area has been left unhedged. The owners, Mark and Helen Lowe, continue to strive to provide quality facilities and maintain standards, and this is reflected in the awards they have won. The New Barn provides a comfortable lounge, a mezzanine bar with bar snacks and a restaurant with extra seating in the conservatory which is home to some exotic and colourful plants. The touring area is divided into bays or groups by hedging and shrubs and all 110 pitches are provided with electricity (16A). Some 82 of these have a hardened surface, some made larger with a further gravel area. An orchard area alive with daffodils in the spring and a conservation area with information on wild flowers and butterflies, and with extended views, completes these environmentally considered amenities. Barn dances are organised on Sundays in high season. This is a well cared for park worthy of consideration. A member of the Best of British group.

Facilities

Seven well equipped, heated en-suite units, one with baby facilities, two suitable for disabled people. Further separate shower, washbasin and toilet facilities. Extra heated block with toilets, washbasins in cabins and hair-care centre. Fully equipped laundry room. Utility room with dishwashing, freezer and battery charging. Dog shower. Motorcaravan services. Recycling bins. Reception with licensed shop. Gas supplies. Bar, bar snacks and restaurant (all April - end Oct, plus Christmas and New Year). Conservation and tourist information room. Games room (table tennis, snooker, pool). 7-acre park area for recreation. Croquet green. Badminton. Volleyball. Large well equipped playground. Caravan storage. Off site: Dainton Park 18-hole golf course is adjacent. Fishing 3 miles. Riding 1 mile. Beach 6 miles.

Open: All year excl. January and February.

Directions

From A381 Newton Abbot - Totnes road, park is signed towards Woodland at Park Hill crossroads and Jet filling station. O.S.GR: SX845671.
GPS: 50.491940, -3.634240

Charges guide

Per unit incl. 2 persons	£ 10.50 - £ 20.00
incl. electricity	£ 11.50 - £ 21.00
extra person	£ 3.25 - £ 5.30
child (4-16 yrs)	£ 1.50 - £ 2.50

Christmas packages available.
No credit cards.

Newton Abbot
Lemonford Caravan Park

Bickington, Newton Abbot TQ12 6JR (Devon) T: **01626 821242**. E: **info@lemonford.co.uk**
alanrogers.com/UK0980

Lemonford is a well-run, neat and tidy site for all ages and families on the southern edge of the National Park, some three miles from both Ashburton and Newton Abbot. It has the look and atmosphere of the 'cultivated' caravan park, close to the main road, yet set in a sheltered, peaceful dip bordered by the pretty River Lemon. There are 85 pitches (around 40 used as seasonal pitches) on level grass and grouped in four areas with some new, fully-serviced pitches added. Most have 12A electricity (some 16A); over 55 have hardstanding. A good pub is within walking distance, along the banks of the river.

Facilities

Two modern toilet blocks, one new, can be heated and provide some large private cabins, a ladies' bathroom (£1 payment) and a family bathroom. The new block has facilities for disabled visitors. Laundry facilities. Shop. Gas supplies. Freezer service. Play area. No commercial vehicles are accepted. Off site: Fishing 4 miles, riding and bicycle hire 3 miles, golf 2 miles. Leisure pool in Newton Abbot.

Open: All year.

Directions

From Exeter, turn off A38 at A382 (Drumbridges) exit signed Newton Abbot, Mortonhampstead. At roundabout take third exit to Bickington. Continue for 3 miles and park is on left at the bottom of the hill. From Plymouth, take A383 (Goodstone) exit, cross A38 and take first left to Bickington to site on right. O.S.GR: SX793723. GPS: 50.5391, -3.704

Charges guide

Per unit incl. 2 persons and electricity	£ 13.00 - £ 19.00

Special low season offers.

Paignton

Whitehill Country Park

Stoke Road, Paignton TQ4 7PF (Devon) T: 01803 782338. E: info@whitehill-park.co.uk

alanrogers.com/UK0860

Whitehill Country Park is beautifully situated in rolling Devon countryside, just 2.5 miles from the nearest beaches. Extending over 40 acres, a definite sense of space characterises this park and 10 acres of ancient woodland are available for walks and attract a great deal of wildlife. Whitehill is a friendly park with 320 large grassy pitches which are located in separate fields around the site with evocative names, such as Nine Acres, Sweethill and Coombe Meadow. Most pitches have electrical connections (16A). Around 60 pitches are used for caravan holiday homes. The park boasts an attractive swimming pool (max. depth 1.3 m) with a children's paddling pool alongside, as well as a good range of other leisure facilities, notably The Hayloft bar (with satellite TV), a café and an extensive decking area for outside eating.

Facilities

Two brand new sanitary blocks include private, individual washing facilities for ladies. Ample laundry facilities. Gas supplies. Shop. Bar. Café (24/5-1/9). Swimming and paddling pools (heated 17/5-1/9). Three play areas. Electronic games. Craft centre for children. Dogs and other pets are not accepted. Off site: Paignton (Zoo and Steam Railway) 2.5 miles. Beach 3 miles. Fishing and golf 2 miles. Riding 4 miles. Torquay, Dartmoor, Quay West Aqua Park. Bus stop at site entrance.

Open: Easter - 30 September.

Directions

Turn left at The Parkers Arms off the A385 Paignton to Totnes road, signed Stoke Gabriel. Site is 1 mile along this road. O.S.GR: SX857587. GPS: 50.417867, -3.609

Charges guide

Per unit incl. 2 persons and electricity	£ 14.50 - £ 27.50
tent pitch incl. 2 persons	£ 12.50 - £ 23.00
extra person	£ 4.00
child	£ 3.00

Camping Cheques accepted.

Paignton

Byslades International Touring Park

Totnes Road, Paignton TQ4 7PY (Devon) T: 01803 555072. E: info@byslades.co.uk

alanrogers.com/UK0865

Byslades is a large, well maintained touring park covering 23 acres on the side of a valley. The site is cut into terraces on the steepest slopes, so that most of the pitches are level. Many of the pitches (grass and hardstanding) have a lovely view across the valley to the fields on the other side. There are 190 pitches, 150 with electricity (10/16A). There is a security barrier at the entrance to the park and CCTV has been installed. There is a large heated outdoor swimming pool, with a special area for toddlers. A café is nearby which also sells bread, milk and a few essentials.

Facilities

Two modern toilet blocks are kept very clean, with some washbasins in private cubicles and free showers (with dividing curtain). Facilities for disabled visitors (access by key). Baby changing facilities in the Ladies. Laundry. Freezer for ice packs. Motorcaravan point. Café with takeaway and basic supplies. Club house with bar. Swimming pool. Play area. Off site: Bus stop near park entrance (Totnes and Paignton). Fishing ajacent. Beach 3 miles.

Open: May - September.

Directions

Leave the A38 near Buckfastleigh (A384) or near South Brent (A385) signed for Totnes. Leave Totnes on the A385 signed for Paignton and the site is about 3 miles from Totnes on the left. O.S.GR: SX845597. GPS: 50.42997, -3.61702

Charges guide

Per unit incl. 2 persons, electricity	£ 8.00 - £ 14.50
extra person	£ 3.00 - £ 5.00
child (3-12 yrs)	£ 2.00 - £ 3.50

65

Paignton

Beverley Park

Goodrington Road, Paignton TQ4 7JE (Devon) T: 01803 661978. E: info@beverley-holidays.co.uk

alanrogers.com/UK0870

Beverley Park, a good quality holiday centre, celebrated its 50th anniversary in 2008. This popular, busy park is attractively landscaped and has marvellous views over Torbay. The pools, a large dance hall, bars and entertainment, are all run in an efficient and orderly manner. The park has 195 caravan holiday homes and 23 lodges, mainly around the central complex. There are 179 touring pitches in the lower areas of the park, all reasonably sheltered, some with views across the bay and some on slightly sloping ground. All pitches can take awnings and 87 have 16A electricity (15 m. cable), 38 have hardstanding and 42 are fully serviced. Tents are accepted and a limited number of tent pitches have electrical connections. The park has a long season and reservations are essential for caravans. Entertainment is organised at Easter and from early May in the Starlight Cabaret bar. There are indoor and outdoor pools, each one heated and supervised. The Oasis fitness centre provides a steam room, jacuzzi, sunbed and an excellent fitness room. The park is in the heart of residential Torbay, with views across the bay to Brixham and Torquay, and sandy beaches less than a mile away. There is a regular local bus service to Paignton, Torbay and Brixham and minibus service to the beach and town. This popular park has lots to offer and is well maintained and run. A member of the Best of British group.

Facilities

Good toilet blocks adjacent to the pitches, well maintained and heated, include roomy showers, some with washbasins en-suite. Baths on payment. Unit for disabled visitors. Facilities for babies. Laundry. Gas supplies. Motorcaravan service point. Large general shop (29/3-29/10). Restaurant, bars and takeaway (all Easter, then 30/4-29/10, and Autumn half-term). Heated pools, outdoor 22/5-4/9, indoor all year. Fitness centre. Tennis. Crazy golf. Playground. Amusement centre. Soft play area. Dogs are not accepted. Off site:Fishing, bicycle hire, riding and golf within 2 miles.

Open: All year.

Directions

Park is south of Paignton in Goodrington Road between A379 coast road and B3203 ring road and is well signed on both. O.S.GR: SX882584. GPS: 50.413533, -3.568667

Charges guide

Per unit incl. 2 persons and electricity	£ 15.00 - £ 32.00
tent pitch incl. 2 persons	£ 12.50 - £ 28.00
extra person	£ 3.50 - £ 4.70

Max. 6 persons per reservation.

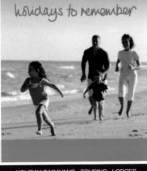
Paignton

Hoburne Torbay

Goodrington, Paignton TQ4 7JP (Devon) T: 01803 558010. E: enquiries@hoburne.co.uk

alanrogers.com/UK1130

Situated to the south of central Paignton, with a short, signed walk to the sea and some sea views of Torbay, this Hoburne park's major interest is a complex of 560 holiday homes (120 to let). However, there are 60 touring pitches (no tents) on flat grass by the entrance. The pitches are of a reasonable size, although with some variation, and all have 10A electricity. The central club complex is the park's best feature, with a good sized heated outdoor pool and a super indoor pool with views across the bay.

Facilities

Two toilet blocks of modern design. Launderette. Shop. Motorcaravan service point. Club room. Restaurant/bar. Takeaway. Heated outdoor pool. Indoor pool with flume. Sauna and steam room. Amusement arcade. TV room. Crazy golf. Adventure playground. Indoor soft adventure play area. Daily children's entertainment. Up to 30 American motorhomes accepted (25 ft. max). Dogs are not accepted.

Open: 14 February - 15 January excl. 2 weeks at Christmas.

Directions

Park is signed from the outer Paignton ring road. Look for left turn into Goodrington Road, then left into Grange Road. O.S.GR: SX890585. GPS: 50.41985, -3.56783

Charges guide

Per unit incl. up to 6 persons	£ 11.50 - £ 27.50

Paignton

Widdicombe Farm Tourist Park

The Ring Road, Compton, Paignton TQ3 1ST (Devon) T: 01803 558325. E: info@widdicombefarm.co.uk
alanrogers.com/UK0900

Widdicombe Farm, an 'adult only' park from 2010, is just three miles from Torquay and with easy access from the A380, well situated for the Torbay area. There are 200 numbered pitches, most with electricity (10A) of which most have hardstanding and 38 are fully serviced. Surrounded by farmland, the pitches are on terraces with open views across the countryside. Many trees and shrubs have been planted and there are tarmac access roads. There may be some background traffic noise but it is not too intrusive. Touring areas are separated into sections for couples, tent campers, etc. A large comfortable bar offers entertainment and barbecued food is served during most entertainment evenings. The site has a relaxed, friendly feel.

Facilities

Three older style toilet blocks are kept very clean. The original heated block near reception is fully equipped and includes facilities for disabled people, dishwashing area and laundry room. Shop and 'Poppy' restaurant (evening meals, breakfasts, cream teas and takeaway) and bar (all Easter, then spring B.H - mid Oct). Certain breeds of dog are not accepted. Caravan storage. Off site: Fishing, bicycle hire, and golf, all within 2 miles.

Open: 24 March - 18 October.

Directions

From Newton Abbot take A380 south for about 5 miles; site is well signed off this road. O.S.GR: SX874641 GPS: 50.467081, -3.586797

Charges guide

Per unit incl. 2 persons	
and electricity	£ 10.50 - £ 22.00
extra person	£ 3.50 - £ 4.00
dog	£ 1.50 - £ 2.00

Bargain breaks available.

Plymouth

Riverside Caravan Park

Leigham Manor Drive, Marsh Mills, Plymouth PL6 8LL (Devon) T: 01752 344122
E: info@riversidecaravanpark.com alanrogers.com/UK0810

As you leave the A38 for Plymouth and negotiate the Marsh Mills roundabout you can have no idea that there is a lush green touring park tucked away from the modern, out-of-town shopping units in a quiet green valley. There are 232 pitches for caravans or motorcaravans, 150 of which have electricity (10A) and 60 are on hardstanding – especially useful as the site is open all year round. There is further provision for 60 tents. Hidden behind a high, evergreen hedge are an attractive swimming pool and a children's pool. A play area is nearby and a pleasant restaurant with bar and games room provide welcome facilities and entertainment in high season. 27 years ago the park was a corn field but, with careful development by its owner, it now provides a welcome oasis from which to explore Dartmoor, to enjoy the amazing views from Plymouth Hoe or even to overnight quietly before catching the ferry to France. The wooded valley sides give way to level grass where the trees and shrubs planted all those years ago have matured to give a park-like feel. The River Plym runs down one side of the site but it is carefully fenced.

Facilities

Three modern, fully equipped toilet blocks include cubicles with toilets and washbasins. Laundry room. Motorcaravan service point. Gas supplies. Basics are kept in reception (more in high season). Bar, restaurant and takeaway (B.Hs and high season) with family entertainment included. Heated swimming pool and children's pool. Games room with TV. Play area. Off site: Fishing possible in River Plym. Sea fishing 3.5 miles. Golf and riding 5 miles. Bicycle hire and boat launching 3.5 miles. Beach 10 miles. Dry ski slope and supermarket within walking distance. Bus stop 10 minutes.

Open: All year.

Directions

From the A38 Marsh Mills roundabout for Plymouth take the third exit. After a few yards turn left following caravan signs, then right alongside the River Plym to the park. O.S.GR: SX518576. GPS: 50.398167, -4.087333

Charges guide

Per person	£ 3.25 - £ 5.50
child (3-10 yrs)	£ 1.75 - £ 2.50
pitch incl. electricity	£ 5.50 - £ 7.50
tent pitch	£ 3.50 - £ 6.50
dog or pup tent, extra car or boat	£ 1.00 - £ 2.00

67

Sidmouth

Salcombe Regis Camping & Caravan Park

Salcombe Regis, Sidmouth EX10 0JH (Devon) T: 01395 514303. E: contact@salcombe-regis.co.uk

alanrogers.com/UK1110

On the edge of Salcombe Regis village, 1.5 miles from Sidmouth and less than a mile from the sea. Salcombe Regis Park covers 16 acres of land. It is surrounded by farmland with views of the combe and the sea beyond. The focal point of the main camping area is a large 'village green' where the play area and pitch and putt are located. The reception and pitches are arranged around the green, all connected by a tarmac road. The 110 pitches are level and have their own water supply, with 98 electricity hook-ups (16A). A 25 minute walk across fields takes you to a small secluded beach, although the walk there is fairly steep – we are told there are 129 steps that take you down to the beach! There are many footpaths and coastal walks nearby, protected by the National Trust and with views of Sidmouth and Weston Mouth. Sidmouth town, originally a small fishing town but now a seaside resort, is host to the annual International Folk Festival, where for one week in summer the town is filled with folk artists from all over the world.

Facilities

The traditional style toilet block (to one side of the site and a longer walk for some) is kept spotlessly clean by the resident wardens and includes a bathroom for families and disabled visitors. Shop at reception selling basic supplies and local produce. Dishwashing area under cover. Laundry room with washing machines, dryers and ironing board. Motorcaravan service point. Play area. Pitch and putt. Caravan storage. Torches useful. Off site: Fishing, bicycle hire and golf 1.5 miles. Riding 3 miles. Sidmouth and beach 1.5 miles.

Open: Easter - 28 October.

Directions

Park is well signed on the A3052 Exeter - Lyme Regis road. From the east, take first left after Donkey Sanctuary. From the west proceed up the hill out of Sidford. Do not take first road signed Salcombe Regis, but take the next right at top of hill. Follow road round to site on left after golf range. O.S.GR: SY149892. GPS: 50.695717, -3.205367

Charges guide

Per unit incl. 2 persons	£ 10.50 - £ 15.50
incl. electricity	£ 14.00 - £ 19.00
extra person	£ 3.65
child (5-15 yrs)	£ 2.25

South Molton

Riverside Caravan Park

Marsh Lane, North Molton Road, South Molton EX36 3HQ (Devon) T: 01769 579 269

E: relax@exmoorriverside.co.uk alanrogers.com/UK0745

A very impressive purpose-built campsite beside the River Mole, all the 44 pitches at this park have hardstanding, 16A electricity connection, water, drainage and TV aerial socket. Neat grass, tarmac roads and growing trees and hedges contribute to the attractive, overall impression. The heated toilet block gleams but the highlight must be the chemical disposal point which has its own special house and is tiled with a washbasin (would they were all like that!) The owners, Joy and Nicky Penfold, are not resting on their laurels and are currently developing fishing lakes down by the river and a play area on the opposite bank. The ancient market town of South Molton is a mile away and a bus stops outside the site entrance. Exmoor is on hand to explore, as are the North Devon resorts of Woolacombe, Ilfracombe, Combe Martin and Lynton, not to mention the surfing paradise of Croyde Bay.

Facilities

Modern, fully-equipped and heated toilet block accessed by code. Facilities for disabled visitors. Laundry room. Shop (limited hours in low season). Play area planned. Fishing. Caravan storage. Swimming in river. Off site: Riding 2 miles. Golf 5 miles. Boat launching and beach 12 miles.

Open: All year.

Directions

From M5 exit 27 take the North Devon Link road A361. Near South Molton watch for site sign (direction North Molton). O.S.GR: SS723270. GPS: 51.03086, -3.81871

Charges 2010

Per unit incl. 2 adults and 2 children	£ 10.00 - £ 18.00
incl. electricity	£ 14.00 - £ 17.00
extra person	£ 6.00
large motorcaravan	£ 24.00 - £ 29.00

Sidmouth

Oakdown Touring & Holiday Caravan Park

Weston, Sidmouth EX10 0PT (Devon) T: **01297 680387**. E: enquiries@oakdown.co.uk

alanrogers.com/UK1020

Oakdown is a very attractive, well-planned park and the Franks family and their team continue to work hard to provide a warm welcome. The attention to detail is evident at this award-winning park as soon as you arrive. The park has easy access, beautiful floral displays and a spacious feeling. There are 100 level touring pitches arranged in landscaped bays, screened by a wide range of trees and shrubs and linked by a circular road. All have 10/16A electricity, all have hardstanding and many have water and drainage. A new touring area, Beech Grove, provides a further 50 pitches (all with 16A electricity) and a new, fully-equipped toilet block. There are two bays on the park with 16 caravan holiday homes for rent and Oak Grove, a separate neat area contains 46 privately owned holiday homes. Waste water is dealt with by a Victorian style reed bed which has encouraged more birds and a hide has been established. The field trail, a haven for wild flowers and birds leads to the nearby Donkey Sanctuary. Recent additions include a lake, dew pond and further wild flower areas and there is a 9-hole, par 3 Approach golf course. Continual improvements make this park an excellent choice for visitors with disabilities. A Best of British Group member.

Facilities

The original central toilet block provides well-maintained, fully equipped, heated sanitary facilities. One private cabin for ladies. Two unisex family bathrooms (bath, shower, toilet, washbasin and coin operated entry), double as units for disabled people. Laundry facilities plus free freezer and microwave. New facilities in Beech Grove including full facilities, a room for families and disabled visitors, and a laundry. Motorcaravan service point. New shop (mid-May - mid-Sept). Internet room. Fax service. TV room. Two adventure play areas and castle. No cycling, skate-boarding or kite flying is permitted. Caravan storage. Off site: Riding 6 miles. Golf adjacent. Swimming 1 mile. Beach 2 miles.

Open: 14 March - 2 November.

Directions

Turn south off the A3052 (Exeter - Lyme Regis) road between Sidford and Colyford, 2.5 miles east of the A375 junction and park is on left. O.S.GR: SY167902. GPS: 50.7056, -3.18063

Charges guide

Per unit incl. 2 persons	
and electricity	£ 15.00 - £ 21.25
incl. mains services	£ 20.50 - £ 26.50
extra person (5 yrs and over)	£ 3.00
dog	£ 2.30

Less 70p for senior citizens in low season.

Tavistock

Higher Longford Caravan Park

Moorshop, Tavistock PL19 9LQ (Devon) T: 01822 613360. E: stay@higherlongford.co.uk

alanrogers.com/UK0800

This attractive family run park is situated within the Dartmoor National Park boundaries with views up to the higher slopes of the moor. A neat, sheltered field provides 40 level pitches arranged on each side of a circular access road, with three smaller touring areas for a further 12 units, a small terraced camping field with good views and a seasonal camping field for a further 40. There are 65 electrical hook-ups (16A), several multi-serviced pitches and an area of hardstanding for motorcaravans in poor weather. Some attractive converted cottages form a courtyard area with the farmhouse and reception. Within the 14th-century farmhouse is a small licensed shop with gas and some farm produce, and a takeaway including breakfast items and fresh bread. It adjoins a pleasant, cosy campers' lounge with pool table and TV which is open all day. Higher Longford is an ideal centre for touring Dartmoor, either by car, on foot, or astride a local pony (riding stables nearby). Plymouth and the cross-channel ferries are a 30 minute drive, Tavistock is three miles, with a good market and Goose Fair in October.

Facilities

A heated toilet block provides excellent full en-suite facilities (amongst the best we have seen) plus extra toilets and washbasins. Family bathroom and baby changing. Full laundry facilities. Motorcaravan services. Ice block service. Shop and takeaway (hours limited in winter). Campers' lounge with pool and TV. Large recreation field with adventure play area in centre. Nature area. Adventure trail for children and walks. Caravan storage. Off site: Bus service outside park. Tavistock golf course 1 mile. Bicycle hire 2.5 miles. Game or coarse fishing 3 miles. Riding 5 miles. Beach 15 miles.

Open: All year.

Directions

Park is clearly signed from the B3357 Princetown road, 2 miles from Tavistock. O.S.GR: SX520747. GPS: 50.5535, -4.093717

Charges guide

Per person	£ 3.50 - £ 6.00
child (5-16 yrs)	£ 1.10 - £ 3.00
pitch incl. electricity	£ 4.50 - £ 10.00
tent pitch	£ 5.50 - £ 7.00

Tavistock

Langstone Manor Holiday Park

Moortown, Tavistock PL19 9JZ (Devon) T: 01822 613371. E: web@langstone-manor.co.uk

alanrogers.com/UK0802

Situated on the southwest edge of Dartmoor, this holiday park has been developed in the grounds of the old Langstone Manor house. The touring pitches are tucked into various garden areas with mature trees and flowering shrubs, or in the walled garden area with views over the moor. In all there are 42 level grass pitches which vary in size (30 with 10A electricity). A new camping area has been terraced and has open views over farmland and the moor. You pass through a number of holiday caravans on the way to reception and the touring pitches where you will also find some holiday cottages and flats for rent. The 'pièce de résistance' is the unexpected traditional bar and restaurant in the Manor House, complete with a terrace that catches the evening sun. Open in high season and on demand in low season it has an open fire (if needed). Approaching over a short section of the moor, you realise how well Langstone Manor is situated to explore Dartmoor by foot, by car or on bike (the park has direct access). Tavistock is 3 miles away and there is a wealth of National Trust Houses and Gardens to visit nearby.

Facilities

The toilet block is set to one side of the walled garden area, fully equipped and well maintained. Showers on payment (20p tokens from reception or bar). Fully equipped laundry room . Changing mat for babies in the ladies. Basic supplies kept in reception (order bread the day before). Bar/restaurant. Play area. Off site: Leisure centre and pool 2 miles. Golf 1 mile. Fishing 2 miles. Bicycle hire 3 miles. Boat Launching 10 miles. Sailing 15 miles.

Open: 15 March - 29 October.

Directions

From Tavistock take B3357 Princetown road. After about 2 miles turn right at crossroads (site signed). Pass over cattle grid onto the moor and follow site signs. O.S.GR: SX524738 GPS: 50.5449, -4.084167

Charges guide

Per unit incl. 2 persons and electricity	£ 15.00 - £ 18.00
extra person	£ 4.00
child (3-11 yrs)	£ 3.00
dog	free

Tavistock
Harford Bridge Holiday Park

Peter Tavy, Tavistock PL19 9LS (Devon) T: **01822 810349**. E: enquiry@harfordbridge.co.uk
alanrogers.com/UK0790

Harford Bridge has an interesting history – originally the Wheal Union tin mine until 1850, then used as a farm campsite from 1930 and taken over by the Royal Engineers in 1939. It is now a quiet, rural, mature park inside the Dartmoor National Park. It is bounded by the River Tavy on one side and the lane from the main road to the village of Peter Tavy on the other, with Harford Bridge, a classic granite moorland bridge, at the corner. With 16.5 acres, the park provides 120 touring pitches well spaced on a level grassy meadow with some shade from mature trees and others recently planted; 52 pitches have electrical hook-ups and 10 have 'multi-services', five with hardstanding. Out of season or by booking in advance you may get one of the delightful spots bordering the river (these are without electricity). Some holiday caravans and chalets are neatly landscaped in their own area. At the entrance to the park a central grassy area is left free for games, which is also used by the town band, village fete, etc. While the river (unfenced) will inevitably mesmerise youngsters, a super central adventure play area on a hilly tree knoll will claim them. In early summer there are chicks to watch, horses to make a fuss of and the park ducks are a feature. With its own and the local history, plus its situation, this is a super place to stay.

Facilities

The single toilet block is older in style but fully equipped and well kept, with free hot water and showers all year. Facilities for disabled visitors and babies. Good launderette and drying room. Freezer. Motorcaravan service point. Games room with table tennis and separate TV room. Play area. Tennis court (free). Two communal barbecue areas. Fly fishing (by licence, £3 p/day, £10 p/week). WiFi planned. Off site: Bicycle hire, riding and golf, all within 2.5 miles. West Devon cycle way adjacent to park. Tavistock market twice monthly.

Open: All year.

Directions

Two miles north of Tavistock, off A386 Tavistock - Okehampton road, take the road to Peter Tavy. O.S.GR: SX504768. GPS: 50.5713, -4.114

Charges guide

Per unit incl. 2 persons and electricity	£ 14.25 - £ 18.75
with full services	£ 15.25 - £ 20.25

- Beautiful level sheltered park set in Dartmoor beside the River Tavy with delightful views of the moor
- Riverside camping and other level spacious pitches
- Free hot water and showers
- Luxury self-catering caravan holiday homes and lodge
- Tennis court, table tennis, children's play area, fly fishing, dog exercise field, free roaming ducks
- Nearby horse riding, golf, cinema/theatre, indoor swimming pool, cycle route 27
- Ideally situated for exploring Devon & Cornwall, walking the moor or just relaxing on this beautiful peaceful park
- Parking alongside units. Open all year

HARFORD BRIDGE HOLIDAY PARK

Peter Tavy, Tavistock, Devon PL19 9LS
Tel: 01822 810349 Fax: 01822 810028
Email: enquiry@harfordbridge.co.uk
Website: www.harfordbridge.co.uk
Just 2 miles from Tavistock off A386
Okehampton Road, take Peter Tavy turn

Tavistock
Woodovis Park

Woodovis House, Gulworthy, Tavistock PL19 8NY (Devon) T: **01822 832968**. E: info@woodovis.com
alanrogers.com/UK0805

Woodovis Park is set in the grounds of Woodovis House, owned in the 19th century by a mine captain in the days when the valley had a thriving copper mining industry. It nestles in a sheltered wooded position covering 14 acres, by the edge of the Tamar Valley on the borders of Devon and Cornwall. John and Dorothy Lewis have been running Woodovis Park since 1999, helped by their very welcoming staff. There are 50 good sized pitches, all with 10A electricity. You have a choice of grass, all weather and 'super' pitches (with water, waste and tv hook-ups too). Split over two fields and landscaped inbetween are 35 caravan holiday homes. The whole area is sheltered by thick hedges and woodland, but in places you can see across the valley to Cornwall. An indoor heated swimming pool complete with spa pool and sauna are a welcome attraction. A member of the Best of British group.

Facilities

A purpose built, modern toilet block is fully equipped. Bathroom (coin operated) could be used by disabled people or for babies. Family cubicles. Toilet for disabled visitors at the pool. Fully equipped laundry. Motorcaravan service point. Shop for basics with off licence doubles with reception. Indoor heated pool (no swimming alone), spa and sauna. Good games room including large size 'Connect 4'! Fenced play area. Minigolf. Archery and 'water-walking' organised weekly during school holidays. WiFi. Off site: Pub with restaurant within walking distance. Fishing 1.5 miles. Golf, riding and bicycle hire 3 miles. Boat launching 6 miles. Tavistock 4 miles.

Open: 27 March - 30 October.

Directions

From Tavistock follow A390 for Liskeard. After 3 miles turn right at Gulworthy roundabout signed Chipshop, Lamerton and Caravan Park. After 1 mile entrance is signed on left. O.S.GR: SX431743. GPS: 50.548867, -4.21585

Charges guide

Per person (over 5 yrs)	£ 6.00
pitch incl. electricity	£ 6.00 - £ 20.00
awning	£ 2.00

Teignmouth

Coast View Holiday Park

Torquay Road, Shaldon, Teignmouth TQ14 0BG (Devon) T: **01626 872392**. E: info@coastview.co.uk
alanrogers.com/UK1080

On the coast road between Teignmouth and Torquay with magnificent views over Lyme Bay, this family run park has a section of caravan holiday homes and chalets with the touring area higher on the hillside. There are 18 pitches with hardstanding and 16A electricity, and a number with water in a further area. A level area is kept for motorcaravans. Over 100 pitches for tents are on part sloping, part terraced grass on the hillside with adequate protection from the prevailing southwest winds and marvellous views. To the right of the park entrance is an attractive indoor swimming pool and an entertainment area comprising a clubroom with a bar. Bar meals, snacks and takeaway food are served here. Entertainment is organised each evening and activities in the mornings for children. All these facilities are open all season. Various themed weekends are organised, for example Jazz and Rock and Roll. The park is conveniently located for the beach (1.5 miles) and the coastal footpath is adjacent. Torbay is five miles. A bus service stops at the gates. Good for holidaymakers of all ages, this park offers superb views with a range of facilities.

Facilities	Directions
The modern toilet block is spacious with free hot showers and open washbasins, and includes a baby room. Laundry facilities. Licensed shop for basic provisions. Indoor pool and children's pool. Clubroom with bar, restaurant, takeaway, games room and TV room. Full entertainment programme and themed weekends. Adventure playground and indoor soft play area. Crazy golf. Off site: Beach 1.5 miles. Fishing and golf 1 mile. Riding 3 miles.	From A380 Exeter - Newton Abbot road, take A381 to Teignmouth. On entering town turn right over Shaldon Bridge on B3199 for Torquay. Park is on right in about 1.5 miles. O.S.GR: SX932714. GPS: 50.53455, -3.503167

Open: 15 March - 31 October.

Charges guide

Per unit incl. up to 5 persons and electricity	£ 18.00 - £ 28.00
serviced pitch	£ 25.00 - £ 38.00

Tiverton

Minnows Touring Caravan Park

Sampford Peverell, Tiverton EX16 7EN (Devon) T: **01884 821770**
alanrogers.com/UK0750

Minnows is an attractive, neat small park with views across the Devon countryside, separated from the Grand Western canal by hedging. Easily accessible from the M5, it is suitable as an ideal touring centre for Devon and Somerset, for cycling, walking or canoeing (own landing stage), or simply for breaking a long journey. A small, neat park, open for eight months of the year, it provides 45 level pitches all with 16A electricity and hardstandings for all weather, four with water and waste water. A further 3.5 acres have been added to the park providing space for more and larger pitches, a tent area, a playground and a large field for ball games, etc. The village of Sampford Peverell, with pub and farm shop, is only a half mile walk via the towpath, with Tiverton 7.5 miles. In fact, there are 12 miles of level walking on the towpath or one can take a trip on a horse-drawn barge. The site is also on the Sustran cycle route (Route Three). Tiverton Parkway station (BR) is less than one mile and buses run from the village to Tiverton. Coarse fishing permits for the canal are available from reception. A Caravan Club affiliated site, non-members are also very welcome. There could be some road noise from the adjacent A361.

Facilities	Directions
The heated toilet block has been refurbished with tiled floors, new pressurised showers and 2 cubicles for ladies. It is clean and comfortable with all modern facilities and constant hot water. Facilities for disabled visitors and babies. Laundry with washing machine, dryer and ironing. Motorcaravan service point. Gas supplies. Shop (all season). Newspaper delivery arranged. Play area. Bicycle hire (delivery to site). American RVs accepted (up to 36 ft), advance booking necessary. All year caravan storage. Site gates closed 21.00 and locked 23.00-7.30. Off site: Boat slipway, golf driving range and 9-hole course 400 yds, full course 4 miles. Riding 6 miles.	From M5 junction 27 take A361 signed Tiverton. After 600 yds take first exit signed Sampford Peverell. After 100 yds. turn right at roundabout and cross bridge over A361 to second roundabout. Go straight ahead and park is immediately ahead. From North Devon on A361 go to M5 junction 27 and return back up the A361 as above. O.S.GR: ST042148. GPS: 50.925017, -3.364517

Open: 8 March - 1 November.

Charges guide

Per unit incl. 2 persons and electricity	£ 12.20 - £ 22.95

Credit cards accepted for £10 or more.

Totnes

Woodlands Leisure Park

Blackawton, Totnes TQ9 7DQ (Devon) T: 01803 712598. E: fun@woodlandspark.com

alanrogers.com/UK0840

Woodlands is a pleasant surprise – from the road you have no idea of just what is hidden away deep in the Devon countryside. To achieve this, there has been sympathetic development of farm and woodland to provide a leisure centre, open to the public and with a range of activities and entertainment appealing to all ages. The camping and caravan site overlooks the woodland and the leisure park, taking 350 units on three sloping, grassy fields, the original terraced one maturing well. One of the others has been fully terraced to provide groups of four to eight flat, very spacious pitches (90% with 10A electricity and a shared water tap, drain and rubbish bin). The newest field has 120 pitches (with electricity) designed with a more open feel to provide space for larger groups or rallies. Children (and many energetic parents too!) will thoroughly enjoy a huge variety of imaginative adventure play equipment, amazing water coasters, toboggan runs, the new 'Sea Dragon Swing Ship', a white knuckle monster, the 'Avalanche' and much more, hidden amongst the trees. Those more peacefully inclined can follow woodland walks around the attractive ponds. The 'Empire of the Sea Dragon', an indoor play centre, provides marvellous wet weather facilities comprising five floors of play areas and amazing slides. With a two night stay, campers on the touring park are admitted free of charge to the leisure park. A popular touring park, early reservation is advisable.

Facilities

Three modern, heated toilet blocks, include private bathrooms (coin-operated, 20p) and 16 family shower cubicles. Two laundry rooms. Freezer for ice packs. Baby facilities. The leisure park café provides good value meals and a takeaway service for campers. Café opening hours and camping shop (with gas and basic food supplies) vary according to season and demand. TV and games room. Dogs are accepted on the campsite but not in the leisure park (kennels available). Caravan storage. Off site: The charming town of Dartmouth and the South Hams beaches are near. Fishing 4 miles. Golf 0.5 miles. Riding 5 miles. Beach 4 miles.

Open: Easter - 1 November.

Directions

From A38 at Buckfastleigh, take A384 to Totnes. Before the town centre turn right on A381 Kingsbridge road. After Halwell turn left at Totnes Cross garage, on A3122 to Dartmouth. Park is on right after 2.5 miles. O.S.GR: SX813521. GPS: 50.357898, -3.675001

Charges guide

Per unit incl. 2 persons, electricity	£ 14.50 - £ 21.00
extra person over 2 yrs	£ 6.75
awning or extra small pup tent	£ 2.50
large tent or trailer tent (120 sq ft plus)	£ 2.50
dog (contact site first)	£ 2.50

Free entry to leisure park for stays 2 nights or more.

Woolacombe
Woolacombe Bay Holiday Park

Sandy Lane, Woolacombe EX34 7AH (Devon) T: 01271 870343. E: goodtimes@woolacombe.com

alanrogers.com/UK1070

Woolacombe Bay Holiday Village, and its sister site Golden Coast Holiday Village nearby, are well known holiday parks providing a range of holiday accommodation from caravan holiday homes to luxury lodges, apartments and villas, with many on site amenities including pools, restaurants and bars, and providing a wide range of entertainment. A camping section at the Woolacombe Bay park caters for tents and trailer tents only, so touring visitors can enjoy all the activities and entertainment of both parks. Partly terraced out of the hillside and partly on the hill top with some existing pine trees but with many more trees planted for landscaping, the site has magnificent views out across the bay. Marked and numbered pitches have been provided on grass for 150 tents, 97 with electricity (10/16A). All should be level, having been terraced where necessary and they are connected by gravel roads. Some up and down walking will be needed for the toilet block. A bus service (small charge) runs between the two parks, the third and fourth parks in the group (Twitchen Park and Easewell Farm) and the beach during the main season, although there is a footpath to the beach from the site. The three larger parks have varied entertainment programmes and children's clubs and Woolacombe Bay also boasts a health spa and beauty suite.

Facilities

A smart central toilet block has excellent facilities, including en-suite shower and washrooms and separate toilets, baby facilities, and also a sauna and steam room. Laundry rooms. Two units for disabled visitors. Supermarket. Bars, restaurant and entertainment. Indoor (heated) and outdoor pools with flumes and slides. Sauna and gym. Beauty and holistic treatments. Wide range of sporting activities. Tennis. ATM. Dogs are welcome at Woolacombe Bay but not at Golden Coast. Brand new caravan holiday homes (2009).
Off site: Fishing and riding 1 mile. Beach 1 mile.

Open: 11 May - end October.

Directions

Take A361 Barnstaple - Ilfracombe road through Braunton. Turn left at Mullacott Cross roundabout towards Woolacombe then right towards Mortehoe. Now follow the camping signs by turning left and park is on the left. O.S.GR: SS469443.
GPS: 51.177117, -4.191317

Charges guide

Per caravan or motorcaravan	
incl. all persons	£ 15.00 - £ 55.00
serviced pitch	£ 19.00 - £ 57.50
tent - per person	£ 5.00 - £ 18.30
tent - child (5-15 yrs)	£ 2.50 - £ 9.15
dog (camping only)	£ 1.50

Woolacombe
Twitchen Park

Mortehoe, Woolacombe EX34 7ES (Devon) T: 01271 870848. E: goodtimes@woolacombe.com

alanrogers.com/UK0730

Set in the grounds of an attractive Edwardian country house, Twitchen Park is owned by Woolacombe Bay Holiday Parks. Its main concern lies in holiday caravans and apartments, although it also provides marked pitches, all for touring units, at the top of the park, with some views over the rolling hills to the sea. With a more recently developed touring field, they include 228 pitches with 16A electricity, many with tarmac hardstanding (not always level), mostly arranged around oval access roads in hedged areas. Further non-electric pitches are behind in two open, unmarked fields which are sloping (blocks are thoughtfully provided, stored in neat wooden boxes next to the water points). A smart, modern entertainment complex incorporates a licensed club and family lounge with snacks, a restaurant, disco room for teenagers, cartoon lounge, outdoor pool and smart indoor pool complex. Twitchen is very popular with families with children. If they become bored, there are always the excellent beaches nearby with a footpath down to the sea. All the facilities of Golden Coast and Woolacombe Bay Holiday Villages and Easewell Farm are free to visitors at Twitchen, with a bus (small charge) running regularly between the four parks and to the beach.

Facilities

There are two toilet blocks. Dishwashing and laundry facilities at each block plus a good modern launderette at the central complex. Motorcaravan service point. Shop and takeaway. Club, bars, restaurant and entertainment for adults and children, day and evening. Outdoor pool (heated mid May - mid Sept). Attractive indoor pool with sauna, paddling pool, fountain and a viewing green. Games rooms. Good adventure play area. ATM. American motorhomes are accepted (up to 30 ft). Off site: Beach 1 mile. Golf 1 mile. Fishing, riding and bicycle hire 2 miles.

Open: Easter- end October.

Directions

From Barnstaple take A361 towards Ilfracombe and through Braunton. Turn left at Mullacott Cross roundabout towards Woolacombe and then right towards Mortehoe. Park is on the left before village. O.S.GR: SS465451. GPS: 51.184683, -4.1977

Charges guide

Per caravan or motorcaravan	£ 15.00 - £ 55.00
incl. services	£ 19.00 - £ 57.50
tent - per person	£ 5.00 - £ 18.30
tent - child (5-15 yrs)	£ 2.50 - £ 9.15
dog	£ 1.50
Special offers available.	

CAMPING FROM ONLY £5 per person a night

TOURING FROM ONLY £15 per van a night

endless fun...

Four award winning Holiday Parks set in Devon's breathtaking countryside next to Woolacombe's 3 miles of golden Blue Flag sandy beach!

SEAVIEW Camping, Touring & Supersite Pitches plus Luxury Lodges & Holiday Homes

over 40 FREE activities...

- 10 Heated Indoor & Outdoor Pools
- Waterslides • Health Suite • Playzone
- Nightly Star Cabaret & Entertainment
- Snooker • Crazy Golf • Kid's Clubs
- Kid's Indoor & Outdoor Play Areas
- Tennis • Cinema • Coarse Fishing Ponds
- ... Plus so much more!

...and for just a little more

- 10 Pin Bowling • Affiliated Golf Club
- Waves Ceramic Studio • 17th Century Inn
- Indoor Bowls Rinks • Amusement Arcade
- Restaurants & Bars • WaterWalkerz
- Kiddy Karts • Sports Bar • Climbing Wall
- NEW All-Weather Pitches • Electric Hook-ups
- Laundry Facilities & Shop • Swim Lessons

REGISTER ONLINE FOR LATEST OFFERS!!
woolacombe.com/ar
0844 770 0363
OR TEXT HOLIDAY TO 60800

WOOLACOMBE BAY
HOLIDAY PARKS · NORTH DEVON

Woolacombe
Easewell Farm Holiday Park

Mortehoe, Woolacombe EX34 7EH (Devon) T: 01271 870343. E: goodtimes@woolacombe.com
alanrogers.com/UK0720

Near the sandy beaches of Woolacombe, Easewell Farm is now part of the Woolacombe Bay Holiday Park group who own the Woolacombe Bay, Golden Coast and Twitchen parks. A shuttle bus runs between the four parks and to the beach (tickets £3 per person per holiday). This is a traditional style touring park which during the day is a hive of activity, but the nights are quiet and peaceful. The largest of the camping fields is sloping with superb views across the headland to the sea. Two smaller fields are terraced and one area has hardstandings. Together they provide 302 pitches, 124 with electricity connections (15A) and 20 also with TV and water connections. Pea-shingle all-weather hardstandings have been added. Also available are a lovely four bedroom farmhouse (sleeping ten), a pretty two bedroom cottage (five beds) and a caravan holiday home. The shop is well stocked (gas available), there is a takeaway and restaurant and an attractive bar with patio overlooking a small duck pond. The park has its own very well maintained nine-hole golf course which is popular and has reduced fees for campers. One of the huge redundant farm buildings has been put to excellent use: divided into three areas, it provides table tennis and pool, a skittle alley and two lanes of flat green bowling with changing rooms. Walks to the local village and along the coastal path are easy from the site and a bus to Ilfracombe and Barnstaple stops 100 yards from the entrance.

Facilities

The central toilet block has been regularly upgraded and can be heated. Two washbasins in the ladies have hoses for hair washing, controllable showers (no dividers). Small area with baby bath facilities. Laundry. These facilities are arranged around the farmhouse area and include a very well equipped unit for disabled people with everything in one large room including a hairdryer. Motorcaravan service point. Shop. Bar. Golf. Small heated indoor swimming pool is well used, as are games and TV rooms. Fenced play area with bark base. Indoor skittle alley. In high season only one dog per pitch is allowed. Off site: Fishing or riding 1 mile. Bicycle hire 3 miles. Tarka Trail for walking and riding. Boat trips to Lundy Island.

Open: March - end October.

Directions

From Barnstaple, take A361 Ilfracombe road through Braunton. Turn left at Mullacott Cross roundabout on B3343 to Woolacombe, turning right after 2-3 miles to Mortehoe. Park is on right before village.
O.S.GR: SS465455. GPS: 51.1853, -4.198933

Charges guide

Per caravan or motorcaravan incl. services	£ 14.25 - £ 49.15 £ 17.50 - £ 52.50
tent - per person	£ 4.75 - £ 16.60
tent - child (5-15 yrs)	£ 2.40 - £ 8.30
dog	£ 1.50

Woolacombe
Woolacombe Sands Holiday Park

Beach Road, Woolacombe EX34 7AF (Devon) T: 01271 870569. E: lifesabeach@woolacombe-sands.co.uk
alanrogers.com/UK0735

With sea views and within walking distance of Woolacombe's lovely sandy beach, this family park has been terraced out of the valley side as you drop down into the village. Apart from its smart entrance, it has been left natural. The pond and stream at the bottom are almost hidden with gated access to the National Trust fields across the valley. The 200 terraced level grass pitches all with 10A electricity are accessed by gravel roads with some good up and down walking needed to the toilet blocks (probably not the best environment for disabled people). Some 50 mobile homes and 14 bungalows are in the more central area, and tents tend to be placed on the bottom terraces. The park boasts both indoor and outdoor pools (accessed by code) with a full time attendant. Evenings see Woolly Bear emerge from his 'shack' to entertain children, with adult family entertainment later. A good plus factor is the fact that all facilities open when the site opens. A useful path leads from the site to the beach via the car park and the walk is said to take 15 minutes.

Facilities

Four basic toilet blocks with good hot water are spread amongst the terraces. The newer shower block has separate toilets opposite. Shop. Self-service food bar providing good value meals and breakfast (main season and B.Hs). Two bars and full entertainment programme. Heated indoor and outdoor pools both with paddling pool areas. Fenced play area on bark with plenty of equipment. Ball area with nets. Crazy golf. 'Kingpin' bowling. Off site: Beach 15 minutes walk or 0.5 miles. Riding next door. Golf, bicycle hire and freshwater fishing 0.5 miles.

Open: 1 April - 1 November.

Directions

Follow A361 from Barnstaple through Braunton towards Ilfracombe. At Mullacott Cross roundabout turn left for Woolacombe (B3343). Site clearly signed on left as you go down the hill into the village.
O.S.GR: SS468436. GPS: 51.17145, -4.191833

Charges guide

Per person (incl. electricity)	£ 5.00 - £ 15.00
child (5-16 yrs)	£ 2.50 - £ 7.50
dog	£ 5.00

Easewell holiday park

sit back, relax and enjoy the view...

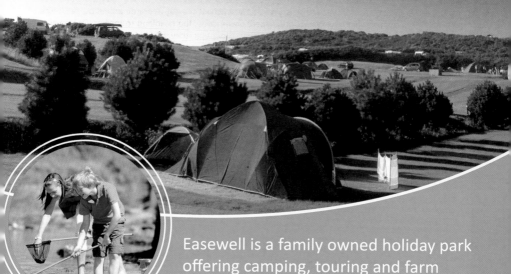

Easewell is a family owned holiday park offering camping, touring and farm cottages, set amidst the beautiful & tranquil North Devon countryside with **STUNNING SEA VIEWS.**

Great facilities

- Indoor Heated Pool
- Indoor Bowls/Skittles
- Snooker
- Club House & Café
- 9 Hole Affiliated Golf Club
- Takeaway & Restaurant
- Adventure Playgrounds
- NEW All-Weather Pitches

- Indoor Games Room
- Dishwashing Area
- Electric Hook-ups
- Super Site Pitches
- Free Hot Showers
- Well Stocked Shop
- Launderette
- 1 Mile to Woolacombe Beach

Register online for latest offers

woolacombe.com/ar

0844 770 0363

or text HOLIDAY to 60800

Easewell Holiday Park & Golf Club, Mortehoe, Woolacombe, Devon

Part of **WOOLAC⬤MBE BAY** Holiday Parks

Woolacombe

Golden Coast Holiday Park

Station Road, Woolacombe EX34 7HW (Devon) T: 01271 870343. E: goodtimes@woolacombe.com
alanrogers.com/UK1075

The Golden Coast Holiday Park is part of the Woolacombe Bay Holiday Parks group that includes Woolacombe Bay, Twitchen Park and Easewell Farm. Golden Coast's main interest is a range of brick-built bungalows, lodges and apartments, plus a variety of caravan holiday homes, all of good quality and well equipped. However, two touring areas also provide 91 pitches, all with electricity and about half with all-weather hardstanding. There are indoor and outdoor pools, spa facilities, a cinema and a range of sports facilities for active visitors. Guests at the park can enjoy extensive entertainment and nightly cabaret and a programme of daily activities is arranged for adults and children. A shuttle bus runs between the four parks and to the beach several times a day (it costs £3 per person per holiday). A visit to the Old Mill Inn should not be missed; it serves bar meals, and has an excellent beer garden with adventure play area for the children. The range of amenities and facilities at this large park will suit families looking for a lively holiday filled with activities and entertainment.

Facilities

A fairly new building provides adequate facilities and was quite clean at the time of our visit. Washing machine and dryer. Large, well stocked supermarket, boutique and beauty salon. Indoor and outdoor swimming pools, outdoor flume, sauna and solarium. Bar, club, Old Mill Inn, restaurant and takeaway. Floodlit tennis court. Adventure playgrounds. Snooker. Games room. Soft play area. Ceramics studio. Learn to swim classes. 9-hole golf course. Indoor and outdoor bowls, ten-pin bowling. Nightly entertainment and cabaret. Activities and clubs for chldren. Fishing. Woodland walks. Dogs are not accepted.
Off site: Woolacombe beach is about 2 miles. For walkers there is the coastal path. Amenities at sister parks available to all visitors, with shuttle bus. Golf and riding 0.5 miles.

Open: 5 February - 2 January.

Directions

From Barnstaple, take A361 (signed Braunton and Ilfracombe). Turn left on B3343 (signed Woolacombe) and follow the road towards the town. The park is on the left near the top of the hill. O.S.GR: SS480435. GPS: 51.1725, -4.172767

Charges guide

Per caravan or motorcaravan	£ 15.00 - £ 55.00
incl. services	£ 19.00 - £ 57.50
tent - per person	£ 5.00 - £ 18.30
tent - per child (5-15 yrs)	£ 2.50 - £ 9.15

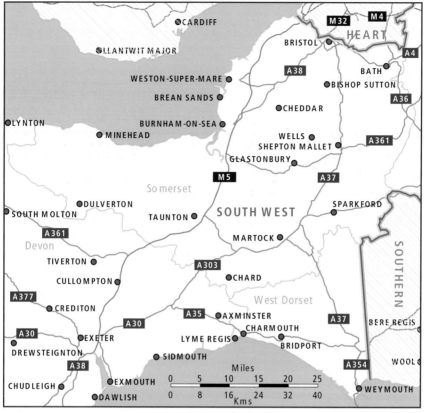

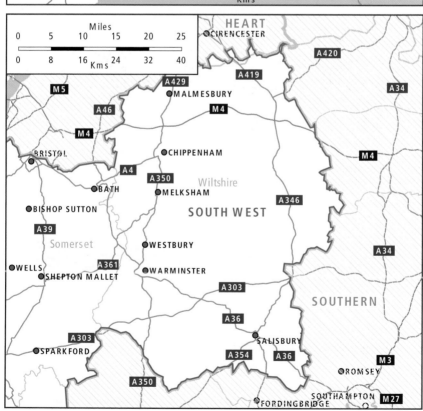

Bath

Newton Mill Camping Park

Newton Road, Bath BA2 9JF (Somerset) T: 01225 333909. E: enquiries@newtonmillpark.co.uk

alanrogers.com/UK1460

In a peaceful valley two miles from the centre of the historic city of Bath and with direct access to the local cycle track network, Newton Mill is an excellent base from which to explore the city and the area. The site accepts 105 tents and also has 90 caravan pitches (with 30 long stay) which are located at the other end of the valley. All of these have hardstandings, with 16A electricity and satellite TV hook-ups. This end of the park is closest to the main Bristol - London railway line, not visually obtrusive but occasional rail noise may be noticeable. The site has been created around an old mill, the bar and restaurant now occupying part of the original building, and there is a modern timber chalet style reception building with a small, well stocked shop. The restaurant (open evenings all year) serves good value, speciality meals. Breakfasts are available (weekends Easter - October, daily in summer). The tent meadow is in an elevated position, or alternatively you may prefer the paddock, a small field alongside the stream which is a car free zone with a separate parking area.

Facilities

Two new heated toilet blocks provide excellent modern facilities with some washbasins in cubicles, free hot showers, bathrooms (on payment), baby rooms and a good suite for disabled campers. Launderette. Basic motorcaravan service point. Shop, bar, restaurant with garden seating area. Play area. Boules court. Fishing. Off site: Bus service into Bath runs every 10 minutes from Twerton village which is a 10 minute walk. Nearby Bristol and Bath Railway Path (a traffic free cycle way) links to the West Bath Riverside Path, and the Kennet and Avon towpath. Thursday market in Twerton.

Open: All year.

See advertisement on page 345

Directions

Site is 2 miles west of Bath city centre, about 1 mile southeast of the roundabout where the A4 meets the A39. From the north take M4 exit 19, turn on to the M32 and almost immediately take A4174 (Avon ring road) for 7.5 miles to the A4. Turn left towards Bath and after 5 miles at second roundabout, take second exit signed Newton St Loe and pass The Globe public house. Site entrance is on the left after about 1 mile. O.S.GR: ST713647. GPS: 51.378133, -2.410817

Charges guide

Per person	£ 5.00
child (3-16 yrs)	£ 2.50
pitch incl. car	£ 3.00 - £ 8.00
awning	£ 2.00
dog	£ 0.75

Bishop Sutton

Bath Chew Valley Caravan Park

Ham Lane, Bishop Sutton BS39 5TZ (Somerset) T: 01275 332127. E: enquiries@bathchewvalley.co.uk

alanrogers.com/UK1510

A small and secluded garden site for adults only, Chew Valley has been developed with much tender love and care by the Betton family and is now affiliated to the Caravan Club. Caravans are sited on neat lawns amongst colourful beds of flowers and the cars are tucked away on the nearby car park, providing a tranquil and restful atmosphere. An area of woodland is adjacent to the tent field (grass pitches) along with an enclosed dog walking area. The warden will assist you in placing your caravan. There are neat hardstandings for all pitches and 27 spacious, fully serviced pitches. This park will particularly appeal to garden lovers. Next to reception there is a good library, also providing tourist information. Chew Valley lake with trout fishing available is about half a mile away on foot, and Blagdon lake is popular for birdwatching. There are several circular walks in the area – visitors may borrow the route plans and a walking stick from reception. Bristol and Bath are within an easy distance and Cheddar Gorge or Longleat make excellent days out. A Best of British group member.

Facilities

The heated toilet block (with a 'home from home' feel), provides all the fittings that make life comfortable. Eight separate en-suite units each with WC, basin and shower. One unit has facilities for disabled visitors. Useful utility room with sinks, spin dryer and ironing facilities, together with a washing machine and tumble dryer for service washes only. Motorcaravan service point. Internet access and WiFi. Off site: Village 100 yds with useful general store, newsagent, two pubs and post office. Supermarkets within 15 minutes drive. Fishing 1 mile. Golf 5 miles. Riding 8 miles. Beach 15 miles.

Open: All year.

Directions

From Bath on A368 turn right opposite Red Lion pub in Bishop Sutton. Continue past small track to the left (50 yds) for a further 50 yds. Park entrance is on the left with neat, clear entrance. O.S.GR: ST584599. GPS: 51.336583, -2.597183

Charges guide

Per unit incl. 2 persons and electricity	£ 21.00 - £ 25.00

Bridport

Freshwater Beach Holiday Park

Burton Bradstock, Bridport DT6 4PT (Dorset) T: 01308 897317. E: enquiries@freshwaterbeach.co.uk

alanrogers.com/UK1780

Family run parks for families with direct access to their own private beach are rare in Britain and this one has the added advantage of being in beautiful coastal countryside in West Dorset. The site is next to the sea and a beach of fine pebbles, sheltered from the wind by pebble banks. The River Bride edges the park and joins the sea here. Approached by a fairly steep access road, the park itself is on level, open ground. The 500 plus touring pitches, 400 with 10A electricity, are on an open, undulating grass field connected by tarmac or hardcore roads. Caravan pitches (10 x 11 m) are marked and evenly spaced in lines. Some tent pitches are in the main field, with others well spaced on a newly terraced extra field. In separate areas there are 270 caravan holiday homes, with 40 for hire. This lively holiday park has an extensive range of facilities which include an outdoor pool, a good value licensed restaurant and newly refurbished bars with an evening entertainment programme in season. Daytime entertainment caters for all ages – don't miss the donkey derby! Footpaths lead to the thatched village of Burton Bradstock or West Bay. The overall impression at Freshwater is of a large, busy holiday park with a friendly reception and happy atmosphere.

Facilities

Two fully equipped toilet blocks serve the caravan fields and a third newer block is in the tent field. It is a good provision for a busy beach park. Facilities for disabled people (Radar key), and a baby care room (key system). Laundry and dishwashing sinks cope well at peak times. Launderette. Bars with wide variety of entertainment and evening shows. Licensed restaurant (weekends only in late season; closed Mondays all season). Good value supermarket and takeaway. Heated and supervised outdoor swimming and paddling pools (15/5-30/10) with lessons available. New indoor games room with pool table, music, TV, amusements and soft drinks bar. Activities for children. Two play areas. High season pony trekking (stables on site). Off site: Golf course 0.5 miles. Fishing possible from Chesil Bank. Abbotsbury Sub-Tropical Gardens and Swannery 8 miles.

Open: 17 March - 12 November.

Directions

Park is immediately west of the village of Burton Bradstock, on the Weymouth - Bridport coast road (B3157). O.S.GR: SY980898.
GPS: 50.70500, -2.73867

Charges guide

Per unit incl. up to 6 persons,	
car and awning	£ 15.00 - £ 33.00
extra person, car or boat	£ 2.00
electricity	£ 2.00
small tent incl. 2 persons	
walking or cycling	£ 4.00 - £ 16.00
dog	£ 2.50

Single sex groups not admitted.

Bridport

Golden Cap Holiday Park

West Dorset Leisure Holidays, Seatown, Chideock, Bridport DT6 6JX (Dorset) T: **01308 422139**
E: **holidays@wdlh.co.uk alanrogers.com/UK1740**

Golden Cap, named after the adjacent high cliff (the highest in southern England) which overlooks Lyme Bay, is only 150 m. from a shingle beach at Seatown and is surrounded by National Trust countryside and the Heritage Coastline. The park is arranged over several fields on the valley floor, sloping gently down towards the sea. It is in two main areas, having once been two parks, each separated into fields with marvellous views around and providing 108 touring pitches. All have electricity and 30 also have hardstanding with drainage and gravel awning area. An extra sloping tent area is used for peak season (torch useful), although it is a five minute walk from here to the toilet blocks and shop. There are 219 caravan holiday homes in their own areas. A coarse fishing lake has been opened and the heated indoor pool at Highlands End (under the same ownership, three miles away) is open for campers at Golden Cap on payment. Beaches are nearby, sea fishing, boat launching, riding or fossil hunting are possible in the area, plus good walks including access to the coastal path.

Facilities

The modern toilet block is of good quality with spacious shower cubicles (some with toilet and washbasin). Facilities for disabled visitors. Baby room. Two other smaller blocks around the park. Laundry room. Motorcaravan service point. Useful and well stocked shop (all season). Gas supplies. Small play area. Fishing lake (day tickets from shop). American motorhomes are not accepted. Off site: Pub with food service close. Beach 150 yds. Golf 2 miles. Bicycle hire, boat launching 3 miles.

Open: 20 March - 8 November.

Directions

Turn off A35 road at Chideock (a bigger village) 3 miles west of Bridport, at sign to Seatown opposite church. Park is less than 1 mile down narrow lane. O.S.GR: SY423919. GPS: 50.715333, -2.821667

Charges guide

Per unit incl. 2 persons	
and electricity	£ 13.25 - £ 22.00
extra person	£ 3.50 - £ 4.00
child (4-17 yrs)	£ 2.00 - £ 2.50
all service pitch	£ 15.25 - £ 24.00
pitch with sea view	£ 19.25 - £ 28.00

Highlands End and Golden Cap Holiday Parks
Tel: 01308 422139 Email: holidays@wdlh.co.uk
Eype, Bridport, Dorset DT6 6AR
www.wdlh.co.uk
A World Heritage Coastline on your doorstep
WEST DORSET LEISURE HOLIDAYS

Bridport

Highlands End Holiday Park

West Dorset Leisure Holidays, Eype, Bridport DT6 6AR (Dorset) T: **01308 422139**. E: **holidays@wdlh.co.uk**
alanrogers.com/UK1750

On slightly sloping ground with superb open views, both coastal and inland, Highlands End is quietly situated on the Dorset Heritage Coastline. With access to the coastal path, a path in front of the park runs along the cliff top and then leads down to a shingle beach a little further along. It is a good quality park with 180 caravan holiday homes, mostly privately owned, and 195 touring pitches in two areas nearest to the sea – one has to travel through the holiday homes to reach them. All have electricity and 45 also offer water, drainage, hardstanding and a gravel awning area. A further area is used for tents in high season. A modern, attractive building houses a lounge bar, good value restaurant with takeaway facility, family room and games room with some musical evenings in high season. The park's amenities also include an excellent, air-conditioned indoor heated pool, a tennis court and pitch and putt (all charged). A well run park and a member of the Best of British group.

Facilities

Two toilet blocks near the touring sections are well maintained and can be heated. Some washbasins in cubicles with toilets, large, roomy showers. Dishwashing room. En-suite facilities for disabled visitors. Baby care room. Laundry room. Motorcaravan service point. Well stocked shop (opening times vary), including gas supplies. Bar and restaurant/takeaway (evenings and Sunday lunch). Tennis (charged). Indoor pool (20 x 9 m), gym, sauna/steam room. Games room. 9-hole pitch and putt. Two adventure play areas. Large sloping field for ball games. All facilities open all season. Off site: Beach 0.5 miles. Bicycle hire and golf 2 miles. Fishing 3 miles.

Open: 20 March - 8 November.

Directions

Follow Bridport bypass on A35 around the town and park is signed to south (Eype turning), down narrow lane. There is a new exit road. O.S.GR: SY452914. GPS: 50.725333, -2.777

Charges guide

Per unit incl. 2 persons	
and electricity	£ 13.25 - £ 22.00
full services and hardstanding	£ 15.25 - £ 24.00
extra person	£ 3.50 - £ 4.00
child (4-17 yrs)	£ 2.00 - £ 2.50
dog	£ 2.00 - £ 2.50

Bridport

Bingham Grange Touring & Camping Park

Melplash, Bridport DT6 3TT (Dorset) T: **01308 488234**. E: **enquiries@binghamgrange.co.uk**

alanrogers.com/UK1770

Bingham Grange is an attractive, purpose-built park for adults only. In a pleasant, rural situation two miles from the market town of Bridport, there are views seaward towards West Bay and inland across Beaminster Downs and Pilsdon Hill. The park provides an area of individual pitches with 10A electricity and over 75 hardstandings, nicely landscaped with shrubs and trees growing between the pitches, plus an open sloping field overlooking the valley with serviced pitches and space for tents. A path is provided to the river which links with the main footpaths for Bridport (20 minutes). Local hostelries are also within reach. A limited bus service runs on the main road. The Brit Valley is an unspoilt area of West Dorset with an ancient heritage and coastal West Bay is only a couple of miles. The facilities at this park are good, having been converted from original farm buildings. The present owners are working hard to maintain and improve them.

Facilities

Well equipped toilet block, with under floor heating with a separate, fully equipped room for the less able with ramped access and 5 luxury shower rooms (also with washbasin and 4 with WC). Laundry room with microwave and freezer. Reception keeps simple supplies. Restaurant serving home cooked food seems to be very popular. Gas available. Only adults (over 18 yrs) are accepted. Off site: Sea fishing and golf 3 miles.

Open: March - end October.

Directions

At the roundabouts on the A35 road, on the east side of Bridport, follow signs for Beaminster on the A3066. After about 2 miles watch for site entrance on the left. O.S.GR: SY482963. GPS: 50.765076, -2.740911

Charges guide

Per unit incl. 2 persons and electricity (10A)	£ 13.00 - £ 28.00
tent pitch incl. 2 persons	£ 12.00 - £ 19.50
extra person	£ 5.00
dog	£ 2.00

'Exclusively for discerning adults in pursuit of sanctuary from 21st century life!'

Tel: 01308 488234

- Award winning toilets & washrooms
- All weather pitches – electric, water, drainage
- Dogs welcome – superb on-site walks
- Meadows – woodland – riverbanks
- Jurassic Coastline nearby @ West Bay
- Excellent loungebar & restaurant with our own talented resident chef

Binghams Farm A3066 Melplash Bridport Dorset DT6 3TT   www.binghamgrange.co.uk

Bristol

Baltic Wharf Caravan Club Site

Cumberland Road, Bristol BS1 6XG (Somerset) T: **01179 268030**. E: **balticwharf@caravanclub.co.uk**

alanrogers.com/UK1440

This excellent Caravan Club site in Bristol's redeveloped dockland is well laid out and maintained to a high standard. It is screened from the road by a high wall with a boatyard on one side and residential apartments on the other, with access via a lockable gate to the Baltic Wharf dockside. The view across the dock towards Clifton village and Bristol is unique and you can even glimpse the suspension bridge. Accessed by a circular tarmac road, the 55 pitches are on stone chippings and are ideal for all year round use (steel pegs are sold at reception). All have electricity (16A) and TV aerial points (reception is poor).

Facilities

The toilet block provides good clean facilities including controllable showers and washbasins in cubicles (heated in winter). Good facilities for disabled visitors, plus toilets and showers for the walking disabled in the main block. Fully equipped laundry room. Motorcaravan service point. Dogs are welcome but there is no dog walking area. Wardens live on the site. Off site: Fishing and boating (permits from Harbour Master's office) 400 yards.

Open: All year.

Directions

From M5, J18, take A4 (Bristol West). Follow signs for Historic Harbour and SS Great Britain under Clifton Suspension Bridge and through Hotwells (5.5 miles). Cross over Dock bridge and site is about 500 yds. on left. From East follow signs for Historic Harbour and SS Great Britain. Site on right just to west of SS Great Britain. Look carefully for the Caravan Club sign. O.S.GR: ST574721. GPS: 51.446533, -2.61425

Charges guide

Per person	£ 4.90 - £ 6.55
child (5-16 yrs)	£ 1.50 - £ 2.95
pitch incl. electricity (non-member)	£ 11.80 - £ 15.30

South West - Somerset, Wiltshire, W Dorset

Brean Sands
Holiday Resort Unity

335

Coast Road, Brean Sands, Burnham-on-Sea TA8 2RB (Somerset) T: **01278 751235**. E: **admin@hru.co.uk**
alanrogers.com/UK1575

Holiday Resort Unity offers everything for everyone, from young children to the 'young at heart'. Apart from the extensive on-site amusements and entertainment programme, campers can also use the swimming pools, funfair and other leisure pursuits at the adjoining Brean Leisure Centre (owned by the same family), some free of charge and others by paying a small fee. Three large touring fields provide pitches that are flat and open, mostly grass but some on concrete hardstandings (motorcaravans up to 30 ft. can be accommodated). Most pitches have 16A electricity hook-ups. A separate warden looks after each camping field. Ready equipped tents and a substantial number of caravan holiday homes are available for rent. Access to the five-mile stretch of sandy beach is via a footpath opposite the site entrance. Fishing (with a licence) is permitted from Unity Lake in the Yellow Field. RJ's is a club with bars, food and nightly entertainment for the whole family. Sarah's Pantry offers takeaway or sit-down meals (including the Sunday roast), while fish and chips are available at Porkers Bar.

Facilities

Three good toilet blocks provide ample facilities and include en-suite units. Some toilets and washbasins have been adapted for people with disabilities (radar key). Well equipped laundries. Motorcaravan service point, recycling station, jet spray to wash vehicles. Well stocked shop. Gas exchange. RJ's Club, Sarah's Pantry and Porkers fish and chip bar. Large adventure play area. Buster's Work Out Gym, Sally's sun beds. Monday market, Sunday car boot sales. All facilities open during high season, most open during mid season and at weekends in low season. Torches advisable at night. Off site: Walking access from park to Brean leisure Centre (swimming pool, funfair etc); riding, cycling, cinema, walks, golf all within walking distance from park. Bus and land-train services vary according to season. Bus to Weston-super-Mare and Cheddar Gorge stops at park gates. Beach 100 m.

Open: 10 February - 20 November.

Directions

From M5 exit 22, follow signs for Burnham-on-Sea (B3140), Berrow and Brean. Holiday Resort Unity is on right along the main street of Brean – it is well signed. Take care as road through Berrow and Brean is rather narrow. O.S.GR: ST290539.
GPS: 51.280483, -3.012217

Charges guide

Per unit incl. 4 persons and electricity	£ 10.00 - £ 36.00
extra person	£ 3.50
dog	£ 3.00

Price includes unit, 4 persons, awning, entertainment/swimming and 'Piglet Club'. Deduct 25% if only two people occupy the pitch. Credit cards accepted (charge of £2 per transaction; no charge for debit cards).

Burnham-on-Sea
Home Farm Holiday Park & Country Club

Edithmead, Burnham-on-Sea TA9 4HD (Somerset) T: **01278 788888**. E: **SITE@hfhp.co.uk**
alanrogers.com/UK1480

Home Farm is neatly and attractively laid out covering 44 acres, and is convenient for those using the M5. The 780 level pitches (including 180 privately owned holiday homes and a number of seasonal units) laid out on level mown grass are all clearly marked, accessed by tarmac roads and divided into various sections, for example an area for those with pets. Including 183 pitches with hardstanding, there are 20 serviced pitches for RVs and motorcaravans. Electrical connections (10A) are available everywhere. A large, modern pool with paved surrounds and a paddling section is neatly walled and a new indoor pool and leisure centre opened in 2009. Tents are not accepted.

Facilities

Two main, refurbished toilet blocks are heated and well situated for touring areas. Hot showers in one block are larger, but minus dividers. Bathrooms (key with £5 deposit). Baby room. Laundry. Facilities for disabled visitors. Dog shower. Shop with groceries, camping accessories and Camping Gaz, restaurants and takeaway (April - October). Bar (all season). Swimming pool (May - Sept). Indoor pool. Play area. ATM. Internet access and WiFi zone. Security patrols at night. Barrier card (£2). Off site: Boat launching 1 mile. Golf 2 miles. Riding 3 miles. Beach 3 miles.

Open: 10 February - 6 January.

Directions

Home Farm is 400 yards from M5 junction 22 and the A38. It is signed from the B3140 into Burnham-on-Sea. O.S.GR: ST328493. GPS: 51.23875, -2.964167

Charges guide

Per unit incl. 2 persons, electricity and awning	£ 9.00 - £ 27.00
extra person	£ 3.25 - £ 5.50
child (4-17 yrs)	£ 1.75 - £ 4.75
dog	£ 1.00 - £ 2.50

Club membership free. Special breaks available.

Burnham-on-Sea
Northam Farm Touring Caravan Park
Brean Sands, Burnham-on-Sea TA8 2SE (Somerset) T: **01278 751244**. E: enquiries@northamfarm.co.uk
alanrogers.com/UK1570

Brean has been a popular holiday destination for decades and many large campsites have evolved. Northam Farm is one of them; it is a large family park with good facilities and an ongoing programme of improvements. Of the 750 pitches, 350 are for seasonal units and these are separated from the four tourist fields. Pitches are large so you won't feel cramped and 252 have block paved hardstanding. There are two play areas for youngsters, a sports field, bicycle track, and cricket pitch for teenagers, and fishing on the lake for adults. The owners and staff are always available to help visitors enjoy their stay. About 500 yards down the road is The Seagull, which is also owned by Northam Farm. Here you'll find an excellent restaurant, bar and nightly live entertainment, even during the low season. A bus stops at the park entrance, or visitors can book a free ride on the bus to Cheddar, famous for its gorge and caves. Alternatively, just down the road is Brean Leisure Park with its swimming complex, funfair, golf and much more.

Facilities	Directions
Three good toilet blocks, well maintained and within reasonable distance of all pitches, provide ample toilets, washbasins (newest block has curtained cubicles) and spacious showers (50p pull cord operation). Bathrooms (£1 charge). Baby room. Rooms for visitors with disabilities (opened by key). Laundry. Motorcaravan service point. Dog shower. Licensed shop well stocked with food, holiday gear and accessories. Snack bar/takeaway. Free entry to live entertainment at The Seagull. Games room. Two play areas. Sports field. Fishing lake. Caravan workshop for repairs and servicing. Caravan storage. Dogs are not accepted in one field. Off site: Burnham-on-Sea and Weston-Super-Mare nearby. Golf, bicycle hire and riding 0.5 miles.	From M5 junction 22 follow signs to Burnham-on-Sea, Berrow and then Brean. Continue through Brean and Northam Farm is on the right, half a mile past Brean Leisure Park. O.S.GR: ST297556. GPS: 51.2949, -3.010167

Charges guide

Per unit incl. 2 persons and electricity	£ 9.25 - £ 22.50
extra person	£ 2.00 - £ 2.50
child (0-15 yrs)	£ 1.00
dog, awning, fishing	free

Open: March - October.

One of the most sought after touring parks in Somerset

Northam Farm
Where the sea meets the countryside
Brean Sands

Telephone:- 01278 751244 Fax:- 01278 751150
enquiries@northamfarm.co.uk | www.northamfarm.co.uk

Burnham-on-Sea
Warren Farm Holiday Centre
Warren Road, Brean Sands, Burnham-on-Sea TA8 2RP (Somerset) T: **01278 751227**
E: enquiries@warren-farm.co.uk alanrogers.com/UK1580

Warren Farm is a popular venue for family campers who want the beach, fun and entertainment. With over 1,000 pitches, the park is divided into several fields, with touring and seasonal pitches kept well apart; Sunnyside, part of Warren Farm, is about 200 yards further down the road and has its own warden. Access roads are wide and all the 565 touring pitches are grassy and level, with 16A electric hook-ups. There are no hardstandings so motorhomes may have difficulties in extremely wet weather. Play equipment is located in a line through the centre of the camping fields – ranch-style wooden fences break up the fields and couples usually park around the perimeter overlooking fields and views of the Mendip Hills.

Facilities	Directions
Several toilet blocks of varying styles provide WCs, showers (on payment) and mostly communal washbasins. Facilities vary depending on which block you are using. Showers are of adequate size, the new building in field 4 has larger ones and hairdressing stations, all have facilities for babies. Facilities for disabled visitors in all the fields. A warden looks after each block. Four laundries. Motorcaravan service points. Two shops, snack bar and Chinese takeaway (opening times vary). Fish bar. Beachcomber Inn. Play equipment for toddlers. Play barn. Sports field. Fishing lake. No dogs in field six. WiFi. Off site: Burnham-on-Sea, Weston-super-Mare, Cheddar, Wells and Glastonbury all close by. Golf and riding 1.5 miles.	Leave M5 at junction 22 and follow the B3140 to Burnham-on-Sea, then to Berrow and Brean. Continue through Brean and Warren Farm is on the right about 1.5 miles past Brean Leisure Park. O.S.GR: ST297564. GPS: 51.302483, -3.009833

Charges guide

Per unit incl. 2 persons and electricity	£ 9.50 - £ 18.50
extra person	£ 2.00
dog	free

Open: 2 April - 31 October.

Chard

Alpine Grove Touring Park

Forton, Chard TA20 4HD (Somerset) T: **01460 63479**. E: **stay@alpinegrovetouringpark.com**
alanrogers.com/UK1415

This peaceful and green site is owned by Richard and Helen Gurd who go the extra mile to ensure you enjoy your stay here. The pitches vary in size (90-120 sq.m) and are on flat ground served by gravel roads giving easy access. Some informally marked pitches are tucked away in dense foliage and are very private. Electricity (10A) is supplied. All the standard facilities are near reception, including a free fenced and heated swimming pool (10 x 5 m). A play area is provided for children under the canopy of mature trees which shade the site.

Facilities

A modest, clean sanitary building provides all the usual facilities. The facilities for disabled campers double as a family bathroom. Reception doubles as the shop selling some fresh food and essentials. Heated swimming pool. Play area. WiFi (charged). Dog sitting service (extra charge). Washing machine and dryers. Play area with trampoline (outside). Off site: Public transport – a half mile walk in Forton. ATM and supermarket at Chard 2 miles.

Open: 14 March - 30 September.

Directions

From M5 exit 25 take the A358 signed Cricket St Thomes Wildlife Park and Chard. From Chard take the Forton road where the site is well signed. From the A35, take A358 via Axminster to Chard, and then Forton. Ignore GPS and approach through Chard. O.S.GR: ST342068. GPS: 50.85779, -2.93597

Charges guide

Per unit incl. 2 persons	£ 11.00 - £ 19.50
incl. 6 persons	£ 13.00 - £ 24.00

Charmouth

Monkton Wyld Farm Caravan Park

Monkton Wyld Farm, Scotts Lane, Charmouth DT6 6DB (Dorset) T: **01297 631131**
E: **holidays@monktonwyld.co.uk** **alanrogers.com/UK1730**

Monkton Wyld Farm is a combination of two sites, the original one developed by Simon and Joanna Kewley, the other a Camping & Caravanning Club site developed by the Kewleys. The family runs both sites together, with the reception and the shop on the club side. Both sites have matured into attractive, comfortable, garden-like parks, with trees and flowering shrubs. Mature trees around the perimeter of the park provide shade. Plenty of room between the 180 pitches gives a feeling of spaciousness. All have 16A electricity and 93 have hardstanding. A woodland walk has been created in 80 acres of the beautiful countryside surrounding the park. On-site facilities are limited but there are two play areas, one with good space for ball games, a climbing frame, trampoline, etc. For a holiday with a difference, try staying in a 'yurt' – the site offers one of these fully-equipped, Mongolian-style tents for rent. There is also a ground floor flat for rent. A select development of caravan holiday homes for private ownership is being developed to one side of the club site.

Facilities

Two well built, heated toilet blocks are fully equipped. Family room with baby changing facilities (can also be accessed by wheelchairs). Laundry area. Gas supplies. Shop (Easter - end Sept). Takeaway (May - Aug). Play areas. Caravan storage. Gate locked at 23.00. Off site: Fishing and riding 2 miles. Bicycle hire, golf and boat launching 3 miles. Shops and local pubs within 1 mile. Charmouth and Lyme Regis 3 miles (buses leave from just along the road to both towns). The X53 Jurassic Coast bus stops at the end of the lane.

Open: 14 March - 10 November.

Directions

Park is signed on A35 between Charmouth and Axminster, about 2.5 miles west of Charmouth. Turn right at Greenway Head (B3165 signed Marshwood) and park is on the left. Approach reception through the Club site entrance. Don't go to Monkton Wyld hamlet – the road is very steep. O.S.GR: SY329966. GPS: 50.765333, -2.9525

Charges guide

Per unit incl. 2 persons and electricity	£ 17.33 - £ 27.89
extra person	£ 7.10 - £ 9.15
child (6-17 yrs)	free - £ 2.54

MONKTON
WYLD

WELCOME TO MONKTON WYLD
TOURING CARAVAN AND CAMPING PARK

High-quality facilities on a beautifully landscaped site, grass or hardstanding available.
Large well-spaced pitches with plenty of room for families to relax and children to play.
Spotless shower and laundry block, family room, large showers.
Three miles to the coast with many and varied attractions nearby.
Ground floor holiday flat - ideal for friends and relatives who don't wish to camp.

www.monktonwyld.co.uk • Tel: 01297 631131 • holidays@monktonwyld.co.uk

Charmouth

Newlands Caravan Park

Charmouth DT6 6RB (Dorset) T: **01297 560259**. E: enq@newlandsholidays.co.uk

alanrogers.com/UK1810

Newlands is well situated on the Jurassic Coast, the first natural world heritage site in England. A family owned park, it is run with care and enthusiasm, occupying a prominent position beside the road into Charmouth village with rural views southwards to the hills across the valley. The terrain is terraced in two fields to provide over 200 well spaced places for touring units, some for seasonal units and over 80 for caravan holiday homes (some for hire). The mainly sloping tent field also has super views towards the sea and Lyme Regis. Electricity (10A) is provided on 160 pitches and 30 have hardstanding, water and drainage. Other accommodation includes smart pine lodges, apartments and motel rooms. All the facilities are located in a modern building to one side of the wide tarmac entrance. The club bar opens each evening and lunch times to suit. Family entertainment includes a children's club during school holidays with Dino Dan, the dinosaur. The indoor pool adjoins the bar area and an adjacent outdoor pool is walled, paved and sheltered. A large play area in the field below the tent field is open dawn to dusk. This is a comfortable site for families with the beach and village within easy walking distance, with some evening and family activity.

Facilities

Two modern, heated toilet blocks (both refurbished) provide roomy showers and adjoining covered dishwashing areas and laundry rooms. Baby room. Well stocked shop (March - Nov). Licensed club bar (limited hours Nov - March). Restaurant (open 18.00-21.00. March - Nov plus Xmas/New Year) including takeaway. Outdoor heated pool (supervised in high season; the entrance is key coded). Indoor pool and jacuzzi (small charge, open all year, limited hours Nov - March). 9-pin bowling alley for hire at £5 per half hour. Play area. Off site: Beach 0.5 miles. Fishing 1 mile. Riding 3 miles. Golf 2 miles. Charmouth is known for its fossil finds and its connection with Jane Austen

Open: 1 February - 1 December (also 27 December - 3 January).

Directions

Approaching from Bridport leave the A35 at first sign for Charmouth at start of the bypass and site almost directly on your left. O.S.GR: SY373935. GPS: 50.7385, -2.889833

Charges guide

Per unit incl. up to 6 persons	
and awning	£ 10.00 - £ 25.00
incl. electricity	£ 15.00 - £ 27.00
serviced pitch	£ 14.00 - £ 30.00
dog (max. 2)	£ 1.00 - £ 3.00
extra pup tent	£ 5.00

Only one van or tent per pitch.
Camping Cheques accepted.

Charmouth
Wood Farm Caravan Park
Axminster Road, Charmouth DT6 6BT (Dorset) T: 01297 560697. E: holidays@woodfarm.co.uk
alanrogers.com/UK1760

Wood Farm is an excellent, family run park, maintained to high standards and with an indoor swimming pool. On sloping, well landscaped ground, it has splendid rural views across the Marshwood Vale. There are 196 pitches for touring units, all with 10A electricity of which 25 are for tents on a grassy, terraced field. The standard pitches are neat, level all-weather pitches with hardstanding, electricity (10A) and TV connections, and provision for awnings. Some are divided by neat, box-like leylandii hedging, some are terraced. There are 57 'premium' pitches with water, waste water and TV connections. Around 80 caravan holiday homes are in separate areas. Excellent provision is made for disabled visitors, although there is considerable up and down walking due to the terrain. Situated on the western side of Charmouth beside the A35 (some road noise may be expected), the park is only a mile or two from Lyme Regis and its beaches. This area is now part of England's first natural World Heritage site, the Jurassic Coast. Wood Farm is part of the Caravan Club's 'affiliated' scheme (non-members are also very welcome). A member of the Best of British group.

Facilities
Four modern, well equipped toilet blocks can be heated and include some washbasins in cubicles, en-suite family rooms charged). Excellent facilities for disabled people. Baby care unit. Two laundry rooms. Motorcaravan service point. Shop by reception. Fish and chip van several times weekly. Good heated indoor pool (charged). Recreation hall. Internet access. Bridge club. Outdoor draughts. Outdoor tennis court. Play field. Two coarse fishing ponds (carp, rudd, roach, tench, perch) adjacent – day and weekly tickets (licence required from park). Off site: Golf 1 mile. Riding 4 miles. Beaches and shops 1 and 2 miles. Use the X53 Jurassic Coast bus to explore the coast.

Open: 13 March - 2 November.

Directions
Park is 0.5 miles west of Charmouth village with access near the roundabout at the A35 and A3052 (Lyme Regis) junction. O.S.GR: SY356940. GPS: 50.74216, -2.91588

Charges guide
Per person	£ 4.50 - £ 6.50
child (5-16 yrs)	£ 2.00 - £ 3.00
pitch incl. 10A electricity	£ 5.00 - £ 10.50
'premium' pitch	£ 10.50 - £ 15.50
pup tent, dog, extra car	£ 2.00

Special senior citizens low season discounts.

Cheddar
Cheddar Bridge Touring Park
334

Draycott Road, Cheddar BS27 3RJ (Somerset) T: 01934 743048. E: enquires@cheddarbridge.co.uk
alanrogers.com/UK1545

Within easy walking distance of Cheddar village, this is an adult only (over 18 yrs) park. A compact site, there are 50 pitches, mostly on level grass, with 45 electric hook-ups (16A) and ten gravel hardstandings. A separate area for a few tents is on the river bank. Reception keeps basic supplies and gas cylinders. Note: the site access is over a fairly narrow bridge with low stone walls, passable for double axle caravans, but more difficult for American RVs and very large motorcaravans. Cheddar village has a small supermarket with ATM, garage, pubs, restaurants and a leisure centre with an indoor pool. Cheddar Gorge is a little further and would make a good day's hike with a packed lunch, without the problems of parking a vehicle in the Gorge itself where most parking is on payment.

Facilities
Attractive heated sanitary block (close to site entrance, some distance from most of the pitches) with washbasins in cubicles, large showers, and family bathroom with shower over the bath. Utility room with dishwashing and laundry sinks, and washer/dryer. Hot water is restricted to 07.00-12.00 and 16.00-21.00. Fishing. Off site: Cheddar Gorge and village. Swimming pool 0.5 miles. Golf 3 miles. Riding 3 miles.

Open: 1 March - end October.

Directions
Site entrance is about 100 yards south of village on A371, on right hand side, next to Cheddar Football Club. O.S.GR: ST461530. GPS: 51.27315, -2.774583

Charges guide
Per unit incl. 2 persons and electricity	£ 7.00 - £ 17.00
extra person	£ 2.00
dog	£ 1.00

Cheddar
Broadway House Caravan & Camping Park
Cheddar BS27 3DB (Somerset) T: **01934 742610**. E: **enquiries@broadwayhouse.uk.com**
alanrogers.com/UK1410

A well maintained park offering a range of facilities on continental lines, Broadway is now part of the Darwin Group. Occupying a gently sloping area at the foot of the Mendips near Cheddar Gorge, the park takes over 300 touring units of all types. From the entrance, after an area of neat caravan holiday homes and a separate area of luxury timber lodges, a series of touring areas graduates upwards, culminating in a tent and overflow rally field. The central access avenue is lined by trees with the groups of pitches on either side separated by ranch style fencing or hedging. All pitches have 16A electricity and 47 on gravel hardstanding have water and drainage. This park aims to cater for the normal active family – single sex groups are actively discouraged. There is a secluded, walled, heated pool (60 x 25 ft.) and paddling pool (open Easter - Sept; unsupervised) with grass sunbathing area and shade from silver birches. A BMX track, adventure play areas and crazy golf will also help to keep children entertained. A nature trail leads from the park – Cheddar Wood is a site of special scientific interest.

Facilities
The large, purpose built toilet block at the start of the touring area. Behind are 10 family shower units with shower, bidet and washbasin, two of which are 'disabled friendly'. Extra facilities with bathroom (coin operated) and a unit for disabled visitors are near reception, with a 'portacabin' type unit (no showers) in the top tent field. Baby room. Well equipped launderette. Motorcaravan service point. Shop. Bar and café. Adventure playground. Barbecue area. Crazy golf. BMX track. Games room. Lodges and caravan holiday homes to rent. Off site: Buses pass the gate. Fishing 0.5 and 5 miles.

Open: March - November.

Directions
From M5 exit 22 follow brown tourist signs towards Cheddar. Park entrance is on the A371 between Axbridge and Cheddar. O.S.GR: ST449547. GPS: 51.288214, -2.792303

Charges guide
Contact the park.
See advertisement on page 345

Cheddar
Bucklegrove Caravan & Camping Park
Wells Road, Rodney Stoke, Cheddar BS27 3UZ (Somerset) T: **01749 870261**. E: **info@bucklegrove.co.uk**
alanrogers.com/UK1550

Bucklegrove is set right in the heart of Somerset on the southern slopes of the Mendip Hills and close to the tourist attractions of Cheddar Gorge, Wookey Hole, and Wells. The 125 touring pitches, 80 of which have 10A electricity connections, are split between two fields joined by a woodland walk. The top slightly undulating field is more suitable for tents and caravans, while the lower field with some short hardstandings is a little more level and would be suitable for caravans and smaller motorhomes. A new play area (for under 14s) has a safety surface and includes a multiplay unit, slide and spring riders. Campers also have a games room and a heated indoor swimming pool (adult only sessions 10.00-11.00 daily). Adjoining the pool is a licensed bar with terrace providing simple bar menus and low-key entertainment mainly during high season or depending on the number of campers on site. A new development includes four privately owned lodges.

Facilities
Two bright and cheerful toilet blocks house all the usual amenities including some washbasins in cubicles and some spacious showers. The larger, heated block near reception also provides bathrooms (50p) with baby changing facilities, and a room for visitors with disabilities. Laundry rooms. Freezer for ice packs. Well stocked shop. Indoor swimming pool and paddling pool with terrace bar. Games room. Play area. Dogs are accepted in low season only. Off site: Riding 2 miles. Golf 3 miles. Fishing 5 miles. Beach at Weston-super-Mare 12 miles. Wookey Hole 2 miles, Wells Cathedral 4 miles, Cheddar 7 miles. A bus to Wells and Cheddar stops at the park entrance.

Open: 1 March - 14 December.

Directions
Take A371 Wells to Cheddar road. Park is on the right about 1 mile past Westbury village. Take care as the road between Wells and Cheddar is rather narrow through some of the villages. O.S.GR: ST490496. GPS: 51.243317, -2.7323

Charges guide
Per unit incl. 2 persons	£ 8.00 - £ 21.00
incl. electricity	£ 12.00 - £ 25.00
extra person	£ 4.00
child (4-17 yrs)	£ 1.00 - £ 3.00
dog (off peak only)	£ 2.00

Chippenham
Piccadilly Caravan Park

Folly Lane West, Lacock, Chippenham SN15 2LP (Wiltshire) T: 01249 730260. E: piccadillylacock@aol.com
alanrogers.com/UK1660

Piccadilly Caravan Park is set in open countryside close to several attractions, notably Longleat, Bath, Salisbury Plain, Stourhead, and Lacock itself. You will receive a warm welcome from the owner at this small, quiet family owned park that is beautifully kept. Well kept shrubs, plants and trees have been landscaped to give the impression of three separate areas and create a very pleasant ambience. There are 40 well spaced, clearly marked pitches, 12 of which have hardstanding, and two good areas for tents. Electrical connections (10A) are available on 34 pitches.

Facilities

The one toilet block is well maintained and equipped, should be adequate in size for peak periods and can be heated in cool weather. Laundry room with baby changing facilities. Ice pack service. Small, bark-based playground and a large, grass ball play area. Limited gas supplies. Papers can be ordered. Off site: Fishing 1 mile. Bicycle hire 6 miles. Riding 4 miles. Golf 3 miles.

Open: Easter/1 April - October.

Directions

Park is signed west off A350 Chippenham - Melksham road (turning to Gastard with caravan symbol) by Lacock village. 300 yds. to park. O.S.GR: ST911683. GPS: 51.4138, -2.129683

Charges guide

Per unit incl. 2 persons and electricity	£ 17.00
extra person (over 5 yrs)	£ 2.00

No credit cards.

Chippenham
Plough Lane Caravan Site

Plough Lane, Kington Langley, Chippenham SN15 5PS (Wiltshire) T: 01249 750146
E: enquiries@ploughlane.co.uk alanrogers.com/UK1680

Catering for adults only, this is a good example of a well designed, quality, modern touring site. The 50 pitches (all for touring units) are attractively laid out over four acres, access roads are gravel and the borders are stocked with well established shrubs and trees. The pitches are half grass, half hardstanding and all have electricity (16A), with 25 having full services. The site entrance has a barrier system for security. This site is an ideal base for visiting Bath and the Cotswolds, Avebury and Stonehenge.

Facilities

The sanitary building is heated, spacious, light and airy, and includes some washbasins in cubicles. Separate en-suite room for disabled visitors with ramp access. Fully equipped heated laundry with two further dishwashing sinks. Max. 2 dogs per unit, a gravel dog walking path is provided. This park is for adults only (over 18 yrs). Barrier card deposit £10. Off site: Supermarket, two public houses, and two garages (both with gas). Golf less than 1 mile.

Open: Easter - October.

Directions

From M4 junction 17 turn south on A350 for 2 miles, left at traffic lights (site signed). From Chippenham head north on A350 (towards M4), approaching traffic lights you need right hand lane (Kington Langley). O.S.GR: ST914764. GPS: 51.486367, -2.1257

Charges guide

Per unit incl. 2 persons and electricity	£ 16.75
extra person (max. 2 extra)	£ 5.00

No credit cards.

Dulverton
Exe Valley Caravan Site

Bridgetown, Dulverton TA22 9JR (Somerset) T: 01643 851432. E: paul@paulmatt.fsnet.co.uk
alanrogers.com/UK1590

Occupying a prime position in a wooded valley alongside the River Exe, within the National Park. Exe Valley Caravan Site is ideally situated for visiting the Doone Valley, Tarr Steps, Dulverton and many other beautiful venues in the area. This four acre 'adult only' campsite is owned and managed by Paul and Christine Matthews. Set beside the River Exe or the millstream, there are 50 large pitches (mostly grass but with some hardstandings at the top end), of which 41 have 10A electricity and TV hook-ups. Reception forms part of the owner's home which is an old mill, complete with water wheel and grindstones that are in working order. Open to visitors every Sunday at 10.00, CCTV has been installed so campers may watch the bat colony in the loft from a screen in the mill. Reception also houses a small shop stocking basic provisions. Fly fishing along the River Exe is possible or at Wimbleball Reservoir just over four miles away. This part of Somerset is a haven for walking, cycling and pony trekking.

Facilities

The refurbished toilet block houses the usual facilities and an en-suite room for disabled visitors (quite short steep ramp to enter). Excellent laundry with washing and drying machines, plus a microwave (free). Motorcaravan service point. Small shop with basic provisions. Bicycle hire. Gas supplies. Free fly fishing. WiFi. This is an adult-only park. Off site: Riding 4 miles. Golf 12 miles. Pub at Bridgetown. Winsford village has a general stores and tea rooms.

Open: 12 March - 18 October.

See advertisement opposite

Directions

Bridgetown is roughly midway between Dunster and Tiverton on the A396. As you enter Bridgetown from Tiverton, look for site sign and turn left on minor road. Site is 100 yards on the right. O.S.GR: SS923332. GPS: 51.0882, -3.53875

Charges guide

Per unit incl. 2 persons and electricity	£ 10.50 - £ 16.50

No credit cards.

Glastonbury
The Old Oaks Touring Park

Wick Farm, Wick, Glastonbury BA6 8JS (Somerset) T: 01458 831437. E: info@theoldoaks.co.uk
alanrogers.com/UK1390

The Old Oaks, an 'adults only' park, is tucked below and hidden from the 'Tor', in a lovely secluded setting with views across to the Mendips. In total there are 100 large pitches in a series of paddocks, the majority with 10A electricity, hardstanding and several with fully serviced (including sewage). Mainly backing on to hedges, they are attractively arranged and interspersed with shrubs and flowers in a circular development or terraced with increasing views. A quiet orchard area or a separated hedged paddock for camping and a larger field with chemical disposal facilities complete the provision. Mature trees and hedging combine with the mellow farm buildings to give a sense of timelessness, tranquility and peace. Whether you fish or not, the pond which is well stocked with carp, roach and tench is worth a visit for its view of the Tor. There is parking for disabled visitors within 25 yards of the pond. In an area steeped in history and legend, this is a very well equipped and maintained park which should meet the needs of the discerning camper or caravanner. A member of the Best of British group.

Facilities

The heated toilet block, converted from the old stables, is of excellent quality and well equipped. Neatly paved outside, it has digital security locks (a public footpath from the Tor passes through the farm). Some washbasins are in cubicles. Two en-suite rooms and a bathroom (£1). Disabled visitors have two rooms. Fully equipped laundry room. Two recycling points. Motorcaravan service facilities. Freezer for ice packs (free). Useful dog wash. Licensed shop for basics (limited hours). Pool table. Library room. Bicycle hire (with helmets). Fishing. Adults only accepted (18 yrs and over). Internet access at reception. Off site: Riding 5 miles. Golf 6 miles. Market day is Tuesday.

Open: All year.

Directions

Park is north off A361 Shepton Mallet - Glastonbury road, 2 miles from Glastonbury. Take narrow unclassified road signed Wick for 1 mile and park is on the left. O.S.GR: ST521394.
GPS: 51.152633, -2.6803

Charges guide

Per unit incl. 2 persons and electricity	£ 18.00 - £ 23.00
with full services	£ 19.00 - £ 25.00
extra person	£ 5.00
dog	£ 1.00

Lyme Regis
Shrubbery Caravan & Camping Park

Rousdon, Lyme Regis DT7 3XW (Dorset) T: 01297 442227. E: info@shrubberypark.co.uk
alanrogers.com/UK1720

Three miles south of historic Lyme Regis in a good situation to explore the Jurassic Coast, this well cared for park has distant views of the surrounding countryside. There are 120 generous pitches with more than enough room to pitch for most units. On slightly sloping, neatly cut grass which undulates in places, they are accessed by tarmac roads and all have 10A electricity. The pitches back on to well cut shrubs or the perimeter trees. A modern reception area is welcoming and stocks basic supplies and local provisions. This is a comfortable park where couples and families with young children are welcomed. The X53 Jurassic coastal bus which runs from Poole to Exeter passes the door. A general store and petrol station are adjacent to the site entrance. In the local area you can search for fossils, visit the donkey sanctuary or ride the miniature train at Pecorama in Beer. The Cob at Lyme Regis evokes memories of 'The French Lieutenant's Woman', whilst the unique Undercliff National Nature Reserve is popular with naturalists and walkers.

Facilities

Excellent heated toilet blocks, the newest (part of the reception building) with en-suite units, bathroom and laundry facilities. Two further blocks nearer the top of the park, fully equipped and well maintained. Facilities for disabled visitors. Simple shop at reception. General store at adjacent fuel station. Play area. Crazy golf. Off site: Beach and boat launching 3 miles. Fishing 1 mile. Golf 3 miles. Riding 5 miles

Open: Mid March - end October.

Directions

From the A35 near Axminster follow the A358 towards Seaton. At T-junction turn left on A3052 signed Rousdon and Lyme Regis. Site entrance is on the left few yards after Rousdon Garage. O.S.GR: SY298913. GPS: 50.71734, -2.99521

Charges guide

Per unit incl. 2 persons	£ 8.75 - £ 14.25
extra person	£ 3.00
child (4-16 yrs)	£ 2.00
electricity	£ 2.75

EXE VALLEY CARAVAN SITE
Within Exmoor National Park
Tel: 01643 851432 www.exevalleycamping.co.uk

Malmesbury

Burton Hill Caravan Park

Arches Lane, Malmesbury SN16 0EH (Wiltshire) T: **01666 826 880**. E: **audrey@burtonhill.co.uk**

alanrogers.com/UK1665

The owners of this park, Audrey and Warren Hateley, tend it with pride. It is a flat, grassy site surrounded by hedges, with open views across farmland on the outskirts of historic Malmesbury. There are 28 numbered touring pitches each with 16A electricity, 8 more for tents also with electricity and 8 without hook ups. It is a short walk (10-15 minutes) along the river bank to the town, its shops, Abbey Gardens, Abbey and 15th century market place. Within easy travelling distance are the towns of Bath, Chippenham, Tetbury, Trowbridge and Bradford-on-Avon.

Facilities	Directions
Modern, well equipped and well maintained toilet block with free hot water. Seperate well equipped facilities for disabled visitors. Washing machine. Off site: Malmesbury also has a sports centre and pool. Golf 6 miles. **Open:** 1 April/Easter - 31 October.	From M4 exit 17 follow the A4129 road towards Cirencester 5 miles. At approach to Malmesbury at international caravan sign, turn left into Arches Lane, and follow signs. O.S.GR: ST933866. GPS: 51.579083, -2.097321

Charges guide	
Per unit incl. 2 persons and electricity	£ 15.50
extra person	£ 2.00 - £ 3.00

Martock

Southfork Caravan Park

Parrett Works, Martock TA12 6AE (Somerset) T: **01935 825661**. E: **southforkcaravans@btconnect.com**

alanrogers.com/UK1420

Don't be put off by the address which is historic – this was once a 17th-century flax mill. Michael and Nancy Broadley now own and run this excellent, modern, well drained site just outside the lovely village of Martock. With 27 touring pitches on grass with a gravel access road (21 with 10A electrical hook-ups and two with water and waste water), it is an orderly, quiet park on two acres of flat, tree lined meadow near the River Parrett. All the expected facilities are close to the entrance and as the owners live on the premises, the park is open all year. There is also an NCC approved caravan repairs/servicing centre.

Facilities	Directions
The heated well maintained toilet block is fully equipped and includes some washbasins in cabins. Laundry room with washing machine and dryer. Shop and limited off-licence with gas and comprehensive camping accessories. Play area. Off site: Fishing (with licences) on the River Parrett a few yards from the park. Golf 5 miles. Bicycle hire 8 miles. Riding 10 miles. Pubs with good food in South Petherton and Martock, less than 2 miles in each direction. **Open:** All year.	From A303 between Ilchester and Ilminster turn north at the roundabout signed South Petherton. At the T-junction in village, turn right (Martock). Park is midway between the two villages (1.5 miles). O.S.GR: ST446187. GPS: 50.965367, -2.789817

Charges guide	
Per unit incl. 2 persons	£ 9.00 - £ 13.00
incl. electricity (10A)	£ 11.50 - £ 15.50
extra person	£ 1.75

Melksham

Devizes Camping & Caravanning Club Site

Spout Lane, Seend, Melksham SN12 6RN (Wiltshire) T: **01380 828839**

alanrogers.com/UK1700

First opened in 1998, this site occupies a level field with gravel roads and centrally located facilities. It is also adjacent to the Kennet and Avon Canal (opened in 1810 and recently extensively restored). The towpath now provides a traffic-free route passing the Caen Hill flight of 29 locks into Devizes (4 miles). In the other direction the towpath runs towards Melksham (also 4 miles). There are 50 hardstanding and 40 grass pitches, 80 with electricity (16A). The Millennium Wood on the site contains more than 1,000 trees. The site is central for visiting many places of interest including the stone circles at Stonehenge and Avebury.

Facilities	Directions
The modern, heated toilet block provides spacious hot showers, washbasins in cubicles, laundry, dishwashing room, and a baby room. Facilities for disabled visitors are in a suite (with alarm system) by reception. Motorcaravan services (in the late arrivals area). Small playground. Reception opens 09.00-10.00 and 16.00-17.30, and stocks basic foods and drinks, snacks and gas supplies, fishing licences and local tourist information. Off site: Melksham Farmers' Market second Friday each month. **Open:** All year.	From Devizes take A361 westbound, and 0.5 miles before Seend village, take A365 towards Melksham. Cross the canal bridge, take next left by 'Three Magpies' and the site entrance is on the right. From M4 junction 17, use A350 to Melksham and A365 to the site. O.S.GR: ST950620. GPS: 51.3565, -2.07225

Charges guide	
Per person	£ 6.30 - £ 7.25
child	£ 2.15 - £ 2.25
pitch (non-member)	£ 5.65

Minehead

Halse Farm Touring Caravan & Camping Park

Winsford, Minehead TA24 7JL (Somerset) T: 01643 851259. E: ar@halsefarm.co.uk

alanrogers.com/UK1360

A truly rural park with beautiful moorland views, you may be lucky enough to glimpse red deer across the valley or be able to see ponies and foals grazing outside the main gate which is adjacent to the moor. Two open, neatly cut fields (level at the top) back onto traditional hedging and slope gently to the middle and bottom where wild flowers predominate. One field provides electricity points (10A) and is used for motorcaravans and caravans, the other is for tents. There is no reception – you leave your unit by the toilet block and walk down to the farm kitchen to book in. The pretty village of Winsford is one mile (footpath from farm) with a post office, shop, pub and restaurant. Mrs Brown has laminated maps available (at a small cost) detailing six walks of varying distances, starting and finishing at the farm. Also available is a list of the wild birds, flowers, etc. to be found on the site. A member of the Countryside Discovery group.

Facilities	Directions
The central toilet block is of good quality and heated. Well equipped and maintained, it includes a toilet, washbasin and shower for visitors with disabilities, washing machine, dryer and iron, and tourist information. Gas is available at the farm. Play equipment. Off site: Fishing 4 miles, bicycle hire 5 miles, riding 2 miles. Tarr Steps and Barle Valley 3 miles. Winsford village 1 mile.	Turn off A396 Tiverton - Minehead road for Winsford (site signed). In Winsford village turn left in front of the Royal Oak (not ver ford) and keep on uphill for 1 mile (sharp bend at the bottom). Cross cattle grid onto moor and turn immediately left to farm. Caravans should avoid Dulverton - keep to the A396 from Bridgetown (signed). O.S.GR: SS898342. GPS: 51.097717, -3.579983

Open: 18 March - 1 November.

Charges guide

Per unit incl. 2 persons and electricity	£ 14.00 - £ 16.00
extra person	£ 6.00 - £ 7.00
child (5-16 yrs)	£ 1.50 - £ 2.00

Minehead

Burrowhayes Farm Caravan & Camping Site

West Luccombe, Porlock, Minehead TA24 8HT (Somerset) T: 01643 862463. E: info@burrowhayes.co.uk

alanrogers.com/UK1370

This delightful park with riding stables on site, is on the edge of Exmoor. The stone packhorse bridge over Horner Water beside the farm entrance sets the tone of the park, which the Dascombe family have created over the last 40 years having previously farmed the land. The farm buildings have been converted into riding stables with escorted rides available (from Easter). Touring and tent pitches are on partly sloping field with marvellous views or a flatter location in the clearing by the river, while 20 caravan holiday homes are in a separate area. Electrical hook-ups are available (16A), although some long leads may be needed. With walking, bird watching, plenty of wild life to observe, pretty Exmoor villages and Lorna Doone country nearby there is much to do. Children can ride, play in the stream or explore the woods at the top of the site. Limited trout fishing is available in Horner Water (NT permit) alongside the park.

Facilities	Directions
The heated toilet block provides controllable hot showers, one washbasin cubicle for each sex, hairdressing and shaving areas, laundry room, unit for disabled visitors and babies, and an indoor dishwashing room. A second older block is opened in high season with extra WCs and washbasins. Motorcaravan service point. Well stocked shop doubles with reception (from 1/4). Dogs must be kept on leads at all times and exercised off site. Off site: Beach 2 miles. Fishing 2 miles. Bicycle hire 5 miles. Golf 6 miles. Minehead 5 miles. Local pub 20 minutes walk.	From A39, 5 miles west of Minehead, take first left past Allerford to Horner and West Luccombe. Site is on right after 400 yards. O.S.GR: SS899461. GPS: 51.203533, -3.5778

Open: 15 March - 31 October.

Charges guide

Per unit incl. 2 persons and electricity	£ 12.50 - £ 16.50
extra person	£ 4.00 - £ 5.00
child (3-15 yrs)	£ 2.00 - £ 2.50
dog	free

www.alanrogers.com for latest campsite news

Minehead

Hoburne Blue Anchor

Blue Anchor Bay, Minehead TA24 6JT (Somerset) T: **01643 821360**. E: **enquiries@hoburne.com**

alanrogers.com/UK1380

Although mainly a holiday park, with almost 300 caravan holiday homes, Blue Anchor nevertheless offers good facilities for 103 touring units. Trailer tents are accepted but not other tents (other than pup tents with a touring booking). Virtually in a separate touring area, the level pitches all have 16A electricity and hardstanding for cars and motorcaravans (with caravans going on the adjacent grass). A feature of the park is a good sized, indoor swimming pool with an area for small children and views of the sea; it is heated and supervised. Part of the Hoburne Group.

Facilities	Directions
Toilet facilities provide large pushbuttonshowers. Launderette in a single block serving just the touring area. Indoor heated swimming pool. Adventure-style play area. Note: an unfenced river runs along one boundary of the park. Crazy golf. Small supermarket/shop with coffee shop (08.00-21.00 in high season, less at other times). American motorhomes accepted (max. 36 ft). Dogs are not accepted. Off site: Beach 100 yds. Riding and bicycle hire 5 miles. **Open:** 1 March - 31 October.	From M5 junction 25, take A358 signed Minehead. After 12 miles turn left onto A39 at Williton. After 4 miles turn right onto B3191 at Carhampton signed Blue Anchor. Park is 1.5 miles on right. O.S.GR: ST024535. GPS: 51.1822, -3.397283

Charges guide

Per unit incl. up to 6 persons,
electricity and awning   £ 9.50 - £ 19.50

Salisbury

Greenhill Farm Caravan & Camping Park

New Road, Landford, Salisbury SP5 2AZ (Wiltshire) T: **01794 324117**. E: **info@greenhillholidays.co.uk**

alanrogers.com/UK1640

Located on the northern edge of the New Forest National Park, this park occupies 14 acres out of a total of 50 acres of beautiful forest owned by the family. It is an uncommercialised hideaway and has two distinctive areas: the 'adult only' area, fenced, gated and set around two small lakes, one of which is reserved for coarse fishing and the 'family' area with a playground, views over the meadow, sightings of deer and a generally open aspect. There are 160 pitches in total, with 50 for tents in a separate hill-top meadow with views over the nearby forest and its own fishing lake.

Facilities	Directions
New toilet block planned; in the interim, Portacabin-style units of varying ages provide facilities. No dedicated facilities for disabled persons. Laundry facilities. Reception/shop. Takeaway in high season. Bicycle hire. Coarse fishing lakes (£3.60 per rod per day). Torches useful. Off site: Landford village has a post office/general store (15 minutes walk). Golf 3 miles. Riding 4 miles. Local attractions include Paultons Park, Breamore House and the New Forest. Several pubs serving meals are close by. Bus stop outside entrance. **Open:** All year.	From M27 exit 2 take A36 north towards Salisbury for about 6 miles. Pass through West Wellow and after passing a B.P. garage on left, take next left into New Road, and continue for 0.9 mile to site entrance on left. O.S.GR: SU264184. GPS: 50.96445, -1.62575

Charges guide

Per unit incl. 2 persons,	
awning and electricity	£ 15.00 - £ 16.50
tent incl. 2 persons	£ 9.00 - £ 13.00
extra person	£ 2.00 - £ 3.50

Salisbury

Coombe Touring Park

Coombe Nurseries Race Plain, Netherhampton, Salisbury SP2 8PN (Wiltshire) T: **01722 328451**

alanrogers.com/UK1650

A true touring park with outstanding views over the Chalke Valley, Coombe is adjacent to Salisbury racecourse. There are 100 spacious pitches all on level, well mown grass, 46 with electricity hook-ups (10A). The 50 tent pitches are generally around the outer perimeter and there are 4 caravan holiday homes to rent. Many pitches are individual and sheltered by hedging. Reception has a small shop and there are supermarkets in Salisbury and pubs in Netherhampton and Coombe Bissett both serving meals.

Facilities	Directions
A well built, modern, centrally heated sanitary unit, provides an ample supply of WCs, spacious pushbutton showers, washbasins in cubicles for the ladies, and a family room (with bath) has facilities for disabled persons, babies and toddlers. Laundry. Small shop (May-Sept). Gas available. Good tourist information chalet. Open grass play area. Off site: Nearby attractions include Wilton House, Wilton Carpet Factory and the Wilton Shopping Village, Salisbury Cathedral, Stonehenge. Golf 400 yards. Riding and tennis in Wilton 2.5 miles. Indoor pool, leisure centre and cinema in Salisbury 4.5 miles. **Open:** 1 January - 20 December.	From A36 two miles west of Salisbury, turn south on A3094 towards Netherhampton and Harnham. After 0.5 miles on sharp left hand bend, turn right to Stratford Tony and Racecourse. Continue to top of hill by racecourse entrance, and turn left on narrow lane behind racecourse for 700 yards to site entrance. O.S.GR: SU098282. GPS: 51.05428, -1.86092

Charges guide

Per unit incl. 2 persons and electricity	£ 15.00
extra person	£ 3.50
child (3-17 yrs)	£ 1.50 - £ 2.00
No credit cards.	

Salisbury

Church Farm Caravan & Camping Park

Sixpenny Handley, Salisbury SP5 5ND (Wiltshire) T: 01725 553005. E: churchfarmcandcpark@yahoo.co.uk
alanrogers.com/UK1655

Sixpenny Handley is a Saxon hilltop village and St Mary's church dates back some 900 years. From the site you can hear the bells and the chimes of its clock. Church Farm, a stone's throw from the village centre, offers 35 partly-sheltered, level, spacious pitches including some hardstandings, all with 16A, arranged around the perimeter of two fields, plus a tent field. It is in an Area of Outstanding Natural Beauty and the views and many walks are an absolute delight. There are many places for the visitor to discover the delights around this junction of Dorset, Hampshire and Wiltshire.

Facilities

New spacious multi-function building houses reception, a seasonal café/bar, and up-to-date heated toilet facilities. Dedicated room for disabled campers. Baby changing. Laundry facilities. Motorcaravan service point. Play area. Two holiday caravans for rent. Off site: Village has some small shops, a small supermarket and Post Office. The Roebuck Inn offers a varied menu. Tennis courts (hire equipment from site). Golf 4 miles. Riding 5 miles. Fishing 10 miles.

Open: All year.

Directions

To avoid the village centre, 1 mile south of Handley Hill roundabout on A354 turn towards Sixpenny Handley, then right by the school and site 300 yards by the church. O.S.GR: ST996173.
GPS: 50.955317, -2.006883

Charges guide

Per unit incl. 2 persons and electricity	£ 15.75 - £ 16.75
extra person	£ 6.50 - £ 7.00

Shepton Mallet

Greenacres Camping

Barrow Lane, North Wootton, Shepton Mallet BA4 4HL (Somerset) T: 01749 890497
E: stay@greenacres-camping.co.uk alanrogers.com/UK1490

Greenacres is a rural site in Somerset countryside for tents, trailer tents and small motorcaravans only. Hidden away below the Mendips and almost at the start of the 'Levels', it is a simple green site – a true haven of peace and quiet. The grass is neatly trimmed over the 4.5 acres and hedged with mature trees, though there is a view of Glastonbury Tor in one direction and of Barrow Hill in the other. All of the 40 pitches are around the perimeter of the park, leaving a central area safe for children to play.

Facilities

The central wooden toilet block is simple but perfectly acceptable and kept clean. Hot showers are accessed directly from the outside. Play equipment, badminton net and play house. The park office (and bicycle hire), is across the lane. New cabin with fridges and freezers for campers' use (free), library and tourist information. Batteries may be charged or borrowed. Dogs are not accepted. Off site: North Wootton (under 1 mile) with large pub/restaurant and a vineyard. Fishing and riding nearby.

Open: March - October.

Directions

From A39 Glastonbury - Wells road turn east at Brownes Garden Centre and follow camping signs. From A361 Glastonbury - Shepton Mallet road follow camp signs from Pilton or Steanbow. (Roads are narrow with few passing places). O.S.GR: ST553416.
GPS: 51.172367, -2.641883

Charges guide

Per person	£ 7.00
child (4-16 yrs)	£ 2.50

No credit cards.

Shepton Mallet

Batcombe Vale Campsite

Batcombe Vale, Shepton Mallet BA4 6BW (Somerset) T: 01749 831207. E: gary.butler1@virgin.net
alanrogers.com/UK1540

Set in a secluded valley with fields gently rising around it, contented cows grazing with watchful buzzards cruising above and views across the distant hills, this is a very special place. Descending slowly down the narrow drive you see the pitches, attractively set and terraced where necessary, in an oval with the lakes below. The grass is left natural around the 32 pitches (20 have 10A electricity) and paths mown where needed. Batcombe Vale House is an attractive, mellow building covered with wisteria, to one side of the valley overlooking the lakes and the 'wilder' landscape.

Facilities

The small rustic toilet block covered in honeysuckle meets all needs, including a freezer and dishwashing sinks. Groundsheet awnings must be lifted daily. Fishing. Caravan storage. One dog per pitch is welcome (no dangerous breeds). Bed and breakfast available in Batcombe Vale House. No commercial vehicles or motorcycle 'packs' - family groups only. Off site: Golf, riding and bicycle hire 5 miles. Bruton (for shops, etc.) is 2 miles. Launderettes at Shepton or Frome.

Open: Easter - end September.

Directions

Bruton is south of Shepton Mallet and Frome and north of Wincanton where the A359 intersects the B3081. Access to the site must be via Evercreech or Bruton (B3081), then follow the brown and white camping signs. Access drive is steep.
O.S.GR: ST684376. GPS: 51.136467, -2.453167

Charges guide

Per unit incl. 2 persons and electricity	£ 19.50
extra person	£ 4.75
child (4-15 yrs)	£ 2.75

No credit cards.

95

Sparkford

Long Hazel Park

High Street, Sparkford, Yeovil BA22 7JH (Somerset) T: 01963 440002. E: longhazelpark@hotmail.com
alanrogers.com/UK1500

Pamela and Alan Walton are really enthusiastic about their neat, small, 'adult-only' park in the Somerset village of Sparkford where they will make you most welcome. This level, landscaped park is surrounded by attractive beech hedging, silver birches and many other ornamental trees and the park has a relaxed, comfortable feel. It provides 50 touring pitches with electrical hook-ups (16A), 40 pitches with hardstanding, some extra long with grass lawns at the side, and the entrance has been widened for easier access. Part of the park is being developed with pine holiday lodges for private ownership.

Facilities

The well equipped toilet block is neat, tidy and heated in winter. Well planned en-suite facilities for visitors with disabilities. Washing machine and dryer. Motorcaravan waste water discharge. Long hardstanding pitches suitable for American style motorhomes. Safe cycle routes and walks available at reception. Caravan storage. Off site: Bus service. Spar shop, post office and McDonalds 400 yards. Village inn 100 yds. Riding or fishing 8 miles. Golf 5 miles.

Open: All year.

Directions

At roundabout on A303 take road into Sparkford and park is signed on the left 100 yds before the Inn. O.S.GR: ST604263. GPS: 51.0344, -2.568633

Charges guide

Per unit incl. 2 persons and electricity	£ 16.00 - £ 18.00
extra person	£ 2.00

No credit cards.

Taunton

Quantock Orchard Caravan Park

Crowcombe, Taunton TA4 4AW (Somerset) T: 01984 618618. E: member@flaxpool.freeserve.co.uk
alanrogers.com/UK1350

Quantock Orchard, nestles at the foot of the Quantocks in quiet countryside, close to many of the attractions of the area. Attractively developed, mature apple trees, recently planted trees, shrubs and pretty flower beds with a nice use of heathers, make a pleasant environment and the clock tower on the wooden sanitary block adds interest. With access from fairly narrow gravel roads, there are 69 touring pitches, part separated by growing shrubs and hedging, of which 40 are for tents. Of various sizes, all touring pitches have 15A electricity hook-ups, 30 have hardstanding, four have TV hook-up and five are fully serviced (two extra large, with patio and barbecue).

Facilities

The central, heated sanitary block is very well maintained. Four showers each for ladies and men. Some washbasins in curtained cubicles for ladies, excellent family bathroom and separate baby rooms. Microwave. Laundry facilities. Facilities for disabled visitors. Well stocked licensed shop. Swimming pool (40 x 20 ft. and open May - Sept). Leisure suite. Games room, Sky TV. Fenced safe-based play area. Caravan storage Oct. - March. Holiday homes for hire. Off site: Coast 5 miles. Bus service 1 minute walk. Pub 3 miles.

Open: All year.

Directions

Park is west off A358 road (Taunton - Minehead), about 1 mile south of Crowcombe village. O.S.GR: ST140363. GPS: 51.1084, -3.22645

Charges guide

Per unit incl. 2 persons and electricity	£ 13.00 - £ 25.00
extra person	£ 4.00
child (3-15 yrs)	£ 2.00 - £ 3.00

Taunton

Waterrow Touring Park

Wiveliscombe, Taunton TA4 2AZ (Somerset) T: 01984 623464. E: waterrowpark@yahoo.co.uk
alanrogers.com/UK1520

Beside the River Tone in a pretty part of South Somerset, Tony and Anne Taylor have enthusiastically developed Waterrow into a charming, landscaped touring park for adults only. Nestling in a little sheltered valley, it is very peaceful and possible for an overnight stop (just over 30 minutes from M5) or ideal as a base for exploring nearby Exmoor and the Brendon Hills. There are 48 touring pitches, all of which are on level hardstandings, including five with full services. All have electricity (16A). A small area has been set aside for tent campers. A member of the Best of British group.

Facilities

A modern, clean toilet unit, well fitted out and with heating, provides WCs and washbasins, some in curtained cubicles. New heated shower block. Facilities for disabled people (key). Laundry facilities. Motorcaravan service point. Limited provisions are available in reception. Order jacket potatoes before lunchtime for the evening for just £1.20. WiFi. Caravan storage. Off site: Fishing 5 miles. Golf 7 miles. Bicycle hire 10 miles. Wiveliscombe 3 miles.

Open: All year.

Directions

From M5 exit 25 take A358 (signed Minehead) round Taunton for 4 miles, then at Staplegrove onto the B3227 for 11.5 miles to Wiveliscombe where straight on at lights to Waterrow (still B3227). Park is on left shortly after the Rock Inn. Do not use Sat Nav. O.S.GR: ST052250. GPS: 51.0165, -3.352717

Charges guide

Per unit incl. 2 persons (adults only) and electricity	£ 14.00 - £ 27.00

Taunton
Cornish Farm Touring Park
Shoreditch, Taunton TA3 7BS (Somerset) T: **01823 327746**. E: **info@cornishfarm.com**
alanrogers.com/UK1340

This neat little park, which opened for its first full season in 2006, is on level ground and conveniently located close to the M5 motorway. There are 49 pitches, all with 10A electricity, of which 25 are on gravel hardstanding. Most pitches are accessed from a gravel road (one-way system) with plenty of fresh water taps, site lighting and some picnic tables. A separate area for tents is close to the toilet block. With its colourful flowerbeds and old apple trees this makes a very pleasant stop-over. Light power cables cross the site and there is some background motorway noise. Maximum length for motorhomes is 30ft, unless by arrangement. To the left are the barns that house the Van Bitz workshops producing security systems for motorcaravans. The centrally situated, modern toilet block is of a high standard including underfloor heating, designed by the owners who are caravanners themselves. There are no other facilities on the park but a cycle path and a footpath will take you into Taunton town centre. The site would make a good base from which to visit Cheddar Gorge, Wookey Hole, and Clarke's shopping village at Street.

Facilities	Directions
One central block with underfloor heating and modern fittings. Large dual purpose room providing facilities for disabled visitors and small children. Dusk to dawn low energy lighting. Laundry room. Dishwashing sinks outside under cover at one end of the building. Motorcaravan service point. Off site: Level cycle/footpath into Taunton (2 miles) which has a castle, museum, and markets. Tesco Express 1 mile. Golf 2 miles. Bicycle hire 2 miles. **Open:** All year.	From M5 exit 25 follow signs for Taunton. At first set of traffic lights turn left signed Corfe (B3170). Take third left into Ilminster Road following signs to Corfe. Bear right at roundabout onto Blackbrook Way. Bear left at next roundabout and follow to T-junction (B3170). Turn right then next left (Killams Drive). Take second left (Killams Ave), and cross motorway bridge. Site entrance is immediately after the bridge. O.S.GR: ST 234 219. GPS: 50.99200, -3.09257

Charges guide

Per unit incl. 2 persons, electricity	£ 13.00 - £ 15.00
extra person (over 5 yrs)	£ 2.00

Taunton
Lowtrow Cross Caravan Site
Upton, Wiveliscombe, Taunton TA4 2DB (Somerset) T: **01398 371199**. E: **info@lowtrowcross.co.uk**
alanrogers.com/UK1355

Situated just inside Exmoor National Park, Lowtrow Cross is a small park for adults only and ideal for dogs owners. It is quietly located on a hillside giving lovely views north towards the Brendon Hills. There are 23 generously sized pitches, of which two are occupied by caravan holiday homes and two are seasonal. An adjacent meadow can be used for tents. There are four hardstandings otherwise the pitches are on sloping grass. There are 17 electricity hook-ups (16A) each with a TV socket (aerial cables on loan). Although there is no bar or restaurant on site there is a pub at the gate which serves excellent food.

Facilities	Directions
Traditional heated, well equipped, toilet block but no facilities for disabled visitors. Excellent laundry room. Freezer and microwave. Small shop in reception; basic foodstuffs, milk, bread, free range eggs, frozen ready meals, toiletries. Off site: Lowtrow Cross Inn at gate. Garage 750 m. Fishing and boating 3 miles. Golf and riding 10 miles. **Open:** 16 March - 31 October. *See advertisement on following page*	From M5 junction 25 follow signs for Minehead (A358) through Taunton. 5 miles from Taunton turn west (left) on B3224 (Raleigh Cross). Shortly after Raleigh Cross Inn turn south on B3190 (Bampton). Site on right in 4 miles just before Upton village. O.S.GR: ST007292. GPS: 51.053342, -3.419923

Charges guide

Per unit incl. 2 persons	£ 10.00 - £ 13.00
electricity (16A)	£ 2.50

Warminster

Longleat Caravan Club Site

Warminster BA12 7NL (Wiltshire) T: **01985 844663**

alanrogers.com/UK1690

What a magnificent situation in which to find a caravan park, amidst all the wonders of the Longleat Estate including the Elizabethan House, gardens designed by Capability Brown and the Safari Park. Visitors can roam the woodlands and enjoy the views, watch the wildlife and marvel at the azaleas, bluebells, etc. according to the season or listen to the occupants of the Safari Park. The site itself, well managed by Caravan Club wardens, is situated in ten acres of lightly-wooded, level grassland within walking distance of the house and gardens. There are 165 generous pitches (139 with hardstanding and 26 on grass), all with 16A electricity connections. Water points and re-cycling bins are neatly walled with low night lighting. Tents are not accepted (except trailer tents).

Facilities

Two heated toilet blocks provide washbasins in cubicles, controllable showers and a vanity section with mirrors and hairdryers. Baby/toddler room, suite for disabled visitors, laundry and dishwashing room and a family room with a DVD player. Two motorcaravan service points. Play area. Office is manned 09.00-18.00 and stocks basic food items, papers can be ordered and gas is available. Paperback exchange library. Fish and chip van calls some evenings. Late arrivals area. Off site: Longleat House and its attractions. Frome 7 miles.

Open: 17 March - 30 October.

Directions

The main entrance to Longleat which caravans must use is signed from the A362 Frome - Warminster road near where it joins the A36 Warminster bypass. Turn into estate and follow Longleat House route through toll booths for 2 miles then follow caravan club signs for 1 mile. There are shorter ways to leave the site. O.S.GR: ST806434. GPS: 51.1907, -2.278517

Charges guide

Per person	£ 4.90 - £ 6.55
child (5-16 yrs)	£ 1.50 - £ 2.95
pitch incl. electricity (non-member)	£ 11.80 - £ 15.35

Wells

Cheddar, Mendip Heights Camping & Caravanning Club Site

Priddy, Wells BA5 3BP (Somerset) T: **01749 870241**. E: cheddar@campingandcaravanningclub.co.uk

alanrogers.com/UK1430

Now owned by the Camping & Caravanning Club, Mendip Heights is a well kept site half a mile from the village. There are tranquil views across the Mendip fields which are characterised by dry stone walling. It has a simple charm with field margins left natural to encourage wildlife and nest boxes in the mature trees edging the three fields which comprise the site. These provide space for 90 units on mostly slightly sloping short grass with 56 electric hook-ups (16A), 36 with hardstanding. Historic Priddy is the highest village in the Mendips and is famed for its annual Sheep Fair in August.

Facilities

The refurbished toilet block with all facilities is bright, cheerful and heated. Two family rooms (one with high and low toilet and shower). Facilities for disabled visitors. Laundry facilities. Motorcaravan service point. The reception/licensed shop doubles as the village shop and is therefore open all season selling groceries, Calor gas, etc. Wendy house, swings and table tennis for children. Torches useful. Off site: Two traditional village pubs with very different characters stand by the village green within walking distance (0.5 miles). Bicycle hire and golf 5 miles. Fishing 6 miles, riding 2 miles.

Open: 1 March - 15 November.

Directions

From M5 exit 21 take A371 to Banwell. Turn left on A368, right on B3134 and right on B3135. After 2 miles turn left at camp sign. From M4 westbound exit 18, A46 to Bath, then A4 towards Bristol. Take A39 for Wells and right at Green Ore traffic lights on B3135; after 5 miles, left at camp sign. From Shepton Mallet, follow A37 north to junction of B3135 and turn left. Continue on B3135 to traffic lights at Green Ore. Straight on, after 5 miles turn left at camp sign. O.S.GR: ST522518. GPS: 51.2636, -2.685383

Charges guide

Per person	£ 6.05 - £ 8.40
child	£ 2.25 - £ 4.80
pitch with services incl. electricity	£ 3.25

Westbury

Brokerswood Country Park

Brokerswood, Westbury BA13 4EH (Wiltshire) T: **01373 822238**. E: info@brokerswood.co.uk
alanrogers.com/UK1630

This countryside campsite is located in an 80-acre country park, with ancient broadleaf woodland, plenty of marked walks, and a woodland railway, which also runs 'Santa Specials' (bookings taken from 1 August). The campsite has 65 pitches arranged around an open meadow area, served by a circular gravel roadway, with low level site lighting. There are 25 hardstanding pitches, and 44 electric hook-ups (10A). Although fairly recently laid-out, the site is maturing well. American RVs and other large units should use the coach entrance and they (and all other arrivals after 18.00) are asked to phone ahead so that arrangements can be made for the barrier. The gift shop has a special Christmas theme from the end of October. The park also has adventure playgrounds and play trails amongst its many activities for the family. Most are free for campers, except for the train. Fishing in the lake is available, ask at reception. Cycling in the park is forbidden. In the interest of environmental conservation it has its own biological waste management system. There are also recycling bins for glass, paper and metal cans.

Facilities

Two well insulated and heated, timber clad buildings are at one end of the site. Some washbasins in cubicles, large, controllable hot showers. Family rooms (on payment). Fully equipped suite for disabled people with ramp and alarm. Laundry and ironing facilities. Motorcaravan services. Gas available. Milk, bread, newspapers to order from the shop in reception. Café serving meals and refreshments all day. Takeaway food service during August. Fishing. Entry barrier (key code). Cycling allowed on site but not in Country Park. Off site: Golf 6 miles. Nearest shops are at Dilton Marsh and Westbury. Longleat House 6 miles. Bath 12 miles.

Open: All year.

Directions

From Trowbridge take A361 south for 2 miles, turning left (east) at Southwick, and follow signs to Country Park. O.S.GR: ST840524. GPS: 51.270283, -2.231417

Charges guide

Per unit incl. 4 persons and electricity	£ 13.00 - £ 28.00
extra person	£ 3.75
child	£ 3.00
dog	£ 1.00

Weston-super-Mare

Slimeridge Farm Touring Park

Links Road, Uphill, Weston-super-Mare BS23 4XY (Somerset) T: **01934 641641**
alanrogers.com/UK1530

This small touring site is next to the beach in Uphill village at the southern end of Weston Bay. There are 56 pitches (many taken on seasonal lets), on level grass with electricity (16A) available, separated from the beach by stone walling. The view across the bay is quite something. However it is worth noting that, because of its close proximity to the beach, the site could be affected by the tide in extreme adverse winter weather conditions. A circular tarmac road connects the marked and numbered pitches which include eight hardstandings for motorcaravans. Arrive between 11.00 and 17.00 hrs only.

Facilities

A modern toilet block with electronic code entry system is well equipped and includes en-suite shower facilities that are also provided for handicapped visitors. Laundry room. Chemical disposal unit also used for waste water. Off site: Post office, general stores and pubs within close walking distance. Golf (note: golfers have right of way to cross the park as the golf course is split by the site).

Open: 1 March - 30 October.

Directions

Site is south of Weston-super-Mare. From A370 follow sign for Uphill village and sands. O.S.GR: ST312588. GPS: 51.323883, -2.989033

Charges guide

Per unit incl. 2 persons, electricity and awning	£ 10.00 - £ 20.00

Min. stay 2 nights at B.Hs.
No credit cards.

99

Weymouth
East Fleet Farm Touring Park
Fleet Lane, Chickerell, Weymouth DT3 4DW (Dorset) T: **01305 785768**. E: **enquiries@eastfleet.co.uk**
alanrogers.com/UK1800

East Fleet Farm has a marvellous situation on part level, part gently sloping meadows leading to the shores of the Fleet, with views across to the famous Chesil Bank and the sea beyond. This park has been developed by the Whitfield family within the confines of their 300-acre organic arable farm in keeping with its surroundings, yet with modern amenities. It is maturing well as bushes and trees grow. The 400 pitches back onto hedges and are a comfortable size so there is no feeling of crowding. Of these, 280 are level and marked with 10/16A electric hook-ups, 100 also having hardstanding. The terraced bar with views over the Fleet was converted from the barn and features original beams and brickwork. Part of the World Heritage Jurassic Coast, the Fleet is a lagoon renowned for its wildlife and popular with bird watchers. The busy resort of Weymouth with its safe bathing beaches and many watersports facilities is only 3 miles away (bicycle hire and boat launching possible). In peak season a regular bus service runs to Weymouth and the nearby Abbotsbury Swannery and Gardens.

Facilities	Directions
Two fully equipped toilet blocks include family rooms. The newest one is very smart in a Norwegian log cabin. En-suite unit for disabled visitors. Laundry room. Motorcaravan service point. Reception plus shop with basic groceries, bread, papers and gas. Bar serving food with terrace (Easter - Sept). Games room. Fenced play area (remember, elsewhere this is a working farm). Games field. Nature watch farm. Off site: Riding and golf 2 miles. Access to the Fleet and coastal path.	Park is signed at traffic lights on B3157 Weymouth - Bridport road, about 3 miles west of Weymouth beside Territorial Army base. Fleet Lane has been widened with plenty of passing places and speed bumps (20 mph). O.S.GR: SY639798. GPS: 50.61927, -2.50040

Open: 15 March - 31 October.

Charges guide

Per unit incl. 2 persons	£ 8.00 - £ 18.00
incl. electricity	£ 12.00 - £ 22.50
extra person	£ 1.00 - £ 4.50
child (5-12 yrs)	£ 0.25 - £ 0.50

Weymouth
Bagwell Farm Touring Park
Chickerell, Weymouth DT3 4EA (Dorset) T: **01305 782575**. E: **ar@bagwellfarm.co.uk**
alanrogers.com/UK1820

A pleasant, large, family park, Bagwell Farm is situated between Weymouth and Abbotsbury, close to Chesil Beach. In a valley, yet with an open aspect, there are 280 numbered touring pitches, some taken up by seasonal units. There are 260 electricity connections (10A) and 9 serviced pitches. Some of the terraced pitches have beautiful views of Chesil Bank and the sea. In addition there is a traditional camping field with a campers' shelter and a barbecue, plus a rally field with electricity hook-ups. An attractive bar, where meals are served, has been converted from farm buildings. A patio overlooks a good pets corner (also open to the public). A new toilet block is now open. The park is only four miles from Weymouth, so the excellent 'Blue Flag' beaches and the other holiday attractions of the resort are easily accessible. This is a useful site that is open all year round.

Facilities	Directions
Traditional style toilet blocks are supplemented by a new heated block. Unisex bathrooms on payment. Laundry. Motorcaravan service point. Shop with off-licence opposite reception (all year). Bar and grill with takeaway (open mid/high seasons, check when booking). Games room. Play area. Pets corner. Caravan storage. Off site: Riding 1 mile. Golf, fishing and bicycle hire 5 miles. Weymouth beach 5 miles with bus service. Abbotsbury with Swannery and Tropical Gardens 4 miles. Two pubs are within walking distance, one in the direction of the marvellous walk from the site to the sea.	Follow the B3157 from Weymouth towards Bridport. Park is 2 miles after passing Chickerell village. The entrance is on the brow of a hill – care is needed. O.S GR: SY627816. GPS: 50.63088, -2.51999

Open: All year.

Charges guide

Per unit incl. 2 persons and electricity	£ 12.50 - £ 22.00
incl. services	£ 14.50 - £ 25.00
extra person	£ 4.00 - £ 5.00
child (5-16 yrs)	£ 1.00 - £ 1.50
dog	£ 1.00

Weymouth
Sea Barn & West Fleet Holiday Farms
Fleet Road, Fleet, Weymouth DT3 4ED (Dorset) T: **01305 782218**. E: **enquiries@seabarnfarm.couk**
alanrogers.com/UK1830

Sea Barn and West Fleet are located just half a mile apart in delightful countryside overlooking the Fleet Lagoon, Chesil Bank and Lyme Bay – all part of the Jurassic coast. Only tents, trailer tents and motorcaravans with tents and awnings are accepted. The parks share some facilities. An outdoor pool and clubhouse are at West Fleet, along with the new smart toilet block. Both have their own reception with well stocked shops. Sea Barn is quieter and popular over a longer period with spectacular views, whereas West Fleet attracts families. Both are popular with birdwatchers, walkers and fishermen. West Fleet has 250 pitches, 112 with electricity, Sea Barn the same number of pitches but only 45 electric hook ups. These are situated in grassy meadows some sloping, some protected by trees and hedging, many with wonderful views.

Facilities
Traditional simple toilet blocks, brightly painted and clean. New block at both sites with en-suite room for disabled visitors and two bathrooms (free). Laundry facilities at both sites. Heated pool at West Fleet (May - Sept). Bigger shop offering wider range at West Fleet which also has the Club House (evenings), in reality an open ended barn and outdoor area which works well (home produced steaks the speciality). Breakfast served. Family entertainment. Adventure play area at Fleet and smaller area at Sea Barn. Games field. Torches useful. Off site: Access to South West Coastal path. Fishing Chesil Bank. Riding 1 mile. Golf, bicycle hire, boat launching and beach all at Weymouth 5 miles. Abbotsbury 7 miles.

Open: March - October.

Directions
From Wemouth take the B3157 coast road for Abbotsbury. Pass Chickerell and turn left at mini-roundabout to Fleet. Pass church on right and continue to top of hill. Sea Barn is to the left, West Fleet to the right. O.S.GR: SY626805.
GPS: 50.62539, -2.53865

Charges guide
Per unit incl. 2 persons	
and electricity	£ 14.00 - £ 23.00
extra person	£ 4.00 - £ 5.00
child (2-15 yrs)	£ 1.00 - £ 3.00
dog (max 2)	£ 1.00 - £ 2.00

Weymouth
Littlesea Holiday Park
Littlesea Holiday Park, Lynch Lane, Weymouth DT4 9DT (Dorset) T: **0871 231 0879**
alanrogers.com/UK1860

With an impressive situation, Littlesea is one of Haven's flagship parks with an amazing range of facilities and overlooking the lagoon and Chesil beach. Do not be put off negotiating the one-way system or the built up area on your approach; much work has gone into upgrading this large park. A total of 800 pitches allows for a good number of privately owned mobile homes with more still for sale and to rent, plus a splendid touring area on the cliff top for 120 units. As with other Haven Parks, there are indoor and outdoor pools, a wide range of sporting activities including a multisport court, and much entertainment for all the family. The wardens for the touring area do a sterling job looking after customers and keeping the purpose-built toilet block immaculate. Among the 120 touring pitches there are 16 with reinforced bases and water taps and these have sea views. Most pitches have 16A electricity. Some small simple tent pitches are perched right on the cliff top. The lagoon is a nature reserve so the nearest beach is at Sandsfoot (2.5 miles). The coastal path passes through the park and from the touring area you look across to the rest of the site with Portland in the distance.

Facilities
The modern toilet block includes facilities for disabled visitors and a family room (£10 deposit for keys). Washing machine and dryer. Launderette. Well stocked shop. Restaurant, café, fish and chip shop, pizza place. Bars. Amusement machines. Indoor (all season) and outdoor pools (28/5-6/9), heated with lifeguards. Adventure play area. Multisports court. Fencing. Archery. Football coaching. Entertainment for all the family. WiFi throughout. Photographer. Off site: Weymouth 6 miles with harbour and beach, (half hourly bus). Beach at Sandsfoot 2.5 miles. Bicycle hire 1 mile. Riding 1.5 miles. Golf 2 miles. Fishing and boat launching 3 miles. Chesil beach 2.5 miles.

Open: 20 March - 3 November.

Directions
From the A35 at Dorchester take the A354 towards Weymouth. On approaching Weymouth turn right at the first roundabout, then the third exit at next roundabout towards the B3157. Take third exit at next roundabout towards Chickerell and Portland. Cross traffic lights and at end of Benvielle Road turn right, then left into Lynch Lane. Park entrance is at the far end of the road. O.S.GR: SY652783.
GPS: 50.606746, -2.489707

Charges guide
Per unit incl. up to 4 persons	
and electricity	£ 50.00 - £ 60.00

See advertisement on page 349

Rich in maritime heri
and historical attract
the Southern region
comprises tranquil Er
countryside boasting
picture-postcard villages,
ancient cities and towns, forr
castles and grand stately homes
coupled with a beautiful coastli
and lively seaside resorts.

THIS REGION INCLUDES: EAST DORSET, HAMPSHIRE,
ISLE OF WIGHT, OXFORDSHIRE, BERKSHIRE AND
BUCKINGHAMSHIRE

The south coast is a popular holiday
destination for those looking for a beach
holiday. Seaside resorts include Swanage,
and Bournemouth, with its seven miles of
golden sand. Also along this coastal stretch
is Durdle Door, a natural arch that has been
cut by the sea, and Europe's largest natural
harbour at Poole Bay. Nearby, the Isle of
Purbeck is not actually an island, but
a promontory of low hills and heathland
that juts out below Poole Harbour. Across
the water is the Isle of Wight, easily
reached via a short ferry trip across the
Solent. Rural Southern England comprises
green rolling hills and scenic wooded
valleys, with numerous walking and bridle
paths passing through picturesque villages
with quintessential English pubs. The New
Forest, well known for its wild roaming
ponies, is a distinctive, peaceful retreat.
The River Thames weaves its way through
the Thames basin and Chilterns area,
passing charming riverside villages, castles,
stately homes and beautiful countryside,
including that around Oxford. This city of
dreaming spires has lovely scenic walks, old
university buildings to explore, plus a huge
selection of restaurants, pubs and shops.
Along the river you can go punting, hire
a rowing boat, or take one of the many
river-boat trips available.

Places of interest

East Dorset: Monkey World in Wareham;
village of Cerne Abbas, with Cerne Giant

Hampshire: historic Winchester; Portsmo
home of the Mary Rose; Southampton
maritime museum.

Isle of Wight: Cowes; Sandown with
Dinosaur Isle; Shipwreck Centre in Ryde;
Smuggling Museum in Ventnor; Carisbro
Castle in Newport.

Oxfordshire: Blenheim Palace; Didcot
Railway Centre; historic market town of
Chipping Norton.

Berkshire: Windsor, with Legoland, Wind
Castle; Reading.

Buckinghamshire: Bletchley Park near
Milton Keynes; county town of Aylesbury
Beaconsfield, once home to Enid Blyton,
now housing the world's first model villa

Did you know?

The Cerne Giant is thought to have
represented a pagan god dating back to
pre 13th century.

Gosport is home to one of the worlds
largest sundials covering 40 metres.

T.E Lawrence 'Lawrence of Arabia' was
a fellow of All Souls College in Oxford ar
lived in Dorset.

Remains of over 20 species of dinosaur h
been recovered on the Isle of Wight.

The annual Olney Pancake Race in Bucks
been running since around 1445.

Author Charles Dickens was born in
Portsmouth, the house where he was bo
is now a museum.

Windsurfing was invented on Hayling Isl
by Peter Chilvers in 1958.

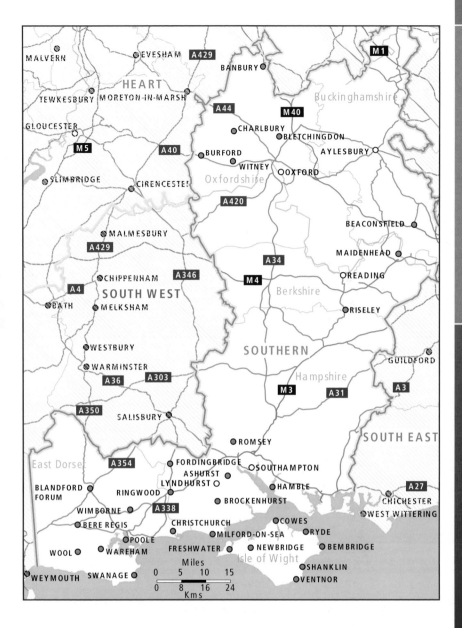

Maps and campsite listings

For this 2010 guide we have changed the way in which we list our parks and also the way in which we help you locate the parks within each region.

We now include a map immediately after our Introduction to that region. These maps show the towns near which one (or more) of our featured parks is located. Within each regional section of the guide, we list these towns and the park(s) in that vicinity in alphabetical order.

You will certainly need more detailed maps for navigation, for example the Ordnance Survey road atlas. We provide O.S. references and G.P.S. coordinates for each park to assist you. Our three indexes will also help you to find a park by its reference number and name, by region and park name, or by the town where the park is situated.

Ashurst

Forest Holidays Ashurst

Forest Holidays, Lyndhurst Road, Ashurst SO4O 7AR (Hampshire) T: **02380 292097**
E: **info@forestholidays.co.uk alanrogers.com/UK2300**

Forest Holidays is a partnership between the Forestry Commission and the Camping & Caravanning Club. An attractive site, Ashurst is on the fringe of the New Forest, set in a mixture of oak woodland and grass heathland which is open to the grazing animals of the Forest. Smaller than the Hollands Wood site (23 acres), it provides 280 pitches, 180 of which have been gravelled to provide semi-hardstanding; otherwise you pitch where you like, applying the 20 ft. rule on ground that can be uneven. There are no electricity connections. Some noise must be expected from the adjacent railway line – the station is just five minutes' walk away.

Facilities

The single well kept central toilet block (may be under pressure in main season) provides everything necessary, including hairdryers and a well equipped unit for visitors with disabilities. Good laundry room. Motorcaravan service point. Freezer pack service and charging of batteries (fee). Camping accessories and charcoal available. Torches useful. Dogs are not accepted. Off site: Nearby pub by footpath across an adjacent field. Shops and local buses within a five minute walk. Guided forest walks are organised during the main season. Golf 4 miles.

Open: 26 March - 27 September.

Directions

From Southampton, follow A35 west through village of Ashurst, continue over railway bridge and site is 200 yards on left. O.S.GR: SU344099.
GPS: 50.88810, -1.52846

Charges guide

Per unit incl. 2 persons	£ 10.00 - £ 26.50
extra person	£ 4.25 - £ 8.50
child	£ 2.25 - £ 4.25

Discounts for families, backpackers, disabled guests and senior citizens.

Banbury

Barnstones Caravan & Camping Park

Great Bourton, Banbury OX17 1QU (Oxfordshire) T: **01295 750289**
alanrogers.com/UK2600

Three miles from Banbury and open all year round, this small, neat park provides an excellent point from which to explore the Cotswolds, Oxford and Stratford-upon-Avon. There are 49 level pitches of which 44 have gravel hardstanding with a grass area for awnings (only breathable groundsheets are allowed) and 10A electricity; 20 of these are fully serviced. Shrubs, flowers and an oval tarmac road convey an attractive, tidy impression throughout. The park provides a pleasant environment for couples and young families, but it is near the main road, so some traffic noise is to be expected. New arrivals should call at the warden's caravan at the park entrance.

Facilities

The good toilet block is small, but very clean, heated and well maintained. It is quite adequate for the number of people it serves. Good tiled, adjustable showers. Laundry rooms. Freezer. Gas supplies. Good enclosed play area. Boules. American motorhomes accepted but call first. Off site: Pub 150 yds. Nearest shop 1 mile. Supermarket, fishing, bicycle hire, golf and riding, all within 3 miles.

Open: All year.

Directions

From M40 take exit 11 for Banbury. Follow signs for Banbury and Southom. On the two small roundabouts follow signs for Southom and Great Bourton. At third roundabout turn right on A423, Southom is 2.5 miles. Turn right signed Great Bourton and Crofredy and site is almost immediately on the right. O.S.GR: SP454454.
GPS: 52.10535, -1.3369

Charges guide

Per unit incl. 2 persons, electricity	£ 11.00 - £ 14.00
extra person (over 5 yrs)	£ 1.50

OAPs less 50p per night. No credit cards.

Banbury

Bo Peep Caravan Park

Aynho Road, Adderbury, Banbury OX17 3NP (Oxfordshire) T: 01295 810605. E: warden@bo-peep.co.uk
alanrogers.com/UK2610

Set amongst 85 acres of farmland and woodland, there is an air of spacious informality about this delightful, friendly park which blends perfectly with the surrounding views. Warm Cotswold stone buildings, dovecotes and extensive planting of trees, shrubs and hedges enhance the natural environment of the park. There are 104 numbered pitches all with 16A electricity for caravans and motorhomes in several areas, each with a different character. A separate 4 acre field for tents provides a further 40 pitches, including 4 electricity points. One area near the central buildings provides eight gravel hardstandings. Gravel roads connect the various touring areas which are screened by hedges and trees. A network of walks along well-kept grass trails have been developed around the park, including a pleasant river walk. Bench seats and waste bags and bins for dogs are provided. A 15-acre field is available for recreational use. Children are welcome but there is no play area or baby changing facilities.

Facilities

The original toilet block has been supplemented by a larger, purpose-built unit, all very clean and heated. Large showers and hairdryers. Laundry rooms. Motorcaravan service point. Low level lighting. Excellent small shop with off-licence, gas and basic supplies. Information centre with armchairs and internet access. Fishing. Caravan storage. Caravan cleaning area. Off site: Golf 1 mile. Riding 10 miles. Banbury 3 miles. Blenheim Palace 15 miles. Silverstone 16 miles. Day trips to Stratford-upon-Avon and Warwick.

Open: 14 March - 26 October.

Directions

Adderbury village is on the A4260 Banbury - Oxford road. From the north on the M40 use exit 11, the A422 (Banbury) then the A4260. At traffic lights in Adderbury turn on B4100 (Aynho). Park is signed 0.5 miles on the right (0.5 mile drive). From the south on the M40 use exit 10 onto the A43, then the B4100 (Aynho and Adderbury). O.S.GR: SP480348. GPS: 52.01585, -1.299433

Charges guide

Per unit incl. 2 persons, electricity	£ 15.00 - £ 28.00
tent incl. 1 or 2 persons	£ 13.00 - £ 15.00
extra person	£ 2.50 - £ 3.00
dog	£ 1.00

No credit cards.

Beaconsfield

Highclere Farm Country Touring Park

Newbarn Lane, Seer Green, Beaconsfield HP9 2QZ (Buckinghamshire) T: 01494 874505
E: highclerepark@aol.com alanrogers.com/UK2750

Only 25 miles from London and 12 miles from Windsor, this is a peaceful park that backs onto fields and woodland. Originally developed around a working farm, the owners continue to keep chickens. There are 95 level pitches all with 10A electricity. Of these 60 with gravel hardstanding are reserved for caravans and motorcaravans, the remainder being mainly used for tents. The atmosphere is friendly but informal, with reception doubling as a small shop supplying freshly laid eggs. At the top of the park is an open play area and a footpath leading to walks in the surrounding fields.

Facilities

The toilet and shower block is fully equipped and can be heated. Large showers (20p). Unit with toilet and washbasin for disabled people. Baby changing. Two new units (in former stables) provide extra luxury facilities including showers at 50p. Launderette. Fridge and freezer. Basic shop in reception. Play area. Off site: Inn serving food 0.25 miles. Golf 0.5 miles. Riding 2 miles. Bicycle hire 3 miles. Fishing 8 miles. Bekonscot Model Village and Milton's Cottage are close.

Open: All year excl. February.

Directions

From M40 exit 2 follow signs for Beaconsfield at first roundabout. Then take A355 towards Amersham and after 1 mile turn right signed Seer Green and Jordans following signs to park. From the north on M25 take exit 18 to Little Chalfont, B44442 to Chalfont St Giles, go through village and park is 1.25 miles on the right. O.S.GR: SU977927. GPS: 51.625617, -0.590867

Charges guide

Per unit incl. 2 persons and electricity	£ 17.50 - £ 21.50
extra person	£ 1.00
tent (one man)	£ 12.00
awning, dog or extra car	free

Bembridge

Whitecliff Bay Holiday Park

Hillway, Whitecliff Bay, Bembridge PO35 5PL (Isle of Wight) T: **01983 872671**
E: **holiday@whitecliff-bay.com alanrogers.com/UK2510**

Whitecliff Bay is a very large complex divided by a road, with a holiday home and chalet park on the right hand side, and a touring site on the left hand side. The large touring site is on a sloping hillside with commanding views over the surrounding countryside. The 659 pitches are spread over three fields, the top and second fields are terraced, but field three (the only one in which dogs are permitted in low season only) is quite level. Half of the pitches have electric hook-ups (16A), and there are around 44 gravel hardstandings, 12 in the top field, the remainder in lowest field. There are 13 individual hedged multi-serviced pitches available, so book early. On the opposite side of the lane, in the holiday home park, you will find all the main entertainment and leisure facilities. These include The Culver Club with a bar and evening entertainment, several snack bars and takeaways, supervised swimming pools (indoor and outdoor), a sauna and sunbed, small gym and soft 'playzone' (under 8s). Close to the outdoor pool a very steep path leads down to a sandy beach, where there is a small café. It is possible to launch a boat from this beach (4-wheel drive vehicle essential, advance booking necessary).

Facilities

Three sanitary units, one on the lower part of the site. The other two are fairly close together, not far from reception and both of these have been refitted to a good standard. Showers (on payment) and a suite (with shower) for disabled people. A second suite with a hip bath/shower is at the lower block with a similar facility to serve as a family room. Laundry with ironing facility. Motorcaravan service point. Small shop with reception. Playground. At the holiday home park: Launderette, hairdresser and second larger shop. The Culver Club. Snack bars. Swimming pool (18 x 18 m, Whitsun - end Aug). Indoor fun pool with jacuzzi, a sauna and sun bed, small gym, a soft play zone (under 8 yrs). Most facilities open March - Oct. Dogs only accepted in lower field outside 20/7-31/8. Fully equipped tents to rent. Off site: Normal bus service from entrance on weekdays, site runs a courtesy minibus at weekends to Bembridge and Sandown. Golf 5 miles. Bicycle hire 4 miles. Riding 2 miles.

Open: 30 March - 1 November.

Directions

Bembridge is at the eastern end of the island. From the A3055 between Ryde and Sandown, turn east at Brading on B3395 for about 2 miles passing the Airfield and Propeller Club, fork right (site signed). Follow signs to site, first entry on right is static area, touring entrance is on left immediately after.
O.S.GR: SZ635865. GPS: 50.67498, -1.09606

Charges guide

Per unit incl. 2 persons	£ 9.85 - £ 17.35
incl. electricity	£ 13.15 - £ 21.25
incl. full services	£ 16.15 - £ 25.50
extra person	£ 4.30 - £ 6.70
child (5-13 yrs)	£ 2.85 - £ 4.40

Bere Regis

Rowlands Wait Touring Park

Rye Hill, Bere Regis BH20 7LP (Dorset) T: 01929 472727. E: enquiries@rowlandswait.co.uk

alanrogers.com/UK2050

Rowlands Wait is in a designated Area of Outstanding Natural Beauty (AONB) and part of the park is officially of Special Scientific Interest (SSSI). The top of the park, edged by mature woods (full of bluebells in spring) is a haven for tents (and squirrels) with marvellous views and provides 30 places in three descending fields. The rest of the park is a little more formal – and nearer to the central toilet block. Most pitches back on to hedging or trees and they are generally level. There are 71 pitches in total with 23 seasonal pitches. Many walks are possible from the park with information leaflets available from reception. It is also possible to walk into the village of Bere Regis. The owners Ivor and Stevie Cargill are keen to welcome nature lovers who enjoy bird watching, walking, and cycling. Sightings of various owls and two pairs of buzzards have been reported on the park. The park is a member of the Countryside Discovery group and is open in winter by arrangement. Rallies are welcome.

Facilities

The refurbished toilet block is fully equipped. New family room and facilities for disabled visitors. Laundry room. Recycling bins. Shop (reduced hours in low season) providing basic essentials and a freezer for ice packs. Play area. Games room. Bicycle hire arranged. Torch useful. Off site: Village (10 minute walk) with shops, two pubs, etc. plus a bus service for Dorchester and Poole. Golf 3 miles. Fishing 5 miles. Riding 9 miles.

Open: All year (16 March - 31 October by arrangement).

Directions

Park is about 0.5 miles south of Bere Regis on the road to Wool. O.S.GR: SY842933. GPS: 50.743683, -2.22405

Charges guide

Per unit incl. 2 persons	£ 11.00 - £ 14.00
incl. electricity	£ 13.00 - £ 16.00
extra person	£ 3.00 - £ 4.00
child (under 16 yrs)	£ 1.50 - £ 2.50
dog	£ 1.00 - £ 2.00

Blandford Forum

The Inside Park Touring Caravan & Camping Park

Blandford Forum DT11 9AD (Dorset) T: 01258 453719. E: mail@theinsidepark.co.uk

alanrogers.com/UK2070

The Inside Park is set in the grounds of an 18th-century country house that burned down in 1941. Family owned and carefully managed alongside an arable farm, this is a must for those interested in local history or arboriculture and it is a haven for wildlife and birds. The nine acre camping field, a little distant, lies in a sheltered, gently sloping dry valley containing superb tree specimens – notably cedars, with walnuts in one part – and a dog graveyard dating back to the early 1700s under a large Cedar of Lebanon. In total there are 125 spacious pitches, 90 with electricity (10A) and some in wooded glades. The six acres adjoining are the old pleasure gardens of the house. The reception/toilet block and games room block are respectively the coach house and stables of the old house. No vehicle access to the park is allowed after 22.30 (there is a separate late arrivals area and car park). Extensive, marked walks are provided through the farmland and a guide is available in the shop.

Facilities

The toilet block provides some washbasins in cubicles, comfortably sized showers and facilities for disabled visitors or mothers and babies. Laundry room. Shop with basics, gas and camping provisions. Spacious games room. Safe based adventure play area. Day kennelling facilities for dogs. Mountain bike course. Winter caravan storage. Off site: Blandford leisure and swimming centre (temporary membership possible) 2 miles. Fishing and riding 2 miles. Golf 3 miles. Beach 25 miles.

Open: Easter - 31 October.

Directions

Park is about 2 miles southwest of Blandford and is signed from roundabout junction of A354 and A350 roads. O.S.GR: ST864045. GPS: 50.841333, -2.19515

Charges 2010

Per unit incl. 2 persons and electricity	£ 17.20 - £ 21.00

Bletchingdon

Greenhill Farm Caravan & Camping Park

Bletchingdon OX5 3BQ (Oxfordshire) T: **01869 351600**. E: **info@greenhill-leisure-park.co.uk**

alanrogers.com/UK2590

On a working farm in a rural setting, this is a newly-established site. The approach is a half mile gravel track down into the valley, past recently planted woodlands, fields and the farm. The reception office with a shop and tourist information is located in the farmhouse. A gravel path continues round the park giving access to 50 pitches, all with 16A electricity and 25 with hardstanding. Growing trees and hedges partition the site and screen the water stands. An adjacent field is available for rallies and there is a second smaller field for tents. Continuing developments include two fishing lakes (carp, roach, bream and tench). One of the farm barns is now a games room.

Facilities

Two new toilet blocks, one in a converted barn with ramp access for facilities for disabled visitors and families. Separate laundry room. Shop (April - Sept). Play area with assault course and basketball hoop. Fishing lakes. Games room which can also be used for meetings. Pets are not accepted 1/10-1/3. Off site: Golf 2 miles. Boat launching and canal walks 1 mile.

Open: All year.

Directions

From M40 exit 9 take A34 to Newbury and Oxford. After 5 miles turn left on B4027 signed Bletchingdon. After 2.5 miles park is on left just past the village. O.S.GR: SP488177. GPS: 51.85754, -1.29142

Charges guide

Per unit incl. 2 persons	£ 12.00 - £ 15.00
extra person (over 4 yrs)	£ 3.00
electricity	£ 3.00

No credit cards.

Brockenhurst

Forest Holidays Hollands Wood

Forest Holidays, Lyndhurst Road, Brockenhurst SO43 7QH (Hampshire) T: **01590 622967**

E: **info@forestholidays.co.uk alanrogers.com/UK2310**

Forest Holidays is a partnership between the Forestry Commission and the Camping & Caravanning Club. This is a large, spacious 168-acre secluded site in a natural woodland setting (mainly oak). It is set in the heart of the New Forest, with an abundance of wildlife. The site is arranged informally with 600 level unmarked pitches but it is stipulated that there must be at least 20 feet between each unit. There are no electrical connections and traffic noise is possible from the A337 which runs alongside one boundary. Brockenhurst village is only half a mile where there are shops, trains and buses.

Facilities

Three refurbished toilet blocks provide all necessary requirements, including for disabled visitors and babies. Good laundry room. All these may be under pressure at peak times. Motorcaravan services. Freezer packs and charging of batteries (fee). Maps and guides. Barbecues allowed (off ground). Milk stocked. Barrier closed 22.30-07.00. Night security. Torches essential. Off site: Bicycle hire and riding 2 miles. Golf 3 miles.

Open: 26 March - 27 September.

Directions

Site entrance is on east side of A337 Lyndhurst - Lymington road, 0.5 miles north of Brockenhurst. O.S.GR: SU303034. GPS: 50.83655, -1.56952

Charges guide

Per unit incl. 2 persons	£ 10.00 - £ 26.50
extra person	£ 4.25 - £ 8.50
child	£ 2.24 - £ 4.25

Various discounts available.

Burford

Wysdom Touring Park

The Bungalow, Burford School, Burford OX18 4JG (Oxfordshire) T: **01993 823207**

alanrogers.com/UK2620

You'll have to go a long way before you find anything else remotely like this site! The land is owned by Burford School and the enterprising caretaker and his wife, caravanners themselves, suggested that they create this wonderful place to raise money for the school (£41,000 raised in 2008/9). Beautifully maintained, it really is like stepping into their own private garden. This 'adults only' park is screened from the main school grounds by trees and provides 25 pitches (six seasonal), separated by hedges, all with electricity (16A) and some have their own tap. Tents are accepted for short stays by arrangement.

Facilities

The older sanitary building is clean and well maintained with two unisex showers (30p token) – there may be a queue at peak times. (Max. 2 dogs per pitch). Tennis courts. Off site: Burford is yards away with its famous hill full of antique shops, old coaching inns and all those 'interesting' shops it is so much fun rooting about in. Burford Golf Club is next door.

Open: All year (excl. 14 December - 5 January).

Directions

From roundabout on A40 at Burford, take A361 towards Lechdale on Thames. Park is a few yards on right signed Burford School. Once in drive watch for narrow entrance to site on right in about 100 yards. O.S.GR: SP250115. GPS: 51.801983, -1.639367

Charges guide

Per unit incl. 2 persons, electricity	£ 10.00 - £ 12.00
extra person	£ 2.00

No credit cards.

Charlbury
Cotswold View Caravan & Camping Park
Enstone Road, Charlbury OX7 3JH (Oxfordshire) T: **01608 810314**. E: bookings@cotswoldview.co.uk
alanrogers.com/UK2580

On the edge of the Cotswolds and surrounded by fine views, this well-run family park offers a warm welcome. Originally a working farm, the touring park and self catering country cottages are situated amongst 54 acres of farmland. Wide gravel or tarmac roads ensure easy access to the 125 pitches (all with 10A electricity) in the ten-acre touring area. The park has been thoughtfully separated by hedges into different areas to enable those with children to be close to play areas, and quieter areas for those wanting to enjoy the peaceful surroundings.

Facilities	Directions
Two well maintained heated toilet blocks provide washbasins in cubicles, showers, two family shower rooms (free), bathrooms (50p) and hairdryers. Good units for disabled people. Baby changing area. Laundry facilities. Motorcaravan service point. Shop and off-licence. Bar. Play areas. Games room. Tennis. Outdoor chess and draughts. Skittle alley. American motorhomes accepted. Security barrier (£5 deposit). Off site: Fishing 1 mile. Golf 7 miles. Riding 10 miles. Boat launching 1 mile.	From A44 Oxford - Chipping Norton road, take B4022 to Charlbury, just south of Enstone. Park is 2 miles on left. O.S.GR: SP365210. GPS: 51.886167, -1.4708

Open: 1 April (or Easter if earlier) - 31 October.

Charges guide	
Per unit incl. 2 persons and electricity	£ 15.00 - £ 19.50
extra person	£ 2.25
child (6-16 yrs)	£ 2.00
dog	free

Christchurch
Grove Farm Meadow Holiday Park
Meadowbank Holidays, Stour Way, Christchurch BH23 2PQ (Dorset) T: **01202 483597**
E: enquiries@meadowbank-holidays.co.uk alanrogers.com/UK2130

Grove Farm Meadow is a quiet, traditional park with caravan holiday homes and a small provision for touring units. The grass flood bank which separates the River Stour from this park provides an attractive pathway. The river bank has been kept natural and is well populated by a range of water birds. It is popular with bird watchers and there is fishing in the river. There are just under 200 caravan holiday homes (75 for hire), sited in regular rows. For touring units there are 41 level pitches, all clearly numbered with electricity (10A), backing on to fencing or hedging and accessed by tarmac roads.

Facilities	Directions
The well kept toilet block provides a bathroom for each sex (50p). Separate toilet and washbasin with ramped access for disabled visitors. Baby room. Spin dryer, iron and board and washing lines provided. Launderette near reception. Well stocked shop (limited hours in low season). Games room. Adventure play area. Fishing (permits from reception). Dogs or other pets are not accepted. Off site: Golf 0.5 miles. Large supermarket 1.5 miles. Beach, boat launching and sailing 2 miles. St Catherine's nature reserve.	From A388 Ringwood - Bournemouth road take B3073 for Christchurch. Turn right at the first roundabout and Stour Way is the third road on the right. O.S.GR: SZ136946. GPS: 50.750336, -1.807938

Open: 1 March - 31 October.

Charges guide	
Per unit incl. 2 persons	£ 8.50 - £ 27.00
large pitch	£ 11.50 - £ 23.00
extra person over 5 yrs	£ 1.00 - £ 2.00
extra car or boat	£ 1.00 - £ 2.00

Cowes
Waverley Park Holiday Centre
51 Old Road, East Cowes PO32 6AW (Isle of Wight) T: **01983 293452**. E: sue@waverley-park.co.uk
alanrogers.com/UK2530

This pleasant small family owned site is set in the grounds of an old country house which was once frequently visited by Dr Arnold, the subject of 'Tom Brown's Schooldays'. The owners have now terraced the grass area for touring units. This has created 31 large and level, well spaced, fully serviced hardstanding pitches all with outstanding views over the Solent. The remaining 14 caravan pitches share a sloping grass area with tents – these have no electricity. To one side there are 75 private and rental holiday homes. At the bottom of the park a gate leads onto the promenade and the pebble beach which is popular with sailors and windsurfers.

Facilities	Directions
At the top of the park, a toilet block provides the usual facilities, including some spacious cubicles with washbasins en-suite. Good suite for disabled people with baby changing. Laundry facilities. Heated outdoor pool. Club with restaurant and bar serving good value meals, plus family entertainment in season (Whitsun - early Sept). Small adventure style playground. Games room. Off site: East Cowes is within walking distance. Bus stop in East Lewes.	Immediately after leaving Southampton - Cowes car ferry, take first left, then right into Old Road, and park entrance is 300 yds on left. O.S.GR: SZ505958. GPS: 50.76088, -1.28366

Open: All year.

Charges 2010	
Per unit incl. 2 persons and electricity	£ 15.00 - £ 21.00

Packages incl. ferry travel and other offers available.

109

Cowes

Thorness Bay Holiday Park

Thorness Bay, Cowes PO31 8NJ (Isle of Wight) T: **01983 523109**. E: holiday.sales@park.resorts.com
alanrogers.com/UK2520

Spread over a large area of rural down and woodland that slopes down to the beach at Thorness Bay, this is a large site with more than 500 holiday homes. The touring area has around 90 pitches, most with electricity (16A) including 27 multi-serviced pitches on gravel hardstandings with electricity, water, drain and TV points. These and some grass pitches are on terraces served by tarmac roads. The remainder are on sloping open grassland either divided by ranch style rails or in an open tent area, and all have views of the surrounding countryside. The main activity centre is located in the holiday home area, a short walk from the touring site. There are activities and entertainment here for all the family.

Facilities	Directions
New toilet block providing showers, WCs and washbasins. Suite for disabled visitors. Baby changing. Laundry facilities. Shop. Indoor pool. Indoor playroom for small children. Adventure playground. Multisport court. Children's club. Off site: The beach is easily accessed from the main entertainment complex. All the attractions of the Island are within easy day-trip distances. Riding within 1 mile. Golf 4 miles.	From East Cowes ferry follow signs to Newport. Follow A3054 (Yarmouth). Continue for about 2.5 miles to crossroads, turning right (north) to Thorness Bay. After about 2 miles, on sharp right hand bend, turn left, site signed. O.S.GR: SZ452926. GPS: 50.731133, -1.360467

Open: Easter - 29 October.

Charges guide

Per unit incl. up to 6 persons	£ 6.00 - £ 35.00
tent pitch	£ 3.00 - £ 27.00

Fordingbridge

Hill Cottage Farm Camping & Caravan Park

Sandleheath Road, Alderholt, Fordingbridge SP6 3EG (Hampshire) T: **01425 650513**
E: hillcottagefarmcaravansite@supanet.com alanrogers.com/UK2360

This established, modern site is set in 47 acres of beautiful countryside on the Dorset and Hampshire border. The 35 pitches, all on hardstandings with electric hook-ups (16A), water taps and drainage are arranged around a circular gravel roadway. Secluded and sheltered, there are views across the surrounding countryside. A field, also with electric hook-ups, alongside the camping area is used for tents and rallies, and has space for ball games and a small playground. Also on site there are two lakes for coarse fishing, and there are many woodland walks in the area. Overall this site is more suitable for adults and younger children – it is not really designed for active teenagers.

Facilities	Directions
A large modern barn-style building provides excellent heated facilities. Laundry room. Facilities for disabled people and babies. Facilities for tent pitches. First floor games room with full size snooker table, two pool tables and darts board, plus a separate function room. Motorcaravan services. Shop. Playground. WiFi. Shepherd's hut for hire. Off site: Village centre with pub, church, Post Office and store is a 20 minute woodland walk.	From Fordingbridge take B3078 westwards for 2 miles to Alderholt. On entering the village, at left hand bend, turn right towards Sandleheath (site signed) and site entrance is about 300 yards on the left. O.S.GR: SU120130. GPS: 50.919017, -1.832783

Open: 1 March - 30 November.

Charges guide

Per unit incl. 2 persons	£ 12.00 - £ 22.00
extra person	£ 5.00
child (0-15 yrs)	£ 2.00 - £ 4.00

Freshwater

Heathfield Farm Camping

Heathfield Road, Freshwater PO40 9SH (Isle of Wight) T: **01983 407822**. E: web@heathfieldcamping.co.uk
alanrogers.com/UK2500

Heathfield is a pleasant contrast to many of the other sites on the Isle of Wight, in that it is a 'no frills' sort of place, very popular with tenters, cyclists and small camper vans. Despite its name, it is no longer a working farm. A large, open meadow provides 60 large, level pitches, 50 with electricity (10A). Two small fenced areas provide traffic free zones for backpackers and cyclists' tents. There is no shop as you are only eight minutes' walk from the centre of Freshwater. The site overlooks Colwell Bay and across the Solent towards Milford-on-Sea and Hurst Castle.

Facilities	Directions
The main toilet unit is housed in a modern, ingeniously customised, 'portacabin' type unit. Baby room. Showers have two pushbutton controls, one for pre-mixed hot water, the other for cold only. A second similar unit has facilities for disabled visitors. Laundry facilities. Motorcaravan service point. Gas supplies. Ice pack service. Play field. Bicycle hire arranged. Off site: Bus stop 200 m. Beach 0.5 miles. Fishing 0.5 miles. Golf 1.25 miles. Riding 3 miles.	From A3054 north of Totland and Colwell turn into Heathfield Road where site is signed. Site entrance is on right after a short distance. O.S.GR: SZ336879. GPS: 50.68940, -1.52704

Open: 1 May - 30 September.

Charges 2010

Per unit incl. 2 persons	£ 10.50 - £ 20.00
extra person	£ 2.00 - £ 7.00
Min. pitch fee July/Aug. £17.	

Fordingbridge

Sandy Balls Holiday Centre

Godshill, Fordingbridge SP6 2JZ (Hampshire) T: 0845 2702248. E: post@sandy-balls.co.uk
alanrogers.com/UK2290

Sandy Balls sits high above the sweep of the Avon river near Fordingbridge, amidst woodland which is protected as a nature reserve. It well deserves the entry it has maintained in these guides for over 30 years and continues to improve and develop. Very well run and open all year, the 120 acre park has many private holiday homes as well as 26 caravan holiday homes and 117 lodges for rent. The touring areas have 233 marked and hedged serviced pitches, for caravans and tents on part-hardstanding and part-grass, with 16A electricity and TV connections. In August there is an additional unmarked tent area. In winter only 50 pitches are available. A woodland leisure trail allows wild animals and birds to be observed in their natural surroundings and the attractions of the New Forest are close at hand. The heart of this holiday centre is the architecturally designed multi-million pound 'village' with its traffic-free piazza. Here you will find the bistro, pub, Guest Services bureau, gift shop, cycle shop, small supermarket and leisure club, all designed to blend in with the forest surroundings and provide space to relax and meet friends. A member of the Best of British Group.

Facilities

Three refurbished toilet blocks have under-floor heating and washbasins in cubicles. One Portacabin-style unit remains as an overflow in the tent field. Toilets for disabled visitors and baby facilities. Excellent central launderette. Motorcaravan service point. Chemical disposal. Entertainment (high season only). Outdoor pool (25/5-30/8). Indoor pool (66 x 30 ft). Well equipped gym, jacuzzi, steam room, sauna and solarium. Tempus therapy centre. Games room. Adventure playground and play areas. Soft play area. Clay modelling tuition and story telling. Teepees and tents for rent. River fishing (permit). Riding stables. Bicycle hire. Archery. Dogs only allowed on certain fields. Off site: Golf 6 miles. Beach 20 miles.

Open: All year.

Directions

Park is well signed 1.5 miles east of Fordingbridge on the B3078 O.S.GR: SU168147.
GPS: 50.930267, -1.7602

Charges guide

Per unit incl. 2 persons and electricity	£ 10.00 - £ 37.00
extra person	free - £ 3.50
child (12-17 yrs)	free - £ 2.00
child (3-11 yrs)	free - £ 1.50
dog	free - £ 3.00

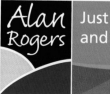

Hamble
Riverside Holidays

Satchell Lane, Hamble, Southampton SO31 4HR (Hampshire) T: **023 8045 3220**
E: **enquiries@riversideholidays.co.uk** **alanrogers.com/UK2315**

What makes Riverside so special is its location; close to the River Hamble, Mecca for the international yachtsman. The site is family-owned and covers five acres surrounded by trees and hedges; it has 125 pitches of which 77 are level for touring caravans and tents with 53 electricity hook-ups (16A). The remaining pitches are used for lodges and residential and static caravans on slightly rising ground, but so well spaced and with plenty of grass they are not too obtrusive. A warden-run log cabin reception, with tourist information, including local bus and rail times, is at the entrance. Hamble village, one mile away, with its cobbled streets, pubs and restaurants, is famed the world over for its association with yachting. This is an ideal base for the Southampton Boat Show, Cowes Week and its very own Hamble Week Regatta. On the marina adjacent to the site, a mere two minutes walk, is Oyster Quay with a bar and restaurant overlooking hundreds of yachts worth millions.

Facilities

The old Portacabin-style unit is clean but not quite up to standard, with a baby changing area but no unit for disabled visitors. However, an additional amenities block has recently been installed. Small laundry room alongside. All these facilities could be under pressure in high season. Bicycle hire. Caravan storage. Off site: Buses and trains 1 mile. Fishing, sea fishing, sailing, supermarket, 1 mile in village. Riding 3 miles. Golf 4 miles. You can catch a small ferry across to Warsash on the other bank or take a boat up to the Upper Hamble Country Park. The New Forest, Winchester and Portsmouth are nearby.

Open: 1 March - 31 October.

Directions

From M27 exit 8 follow signs for Hamble. Take the B3397 with Tesco on the left, continue 1.9 miles through traffic lights until Hound roundabout. After 50 yds turn left into Satchell Lane (signed Mercury Marina) and site is on left in 1 mile.
Q,S. GR: SU484082. GPS: 50.868835, -1.313586

Charges guide

Per unit incl. 2 persons and electricity	£ 15.00 - £ 32.00
extra person	£ 3.50
child (4-16 yrs)	£ 2.50

Camping Cheques accepted.

Maidenhead
Hurley Riverside Park

Hurley, Maidenhead SL6 5NE (Berkshire) T: **01628 824493**. E: **info@hurleyriversidepark.co.uk**
alanrogers.com/UK2700

On the banks of the Thames, not far from Henley-on-Thames, you will find the picturesque village of Hurley where some buildings date back to 1086. Just outside the village is Hurley Riverside Park providing facilities for holiday home, touring units and moorings for boats. The touring area is flat and separated into smaller fields. With the pitches arranged around the outside of each field and the centre left free, the park has a spacious feel. There are 138 touring pitches with 10A electricity including 12 fully serviced on long hardstandings. A camping field provides a further 62 pitches including six electric hook-ups. A very popular park, there is also a large rally field. You can enjoy walks along the banks of the Thames or visit the various pubs and restaurants in the village for a good meal and a pint. Nearby Windsor has its famous castle or for younger members of the family, Windsor is the home of Legoland. At Henley you can watch the regatta. Alternatively, you can just relax in the peaceful settings of the site.

Facilities

Three wooden toilet blocks (raised on legs) include a very good new unisex block with private bathrooms (shower, washbasin, toilet). The other blocks have been renovated and are well equipped. Separate shower and toilet facilities for disabled visitors. Baby area. Laundry. Motorcaravan service point. Shop at reception. Fishing. WiFi. Temporary moorings. Off site: Golf 5 miles. Riding 10 miles. Legoland at Windsor, Thorpe Park.

Open: 1 March - 31 October.

Directions

From M4 exit 8/9 take A404M towards Wycombe. After 3 miles take A4130 (Henley). Go down steep hill (Hurley village signed on right) - ignore this turning and take next right (site signed from here).
O.S.GR: SU825838. GPS: 51.5466, -0.8248

Charges guide

Per unit incl. 2 persons	£ 10.00 - £ 20.00
full services	£ 13.00 - £ 21.00
extra person	£ 2.00
child (5-17 yrs)	£ 1.50
dog	£ 2.00

Newbridge
The Orchards Holiday Caravan & Camping Park
Newbridge, Yarmouth PO41 0TS (Isle of Wight) T: **01983 531331**. E: info@orchards-holiday-park.co.uk
alanrogers.com/UK2450

In a village situation in the quieter western part of the island, The Orchards Holiday Park, a park for all seasons, has panoramic views of rolling countryside and the Solent. The park's neat 11-acre touring area has 175 marked pitches for tents, caravans and motorhomes, broken up by apple trees, mature hedges and fences. All pitches have electricity, 62 have hardstandings and 22 are 'all service' pitches, also with hardstanding. A meeting room is suitable for small rallies. A separate area contains 64 caravan holiday homes. The Orchards is a good base from which to explore the island and there are two beaches within five miles. The scenic harbour of Yarmouth is five minutes away, as are the attractions of Fort Victoria and Chessil Pottery, with bird watching at Newtown Creek. Osbourne House is 20 minutes away. There are walking and cycling routes from the park with leaflets available from reception. The park is part of the Caravan Club's affiliated scheme. A member of the Best of British group.

Facilities
An excellent new Facilities Centre provides 24 shower and washbasin cubicles, a family bathroom, 2 family shower rooms, fully accessible facilities, spacious laundry and ironing area, walkers' drying room, baby changing room, campers' kitchen area and indoor washing up area all with underfloor heating. Shop. Gas supplies. Indoor heated pool (Feb - Dec). Outdoor heated pool (May - Sept). Licensed coffee shop. Takeaway (mid March - Sept). Play areas. TV and amusements rooms. Off site: Bus stop at entrance. Membership for village social club. Discount at Freshwater golf club, 4 miles.

Open: All year excl. 3 January - 15 February.

Directions
Park is in Newbridge village, signed north from B3401 (Yarmouth - Newport) road. O.S.GR: SZ411878. GPS: 50.687967, -1.419967

Charges guide
Per unit incl. 2 persons
and electricity   £ 15.00 - £ 25.00
No pitch fee for hikers or cyclists.
Packages incl. ferry travel - ring park for best deal.
Camping Cheques accepted.

Milford-on-Sea

Lytton Lawn Touring Park

Lymore Lane, Milford-on-Sea SO41 0TX (Hampshire) T: **01590 648331**. E: **holidays@shorefield.co.uk**
alanrogers.com/UK2280

Lytton Lawn is the touring arm of Shorefield Country Park, a nearby holiday home park and leisure centre. Set in eight acres, it provides 135 marked pitches. These include 53 'premier' hardstanding pitches (16A electricity, pitch light, water and waste water outlet) in a grassy, hedged area – this section with its heated toilet block is open for a longer season. The other pitches, all with electricity, are in the adjoining, but separate, gently sloping field, edged with mature trees and hedges and with a further toilet block. The larger reception and a well stocked shop make this a good, comfortable, self-sufficient site. Visitors to Lytton Lawn are entitled to use the comprehensive leisure facilities at Shorefield itself (2.5 miles away). These include a very attractive indoor pool, solarium, sauna and spa, fitness classes and treatments, all weather tennis courts, outdoor pools, restaurant facilities including a bistro, and entertainment and activity programmes. These are of a very good standard and mostly free (extra charges are made for certain activities). These include the 'Reflections' day spa and 'Expressions' hair salon.

Facilities

Two modern toilet blocks are well fitted. Washing machine and dryer. Baby changing. Facilities for disabled visitors (Radar key). Motorcaravan service point. Shop (all year). Small fenced play area and hedged field with goal posts. Euro tents for rent. Only one dog per pitch is accepted. Off site: Facilities of Shorefield including pool and bistro (Easter- 2 Nov). Village pub 10 minutes walk. Golf, riding, coarse fishing (all within 3 miles), sailing, windsurfing and boat launching facilities (1.5 miles). The New Forest, Isle of Wight, Bournemouth, Southampton and the beach at Milford on Sea are near.

Open: All year excl. 2 January - 6 February.

See advertisement opposite

Directions

From M27 follow signs for Lyndhurst and Lymington on A337. Continue towards New Milton and Lytton Lawn is signed at Everton; Shorefield is signed at Downton. O.S.GR: SZ293937.
GPS: 50.73497, -1.61803

Charges guide

Per unit incl. all persons and electricity,	£ 11.00 - £ 34.00
premier pitch incl. water, drainage and TV connection	£ 13.50 - £ 37.50
dog (1 only)	£ 1.50 - £ 3.00

Less 40% Mon - Thurs in certain periods.
Min. weekly charge at busy times.

Poole

Sandford Caravan Park

Organford Road, Holton Heath, Poole BH16 6JZ (Dorset) T: **01202 631600**
E: **enquiries@parkdeanholidays.co.uk alanrogers.com/UK2100**

Sandford Park is an 'all singing, all dancing' park with a wide range of facilities near the popular coastal areas of Dorset. It has a large permanent section with caravan holiday homes and lodges. However, the touring section is in an attractive secluded area and can accommodate around 354 units of any type. The pitches are mainly on level grass, either with mature evergreen hedging, or in a more open style area broken up by shrubs. All have 10A electrical connections and 13 are fully serviced. Early booking is advisable. Sandford is a large, very busy holiday park with a wide range of entertainment. The central complex, the Plaza, contains a variety of bars and restaurants (book in busy periods) and a large hall with stage and dance floor. The daily entertainment programme caters for different tastes and age groups. There is provision for simple hot meals and takeaways elsewhere on site in peak season. The 25 m. heated and supervised outdoor swimming pool (May - Oct) and a very large play pool, ideal for children, are attractively situated with a snack bar and terraced area close by. There is also an impressive, heated and supervised indoor pool.

Facilities

Three toilet blocks also include facilities for disabled visitors and babies. Large launderette. Ladies' hairdresser. Bars, restaurants. TV lounges. Outdoor swimming pool (May-Sept) and indoor pool. Large supermarket and other shops, including well stocked camping accessory shop. Supervised soft indoor play area (April - Oct and Christmas). Playground. Tennis court. Multisport court. Table tennis. Two short mat bowling greens (outdoor). Crazy golf. Bicycle hire. One dog walk. Off site: Beach 9 miles. Golf 3 miles.

Open: March - November.

Directions

From the A351 (Wareham - Poole) road turn west at traffic lights in Holton Heath (signed Organford and Sandford Park). Park is on left after about 50 yards. Touring pitch reception is at the top of the park. O.S.GR: SY940913. GPS: 50.720067, -2.085533

Charges guide

Per unit incl. up to 6 persons	£ 13.00 - £ 31.00
incl. electricity	£ 16.00 - £ 34.00
serviced pitch	£ 18.00 - £ 36.00
dog (max 2)	£ 3.00 - £ 5.00

Southern England

Poole

Beacon Hill Touring Park

Blandford Road North, Poole BH16 6AB (Dorset) T: 01202 631631
E: bookings@beaconhilltouringpark.co.uk alanrogers.com/UK2180

Beacon Hill is located in a marvellous, natural environment of partly wooded heathland, with certain areas of designated habitation for protected species such as sand lizards and the Dartford Warbler, but there is also easy access to main routes. Wildlife ponds encourage dragonflies and other species but fishing is also possible. Conservation is obviously important in such a special area but one can ramble at will over the 30 acres with the hilltop walk a must. Grassy open spaces provide 170 pitches, 151 with 10A electricity, on sandy grass which is sometimes uneven. Of these, 50 are for tents only and a few are seasonal. The undulating nature of land and the trees allows for discrete areas to be allocated for varying needs, for example young families near the play area, families with teenagers close to the bar/games room, those with dogs near the dog walking area, and young people further away. The park provides a wide range of facilities, including an open air swimming pool and a tennis court. It is well situated for beaches, Poole harbour and ferries for France or the Channel Isles.

Facilities

Two fully equipped toilet blocks include facilities for disabled people. Laundry facilities. Well stocked shop at reception. Coffee bar and takeaway (main season). Bar (July/Aug, B.Hs, half-terms). Heated swimming pool (mid May - Sept). All-weather tennis court (charges). Adventure play areas including a hideaway. Games room with pool tables and amusement machines. TV room. Internet (WiFi). Fishing (charges). Off site: Poole harbour and ferries 3 miles. Riding 2 miles. Bicycle hire 3 miles. Brownsea Island, Studland beach with Sandbanks ferry and the Purbecks near.

Open: 17 March - end September.

Directions

Park is about 3 miles north of Poole. Take the A350 (towards Blandford) at roundabout where A350 joins A35. Park signed to the right (northeast) after about 400 yards. O.S.GR: SY977945. GPS: 50.74953, -2.03446

Charges guide

Per person	£ 3.50 - £ 6.25
child (under 16 yrs)	£ 2.50
pitch	£ 3.00 - £ 18.00
awning	£ 1.00 - £ 2.50
electricity	£ 2.00

www.beaconhilltouringpark.co.uk | bookings@beaconhilltouringpark.co.uk

A campsite offering pitches for tents, caravans, motorhomes ideally situated for Poole ferries, Bournemouth, the New Forest and Dorset. Family run Beacon Hill park enjoys the beauty of 30 Acres of partly wooded heathland, together with a wide selection of wildlife.

Blanford Road North, Poole, Dorset BHI6 6AB   On the A350 1/4 mile north of the junction with the A35, approximately 3 miles north of Poole

Poole

Pear Tree Holiday Park

Organford Road, Holton Heath, Poole BH16 6LA (Dorset) T: 01202 622434. E: enquiries@peartreepark.co.uk
alanrogers.com/UK2110

Pear Tree is a neat, landscaped and well cared for park welcoming families with young children and couples only. Set in 7.5 acres, with mature trees and views across to Wareham Forest, there are 155 pitches in total, of which around 90 are for touring with hardstanding, electricity (10A), water and drainage. Only breathable groundsheets are permitted for awnings. The tent area is a tranquil, secluded spot with many mature trees. Reception, incorporating tourist information and a small shop supplying milk, bread, gas and other basics, is at the park entrance. The gates (with key) are closed at dusk, although latecomers are admitted. A large, hedged, separate play field is at the top of the park with swings, climbing frame, trampolines and ball games area, all for younger children. A bus service stops outside for Wareham (2.5 miles) or Poole (5 miles). There is a walk from the back of the park into Wareham Forest.

Facilities

The main heated toilet block (opened by key) provides some washbasins in cubicles, baby changing unit and two WCs for disabled visitors. Separate small block near the tent area. All is kept spotlessly clean. Shop (basics only). Play area. All year caravan storage. Off site: The Clay Pipe Inn 500 m. Bicycle hire 0.5 miles. Golf 2.5 miles. Riding 5 miles. Beach 9 miles.

Open: 1 March - 31 October.

See advertisement on page 345

Directions

From the A351 (Wareham - Poole) road, turn west at traffic lights in Holton Heath (signed Organford and Sandford Caravan Park). Park is on left after about 550 m. past Sandford Park and the Clay Pipe Inn. O.S.GR: SY940915. GPS: 50.724033, -2.086967

Charges guide

Per unit incl. 2 persons	£ 16.00 - £ 24.00
tent pitch with electricity	£ 16.00 - £ 22.00
extra person	£ 4.00 - £ 6.00
child (5-16 yrs)	£ 1.50 - £ 2.00
Security key deposit £20 (refundable).	

Poole
South Lytchett Manor Caravan & Camping Park

Dorset Road, Lytchett Minster, Poole BH16 6JB (Dorset) T: 01202 622577. E: info@southlytchettmanor.co.uk

alanrogers.com/UK2120

Close to Poole, the Isle of Purbeck and the Jurassic Coast, Lytchett Manor is a quiet, attractive, rural campsite with views over the surrounding countryside. There are 150 pitches laid out in fields at either end of the site – one for tents, one for tents or caravans – and a long main drive connecting them. It has been extensively renovated by the new owners, Joanne and David Bridgen, with new hardstandings, toilet blocks and electricity system. There are 40 hardstandings (some used by seasonal units). All pitches have electricity (10A) and 78 have TV aerial connections. Water points are plentiful and the three heated toilet blocks have facilities for all needs. This park will suit those who are looking for a quiet holiday or to visit the many attractions in this part of Dorset. Although there are no such facilities on site, there are two pubs within a mile and a local craft centre (300 yards) has some evening events.

Facilities

Three modern, heated toilet blocks include private cabins, en-suite facilities for disabled people, family rooms and dishwashing sinks. Motorcaravan service point. Laundry. Shop in reception for basics, off licence and gas. Games room with TV. Internet. Large grass playing field. New play area. Bicycle hire. WiFi. Off site: Shops, pubs, ATM 1 mile. Beach and sailing 2 miles. Golf, fishing and riding 3 miles. Ferry port 3 miles.

Open: 1 March - 2 January.

Directions

At the roundabout at the end of the dual carriageway on the A35 to the west of Poole turn north on the B3067 to Lytchett Minster. Go through village and site is on the left half a mile past the church, through imposing wrought iron gates. O.S.GR: SY966934. GPS: 50.73959, -2.05542

Charges guide

Per unit incl. 2 persons and electricity	£ 16.50 - £ 23.50
extra person	£ 5.00 - £ 7.50
child (3-14 yrs)	£ 2.50 - £ 3.75
dog	£ 1.00

Ringwood

Shamba Holidays

Ringwood Road, St Leonards, Ringwood BH24 2SB (Hampshire) T: **01202 873302**
E: enquiries@shambaholidays.co.uk **alanrogers.com/UK2340**

Shamba is a family run, very modern park, although the aim remains to create a relaxed, pleasant atmosphere. There are 150 pitches, most of which are used for touring units, 45 are on a seasonal basis. Surrounded by trees, the camping area is on flat, open grass with electricity (10/16A) available on all pitches. A Scandinavian style building forms the focal point and here you will find reception, a bar/restaurant, a takeaway and a shop. The indoor swimming pool has walls and a roof which can be opened in good weather. The park's location is excellent for a short stop-over but well worth a longer stay for a family holiday. Bournemouth with its shops and beaches is eight miles, while the delights of the New Forest and Dorset are within easy reach.

Facilities

Sanitary facilities with underfloor heating include modern showers, washbasins and toilets and family changing rooms. Baby rooms with bath and facilities for disabled visitors. Launderette. Motorcaravan service point. Bar with meals and takeaway. Indoor swimming pool (12 x 6 m, heated) and children's pool. Large children's play area. Amusements room. Adjacent field for dog walking and football/sports pitch. Off site: Riding 1 mile. Golf 2 miles. Fishing and bicycle hire 2.5 miles. Ringwood 2.5 miles. Moors Valley Country Park 1 mile. Beach 8 miles.

Open: 1 March - 31 October.

Directions

Take the A31 westbound from Ringwood, after 3 miles, at second roundabout, turn back on yourself and after only 20 m. turn left at the park sign. O.S.GR: SU104026. GPS: 50.825067, -1.853117

Charges guide

Per unit incl. 2 persons, electricity	£ 18.00 - £ 28.00
extra person	£ 3.00
child (6-13 yrs)	£ 2.50
dog	£ 2.50

Camping Cheques accepted.

Ringwood

Forest Edge Holiday Park

229 Ringwood Road, St Leonards, Ringwood BH242SD (Hampshire) T: **01590 648331**
E: holidays@shorefield.co.uk **alanrogers.com/UK2285**

This popular family park is part of the Shorefield Group. Offering 120 pitches for tents and touring holidays and eight caravan holiday homes, it is complemented by the leisure facilities available at Oakdene Forest Park (which is no longer taking any touring units). There is easy access to the level, marked pitches, each with 16A electricity hook-ups. The cheerful, flowery reception and well stocked shop help create a friendly and relaxed atmosphere. Picnic tables are dotted about the park giving it a country feel. A short walk through Hurn Forest (less than a mile) leads to Oakdene and its new clubhouse and entertainment centre. Visitors at Forest Edge may use the bar, restaurant, large pools, games room and other free entertainment which is ideal for families not wishing to travel too far. The location of Forest Edge is ideal for visiting Bournemouth, the New Forest and the attractions of Dorset.

Facilities

The toilet block provides clean but fairly standard facilities. Unit for disabled visitors. Baby area. These facilities may be under pressure in high season. Laundry in a separate room near the children's adventure play area. Gas supplies. Shop with off-licence. Heated outdoor swimming pool (Whitsun - Sept, weekends only plus school holidays). Football and netball court. Games room. Off site: Riding 1 mile. Fishing 1 mile. Golf 1 mile. Beach 7 miles.

Open: 1 February - 3 January.
See advertisement on page 115

Directions

Take the A31 westbound from Ringwood. After 3 miles and two roundabouts, turn left at the second roundabout into Boundary Lane (before reaching Oakdene). Site is signed. O.S.GR: SU105024. GPS: 50.82137, -1.84989

Charges guide

Per unit incl. 6 persons	£ 9.50 - £ 28.00
incl. electricity	£ 11.50 - £ 34.00
dog	£ 1.50 - £ 3.00

Ringwood

Red Shoot Camping Park

Linwood, Ringwood BH24 3QT (Hampshire) T: **01425 473789**. E: enquiries@redshoot-campingpark.com
alanrogers.com/**UK2350**

Red Shoot is set on four acres of open, slightly sloping, level grass, in the heart of the New Forest. A simple, rural retreat with panoramic views of the surrounding countryside and forest, it is very popular in high season. There are 120 good sized pitches, 45 with electrical hook-ups (10A), served by a circular gravel road. There is no site lighting so a torch would be useful. The adjacent Red Shoot Inn (under separate ownership) serves hot or cold meals and brews its own real ales – Forest Gold and Tom's Tipple. There are ample opportunities for walking, cycling and naturalist pursuits in the area. Local attractions include watersports at the New Forest Water Park near Ringwood, a Doll Museum in Fordingbridge, cider making in Burley, and Breamore House just north of Fordingbridge. Nearby Ringwood has a market on Wednesdays.

Facilities

The sanitary facilities have been upgraded to a high standard with under-floor heating, including a family shower room, baby bath and changing area. Well equipped laundry room. Good unit for disabled visitors. Very well stocked, licensed shop. Fenced adventure style playground. Off site: Fishing 5 miles. Riding 6 miles. Golf 7 miles. Beach 12 miles.

Open: 1 March - 31 October.

Directions

From A338 about 1.75 miles north of Ringwood, turn east (signed Linwood and Moyles Court). Follow signs, over a staggered crossroads, and continue straight on for another 1.75 miles to Red Shoot Inn. O.S.GR: SU188095. GPS: 50.883917, -1.7347

Charges guide

Per unit incl. 2 persons and electricity	£ 19.00 - £ 28.00
extra person	£ 6.90
child (3-14 yrs)	£ 3.75
dog	£ 1.00
Min. pitch charge £11.50.	

Romsey

Hill Farm Caravan Park

Branches Lane, Sherfield English, Romsey SO51 6FH (Hampshire) T: **01794 340402**. E: gjb@hillfarmpark.com
alanrogers.com/**UK2380**

This 11-acre rural park is ideal for those seeking a quiet base but one that is within easy reach of all the main tourist attractions of Hampshire and Dorset. There are 92 pitches, of which 30 for seasonal units are located in a separate area. The touring area is a large open field surrounded by trees and hedges. All pitches are well marked, numbered and mainly level. All have electric hook-ups (6/10A), 20 pitches are fully serviced and some are available with hardstanding. Adding to the attractiveness of the site is a pitch and putt golf course, set in a sizeable and well landscaped area. For anyone interested in roses, nearby Mottisfont Abbey (National Trust) has a unique collection of old fashioned varieties and during the summer open-air plays, films and concerts take place here. The New Forest with Beaulieu Estate and National Motor Museum is just a short drive away. A trip to the Isle of Wight makes a good excursion – the ferry terminal is within a 30-minute drive.

Facilities

Two very clean, traditionally built toilet blocks include washbasins, both open style and in cubicles, and controllable showers. Facilities for babies and disabled visitors. Motorcaravan service point. Shop in reception for gas supplies and basics. Bread and pasties are cooked on the premises. Snack bar serves breakfast and takeaway meals. Play area. Pitch and putt golf. Off site: Riding and fishing 3 miles. Bicycle hire 15 miles. Bournemouth and Southampton for shopping, leisure and family entertainment nearby. Golf 3 miles.

Open: 1 March - 31 October.

Directions

From Romsey, drive north on the A27 for 3.5 miles, turning right into Branches Lane and site is a further 0.5 miles on right. O.S.GR: SU235300. GPS: 51.00627, -1.57682

Charges guide

Per unit incl. 2 persons and electricity	£ 14.00 - £ 26.00
extra person	£ 4.00
child (4-17 yrs)	£ 2.00 - £ 3.00
Minimum booking requirement for B.Hs, July and August weekends.	
No credit cards.	

Riseley
Wellington Country Park

Riseley, Reading RG7 1SP (Berkshire) T: **01189 326444**. E: info@wellington-country-park.co.uk
alanrogers.com/UK2690

Wellington Country Park is open to all on payment of an entry fee (entry for campers is included in pitch fees) and many visit it for a day out. It contains play areas for children, nature trails, a deer park, crazy golf and a miniature railway. The camping site is situated in woodland within the 350 acre park. There are 72 pitches, 10 with hardstanding, 57 with electricity hook-ups (6A) and 15 tent pitches. A few 'Premium' pitches are larger, more private and have picnic tables. It is a very pleasant setting and once the Country Park closes at 18.00 all is very quiet. You should aim to arrive before 17.30 when the main park reception centre closes. Access to the site is through a locked gate (key from reception). The design of the site with individual pitches and some small groups all within woodland clearings gives a very rustic and relaxed ambience. A warden lives on the site.

Facilities

The central toilet block provides traditional style facilities including washbasins in cubicles and well equipped showers with good dry areas. Ample laundry. Shop stocks basics. Gas supplies. Country Park with fishing, nature walks, crazy golf and play areas. Family events. Torch useful. Off site: Wellington Farm Shop 0.5 miles. Bus service at Risley 2 miles. Legoland and Windsor 30 minutes drive. Riding 1 mile. Golf 6 miles.

Open: 3 March - 9 November.

Directions

Park is signed at Riseley, off the A33 between Reading and Basingstoke. From the M4 take exit 11 and park is 4 miles south off the second roundabout (signed). From the M3 use exit 8 and follow the A33 for 7 miles towards Reading. Turn right at the roundabout after the Wellington monument and park is at the next roundabout. O.S.GR: SU727628.
GPS: 51.3592, -0.961167

Charges guide

Per unit incl. 2 persons	£ 17.50 - £ 22.00
extra person	£ 4.00
child (3-15 yrs)	£ 3.00
dog	£ 1.00

Wellington Country Park
is situated within beautiful woodlands on the Hampshire/Berkshire border near Reading. Facilities include toilets, free showers, electric shaving points, hair driers and laundry. Campers enjoy 'FREE' access to all Park facilities.
Please see website for full details.
www.wellington-country-park.co.uk
Email:- info@wellington-country-park.co.uk
Tel:- 01189 326444

Ryde
Whitefield Forest Touring Park

Brading Road, Ryde PO33 1QL (Isle of Wight) T: **01983 617069**. E: pat&louise@whitefieldforest.co.uk
alanrogers.com/UK2495

This new, family run park, opened in May 2007, has been sympathetically developed by the owners working closely with the Forestry Commission to maintain the natural beauty of the ancient woodland, Whitefield Forest. There is a mixture of well drained all-weather hardstanding and grass pitches, (70 in total) all with 16A electricity hook up. Varying in size (100-170 sq.m), the pitches are level and sheltered with some on terraces. They are all suitable for tents, caravans and motorcaravans. There is good access to the park and the pitches. Some slight road noise is audible from a few pitches. The park is suitable for families and pre-teen children who want a peaceful relaxing holiday. The nearby towns of Ryde, Shanklin and Sandown provide evening entertainment.

Facilities

The excellent well appointed heated toilet block has private cubicles, hairdryers and razor points. Family shower rooms. Baby changing and facilities for people with disabilities. Laundry room with free ironing (iron from reception). Motorcaravan service point. Paperback book exchange. Adventure type play area with bark surface for children over 5 yrs. Suitable for American style motorhomes and twin axle caravans. Off site: Network of public footpaths from the site. Golf 1 km. Riding, fishing and boat launching 3 km. Bicycle hire 4 km. Beach 3 km. Supermarket 1 km.

Open: Easter - 5 October.

Directions

From Fishbourne and East Cowes follow A3054 to Ryde. Follow the A3055 to Brading. Site is 800 yds. on left (signed) after Tesco roundabout. From Yarmouth follow A3054 to Newport, then to Ryde. Follow the A3055 to Brading and as above. O.S.GR: SZ606894. GPS: 50.70044, -1.14572

Charges 2010

Per unit incl. 2 persons and electricity	£ 11.50 - £ 17.50

Ryde

Nodes Point Holiday Park

Saint Helens, Ryde PO33 1YA (Isle of Wight) T: **01983 872401**. E: holiday.sales@park-resorts.com
alanrogers.com/UK2515

In a spectacular position, Nodes Point overlooks Bembridge Bay and is set in 65 acres of parkland running down to the beach. This is a park of 200 holiday homes with a separate area for 70 touring caravans. There is a further large dedicated field for up to 200 tents which runs down to the beach. The caravan pitches are large, level and numbered, all with electricity hook-ups (16A) and including 25 fully serviced (hardstanding, water, electricity and TV point). A one-way circular tarmac road leads you round the site which is landscaped and has been cultivated with wildlife in mind. A permanent warden lives in this same area to assist. Alongside are 30 park-owned rented tents, all well sited and maintained. The latest modern toilet block supplements two older ones and a Portacabin unit – together these are ample. The rest of the facilities and entertainment are in the holiday home area, a few minutes walk away. There is a large stage area for discos and spectacular cabaret shows. With these and the park's location by the beach, Nodes Point makes for a good family holiday.

Facilities	Directions
Together, the toilet blocks have WCs, open washbasins, showers, a family shower room and two baths. Baby room. Suite for disabled persons. Launderette. Shop. Bar. Restaurant and takeaway. Indoor pool. Adventure playground. Clubs for children. Entertainment. Archery. Riding. ATM. Off site: Fishing and boat launching 2 miles. Golf 3 miles.	From Ryde, take the A3055. At Bishop Lovett School (on the left), go straight ahead onto B3330 towards St Helens. After about 2 miles, as road curves right, turn left into signed entrance. O.S.GR:SZ631896. GPS: 50.705417, -1.105283

Open: Easter - 29 October.

Charges guide

Per unit incl. up to 6 persons	£ 3.00 - £ 37.00
dog	£ 1.00 - £ 3.00

Shanklin

Lower Hyde Holiday Park

Landguard Road, Shanklin PO37 7LL (Isle of Wight) T: **01983 866131**. E: holiday.sales@park-resorts.com
alanrogers.com/UK2475

This site is located on the edge of Shanklin, within walking distance of shops and services and only 1.5 miles from the beach. Lower Hyde is a large holiday park complex with around 200 caravan holiday homes for rent and 114 privately owned. The separate touring area has 115 well-spaced and numbered pitches, 85 with 16A electricity of which 26 are fully serviced. This area is in an elevated position with good views over the surrounding countryside. The pitches are large and flat, easily accessed, with tarmac roads and low-level lighting. Landscaping is good, with much wildlife planting throughout. There is a permanent warden for the tourers. This section has a modern toilet block but the rest of the facilities and entertainment are in the holiday home area, near reception, a few minutes walk. This is a lively site with a large dedicated stage area for discos and spectacular cabaret shows.

Facilities	Directions
The new toilet block has WCs, open washbasins, showers, a family shower room and two bathrooms. Separate baby room. Suite for disabled persons. Launderette. Shop. Bar. Restaurant and takeaway. Indoor and outdoor pools. Adventure playground. Children's clubs. Entertainment. Multicourt. Soccer. Archery. Fencing. Tennis. ATM. Off site: Fishing and boat launching 1.5 miles. Golf 2.5 miles. Riding and bicycle hire 5 miles.	From East Cowes ferry terminal take A3021 for about 2.5 miles to roundabout and turn right on A3054 to Newport. From Newport take A3020 towards Sandown and Shanklin. After 1.5 miles (at Blackwater) continue straight on joining A3056 to Sandown. Pass Safeway, and shortly afterwards, turn right into Whitecross Lane (signed Landguard Camping). Keep straight on past Landguard. Site is on right in 1 mile. O.S.GR:SZ576817. GPS: 50.633317, -1.180983

Open: 2 April - 29 October.

Charges guide

Per unit incl. up to 6 persons	£ 3.00 - £ 37.00

Shanklin

Ninham Country Holidays

You might also like to consider...

121

Wareham
Wareham Forest Tourist Park

North Trigon, Wareham BH20 7NZ (Dorset) T: **01929 551393**. E: holiday@warehamforest.co.uk
alanrogers.com/UK2030

This peacefully located and spacious park, on the edge of Wareham Forest, has 200 pitches and is continually being upgraded by its enthusiastic owners, Tony and Sarah Birch. The focal point of the park is the modern reception and shop, located by the pools. Four main areas provide a wide choice of touring pitches from grass to hardstanding and luxury, all with 16A electricity. Tenters have their own choice of open field or pinewood. The site has provided direct access for walkers into the forest or the seven miles of the Sika cycle trail may be used. The lovely market town of Wareham is accessible by bike without having to use the roads. This park has an almost continental feel, with plenty of space. Even when it is busy, it is calm and peaceful in its forest setting. In low season you may be lucky enough to spot the herd of Sika deer which live in the forest. The park is well situated to explore the Dorset coast and Thomas Hardy country. A member of the Best of British Group.

Facilities

Two well maintained toilet blocks are of a good standard with some washbasins in cubicles for ladies. The block used in the winter months is centrally heated. Facilities for disabled people. Well equipped laundry rooms. Motorcaravan service point. Small licensed shop with gas. Swimming pool (60 x 20 ft), heated 20/5-15/9. Large adventure play area. Barrier closed 23.00-07.00. Resident wardens on site. Caravan storage. WiFi. Off site: Cycle trail and walking in the forest. Bicycle hire and golf 3 miles. Fishing 5 miles. Riding 8 miles.

Open: All year.

Directions

From A31 Bere Regis, follow A35 towards Poole for 0.5 miles and site is well signed to the right for a further 1.5 miles towards Wareham. O.S.GR: SY899903. GPS: 50.721733, -2.156217

Charges guide

Per unit incl. 2 persons and electricity	£ 15.00 - £ 27.00
'superior' pitch fully serviced	£ 17.00 - £ 29.25
extra person	£ 2.75 - £ 4.75
child (5-15 yrs)	£ 2.00 - £ 3.00
dog	free - £ 1.50

Couples and families only.

Swanage
Ulwell Cottage Caravan Park

Ulwell, Swanage BH19 3DG (Dorset) T: **01929 422823**. E: enq@ulwellcottagepark.co.uk
alanrogers.com/UK2020

Nestling under the Purbeck Hills on the edge of Swanage, in the Dorset and East Devon Coast World Heritage Site, Ulwell Cottage is a family run holiday park with an indoor pool and wide range of facilities. A good proportion of the park is taken by caravan holiday homes (140), but an attractive, undulating area accessed by tarmac roads is given over to 77 numbered touring pitches interspersed with trees and shrubs. All have electricity (16A) and eight are fully serviced. The colourful entrance area is home to the Village Inn with a courtyard adjoining the heated, supervised indoor pool complex (both open all year and open to the public) and modern reception. The hill above the touring area, Nine Barrow Down, is a Site of Special Scientific Interest for butterflies and overlooks Round Down. It is possible to walk to Corfe Castle this way. With Brownsea Island, Studland Bay, Corfe village and the Swanage Railway close by, Ulwell Cottage makes a marvellous centre for holidays.

Facilities

The modern, cheerful toilet block at the top of the site is heated and includes a unit for disabled visitors. An older block in the holiday home section has been converted to family rooms. Both are well equipped. Laundry room and baby sinks in the upper block. Well stocked shop with gas (Easter - mid Sept). Bar snacks and restaurant meals with family room. Takeaway (July/Aug). Indoor pool with lifeguard (times vary acc. to season). Playing fields and play areas. Off site: Beach 1 mile. Fishing and golf 1 mile. Bicycle hire, sailing and riding 2 miles.

Open: 1 March - 7 January.

Directions

From A351 Wareham - Swanage road, turn onto B3351 Studland road just before Corfe Castle. Follow signs to right (southeast) for Swanage and drop down to Ulwell. Park is on right about 100 yards after 40 mph. sign. O.S.GR: SZ019809. GPS: 50.626460, -1.969403

Charges guide

Per unit incl. up to 6 persons	£ 18.50 - £ 36.70
full services incl. hardstanding	£ 21.00 - £ 39.00
extra tent, car or boat	£ 2.50

Less £2 for two persons only, less £1 for three persons.

Ventnor

Appuldurcombe Gardens Holiday Park

Wroxall, Ventnor PO38 3EP (Isle of Wight) T: 01983 852597. E: info@appuldurcombegardens.co.uk
alanrogers.com/UK2480

Originally part of the grounds of an historic house, this pretty family holiday park is situated in 14 acres of beautiful countryside in the valley of Stenbury Downs and St Martin's Downs, close to the sandy beaches at Sandown, Shanklin and Ventnor. The camping field is set in a grassy meadow through which a stream meanders, with a tranquil seating area close by. With hard access roads, there are 100 spacious marked pitches for touring units and tents, 70 of which have electricity hook-ups (10A). The old walled orchard contains 40 good quality caravan holiday homes. Here also is the access friendly Orchard Lodge (all accommodation on one level with ramp access to outside), plus two self contained apartments. In an area of outstanding natural beauty, it is an ideal spot for bird watching and horse riding. For walkers and cyclists there is an excellent network of footpaths and cycle paths.

Facilities

Two good toilet blocks (access by key) are fully tiled with free hot water throughout. Facilities for visitors with disabilities. Launderette. Shop (fresh baguettes baked daily) and café. Bar and family entertainment room. All amenities open from Spring B.H. Large outdoor swimming pool and toddlers' pool (May - early Sept). Play area. Pitch and putt. Crazy golf. Off site: Fishing, golf, riding, bicycle hire, boat launching, beach, sailing, all within 2-3 miles.

Open: All year excl. mid December - mid January.

Directions

Do not use Sat Nav instructions, road with restricted access nearby. From Newport take A3020 towards Shanklin and Ventnor. Travel through Blackwater, Rookley, Godshill and Sandford. At Whiteley Bank roundabout turn right towards Wroxhall (B3320). Pass Donkey Sanctuary and turn right into Appuldurcombe Road. Park entrance is second on the right, 150 yards along this road. O.S.GR: SZ548803. GPS: 50.61891, -1.22657

Charges guide

Per person	£ 5.00 - £ 7.50
child (3-14 yrs)	£ 1.50 - £ 3.75
serviced pitch	£ 2.50
dog	£ 1.00 - £ 1.50

Wimborne

Wilksworth Farm Caravan Park

Cranborne Road, Wimborne BH21 4HW (Dorset) T: 01202 885467
E: rayandwendy@wilksworthfarmcaravanpark.co.uk alanrogers.com/UK2060

First opened by the parents of the present owners, the careful and sympathetic development of Wilksworth continues with the aim of providing all the 'mod cons' yet remain in keeping with the environment. It is a spacious, quiet park, well suited for families with a heated outdoor pool which has been totally refurbished in a beautiful Spanish style. The rural situation is lovely, just outside Wimborne and around 12 miles from the beaches between Poole and Bournemouth. The park takes 65 caravans and 25 tents mainly on grass. All pitches have electricity, ten also have water and drainage. There are 77 privately owned caravan holiday homes in a separate area. With a duck pond at the entrance, the park has been well planned on good quality ground with fairly level grass and some views. Facilities are in attractively converted farm buildings designed to be in keeping with the listed status of the other buildings. A heated swimming pool and a tennis court are on the far side of the touring area.

Facilities

The central, well equipped toilet block has underfloor heating, washbasins in cubicles, a family bathroom and a shower/bath for children with baby changing. Facilities for disabled visitors. Laundry room. Modern reception and shop (basics only, limited hours, Easter - 30 Sept). Gas supplies. Freezer for ice packs. Attractive coffee shop serving simple meals with takeaway service (weekends and B.Hs. only outside the main season). Heated 40 x 20 ft. swimming pool (unsupervised, but walled and gated, May-Sept). Small paddling pool with slide. Adventure play area. BMX track. Golf practice net. Two tennis courts, one full and one short size. Games room. Winter caravan storage. Off site: Golf, fishing and riding 3 miles. Kingston Lacy (NT) 3 miles and Wimborne town centre 1 mile. Beach 12 miles.

Open: Easter/1 April - 30 October.

Directions

Park is 1 mile north of Wimborne, west off the B3078 road to Cranborne. O.S.GR: SU010019. GPS: 50.8167, -1.9904

Charges guide

Per unit incl. 2 persons and electricity	£ 14.00 - £ 24.00
extra person	£ 3.00
child	£ 2.00
full services	£ 2.00
dog	£ 1.00

No credit cards.

Wimborne

Merley Court Touring Park

Merley, Wimborne BH21 3AA (Dorset) T: 01590 648331. E: holidays@shorefield.co.uk

alanrogers.com/UK2080

Merley Court is the latest addition to the Shorefield Group and all aspects of this well planned, attractively landscaped park are constantly maintained to the highest of standards. Tarmac roads connect 179 touring pitches, 162 of which have 16A electricity, on neat lawns or one of the many hardstandings. This provision includes 20 serviced pitches with water, waste disposal and satellite TV. The entire park is interspersed with a variety of shrubs, plants and the odd ornamental urn. Some attractive tent pitches are to be found in a small wooded valley. A well furnished club complex provides a lounge bar where meals are available. There is also a snack bar, takeaway, large games room with pool tables and a family room leading onto a spacious sheltered patio. This in turn leads to the paved walled swimming pool area. There are woodland walks (including dog walks) directly from the site connecting to the disused railway line where nature has returned with an abundance of wild flowers, which in turn leads to Delph woods with designated nature trails. A member of the Best of British group.

Facilities

Three heated toilet blocks, two with showers, are of good quality. Separate facilities for disabled visitors and babies. Dishwashing and laundry facilities. Motorcaravan service point. Shop with caravan accessories and gas. Café and takeaway. Bar with food (limited hours in low and mid season). Outdoor pool (30 x 20 ft) with children's section open mid May - mid Sept. Tennis and short tennis courts. Table tennis. Play area. Games room with pool tables. Tourist information. Barrier card £5 deposit. Off site: Fishing, riding and golf all within 2 miles. Bicycle hire 5 miles. Poole 5 miles, Bournemouth 8 miles. Tower Park leisure and entertainment centre is nearby, Kingston Lacy House, Knoll Gardens, Brownsea Island and the Moors Valley Country Park are also near.

Open: All year excl. 2 January - 6 February.

Directions

Site clearly signed at the junction of the A31 and A349 roads (roundabout) on the Wimborne bypass. O.S.GR: ST008984. GPS: 50.785733, -1.98525

Charges guide

Per unit incl. 2 persons and electricity	£ 13.50 - £ 35.00
all service pitch	£ 19.00 - £ 40.00
extra person	£ 4.00

No extra pup tent as well as awning.

See advertisement on page 115

Wimborne

Woolsbridge Manor Farm Caravan Park

Three Legged Cross, Wimborne BH21 6RA (Dorset) T: 01202 826369. E: woolsbridge@btconnect.com

alanrogers.com/UK2150

Close to the Moors Valley Country Park, this friendly, family run site is within easy reach of the south coast, the resorts of Christchurch, Bournemouth and Poole, and the ancient market town of Wimborne Minster. Entry is restricted to couples and families. The seven-acre camping meadow has 101 large level pitches (51 seasonal) all with electricity (16A) and arranged on either side of a central tarmac road. Reception has a well stocked shop and a good selection of tourist information. The site is part of a working beef cattle farm, so parents should be aware of moving farm machinery and tractors. A cycleway/footpath crosses the fields to the Country Park – very safe for children – where amenities include coarse fishing, golf, steam railway, bicycle hire, a tea room and a country shop.

Facilities

The neat, refurbished toilet block is well maintained and has ample facilities. Four newly built family rooms each with shower, WC, basin, handrails and ramped access provided for disabled people, babies and toddlers. Washing machine, dryer and ironing facilities. Shop. Gas. Playground. Fishing. American RVs accepted, advance booking appreciated. Torches useful. Caravan storage. Off site: Old Barn Farm inn and restaurant 400 m. Riding, golf and bicycle hire 0.5 miles. Boat launching and sailing 5 miles.

Open: Easter - 31 October.

Directions

From Ringwood take A31 southwest to the large Ashley Heath roundabout (Junction of A31 and A338 to Bournemouth). Take left hand slip road up to roundabout, avoiding underpass, and turn right (north) onto unclassified road signed for Three Legged Cross, Ashley Heath, Horton and Moors Valley Country Park. Follow signs to Country Park (2 miles), pass the park entrance on right, continue for another 400 yards to campsite entrance (well signed on right). O.S.GR: SZ 099052. GPS: 50.842982, -1.859982

Charges guide

Per unit incl. 2 persons and electricity	£ 15.50 - £ 20.50
extra person	£ 5.50 - £ 6.00
child (under 16 yrs)	£ 3.50 - £ 4.00
dog	£ 1.50 - £ 2.00
awning or extra car	£ 2.50

Witney

Lincoln Farm Park

High Street, Standlake, Witney OX29 7RH (Oxfordshire) T: 01865 300239. E: info@lincolnfarmpark.co.uk
alanrogers.com/UK2570

From its immaculately tended grounds and quality facilities, to the efficient and friendly staff, this park is a credit to its owner. Situated in a small, quiet village, it is well set back and screened by mature trees, with wide gravel roads, hedged enclosures, brick pathways and good lighting. All 90 numbered, level touring pitches are generously sized and have electrical connections (10/16A), 75 with gravel hardstanding and grass for awnings, and 22 are fully serviced (fresh and waste water, electricity and satellite TV). Gazebos or extra tents are not permitted on pitches. Although only a relatively small site its leisure facilities are quite outstanding. The indoor leisure centre boasts two heated pools plus a pool for toddlers, spa pools, saunas, steam room, sun bed and a fitness suite. Charges for all of these are modest, and outside of the open sessions everything can be hired privately by the hour. Oxford and the Cotswolds are conveniently close. A member of the Best of British group.

Facilities

Two heated toilet blocks are well maintained and extremely clean, with showers and washbasins in cubicles. A well equipped, separate unit for disabled people. Two family bathrooms (with baby bath and changing facilities). Laundry facilities, freezers, fridges and microwaves. Motorcaravan service point. Shop (basic supplies). Information kiosk. Outdoor chess/draughts, putting green and adventure play area. Indoor swimming pools. WiFi. Off site: Fishing (lake and river) 300 yds - 5 miles, riding centre and water sports nearby. Golf 5 miles.

Open: 1 February - mid November.

Directions

Take A415 Witney - Abingdon road and turn into Standlake High Street by garage; park is 300 yds on the right. O.S.GR: SP396029.
GPS: 51.7232, -1.428783

Charges guide

Per unit incl. 2 persons and electricity	£ 13.95 - £ 24.95
extra person	£ 3.00
child (5-14 yrs)	£ 2.00
dog	£ 1.25

Low season offers.

Wool

Whitemead Caravan Park

East Burton Road, Wool BH20 6HG (Dorset) T: 01929 462241. E: whitemeadcp@aol.com
alanrogers.com/UK2090

The Church family continue to make improvements to this attractive little park which is within walking distance of the village of Wool, between Dorchester and Wareham. Very natural and with open views over the Frome Valley water meadows, it provides 95 numbered pitches on flat grass sloping gently north and is orchard-like in parts. The 76 touring pitches are well spaced, mostly backing onto hedges or fences and all have electrical connections (10A). All roads are now tarmac. There are no caravan holiday homes but 20 pitches are seasonal. There may be some rail noise but this is not intrusive at night. The park is 4.5 miles from the nearest beach at Lulworth and is handily placed for many attractions in this part of Dorset (railway station and main route bus stop is within 400 yards).

Facilities

The toilet block provides showers, private cubicles, a baby room, dishwashing and laundry sinks, washing machine and dryer. Shop (limited hours) with off-licence, gas supplies and information room/library. Games room with pool table and darts. Playground. Caravan storage. WiFi in games room. Off site: The Ship Inn is 300 yards. Riding, fishing and golf 3 miles. Bicycle hire 2 miles.

Open: 15 March - 31 October.

Directions

Turn off main A352 on eastern edge of Wool, just north of level crossing, onto East Burton road. Site is 350 yards. on right. O.S.GR: SY841871.
GPS: 50.68164, -2.22595

Charges guide

Per unit with 2 persons and electricity	£ 11.75 - £ 18.50
extra person (over 5 yrs)	£ 3.50
dog	£ 0.75 - £ 2.00

No credit cards.

www.alanrogers.com for latest campsite news

Land of 1066, the South East is brimming with historical sights as castles, stately homes and cathedrals abound. It also boasts miles of footpaths and cycle routes through some of the best landscapes in England, passing chalk downland, wooded valleys and dramatic white-faced cliffs.

THE SOUTH EAST COMPRISES: EAST SUSSEX, WEST SUSSEX, SURREY AND KENT

The chalk countryside of golden downland in Sussex offers many opportunities for an active holiday, from walking and cycling to more adventurous pursuits such as rock climbing or ballooning. Once an ancient forest, much of the Weald is now taken up with farmland, but some areas still remain, including Ashdown Forest, a walker's paradise with stunning views of the High Weald and South Downs. The many rivers of the county have cut their way through gaps in the chalk landscape, ending spectacularly in white cliffs on the coast. Here you will find the Regency resorts of Bognor Regis and Brighton, with its Royal Pavilion, famous pier and quirky shops. Often referred to as the 'Garden of England', Kent is a richly fertile region flourishing with hop gardens, fruit orchards and flowers. It is also home to the world renowned Canterbury Cathedral, several splendid castles, hidden towns, and quaint villages with oast houses. Surrey too boasts a rich heritage with numerous stately homes and National Trust sites plus large areas of ancient woodland. With a network of rivers, an enjoyable way to explore the beautiful countryside is by boat, stopping off at a riverside pub – or two!

Places of interest

East Sussex: Runnymede; Thorpe Park in Chertsey; Bexhill; historical towns of Hastings and St Leonards.

West Sussex: Eastbourne; Chichester; Bognor Regis; Arundel, with castle; Littlehampton.

Surrey: Guildford castle and cathedral; Mole Valley; Royal Horticultural Society's gardens at Wisley; Chessington World of Adventures; Dorking, a renowned centre for antiques.

Kent: Leeds Castle and gardens, the oldest stately home in the country; Canterbury, a designated World Heritage Site; Dover, with museum and castle; traditional seaside resort of Folkstone; Hever Castle in Sevenoaks; market town of Maidstone; Isle of Thanet incorporating Margate, Broadstairs and Ramsgate.

Did you know?

Hastings is home to Britain's first Norman castle, built by William the Conqueror.

Some of England's finest writers have found inspiration from living in Sussex – Rudyard Kipling, Sir Arthur Conan Doyle and A.A.Milne.

Bexhill housed one of the country's first cinemas and was the first to permit 'risqué' mixed sea bathing.

The world famous Mclaren F1 racing team has its base in Woking.

Runnymede takes its name from the meadow where the Magna Carta, the great charter of English liberties, was sealed by King John in 1215.

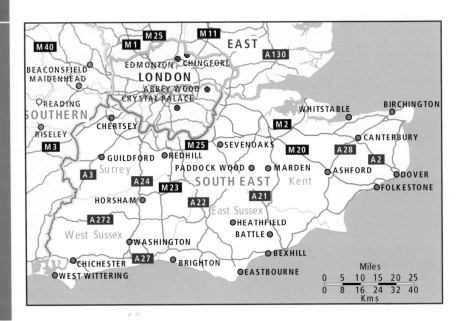

Maps and campsite listings

For this 2010 guide we have changed the way in which we list our parks and also the way in which we help you locate the parks within each region.

We now include a map immediately after our Introduction to that region. These maps show the towns near which one (or more) of our featured parks is located. Within each regional section of the guide, we list these towns and the park(s) in that vicinity in alphabetical order.

You will certainly need more detailed maps for navigation, for example the Ordnance Survey road atlas. We provide O.S. references and G.P.S. coordinates for each park to assist you. Our three indexes will also help you to find a park by its reference number and name, by region and park name, or by the town where the park is situated.

Ashford

Broadhembury Caravan & Camping Park
Steeds Lane, Kingsnorth, Ashford TN26 1NQ (Kent) T: **01233 620859**. E: **holidaypark@broadhembury.co.uk**
alanrogers.com/UK3040

In quiet countryside just outside Ashford and within easy reach of Dover, Folkestone and the Kent coast, this sheltered park is attractively landscaped. It takes 65 touring units of any type with several seasonal units and 25 caravan holiday homes (five for hire) in separate areas. The well kept pitches are on level grass and backed by tall, neat hedges, with over 50 electricity connections (10A). In addition, four pitches are fully serviced including16A electricity and eight more have double hardstanding plus a grass area for an awning. The welcome is friendly at this popular park and it is often full in the main season, with a good proportion of continental visitors, so reservation is advisable. Thoughtfully considered amenities include a very good toilet block, well equipped campers' kitchen and provision for children of all ages. Security arrangements are excellent. A member of the Best of British group.

Facilities
The toilet block is well equipped including underfloor heating and is kept very clean. Private cabins. High quality facilities for disabled visitors. Well equipped laundry room. Good campers' kitchen with microwaves, fridge and freezer, all free of charge. Motorcaravan service point. Well stocked shop (bread and papers to order). Internet access. TV and pool room, games room. Two play areas. Dog exercise field – up to two dogs per pitch are accepted. Off site: Fishing 300 m. Golf 1 mile. Riding 2 miles. Bicycle hire 3 miles.

Open: All year.

Directions
From M20 junction 10 take A2070. After 2 miles follow sign for Kingsnorth. Turn left at second crossroads in Kingsnorth village. O.S.GR: TR010382. GPS: 51.10647, 0.86809

Charges guide
Per unit incl. 2 persons, electricity	£ 18.00 - £ 22.00
extra person	£ 2.00 - £ 5.00
tent incl. 2 persons	£ 16.00 - £ 20.00
Less 10% for bookings of 7 nights or more.	

Battle

Crazy Lane Tourist Caravan Park

Crazy Lane, Sedlescombe, Battle TN33 0QT (East Sussex) T: **01424 870147**. E: **info@crazylane.co.uk**
alanrogers.com/UK2960

This simple, neat two-acre park has just 36 pitches arranged on grassy terraces, all with electricity (5/10A) and four with hardstanding. Many pitches are used by seasonal units so it may be best to phone to make sure space is available before travelling long distances. With easy access from the A21 (perhaps some background road noise), the park is set in the heart of '1066 country' with its historical links. Other local attractions within easy reach include the pretty village of Sedlescombe, a steam railway, an organic vineyard and the seaside at Hastings. This is an ideal park for couples.

Facilities

New solar heated toilet facilities are unisex providing excellent private rooms, each with WC, shower and washbasin. Laundry facilities. Shop at reception. Caravan storage. Off site: Golf 0.5 miles. Riding 2 miles. Fishing 3.5 miles. Bus stop and pub in the village. The fascinating towns of Battle and Rye, plus Hastings (6.5 miles) with its beaches, markets and Heritage Shipwreck Centre.

Open: March - October.

Directions

From the A21, 6 miles north of Hastings and 100 yards south of junction with B2244 (to Sedlescombe), turn right into Crazy Lane. Site is immediately on the right. O.S.GR: TQ782170. GPS: 50.92453, 0.53495

Charges guide

Per unit incl. 2 persons and electricity	£ 15.00 - £ 18.00
extra person over 8 yrs	£ 1.00
dog	£ 1.00

No credit cards.

Crazy Lane Tourist Park

Whydown Farm, Crazy Lane, Sedlescombe Battle TN33 0QT East Sussex
Tel/Fax: +44 (0)1424 870147 • info@crazylane.co.uk

WELCOME!
Gill and Ron Morgan would like to welcome you to Crazy Lane Tourist Caravan Park. This family-run park is in a quiet, secluded, sun-trapped valley in the heart of '1066' country within easy reach of beach and historical sites.

Bexhill

Kloofs Camping & Caravan Park

Sandhurst Lane, Whydown, Bexhill-on-Sea TN39 4RG (East Sussex) T: **01424 845669**
E: **camping@kloofs.com alanrogers.com/UK2955**

This peaceful and rural park is situated in a quiet country lane with countryside views yet within easy reach of several well known towns on the East Sussex coast. Set in three acres, Kloofs is owned and run by Terry and Helen Griggs who have taken great care in making this a most attractive and well maintained park. There are 40 level, generously sized touring pitches, divided into two areas, and a combination of grass and hardstanding making them suitable for all-weather touring. It is evident that considerable investment has been made to ensure visitors have a comfortable stay. The lower field, surrounded by hedging and trees offers some landscaped pitches which are divided by their own private trellised garden area, complete with picnic table. Pitches for caravans and motorcaravans are terraced, easy to access and surrounded by hedges and mature trees which provide shade. Most pitches have electric hook-ups and a water tap, some also have waste water drainage. This is an ideal location for a quiet and relaxing break and for visiting the attractions of the South Coast. Very large units would find the narrow lanes to the park a challenge.

Facilities

One main, centrally heated toilet block is modern and spotlessly clean. Washbasins in cubicles and spacious hot showers. Large shower room for families and good en-suite facility for disabled visitors (key from reception). A new paddock service block is partially completed and will provide further toilet and shower facilities also suitable for disabled visitors. Heated kitchen area. Washing machine, dryer, iron and board. Small shop in reception for basic requirements and camping gas. Wooden adventure style play area, fenced. Small library. Off site: Footpath from site to local village for pubs and other eating places 1.4 miles. Beach 2 miles. Bexhill-on-Sea 3 miles. Battle 6 miles. Hastings 8 miles. Eastbourne 11 miles. Watersports, golf, riding and fishing all nearby.

Open: All year.

Directions

From the north (Battle, Catsfield, Ninfield), take A269 and turn right into Pear Tree Lane, then right at crossroads. Sandhurst Lane is 300 m. on the left and site is signed a short way down on the right. From east (Hastings), take A259 to Little Common roundabout. Turn off right into Pear Tree Lane, then left at crossroads. Then as above. From west (Eastbourne), take A259 to Little Common roundabout. Turn left into Pear Tree Lane, then left at crossroads. Then as above. O.S.GR: TQ708090. GPS: 50.8560, 0.4271

Charges guide

Per person	£ 5.50
child (5-17 yrs)	£ 2.50
pitch incl. electricity and water	£ 7.00 - £ 14.00
small tent	£ 6.00

Battle

Brakes Coppice Park

Forewood Lane, Crowhurst, Battle TN33 9AB (East Sussex) T: **01424 830322**. E: **brakesco@btinternet.com**

alanrogers.com/UK2965

Brakes Coppice Park is a small and secluded site set in woodland just a mile away from historic Battle. Reached by an uneven, winding private track, it is signed to prevent visitors taking a wrong turn to the nearby farm of the same name. The site has 30 grassy pitches, 21 with 6A electricity and TV aerial points, in a gently sloping field. An adjacent area of 15 small pitches has been set aside for adults only. A further area near a small fishing lake provides a few extra pitches. As well as fishing, visitors can enjoy walking in the surrounding woods. There is a wooden play area for younger children in the centre of the main field. The reception building at the site entrance also doubles as the shop and is stocked with basic essentials. Barbecues can be borrowed and a wealth of information about the attractions of East Sussex and 1066 country can be found here.

Facilities

The single toilet block is very basic with coin operated showers (one for men, one for ladies). Facilities for disabled visitors. Laundry. Shop. Gas supplies. Fishing permits from reception. Off site: Pubs and shops in Crowhurst and Battle. Crowhurst station 10 minutes walk.

Open: 1 March - 31 October.

Directions

From Battle follow the A2100 towards Hastings for about 2 miles. Turn right on Telham Lane (signed Crowhurst). Continue into Foreword Lane and turn left on private track shortly after passing sign for Crowhurst village. O.S.GR: TQ764131.
GPS: 50.89065, 0.507083

Charges guide

Per unit incl. 2 persons	£ 12.00 - £ 14.00
incl. electricity	£ 14.00 - £ 16.00
extra person	£ 2.50
child (5-15 yrs)	£ 0.75
dog	£ 0.25

Brakes Coppice Park

Forewood Lane, Crowhurst, Nr. Battle, East Sussex TN33 9AB
Tel: +44 (0) 1424 830322
www.brakescoppicepark.co.uk
brakesco@btinternet.com

O.S. 199 TQ

Open Mar—Oct

Camping for tents, caravans & motorhomes (serviced pitches available) with full facilities (inc. disabled) on a beautiful 3-acre site surrounded by woodland with a small fishing lake.

Birchington

Quex Caravan Park

Park Road, Birchington CT7 0BL (Kent) T: **01843 841273**. E: **info@keatfarm.co.uk**

alanrogers.com/UK3110

Although there is a large number of privately owned holiday homes at Quex, they do not intrude on the touring area which is in a sheltered glade under tall trees. Here there are 40 shady touring pitches all with electricity hook-ups (16A). This park does not accept tents. This is an attractive and well maintained park, which is well located for the Thanet coast. Local attractions include Quex House and gardens and, of course, the popular seaside resorts of Margate, Ramsgate and Broadstairs. Reception provides a good selection of tourist information and can provide a map of the local area. A member of the Best of British group.

Facilities

The central sanitary unit is in a heated chalet style building with all the usual facilities. Laundry room with sink, washing machine and dryer. Well stocked shop. Playground. Café. Takeaway. More than one dog per pitch is accepted by prior arrangement only. Off site: Supermarkets close by. Fishing, golf and riding 3 miles.

Open: 7 March - 7 November.

Directions

From roundabout at junction of A28 and A299, take A28 east towards Birchington and Margate. At Birchington carry straight on at roundabout by church, then take next right, then right again, and left at mini-roundabout. Site is on right in half a mile (well signed). O.S.GR: TR320685.
GPS: 51.367583, 1.3324

Charges guide

Per unit incl. 2 persons and electricity	£ 15.25 - £ 18.75
unit over 7 metres incl. electricity	£ 20.00 - £ 25.00
extra person	£ 3.00 - £ 3.50
child (5-16 yrs)	£ 2.00 - £ 2.25
dog	£ 1.50

Brighton
Sheepcote Valley Caravan Club Site
East Brighton Park, Brighton BN2 5TS (East Sussex) T: 01273 626546

alanrogers.com/UK2930

Brighton is without doubt the South of England's most popular seaside resort and the Caravan Club's Sheepcote Valley Site is a first class base from which to enjoy the many and diverse attractions both in the town and this area of the south coast. A wide tarmac road winds its way through the site from reception, with gravel pitches on either side, leading to terraces with grass pitches on the lower slopes of the valley. The 169 pitches all have electricity (16A), 85 have hardstanding and 11 have water, drainage and TV sockets. Three grass terraces are for tents and these have hard parking nearby as a low fence prevents cars being taken onto the camping areas.

Facilities

Two heated sanitary blocks include all washbasins in private cabins. In the main season a third timber-clad building provides additional services near the tent area. Well equipped room for wheelchair users, another one for walking disabled and two baby and toddler wash rooms. Laundry facilities. Motorcaravan service point. Gas available. Milk and bread from reception. Play area with safety base. Off site: Brighton is 2 miles with a bus service from the entry road. Extensive recreation grounds adjacent.

Open: All year.

Directions

From the north (London) on M23/A23, join A27 (Lewes). Immediately after passing University on left, exit via slip road for B2123 (Falmer). At roundabout turn right on B2123. Continue for 2 miles then turn right by Downs Hotel into Warren Ave. After 1 mile turn left at lights into Wilson Ave. In 1.75 miles at foot of hill (just before lights) turn left and follow lane to site. O.S.GR: TQ341043. GPS: 50.82340, -0.12927

Charges guide

Per person	£ 4.90 - £ 6.60
pitch (non-member)	£ 11.80 - £ 15.35

Canterbury
Yew Tree Park
Stone Street, Petham, Canterbury CT4 5PL (Kent) T: 01227 700306. E: info@yewtreepark.com

alanrogers.com/UK3060

Yew Tree Park is a small, quiet site located in the heart of the Kent countryside overlooking the Chartham Downs. Just five miles south of Canterbury and eight miles north of the M20, it is ideally placed either to explore the delights of the ancient city or the many attractions of eastern and coastal Kent. Its nearness to the Channel ports also makes it useful for a night stop on the way to, or on return from, the continent. With some caravan holiday homes, the site also has 45 pitches for tourers and tents.

Facilities

Two brick-built sanitary blocks (one for each sex) can be heated. Washbasins (H&C) and four showers (on payment). Extra toilets on the edge of the camping area. Toilet/shower room for families or disabled visitors. Laundry and dishwashing sinks, plus a washing machine, dryer and iron. Gas supplies. Outdoor heated swimming pool (53 x 30 ft; June - Sept). Play area. WiFi. Torches may be useful. Dogs are not accepted. Off site: Riding 4 miles. Golf 6 miles. Bicycle hire 5 miles. The County cricket ground is 4 miles.

Open: Easter - mid October.

Directions

Park is on B2068 Canterbury - Folkestone road. From south, take exit 11 from the M20. From Canterbury, ignore signs to Petham and Waltham on B2068 and continue towards Folkestone. From either direction, turn into road beside the Chequers Inn, turn left into park and follow road to owners' house/reception. O.S.GR: TR138507. GPS: 51.2168, 1.058183

Charges guide

Per unit incl. 2 persons, electricity	£ 15.30 - £ 20.30
extra person	£ 4.00 - £ 5.00

Canterbury
Canterbury Camping & Caravanning Club Site
Bekesbourne Lane, Canterbury CT3 4AB (Kent) T: 01227 463216

E: canterbury@campingandcaravanningclub.co.uk alanrogers.com/UK3070

Situated just off the A257 Sandwich road, about 1.5 miles from the centre of Canterbury, this site is an ideal base for exploring Canterbury and the north Kent coast, as well as being a good stop-over to and from the Dover ferries, and the Folkestone Channel Tunnel terminal. There are 200 pitches, 86 with electric hook-ups (10A) and, except at the very height of the season, you are likely to find a pitch, although not necessarily with electricity. Most of the pitches are on well kept grass with hundreds of saplings planted, but there are also 21 pitches with hardstanding (more are planned).

Facilities

Two modern toilet blocks, the main one with a laundry room. Motorcaravan service point. Reception stocks a small range of essential foods, milk and gas. Excellent tourist information room. Play area with equipment on bark chippings. Off site: Golf adjacent. Bicycle hire 2 miles.

Open: All year.

Directions

From A2 take Canterbury exit for Sandwich on the A257. After passing Howe military barracks turn right into Bekesbourne Lane opposite golf course. O.S.GR: TR172577. GPS: 51.2769, 1.113533

Charges guide

Per person	£ 4.90 - £ 7.25
child (6-18 yrs)	£ 2.15 - £ 2.25
pitch (non-member)	£ 5.65

131

Chertsey

Chertsey Camping & Caravanning Club Site

Bridge Road, Chertsey KT16 8JX (Surrey) T: **01932 562405**
alanrogers.com/UK2810

This long-established site (1926) is splendidly located on the banks of the River Thames, only a few minutes walk from the shops and amenities of Chertsey. A flagship site for the Club, it was totally redeveloped a few years ago at a cost of over £1 million pounds. There are 200 pitches including 50 new serviced pitches with hardstanding and 16A electricity and 15 'super service' pitches which have TV aerial points, water and waste drainage. The work included a new road system, heated toilet blocks with facilities for disabled visitors, recreation hall and much more. There has been extensive landscaping and the existing Thames creek has been extended to flow through the site with marshland areas to support the local wildlife environment. When possible, energy saving devices have been used.

Facilities

The well equipped toilet blocks can be heated and include washbasins in cabins and facilities for disabled visitors. Hairdryers. Laundry. Motorcaravan service point. Well stocked shop for essentials and gas (08.00-11.00 and 16.00-18.00). Recreation hall. Play area on bark. Fishing (adults £1.70, NRA licence needed). Short dog walk areas. Caravan storage. Torches are necessary. Off site: Bus service in Chertsey 1.5 miles. Trains in Weybridge 3 miles. Golf and bicycle hire 1 mile.

Open: All year.

Directions

Suggested: from M25 use junction 11. Turn left at roundabout on A317 towards Shepperton and continue to second set of traffic lights. Turn right then almost immediately left watching for green Club camp sign just before Chertsey bridge; the opening is narrow. O.S.GR: TQ052667. GPS: 51.38993, -0.48966

Charges guide

Per person	£ 6.65 - £ 9.25
child (6-18 yrs)	£ 2.45 - £ 5.30
non-member pitch fee	£ 6.00

Chichester

Warner Farm Touring Park

Warner Lane, Selsey, Chichester PO20 9EL (West Sussex) T: **01243 604499**. E: **touring@bunnleisure.co.uk**
alanrogers.com/UK2885

This site is a member of the Bunn Holiday Villages group, owners of several large holiday home parks which surround the pretty holiday town of Selsey. Warner Farm is a top quality touring park with 250 large grassy pitches, 165 of which have electrical connections. Pitches have a generally open aspect and there is a large area at the back of the site, the 'Artichoke Field', which offers an unmarked camping area, as well as providing picnic tables and barbecues. There are 35 serviced pitches with electricity, water and waste water. The site is modern and well maintained, and benefits from free access to the extensive leisure facilities on offer at the neighbouring holiday villages. These include the Oasis Pool and Leisure Complex with two indoor pools, a fun fair, a number of bars and restaurants and a lively 'top name' entertainment programme and kid's club. Surprisingly perhaps, the site retains a pleasant rural feel with plenty of space despite its proximity to the sea and the resort of Selsey.

Facilities

Modern toilet block with facilities for disabled visitors. Preset showers in large cubicles. Washing machines and dryers. Small shop. Play area. Multisport area. Communal barbecue areas, picnic tables and dog walking area. Free shuttle bus to neighbouring parks. Off site: Nearest beach 900 m. Oasis Pool and Leisure Complex, indoor pools, fun fair, bars, restaurants, entertainment and kid's club. Bicycle hire. Tennis.

Open: 1 March - 30 October.

Directions

Head for Chichester on the A27. At the Whyke roundabout join the B2145 and follow signs to Selsey. At Selsey go across mini-roundabout and continue past entrance to Bunn Leisure. After next mini-roundabout take second right into School Lane, right again into Paddock Lane and then first left into Warner Lane. Follow signs to park. O.S.GR: SZ846939. GPS: 50.73815, -0.79913

Charges guide

Per unit incl. up to 4 persons and electricity	£ 19.50 - £ 33.50
extra person	£ 5.00 - £ 7.50

Chichester

Lakeside Holiday Park

You might also like to consider...

Chichester

Chichester Camping & Caravanning Club

345 Main Road, Southbourne, Chichester PO10 8JH (West Sussex) T: **01243 373202**
alanrogers.com/UK2320

This small, neat site is just to the west of Chichester and north of Bosham harbour. Formerly an orchard, it is rectangular in shape with 58 pitches on flat, well mown lawns on either side of gravel roads. All pitches have 16A electricity, 42 with level hardstanding. Although the A27 bypass takes most of the through traffic, the site is by the main A259 road so there may be some traffic noise in some parts (not busy at night). Opposite the park are orchards through which paths lead to the seashore. Arrival must be before 20.00 unless prior arrangements have been made with the site manager. Unfortunately there is no parking outside or overnight area for late arrivals.

Facilities

The well designed, brick built toilet block is of first class quality. Fully tiled and heated in cool weather, with facilities for people with disabilities (access by key). Washing machines and dryers. Gas supplies. WiFi (charged). No ball games permitted. Dogs can be walked in the lane opposite the entrance. Off site: Shops, restaurants and pubs within easy walking distance in the nearby village and the park is on a main bus route. Chichester has a leisure centre and market day is Wednesday. Excellent caravan shop nearby. Bicycle hire 1 mile. Fishing or golf 5 miles, riding 6 miles.

Open: February - November.

Directions

Park is on A259 Chichester - Havant road at Southbourne, 750 yards west of Chichester Caravans. Coming from the west, it is 2.8 miles from the A27/A259 junction near Havant. O.S.GR: SU774056. GPS: 50.84498, -0.90299

Charges year

Per person	£ 7.10 - £ 9.15
child (6-18 yrs)	£ 2.45 - £ 2.54
pitch (non-member)	£ 6.46

Dover

Hawthorn Farm Caravan & Camping Site

Martin Mill, Dover CT15 5LA (Kent) T: **01304 852658**. E: **info@keatfarm.co.uk**
alanrogers.com/UK3100

Hawthorn Farm is a large, relaxed park near Dover. Set in 27 acres, it is an extensive park taking 226 touring units of any type on several large meadows which could accommodate far more, plus 160 privately owned caravan holiday homes in their own areas. Campers not requiring electricity choose their own spot, most staying near the toilet blocks, leaving the farthest fields to those liking solitude. There are 112 pitches with electricity (10/16A), 46 of which are large and separated by hedges, the remainder in glades on either side of tarmac roads. There are 15 new hardstandings available. A well run, relaxed park with plenty of room, mature hedging and trees make an attractive environment. A torch would be useful. Being only four miles from Dover docks, it is a very useful park for those using the ferries and is popular with continental visitors. Close to the sea at St Margaret's Bay, it is a fairly quiet situation apart from some rail noise (no trains 23.30 - 05.30). A member of the Best of British group.

Facilities

Two heated toilet blocks are well equipped and of good quality. Facilities for disabled visitors. Baby room. Launderette. Motorcaravan services. Breakfast and other meals are served at the shop (all season). Gates close at 20.00 (22.00 in July and August), £10 deposit for card. Caravan storage. Off site: Riding 0.5 miles. Golf 3 miles. Bicycle hire, fishing and boat launching 4 miles. Martin Mill railway station 500 yds.

Open: 1 March - 31 October.

Directions

Park is north of the A258 road (Dover - Deal), with signs to park and Martin Mill where you turn off about 4 miles from Dover. O.S.GR: TR341464. GPS: 51.16855, 1.346333

Charges guide

Per unit incl. 2 persons and electricity	£ 15.25 - £ 25.00
extra person	£ 3.00 - £ 3.50
child (5-16 yrs)	£ 2.00 - £ 2.25
dog	£ 1.50

Less 10% for 4 nights booked (and paid for on arrival).

South East England

Eastbourne

Bay View Park

Old Martello Road, Pevensey Bay BN24 6DX (East Sussex) T: 01323 768688. E: holidays@bay-view.co.uk

alanrogers.com/UK2920

335

This friendly beachside park is located at the end of a private road right beside the beautiful Sussex coast and its pebble beach and the park's own brand new 9-hole, par-3 golf course. Two separate areas of grass (some areas are a little uneven) are surrounded by low banks and hedges to give shelter if it is windy. Careful use of wooden fencing adds to the attractiveness, whilst also keeping the rabbits off the flowers. The 94 touring pitches (80 sq.m, most with 16A electricity and some with hardstanding) are neatly marked and numbered. Several caravan holiday homes for hire are positioned at the back of the park. The golf course clubhouse provides tea, coffee and snacks. Visitors can enjoy all the attractions of Sussex, as well as swimming, fishing and windsurfing. This is an ideal park for a family beach holiday. A cycle path leads along the coast to Pevensey Bay and Eastbourne's Sovereign Harbour marina with its shops, restaurants and cinema.

Facilities

Each area has toilet facilities, one a new, fully equipped block with private cubicles (shower, washbasin and WC) and facilities for babies and disabled visitors. Heated when required, both blocks are kept very clean. Fully equipped laundry room. Motorcaravan services. Well stocked shop (open long hours as the managers live on site). Golf (9-hole, par 3). Clubhouse for tea, coffee and snacks. Gas. Popular, fenced play area (10 yrs and under). Winter caravan storage. Off site: Sailing club. Sea fishing. Indoor swimming pool 1 mile.

Open: 1 March - 31 October.

Directions

From the A27/A259 roundabout at Pevensey take A259 through Pevensey Bay. Park and golf course are signed after 1 mile (private access road) to the left, 2 miles east of Eastbourne. O.S.GR: TQ648028. GPS: 50.79998, 0.33797

Charges guide

Per unit incl. 1 or 2 persons and electricity	£ 18.50 - £ 21.00
extra person	£ 2.50
child (5-16 yrs)	£ 2.00
dog	£ 1.00

Tel:	01323 768688
Fax:	01323 769637
E-mail:	holidays@bay-view.co.uk
Web:	www.bay-view.co.uk

BAY VIEW PARK
HOLIDAY HOMES, TOURING AND CAMPING

Award-winning caravan and camping park
next to the beach on Eastbourne's sunshine coast

AA

Eastbourne

Fairfields Farm Caravan & Camping Park

Eastbourne Road, Westham, Pevensey BN24 5NG (East Sussex) T: 01323 763165
E: enquiries@fairfieldsfarm.com alanrogers.com/UK2915

Part of a working, family-run farm, this is a simple peaceful park which is ideally located to enjoy the Sussex countryside and coast, just a short distance from Eastbourne. A single, rectangular meadow is split by a line of attractive silver birch trees and provides 66 large pitches, all but four with electricity connections. The farm and its rural landscape stretch towards the sea at Pevensey Bay and you can walk through the fields to the beach. Beyond the camping field there is a duck pond with grassy surrounds and picnic benches, pens with numerous small animals and pets and a pleasant walk to a fishing lake. Children are invited to feed the animals (with special food on sale). Within walking distance are the villages of Westham and Pevensey with a choice of pubs and restaurants, as well as Pevensey Castle which has a history spanning 16 centuries. Eastbourne has a promenade and beautiful beaches with a new retail complex and cinema at the Sovereign Centre.

Facilities

The single, central toilet block is traditional in style and very clean. Toilet for disabled visitors. Laundry facilities. Farm shop. Small animals and pets. Fishing lake (licence required). Off site: Pubs, restaurants and fish and chip shop within walking distance. Beach 1.5 miles. Golf 4 miles. Eastbourne 5 miles.

Open: 1 April - 31 October.

Directions

From the roundabout junction of the A27 and the A259 (Little Chef and petrol station) take exit to Pevensey and the Castle. Go around the castle walls and into Westham village. At end of high street turn left (B2191), over level crossing and park is on left. O.S.GR: TQ639041. GPS: 50.81358, 0.32448

Charges guide

Per unit incl. 2 persons	£ 11.50 - £ 13.00
incl. electricity	£ 15.00 - £ 16.50
extra person	£ 3.00
child (3-13 yrs)	£ 1.50
dog	£ 1.00

Folkestone
Black Horse Farm Caravan Club Site
385 Canterbury Road, Densole, Folkestone CT18 7BG (Kent) T: **01303 892665**
alanrogers.com/UK3090

This neat, tidy and attractive six-acre park, owned by the Caravan Club, is situated amidst farming country in the village of Densole on the Downs just four miles north of Folkestone, eight west of Dover and 11 south of Canterbury. Accessed directly from the A260, the tarmac entrance road leads past reception towards the top field which has gravel hardstanding pitches with a grass area for awnings (possibly some road noise), past hedging to the smaller middle area with eight hardstandings, then to the large bottom field which has been redeveloped to give 140 large pitches (including 15 for tents and some extra large for American style motorhomes), all with electricity (16A).

Facilities	Directions
The carefully thought out and well constructed toilet blocks, one below reception and the other at the far end of the site, have washbasins in private cabins with curtains, good sized shower compartments, a baby room and facilities for disabled visitors, laundry and dishwashing facilities, all well heated in cool weather. Motorcaravan service point. Gas supplies. Play area. Caravan storage. Off site: Riding 1 mile. Golf and fishing 5 miles.	Directly by the A260 Folkestone - Canterbury road, 2 miles north of junction with A20. Follow signs for Canterbury. O.S.GR: TR211418. GPS: 51.132617, 1.158483

Open: All year.

Charges guide

Per person	£ 3.90 - £ 5.50
child (5-16 yrs)	£ 1.30 - £ 2.10
pitch incl. electricity (non-member)	£ 11.20 - £ 13.95

Folkestone
Little Satmar Holiday Park
Winehouse Lane, Capel-le-Ferne, Folkestone CT18 7JF (Kent) T: **01303 251188**. E: **info@keatfarm.co.uk**
alanrogers.com/UK3095

Capel-le-Ferne is a relatively little known seaside town midway between Dover and Folkestone. Little Satmar is a quiet site a short walk from the delightful cliff top paths which run between these towns and which offer fine views across the English Channel. The site is a member of the Keat Farm group and is located about a mile from the village. There are 61 touring pitches, 51 of which have electricity (10A). The pitches generally have a sunny, open setting, a few with rather more shade. Privately owned mobile homes occupy 78 pitches between the entrance to the site and reception, but these are quite separate from the touring field.

Facilities	Directions
Two toilet blocks (one in a Portacabin-style unit) are modern and kept very clean and the main block has now been fitted with heating. Washing and drying machines. Shop (with gas). Play area. For more than 1 dog per unit, contact park. Off site: Bus at end of lane to Dover and Folkestone. Port Lympne Zoo, seafront funpark nearby.	Leave A20 Dover - Folkestone road at Capel-le-Ferne exit and follow signs to the village. Site is clearly signed to right after about 0.75 miles. O.S GR: TR256393. GPS: 51.101917, 1.222933

Open: 1 March - 31 October.

Charges guide

Per unit incl. 2 persons and electricity	£ 15.25 - £ 25.00
extra person	£ 2.00 - £ 3.50

Guildford
Horsley Camping & Caravanning Club Site
Ockham Road North, East Horsley KT24 6PE (Surrey) T: **01483 283273**
alanrogers.com/UK2820

London and all the sights are only 40 minutes away by train, yet Horsley is a delightful, quiet unspoilt site with a good duck and goose population on its part lily covered lake (unfenced). It provides 130 pitches, of which 83 have 10A electrical connections and 42 are all weather pitches (most with electricity). 17 pitches are around the bank of the lake, the rest further back in three hedged, grass fields with mostly level ground but with some slope in places. A new area has been developed in woodland. There is a range of mature trees and a woodland dog walk area (may be muddy).

Facilities	Directions
Two purpose built, heated toilet blocks with good design and fittings, with some washbasins in cabins, a Belfast sink and parent and child room with vanity style basin, toilet and wide surface area. Laundry room and new drying areas. Well designed facilities for disabled people. Small shop in reception. Play area. Fishing is possible from May (adult £5.20/children £2.60 per day, NRA licence required). Off site: Shops and the station are 1 mile. Pubs 1.5 - 2 miles. Golf 1.5 miles. Riding 2 miles.	From M25 exit 10 towards Guildford, after 0.5 miles take first left B2039 to Ockham and East Horsley, continuing through Ockham towards East Horsley. After 2 miles start to watch for brown site sign - not easy to see - and site is on right in 2.5 miles. O.S.GR: TQ083552. GPS: 51.28640, -0.44502

Open: March - October.

Charges guide

Per person	£ 6.60 - £ 8.60
child (6-18 yrs)	£ 2.25 - £ 2.35
non-member pitch fee	£ 6.00

(135)

Heathfield

Horam Manor Touring Park

Horam, Heathfield TN21 0YD (East Sussex) T: **01435 813662**. E: camp@horam-manor.co.uk
alanrogers.com/UK2900

In the heart of the Sussex countryside, this rural touring park is part of (but under separate management from) Horam Manor which has a farm museum, nature trail and several fishing lakes. The 90 generously sized, numbered pitches, 54 with electricity, are on two open meadows. The area nearer reception has an undulating surface, the second field is flatter, but slopes – levelling blocks are needed for motorcaravans. Both areas are ringed with a variety of mainly tall trees. The whole park, back from the main Eastbourne to Tunbridge Wells road, is a haven of peace and tranquillity, although in high season it naturally becomes very busy. The site has no shop but the village is very close, with supermarkets in Heathfield (three miles). Two inns are within walking distance and the Lakeside cafe at the Farm Centre serves drinks and snacks (09.30 - 17.00). The Craft Centre to the side of the site has some interesting exhibits, farm machinery and riding stables. The nature trail has walks ranging from 30 to 90 minutes in length (written guide available). Fishing is possible in ten lakes on the estate.

Facilities

The well built toilet block (unheated) is fully equipped and is said to be cleaned four times daily. Some curtained cubicles. Family room (access by key from reception) with shower, washbasin, toilet and baby bath, suitable also for disabled visitors (not good for wheelchairs). Laundry. Gas supplies. Very simple fenced play area (under 12 yrs). WiFi. Off site: Horam Manor adjacent with café, fishing and riding. Shops and inns within walking distance. Tennis (small fee) 200 yds. Golf within 1 mile. The coastal towns of Brighton, Hastings and Eastbourne are within easy reach, as is the famous Pantiles at Tunbridge Wells.

Open: 1 March - 31 October.

Directions

Horam is on the A267 between Tunbridge Wells and Eastbourne and entry to the park is signed at the recreation ground at southern edge of the village. O.S.GR: TQ577169. GPS: 50.931783, 0.240167

Charges guide

Per unit incl. 2 adults, 2 children	
and electricity	£ 17.75 - £ 19.35
extra person	£ 6.00
extra child	£ 2.50
No credit cards.	

Horsham

Honeybridge Park

Honeybridge Lane, Dial Post, Horsham RH13 8NX (West Sussex) T: **01403 710923**
E: enquiries@honeybridgepark.co.uk alanrogers.com/UK2940

This 15-acre park is situated amidst beautiful woodlands and countryside on the edge of the South Downs, within an Area of Outstanding Natural Beauty. Of the 200 pitches, 147 are for touring, some are on hardstandings and the majority have electric hook-ups (16A). Some pitches are hedged for privacy, others are on slightly sloping grass, well spaced and generously sized. The reception building houses a licensed shop. A large wooden, adventure-style playground is provided for children away from the pitches, and simple family entertainment is organised on special occasions. A large games room provides darts, table tennis, pool, free use of many board games and a library. The tourist information centre is also here. This site is ideally situated for visiting the South Downs with its many attractive villages and the popular coastal resorts.

Facilities

Modern toilet facilities are heated in cool weather and include spacious facilities for disabled visitors (radar key). Laundry facilities. Motorcaravan service point. Licensed shop. Play area. Games room with library. Security barrier (card access) is locked 23.00-07.00. Off site: Bus 0.5 miles. Pub/restaurant in nearby Dial Post village. Old Barn Nurseries serves meals during the day. Billingshurst and Horsham are both 8 miles. Fishing 1 mile. Golf 10 miles. Riding 5 miles. Beach at Worthing 10 miles.

Open: All year.

Directions

Two miles south of the junction of A24 and A272 at Dial Post, turn east by Old Barn Nurseries. Follow signs to site (about 0.5 miles). O.S.GR: TQ153183. GPS: 50.94864, -0.35274

Charges guide

Per unit incl. 2 persons	
and electricity	£ 17.00 - £ 23.00
extra person	£ 3.00 - £ 6.00
child (5-14 yrs)	£ 2.50
dog	£ 1.25
Senior citizen discounts.	
Barrier pass (£10 deposit).	

Marden
Tanner Farm Touring Caravan & Camping Park

Goudhurst Road, Marden TN12 9ND (Kent) T: **01622 832399**. E: enquiries@tannerfarmpark.co.uk

alanrogers.com/UK3030

Tanner Farm is a top-class, quality park, developed as part of a family working farm in the heart of the Weald of Kent. It is surrounded by orchards, oast houses, lovely countryside and delightful small villages and the owners are much concerned with conserving the natural beauty of the environment. The park extends over 15 acres, most of which is level and part a gentle slope. The grass meadowland, which units back onto, has been semi-landscaped by planting saplings, etc. , as the owners do not wish to regiment pitches into rows. There are 100 pitches, all with 16A electricity, 38 with hardstanding, 27 with water tap and 15 with waste water point also. Places are numbered but not marked, allowing plenty of space between units which, with large open areas, gives a pleasant, comfortable atmosphere. Visitors are welcome to walk around the farm and see the Shire horses and other animals. The farm drive links the park with the B2079 and a group of refurbished oast houses (listed heritage buildings) with a duck pond in front, along with pigs, pygmy goats, lambs, etc. make a focal point. The park is a member of the Caravan Club's 'Affiliated Site' scheme (although non-members are also very welcome), Best of British and Countryside Discovery groups.

Facilities

Two heated, well cared for sanitary units include some washbasins in private cubicles in both units. Purpose built facilities for disabled visitors. Bathroom (£1 token) and baby facilities in the newer block (this block is not opened Nov - Easter). Small launderette. Motorcaravan service point. New reception, shop and tourist information building (opening hours and stock limited in winter). Gas supplies. Off site: Riding and golf within 6 miles, leisure centres and sailing facilities near and good shopping facilities at Maidstone and Tunbridge Wells. Many National Trust attractions in the area (Sissinghurst, Scotney Castle, Bodiam Castle).

Open: All year.

Directions

Park is 2.5 miles south of Marden on B2079 towards Goudhurst. O.S.GR: TQ732417.
GPS: 51.1471, 0.47482

Charges guide

Per person	£ 3.50 - £ 5.50
child (5-16 yrs)	£ 1.30 - £ 2.15
pitch incl. electriciry	£ 5.30 - £ 8.10
tent pitch	£ 4.50 - £ 5.50

Only one car per pitch permitted.

Paddock Wood
The Hop Farm Touring & Camping Park

Maidstone Road, Paddock Wood TN12 6PY (Kent) T: **01892 838161**. E: touring@thehopfarm.co.uk

alanrogers.com/UK3055

Set in 400 acres of the Garden of England, The Hop Farm is a popular family visitor attraction. There are plenty of activities to entertain children including adventure play areas (indoor and outdoor), a driving school, funfair rides, the Magic Factory and the Great Goblin Hunt. This is also the venue for many special events throughout the summer including music festivals, shows and other gatherings. To one side and overlooking all this activity and the attractive cluster of oasts is the touring park which provides over 300 grass and hardstanding pitches on flat, open fields. Electricity (16A) and water are available. There is also plenty more space for tents. The single toilet block is clean and provides straightforward, simple facilities. It can be supplemented by Portacabin units when events bring extra campers. Entry to the visitor attraction is half price for campers and here are the Shires Restaurant and the Happy Hopper's café. This park will suit those looking to enjoy the visitor attraction or attend one of the events.

Facilities

Brick built toilet block with open washbasins, preset showers (with curtain) and toilets. Further portacabin style units when the park is full for events. Small shop for essentials. Restaurant and café at the visitor attraction (half price entry for campers). Dogs accepted but not permitted inside the visitor attraction. Activities and entertainment at the visitor attraction. Off site: Shops, restaurants and golf courses nearby.

Open: March - November.

Directions

The Hop Farm is located on the A228 near Paddock Wood. Follow the brown tourist signs from exit 4 of the M20 or exit 5 of the M25 onto the A21 south. O.S.GR: TQ674472. GPS: 51.200725, 0.39333

Charges 2009

Per unit incl. 2 persons	£ 12.00 - £ 16.00
extra person (over 3 yrs)	£ 3.00
electricity	£ 4.00

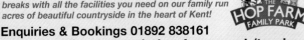

Redhill

Alderstead Heath Caravan Club Site

Dean Lane, Merstham, Redhill RH1 3AH (Surrey) T: 01737 644629
alanrogers.com/UK2800

Alderstead Heath is a surprisingly rural site given that it lies just 25 minutes from central London by train. It is also well located for exploring the North Downs and is situated on the Pilgrim's Way. There are 150 pitches, all with 16A electrical connections. Most pitches are on well kept grass, but there are also 59 hardstandings. Given the proximity of the M25 and M23 motorways, there is a certain amount of background traffic noise in parts of the site. An attractive wooded area surrounds the site and concrete tracks there were laid during the war for tanks in preparation for the D-Day landings.

Facilities

Two well-maintained toilet blocks, include a parent and toddler bathroom. The main block houses facilities for disabled visitors. Motorcaravan service point. Reception stocks a small range of essential foods, milk and gas. Small playing field. Good tourist information room. Off site: Golf 2 miles, Fishing 3 miles.

Open: All year.

Directions

Leave M25 at exit 8 and join A217 signed Reigate. Fork left after 300 yards (signed Merstham). After a further 2.5 miles turn left at T-junction and join the A23. After 500 yards turn right into Shepherd's Hill and after 1 mile turn left into Dean Lane. Site is on the right after 175 yards. O.S.GR: TQ290557. GPS: 51.28648, -0.15084

Charges guide

Per person	£ 3.90 - £ 5.40
child (5-16 yrs)	£ 1.30 - £ 2.10
pitch (non-member)	£ 11.20 - £ 13.95

Sevenoaks

Gate House Wood Touring Park

Ford Lane, Wrotham Heath, Sevenoaks TN15 7SD (Kent) T: 01732 843062
E: gatehousewood@btinternet.com alanrogers.com/UK3120

This sheltered park has been created in a former quarry where all the pitches are on well drained grass. A spacious paved entrance with a new reception building and well stocked shop, leads on to the park itself. The 54 pitches are level and open with a few small trees, two brick built barbecue units, and 36 electric hook-ups (10A). A playground has swings, seesaw and a slide, all set on a safety base, and the entire site is enclosed by grassy banks on three sides, with a wild flower walk around the top. Local attractions include Brands Hatch Circuit (four miles), the International Karting Circuit at Buckmore Park (seven miles), and the nearby Country Park at West Malling.

Facilities

Comprehensive toilet facilities are smart and well maintained, including a well equipped room which is designed for disabled people. The laundry and dishwashing room is at one end of the modern heated building. No dogs or other pets. Caravans/motorcaravans greater than 25 ft. overall are not admitted. Commercial vehicles are not accepted. Off site: Within walking distance are three pubs and a good Cantonese restaurant. Trains run to London Victoria from Borough Green (2 miles). Golf 1 mile. Riding 3 miles. Fishing 7 miles.

Open: 1 March - 31 October.

Directions

From M26 junction 2a, take A20 eastwards towards Wrotham Heath and Maidstone. Just past junction with A25, and opposite the Royal Oak pub, turn left into Ford Lane, and park is immediately on left. O.S.GR: TQ630580. GPS: 51.300133, 0.345383

Charges guide

Per unit incl. 2 persons and electricity	£ 15.50 - £ 17.00
extra person	£ 2.50
child (3-12 yrs)	£ 2.00
No credit cards.	

Washington
Washington Caravan & Camping Park
Old London Road, Washington RH20 4AJ (West Sussex) T: **01903 892869**. E: **washcamp@amserve.com**
alanrogers.com/UK2950

Washington is a pleasant campsite to the north of Worthing with a bias towards tenting families. It provides only 21 hardstanding pitches for caravans or motorcaravans, and a large gently sloping grassy field with enough space for 80 tents. The 23 electric hook-ups (16A) are on slot meters (50p). There is some road noise from the A24. There is an equestrian centre adjacent to the campsite offering stabling and paddock facilities. There are excellent riding opportunities on the bridle paths of the South Downs Way. Local attractions (all with free admission, check opening times) include Highdown Chalk Gardens at Worthing, Nutbourne Vineyard near Pulborough, and Steyning Museum.

Facilities	Directions
A heated wooden chalet style building houses the sanitary facilities including spacious shower rooms (20p) and indoor dishwashing and laundry facilities. No on-site shop but eggs, bread, butter and milk can be obtained from the reception office. Drinks machine and freezer. Off site: Bus stop 200 yds in village. Eating out options include the local pub and a nearby restaurant. Beach 9 miles.	Site entrance is just east of the junction of A24 and A283 at Washington, 6 miles north of Worthing. O.S.GR: TQ122134. GPS: 50.90875, -0.4056

Open: All year.

Charges guide

Per unit incl. 2 persons	£ 19.00
extra person	£ 4.00
electricity on meter	£ 0.50

West Wittering
Nunnington Farm Campsite
Rookwood Road, West Wittering PO20 8LZ (West Sussex) T: **01243 514013**
E: nunningtonfarm@hotmail.com **alanrogers.com/UK2895**

This no-frills, basic, family run farm site for touring units only can be found on the coast a mere seven miles from Chichester. There are 147 touring pitches, 77 with 15A electricity connections. The pitches are large, level and grassy, providing a comfortable feeling, even when the site is full. The safe, sandy beaches of The Witterings, only a mile away, make this an especially good venue for families in the holidays and a quieter one for off-season visitors. The easily accessible pets corner is an attraction for children of all ages. Visitors with tents are very welcome here and a second field is opened in busy periods, but with no electricity.

Facilities	Directions
Three rather dated but clean, central toilet blocks provide all facilities including showers in cubicles, open washbasins, baby bath, washing machines and ramped facilities for disabled visitors (key access). Gates closed 23.00-07.00. Off site: Local shops 300 yds. Bus service to Chichester every 30 minutes. Beach and boat mooring 1 mile. Bicycle hire 2 miles. Golf 3 miles.	From A27 at Chichester, take A286 signed The Witterings and continue to roundabout. Take second exit on B2179 for West Wittering and site is on left after 2 miles. O.S.GR: SZ785988. GPS: 50.78377, -0.88588

Open: Easter - 2nd week October.

Charges guide

Per unit incl. 2 persons	£ 13.00 - £ 18.00
extra person	£ 2.00
child (under 17 yrs)	£ 0.50
No credit cards.	

Kent holiday parks
Park Holidays
You might also like to consider...

336

(139)

The largest city in Euro covering over 600 squ miles, London is jam packed with hundreds of magnificent museum impressive art galleries, historic buildings and monum beautiful parks, bustling shoppin centres and markets; it really has something to offer everyone.

WE HAVE CHOSEN FOUR PARKS WHICH HAVE EASY ACCESS TO CENTRAL LONDON, INCLUDING ONE IN HERTFORDSHIRE

Despite its size, London is relatively easy to explore, largely thanks to the efficient underground service. Buses are also very useful and allow you to see the famous sights as you travel, in particular, the open-top tourist buses which ply the streets offer a good introduction to the city. Among London's many landmarks are the Tower of London, Trafalgar Square, Piccadilly Circus, Buckingham Palace, Big Ben and the Houses of Parliament, to name but a few! Running through the heart of London is the River Thames, dividing north and south; over the years many attractions, restaurants and chic bars have appeared along its banks. Being one of the most multicultural cities in the world, there is a huge choice of restaurants offering a diverse variety of cuisine; food markets are dotted all around the capital. Shopping is another major feature of the city, from the famous Harrods store and Harvey Nichols, to commercial Oxford Street and the street markets of Camden town and Portobello Road. If all the crowds become too much then head to one of London's beautiful parks such as St James' Park next to Buckingham Palace, or Hyde Park, where you can take a boat trip along the Serpentine.

Places of interest

London Eye: world's highest observation wheel, reaching 450 feet. With 32 capsule carrying 25 passengers in each, it offers breathtaking views.

Madame Tussaud's: huge collection of wax figures.

Tate Modern: contemporary art gallery housed in a transformed Bankside Power Station.

Victoria & Albert Museum: decorative art and design from around the world.

Kew Gardens: beautiful botanical gardens with over 40,000 varieties of plants.

London Dungeon: a grisly house of horror

Hampton Court Palace: one the best palac in Britain, with maze.

British Museum: houses a treasure trove o objects from all over the globe.

Did you know?

One in eight of the UK population live in London and over 200 languages are spoke

The London Underground dates back to 1863 when the first underground railway was opened, from Paddington to Farringd Street. Today, 150,000 people an hour ent the Tube network.

Founded in 1753 the British Museum is th oldest public museum in the world.

With 345 steps to the top, the Monument marks the start of the Great Fire of Londo

London has over 18,000 Licensed Taxis.

At over 900 years old, the Tower of Londo has been a palace, prison, treasury, arsena and even a zoo. It is now home to the Crown Jewels, which have been housed there since the 14th century.

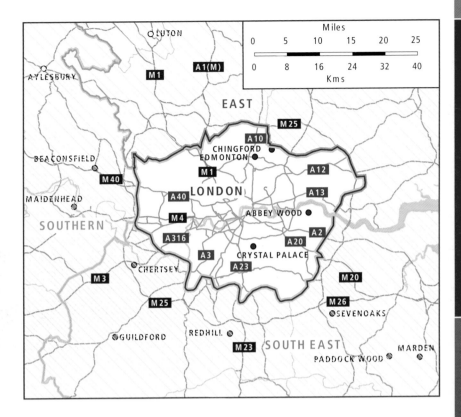

Abbey Wood

Abbey Wood Caravan Club Site

Federation Road, Abbey Wood, London SE2 0LS T: **020 8311 7708**

alanrogers.com/UK3260

Situated close to Abbey Wood, it is hard to believe that this park is in London and the wardens have made every effort to create an attractive environment. There are 120 level caravan pitches all with 16A electricity and TV aerial connections. Of these, 64 have hardstandings. A large tent area provides an additional 100 pitches. Many pitches benefit from shade by mature trees. A secure fence around the perimeter is linked to close circuit TV cameras for security and just outside is a late arrivals area with electric and toilets; also protected by cameras. This park attracts many UK and overseas visitors as it offers a very good base from which to visit central London. A train service runs every 15 minutes from Abbey Wood station (five minutes' walk) to either Charing Cross or Cannon Street.

Facilities

Three modern, fully equipped toilet blocks, two with underfloor heating, one designed to be open all year, include washbasins in cubicles, generous showers, baby/toddler washroom, laundry equipment and dishwashing sinks. Good private facilities for disabled visitors. Motorcaravan service point. Gas. Bread, milk and cold drinks from reception (high season). Play area. Good travel and information centre can provide tickets for travel and tourist attractions. Off site: Sports centre 1 mile. Golf 4 miles.

Open: All year.

Directions

From east on M2/A2 or from central London: on A2 (third exit) turn off at A221 into Danson Road (signed Bexleyheath, Welling and Sidcup). Follow sign Bexleyheath to Crook Log (A207 junction); at traffic lights turn right and immediately left into Brampton Road. In 1.5 miles at traffic lights turn left into Bostal Road (A206); in 0.75 miles at traffic lights turn right into Basildon Road (B213). In 300 yds. turn right into McLeod Road, in about 0.5 miles at roundabout turn right into Knee Hill; in 100 yds. turn right (second right) into Federation Road. Site on left in 50 yds. From M25, north, west or south approach: leave at junction 2 onto A2 (signed London), then as above. O.S.GR: TQ472785. GPS: 51.48693, 0.11757

Charges guide

Per person	£ 4.90 - £ 6.60
child (5-16 yrs)	£ 1.50 - £ 2.95
pitch incl. electricity (non-member)	£ 11.80 - £ 15.35

Tent campers apply to site.

Crystal Palace

Crystal Palace Caravan Club Site

Crystal Palace Parade, London SE19 1UF T: 020 8778 7155

alanrogers.com/UK3270

The Caravan Club's site at Crystal Palace in south London provides easy access to the city centre and all its many attractions. The pitches are pleasantly arranged in terraces overlooking the ruins of the old Crystal Palace, its park and National Sports Centre. It is surprisingly quiet given its location (with the exception of police sirens and over-flying aircraft). In peak season advance booking is always necessary. Most pitches are on gravel hardstanding, so it is particularly useful for out of season stays. There are places for 126 caravans or motorcaravans, all with electricity (16A). Tents are placed on the site's well mown lawns near reception, where there are four additional electric points. The Crystal Palace park is extensive and provides open spaces for strolls or picnics and plenty of activities for children. The Sports Centre has two swimming pools, tennis and squash courts and gym facilities, with national events in a variety of sports at certain times. An area at the site entrance should be used for arrivals after 20.00.

Facilities

The main toilet block can be heated in cool weather with curtained washbasins for ladies. Another block provides basic unisex showers and toilets. Facilities for disabled visitors. Laundry room. Dishwashing sinks and rubbish bins. Motorcaravan service facilities. Gas available. Off site: Shops, pubs, etc. 400 yards. Many buses stop outside the site, including services to central London.

Open: All year.

Directions

On A205 South Circular road travelling east, pass Dulwich College and golf course on right, turn right at traffic lights. Within 400 yards, at traffic lights, turn right into Sydenham Hill. In 350 yds. at roundabout turn left. Site is 1 mile opposite mini-roundabouts. Travelling west on A205 South Circular, immediately after passing under Catford railway bridge, keep left onto A212 (Crystal Palace). After 2.75 miles, site is on left. O.S.GR: TQ341724. GPS: 51.42587, -0.07379

Charges guide

Per person	£ 4.90 - £ 6.60
child (5-16 yrs)	£ 1.50 - £ 2.95
pitch incl. electricity (non-member)	£ 11.80 - £ 15.35
Tent campers apply to site.	

Chingford

Lee Valley Campsite

Sewardstone Road, Chingford, London E4 7RA T: 020 8529 5689. E: scs@leevalleypark.org.uk

alanrogers.com/UK3250

This attractive site provides an excellent base from which to visit London, having both easy access to the M25 and excellent public transport links into the centre of London. Close to Epping Forest in the heart of the Lee Valley, this site is on a hillside overlooking the King George reservoir in a very pleasant and relaxed setting. Like its sister sites, it is understandably very popular with foreign tourers. With capacity for 200 units the site is mostly level, with several bush sheltered avenues and plenty of trees throughout providing shade. There are 20 pitches with tarmac hardstanding and 100 with electricity (10A). American motorhomes are not accepted. Just outside the gate is the bus stop (reception have full details of good value Travel Card schemes). The bus (no. 215) will take you to Walthamstow Central Underground station from where a frequent service runs to central London. Alternatively you can park at South Woodford or Chingford stations and use the train for London visits. Staff are very pleasant and helpful.

Facilities

Three blocks offer good facilities (one is heated in low season), all recently totally refurbished. Good en-suite room for disabled visitors. Baby changing area. Dishwashing, Laundry. Motorcaravan service point. Well stocked shop. Gas available. Playground. Off site: Fishing 500 yards. Shops within 2 miles. Riding 1 mile. 9-hole golf 1 mile, 18-hole golf 3 miles. Waltham Abbey 3 miles. River Lee Country Park and Epping Forest nearby.

Open: 1 April - 4 November.

Directions

From M25 take exit 26 on A112 to Chingford and site is on right in 3 miles. From A10 take A110 (Chingford). After passing between reservoirs, at next traffic lights turn left on A112. Site on left after 2 miles. O.S. GR: TQ378970. GPS: 51.653983, -0.006517

Charges guide

Per person	£ 6.45
child (under 16 yrs)	£ 2.90
electricity	£ 2.80
dog	£ 1.65
Min charge £8.60 per unit/night	

Edmonton

Lee Valley Camping & Caravanning Park

Meridian Way, Edmonton, London N9 0AR T: **020 8803 6900**. E: **leisurecentre@leevalleypark.org.uk**

alanrogers.com/**UK3230**

Certainly one of the only sites in this guide with a multiplex cinema just outside the gate, you are greeted here by a very attractive entrance with flower displays. The site offers 140 spacious level pitches, with hardstandings and 100 with electricity hook-ups. The pitches are well laid out around a large field and there is a tent area just behind two grassy mounds. The grass and gardens are well trimmed and kept very tidy. The site also offers hook-up points for tents. The adjacent sports complex is being rebuilt and will be used for the 2012 Olympics. The cinema complex incorporates a pizza restaurant, and from here you can hop on a bus to Edmonton Green or Ponders End station from where there is a regular service into central London (journey time around 40 minutes). The friendly site managers are pleased to provide detailed information about the various Travel Card schemes available. Alternatively, historic Waltham Abbey, Epping Forest and the 1,000 acre River Lee Country Park are all within easy access. This is a popular site, very well looked after and kept clean and tidy by site managers, this is a peaceful stop within easy reach of the city.

Facilities

Two modern, heated toilet blocks include spacious showers and two large en-suite units for disabled people. Baby changing area. All facilities are accessed by combination locks. Dishwashing. Laundry. Motorcaravan service point. New barbecue area. Kitchen. Shop. Play area. badminton. Off site: Cinema at entrance. Supermarket 0.5 miles. Fishing 0.5 miles. Golf adjacent. Riding 4 miles.

Open: All year excl. Christmas, Boxing Day and New Year.

Directions

From M25 take exit 25. Follow signs for the city. At the first set of traffic lights turn left (Freezywater). Continue on for about 6 miles. Follow signs for Lee Valley Leisure Complex. After roundabout (where A110 crosses), turn left at second set of traffic lights onto the complex. Follow site signs.
O.S.GR: TQ357940. GPS: 51.632383, -0.038383

Charges guide

Per unit incl. 2 persons and electricity	£ 17.70
extra person	£ 7.10
child (5-16 yrs)	£ 3.10

Min. charge £ 9.60

(143)

The East of England is a perfect mix of soft and gentle countryside, ancient cities, historical towns, and storybook villages. Its coastline is largely untouched and studded with nature reserves, ideal for bird-watching, while the traditional beach resorts offer old-fashioned seaside fun.

THIS REGION INCLUDES THE COUNTIES OF ESSEX, SUFFOLK, NORFOLK, CAMBRIDGESHIRE, HERTFORDSHIRE AND BEDFORDSHIRE

Bedfordshire and Hertfordshire are the smallest counties in the region, with peaceful canals, undulating countryside with chalk downs, and some of the greatest stately homes in the country. Essex is full of quaint villages with a smattering of old towns and traditional seasides resorts, including Colchester and Southend-on-Sea. The river Cam winds its way through Cambridgeshire; punting along the river in Cambridge is a good way to relax and take in the many famous university buildings that dominate the waterfront along the 'Backs'. Further along the river is the ancient cathedral city of Ely, once an island before the Fen drainage. The flat Fenland has a network of rivers and canals, ideal for narrowboat trips, as are the Norfolk Broads. Norfolk itself is very flat, sparsely populated and tranquil, popular with walkers and cyclists, while the numerous nature reserves attract a variety of wildlife. It also has a beautiful coastline; the seaside towns of Great Yarmouth and Hunstanton are major draws. This unspoilt coastline stretches into Suffolk, 'Constable Country'. Full of space, with picturesque villages set amongst lush green countryside, dotted with timbered cottages and ruined abbeys, the county is home to Newmarket, the horse racing capital of the world.

Places of interest

Essex: Clacton-on-Sea; Walton-on-the-Naze with nature reserve; Colchester, Epping; Chelmsford.

Suffolk: Ipswich; Felixstowe; Lowestoft; Bury St Edmonds; village of Clare with country park.

Norfolk: Norwich, seaside resort of Cromer, old fishing village of Sheringham, Sandringham Palace near King's Lynn; Banham Zoo.

Cambridgeshire: King's College and Chapel in Cambridge plus Fitzwilliam Museum; Peterborough; Imperial War Museum in Duxford; Huntingdon; Wildfowl & Wetland Trust near Wisbech.

Hertfordshire: St Albans; stately homes and gardens of Knebworth House and Hatfield House.

Bedfordshire: Bedford, Woburn with Abbey and safari park; Whipsnade Wild Animal Park; Shuttleworth Collection near Biggleswade.

Did you know?

Newmarket has been recognised as the Headquarters of Racing for over 300 years.

The highest point of the East of England is the Dunstable Downs at 244 metres.

Colchester is Britain's oldest recorded town with Europe's largest Norman Castle keep.

The artist John Constable was born in 1776 in the village of East Bergholt. Nearby Flatford Mill, was portrayed in his most famous scene 'The Haywain'.

Peterhouse is the first Cambridge college, founded in 1284 by the Bishop of Ely.

Epping Forest was the haunt of the renowned highwayman, Dick Turpin.

Aldeburgh

Church Farm Holiday Park

Church Farm Road, Aldeburgh IP15 5DW (Suffolk) T: **01728 453433**. E: aldeburgh@amberleisure.com
alanrogers.com/UK3350

This area of the Suffolk coast has always been a popular destination for visitors and Church Farm Holiday Park has an enviable location on the outskirts of Aldeburgh. The park includes a large area designated for caravan holiday homes as well as a separate touring area situated to the front of the park. The touring area provides 85 pitches for caravans and motorhomes (tents and trailer tents are not accepted). Pitches are separated by attractive hedging that blends in well with the natural environment. 62 pitches have access to 16A electricity, as well as own water taps and a shared waste outlet (one between two pitches). The park lies opposite a shingle beach (to the south of Thorpeness) and is adjacent to a nature reserve, a haven for birds and other wildlife. The town of Aldeburgh is only 15 minutes' walk away, where there are many pubs, restaurants and takeaways. Fresh local seafood is also available along the seafront, seven days a week. This is a quiet park with no facilities for children on site, but close to the beach and amenities in Aldeburgh.

Facilities

The single toilet block has been fully upgraded with heating, free showers, toilets and washbasins (entry card with deposit). Access to the toilets and showers are via two steps, making it unsuitable for wheelchair users. However ambulant toilets are provided. Laundry room. Gas supplies. Off site: Bus service 0.5-1 mile. Shops, pubs, etc. 15 minutes walk. Beach 5 minutes walk. Fishing and bicycle hire 1 mile. Riding 6 miles.

Open: Easter - 31 October.

Directions

On arrival at Aldeburgh, site is signed at roundabout in the direction of Thorpeness. Where road meets seafront, site is on left. From town centre follow road along seafront to site on left at end of town. O.S.GR: TM465572. GPS: 52.15827, 1.60330

Charges guide

Per pitch incl. all persons	£ 20.00 - £ 24.00
incl. services	£ 24.00 - £ 28.00
Cheques are not accepted.	

Banham
Applewood Caravan & Camping Park
Banham Zoo, The Grove, Banham NR16 2HE (Norfolk) T: 01953 888370. E: info@banhamzoo.co.uk
alanrogers.com/UK3385

Applewood is a 13-acre touring park, adjacent to the famous Banham Zoo, the residents of which are the only thing that may disturb your relaxation while on this park (but they do not usually rise until 08.00). Visitors to the park receive a special price for admission to the Zoo. At weekends, one of Norfolk's largest car boot sales is held at the arena area alongside the site. Applewood has 100 pitches, 70 with electric hook-ups (10A). They are spread amongst 13 areas, each separated by high, established hedges which offer privacy and seclusion. There is a large rally field and a function room. The Appleyard, two minutes walk from the park provides a Spar shop, Huckleberry's restaurant and gift shops. The village with its pub is also within walking distance.

Facilities

Two toilet blocks, one new and one refurbished provide good, clean and spacious facilities. Room for disabled visitors. Laundry. Motorcaravan service point. Accessory shop, rally field and function room. Gas supplies. Off site: Zoo and The Appleyard with shop and restaurant. Snetterton race circuit 3 miles. Norwich 15 miles.

Open: 13 February - 31 October.

Directions

From Attleborough on the A11 take B1077 to New Buckenham and Banham Zoo. Follow road to T-junction with B1113 and turn right signed Banham. Follow through village and park is on the left at top of hill. O.S.GR: TM058871. GPS: 52.44636, 1.02514

Charges guide

Per person incl. electricity   £ 15.95 - £ 19.95

Bury Saint Edmunds
The Dell Caravan & Camping Park
Beyton Road, Thurston, Bury Saint Edmunds IP31 3RB (Suffolk) T: 01359 270121
E: thedellcaravanpark@btinternet.com alanrogers.com/UK3345

Close to the A14 and surrounded by farmland, this small touring site, four miles east of Bury St Edmunds, provides a convenient base to explore the nearby town and surrounding villages or as a stopover point. The current owners have created 60 spacious pitches within the main touring area, divided into two sections – one of which is reserved for adults only. All pitches have electricity (10A). A separate field with a further ten pitches situated under trees is available for contractors working locally, as well as any visitors who prefer shaded areas. The main touring field has some shade from well maintained hedges and the trees bordering the site. All pitches have access to the site's facilities. Food is available from local village pubs within two miles of the park. There is some noise from the nearby A14, especially to the south side of the park, but otherwise the site provides a quiet base for tourers to explore the area.

Facilities

Excellent and ample toilet and spacious shower facilities (free) are provided within a purpose built sanitary block. Ladies' toilets include a private bathroom and toilet. Family bathroom with bath, shower and baby changing facilities (charged). Separate toilet/shower for disabled visitors. Laundry room. Off site: Bus service to Bury St Edmonds from outside park. Fishing, golf and riding 3 miles. Local pubs and restaurants in Thurston and neighbouring villages.

Open: All year.

Directions

From the A14 take exit for Thurston and Beyton, 4 miles east of Bury St Edmunds. Follow signs to Thurston. Park is on the left, shortly after arriving at Thurston and signed from Beyton. O.S.GR: TL928640. GPS: 52.24053, 0.82437

Charges guide

Per unit incl. 2 persons
and electricity   £ 14.00 - £ 17.00

Cambridge
Highfield Farm Touring Park

Long Road, Comberton, Cambridge CB23 7DG (Cambridgeshire) T: 01223 262308
E: enquiries@highfieldfarmtouringpark.co.uk alanrogers.com/UK3560

Situated five miles from Cambridge, this eight-acre park is set in a delightfully quiet touring location yet close to major routes around Cambridge. The welcome is always warm from the friendly family owners. The facilities are of high quality and the grass and hedges are well cared for. Divided into five enclosures by conifers hedges, there are also shady glades for those who wish to retreat even further; plus one enclosure is reserved for those without children. Offering 60 numbered pitches for caravans or motorcaravans, and 60 for tents, pitching is around the outer edges. As a result, the park never looks crowded even when fully booked (which is frequently the case). All pitches have 10A electricity, 50 have gravel hardstanding, and most are level. A good dog walk is provided, which can be extended to a pleasant 1.5 mile walk, with seats, around the farm perimeter. A member of the Best of British group.

Facilities

Three heated toilet blocks provide more than adequate coverage and good facilities (showers 10p), all very clean and well maintained. Baby room but no dedicated provision for disabled visitors, although one block has extra wide doors and easy access. Laundry room. Small play area. Good shop. Motorcaravan service point. Excellent tourist information room. Bicycle hire. Gates closed midnight to 07.30. Off site: Comberton village 0.5 miles. Golf 2 miles. Fishing 3.5 miles. Cambridge 5 miles. Duxford War Museum and National Trust properties.

Open: 23 March - 31 October.

Directions

From M11 exit 12, take A603 towards Sandy. After 0.5 miles turn right, B1046 to Comberton. Turn right just before village signed Madingley (also caravan sign). Site on right just north of village.
O.S GR: TL391571. GPS: 52.186338, 0.014413

Charges guide

Per unit incl. 2 persons	£ 9.50 - £ 12.00
hiker or cyclist incl. tent	£ 8.25 - £ 9.75
extra person	£ 3.00
child (5-16 yrs)	£ 2.00
electricity	£ 2.50

No credit cards.

A warm welcome awaits you at our popular award winning park with its excellent facilities, set in peaceful farming countryside. It is close to the historic University City of Cambridge, the Imperial War Museum, Duxford and ideally suited for touring East Anglia.

Comberton, Cambridge CB23 7DG Tel/Fax: 01223 262308
www.highfieldfarmtouringpark.co.uk

Clacton-on-Sea
Homestead Lake Park
Thorpe Road, Weeley, Clacton-on-Sea CO16 9JN (Essex) T: 01255 833492
E: lakepark@homesteadcaravans.co.uk alanrogers.com/UK3300

This well laid out, 25-acre park was opened in 2002. It is hidden from the road at the rear of Homestead Caravans sales areas and workshops in the countryside of the Tendring district, at Weeley near Clacton. It offers 50 fully serviced hardstanding pitches on gently sloping ground overlooking a fishing lake and recently built holiday lodge accommodation on the other side of the lake. Tents accepted for short stays only on a limited number of pitches. The park makes an ideal spot to stay either for fishing or a relaxing weekend, or as a base for touring this part of Essex. A special area has been added to allow wheelchair users to fish. You could even arrange for your caravan to be serviced or repairs to be made while you stay. Homestead also have a large accessories superstore. Breakfast is recommended at the café as a start to your day.

Facilities

The toilet block offers clean and spacious facilities including an en-suite unit for disabled visitors. Baby changing facilities. Shop. Coffee shop and snack bar. Fishing lake. Woodland walks. Caravan sales, workshops and accessory shop.

Open: 1 March - 31 October.

Directions

From Colchester take A120, then A133 signed Clacton. At roundabout, turn left on B1033 into Weeley and site and showrooms are on left just past council offices. O.S GR: TM149225.
GPS: 51.85989, 1.12021

Charges guide

Per unit incl. 2 persons and electricity	£ 14.00 - £ 19.00
extra person	£ 3.00
child (under 18 yrs)	£ 1.00
dog	£ 1.00

Clacton-on-Sea
Seawick Holiday Park
You might also like to consider...

336

Colchester
Fen Farm Caravan & Camping Site
East Mersea, Colchester CO5 8FE (Essex) T: 01206 383275. E: fenfarm@talk21.com
alanrogers.com/UK3290

Tents were first pitched at Fen Farm in 1923 and since then the park has 'grown rather than developed' – something of which owners Ralph and Wenda Lord are proud. Most of the 90 pitches are unmarked, on grass and within two touring areas, either side of an area for over 80 holiday homes. All pitches have electricity connections and some have hardstanding and are fully serviced. A limited number of touring pitches are available on the smaller field, with outstanding views and direct access to the beach. This is an attractive well laid out site with trees and two ponds. The site provides facilities for launching boats from the seashore and it is popular with water skiers and windsurfers. Jet skis are not allowed. There are also many opportunities for walking, either inland or along the beach.

Facilities

The toilet block in the main touring field includes a family room and shower/toilet for disabled visitors. Laundry room. The block in Heron Bay area also has facilities for disabled visitors. Basic supplies from van from local shop (daily high season, weekends low season). Mobile shop for papers, bread and milk (weekends in summer). Gas supplies. Play area. Caravan and boat storage. Off site: Shop 1.5 miles. 'Pick your own' fruit farm and tea room.

Open: 1 March - 31 October.

Directions

From Colchester, take B1025 to Mersea Island. After crossing causeway bridge, take left fork to East Mersea. Follow road for 2.75 miles to 'Dog and Pheasant' pub. Site entrance is next right. O.S.GR: TM058144. GPS: 51.78996, 0.98460

Charges guide

Per pitch incl. awning	£ 18.00 - £ 20.00
extra car	£ 5.00

Cromer

Woodhill Park

Cromer Road, East Runton, Cromer NR27 9PX (Norfolk) T: 01263 512242. E: info@woodhill-park.com

alanrogers.com/UK3500

Woodhill is a seaside site with good views and a traditional atmosphere. It is situated on the cliff top, in a large gently sloping open grassy field, with 300 marked touring pitches. Of these, 210 have electricity (16A), seven are fully serviced and many have wonderful views over the surrounding countryside. A small number of holiday homes which are located nearer to the cliff edge have the best sea views, although perhaps at times a little bracing! Although the site is fenced there is access to the cliff top path (watch young children). It is possible locally to take a boat trip to see the seals off Blakeney Point. Nearby attractions include the Shire Horse Centre at West Runton and the North Norfolk Steam Railway.

Facilities

The three sanitary units are fully equipped but could be a little short of showers at peak times. Laundry with washing machines and dryer (iron from reception). Fully equipped unit for disabled persons. Well stocked shop (19/3-31/8). Good, large adventure playground and plenty of space for ball games. Crazy golf. Giant chess and golf course adjacent to the site. Off site: Beach 0.5 miles. Fishing 1 mile. Bicycle hire, golf and riding 2 miles.

Open: 19 March - 31 October.

Directions

Site is beside the A149 coast road between East and West Runton. O.S.GR: TG190420.
GPS: 52.93307, 1.27664

Charges guide

Per unit incl. 2 persons	
and electricity	£ 14.80 - £ 17.65
extra person	£ 2.50
child (4-16 yrs)	£ 1.00
dog	£ 2.00 - £ 3.50

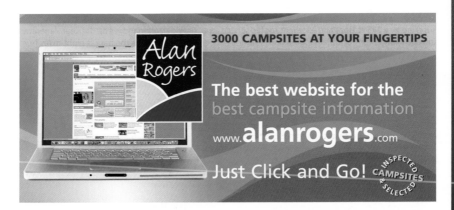

East Harling
The Dower House Touring Park
Thetford Forest, East Harling NR16 2SE (Norfolk) T: 01953 717314. E: info@dowerhouse.co.uk
alanrogers.com/UK3390

Set on 20 acres in the heart of Britain's largest forest on the Suffolk and Norfolk borders, The Dower House provides quiet woodland walks and cycle ways, with an abundance of wildlife. David and Karen Bushell, owners for many years, continue to upgrade the facilities without compromising the park's natural features. There are 160 really large pitches with electricity available (10A). Most are level, although given the forest location there are a few tree roots. A fourth field provides 60 pitches for tents. Six pitches for visitors with mobility problems are linked by a path to the main facilities. The Dower House, as well as being the owners' home, houses a pleasant bar that also serves bar food (weekends only in low season) and a takeaway. A pleasant patio area is used for occasional entertainment at weekends. A torch is necessary as there is no site lighting other than at the facilities.

Facilities
Two toilet blocks. A small, refurbished one near the entrance and a larger one with a baby room. A separate building houses the showers (five for each sex) and a unit for disabled people. Dishwashing room, including a lower sink for children or disabled people. Laundry room with washing machine and dryer. Separate licensed shop doubling as reception and open daily in the season, on request at other times. Gas supplies. Information room. TV and quiet rooms (no games machines). New heated outdoor swimming pool (25/5-2/9, under 15s must be with an adult). Paddling pool. Caravan storage. Torches necessary. Off site: Fishing nearby 1.5 miles. Snetterton motor racing circuit and Sunday market 2-3 miles.

Open: 15 March - 29 September.

Directions
From A11 (Thetford - Norwich) road, 7 miles from Thetford, turn right on B1111 towards East Harling. Turn right at church and right at T-junction; park is on right. From A1066 Thetford - Diss road take left fork signed East Harling. Ignore signs for Forestry Commission site and park is next on left. Follow long drive (unmade road) for about 1 mile - keep speed down. O.S GR: TL969853. GPS: 52.42829, 0.89631

Charges guide

Per unit incl. 2 persons	£ 11.50 - £ 19.95
incl. electricity	£ 14.50 - £ 23.25
extra person	£ 3.50 - £ 4.00
child (4-17 yrs)	£ 1.25 - £ 2.00

No charge for awnings or dogs.

Fakenham
The Old Brick Kilns Caravan & Camping Park
Little Barney Lane, Barney, Fakenham NR21 0NL (Norfolk) T: 01328 878305. E: enquiries@old-brick-kilns.co.uk
alanrogers.com/UK3400

This is a tranquil, family run park and a friendly, helpful atmosphere prevails. The park's development on the site of old brick kilns has resulted in land on varying levels. This provides areas of level, well drained pitches (e.g. the Dell, the Orchard) all of which are on hardstanding. There are 65 pitches in total, all with electricity (16A), including a newer area with serviced pitches. Banks around the park and a wide range of trees and shrubs provide shelter and are home for a variety of wildlife. There are garden areas, including a butterfly garden, and a conservation pond is the central feature. Drinking water is supplied by a 285 ft. bore and excellent roofed service areas provide water and waste disposal. Amenities include a large, comfortable bar area and restaurant, open at weekends. As the park is eight miles from the coast, it is ideally situated to explore North Norfolk. A member of the Best of British group.

Facilities
Smart, heated toilet blocks provide very good, clean facilities with washbasins in curtained cubicles. Baby room. Facilities for disabled people (unisex; Radar key). Laundry room. Motorcaravan service point. Good shop with gas supplies. Bar/restaurant (weekends) with patio area outside with barbecue. TV and games room. Giant chess. Small library. Fenced play area. Fishing (purpose-built platforms). Internet access. B&B also available. Strictly no arrivals until after 13.00. Caravan storage. Off site: Riding 6 miles. Golf 5 or 8 miles. Thursford collection 2 miles.

Open: All year excl. 7 January - 1 March.

Directions
From Fakenham take A148 Cromer road. After 6 miles, at Thursford, fork right on B1354 Melton Constable road. In 300 yds, turn right, signed Barney, and then first left along a narrow country lane with passing places, for 0.75 miles. O.S.GR: TG004332. GPS: 52.85804, 0.97583

Charges guide

Per unit incl. 2 persons and electricity	£ 14.50 - £ 18.50
'super pitch' plus	£ 2.50 - £ 3.50
extra person	£ 3.00
child (up to 15 yrs)	£ 1.00 - £ 2.00
dog (max. 2)	£ 0.75

Great Yarmouth
Clippesby Hall
Clippesby, Great Yarmouth NR29 3BL (Norfolk) T: 01493 367800. E: holidays@clippesby.com
alanrogers.com/UK3485

Set in the heart of the Broads National Park this is a spacious, high quality park where you can be sure of a warm welcome from the Lindsay family who have lived in the Hall for many years. Clippesby offers the choice of pitching amongst the shady woodland, on the gently sloping lawns of the Hall with colourful mature trees and shrubs or in a new area, 'The Meadow' which offers fully serviced pitches with hardstanding. The 100 pitches are well spaced and clearly numbered (70 have 10A electricity). Children can roam at will in safety, and parents can relax and unwind at this beautiful park. Facilities include a sunken grass tennis court, a play area, a timber adventure playground, a football pitch and family golf with a seaside theme. There is also a small, heated simming pool with a separate paddling pool. The Muskett Arms with a comfortable family bar and a sheltered courtyard, provides fresh, home-cooked meals, music nights and family entertainment. Susie's Coffee Shop has a good selection of food during the day. Off-site, the Broads and Great Yarmouth on your doorstep are waiting to be explored.

Facilities

Three timbered heated toilet blocks provide very clean, modern facilities. Some cabins with washbasin and WC. En-suite room for disabled visitors. Family room with bath and baby changing. Laundry. Gas. Shop (Easter - end Oct). Café and family bar/restaurant (early May - end Oct). Pizza takeaway. Small swimming pool and paddling pool (end May - end Sept). Adventure play area. Football. Bicycle hire. Max. 1 dog per pitch. Dog walk. WiFi. Off site: Fishing and boat launching 2 miles. Riding 3 miles. Golf, beach and sailing 5 miles. Great Yarmouth 7 miles. Norwich 15 miles.

Open: 1 April - 31 October.

Directions

From the A47 Norwich - Great Yarmouth road at Acle roundabout take exit for Filby (A1064). After 1.5 miles fork left on B1152 signed Potter Heigham. Take first left and park is 100 yards on the right.
O.S.GR: TG423145. GPS: 52.67283, 1.58299

Charges guide

Per unit incl. 2 persons	
and electricity	£ 13.25 - £ 27.75
extra person	£ 2.50 - £ 5.00
dog (max. 1)	£ 3.50

Great Yarmouth
Rose Farm Touring Park
Stepshort, Belton, Great Yarmouth NR31 9JS (Norfolk) T: 01493 780896
E: myhra@rosefarmtouringpark.fsnet.co.uk alanrogers.com/UK3382

This part of Norfolk is well known for its seaside attractions and the campsites which combine caravan holiday homes and touring pitches. Rose Farm caters for another type of camping holiday, offering space with the peace and tranquillity that you may not be expecting in this particular area! Spread over eight acres, the park is split into two separate fields. The first is large and open, surrounded by fencing and hedges, with pitches around the edge. The second field is long with pitching on either side.

Facilities

The two excellent blocks offer super facilities. The newer block is in Norwegian style, with a very modern fresh and spacious interior. Showers are good with changing space, washbasins are open or in cubicles. The laundry is in the first block along with an iron and ironing board. Facilities for disabled visitors (pitching can be arranged in advance). Adventure playground. TV room. Dog walk. Internet access. Off site: Shops nearby. Fishing and golf 3 miles. Riding and bicycle hire 4 miles. Beach 5 miles.

Open: All year.

Directions

From Great Yarmouth and Gorleston take the A143 signed Beccles and Diss. At dual carriageway (Bradwell) take immediate right to Burgh Castle, take next right, site on right in 25 yards.
O.S.GR: TG486033. GPS: 52.57136, 1.66876

Charges guide

Per unit incl. 2 persons	
and electricity	£ 14.00 - £ 19.00
tent with 2 persons	£ 12.00 - £ 17.00
extra person	£ 2.50

Special offers available. No credit cards.

Great Yarmouth

The Grange Touring Park

Ormesby St Margaret, Great Yarmouth NR29 3QG (Norfolk) T: 01493 730306. E: info@grangetouring.co.uk
alanrogers.com/UK3490

The appearance of this family touring site is that of a garden, with hanging baskets, flowerbeds, bluebells and daffodils under the trees in spring, all carefully tended by the resident wardens. There are 70 level pitches with electricity (16A), 13 with hardstanding, and ten pitches for tents, all arranged on well trimmed grass with tarmac access roads. Adjacent to the campsite is The Grange – a free house offering meals, beers and real ale, plus children's play equipment (open all year). The site owner also has a holiday campsite at Hemsby (four miles) with its own wide sandy beach, which guests at The Grange are welcome to use. The nearest beach is a mile away and local attractions include Caister Castle and Motor Museum and Norfolk Rare Breed Centre. Great Yarmouth Centre with many attractions and The Broads are within five miles.

Facilities

A modern, heated toilet building is spacious and well maintained, housing all the usual facilities including free showers. Baby room in the ladies'. Laundry room with washing machine and dryer. Washing lines are at the rear of the building. Gas supplies. Swings for children. Internet café and WiFi (£2 per hour). Off site: Bus service 250 yds. Beach, shops and supermarket 1 mile. Riding 2 miles. Golf 3 miles. Fishing 4 miles. Great Yarmouth 5 minutes drive.

Open: 20 March - 1 October.

Directions

Site is just north of Great Yarmouth. Entrance is just south of the roundabout at the northern edge of the Caister bypass, O.S.GR: TG512141. GPS: 52.66812, 1.71097

Charges guide

Per unit incl. up to 4 persons and electricity	£ 13.00 - £ 19.00
extra person (over 5 yrs)	£ 3.50
awning	£ 3.00

THE GRANGE TOURING PARK	This level grassy park will accommodate seventy touring outfits and tents and adjoins the grounds of the Grange Free House. It is very conveniently situated as a touring centre for Great Yarmouth, the Norfolk Broads and the historic Cathedral City of Norwich. We are approximately one mile from the beach.
Yarmouth Road, Ormesby St. Margaret, Great Yarmouth, Norfolk NR29 3QG www.grangetouring.co.uk info@grangetouring.co.uk Tel: 01493 730306 - 01493 730023 Fax: 01493 730188	

Great Yarmouth

Long Beach Caravan Park

Long Beach, Hemsby, Great Yarmouth NR29 4JD (Norfolk) T: 01493 730023. E: info@long-beach.co.uk
alanrogers.com/UK3492

This is a large caravan park alongside the sandy dunes bordering the sea. There are 270 reasonably level grassy pitches with 150 for touring, 90 with electricity (10-16A). About 30 touring pitches, open all season, are in the Long Beach site dotted amongst the static caravans close to all the main facilities. Most of the touring pitches are in the Hemsby Touring Park, a few hundred yards further inland and only open during school holidays. Here there are two large grassy fields with little shade and many of these pitches are a long way from the toilet block and other facilities. The beach and dunes extend for many miles along the coast offering plenty of opportunity for walking, beach activities and fun in the local amusement arcades. The nearby nature reserve is within walking distance. Not far away is the small seaside resort of Hemsby, the popular Great Yarmouth, the historic cathedral city of Norwich and the famous Norfolk Broads. There is a busy entertainment programme in July and August.

Facilities

Several small old but clean toilet blocks in main section plus one modern toilet block in the Hemsby section offering all necessary facilities. Shop, bar, restaurant, games room (open all season) in main section. Beach with miles of sand dunes. Play area. Sea fishing. WiFi (charge). Off site: Hemsby close by. Bicycle hire (800 yds). Great Yarmouth 5 miles, Norwich 18 miles.

Open: 14 March - 4 November.

Directions

Hemsby is 5 miles north of Great Yarmouth. Leave Great Yarmouth on the A149, bypass Caister and at Hemsby turn east towards beach and site. O.S.GR: TG502178. GPS: 52.7017, 1.7028

Charges guide

Per unit incl. 4 persons and electricity	£ 13.00 - £ 22.50

High season minimum stay 7 days (Sat-Sat).

Great Yarmouth
Breydon Water Holiday Park
Butt Lane, Burgh Castle, Great Yarmouth NR31 9QB (Norfolk) T: **01493 780357**
E: breydon.water@park-resorts.com **alanrogers.com/UK3510**

Owned by the Park Resorts group, these well established holiday parks (formerly Liffens Holiday Park and Welcome Holiday Centre) are in a semi-rural area on the edge of the Norfolk Broads within easy reach of Great Yarmouth. Breydon Water Holiday Park comprises the two parks, now named Bure Village (caravan holiday homes only) and Yare Village, which are just a short walk apart along a country lane. Visitors at each park may use the facilities at the other. Yare Village has over 500 pitches which include 211 touring pitches (168 with 16A electricity) on a separate open, level and grassy area. The remaining pitches are used for caravan holiday homes, most privately owned, some for rent.

Facilities

Two toilet blocks offer clean, spacious, but fairly standard facilities. Unit for disabled persons. Baby room. Laundry. Shop and post office. Entertainment complex with restaurant, two bars and takeaway. Swimming and paddling pools (29/5-31/8). Play area. Play field. Tennis. Off site: At Bure Village: indoor pool, gym, solarium, amusements and supermarket. Fishing 400 yds. Golf 3 miles. Riding 8 miles.

Open: 1 March - 31 October.

Directions

From Great Yarmouth take A143 signed Beccles. From the dual-carriageway at Bradwell turn right signed Burgh Castle into New Road. At mini-roundabout turn right into Butt Lane and follow this road for 1 mile to park on the left (care needed due to parked vehicles). O.S.GR: TM490050. GPS: 52.58653, 1.65962

Charges guide

Per unit with electricity	£ 5.00 - £ 28.00

Harleston
Little Lakeland Caravan Park
Wortwell, Harleston IP20 0EL (Norfolk) T: **01986 788646**. E: **information@littlelakeland.co.uk**
alanrogers.com/UK3480

This peaceful hideaway with its own fishing lake is tucked behind the houses and gardens that border the village main street. It is a traditional, mature little park with just 58 pitches. There are several caravan holiday homes and long stay units, but there should always be around 22 places with 10A electricity for touring units. The pitches are mostly individual ones separated by mature hedges and trees giving varying amounts of shade. Fishing in the attractive lake is free of charge and solely for the use of campers (bream, tench, roach, perch and carp). A member of the Countryside Discovery Group.

Facilities

A modern, heated toilet block provides washbasins all in cubicles for ladies, and one for men. Fully equipped laundry. Separate en-suite room for disabled visitors also has facilities for baby changing. A further unit (also heated) by reception provides a shower, WC and basin per sex and is used mostly in the colder months. Reception stocks gas, newspapers and some essentials. Small play area. Fishing (max. 4 rods per unit). WiFi (charged). Off site: Bus service on the main road 250 yds. Pub (with food) 500 yds. Golf and bicycle hire 4 miles. Riding 6 miles. Diss 12 miles. Beccles 13 miles.

Open: 15 March - 31 October.

Directions

Approaching from Diss, leave A143 at roundabout signed Wortwell. Continue to village, pass 'The Bell' public house, a garage on the right, then turn right at first bungalow (Little Lakeland Lodge) watching carefully for signs. Site is down lane, 250 yards on right. O.S.GR: TM270850. GPS: 52.41628, 1.35282

Charges guide

Per unit incl. 2 persons	£ 11.90 - £ 14.50
incl. electricity	£ 14.40 - £ 17.00
extra person	£ 1.75 - £ 3.00
No credit cards.	

Hunstanton
Searles Leisure Resort
South Beach Road, Hunstanton PE36 5BB (Norfolk) T: **01485 534211**. E: **bookings@searles.co.uk**
alanrogers.com/UK3520

This 'all-in' family holiday park on the North Norfolk coast offers everything you need for that seaside family holiday. With the beach within walking distance, the covered 'town plaza' including a sports bar, Chinese restaurant and Mediterranean café, pools, a golf course, fishing lakes and bowling greens, there should be something to entertain everyone. Although now a major caravan holiday home park, for more than 50 years touring pitches have remained important on this site. Spacious pitches separated by hedges, either fully serviced, with electricity or not, are set in seven different areas of the park.

Facilities

Three large toilet blocks offer clean and tidy facilities with background music adding that little extra. Washbasins in cubicles. En-suite rooms in all blocks for disabled visitors. Baby room. Laundry. Food hall. Restaurants, bars and cafés. Hair and beauty salon. Indoor and outdoor heated swimming pools. Gym. Tennis. Soft play area. Golf (9-hole course, driving range and putting course). Fishing lake. Bicycle hire. Off site: Beach 200 m. Hunstanton 0.5 miles.

Open: All year.

Directions

On the A149 from Kings Lynn take Hunstanton exit at roundabout. At next roundabout take second exit then immediate left into site. O.S.GR: TF670401. GPS: 52.93033, 0.48289

Charges guide

Per pitch	£ 14.00 - £ 45.00
fully serviced pitch	£ 17.00 - £ 45.00
dog	£ 2.50

Huntingdon

Wyton Lakes Holiday Park

Banks End, Wyton, Huntingdon PE28 2AA (Cambridgeshire) T: **01480 412715**. E: **loupeter@supanet.com**
alanrogers.com/UK3555

Wyton Lakes is a family run, adults only park with four well stocked fishing lakes, very close to the River Great Ouse, between Huntingdon and St Ives. There are 52 level pitches of medium size with 40 for caravans and motorhomes and 12 for tents. The tent pitches are on grass and have no electricity. The other pitches are mainly on hardstanding with grass for awnings and all have electricity and a water tap. Most of the pitches border the lakes making fishing possible from the pitch. Well placed as a centre for touring, the park has easy access for large outfits. The old market towns of Huntingdon and St Ives are only three miles away and the delightful village of Houghton with its old mill, pub and riverside walks is just one mile. Just across the road is a large garden centre complete with restaurant and coffee shop.

Facilities

Heated toilet block with all necessary facilities including those for campers with disabilities. Coarse lake and river fishing on payment (carp, bream, tench, perch, roach and rudd, up to 30 lb). Riverside walks. Off site: Garden centre, restaurant and coffee shop opposite entrance. Interesting old village Houghton, pub, shop, National Trust Mill, riverside walks, 1 mile. St Ives, Huntingdon, 3 miles. Boat hire, golf, 3 miles. Huntingdon Race Course 4 miles. Paxton Pits Nature Reserves, Hinchingbrooke Park.

Open: 4 April - 26 October.

Directions

From the A14 take exit 26 (St Ives). Take A1096 north towards St Ives over four roundabouts. Turn left onto A1123, signed Huntingdon and site entrance is on the left in about 2 miles opposite garden centre.
O.S.GR: TL269725. GPS: 52.33664, -0.13872

Charges guide

Per unit incl. 2 persons, electricity	£ 15.00
tent pitch incl. 2 adults	£ 12.00 - £ 14.00
extra adult	£ 2.00

Adults only (over 18 yrs).
No credit cards.

Wyton Lakes Holiday Park is a family run **ADULTS ONLY** park set in 12½ acres offering 4 well stocked fishing lakes. Enjoy fishing or just sitting watching the wildlife and boats go by.
Tel: 01480 412715   Email : loupeter@supanet.com
www.wytonlakes.com

Ipswich

Low House Touring Caravan Centre

Bucklesham Road, Foxhall, Ipswich IP10 0AU (Suffolk) T: **01473 659437**. E: **low.house@btinternet.com**
alanrogers.com/UK3310

Set in a sheltered 3.5 acres, this site has 30 level, grass pitches and an abundance of shrubs and flowers. The park has been divided into two areas bordered by mature trees and the grounds are well maintained. There are many different varieties of trees with a tree walk leading round two sides of the park. All the pitches have electrical connections (10/16A) and they back onto trees that provide plenty of shade and the opportunity to observe a range of wildlife. A good bus service to Ipswich stops nearby. Low House lies between Felixstowe (eight miles) and Ipswich (four miles) and would be a useful stopover for the Felixstowe port or Harwich.

Facilities

The older style, heated sanitary block is spotlessly clean with hot showers (50p). No on-site provisions but a supermarket is 2 miles (towards Ipswich). Frozen goods can be stored. Calor gas is available. Small, secure play area. Pet area with rabbit, hens and guinea fowl. Off site: Pub in Bucklesham village (1.5 miles) and other good pubs nearby. Golf 2 miles.

Open: All year.

Directions

Turn off A14 (was A45) Ipswich ring road (south) via slip road onto A1156 (signed Ipswich East). Follow road over bridge crossing over the A45 and almost immediately turn right (no sign). After 0.5 miles turn right again (signed Bucklesham) and site is on left after 400 yards. O.S.GR: TM225423.
GPS: 52.03402, 1.24507

Charges guide

Per unit incl. 2 adults, 2 children and electricity	£ 14.00
extra person	£ 3.00
child (5-14 yrs)	£ 2.00

No credit cards.

Ipswich
Orwell Meadows Leisure Park

Priory Lane, Ipswich IP10 0JS (Suffolk) T: **01473 726666**. E: recept@orwellmeadows.co.uk
alanrogers.com/UK3315

This popular, family park is set on the edge of the Orwell Country Park near Ipswich with its many miles of walks and the famous Orwell Bridge with views of the Suffolk countryside. The park is run by David and Sally Miles and offers an ideal spot for a family holiday with an outdoor swimming pool and a good clubhouse with a bar, restaurant and a shop. Spacious pitches are around the edges of several separate meadows (surrounded on three sides by earth banks), all offering 16A electricity hook-ups.

Facilities
The modern toilet block includes clean and spacious showers. It is kept to a very high standard. En-suite facilities for disabled visitors. Well stocked shop. Bar and restaurant. Outdoor pool. Play area. TV/family room. Max. two dogs per unit.

Open: March - January.

Directions
From A14 Ipswich bypass take Nacton/Ipswich exit (north of the A14) and follow signs for Orwell Country Park (narrow lane). Cross single track bridge over the A14 to site entrance 20 yards on left. Follow signs past house, park on left and walk back to reception. O.S.GR: TM190408. GPS: 52.02044, 1.19161

Charges guide
Per unit incl. 2 persons and electricity	£ 15.00 - £ 17.00
extra person	£ 4.00 - £ 6.00

Ipswich
The Oaks Caravan Park

Chapel Road, Bucklesham, Ipswich IP10 0BT (Suffolk) T: **01394 448837**. E: oakscaravanpark@aol.com
alanrogers.com/UK3325

Situated between Felixstowe and Ipswich and with views over open farmland, this pleasant 'adult only' touring park provides access to the surrounding countryside and towns, including the River Deben, Woodbridge and the Suffolk Heritage coast. Since opening in the summer of 2003, the park continues to attract many repeat visitors. Trees and shrubs planted around the perimeter and across the length of the site are now maturing, creating screening and shade for the 89 marked touring pitches. There are 79 electricity hook-ups and the well maintained grass pitches are laid out either side of an oval path.

Facilities
The single modern sanitary block provides bright and clean toilet and shower facilities, as well as a covered dishwashing area and motorcaravan point. Facilities for disabled people are planned. Gas is available at reception. Bicycle hire. Off site: Bus service outside park. Minibus service in the evenings by prior arrangement to nearby local pubs/restaurants, fish and chips Friday evenings. Riding 1 mile. Fishing less than 1 mile. Golf 4 miles. Beach 5 miles.

Open: 1 April - 31 October.

Directions
Site is between Bucklesham and Kirton. From the A12 (south) or A14(12) (north) take A14 towards Felixstowe. Continue for 5 miles and turn left signed Bucklesham and Brightwell. Continue for 1 mile, past Tenth Road on the left, take next right signed Kirton and Newbourne. Park is on the right in 550 yds. O.S.GR: TM261411. GPS: 52.02210, 1.29913

Charges guide
Per unit incl. 2 persons, electricity	£ 13.00 - £ 15.00
tent incl. 2 persons	£ 12.00
extra person	£ 2.50

Ipswich
Westwood Park Caravan Park

Old Felixstowe Road, Bucklesham, Ipswich IP10 0BW (Suffolk) T: **01473 659637**
E: westwoodcaravanpark@bt-connect.co.uk **alanrogers.com/UK3335**

This new park opened in Easter 2007 and has been developed on land previously owned by the neighbouring farm. The park is situated between Felixstowe and Ipswich and is within easy reach of the River Deben and Woodbridge. The 90 level grass pitches are of varying size to accommodate both small and large caravans, motorhomes and tents. All pitches have 16A electricity. The planting of hedges should ensure separation of individual pitches as the park develops.

Facilities
A brand new, but traditionally built, toilet block in the centre of the park includes facilities for disabled visitors (£5 deposit for key). Laundry. Purpose built reception provides local information and sells a limited range of provisions e.g. milk (plus bread and papers at B.Hs and high season). Grass play area for children. Off site: Free range eggs from a farm (short walk). Pubs serving meals in Bucklesham and surrounding villages. Fishing 2 miles. Golf 4 miles. Beach 5 miles. Bus service to Ipswich nearby.

Open: All year excl. 16 January - 28 February.

Directions
Site is near Bucklesham. From the A12 (south) or the A14(12) (north) take A14 towards Felixstowe. Go on for 5 miles and turn left signed Kirton, Bucklesham and Brightwell. Continue for about 1 mile: Park is on the right, immediately after Tenth Road on the left. O.S.GR: TN253411. GPS: 52.02316, 1.28389

Charges 2010
Per unit incl. 2 persons and electricity	£ 18.00 - £ 20.00

155

Kings Lynn
The Garden Caravan Site

Barmer Hall, Syderstone, Kings Lynn PE31 8SR (Norfolk) T: **01485 578220**. E: **nigel@mason96.fsnet.co.uk**
alanrogers.com/UK3460

In the quiet Norfolk countryside, this imaginative touring park is set in an enclosed walled garden. Sheltered from the winds by the high walls and a sun trap, visitors can relax in peace and tranquillity. Attractive mature trees, shrubs and climbers provide shade at various times of the day. The Mason family run the site in a relaxed way and the atmosphere is superb. There are 30 pitches, all with electricity (16A) and TV hook-up (own lead required). Some are slightly slopping and will require blocks. Reception is housed in a small kiosk (not always manned, so pitch yourself and pay later).

Facilities	Directions
The single toilet block (heated when necessary) includes very spacious hot showers and free hot water. Dishwashing sinks are under cover at one end of the building. No shop, but gas (not 'Camping Gaz'), ices, soft drinks and free range fresh eggs are usually available. Off site: Bicycle hire 4 miles. Riding 6 miles. Golf 10 miles. Norfolk Lavender, Langham Glass or the Thursford collection of steam engines and mechanical organs.	About 6 miles west of Fakenham turn off A148 at Fourwinds Garage to Docking and Hunstanton on the B1454. After a further 4 miles turn to Barmer Hall (site signed). Road is marked 'unsuitable for motor vehicles' but ignore and follow past and behind the Hall and farm buildings. O.S.GR: TF810330. GPS: 52.86414, 0.69116

Open: 1 March - 1 November.

Charges guide

Per unit incl. 2 persons and electricity	£ 15.50 - £ 18.50
extra person	£ 6.50 - £ 8.00
No credit cards.	

Lowestoft
Kessingland Beach Holiday Park

Kessingland, Lowestoft NR33 7RN (Suffolk) T: **01502 740636**
E: **holidaysales.kessinglandbeach@park-resorts.com alanrogers.com/UK3370**

Set near the most easterly point in the UK, this park offers all you need for that total family holiday experience, including, bowling, pool tables, an amusement arcade, indoor and outdoor swimming pools and evening entertainment. If you so wish you need never leave Kessingland Beach until your holiday ends. Although mainly a large park for static caravan holiday homes, there is a touring area to the west of the park with quite spacious pitching. Electricity hook-ups are available.

Facilities	Directions
The toilet block has been refurbished, but access is unsuitable for wheelchairs. Laundry. Shop. Bars, restaurants, fish and chips. Entertainment complex. Indoor and outdoor swimming pools. New all-weather sports court. Adventure play area. Tennis courts. Amusements. Crazy golf. Bicycle hire. Off site: Beach and sea fishing 100 yds. Golf and riding 3 miles.	From Lowestoft, north, on A12 ignore first turning to Kessingland village and continue along A12 to next roundabout. Take left turning on roundabout signed Kessingland Beach. From A12 south, turn right at roundabout signed Kessingland Beach. At beach take sharp right continuing along to park entrance (narrow road). O.S.GR: TM535859. GPS: 52.40715, 1.72470

Open: 20 March - 26 October.

Charges guide

Per caravan or motorcaravan incl. electricity	£ 6.00 - £ 29.00
tent pitch	£ 3.00 - £ 26.00

Mundesley-on-Sea
Sandy Gulls Caravan Park

Cromer Road, Mundesley-on-Sea NR11 8DF (Norfolk) T: **01263 720513**
alanrogers.com/UK3410

This is a super, adults only clifftop hideaway on the outskirts of Mundesley-on-Sea. One of the only clifftop parks with space for touring units on this coastline, there are panoramic views from every pitch. All 35 pitches have electricity and TV aerial hook-ups. Some are on hardstanding, others are slightly sloping on grass (chocks advised). Primarily a caravan holiday home park, there are units to rent. Facilities are excellent and well maintained. Access to the Blue Flag beach is via a large tarmac ramp. The village of Mundesley is only a mile away with a nine-hole golf course and a wide variety of shops and pubs. There is much to see and do in this area of Norfolk with a steam railway further along the coast. North Walsham is within easy reach and has a good array of shops and supermarkets.

Facilities	Directions
The toilet block is modern and spacious offering large shower rooms and open washbasins, all kept very clean. Facilities for disabled visitors planned. Shops, pubs and restaurants nearby. Off site: Village 1 mile. Tennis, boat launching, riding and golf nearby.	Site is 1 mile north of Mundesley (4 miles south of Cromer) on the main coast road. O.S.GR: TG302373. GPS: 52.88457, 1.42074

Open: March - November.

Charges guide

Per unit incl. up to 4 persons and electricity	£ 12.00 - £ 21.00

North Walsham

Two Mills Touring Park

Yarmouth Road, North Walsham NR28 9NA (Norfolk) T: 01692 405829. E: enquiries@twomills.co.uk
alanrogers.com/UK3420

Two Mills is a quiet site for adults only. Set in the bowl of a former quarry, the park is a real sun trap, both secluded and sheltered, with bird song to be heard at all times of the day. Neatly maintained with natural areas, varied trees, wild flowers and birds, the owners, Barbara and Ray Barnes, want to add their own touches to this popular park. Following the purchase of an adjacent field, there are now 81 level pitches for tourers, including 56 serviced pitches (patio, water and waste water drainage), 48 all weather gravel. All are generously sized and have electricity (10/16A). A member of the Best of British group.

Facilities

Neat, clean central toilet block can be heated and includes some washbasins in cabins, en-suite facilities for disabled people, laundry and dishwashing rooms. Small shop at reception. TV room with tea and coffee facilities. Dogs are accepted by arrangement only. Only adults are accepted. Off site: Hotel/pub 100 yds. Town 20 minutes walk. Fishing or golf 5 miles. Bicycle hire 1.5 miles. The coast is 5 miles.

Open: All year excl. 2 January - 1 March.

Directions

From A149 Stalham - North Walsham road, watch for caravan sign 1.5 miles before North Walsham (also signed White Horse Common). The road runs parallel to the A149 and site is on right after 1.25 miles. From North Walsham take Old Yarrmouth road past hospital, and park is on left after 1 mile. O.S.GR: TG292287. GPS: 52.80384, 1.40360

Charges guide

Per unit incl. 2 persons and electricity	£ 14.50 - £ 21.00
extra person	£ 2.50

Norwich

Deer's Glade Caravan & Camping Park

White Post Road, Hanworth, Norwich NR11 7HN (Norfolk) T: 01263 768633. E: info@deersglade.co.uk
alanrogers.com/UK3455

In 2003, David and Heather Attew decided that they had an area that would make a superb setting for a caravan park and that they could give up farming. In early 2004 after much hard work, they opened this top quality park and it has since developed into a very popular site. Not far from the Norfolk Broads and close to the East Anglian coast, the park is open all year round. There are 125 level pitches (some with hardstandings), all with 16A electricity and 100 with TV aerial points. New hedging between pitches is becoming established. Internet access is possible from all the pitches. Amenities are of a high standard and include two toilet blocks, a play area, small shop and a popular, well stocked fishing lake. As its name suggests, you would not be surprised to wake and see deer wandering on this park and in the surrounding woodland areas. If you do miss them, a short walk will take you to Gunton Park where deer are bred and wander in herds.

Facilities

Two spacious new toilet blocks are of a high standard and include vanity style washbasins for ladies, a room for disabled visitors or families, dishwashing room and a laundry. Motorcaravan service point. Licensed shop (all year). Play area. Fishing lake (charge). Bicycle hire. Caravan valet service. Free minibus to local tavern. Off site: Bus service under 1 mile. Pub 1.5 miles. Woodland walks. Riding 2 miles. Beach, golf 5 miles.

Open: All year.

Directions

From Norwich take A140 towards Cromer and 5 miles after Aylsham turn right towards Suffield Park (White Post Road). Park is 0.5 miles on the right. O.S.GR: TG214340. GPS: 52.85781, 1.28765

Charges guide

Per person	£ 5.00 - £ 7.50
child	£ 1.75 - £ 2.75
dog	£ 1.00

Family deals available.

www.alanrogers.com for latest campsite news

Norwich

Little Haven Caravan & Camping Park

The Street, Erpingham, Norwich NR11 7QD (Norfolk) T: **01263 768959**. E: **patlhaven@tiscali.co.uk**
alanrogers.com/UK3450

Within easy reach of the coast and the Broads, this is an attractive, peaceful little site with good facilities. Only adults are accepted. There are 24 grassy pitches, all with electricity (16A) and six with hardstanding. They are arranged around the outside of a gravel access road with a central lawn and decorative pergola, a neat little garden and a seating area. There is no shop, but two pubs serving food and traditional ales are within walking distance. An ideal base for cycling and walking or just relaxing.

Facilities

The well maintained toilet unit is heated and includes spacious hot showers and a covered dishwashing and laundry area. Facilities for disabled people are planned. Gas available. Site is unsuitable for American motorhomes. Note: This is an adults only park. Off site: Bus service on the main A140 road. Riding 1 mile. Fishing 3 miles. Bicycle hire 5 miles. Beach 6 miles. Golf 10 miles.

Open: 1 March - 31 October.

Directions

From A140 Cromer - Norwich road, going south towards Aylsham and 3 miles south of Roughton, past the Horseshoes pub, take first turning right signed Erpingham 2 miles (narrow). Site is 175 yards on right. O.S.GR: TG190320. GPS: 52.84208, 1.27090

Charges guide

Per unit incl. 2 persons, electricity and awning	£ 11.00

No credit cards.

Peterborough

Ferry Meadows Caravan Club Site

Ham Lane, Peterborough PE2 5UU (Cambridgeshire) T: **01733 233526**
alanrogers.com/UK3580

Three miles from bustling Peterborough and closer still to the East of England Showground, the immaculate Ferry Meadows is an ideal family holiday site occupying 30 acres of the 500 acre Nene Country Park. Open all year the site provides 252 pitches (16A electricity) – 160 grass pitches on one side of the park, informally laid out in small groups and surrounded by a variety of mature trees, and 94 gravel hardstandings just across the road for caravans and motorcaravans. A very small area (no electricity) is reserved for up to ten tents. Families with children may prefer the grass area.

Facilities

Two modern, well appointed and heated toilet blocks are of the usual high standard, with en-suite facilities for disabled visitors in one block. Baby/toddler washroom. Laundry room. Motorcaravan service point. The office stocks basic provisions. Tourist information room. Good play areas. TV socket and lead. WiFi in one area. Off site: Wheelchair hire in Nene Park. Steam railway 500 yards. Bus Service 800 yards. Pitch and putt 800 yards. Nearest shops 1 mile. Restaurants within 0.5 miles. Peterborough, lido, night clubs and supermarkets 3 miles.

Open: All year.

Directions

From south on A1, do not turn onto A1139, but turn left, 1 mile on, at next junction (signed Showground, Chesterton, Alwalton) and left onto the A605 (Peterborough). Straight on at three roundabouts (Nene Park). At fourth roundabout, left into Ham Lane (Nene Park and Ferry Meadows). Site is on the left 300 yards beyond level crossing. O.S.GR: TL151972. GPS: 52.55789, -0.30221

Charges guide

Per person	£ 4.50 - £ 6.00
pitch incl. electricity (non-member)	£ 11.70 - £ 14.55

Pidley

Stroud Hill Park

Fen Road, Pidley PE28 3DE (Cambridgeshire) T: **01487 741333**. E: **stroudhillpark@btconnect.com**
alanrogers.com/UK3575

Opened in 2003 as an all year round, adult only site Stroud Hill Park is a well-designed, high quality park; a credit to its owners, David and Jayne Newman. The park has been landscaped to create a terraced effect and now incorporates a large fishing lake. There are no half measures here and everything has been well thought out. There are 60 large, slightly sloping pitches, of which 44 are hardstanding, and fully serviced with electricity (16A), fresh water and drainage. The hedges and shrubs around the site are young and need time to mature, but an atmosphere and character has quickly developed. Affiliated to the Caravan Club, non-members are equally welcome.

Facilities

Toilets and spacious en-suite shower facilities are located in the main building along with a very well equipped room for disabled visitors. Good size laundry room. Small, licensed shop stocks basic provisions, home-made cakes, local produce, gas and camping accessories. Attractive bar and café/restaurant. Fishing (£5 per day). All-weather tennis court. Off site: Golf adjacent. Rding 0.5 miles. Cambridge, Ely, Huntingdon and St Ives within easy reach.

Open: All year.

Directions

Leave A1 near Huntingdon, take A14 east. Leave A14 at A141, signed March. In Warboys, at roundabout, turn right on B1040 signed Pidley. In Pidley turn left just beyond church, Fen Road. Site is about 1 mile on right. O.S.GR: TL335787. GPS: 52.38926, -0.03966

Charges guide

Per unit incl. 2 persons and electricity	£ 23.50 - £ 26.00
extra person	£ 2.50

Sheringham
Kelling Heath Holiday Park

Weybourne, Holt, Sheringham NR25 7HW (Norfolk) T: 01263 588181. E: info@kellingheath.co.uk
alanrogers.com/UK3430

Not many parks can boast their own railway station and Kelling Heath's own halt on the North Norfolk Steam Railway gives access to shopping in Holt or the beach at Sheringham. Set in 250 acres of woodland and heathland overlooking the north Norfolk coast, this spacious holiday park offers freedom and relaxation with 300 touring pitches, all with 16A electricity (some are fully serviced) in four different zones. Pitching is good on quite firm, level grass (no hardstanding). Together with 384 caravan holiday homes (36 to let, the rest privately owned), they blend easily into the part-wooded, part-open heath. A wide range of facilities provides activities for all ages. 'The Forge' has an entertainment bar, an adult only bar and a family room, with comprehensive entertainment all season. 'Fitness Express' provides an indoor pool, spa pool, sauna, steam rooms and gym. An adventure playground with assault course is near. The reception area is attractively paved to provide a 'village store' and an open air bandstand where one can sit and enjoy the atmosphere. The park's natural environment allows for woodland walks, a nature trail and cycling trails, and a small lake for fishing (permit). Other amenities include two tennis courts, a small, outdoor heated fun pool and play areas (some rather hidden from the pitches).

Facilities

Three toilet blocks serve the touring pitches, one heated and with a conservatory providing covered access all year to disabled people, baby room and dishwashing and laundry sinks. All blocks have a few washbasins in private cubicles, baby baths and, in season, a nappy disposal service. Laundry facilities. Shop. Gas supplies. Bar, restaurant and takeaway. Indoor leisure centre with pool (19 x 9 m), gym, etc. with trained staff (membership on either daily or weekly basis). Outdoor pool (main season). Adventure play area. Tennis. Fishing. Bicycle hire. Entertainment. Environmental 'Acorn Club' for children. Torches useful. Off site: The coast and the Norfolk Broads National Park are nearby.

Open: 10 February - 12 December.

Directions

On A148 road from Holt to Cromer, after High Kelling, turn left just before Bodham village (international sign) signed Weybourne. Follow road for about 1 mile to park O.S.GR: TG117418. GPS: 52.92847, 1.13663

Charges guide

Per unit incl. electricity	£ 16.75 - £ 33.00
with full services	£ 21.75 - £ 35.50
dog (max. 2)	£ 3.00 - £ 5.00
awning	£ 2.00 - £ 5.00

Min 7 day stay in high season.
No single sex groups.

Sheringham
Woodlands Caravan Park
Holt Road, Upper Sheringham NR26 8TU (Norfolk) T: **01263 823802**
E: **enquiries@woodlandscaravanpark.co.uk alanrogers.com/UK3435**

This pleasantly wooded caravan park is set in the beautiful surroundings of North Norfolk's protected heathland, next to Sheringham Park (National Trust). There are many lovely walks all around the area, including one to the beach (1.5 miles). The park is within easy reach of Holt, Cromer and Sheringham, with the major bird watching areas of Blakeney, Cley and Salthouse also within 30 minutes drive. There are 225 touring pitches in two main areas for caravans and motorcaravans (tents are not accepted). Electricity (10A) is available to most. The excellent Pinewood Park Leisure Club is adjacent to the park offering swimming and other fitness facilities at a discounted rate for those staying at Woodlands.

Facilities
Three well maintained toilet blocks provide good facilities and include facilities for disabled visitors, baby changing and laundry. Well stocked shop. Gas supplies. Lounge bar and family bar with musical entertainment most weekends. Barbecues. Play area (2 acres, fenced and gated). Pinewood Park Leisure Club with indoor pool, gym, sauna etc. Off site: Golf and bicycle hire 1.5 miles. Fishing and riding 3 miles.

Open: March - October.

Directions
From Cromer on the A148 towards Holt, pass signs for Sheringham Park and site is on right just before Bodham village. From Holt on A148 just after Bodham, site is on left, well signed. O.S.GR: TG130409. GPS: 52.92363, 1.19444

Charges guide
Per unit incl. electricity	£ 15.50 - £ 18.50
awning	£ 2.50

WOODLANDS CARAVAN PARK
North Norfolk Coast
Woodlands Caravan Park is situated in a pleasantly wooded site in the most historical and beautiful conservation area of Norfolk. It is ideally placed for the North Norfolk Coast and has extensive onsite facilities including a leisure club with 25m indoor swimming pool, gym and six rink indoor bowling green

Holt Road, Upper Sheringham, Norfolk NR26 8TU
Tel: 01263 823802 www.woodlandscaravanpark.co.uk
 Online Booking

Swaffham
Breckland Meadows Touring Park
Lynn Road, Swaffham PE37 7PT (Norfolk) T: **01760 721246**. E: **info@brecklandmeadows.co.uk**
alanrogers.com/UK3470

Within easy reach of the historic market town of Swaffham, this 'adult only' park offers peace and tranquillity and would make a good base to explore East Anglia and the local area. There are just 45 pitches, 25 on hardstanding, the remainder on fairly level, neat grass. All have 16A electricity. There are two main roads close to the park but well established hedges and trees help minimise any noise. The Swaefas Way runs alongside the park and from this walkers can access the famous Peddars Way.

Facilities
The neat, well cared for toilet block provides all the usual facilities, including spacious showers and a separate toilet and washbasin unit for disabled visitors. Laundry room. Gas supplies. WiFi. Off site: Town 0.5 miles. Bicycle hire 1 mile. Golf 2 miles. Riding 4 miles. Fishing 5 miles.

Open: All year.

Directions
Park is just west of Swaffham on the old A47, about 1 mile from the town centre. O.S.GR: TF809094. GPS: 52.65115, 0.67687

Charges guide
Per unit incl. 2 persons, electricity	£ 11.75 - £ 13.50
extra person	£ 3.00
No credit cards.	

Woodbridge
The Moon & Sixpence
Newbourne Road, Waldringfield, Woodbridge IP12 4PP (Suffolk) T: 01473 736650
E: info@moonandsixpence.eu alanrogers.com/UK3320

This excellent site offers 60 large touring pitches that are positioned in the centre of an established and very spacious caravan holiday home park. The site is extremely well maintained and all the 60 touring pitches are equipped with 5A electricity, TV point, water tap and a drain. In the centre of the site and easily accessible to all, is an unsupervised lake with a sandy beach. An area at one end of the lake is set aside for ten pitches for adults only, all with views of the lake.

Facilities

Exceptionally well finished, centrally placed unisex sanitary block consists of 11 fully equipped private rooms containing a selection of WCs, washbasins and showers and baths. No specific facilities for disabled visitors but access to the block is via a ramp. Laundry facilities. Well stocked shop. Bar and restaurant (main season). TV room. Two adventure play areas. Dog walk trails. Off site: Boat launching 2 miles. Fishing 2 miles, bicycle hire and riding 5 miles.

Open: 1 April - 31 October.

Directions

From the A12 (Ipswich - Lowestoft) turn right at roundabout, towards Waldringfield and follow signs to site. Turn left at Waldringfield Golf Club to site on the left. O.S.GR: TM260457. GPS: 52.06252, 1.29858

Charges 2010

Per person (over 2 yrs) incl. unit and services	£ 9.00 - £ 15.00

Min. charges apply. Max. length 6.5 m.

Woodbridge
Moat Barn Touring Caravan Park
Dallinghoo Road, Bredfield, Woodbridge IP13 6BD (Suffolk) T: 01473 737520
alanrogers.com/UK3330

Mike Allen opened this small touring park in April 2000 on the Suffolk Heritage Cycle Route, and also the Hull - Harwich National Cycle Route. The main touring area is bordered by established hedging and incorporates a circular roadway. The park currently provides 25 level grass pitches, all with electricity (10A), and there are plans to extend the number of pitches to 34. The park is popular with both walkers and cyclists and provides a tranquil environment to explore nearby Woodbridge and surrounding areas. The park has limited provision for large units. There are no facilities for children.

Facilities

The well equipped sanitary block can be heated. A separate unit houses a dishwashing sink. Motorcaravan service point. Bicycle hire. Laundry and shop planned. Off site: Nearby pub serving food. Public footpath.

Open: 1 March - 15 January.

Directions

Park is midway between Woodbridge and Wickham Market. From A12 take turning signed Bredfield (left from south, right from north). In Bredfield turn right and follow road past pub and church. Continue through bends and site entrance is on left in 200 yds. O.S.GR: TM270537. GPS: 52.13510, 1.31710

Charges guide

Per unit incl. 2 persons and electricity	£ 14.00

Woodbridge
Run Cottage Touring Park
Alderton Road, Hollesey, Woodbridge IP12 3RQ (Suffolk) T: 01394 411309. E: contact@run-cottage.co.uk
alanrogers.com/UK3322

This small and very attractive 20 pitch site in the heart of unspoilt Suffolk countryside offers an opportunity to explore many of the local attractions on Suffolk's 'Heritage Coast'. Facilities on the site are limited but certainly adequate and the resident owners, Michele and Andy Stebbens, are always available to ensure that you have an enjoyable stay. The site is open all year round and all pitches have 10A electricity, with six on hardstanding. This is a popular site and advance booking is strongly recommended. Local attractions include Sutton Hoo, Orford Castle and Framlingham Castle. The market town of Woodbridge is only six miles away. Within a short drive are the pretty coastal towns of Southwold, Dunwich, Orford and Aldeborough.

Facilities

New, well finished sanitary block is easily accessed and is well equipped. Reception contains a comprehensive selection of tourist leaflets and details of local attractions. Off site: Excellent pubs and restaurants within 1 mile. Riding 1 mile. Beach 1.5 miles. Fishing 1.5 miles. Golf and bicycle hire 5 miles.

Open: All year.

Directions

From A12 turn right at roundabout at Melton onto A1152 (Bawdsey, Orford). In 1.5 miles, at roundabout, turn right onto B1083 (Bawdsey). In 0.75 miles take left fork to Hollesley. At Duck Corner crossroads, turn right and through village to site on the left, 100 yds past Red Brick Bridge. Don't follow SatNav directions. O.S.GR: TM351442. GPS: 52.04503, 1.42683

Charges guide

Per unit incl. 2 persons and electricity	£ 16.00
tent incl. 2 persons	£ 14.00
extra person (over 3 yrs)	£ 2.50

Spanning central Eng
from the ancient bor
of Wales on the wes
across to Lincolnshire
the east coast, the Heart
England is rich in glorious ro
countryside, magnificent castles
stately houses and beautiful ga

THE REGION COMPRISES LINCOLNSHIRE, RUTLAND, NORTHAMPTONSHIRE, NOTTINGHAMSHIRE, WEST MIDLANDS, DERBYSHIRE, STAFFORDSHIRE, LEICESTERSHIRE, WARWICKSHIRE, HEREFORDSHIRE, WORCESTERSHIRE, GLOUCESTERSHIRE & SHROPSHIRE

The charming and diverse countryside of the Heart of England includes: the Lincolnshire Wolds, with the dramatic open landscape of the Fens; the ragged crags, dales and moorland of the Peak District National Park in Derbyshire and Staffordshire; the heathered hilltops of Shropshire; the famous Sherwood Forest, in the heart of Nottinghamshire; and the miles of lush green countryside of Herefordshire, dotted with black and white timber houses. Rutland Water is a mecca for watersports and the whole region offers superb opportunities for walking, cycling and more daring activities such as rock climbing and caving. The Cotswolds to the west of the region is the largest area of Outstanding Natural Beauty in England and Wales. Here you will find many traditional English villages, with charming country pubs and cottage gardens. Another significant feature of the region are the rivers and canals. Passing pretty towns and villages, a large canal network threads its way through the area, weaving through the Lincolnshire Fens, past the waterside bars and restaurants of Birmingham and along to estuaries of the rivers of Severn and Avon.

Places of interest

Lincolnshire: Belvoir Castle near Grantha

Rutland: market towns of Oakham and Uppingham.

Northamptonshire: Silverstone; Althorp Ho

Nottinghamshire: Nottingham Castle.

West Midlands: Birmingham; Cadbury W

Derbyshire: Bakewell; Buxton; Chatsworth House.

Staffordshire: Alton Towers; Stoke-on-Tre

Leicestershire: Snibston Discovery Park; Twycross Zoo.

Warwickshire: Warwick Castle; Stratford-upon-Avon.

Herefordshire: Hereford Cathedral.

Worcestershire: West Midland Safari Par

Gloucestershire: Sudeley Castle; Chelten

Shropshire: Shrewsbury and Whitchurch

Did you know?

Herefordshire is one of the largest apple cider producers in the world.

The World Toe Wrestling Championship held every June in Wetton, is a registere international sport.

The hollow trunk of the 'Mighty Tree' in Sherwood Forest is reputedly where Rob Hood and his Merry Men hid from the Sheriff of Nottingham.

Quite different from the more familiar ta the Bakewell pudding was first created the 1860s.

Rutland is the smallest county in Britain, measuring just 16 miles by 16 miles.

The Peak District contains over 50 reser including Ladybower, where the bouncin bomb used in World War II was tested.

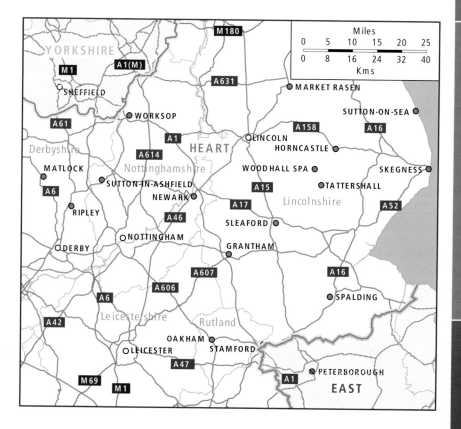

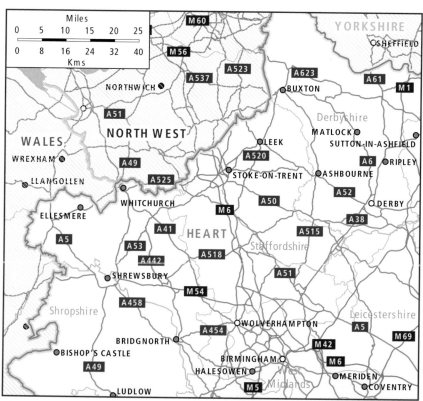

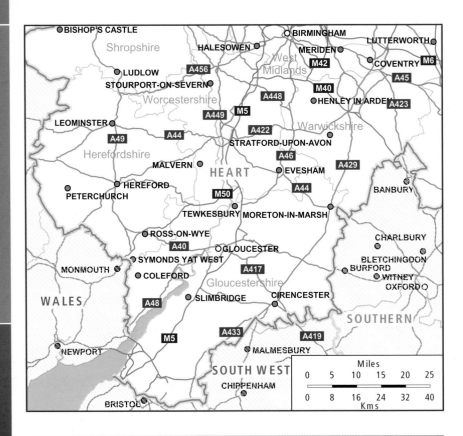

Ashbourne

Callow Top Holiday Park

Buxton Road, Sandybrook, Ashbourne DE6 2AQ (Derbyshire) T: **01335 344020**. E: **enquiry@callowtop.co.uk**
alanrogers.com/UK3855

Situated just north of the market town of Ashbourne, Callow Top nestles within an elevated country setting. The park's location makes it well placed to allow visitors to explore the picturesque villages, bustling market towns and the many attractions of the Peak District. It is ideal for both walking and cycling holidays. Spread over seven separate areas, there are 200 flat pitches of which 100 are for touring units. Those on hardstanding have 10A electricity, the grass pitches have no power supply. Water points tend to be rather scarce. Some of the pitches are rather small and on these, cars are parked away from the pitch. The focal point of the park is an old farmhouse which has been converted into an 'Olde English' style inn/restaurant serving real ale brewed in its own brewery and a good selection of pub food. The Inn also has a family room and a large beer garden. There are also cottages and caravan holiday homes for rent. Dove Dale, Tissington and High Peak trails and the Manifold Valley are nearby.

Facilities

Three heated toilet blocks (only one open in low season) provide unisex showers (20p). Toilet for disabled visitors. Laundry room. Chemical disposal point but no motorcaravan service point. Calor gas. Shop. Inn/restaurant. Snack bar and takeaway. Heated swimming and paddling pools (May - Sept). Bicycle hire. Games room. Play area. Entertainment (w/ends and high season). Fishing. Winter caravan storage. Off site: Golf 1.5 miles. Riding 3 miles. Ashbourne (supermarket etc) 1 mile. Carsington Water (boat launching) 4 miles. Alton Towers 10 miles.

Open: 14 March - 9 November.

Directions

At Sandybrook, 0.5 miles north of Ashbourne, turn left off the A515 (Ashbourne - Buxton) into site road. Site is signed. O.S.GR: SK179483.
GPS: 53.02693, -1.74646

Charges guide

Per unit incl. 2 persons	£ 14.50 - £ 17.50
incl. hardstanding and electricity	£ 18.00 - £ 21.00
extra person	£ 2.50
child (4-16 yrs)	£ 1.50

Ashbourne

Rivendale Caravan & Leisure Park

Buxton Road, Alsop-en-le-Dale, Ashbourne DE6 1QU (Derbyshire) T: **01335 310311**
E: enquiries@rivendalecaravanpark.co.uk **alanrogers.com/UK3850**

This unusual park has been developed in the bowl of a hill quarry which was last worked over 50 years ago. The steep quarry walls shelter three sides with marvellous views over the Peak National Park countryside to the south. A wide access road passes the renovated stone building which houses reception, a shop, bar and a café/restaurant. It gently climbs to a horseshoe shaped area providing 136 pitches some of which are rather small but most are of a generous size, with 16A electricity. The pitches are a mixture of hardstanding and grass, and are divided by shrubs. A further, open, marked grass area is accessed by hardcore roads. All the pitches are within easy reach of the central stone-built toilet block which is in keeping with the environment and thoughtfully provided with under-floor heating. The park takes up about 11 acres and a further 26 acres belong to the owners with certain parts suitable for walking – a must to appreciate the Derbyshire countryside with its dry stone walls, wild flowers and a little more of the quarry history. The park is situated almost on the Tissington Trail for walking or off road cycling and linking with the High Peak and Monsal Dale Trail. Other spectacular walks and cycle rides run along the Manifold, Wye and Dove valleys.

Facilities

First rate toilet facilities include some washbasins in cubicles for ladies, and an excellent en-suite room for disabled visitors. Laundry room. Glass and paper recycling bins. Shop (all essentials). Bar (evenings) and café with home-made and local food (open mornings, lunch and evenings, both with limited opening in low season). Packed lunches from reception. Special events monthly and games in main season. Hot tubs for hire, delivered to your pitch. Accommodation for hire. WiFi. Off site: Bicycle hire and riding 5 miles. Sailing and boat launching 8 miles. Fishing and golf 10 miles. Alton Towers 35 minutes drive. Chatsworth House and Gardens, Heights of Abraham and Guillivers Kingdom near.

Open: All year excl. 9 January - 2 February.

Directions

Park is 7 miles north of Ashbourne on the A515 to Buxton, on the eastern side of the road. It is well signed between the turnings east to Alsop Moor and Matlock (A5012), but take care as this is a very fast section of the A515. O.S.GR: SK161566. GPS: 53.106383, -1.760567

Charges guide

Per unit incl. 2 persons and electricity	£ 14.50 - £ 19.00
extra person	£ 2.50
child (4-15 yrs)	£ 2.00
dog	£ 1.00

Camping Cheques accepted.

Bishop's Castle

The Green Caravan Park

Wentnor, Bishop's Castle SY9 5EF (Shropshire) T: **01588 650605**. E: karen@greencaravanpark.co.uk
alanrogers.com/UK4440

Remotely situated in a pleasant valley, in a designated Area of Outstanding Natural Beauty, and sandwiched between the Stipperstones and The Long Mynd, the Green would make an ideal base for some serious walking or cycling. The 15-acre site is very natural, and is divided into several fields. There are 160 pitches, taking 40 seasonal units, and around 20 holiday homes, with approximately 140 pitches for tourists (42 with 16A electric hook-ups). The main field has some hardstandings. The East Onny is a small, shallow river which runs through the site, much enjoyed by the youngsters.

Facilities

One main sanitary block, rather austere in appearance, built into the side of a large barn. However it provides adequate and plentiful facilities with spacious new hot showers (on payment) and laundry facilities, but there is no dedicated unit for disabled people. Small shop with reception. Playground. Gazebos by prior arrangement. Off site: Four pubs within 3 miles. Fishing 3 miles. Riding 4 miles. Bishops Castle with museums. Leisure Centre. Stapely Hill historic trail. Gliding club.

Open: Easter - 31 October.

Directions

Wentnor lies southwest of Shrewsbury, and to the west of Church Stretton. From Shrewsbury take A488 south for 21 miles. At Lydham Heath turn east on A489 for 0.75 miles, then north on minor road (Wentnor and campsite). Follow signs for 3 miles. Site immediately after The Inn on the Green. O.S.GR: SO381933. GPS: 52.53375, -2.91375

Charges guide

Per unit incl. 2 persons and electricity	£ 13.50 - £ 15.00
extra person	£ 3.00
child (3-14 yrs)	£ 2.50
dog	£ 1.00

Bridgnorth

Stanmore Hall Touring Park

Stourbridge Road, Bridgnorth WV15 6DT (Shropshire) T: 01746 761761. E: stanmore@morris-leisure.co.uk

alanrogers.com/UK4400

This good quality park is situated in the former grounds of Stanmore Hall, where the huge lily pond, fine mature trees and beautifully manicured lawns give a mark of quality. There are 135 generously sized pitches, 130 with 16A electricity including 30 hardstanding 'super' pitches with TV connections. A limited number of 'standard' hardstanding pitches are also available, but most are on grass. Some pitches are reserved for adult only use (over 18 years). Access and internal roads are tarmac; site lighting is adequate and reassuring. Reception is located within the shop. A member of the Caravan Club's 'managed under contract' scheme, non-members are also very welcome at this park.

Facilities	Directions
Access to the centrally heated sanitary block is by key. Facilities are excellent and incude a room for disabled people and baby care. Full laundry facilities. Motorcaravan service points. Shop, including caravan accessories and repair items. Play area. Dogs are limited to two per unit. Off site: Fishing 1.5 miles. Golf and Riding 2 miles.	Site is 1.5 miles from Bridgnorth on the A458 (signed Stourbridge). O.S.GR: SO744922. GPS: 52.52715, -2.378617

Open: All year.

Charges guide

Per unit with 2 persons, electricity	£ 18.10 - £ 23.30
extra person	£ 5.00 - £ 6.40

Buxton

Lime Tree Park

Dukes Drive, Buxton SK17 9RP (Derbyshire) T: 01298 22988. E: info@limetreeparkbuxton.co.uk

alanrogers.com/UK3840

A select park with high quality, modern facilities, Lime Tree is in a convenient, edge of town location that makes a very good base for touring the Peak District. There are 99 pitches including 36 seasonal, 28 privately owned mobile homes and 12 caravan holiday homes to rent. The 64 with 10A electricity (hardstandings available) and an area for tents (some terracing but mainly sloping ground) are on the two upper terraces which have the best views but are slightly more exposed. Below are areas set aside for late arrivals and the mobile homes. With good views, the park is situated next to a thickly wooded, limestone gorge and a magnificent old railway viaduct provides a dramatic backdrop.

Facilities	Directions
A modern toilet building serves the caravan and motorcaravan area, including some washbasins in cubicles, controllable showers, a baby room with the very latest design of baby bath, and a family room with facilities for disabled people. The refitted original unit serves the tent area. Both units can be heated and have top quality fittings. Laundry room with washing machine and dryer. Motorcaravan service area. Shop. Basic play area. Games/TV room. Off site: T Fishing, bicycle hire, sailing and boat launching 5 miles. Alton Towers 22 miles.	Park is on outskirts of Buxton and is signed from A515 Buxton - Ashbourne road 1 mile south of town. From town, immediately after hospital bear sharp left into Dukes Drive, go under railway viaduct and site is on the right. From south watch out for sharp turn right at foot of hill (signed in advance). O.S.GR: SK069725. GPS: 53.250230, -1.896673

Open: 1 March - 31 October.

Charges guide

Per unit incl. 2 persons and electricity	£ 20.00
extra person	£ 6.00
child (5-15 yrs)	£ 3.00

Buxton

Clover Fields Touring Caravan Park

1 Heath View, Harpur Hill, Buxton SK17 9PU (Derbyshire) T: 01298 78731. E: cloverfields@tiscali.co.uk

alanrogers.com/UK3845

Stephen and Jan Redfern are more than happy to welcome you to their family owned park. It is located on the outskirts of the beautiful spa town of Buxton within easy reach of the magnificent Peak District National Park. You will be able to relax here in the 'away from it all' atmosphere. There are just 25 pitches, part hardstanding and part grass, all with 16A electricity, a water tap and a barbecue. They are divided by low hedges which have yet to mature. There is also a large field for tents. There is a little noise from the adjacent road. The site has its own animals which are happy to be spoiled by visitors.

Facilities	Directions
The toilet and shower block is modern and clean. Facilities for disabled visitors. Gas. Laundry room. Motorcaravan service point. Small shop selling essentials, home made jam and chutney and caravan accessories. Newspapers and milk delivered to your pitch. Towing and pitching courses. Small library. Torches recommended. Off site: Supermarket and fish and chip shop in Buxton. Opera House and Pavilion. Golf 3 miles. Riding 6 miles. Bicycle hire 6 miles.	From Buxton, at Harpur Hill just to the southeast, turn right off the A515 (Buxton - Ashbourne) onto the B5053. Turn immediately right towards Harpur Hill. Site is 0.5 miles on the left. O.S.GR: SK075704. GPS: 53.23066, -1.8878

Open: All year.

Charges guide

Per unit incl. 2 persons and electricity	£ 14.00
extra person (over 5 yrs)	£ 4.00
No credit cards.	

Buxton
Longnor Wood Holiday Park

Newtown, Longnor, Buxton SK17 0NG (Derbyshire) T: **01298 83648**. E: info@longnorwood.co.uk
alanrogers.com/UK3980

A secluded rural location, deep in the heart of the Peak District, Longnor Wood is an 'adult only' park (over 18 yrs) and an ideal environment for a relaxing break from the outside world. It is a good base for walking, red deer and bird watching (barn owls) and serious cycling – the area is very hilly. There are 47 touring pitches plus an additional 13 pitches for holiday homes. Pitches are level, some on small terraces, all with 10A electric hook-ups. There are 17 with multi-services (electricity, water, waste water and TV connections) and 40 on half hardstanding and half grass.

Facilities	Directions
The single heated building has modern facilities and includes cubicles with a toilet and washbasin and spacious showers. Freezer for ice packs and a microwave oven (donations to charity). Laundry facilities. Reception stocks basics. Putting green, badminton and boules. Dogs accepted, max. 2. RVs accepted by appointment. WiFi. Off site: Markets in Buxton 6 miles (Tues/Sat). Riding 4 miles. Fishing 5 miles. Bicycle hire 6.5 miles. Golf 8 miles.	Longnor village is on the B5053, about 6 miles south of Buxton. At crossroads in village square, turn right. Take left turn after 1.25 miles and then immediately right. Also signed from the A53 between Leek and Buxton, turning next at the Winking Man pub. O.S.GR: SK072640. GPS: 53.17086, -1.90042

Open: All year excl. 11 January - 28 February.

Charges guide

Per unit incl. 2 persons, electricity	£ 19.00 - £ 20.00
extra person	£ 6.00

Cirencester
Hoburne Cotswold

Broadway Lane, South Cerney, Cirencester GL7 5UQ (Gloucestershire) T: **01285 860216**
E: enquiries@hoburne.co.uk **alanrogers.com/UK4100**

Since this park is adjacent to the Cotswold Water Park, those staying here will have easy access to the varied watersports available. On the park itself there is a lake with pedaloes and canoes for hire. Its wide range of other amenities includes outdoor and indoor heated swimming pools and an impressive indoor leisure complex. There are 200 well marked touring pitches for any type of unit, all with hardstanding (only fairly level) and a grass surround for awning or tent; 90 are serviced 'super' pitches. Of good size but with nothing between them, all have electricity (some need long leads). Part of the Hoburne group.

Facilities	Directions
Six small toilet blocks are clean and well maintained. Baby room. Basic facilities for disabled visitors. The site has heavy weekend trade. Launderette. Supermarket. Indoor leisure complex including pool, spa bath, sauna, steam room and sun bed. Outdoor pool (Whitsun - early Sept). Clubhouse with bar, food and entertainment. Tennis. Adventure playground. Crazy golf. Fishing lake. Dogs are not accepted.	Three miles southeast of Cirencester on A419, turn west towards Cotswold Water Park at new roundabout on bypass onto B4696. Take second right and follow signs. O.S.GR: SU055957. GPS: 51.66018, -1.91910

Open: March - October.

Charges guide

Per unit incl. max. 6 persons	£ 12.50 - £ 32.00

Cleethorpes
Thorpe Park Holiday Centre

Humberston, Cleethorpes DN35 0PW (Lincolnshire) T: **01472 813395**
alanrogers.com/UK3655

Thorpe Park is a Haven Holiday Park at Cleethorpes on the north Lincolnshire coast. The touring site, although part of one of the largest caravan holiday parks in Europe, is neat and compact. There are 69 landscaped 'Euro' pitches with brick-built hardstandings, electricity, water and drain and a further 55 in an open area, most with electricity available. There is direct access to the beach from one corner of the site and the park's main entertainment complex is a short walk away. A shuttle 'train' will take you to more distant parts of the park, including a nine-hole golf course. Outside the park there are shops within walking distance, not to mention Pleasure Island, and buses run the couple of miles into Cleethorpes with its shops, bars, restaurants and entertainment.

Facilities	Directions
Two modern toilet blocks. The newer, smaller block in the open area has fairly basic shower cubicles and open washbasins. Motorcaravan services. Supermarket. Fish & Chips. Launderette. Bicycle and buggy hire. Entertainment complex including 'Showbar', café bar, amusements and games room. Heated indoor pool and outdoor flumes, splash zone. Play area. Crazy golf. Tennis. Fishing lakes. Wild flower meadow. 9-hole and family golf courses.	Cleethorpes is 2 miles southeast of Grimsby and 60 miles east of Doncaster. From M180 take A180 to Grimsby, turn south on A16 towards Louth, then east on A1098 to Humberston and follow signs for Pleasure Island and Holiday Parks. Park is to right at roundabout. O.S.GR: TA328059. GPS: 53.533178, 0.003272

Open: Easter - 2 November.

See advertisement on page 349

Charges guide

Per unit incl. up to 4 persons	£ 10.00 - £ 86.00
extra person	£ 2.00 - £ 3.00

167

Coleford

Forest Holidays Christchurch

Bracelands Drive, Christchurch, Coleford GL16 7NN (Gloucestershire) T: **01594 837258**
E: **info@forestholidays.co.uk** **alanrogers.com/UK4160**

Forest Holidays is a partnership between the Forestry Commission and The Camping and Caravanning Club. With 280 unmarked pitches, this 20 acre site occupies an undulating, open grassy area in the heart of the Forest of Dean. There are around 60 seasonal units, seven hardstandings and 95 pitches with electrical hook-ups (10A). The reception also houses a well stocked licensed shop and has a good selection of tourist information, including a leaflet about the local forest trails. Tenters will appreciate the large pavilion in the centre of the site, a large common room with a wood burning stove, tables and chairs – an ideal retreat if the weather proves inclement. Symonds Yat Rock is within walking distance with spectacular views over the Wye Valley and also nearby are Clearwell Caves, ancient iron mines and Dean Forest Railway.

Facilities

Four sanitary units, two fairly modern with spacious well equipped showers, some vanity style basins with dividers, plus two much older units with WCs and washbasins only. The central block has a laundry and dishwashing room. Units for disabled people and baby changing in two blocks. Adventure playground on bark. Dogs are not accepted. Off site: Fishing and swimming 1 mile. Coleford 1.5 miles. Golf 2 miles. Bicycle hire 3 miles. Ross-on-Wye 8 miles. Riding 10 miles.

Open: All year.

Directions

From Monmouth take the A4136 east for 5 miles turning north at crossroads at Pike House Inn and site is on the left after 0.5 miles. From centre of Coleford take road towards Monmouth, turning right to Symonds Yat and Berry Hill (site signed). O.S.GR: SO569129. GPS: 51.813333, -2.62735

Charges guide

| Per unit incl. 2 persons | £ 8.00 - £ 19.50 |
| extra person | £ 4.25 - £ 6.25 |

Coventry

Hollyfast Caravan Park

Wall Hill Road, Allesley, Coventry CV5 9EL (Warwickshire) T: **02476 336411**
E: **sales@hollyfastcaravanpark.co.uk** **alanrogers.com/UK4075**

Hollyfast is situated in beautiful countryside on the outskirts of Coventry, part of the park being set within a lovely woodland area giving peace and tranquillity all year round. Located on the Birmingham side of Coventry, this means a five minute drive into the centre of Coventry and just a ten minute drive to Birmingham's National Exhibition Centre. You will receive a friendly welcome and be directed to a very clean and well spaced site with 40 pitches of varying sizes with 16A electricity connections. You may be asked to park your car on a nearby car park.

Facilities

The modern toilet block provides simple clean facilities with good sized showers (3 per sex) and open washbasins. Toilet and shower for disabled campers. Games room. Club house for rallies. Deposit for barrier (£25). Off site: The local area has shops, three pubs (hot and cold food), a golf course and a riding centre. Bus stop 1 mile for Coventry. Interesting British Road Transport museum. Birmingham, Stratford-upon-Avon, Leamington Spa and Warwick are within driving distance.

Open: All year.

Directions

From M1/M45 (or the M40/A46, or M69/A46) take A45 towards Birmingham. Turn right on A4114 and follow brown and white caravan signs. After turning by the White Lion pub, site is 0.5 miles on the left. From the north take M6 north of Birmingham or the M1 north (Nottingham) follow M42 to NEC, A45 towards Coventry and onto A4114 and as above. O.S.GR: SP303831. GPS: 52.44588, -1.55572

Charges guide

| Per unit incl. 2 persons and electricity | £ 14.50 - £ 19.00 |
| extra person | £ 1.50 - £ 2.50 |

Ellesmere

Fernwood Caravan Park

Lyneal, Ellesmere SY12 0QF (Shropshire) T: **01948 710221**. E: **enquiries@fernwoodpark.co.uk**

alanrogers.com/UK4380

Fernwood is set in an area known as the Shropshire 'Lake District' – the mere at Ellesmere is the largest of nine meres – and the picturesque Shropshire Union Canal is only a few minutes walk. The park itself is a real oasis of calm and rural tranquillity with its floral landscaping, setting and attention to detail all of a very high standard, and the planted and natural vegetation blend harmoniously. In addition to 165 caravan holiday homes, used normally only by their owners, the park takes 30 caravans, motorcaravans or trailer tents (but not other tents) in several well cut, grassy enclosures (including 30 seasonal long stay). Some are in light woodland, others in more open, but still relatively sheltered situations. All pitches have electricity and six have water and drainage. One area is set aside for adults only. Siting is made by the management and there is always generous spacing, even when the site is full.

Facilities

The small toilet block for tourers has background heating for cooler days and includes some washbasins in cabins and limited facilities for disabled people. No dishwashing sinks. Basic motorcaravan services. Laundry room near shop and adjacent are WCs for ladies and men. Shop doubles as reception (from 1/4-30/10, hours vary). Coarse fishing lake. 40 acres of woodland for walking. Play area on grass.

Open: 1 March - 30 November.

Directions

Park is just northeast of Lyneal village, signed southwest off the B5063 Ellesmere - Wem road, 1.5 miles from junction of the B5063 with the A495. O.S.GR: SJ452338. GPS: 52.899167, -2.816017

Charges guide

Per unit incl. 2 persons, electricity	£ 19.00 - £ 24.00
multi-service pitch	£ 3.50
awning	free - £ 3.00

One night free for every 7 booked in advance.

FERNWOOD CARAVAN PARK

- ESTABLISHED FAMILY-RUN PARK
- PEACEFUL WOODLAND SETTING
- TOURERS WELCOME
- ALL PITCHES HAVE ELECTRICAL HOOK-UPS
- PICTURESQUE LAKE
- CHILDRENS PLAY AREA
- SHOP
- LAUNDRY

LYNEAL
NR. ELLESMERE
SHROPSHIRE SY12 0QF

www.ranch.co.uk/fernwood.htm

TEL: (01948) 710221

Evesham

Ranch Caravan Park

Honeybourne, Evesham WR11 7PR (Worcestershire) T: **01386 830744**. E: **enquiries@ranch.co.uk**

alanrogers.com/UK4180

Set in the Vale of Evesham, Ranch lies not far from both Evesham and Broadway in quiet rural surroundings of 50 acres and just half an hour's drive from Stratford-on-Avon. The park takes 120 touring units – caravans, motorcaravans or trailer tents, but not other tents – on flat, partly undulating, hedged meadows with well mown grass and a spacious feel. The pitches are not marked but the staff position units. All have electrical connections (10A) and there are 20 hardstandings including eight fully serviced pitches (electricity, TV, water and drainage). There are 169 caravan holiday homes in their own section. The Vale of Evesham is noted for being a sheltered area growing fruit and other produce from early spring through to late autumn.

Facilities

Two very well appointed, modern sanitary blocks with free hot showers and heating. Motorcaravan service point. Shop. Clubhouse (weekends only in early and late season) offering wide range of good value meals and entertainment is arranged at B.H weekends and Saturdays in school holidays. Heated pool (55 x 30 ft; June - Sept). Gym and sauna. Games room with TV. Playground. Off site: Riding and bicycle hire 2 miles. Fishing 4 miles. Golf 6 miles.

Open: 1 March - 30 November.

See advertisement opposite

Directions

From A46 Evesham take B4035 towards Chipping Campden. After Badsey and Bretforton follow signs for Honeybourne down unclassified road (Ryknild Street, Roman road). Park is through village on left by station. O.S.GR: SP112444. GPS: 52.09722, -1.83124

Charges guide

Per unit incl. 2 persons, electricity	£ 19.00 - £ 24.00
incl. water and drainage	£ 22.50 - £ 27.50
extra person (over 5 yrs)	free - £ 4.00
dog	free - £ 2.50

One free night for every 7 booked.

169

Evesham

Weir Meadow Holiday Park

Lower Leys, Evesham WR11 3AA (Worcestershire) T: **01386 442417**

alanrogers.com/UK4185

On entering this park you drive through neat caravan holiday homes surrounded by flowers and shrubs, but his does not prepare you for the view which opens in front of you of 27 touring pitches set out on the banks of the river Avon with splendid vistas of the narrow boats on the river and of the weir itself. The park has 130 caravan holiday homes, eight caravans for hire and 27 touring pitches. Pitches are clearly marked off the tarmac roads and all have electricity. Units over 9 m. may have access problems. There are no facilities for children, but some can be found in the town centre of Evesham, only five minutes' walk away. Visitors to the park should be aware of the dangers of the river and these are clearly signed and the necessary safety equipment provided. Advance booking is necessary most of the year.

Facilities	Directions
Well kept toilet block includes provision for disabled visitors. Excellent laundry area. Barbecue area. Fishing is available (in season with the necessary licence) at £5 per day. Off site: All town centre facilities nearby. River walks. **Open:** 1 March - 31 October.	From the A44 follow signs for Evesham town centre. Go straight across two roundabouts, turn right at second set of traffic lights, then in 80 m. turn left. Site is clearly marked from the A44. O.S.GR: SP041438. GPS: 52.093817, -1.939033

Charges guide	
Per unit incl. 2 persons and electricity	£ 17.00 - £ 24.00

Grantham

Woodland Waters

Willoughby Road, Ancaster, Grantham NG32 3RT (Lincolnshire) T: **01400 230888**

E: **info@woodlandwaters.co.uk** alanrogers.com/UK3765

This attractive holiday park occupies 70 acres of woodland, gently sloping grassland and lakes, with the caravan park itself taking up about 20 of them. The site has 120 pitches although only 60 are regularly used (all with 10A electricity and water taps nearby). There is a rally field of 20 pitches with hook-ups, plus areas for camping and those not requiring hook-ups. The land slopes gently down to the 14-acre lake and the pitches nearer the water are more level, although probably not suitable for those with younger children since there is no fencing.

Facilities	Directions
A single, modern, heated toilet block is well maintained and kept clean. Washbasins (in cubicles for ladies) and free showers (controllable for ladies, push-button for men). A second block will provide extra facilities when the additional camping areas are fully occupied. Small laundry. Motorcaravan service point. Bar and restaurant with takeaway. Play area. Fishing. Off site: Limited bus service near entrance. Shop and trains in village 1 mile. Go-karting and paint-ball 1 mile. Golf 3 miles. Riding 6 miles. **Open:** All year.	Ancaster is 8 miles northeast of Grantham and 19 miles south of Lincoln. The park entrance is off the A153 Grantham - Sleaford road, 600 yards west of the junction with the B6403 High Dyke road (Ermine Street). O.S.GR: SK973437. GPS: 52.98053, -0.54698

Charges guide	
Per unit incl. up to 4 persons	£ 12.00 - £ 14.00
incl. electricity	£ 15.00 - £ 17.00
extra person	£ 1.00 - £ 2.00

Halesowen

Clent Hills Camping & Caravanning Club Site

Fieldhouse Lane, Romsley, Halesowen B62 0NH (West Midlands) T: **01562 710015**

alanrogers.com/UK4040

Conveniently close to Birmingham and only a couple of miles or so off the M5/M42 intersection, this site is a real surprise in terms of being quiet and peaceful and very pretty with good views. Its only disadvantage is that it is on sloping ground, but the present, very helpful holiday site managers are happy to assist in pitching anyone who has a problem in getting level (mainly motorcaravanners); in fact, there are some level pitches and these are all earmarked for motorcaravans. The 95 pitches are all of a good size, 74 with electrical connections (10/16A) and 17 with hardstanding.

Facilities	Directions
The central sanitary toilet block can be heated and provides the latest facilities, including washbasins in cabins, hairdryers, baby room and a toilet and shower for disabled people. It was spotless when last visited. Washing machine, dryer and ironing facilities. Small play area with rubber safety surface. Gas supplies. Caravan storage. Off site: Riding 1 mile. Fishing 3 miles. Golf 7 miles. **Open:** March - November.	From M5 junction 4 take A491, branch right to Romsley on B4551 and watch for site signs in Romsley village by shops. Site is on left. O.S.GR: SO955795. GPS: 52.41469, -2.06814

Charges guide	
Per person	£ 4.90 - £ 7.25
child (6-18 yrs)	£ 2.15 - £ 2.15
non-member pitch fee	£ 5.65

Henley-in-Arden
Island Meadow Caravan Park
The Mill House, Aston Cantlow, Henley-in-Arden B95 6JP (Warwickshire) T: **01789 488273**
E: holiday@islandmeadowcaravanpark.co.uk **alanrogers.com/UK4090**

This peaceful, traditional, family run site is in a rural location, surrounded by the River Alne and its mill race. A good base for walking, cycling and bird watching, it has 80 pitches in total, with 56 holiday homes (four for rent) located around the perimeter. The 24 touring pitches are on the spacious, central grassy area of the site, all have 10A electric hook-ups. Only environmentally friendly groundsheets are permitted. Note: The site is on an island with obvious hazards for small children. There is an excellent playground in the village centre (five minutes walk via footpath across Mill Meadow).

Facilities

Two sanitary units, both heated. The original provides adequate WCs and washbasins for men, and the more modern unit has been provided for women, with a separate access shower unit for the men, and a suite for disabled visitors. Laundry facilities. The millpond and its weir offer good coarse fishing. Off site: The village has its own 'club' (campers welcome) and the local pub serves a good range of meals. Golf 3 miles, riding 4.5 miles, bicycle hire 6 miles. Warwick Castle. Stratford-upon-Avon. Mary Arden's house in Wilmcote is only 1 mile from the site. Buses from village to Alcester and Stratford, including a late night service.

Open: 1 March - 31 October.

Directions

From A46 (Stratford - Alcester) follow signs for Mary Arden's House. At Wilmcote follow signs to Aston Cantlow and site. O.S.GR: SP136598.
GPS: 52.23549, -1.80265

Charges guide

Per unit incl. 2 persons and electricity	£ 17.50
extra person	£ 2.00
child (5-12 yrs)	£ 1.00
tent (2 man)	£ 14.00

Gazebos only by prior arrangement.
No credit cards.

Hereford
Lucksall Caravan & Camping Park
Mordiford, Hereford HR1 4LP (Herefordshire) T: **01432 870213**. E: karen@lucksallpark.co.uk
alanrogers.com/UK4310

Set in around 17 acres on the bank of the River Wye and benefiting from improvements by the new owners, Lucksall has 80 large, well spaced and level touring pitches, of which 80 have 16A electricity and 30 have hardstanding. The river is open to the site but lifebelts and safety messages are in evidence. Canoes are available for hire – or bring your own – and fishing permits may be obtained from reception. A large, fenced new playground and a large grassy area for games are provided. The site shop is well stocked with a variety of goods and gas. A member of the Countryside Discovery group.

Facilities

The main sanitary facilities provide showers (20p) and a separate unit for disabled visitors with ramped entrance, WC, washbasin, shower, hairdryers and hand-dryer. New laundry room. A smaller, refurbished, now c/heated open all times shop (basics only). Fishing. Canoeing. Site barrier (2.13 m. height limit) locked 21.00-09.00 hrs. Off site: Golf 5 miles. Bicycle hire 9 miles.

Open: 1 March - 30 November.

Directions

Between Mordiford and Fownhope, 5 miles southeast of Hereford on B4224, the park is well signed. O.S.GR: SO571355. GPS: 52.02370, -2.63053

Charges guide

Per unit incl. 2 persons	£ 11.00 - £ 14.50
extra person (over 5 yrs)	£ 2.00 - £ 3.00
awning	£ 1.50 - £ 2.00

Hereford
The Millpond Touring Caravans & Camping
Little Tarrington, Hereford HR1 4JA (Herefordshire) T: **01432 890243**. E: enquiries@millpond.co.uk
alanrogers.com/UK4330

This peaceful little site with its own fishing lake is set in 30 acres of countryside. Opened for the first time in 1997, it has 40 large pitches on open grassland, all with electricity hook-ups (10A) and 15 pitches for tents in an adjacent field. Special attention has been made to providing good facilities for disabled visitors. The large fishing lake (unfenced) is well stocked with coarse fish, has facilities for disabled fishermen and offers reduced rates for campers. Site lighting is minimal (local authority regulations) so a torch might be useful for tents. There may be a little noise at times from a railway track nearby.

Facilities

A modern building houses heated sanitary facilities, laundry and dishwashing sinks, baby changing surface, an upgraded unit for disabled persons (with wet room shower) and a common room with a massive supply of tourist information, wildlife charts and walking guides. Site is currently not really suitable for American motorhomes. Off site: The local pub is a 10 minute walk, but there is no shop in the village.

Open: 1 March - 31 October.

Directions

Little Tarrington is midway between Hereford and Ledbury. The site is just north of A438 on eastern edge of Tarrington village (signed).
O.S.GR: SO627409. GPS: 52.06768, -2.54856

Charges guide

Per unit incl. 2 persons, awning,	
electricity and 1 pet	£ 13.00 - £ 16.00
extra person	£ 3.00

Horncastle

Ashby Park

West Ashby, Horncastle LN9 5PP (Lincolnshire) T: 01507 527966. E: ashbyparklakes@aol.com

alanrogers.com/UK3680

Ashby Park is a pleasant, well run site located in 70 acres of former gravel pits that now provide seven attractive fishing lakes. There is a series of clearings occupied by privately owned caravan holiday homes and by 77 touring pitches. Most are on grass, but some have hardstanding. All have access to electricity (16A) and 12 super pitches also have hardstanding, water tap and waste water drain. Lakeside pitches will no doubt appeal to anglers, whereas families with young children will probably prefer to be further away from the lakes, which are inevitably unfenced. This is a peaceful site in an interesting area.

Facilities

Three toilet blocks are well maintained and equipped, with open style washbasins and controllable showers; all hot water is metered (20p). Good en-suite facilities for disabled visitors. Laundry room with washing machine and dryer. Limited dishwashing (in the new block - a long walk from lakeside pitches). Motorcaravan service point. Gas supplies. Fishing (day ticket £4.50). Off site: Golf 0.5 miles. Riding 5 miles. Sailing and lakeside beach 6 miles. Seaside beaches 20 miles. Shops, pubs and restaurants in Horncastle 2 miles.

Open: 1 March - 30 November.

Directions

Horncastle is 20 miles east of Lincoln. From the A153 Sleaford - Louth road, turn west 1.6 miles north of the town along Docking Lane and follow signs to site in 0.8 miles. O.S.GR: TF251724. GPS: 53.233293, -0.122426

Charges guide

Per unit incl. 2 adults, 2 children	£ 11.50
incl. electricity	£ 15.00
serviced pitch	£ 18.50 - £ 20.00

Leek

Glencote Caravan Park

Station Road, Cheddleton, Leek ST13 7EE (Staffordshire) T: 01538 360745. E: canistay@glencote.co.uk

alanrogers.com/UK3970

At the entrance to the Churnet Valley, three miles south of the market town of Leek, Glencote is a pleasant, family run park of six acres. It has 88 numbered touring pitches set on flat grass, all have patio style hardstandings with tarmac access roads, electrical connections (16A) and a dedicated water supply. Pretty flowerbeds and trees make a very pleasant environment. An attractive, sunken play area, on grass and bark with an abundance of shrubs and flowers, sits alongside the small (fenced) coarse fishing pool.

Facilities

The toilet block is centrally situated and can be heated. Facilities include one private cabin for ladies, a combined shower and toilet for disabled visitors, a small laundry room, and two dishwashing sinks under cover. Gas supplies. Max. 2 dogs per unit. Internet. Off site: Small supermarket and post office in Cheddleton 0.5 miles. Variety of inns within walking distance. Golf 4 miles. Bicycle hire 5 miles. Riding 10 miles.

Open: 1 February - end December.

Directions

Park is signed off A520 Leek - Stone road, 3.5 miles south of Leek on northern edge of Cheddleton Village. O.S.GR: SJ982524. GPS: 53.07072, -2.03389

Charges guide

Per unit incl. 2 persons and electricity	£ 21.50
extra person	£ 5.00
child (5-16 yrs)	£ 2.50
dog	£ 1.00
Min. stay of 3 nights at B.Hs.	

Leominster

Townsend Touring & Caravan Park

Townsend Farm, Pembridge, Leominster HR6 9HB (Herefordshire) T: 01544 388527 E: info@townsend-farm.co.uk alanrogers.com/UK4345

Opened in 2002, this is a modern, family run campsite. It provides tarmac roads, good site lighting, well spaced pitches and a drive-over motorcaravan service point, with plenty of open space and a small fishing lake (with ducks and completely unfenced). There are 60 pitches in total, 20 with gravel hardstanding, the remainder on grass, and all have access to electricity hook-up (16A), water and drainage. Reception is at the Farm Shop by the entrance; this is a real treat as it stocks a wide variety of fresh fruit and vegetables, eggs and has a butchery section with farm-produced meats. Pembridge is known as the capital of the Black and White Villages. A member of the Best of British group.

Facilities

A modern building with blown air heating, accessed through a foyer with public telephone and tourist information. It is surrounded by wide decking with ramps giving good access for wheelchairs to all facilities including the dishwashing area and laundry room. Inside are spacious controllable showers, some washbasins in cubicles, a suite for disabled guests, family bathroom and baby changing facilities. Off site: Riding and bicycle hire 0.5 miles. Kington 5 miles, Leominster 7 miles. Golf 7 miles.

Open: 1 March - 15 January.

Directions

Site is beside the A44, 7 miles west of Leominster. Site is just inside the 30 mph. speed limit on the eastern edge of Pembridge village. O.S.GR: SO385580. GPS: 52.21846, -2.89045

Charges guide

Per unit incl. 2 persons	£ 9.00 - £ 15.00
incl. electricity, water and drainage	£ 12.00 - £ 18.00
extra person	£ 3.00
child (5-15 yrs)	£ 1.50
awning or pup tent	£ 2.00

Ludlow

Westbrook Park

Little Hereford, Ludlow SY8 4AU (Shropshire) T: **01584 711280**. E: info@bestparks.co.uk

alanrogers.com/UK4390

A beautifully kept, traditional, quiet touring campsite in a 'working' cider apple orchard, Westbrook Park is bordered on one side by the River Teme and within walking distance of the village and pub. There are 52 level pitches with 16A electric hook-ups, gravel or concrete/gravel all-weather hardstandings with water and waste water drain. Some pitches have semi-shade, other have none. Satellite TV hook-ups are available to all pitches. A footpath along the river bank in one direction leads to the Temeside Inn which serves hot meals. There is a pleasant riverside walk and dog walk in the other direction.

Facilities	Directions
A modern, timber clad, heated toilet block provides spacious hot showers (10p for 7 minutes), washbasins in curtained cubicles, a basic laundry room and dishwashing sinks. Facilities for disabled people (WC and basin). Gas supplies. Playground. Fishing (£4 per day). Riverside walks. No gazebos. No cycling. Off site: Burford House Gardens. Croft Castle. Market towns of Tenbury Wells, Leominster, Ludlow. Golf 3 miles. Riding and bicycle hire 5 miles.	From A49 midway between Ludlow and Leominster, turn east at Woofferton on A456 (Tenbury Wells, Kidderminster). After 2 miles turn right just before river bridge and Temeside Inn. Turn left after 150 yds. Park is on left. O.S.GR: SU547679. GPS: 52.307377, -2.665815

Open: 1 March - 30 November.

Charges 2010

Per unit incl. 2 persons	
and electricity	£ 15.00 - £ 20.00
extra person	£ 4.00
child (4-10 yrs)	£ 2.00
dog	£ 1.00

Lutterworth

Stanford Hall Caravan Park

Stanford Road, Swinford, Lutterworth LE17 6DH (Leicestershire) T: **01788 860387**

E: stanfordpark@yahoo.co.uk **alanrogers.com/UK3890**

This picturesque and tranquil site is ideally situated for an overnight stop where you are guaranteed a warm welcome and a pleasant stay. Formerly a Caravan Club site, it is set in the rural grounds of the Stanford Hall Estate, just a mile from the M1. There are 123 pitches (30 of which are seasonal), 80 on grass and 43 on hardstanding, all with 16A electricity. There are no shower or toilet facilities on the park, so your unit must be self contained. The site experiences high levels of repeat bookings so you are advised to contact them in advance of busy weekends to avoid being disappointed. Dogs are welcome but must be kept on a lead on the main site. A designated dog walk has been established through part of the estate woodland. Visitors staying on site (for two nights or more) receive free admission to the grounds of Stanford Hall during normal opening times, except on certain event days. There is a small charge for admission to the house.

Facilities	Directions
There are no toilets or shower facilities on site which means each unit must be totally self-contained. Tents are not accepted. A small shop sells basics. Newspapers can be ordered daily. Motorcaravan services. Picnic tables. Information room. Off site: Supermarkets and banks in Lutterworth. Warwick Castle 25 miles. NEC, Birmingham 30 miles. Stratford Upon Avon 35 miles. Silverstone, Rockingham and Mallory Race Circuits and Althorpe are all within easy reach. Good location for walking and fishing. Jurassic Walk and the Grand Union Canal nearby.	From the north on the M1 and from the M6 leave at exit 19 and at roundabout take first exit, signed Swinford, and follow signs for Stanford Hall. Site is on the left on Stanford Road. From the east on the A14, at the junction with M1 roundabout, take exit to Swinford. From south on the M1, leave at exit 18 onto A428, A5 north and then follow signs for Stanford Hall. O.S.GR: SK820133. GPS: 52.406493, -1.149361

Open: All year.

Charges guide

Per unit incl. 2 adults,	
2 children and electricity	£ 12.00
extra person	£ 1.50
dog	free

Malvern

Kingsgreen Caravan Park

Kingsgreen, Berrow, Malvern WR13 6AQ (Worcestershire) T: 01531 650272
alanrogers.com/UK4190

A friendly and extremely well kept site with views of the Malvern Hills, Kingsgreen has an attractive rural location. An ideal site for adults who like the quiet life, there are no amusements for children. The surrounding countryside is ideal for walking or cycling, and the small, fenced fishing lakes on the site are well stocked (£4 per day). There are 45 level, grass and gravel pitches, all with electricity (16A), plus an additional area for tents. Some old orchard trees provide a little shade in parts.

Facilities

Modern heated toilet facilities (key on deposit) provide hot showers (25p token from reception) and a separate unit for disabled people (WC and washbasin). Laundry room with washing machine, dryer, sink and iron and board (all metered). Gas. Fishing. Off site: Nearest shop and pub 1.5 miles. Riding 3 miles. Golf 5 miles.

Open: 1 March - 31 October.

Directions

From M50 exit 2, take A417 (Gloucester), then first left, where site is signed, also signed the Malverns, back over the motorway. Site is 2 miles from the M50. O.S.GR: SO767338. GPS: 52.00262, -2.33849

Charges guide

| Per unit incl. 2 persons and electricity | £ 13.50 - £ 17.50 |
| extra person (over 2 yrs) | £ 1.50 |

VAT not included. No credit cards.

Market Rasen

Walesby Woodlands Caravan Park

Walesby, Market Rasen LN8 3UN (Lincolnshire) T: 01673 843285. E: walesbywoodlands@talk21.com
alanrogers.com/UK3660

Surrounded by mature Forestry Commission woodland, this small family-run, no-frills touring park is mainly very peaceful (if the wind is in a certain direction trains may be heard in the distance). The owners, Paul and Christine Burrows will make you very welcome. There are 60 well spaced pitches, 52 with 10A electricity, marked out in a single, mainly flat, grassy field divided by a central gravel road and with a double row of trees providing useful visual screening. Market Rasen is about a mile away and within easy driving distance, are Lincoln, Skegness and, of course, the Lincolnshire Wolds.

Facilities

The single, heated toilet block (£5 deposit charged for the key) is spacious and ample for the site. Pushbutton showers. Open style washbasins. Toilet facilities for disabled people. Laundry room. Basics in reception. Coffee shop open at busy weekends. Battery charging. Gas. Bicycle hire. No kite flying. Winter caravan storage. Off site: Golf 1.5 miles. Riding 2 miles. Fishing 3 miles. Shops, supermarkets, pubs and restaurants 1-2 miles. Racecourse 2 miles. Lincoln 17 miles. Beach (at Cleethorpes) 20 miles.

Open: 1 March - 31 October, plus Christmas and New Year.

Directions

Market Rasen is on the A46, 17 miles northeast of Lincoln. Park is just over a mile northeast of the town. Take the B1203 towards Tealby, then turn left about half a mile along Walesby Road. Site is on the left and is signed from all the main approach roads to town. O.S.GR: TF117907. GPS: 53.40135, -0.321

Charges guide

| Per unit incl. 2 persons and electricity | £ 16.00 - £ 18.00 |
| extra person | £ 1.50 - £ 2.00 |

Matlock

Lickpenny Touring Park

Lickpenny Lane, Tansley, Matlock DE4 5GF (Derbyshire) T: 01629 583040. E: lickpenny@btinternet.com
alanrogers.com/UK3815

This spacious caravan park on a hill above Matlock has 122 terraced pitches, all on hardstandings (no tents) and with electricity (16A). Of these, 100 are touring pitches, 27 of which are fully serviced and 22 are seasonal. There are rows of mature trees and pitches are large and separated by shrubs and bushes. The enthusiastic owners have taken full advantage of the fact that this was previously a market garden and are continuing to work very hard to maintain high standards and improve facilities. Recreational grassy areas are well tended, whilst the top corner of the park has been kept as woodland.

Facilities

Two well equipped, heated toilet blocks include free controllable showers and some washbasins in cubicles. Good facilities for disabled people. Family room with small bath, toilet and washbasin. Laundry room with washing machines, dryers, irons and ironing boards. Motorcaravan service point. Security barrier with keypad access at all times. Off site: Bus service from end of the road. Riding 1 mile. Fishing 3 miles. Golf 4 miles. Bicycle hire 6 miles. Woodland walk to Garden Centre with restaurant serving snacks and lunches (200 yards).

Open: All year.

Directions

Matlock is 18 miles west of the M1 at exit 28. From motorway, follow signs for Matlock on A38, A61 and A615. After 5 miles on A615 turn north on Lickpenny Lane to site (signed). From Matlock take A615; after Tansley fork left on B6014 (Clay Cross) and turn right at top of hill after Garden Centre. O.S.GR: SK339598. GPS: 53.134533, -1.490483

Charges guide

| Per unit incl. 2 persons and electricity | £ 19.50 - £ 22.50 |
| extra person | £ 2.00 - £ 4.00 |

Meriden
Somers Wood Caravan Park

Somers Road, Meriden CV7 7PL (Warwickshire) T: 01676 522978. E: enquiries@somerswood.co.uk
alanrogers.com/UK4070

Somers Wood is a quiet, peaceful park, attractively situated amongst pine trees. This is a very pleasant park which only accepts adults and does not take tents. It is especially useful for those visiting the various shows at the NEC when it can get very busy. From the reception building at the entrance, an oval gravel road provides access to 48 pitches, all on hardstanding and with 10A electricity hook-ups. Areas of woodland surround the site and partition it into small intimate areas that create a rural feel.

Facilities

The central, heated, completely refurbished (private cabins), sanitary block is fully equipped, and a facility for the disabled has been added. Shower cubicles are especially large. Two dishwashing sinks on the veranda area. Laundry service at reception. WiFi on payment. Off site: Local shops and restaurant less than 1 mile and visitors also welcome to use the bar and restaurant at the golf club next door.

Open: 1 February - 3 January.

Directions

From M42 exit 6 (NEC) take A45 towards Coventry. Keep in left lane down to roundabout and exit on A452 (signed Leamington/Meriden), then turn left into Hampton Lane at the next roundabout. Site is signed with golf and fishing centres on the left. O.S.GR: SP228819. GPS: 52.43930, -1.66947

Charges guide

Per unit incl. 2 persons and electricity	£ 20.00 - £ 23.00
extra person	£ 3.00

Moreton-in-Marsh
Moreton-in-Marsh Caravan Club Site

Bourton Road, Moreton-in-Marsh GL56 0BT (Gloucestershire) T: 01608 650519
alanrogers.com/UK4130

This excellent, busy, but rural, tree-surrounded site in the heart of the Cotswolds offers the most one could hope for from a camping holiday. Only 250 yards from the town, there is plenty of choice for food and pubs. The site has 182 pitches, all with electricity (16A) and TV sockets, 172 with hardstanding. Milk, and ice-cream are available from reception. Adjacent to a dog exercise field is a recently updated play area, crazy golf and a boules pitch. In an adjoining field there is plenty of room for ball games. Kite flying is not allowed because of low power cables. Tents are not accepted.

Facilities

The two toilet blocks have been completely renovated and offer excellent facilities. Both have a large room for disabled people and babies. Small toilet and bath with seat for children. Large laundry. Play area. Boules. Internet access. Off site: Shops, pubs and restaurants 400 yards. Golf 7 miles. Nearby are the Cotswold Falconry Centre, Hidcote Manor Gardens and the Rollright Stones.

Open: All year.

Directions

From Evesham on A44, site on left after Bourton-on-the-Hill village, 150 yards before town sign. From Moreton-in-Marsh take A44 towards Evesham and site is on right, 150 yards past the Wellington museum. O.S.GR: SP200323. GPS: 51.98875, -1.710833

Charges guide

Per person	£ 4.90 - £ 6.33
pitch incl. electricity (non-member)	£ 11.80 - £ 15.50

Newark
Smeaton's Lakes Touring Caravan & Fishing Park

Great North Road, South Muskham, Newark-on-Trent NG23 6ED (Nottinghamshire) T: 01636 605088
E: lesley@smeatonslakes.co.uk alanrogers.com/UK3940

This 82-acre site is really ideal for anglers, with four fishing lakes (coarse, carp and pike) and river fishing on the Trent. There are 130 pitches of which 100 have electricity connections (16A). Non-anglers might choose this park if visiting antique fairs or events at nearby Newark Showground, or Newark town (1 mile) with its castle, air museum and various weekly markets. During your stay, you might visit Southwell Cathedral, Sherwood Forest, Clumber Park, Lincoln with its castle and cathedral or Nottingham with its Lace Hall, Castle and Caves.

Facilities

Two toilet blocks (with keypad access) are heated and include a good unit for disabled people, but no laundry room. Laundry and dishwashing sinks are outside. Reception keeps gas, soft drinks, dairy produce, etc. and newspapers can be ordered. On-site concessions for lake and river fishing. Entry barrier with key access. Security cameras and night-time height barrier (about 6 ft). Off site: Bus stop at the end of the entry lane - buses run into Newark every hour until 10 pm. Riding and boat launching 2 miles. Golf 3 miles.

Open: All year.

Directions

Park is a mile north of Newark on the old Great North Road. From south on A1, take A46 west (signed Newark, then Leicester) and turn north on the A6065/A616 towards South Muskham. From southwest (M1/A46) turn north off Newark bypass on A6065/A616 as above. From north on A1 leave B6325 (Newark) continue south through South Muskham and follow signs for Newark. GPS: 53.0936, -0.820667

Charges guide

Per unit incl. 2 persons	£ 12.00 - £ 13.00
with electricity (16A)	£ 15.00 - £ 18.00
extra person	£ 1.50 - £ 3.00

Newark
Milestone Caravan Park

Great North Road, Cromwell, Newark NG23 6JE (Nottinghamshire) T: **01636 821244**
E: **enquiries@milestonepark.co.uk alanrogers.com/UK3945**

Situated just off the A1 north of Newark, Milestone has a good deal more to offer than simply a stopover option. Its 91 good-sized, level touring pitches all have electricity (16A) and nearby water points. Grass pitches are available, but most are all-weather in a variety of locations. Five are outside the barrier for those in transit (although key access is always available), then comes a pleasantly landscaped area and finally terraces overlooking an attractive fishing lake. An embankment built to muffle traffic noise provides a pleasant grassed walk with views across an adjoining lake and the surrounding countryside. This is a Caravan Club affiliated site. The site is convenient for Newark's Antiques Fairs and showground events and the historic town has a 12th century castle, an Air Museum, two other museums and an art gallery, as well as three markets a week. Southwell with its Minster and its racecourse is only ten miles away, while Lincoln, Sherwood Forest, Clumber Park and Nottingham are not much further.

Facilities

Two heated toilet blocks provide pushbutton showers and open-style washbasins (may be under pressure at busy times). Excellent en-suite facilities for disabled visitors. Washing machine, dryer and ironing facilities. Motorcaravan service points. Comprehensive tourist information, guides and children's quiz sheets on the site's wildlife. Fishing (£3 a day). Lakeside cabin with nature and fishing displays). Off site: Large fishing lake . Village has shop, small brewery and buses to Newark. Riding and boat launching 3 miles. Golf 5 miles. Bicycle hire at Sherwood Forest 12 miles.

Open: All year.

Directions

From the south on A1, 3.7 miles after A46 junction, take slip road to Cromwell and site is on the left after the village. From the north on A1, 9 miles after Markham Moor junction, take slip road for Cromwell, turn right over bridge and right again to site. O.S.GR: SK798620. GPS: 53.1494, -0.8077

Charges guide

Per unit incl. 2 persons	
and electricity	£ 14.00 - £ 17.00
extra person	£ 4.60 - £ 6.10
child	£ 1.50 - £ 2.50

Newark
Orchard Park

Marnham Road, Tuxford, Newark NG22 0PY (Nottinghamshire) T: **01777 870228**
E: **info@orchardcaravanpark.co.uk alanrogers.com/UK3950**

This well established family run touring and caravan park has been created in an old fruit orchard in a quiet location, yet is very convenient for the A1. It has a friendly feel, with just 65 pitches, all with electricity (10A), 34 with hardstanding and 20 occupied by seasonal units. There is also a spacious camping field with good views. Reception is at the owner's house with a nearby cabin with information on attractions including Sundown Adventureland, Laxton Medieval village and Victorian Times, Rufford Abbey, Clumber Park, Sherwood Forest and the Robin Hood Centre.

Facilities

The heated toilet block has pushbutton showers, open-style washbasins and a well equipped room for disabled visitors. Laundry with washing machines, dryer and dishwashing sinks, free spin dryer, iron and freezer for ice packs. Small shop with basics and gas. Picnic area. Excellent children's adventure trail and nature walk. Apples, pears and blackberries can be picked in season. WiFi available on most of site (£4 per weekend). Off site: Pub 0.5 miles, shops 1 mile. Riding 3 miles. Fishing 4 miles. Bicycle hire and golf 10 miles.

Open: March - October.

Directions

Tuxford is 15 miles north of Newark and 18 miles west of Lincoln. The Park lies to the east of the A1. Leave at signs for Tuxford and turn east on A6075 towards Lincoln (A57), continue through village and turn south towards Marnham for 0.5 miles. Site is on right 0.5 miles after railway bridge (well signed). O.S.GR: SK750710. GPS: 53.2296, -0.8695

Charges guide

Per unit incl. 2 persons	
and electricity	£ 16.00 - £ 19.00
extra person	£ 4.00
child (4-12 yrs)	£ 1.00
Book for 7 nights, pay for 6.	

Oakham

Greendale Farm Caravan & Camping Park

Pickwell Lane, Whissendine, Oakham LE15 7LB (Rutland) T: 01664 474516. E: enq@rutlandgreendale.co.uk
alanrogers.com/UK3904

This is a delightful little, adult only park set in rolling countryside, ideal for those seeking peace and tranquillity. It is very eco-friendly and extremely well appointed for such a small site. There are only 13 pitches, all with 10 or 16A electricity, so it is worth checking availability! Reception, the shop and the toilet facilities are housed in a modern building adjoining the owners' house. The shop is well stocked with essentials and local produce. Cooked breakfasts are available on Sundays. It also has one of the best presented and most comprehensive information displays we have seen on any campsite. This includes charts for visitors to record birds seen on the park – the list is impressive – walking and cycle routes and pub menus. There are taster sessions for would-be artists (the office is decorated with the paintings produced by previous visitors) and photographers, all free in April and May. There is limited space for large units. Arrivals are not accepted before 13.00.

Facilities

Each of the two rooms of the toilet block has a power shower, WCs and two washbasins (cubicles for the ladies). All is beautifully appointed and immaculately kept. Washing machine, tumble dryer and spin dryer. Chemical disposal and nearby sluicing point. Small open air swimming pool (6 x 3 m; £1 charge), heated by solar-panels, with summer house. Two bicycles for hire. WiFi (charged). Off site: Village with bus service 0.5 mile. Supermarket in Oakham 4 mile. Fishing 3 miles. Riding 4 miles. Golf 8 miles. Sailing, bird-watching, walking, cycling (and bicycle hire) and fishing at Rutland Water 8 miles. Barnsdale Garden 8 miles.

Open: 15 April - 30 September.

Directions

Oakham is 20 miles east of Leicester and Whissendine is just off the A606 Oakham - Melton Mowbray road. Approach park from this road and NOT through the village. From Oakham ignore the first turning to Whissendine, continue 2 miles and turn right at campsite sign. From Melton ignore first two turnings to Whissendine; turn left 0.6 mile after Rutland sign (at campsite sign). Park is on right in 0.6 mile.
O.S.GR:SK819133. GPS: 52.711833, -0.788617

Charges guide

Per unit incl. two adults	
and electricity	£ 17.00 - £ 22.00
extra person	£ 4.00
dog	£ 1.00

Peterchurch

Poston Mill Caravan Park

Peterchurch HR2 0SF (Herefordshire) T: 01981 550225. E: enquiries@poston-mill.co.uk
alanrogers.com/UK4300

Set in the heart of the Golden Valley, Poston Mill Park is a pleasant, neat park in farmland a mile from the delightful village of Peterchurch. It is an ideal location for relaxation or exploring. There are currently 43 touring pitches set on level grass or hardstanding with mature trees and conifers around the perimeter of the park. All the pitches are fully serviced with electricity (16A), water and TV connections (leads to hire). An attractive walk along one side of the park, edging the River Dore (fishing available), follows the line of the old Golden Valley railway. Adjoining the park is 'The Mill' restaurant and Fraser's Farm Shop. There is a footpath from the park over the fields. Peterchurch village is only one mile. Holiday cottages and caravan holiday homes are available to rent. A member of the Best of British group.

Facilities

One central sanitary block with a smaller, refurbished block near the holiday home area which includes private cubicles. Both are fully equipped and include units for disabled people and families. Laundry rooms. Motorcaravan service point. Play area. Pitch and putt. Tennis, pétanque and croquet. Golf driving range. Games room. Winter caravan storage. Off site: Riding 3 miles. Bicycle hire 10 miles. Fishing and walking.

Open: All year.

Directions

Park is 1 mile southeast of Peterchurch on the B4348 road. O.S.GR: SO356371. GPS: 52.03519, -2.94637

Charges guide

Per unit incl. 2 persons	
and electricity	£ 15.00 - £ 20.00
extra person	£ 3.00
child (4-10 yrs)	£ 1.50
awning	£ 2.00
dog	£ 1.00
Min. charge at B.Hs. 5 nights.	

Ripley
Golden Valley Caravan & Camping Park
Coach Road, Golden Valley, Ripley DE55 4ES (Derbyshire) T: **01773 513881**
E: enquiries@goldenvalleycaravanpark.co.uk **alanrogers.com/UK3865**

Golden Valley Caravan & Camping Park is located in the beautiful hamlet of Golden Valley alongside the Cromford Canal in the Amber Valley area of the Peak District. The site is situated within 26 acres of historic woodland which was once a thriving industrial centre for coal, iron foundries and canal workers on the adjacent Canal. This secluded woodland site has just 40 pitches on grass or hardstanding for motorcaravans or caravans. There are 24 with independent water supply, electrical connection and mains drainage. There are also two wooded areas for tents and a communal barbecue area. A small fishing pond is available containing carp and it is visited by kingfishers, dragonflies and ducks. The pond is securely fenced to avoid access by young children. There is a great deal of interest in the area including the Midland Railway centre (reduced fares for campers) and many footpaths and cycle ways, including the Cromford canal towpath, and of course throughout the magnificent Peak District National Park.

Facilities
A centrally positioned, heated utility block provides free showers and toilets, facilities for disabled visitors, a laundry room, heated jacuzzi, an indoor playroom and a gym. Bar and café (July/Aug and weekends). Fishing pond. Woodland walks. Play area. Tourist information. Off site: Midland Railway Centre. Denby Pottery. Derby 7 miles. Nottingham 15 miles. Walking/cycling in the Peak District National Park.

Open: All year.

Directions
Leave the M1 at exit 26 and follow signs for Matlock and Ripley (A610). Upon arrival at Codnor, turn right at the traffic lights and then first right onto the Alfreton Road. After a further 2 miles turn left before passing the Newlands Inn to join Coach Road. Site entrance is on the left. O.S.GR: SK424512. GPS: 53.05669, -1.37267

Charges guide
Per unit incl. 2 persons and electricity	£ 20.00 - £ 26.00
extra person	£ 5.00 - £ 10.00
child (1-16 yrs)	£ 3.00
dog	£ 2.00

Ross-on-Wye
Broadmeadow Caravan & Camping Park
Broadmeadows, Ross-on-Wye HR9 7BW (Herefordshire) T: **01989 768076**. E: **broadm4811@aol.com**
alanrogers.com/UK4320

This modern, spacious park with open views and its own fishing lake, is conveniently located for the town of Ross-on-Wye. The town centre is within easy walking distance. The approach to the site is unusual, but persevere and you will find one of the best laid out, immaculately maintained sites with facilities of the very highest quality. There are 150 large pitches on level, open grass, and the site is especially good for tents. Each set of four pitches has a service post with water, drain, electricity points (16A) and lighting. Although the A40 relief road is at the eastern end of the site, the traffic noise should not be too intrusive (but tenters be aware). This is a good base for touring Herefordshire, the Wye Valley or the Forest of Dean.

Facilities
Two superb modern sanitary buildings are fully equipped, including hairdryers, baby rooms, family bathrooms each with WC, basin and bath, and a comprehensive unit for disabled visitors. Dishwashing room and laundry at each building. Basic motorcaravan service point. Entrance barrier and keypad entry system. Small part-fenced playground. Well fenced fishing lake (coarse fishing £7.50 per rod per day). Off site: Supermarket 200 m. Bicycle hire in town. Golf 3 miles. Riding 8 miles.

Open: Easter/1 April - 30 September.

Directions
From A40 relief road turn into Ross at roundabout, take first right into industrial estate, then right in 0.5 miles before supermarket, where site is signed. O.S.GR: SO610240. GPS: 51.91657, -2.57489

Charges guide
Per person	£ 4.00
child (2-9 yrs)	£ 2.50
pitch	£ 8.00 - £ 10.50
incl. electricity	£ 11.00 - £ 13.50
dog	£ 1.50

Shrewsbury

Beaconsfield Farm Caravan Park

Battlefield, Shrewsbury SY4 4AA (Shropshire) T: **01939 210370**. E: **mail@beaconsfield-farm.co.uk**
alanrogers.com/UK4410

Just north of the historic market town, a drive of half a mile through open fields leads to this purpose-designed park for adults only (21 yrs). It is neatly laid out in a rural situation, with a well stocked trout fishing lake and a small coarse pool forming the main feature. The ground has been levelled and grassed to provide 80 well spaced pitches, 50 are 'de-luxe' hardstanding pitches. All have 10A electricity connections. Two further areas accommodate 36 caravan holiday homes. The park is well lit with a circular tarmac access road. A large timber chalet-style building provides reception and a coffee shop. The 'Bothy' is an à la carte restaurant serving local produce. Limousins and pedigree Suffolk sheep graze in neighbouring fields and a 'park and ride' scheme operates nearby for those interested in Shrewsbury and its medieval past, bought to life by the Brother Cadfael novels. This is a top class park, maturing by the year. A member of the Best of British Group.

Facilities

Heated toilet facilities (£2 key deposit) are of excellent quality, with roomy, preset showers and hairdryers. Excellent unit for disabled visitors. Laundry facilities. Motorcaravan services. Restaurant. Indoor heated swimming pool with daily open sessions (£3 per person, incl. steam room) and to hire privately at other times. Small library. Security barrier and CCTV. WiFi. Only two dogs per unit are accepted. An adult only park. Car hire available. Accommodation for hire. Off site: Bicycle hire and golf 2 miles. Riding 7 miles.

Open: All year.

Directions

Site is north of Shrewsbury and off the A49 Whitchurch road just before Hadnall. Turn opposite the New Inn at camping sign towards Astley and park entrance is 400 m. on right. O.S.GR: SJ525195. GPS: 52.770917, -2.704817

Charges guide

Per unit incl. 2 persons and electricity	£ 18.00 - £ 22.00
extra adults	£ 4.00
dog (max. 2)	£ 1.50

Last arrivals 19.00 (20.00 Fridays).

Shrewsbury

Oxon Hall Touring Park

Welshpool Road, Shrewsbury SY3 5FB (Shropshire) T: **01743 340868**. E: **oxon@morris-leisure.co.uk**
alanrogers.com/UK4430

Oxon Hall is a purpose-built park, well situated for visiting Shrewsbury. It is under the same ownership as Stanmore Hall (no. 4400) and has been developed from a green field site by an experienced park operator to a very high standard. The site has matured well and the trees and shrubs now provide some shade and shelter. Of the 120 pitches, half are all weather, full service pitches (fresh and waste water facilities, TV hook-up), the others being either grass or with hardstanding. An area is set aside as an 'adults only' section. Most pitches have 16A electricity hook-ups, some pitches for large units have 32A. Some extra long hardstandings are provided for American motorhomes. Entry to the park is controlled by electronic barriers. Virtually adjacent to the park is the Oxon 'park and ride' which makes a trip into Shrewsbury, some two miles away, very simple. The famous Ironbridge Gorge Museum and the mysteries of the Welsh Borders are all easy day trips from this excellent base. A member of the Best of British group.

Facilities

Toilet facilities here are first rate with washbasins in cubicles, ample showers, baby room, facilities for disabled visitors, dishwashing room and laundry, all situated at the entrance in a centrally heated building which also houses reception and the shop - perhaps a hike from some of the pitches. Motorcaravan service point. Up to two dogs per pitch. Deposit for toilet block key £5. Off site: Supermarket within walking distance. Golf, riding and fishing nearby.

Open: All year.

Directions

From junction of A5 and A458, west of Shrewsbury, follow signs for Oxon 'park and ride'. Park is signed just 0.5 miles from junction. O.S.GR: SJ457134. GPS: 52.7154, -2.804917

Charges guide

Per person	£ 5.50 - £ 5.90
child (5-15 yrs)	£ 2.20
standard grass pitch	£ 7.60 - £ 9.50
dog (max. 2)	£ 1.00

Heart of England

Skegness

Skegness Sands Touring Site

Winthorpe Avenue, Skegness PE25 1QZ (Lincolnshire) T: 01754 761484. E: info@skegness-sands.com
alanrogers.com/UK3730

This very well organised touring site is part of a much larger caravan holiday home park, but has its own entrance. It is a modern, well appointed site adjacent to the promenade and beach. There are 85 pitches, all level and with electricity (16A); 45 are grass and 37 gravel hardstandings, four of which are fully serviced. Site lighting is good throughout and there are regular security patrols. The gate to the promenade is kept locked at all times; campers can obtain a key. Local attractions include Funcoast World, Fantasy Island, Hardy's Animal Farm, a seal sanctuary and Gibraltar Point National Nature Reserve. The site is a Caravan Club 'Affiliated Site', members and non-members are all made welcome.

Facilities

The good quality, heated toilet block includes washbasins in curtained cubicles plus three family shower rooms with WC and washbasin and a well equipped room for disabled people. Laundry room. Gas supplies. Hairdressing salon. Indoor heated swimming pool (Spr. B.H - 30 Sept; charged). Small modern playground. Off site: Well stocked shop/post office 500 m. Pubs, fast food outlets and a supermarket are all within easy walking distance. Bus service to Skegness and Ingoldmells 500 m. Fishing 1 mile. Golf 2 miles. Bicycle hire 2.5 miles. Riding 5 miles. Also stock car racing and ten-pin bowling.

Open: All year.

Directions

Site is off the A52 Boston - Skegness - Mablethorpe road, 1.75 miles north of Skegness town centre. Turn east opposite 'Garden City' pub into Winthorpe Avenue and site entrance is on the left at far end of road. New arrivals please contact site if unable to arrive before 17.00. O.S.GR: TF570640.
GPS: 53.1668, 0.3495

Charges guide

Per person	£ 4.60 - £ 6.35
child (5-16 yrs)	£ 1.50 - £ 2.50
pitch	£ 4.80 - £ 15.10

Sleaford

Low Farm Touring & Caravan Park

Spring Lane, Folkingham, Sleaford NG34 0SJ (Lincolnshire) T: 01529 497322. E: lowfarmpark@sky.com
alanrogers.com/UK3770

This quiet secluded park is a lovely spot either just to relax or to tour the Lincolnshire countryside. Jane and Nigel Stevens continue to work hard to make this site a pleasant place to stay and have a well laid out park offering good quality facilities which are very clean and tidy. The site offers 36 touring pitches with electricity hook-ups (10 or 16A) and a field for tents and small rallies. Some hardstandings are available. The site is on the edge of the village of Folkingham with a pub (serving food) and a couple of small shops. There are some pleasant walks around the village which is set in attractive Lincolnshire countryside. Larger shops and places of interest are in and around Bourne (nine miles), Sleaford (ten miles), Grantham (14 miles), Lincoln and Peterborough (both 26 miles).

Facilities

Central, well maintained toilet block with controllable free showers and open style washbasins. Washing machine. Reception is at the owners' house but nearby is a tourist information room with toilets. Large field where children can play (also sometimes used by tenters). Off site: Fishing 2 miles. Golf 6 miles. Riding 7 miles.

Open: Easter - 30 September.

Directions

Folkingham is 26 miles south of Lincoln on the A15 to Peterborough, 2 miles south of the roundabout junction with the A52 (Nottingham/Grantham - Boston). Park is on southern edge of village; at foot of hill at campsite sign, turn west and site is at end of lane. O.S.GR: TF070333. GPS: 52.88685, -0.411167

Charges guide

Per unit incl. 2 persons and electricity	£ 12.00 - £ 15.00
No credit cards.	

Slimbridge
Tudor Caravan & Camping Park

Shepherds Patch, Slimbridge GL2 7BP (Gloucestershire) T: 01453 890483. E: info@tudorcaravanpark.co.uk

alanrogers.com/UK4170

This traditional style campsite is adjacent to the Gloucester - Sharpness Canal. Located behind the Tudor Arms public house, a gate clearly identifies the entrance and reception is up a short path on the left. There are many trees and hedges, particularly surrounding the site, so the canal is not visible. Attractively laid out on two separate fields, there are 75 pitches, all with electric hook-ups (16A), and 35 with hardstanding. The old orchard is for long stay or 'adult only' units, with some concrete wheel track hardstands, and a more open grassy meadow is for family touring units. The adjacent pub has a restaurant and bar (2007 CAMRA award winner) and just across the road, beside the canal, is a café and shop where boats can be hired. This is a delightful, peaceful park with plenty to offer: walking, fishing and boating, not to mention ornithology – the Wildfowl and Wetlands Centre founded by Sir Peter Scott at Slimbridge is only 800 yards away.

Facilities

The toilet building located to one side of the orchard, provides all the usual facilities including push button hot showers and it can be heated in cool weather. No facilities for disabled persons at present but a new block is planned in the meadow which will include facilities for disabled people and babies. Gas available. Some site lighting but a torch would be useful. Gate locked 22.30-07.00. Off site: Meals at the Tudor Arms pub. Shop and cafe in boatyard opposite the site (Easter-Sept), also serves breakfasts. Fishing adjacent. Towpath walks. Berkeley Castle, Frampton and Stroud.

Open: All year.

Directions

From A38 by the junction with A4135 (Dursley), turn west, signed WWT Wetlands Centre Slimbridge. Continue for 1.5 miles turning left into car park of the Tudor Arms. Site entrance is at rear of car park. O.S.GR: SO728042. GPS: 51.735533, -2.395817

Charges guide

Per unit incl. 2 persons	£ 11.00 - £ 15.00
extra person	£ 2.00
child (under 12 yrs)	£ 1.00
electricity	£ 2.25 - £ 2.50

No credit cards.

Spalding
Foreman's Bridge Caravan Park

Sutton Saint James, Spalding PE12 0HU (Lincolnshire) T: 01945 440346. E: foremansbridge@btconnect.com

alanrogers.com/UK3750

Foreman's Bridge is a compact park occupying a large, level and grassy meadow surrounded by trees and high hedges which give it a very secluded feel. The park has 42 level pitches, of which 24 are now occupied by caravan holiday homes (seven for rent). The remainder are touring pitches, all with electricity (16A) and gravel hardstanding. Up to half of these are occupied on a seasonal basis. The park could be a useful base from which to explore the Fens and to visit Spalding, famous for its annual flower festival held at the beginning of May. At times there can be noise from military aircraft.

Facilities

The modern, brick-built toilet unit is spacious and kept clean, providing really large individual shower rooms with seats and washbasins (showers on payment). Laundry room. Gas. Fishing possible in the river running past the entrance. Bicycle hire. Two cottages to rent. Winter caravan storage. Off site: Small shop in village 1 mile. Golf 3 miles. Riding 8 miles. Coast 12 miles (The Wash); nearest beach 32 miles.

Open: 1 March - 15 January.

Directions

Sutton St James is 26 miles northeast of Peterborough and 17 miles west of Kings Lynn. From A17 Spalding - Kings Lynn road turn south on B1390 at Long Sutton towards Sutton St James for about 2 miles. Site entrance is on the left immediately after the bridge. O.S.GR: TF410198. GPS: 52.75785, 0.088

Charges guide

Per unit incl. 2 persons and electricity	£ 14.00
extra person	£ 3.00
child	£ 2.00
dog	£ 1.00

No credit cards.

Stamford

Tallington Lakes Camping & Caravanning

Barholm Road, Tallington, Stamford PE9 4RJ (Lincolnshire) T: **01778 347000**. E: **info@tallington.com**
alanrogers.com/UK3760

The 160 acre site spreads around a series of lakes that provide for many watersport activities including water-ski (slalom and jump courses), jet-ski, sailing (sailboards and dinghies) and angling. The touring campsite has 118 pitches, of which 106 have electric hook-ups (10A), and 11 are on hardstandings. Major roads are tarmac, with gravel roads serving the pitches, and maturing hedges and shrubs separate the rows. The complex also has eight mobile homes for hire and there are some 200 privately-owned holiday homes. Local places of interest are Stamford Museum, Burghley House, Sacrewell Farm and Country Centre and the Nene Valley Railway.

Facilities

The heated sanitary unit has facilities for babies, small children and disabled visitors. Additional WCs and showers (also used by the water skiers). Laundry and dishwashing facilities. Motorcaravan service point. Bar and restaurant. Swimming and paddling pools. Climbing wall. Go-karting. Watersports. Fishing. Dry-ski slope, snowboard centre and tennis. Small, well fenced, adventure style playground (age 5-12 yrs). Key-card for toilet unit and barrier (£10 refundable deposit). Off site: Bus stop 1 mile. Golf, riding and bicycle hire 5 miles.

Open: 1 March - 31 January.

Directions

From A16, midway between Stamford and Market Deeping, just east of the railway crossing at Tallington, turn north into Barholm Road and site entrance is on the right (site is signed). O.S.GR: TF085090. GPS: 52.67007, -0.37940

Charges guide

Per person	£ 2.00
pitch	£ 6.00
electricity	£ 2.00
awning or pup tent	£ 1.50
dog (max. 2 per unit)	£ 1.00

Stourport-on-Severn

Lickhill Manor Caravan Park

Lower Lickhill Road, Stourport-on-Severn DY13 8RL (Worcestershire) T: **01299 871041**
E: **excellent@lickhillmanor.co.uk alanrogers.com/UK4210**

Lickhill Manor is a well managed touring and holiday site within easy walking distance of the town centre via a footpath along the River Severn which lies a short distance below the site. There are opportunities for fishing and boating. The touring area has 70 marked, level, pitches accessed via tarmac roads, all with electricity (10/16A). The 124 holiday homes, well screened from the touring area, are not visually intrusive, and there is a separate rally field (with 64 hook-ups). There is an excellent play area for children and the park has recently created wildlife ponds and planted over 1,000 native trees and shrubs. This park has matured into one of the best in the area. Stourport is a lively bustling town with some splendid public parks, amusements and sports facilities. Kidderminster, the Forestry Commission Visitors' Centre at Bewdley, the Severn Valley Railway and West Midland Safari Park are a short drive from the site.

Facilities

A second sanitary building serves the touring pitches and complements the older unit at the other end of the park. This heated building provides good, modern facilities including a well equipped suite for disabled guests which doubles as a family washroom with facilities for baby changing. Drive over motorcaravan service point. Recycling bins. Gas supplies. Children's play park in separate family area. Off site: Shops and pub 10 minutes walk. Riding 1 mile. Bicycle hire 3 miles. Golf 5 miles.

Open: All year.

Directions

From the A451 in Stourport take B4195 northwest towards Bewdley. After 1 mile turn left at crossroads (traffic lights), into Lickhill Road North where site is signed. O.S.GR: SO790730. GPS: 52.34360, -2.29798

Charges guide

Per unit incl. 4 persons and electricity	£ 15.00 - £ 21.00
2 person tent	£ 11.00
extra person over 2 yrs	£ 2.00
dog	£ 1.00

Weekly rates available. Senior citizen discounts.

Stratford-upon-Avon

Riverside Caravan Park

Tiddington Road, Tiddington, Stratford-upon-Avon CV37 7AB (Warwickshire) T: **01789 292312**
E: info@stratfordcaravans.co.uk **alanrogers.com/UK4080**

On the bank of the River Avon, this spacious site has about 250 pitches in total, and about 100 privately owned mobile homes. The 125 touring pitches (no tents) are on level grass, all with electric hook-ups (16A). There is a small shop and cafe on site, which serves breakfasts and takeaways in addition to stocking a good selection of basic supplies. A clubhouse that incorporates a bar, playground, games room and TV room is on the adjacent Rayford Park which is under the same management. There is a possible flood risk during periods of inclement weather. A river taxi runs to Stratford.

Facilities

The main toilet unit has been re-fitted to modern standards and is bright and comfortable with central heating. Spacious preset showers, some washbasins in cubicles, with a child-size toilet and shower in the ladies. Facilities for disabled guests. Utility room with dishwashing and laundry facilities. Slipway and fishing. Courtesy river launch to Stratford. Gas supplies. No commercial vehicles are accepted. Off site: Shakespeare.

Open: 1 April - 31 October.

Directions

From Stratford take B4086 towards Wellesbourne. Site entrance is on left, after one mile, just before Tiddington village (ignore entrance to Rayford Park C.P.). O.S.GR: SP219559. GPS: 52.20023, -1.68213

Charges guide

Per unit incl. 2 persons	
and electricity	£ 15.00 - £ 18.00
extra person	£ 1.50
child (4-15 yrs)	£ 1.00
dog	£ 1.00

Sutton-in-Ashfield

Teversal Camping & Caravanning Club Site

Silverhill Lane, Teversal, Sutton-in-Ashfield NG17 3JJ (Nottinghamshire) T: **01623 551838**
E: teversal@thefriendlyclub.co.uk **alanrogers.com/UK3910**

Formerly known as Shardaroba, this attractive, six-acre campsite has 126 pitches. A paradise for walkers and cyclists, it has a peaceful village location, and yet is surprisingly close to the motorway network. The site is beautifully kept and has won recent awards. Many of the spacious touring pitches are on hardstandings, arranged in well spaced rows surrounded by areas of grass and flower beds. All have electric hook-ups (16A), and 16 are multi-serviced. A grassed area for campers has a patio nearby with tables and chairs. Adjacent is an attractive country park – the highest point in Nottinghamshire.

Facilities

Two excellent, well equipped, heated toilet blocks with spacious showers, and family room. Shower room and toilet/wash room for disabled visitors. Separate laundry. Separate building with six full suites (3 male and 3 female with WC, washbasin, shower) and unisex toilet/washbasin next to camping area. Motorcaravan service point. Shop with basics. Calor gas. Playground. Recycling facilities. Off site: Riding 200 yds. Golf 800 yds. Fishing, bicycle hire, pub, bakery, chip shop and general stores all within 1 mile. Sailing 2 miles. Teversal Manor. Hardwick Hall.

Open: All year.

Directions

Teversal is central in a triangle formed by M1 junctions 28 and 29, and Mansfield. Site is signed off B6014 at western end of the village, turning north by the Carnarvon Arms into Silverhill Lane. Site entrance is 300 yds. on left. O.S.GR: SK485625. GPS: 53.148517, -1.295833

Charges guide

Per person	£ 6.60 - £ 7.60
child	£ 2.25 - £ 2.35
pitch (non member)	£ 6.00

Stoke-on-Trent

The Star Camping & Caravan Park

You might also like to consider...

Sutton-on-Sea

Cherry Tree Site

Huttoft Road, Sutton-on-Sea LN12 2RU (Lincolnshire) T: **01507 441626**. E: info@cherrytreesite.co.uk
alanrogers.com/UK3650

This is a delightful, tranquil, 'adults only' site and is a fine example of a small, good value touring park. It is a 15-minute walk from a Blue Flag beach and a short drive from some of the attractive villages of the Lincolnshire Wolds. A very warm welcome awaits from Geoff and Margaret Murray whose attention to detail is evident everywhere. The site is level, the grass is neatly trimmed and well drained, and screening is provided by lines of evergreen hedging. There are 40 good sized touring pitches, all with 10A electricity and hardstanding (no tents) and ten with water and waste water drain.

Facilities	Directions
The brick-built toilet block, recently extended and refurbished to a high standard, can be heated and is immaculately kept. Controllable hot showers, hairdryers. En-suite unit for disabled visitors (Radar key). Combined dishwashing and laundry room. Neat reception and separate tourist information cabin. Gas. Off site: Riding adjacent. Shop and pub 0.6 miles. Beach 1.5 miles. Tennis, bowls and fishing 1.5 miles. Golf 2 miles. Fantasy Island 10 miles. Skegness 12 miles.	Sutton-on-Sea is 15 miles north of Skegness and 40 miles east of Lincoln. The site is 1.5 miles south of the town on A52 coast road, with the entrance leading off a lay-by on the east. O.S.GR: TF518828. GPS: 53.29292, 0.28439

Open: 5 March - 30 October.

Charges guide

Per unit incl. 2 persons, electricity	£ 15.00 - £ 21.00
extra person	£ 3.50
dog	£ 0.50
Min. stay 3 nights at B.Hs.	

Symonds Yat West

Doward Park Camp Site

Great Doward, Symonds Yat West HR9 6BP (Herefordshire) T: **01600 890438**
E: enquiries@dowardpark.co.uk alanrogers.com/UK4360

Created around 1997 in a disused quarry, this is a very pleasant, peaceful little site, partially terraced and in a sheltered location. The access roads and the physical proportions of the site make it suitable only for tents, trailer tents and campervans. This site is popular with couples and young families, but possibly has nothing to offer teenagers. The 33 pitches are mostly on grass (with six hardstandings used by seasonal units when we visited) and there are 11 electric hook-ups (16A) for touring units. There are two hardstanding pitches for motorcaravan up to 23 feet in length.

Facilities	Directions
A neat central building provides the usual facilities including refurbished hot showers, dishwashing sinks and a freezer for ice packs. Small shop selling basic supplies. Torches are advisable. Only tents, trailer tents and campervans are accepted. Off site: Variety of inns at both Symonds Yat West and East all offering meals. Shops and services in Monmouth 4 miles. Fishing 1 miles. Golf 4 miles. Bicycle hire 10 miles.	From A40 between Ross-on-Wye and Monmouth, turn for Symonds Yat West, and follow signs for Doward Park and Biblins. Turn into narrow lane for about 1 mile and site is on right, on sharp left hand bend. O.S.GR: SO548157. GPS: 51.838517, -2.657

Open: 15 March - 31 October.

Charges guide

Per unit incl. 2 persons, electricity	£ 15.50 - £ 17.50
extra person	£ 2.00 - £ 2.50
dog	£ 1.00

Tattershall

Willow Holt Camping & Caravan Park

Lodge Road, Tattershall LN4 4JS (Lincolnshire) T: **01526 343111**. E: enquiries@willowholt.co.uk
alanrogers.com/UK3675

Willow Holt is a pleasant park with plenty of potential. It will appeal, in particular, to fishing enthusiasts and to those who would like a quiet location from which to explore this interesting corner of Lincolnshire with its RAF associations. It covers some 25 acres of woodland and former gravel pits, with the camping areas on flat land alongside the large lake. There are 60 pitches occupied on a seasonal basis but a further 47 are available for touring units. All have 10A electricity and water taps close by. An area without electricity is available for tents.

Facilities	Directions
The toilet block is small and must be under considerable pressure at busy times. Showers are preset and hot water is free to the open style basins and dishwashing sinks. Motorcaravan service point. Laundry room with washing machines, dryers and iron/ironing board. No facilities for disabled visitors or for babies and young children. Free fishing (permit required). Off site: Golf and riding 2.5 miles. Shops, pubs and restaurants in Tattershall (1.5 miles) and Woodhall Spa (2.5 miles). Beaches 30 miles.	Tattershall is 20 miles southeast of Lincoln on the A153 Sleaford - Horncastle/Louth road. Site is 1.5 miles north of town; from Market Place follow brown campsite sign along Lodge Road. Entrance is on left before junction with B1192 to Woodhall Spa. O.S.GR: TF201592. GPS: 53.116664, -0.206652

Open: 15 March - 31 October.

Charges guide

Per unit incl. 2 persons	£ 10.00 - £ 14.00
incl. electricity	£ 12.00 - £ 16.00
extra person	£ 1.00 - £ 2.00

Tewkesbury
Winchcombe Camping & Caravanning Club Site
Brooklands Farm, Alderton, Tewkesbury GL20 8NX (Gloucestershire) T: 01242 620259
alanrogers.com/UK4140

This is a popular, quiet site in a rural location, close to the Cotswold attractions. Some pitches surround a small coarse fishing lake, with others in a more recently developed area with open views over the surrounding countryside. In total there are 80 pitches, 53 with electric hook-ups (10A) and 42 with gravel hardstanding. The reception building flanks a small gravel courtyard car park and late arrivals area approached from a tarmac drive. Future plans include the addition of lodges, an extended camping area and a new toilet block. Places to visit include Gloucester Docks and the National Waterways Museum, whilst south of Gloucester are Owlpen Manor near Uley, and the Painswick Rococo Garden. The Wildfowl and Wetlands Trust at Slimbridge, first opened in 1946 by Sir Peter Scott is also well worth a visit. Closer to the site is the GWR (Gloucester Warwickshire Railway) at Toddington or Winchcombe.

Facilities	Directions
The main, heated sanitary unit, kept very clean and tidy by the wardens, is well equipped. To the rear of the site is a small, 'portacabin' style sanitary unit (also heated). Well equipped unit for disabled people. Laundry facilities. Gas supplies. Large games room with bowling alley. Small outdoor play area. Off site: Several pubs and restaurants in the area. Golf 7 miles.	From M5 exit 9, take A46 Evesham road for 3 miles to Toddington roundabout, then the B4077 towards Stow-on-the-Wold for a further 3 miles to the site entrance. Ignore signs for Alderton village. O.S.GR: SP 007324. GPS: 51.9904, -1.990683

Open: 16 March - 15 January.

Charges guide

Per person	£ 6.30 - £ 7.25
child (5-16 yrs)	£ 2.15 - £ 2.25
non-member pitch fee	£ 5.65

Tewkesbury
Croft Farm Water & Leisure Park
Bredon's Hardwick, Tewkesbury GL20 7EE (Gloucestershire) T: 01684 772321
E: enquiries@croftfarmleisure.co.uk alanrogers.com/UK4150

Croft Farm is an AALA licensed Watersports Centre with Royal Yachting Association-approved tuition available for windsurfing, sailing, kayaking and canoeing. The lakeside campsite has around 96 level pitches, with 80 electric hook-ups (10A), but there are many seasonal units, leaving around 36 pitches for tourists, plus some tent pitches. There are 36 gravel hardstandings but very little shade or shelter. 'Gym and Tonic' is a fully equipped gymnasium with qualified instructors, sunbed and sauna. Sports massage, aromatherapy and beauty treatments are available by appointment. Activity holidays for families and groups are organised. Campers can use their own non-powered boats on the lake with reduced launch fees and there is free fishing. Climb Bredon Hill (two miles) for a panoramic view of the Severn and Avon Valleys. Places of interest include Bredon Barn, pottery and church, Beckford Silk Mill and Tewkesbury Abbey.

Facilities	Directions
A new building (open in summer) has excellent facilities with spacious hot showers, plus some dishwashing sinks. A heated unit in the main building is always open and best for cooler months; this provides further WCs, washbasins and showers, laundry and facilities for disabled persons. Gas. Cafe/bar (Fri-Sun low season, daily at other times). Takeaway. Gym. Playground. Fishing. Barrier and toilet block key (£5 deposit). Off site: Pub opposite. Tewkesbury 1.5 miles. Golf 3 miles. Riding 8 miles.	Bredon's Hardwick is midway between Tewkesbury and Bredon on B4080. Site entrance opposite 'Cross Keys Inn'. From M5 exit 9 take A438 (Tewkesbury), at first traffic lights turn right into Shannon Way. Turn right at next lights, cross M-way bridge. Turn left (housing estate) and cross second M-way bridge. At T-junction turn right on B4080, site is immediately on left. O.S.GR: SO912353. GPS: 52.015967, -2.130267

Open: All year, excl. January and February.

Charges guide

Per unit incl. 2 persons and awning	£ 14.00
extra person (over 3 yrs)	£ 3.00
electricity	£ 2.00
dog	£ 0.75

Discount 10% for 8 nights or more (excl. July, August and B.Hs).

Woodhall Spa

Glen Lodge Touring Park

Glen Lodge, Edlington Moor, Woodhall Spa LN10 6UL (Lincolnshire) T: **01526 353523**
alanrogers.com/UK3692

This quiet, attractive and spacious site is ideal for couples and families who enjoy the rural lifestyle, yet it is only just over a mile from the thriving village of Woodhall Spa which retains much of its old-fashioned charm. All 35 pitches have hardstanding and 10A electricity hook-ups (one or two appeared to need long leads) and are served by shingle roads with some street lighting. The grass and flowerbeds are obviously tended by someone who enjoys gardening. In fact, the whole park has a much-loved feel. Behind the pitches, on one side of the park, is an attractive lawned area with trees and shrubs, whilst on the other side is a field where ball games are permitted. Woodhall Spa has two modern supermarkets and a good range of traditional shops, as well as tearooms, restaurants and pubs. There is also a delightful, old-style cinema called the Kinema in the Woods. Places to visit in the area include the Battle of Britain Memorial Flight, Tattershall Castle, Horncastle with its antiques centre and the city of Lincoln. Skegness is only 26 miles away.

Facilities	Directions
The modern heated toilet block (key-pad access) is kept spotlessly clean with controllable showers, vanity style washbasins and piped music. En-suite facilities for disabled visitors. Washing machine and dryer. Off site: Pub serving good food 0.5 miles, Open air pool, tennis and bowls 1 mile. Shops in village 1.5 miles. Golf and fishing 2 miles. Tattershall Castle 5 miles. Riding 6 miles. Horncastle 6 miles.	Woodhall Spa is 18 miles southeast of Lincoln. From mini-roundabout in village turn northeast towards Bardney on B1190 (Stixwould Road) past Petwood Hotel. In just over 1 mile at sharp left bend, turn right. Site is 300 yards on left. O.S.GR: TF189647. GPS: 53.166233, -0.22

Open: 1 March - 30 November.

Charges guide

Per unit incl. 2 persons and electricity	£ 14.50
extra person (over 4 yrs)	£ 3.00

No credit cards.
Discount for over 65s Monday - Thursday.

Woodhall Spa

Bainland Country Park

Horncastle Road, Woodhall Spa LN10 6UX (Lincolnshire) T: **01526 352903**. E: **bookings@bainland.co.uk**
alanrogers.com/UK3690

A family park with many amenities, Bainland has 170 spacious, level pitches in hedged bays (120 touring pitches) grouped in circles and islands and linked by curving roads. There are 51 fully serviced pitches with hardstanding, honeycombed for awning, individual water, drainage and chemical disposal, 16A electricity and TV aerial hook-ups. The remainder of the pitches are either on gravel hardstanding or level grass, all with 10A electricity. The friendly reception is housed in a pleasant Swiss-style building together with the heated indoor pool and jacuzzi, a bistro and spacious bar area. These overlook the 18-hole, par-3 golf course and outdoor bowls area. Bainland is 1.5 miles away, with its old fashioned charm and Dambusters associations, yet deep in the heart of the Lincolnshire Wolds, surrounded by mature trees and with direct access to woods for walking dogs. A member of the Best of British group.

Facilities	Directions
Three modern, well equipped, heated toilet blocks including unisex en-suite shower rooms, family bathroom, a baby room, fully equipped unit for disabled visitors. Laundry room. Motorcaravan service points. Licensed shop (Feb - Dec). Bistro and bar. Indoor pool (under 16s must be accompanied by an adult). Adventure playground. Crazy golf. Croquet. Trampolines. Games room. Soft play area. Floodlit tennis dome with 3-4 courts including badminton (the dome comes off in the summer). Par 3, 18-hole golf. Bowls. Leisure activities, including the pool, are individually booked and paid for at reception. Some entertainment in high season. WiFi (free). Winter caravan storage. Off site: Fishing and boat launching 3 miles. Sailing 5 miles. Tattershall Castle 5 miles. Riding and bicycle hire 6 miles.	Woodhall Spa is 18 miles southeast of Lincoln. The entrance to the park is off B1191 Horncastle road 1.5 miles northeast of the village centre and is clearly signed. O.S.GR: TF214637. GPS: 53.158617, -0.183517

Open: All year (in winter, 'super' pitches only).

Charges guide

Per unit incl. 2 persons and electricity	£ 15.00 - £ 32.00
serviced pitch, plus	£ 1.00 - £ 7.00
extra person	£ 2.00 - £ 5.00
child (5-12 yrs)	£ 2.00 - £ 3.00

Special rate for firework display (min. 2 nights, 4/5 Nov).
Discounts for senior citizens.

Whitchurch

Green Lane Farm Caravan & Campsite

Green Lane, Prees, Whitchurch SY13 2AH (Shropshire) T: 01948 840460. E: greenlanefarm@tiscali.co.uk

alanrogers.com/UK4415

Green Lane Farm is a small family run site in the heart of the countryside. Pitches are set on a flat open field, surrounded by trees and hedges and provide a relaxing and really quiet place to stay with no traffic noise to disturb the tranquillity. A gravel track leads into the site and after 30 yards becomes grass encircling the field. The 23 grass pitches are situated around the outside with an attractive group of shrubs beside each electric hook-up stand. There is space for tents in the central area together with play equipment and picnic tables. Although this is a secluded site with the nearest shop being over one mile away, it is convenient for the many nearby attractions. On-site facilities are limited but can be found in the nearby village or in the town of Whitchurch five miles away.

Facilities

The recently built sanitary block provides washbasins and showers (only one toilet for men and two for ladies). Large separate toilet and shower for disabled visitors. Play area. Football. Tourist information. Torches useful. Off site: Pubs, shop, garage, takeaway, and club in Prees village, just over a mile away. The site is central to many attractions and activities. Fishing and golf 2 miles. Ironbridge, Telford, Shrewsbury and RAF Cosford are nearby.

Open: 1 March - 31 October.

Directions

The easiest route is from the A41; 4 miles south of Whitchurch turn west signed Prees. In 200 yards turn right and site is on the right in 200 yards. On the A49 turn east to Prees. At the crossroads in Prees turn right towards the church. Turn left at the church. Site is 1 mile on the left. GPS: 52.90279, -2.65914

Charges guide

Per unit incl. electricity	£ 15.00
awning	£ 1.00

No credit cards.

Worksop

Riverside Caravan Park

Central Avenue, Worksop S80 1ER (Nottinghamshire) T: 01909 474118

alanrogers.com/UK3920

A town centre touring park, adjacent to the Worksop cricket ground, this excellent site is attractive and surprisingly peaceful. Riverside is within easy walking distance of the town centre pedestrian precinct and shops, and the Chesterfield Canal runs close to its northern side offering delightful towpath walks or fishing (children would need to be watched). For those who cannot resist the thwack of leather on willow, this site is ideal. Of the 60 marked level pitches, ten are seasonal and 43 are for touring, mainly on gravel hardstanding, seven are on grass and some are separated by trees and low rails, and all have electric hook-ups. There is good site lighting. Attractions in the area include Creswell Crags, Clumber Park, the Dukeries Cycle Trail, Thoresby Park and Gallery and Rufford Mill Craft Centre and Country Park.

Facilities

The single sanitary unit near reception can be heated and has all the usual facilities, although showers are on payment (20p). No laundry. Motorcaravan service point. Off site: Fishing 0.5 miles. Several golf courses 1 mile. Bicycle hire 4 miles. Squash and flat or crown green bowling nearby. Campers are made very welcome at the cricket ground clubhouse. One of Worksop's most interesting buildings, the medieval Priory Gatehouse, is open free of charge. Market days are Wednesday, Friday and Saturday.

Open: All year.

Directions

Worksop is 7 miles west of the M1 at junction 30 and 4 miles east of the A1. Easiest approach is from A57/A60 roundabout west of the town – third roundabout from the A1. Turn east (at Little Chef) on B6024 towards town centre. Site is well signed. Turn left into Cricket Ground taking care at sharp left turn after bridge. Site entrance is to the left of clubhouse. O.S.GR: SK580790. GPS: 53.30600, -1.12867

Charges guide

Per unit incl. 2 persons, awning and electricity (10A)	£ 16.00

A beautiful and varie
region of rolling hills
and undulating moor
Yorkshire has an histo
past with a wealth of n
attractions. Its landscape h
inspired famous authors and be
the setting for some of Britain's
best-loved television programme

THE REGION IS DIVIDED INTO NORTH, SOUTH, EAST AND WEST YORKSHIRE

The major attractions of this region are the parks: the Yorkshire Dales National Park is comprised of 680 square miles of unspoilt countryside with high fells, winding rivers, ancient castles and outstanding views of the surrounding landscapes; the Peak District is noted for its rocky peaks and limestone plateau; while the North York Moors National Park has miles of open, heather covered moorland and pretty villages in its valleys. These areas are ideal places for walking, cycling, horse riding and climbing. Or if you prefer to relax and take in the scenery, the North Yorkshire Moors Railway, starting at Pickering, is one of the many steam railways in the region. On the coast, traditional family resorts like Scarborough, Bridlington and Cleethorpes offer the holidaymaker a wide range of activities. Also by the sea is Kingston Upon Hull, a maritime city with powerful links to Britain's proud seafaring tradition, and the picturesque fishing port of Whitby, once home to Captain James Cook. Elsewhere in the region are the vibrant cities of York, with its wealth of ancient sites including the Minster, Leeds and Sheffield plus the busy market town of Doncaster.

Places of interest

North: Harrogate; Wensleydale Creamery in Hawes; Jorvik Viking Centre in York; Lightwater Valley Theme Park, near Ripon Castle Howard near York: Flamingo Land Theme Park and Zoo in Malton; Skipton Castle.

South: Hatfield Waterpark near Doncaster Tropical Butterfly House and Wildlife Cen in Anston; Sheffield Ski Village, Europe's biggest artificial ski resort; Magna science adventure centre in Rotherham.

East: Bempton Cliffs RSPB Nature Reserve near Bridlington, England's largest seabird colony; market town of Beverly; Captain Cook Museum in Whitby; Scarborough Millennium.

West: Bolling Hall in Bradford; Royal Armouries Museum in Leeds; 'Brontë Country' and village of Haworth; Pontefr

Did you know?

The comedy series Last of the Summer W is filmed in the Pennine town of Holmfirt and its surrounding countryside.

York is the oldest city in Yorkshire, found in AD71. The Minster is the largest Goth Cathedral in Northern Europe.

Pontefract has been growing liquorice since medieval times, it is believed that Pontefract cakes were made by the mon for medicinal purposes.

The Tan Hill Inn is the highest pub in England at 528 metres above sea level.

Dick Turpin, the notorious 17th century highwayman, lived in Pontefract.

Rudston is said to be the oldest inhabited village in England, named after the Rood Stone, a mysterious 4000 year old mono

Yorkshire

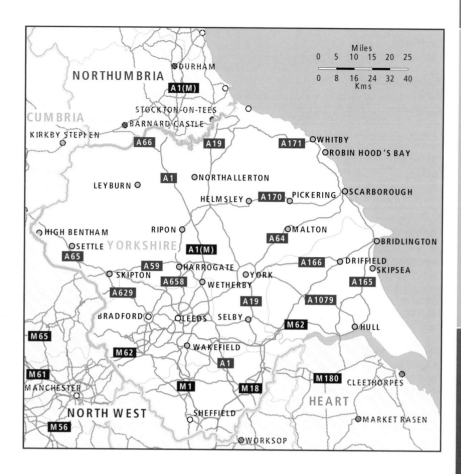

Bridlington
South Cliff Caravan Park
Wilsthorpe, Bridlington YO15 3QN (East Yorkshire) T: **01262 671051**. E: **southcliff@eastriding.gov.uk**
alanrogers.com/UK4498

This traditional style caravan park is part of a large complex owned and operated by the East Riding of Yorkshire Council. There are 184 touring pitches, each with an electricity post (16A); 20 for tents, the remainder with hardstanding surrounded by grass or, in a few cases, extended to the road. Many of them lie back from the road, so access for larger units can be tricky when the site is full. Direct access to the seafront is through the vast caravan holiday home park and from there a 'land train' runs a mile along the shore to Bridlington.

Facilities
Two toilet blocks (one traditional, one new) provide pushbutton showers, open washbasins (a few in cubicles for ladies). Excellent en-suite units for disabled visitors. Three bathrooms with washbasins and baby changing facilities. No motorcaravan service point. Franchised facilities: launderette (washing machines and dryers). Well stocked shop (1/3-8/10); fish and chip shop (busy at times). Leisure complex (bar, restaurant, clubroom, games room) offering entertainment evenings in high season and monthly themed weekends (outside August). Dogs are not accepted (except 'assistance dogs'). Off site: Golf 0.5 m. Beach (by car), riding, sailing, boat launching and bicycle hire 1 mile. Shops, pubs and restaurants within 2 miles.

Open: 1 March - 30 November.

Directions
Bridlington is 40 miles east of York via the A166/A614. From M62 exit 37, take A614 to Bridlington. Before Carnaby turn east to join the A165 to Bridlington South. From the Humber Bridge take the A164 to Beverley, then A165 to Bridlington. Site is signed from A165 at Wilsthorpe. O.S.GR: TA166648.
GPS: 54.0641, -0.2132

Charges guide
Per unit incl. up to 5 persons	£ 18.00 - £ 21.00
extra person	£ 1.00

Discounts in low season and mid seasons.

Driffield

Thorpe Hall Caravan & Camping Site

Rudston, Driffield YO25 4JE (East Yorkshire) T: 01262 420393. E: caravansite@thorpehall.co.uk

alanrogers.com/UK4510

Just outside the village of Rudston, in the grounds of Thorpe Hall, this pleasant small touring park is 4.5 miles from the sea at Bridlington. Enthusiastically managed by Jayne Chatterton, it is set on flat grass, largely enclosed by the old kitchen garden wall. The 90 pitches are numbered and well spaced with 78 electrical hook-ups (16A) and TV connections. A separate area takes tents and there are no caravan holiday homes. There is always a chance of finding space, though it is best to book for B.Hs and peak weeks. Information sheets on a range of local walks are provided.

Facilities

The solid, central toilet block has been completely refurbished and can be heated. Some washbasins are in cabins. Refurbished bathroom for disabled visitors and families with young children (deposit for key). Launderette. Small shop with gas, essentials and local produce. Games room. TV room. Coarse fishing lake. WiFi. Off site: Bicycle hire, golf and boat launching at Bridlington 4.5 miles. Riding 2 miles. Footpath to village.

Open: 1 March - 31 October.

Directions

Site is by the B1253 road, 4.5 miles from Bridlington, on east side of Rudston. O.S.GR: TA105676. GPS: 54.093817, -0.3125

Charges guide

Per unit incl. 2 adults, 3 children and electricity	£ 14.50 - £ 27.50
tent pitch incl. 2 persons	£ 10.50 - £ 23.50

Discounts available.

Harrogate

Rudding Holiday Park

Follifoot, Harrogate HG3 1JH (North Yorkshire) T: 01423 870439. E: holiday-park@ruddingpark.com

alanrogers.com/UK4710

The extensive part wooded, part open grounds of Rudding Park are very attractive, peaceful and well laid out. One camping area is sloping but terraces provide level pitches and further pitches are in the very sheltered old walled garden. All 141 touring pitches have electricity (10/16A) and 49 'super pitches' are fully serviced. Further pitches are let on a seasonal basis and a separate area contains 96 owner-occupied caravan holiday homes and chalets. On the outer edge of the park is 'The Deer House', a family pub serving bar meals, open twice daily during B.Hs and school holidays, otherwise only at weekends.

Facilities

Two toilet blocks (heated when necessary and may be under pressure at peak times), some washbasins in cabins, baby room and bathroom. Laundry rooms. Facilities for disabled visitors. Motorcaravan service point. Shop (1/3-4/11). Gas. Restaurant and bar. Heated outdoor pool (25/5-30/8), supervised (extra charge). Adventure play area. Football pitch. Games room. Golf. Off site: Riding 1 mile. Fishing 2 miles. Buses to Knaresborough and Harrogate.

Open: 1 March - 31 January.

Directions

Park is 3 miles southeast of Harrogate, clearly signed north of the A658 and west of the A661. O.S.GR: SE333528. GPS: 53.97307, -1.49720

Charges guide

Per unit incl. 4 persons and electricity	£ 16.50 - £ 33.00
extra person	£ 4.00 - £ 9.00
child (5-16 yrs)	£ 2.00 - £ 6.00
dog	£ 1.50

Harrogate

Ripley Caravan Park

Ripley, Harrogate HG3 3AU (North Yorkshire) T: 01423 770050. E: ripleycaravanpark@talk21.com

alanrogers.com/UK4630

Peter and Valerie House are the friendly, resident owners of Ripley Park, an 18-acre grass caravan park with an indoor heated pool. It accommodates 100 touring units and 40 caravan holiday homes on fairly level grass which undulates in parts. Connected by a gravel road, some pitches are marked, others carefully spaced. There are 130 electricity connections (10A) and 20 hardstandings. The owners have planted 2,000 trees which are developing well to provide individual areas and shelter. A pond with ducks provides an attractive feature. The park is situated at the gateway to the Yorkshire Dales National Park.

Facilities

The central, attractively designed toilet block can be heated and provides smart facilities including washbasins in curtained cubicles, 4 new individual wash facilities, a baby bath and a separate unit with a shower for disabled people. Small laundry. Motorcaravan service point. Shop (limited hours in low seasons). Games room with TV. Nursery playroom. Adventure play equipment. Football area. Heated indoor pool (£1 per person) and sauna. Up to two dogs per unit are welcome unless by prior arrangement. Off site: Fishing, riding and golf 3 miles. Bus 150 yds.

Open: Easter - 31 October.

Directions

About 4 miles north of Harrogate, park access is 150 yds. down the B6165 Knaresborough road from its roundabout junction with the A61. O.S.GR: SE291601. GPS: 54.0369, -1.558833

Charges guide

Per unit incl. 2 persons and electricity	£ 13.75 - £ 15.75

Helmsley

Foxholme Touring Caravan & Camping Park

Harome, Helmsley YO62 5JG (North Yorkshire) T: **01439 771696**
alanrogers.com/UK4580

Foxholme is now an 'adult only' park. With only 60 pitches for caravans and a large field for tents, it is unusual in that nearly all the pitches are individual ones in clearings in the quite dense coniferous plantation. The trees give much shade and quite a lot of privacy (manoeuvring may be difficult on some of the pitches). All pitches have electricity (6A, a few need long leads) and six places have hardstanding. Some picnic tables are provided. There are 30 pitches for tourers, the remainder being taken by seasonal units. The site is managed by a warden. Reception opening times are limited, but very basic provisions are kept. The park is set in quiet countryside and would be a good base for touring, being within striking distance of the moors, the coast and York. There are no on-site activities. There is site lighting, but a torch would be useful.

Facilities

The toilet block is an older style building and is clean but basic. Laundry facilities and a washing up area. Two further small blocks provide WCs only in other parts of the park. Motorcaravan service point. Caravan storage. Off site: The nearest shops are at Helmsley and Kirkbymoorside, both about 4 miles away, where there is also bicycle hire. Riding and golf also 4 miles.

Open: Easter - 31 October.

Directions

Turn south off the A170 between villages of Beadlam (to west) and Nawton (to east) at sign to Ryedale School, then 1 mile to park on left (passing another park on right). From east ignore first camp sign at turning before Nawton. From west turn right 400 yards east of Helmsley, signed Harome, turn left at church, go through village and follow camp signs. O.S.GR: SE661831. Sat Nav postcode: YO62 7SD GPS: 54.23745, -0.990333

Charges guide

Per unit incl. 2 persons and electricity	£ 20.00

No credit cards.

High Bentham

Riverside Caravan Park

High Bentham LA2 7FJ (North Yorkshire) T: **01524 261272**. E: info@riversidecaravanpark.co.uk
alanrogers.com/UK4715

The pretty, tree lined approach to Riverside leads into an attractive park, owned by the Marshall family for over 30 years. Nestling in beautiful countryside, alongside the River Wenning, the park has easy access to the Yorkshire Dales and the Lake District. There are 49 marked, level grass touring pitches with 10A electricity and TV hook-ups. In addition there are 12 'super' pitches on tarmac. An area has been developed for 50 seasonal pitches on gravel. Located away from the touring area are 206 privately owned holiday homes. Tents are not accepted.

Facilities

The modern toilet block with underfloor heating is centrally situated. Washbasin cubicles. Unisex showers in a separate area. Toilet and shower room for disabled visitors (radar key) also doubles as a family shower room (charged). Motorcaravan services. Caravan storage. Outdoor play area for younger children, large field for ball games. Family games room. The river can be used for fishing (permit from reception) swimming and small boats. Off site: Golf and horse-riding nearby.

Open: All year excl. 15-28 December.

Directions

Leave the M6 at exit 34, and head east on the A683 towards Kirkby Lonsdale. After about 5 miles take B6480 signed to High Bentham. At the Black Bull Hotel follow the caravan signs. The park entrance is on the right after crossing the river bridge. O.S.GR: SD662687. GPS: 54.11311, -2.51066

Charges guide

Per unit incl. 2 persons and electricity	£ 17.50 - £ 20.50
extra person	£ 2.50 - £ 4.50

Min. charge per night £ 15.90.

191

Hull

Burton Constable Holiday Park & Arboretum

The Old Lodges, Sproatley, Hull HU11 4LN (East Yorkshire) T: **01964 562508**. E: **info@burtonconstable.co.uk**
alanrogers.com/UK4500

This park is in the grounds of the stately home of Burton Constable, and consequently the entrance is most impressive – one of the gatehouses acts as reception and tourist information room. The 90-acre campsite is part of the 300-acre park which was landscaped by Capability Brown in the 18th century and with well trimmed grass and hedges, it has a spacious feel. All 160 touring pitches have 10A electricity, there is a separate field for tents and a large hardstanding area providing electricity, water and drainage for six motorcaravans. All the pitches overlook two small lakes (unfenced). Both of these are used for fishing (permits at reception), one for boating (bring your own, but no engines). Privately owned caravan holiday homes are quite separate and do not intrude.

Facilities	Directions
Two heated toilet blocks – one older and small with unisex showers, the central newer block including a laundry room with baby changing. Well equipped room for disabled visitors (Radar key). Shop in the mobile home area. Bar with family room and tables outside overlooking the lakes. Good adventure play area. Off site: Sproatley (1 mile) has pubs, a shop and the occasional bus. Hull 7 miles. Golf 4 miles. Riding 3 miles.	From south via the M62 or Humber Bridge, take A63 into Hull, then follow signs to A165 Bridlington. On eastern outskirts of Hull follow B1238 signed Aldborough. At Sproatley, site is signed to left. From the north and Beverley, take A1035 to Hornsea. At roundabout with A165 (Hull - Bridlington) follow signs to Burton Constable for about 8 miles. Pass the Hall to Sproatley, then follow caravan signs. O.S.GR: TA186357. GPS: 53.80265, -0.199
Open: 1 March - 31 October.	

Charges guide

Per unit incl. 2 persons	
and electricity	£ 14.50 - £ 26.00
extra person	£ 2.00

Leyburn

Constable Burton Hall Caravan Park

Constable Burton Hall, Leyburn DL8 5LJ (North Yorkshire) T: **01677 450428**
E: **thomasknowles@btconnect.com alanrogers.com/UK4690**

This tranquil park is in beautiful Wensleydale and the emphasis is on peace and quiet, the wardens working to provide a relaxing environment. Being in the grounds of the Hall, it has a spacious, park-like feel to it. On part level, and some a little uneven, well-maintained grass, the 120 pitches (40 for touring units) are of a good size and all have electrical connections (10A). There are no pitches for tents. There is no shop on site but nearby Leyburn will provide all your needs. Opposite the park entrance is the Wyvill Arms for bar meals. Ball games are not permitted on site and there is no play area. The gardens of the Hall are open to the public, with a collection of maples and terraced gardens developed by Mrs Vida Burton. The park is ideally placed for visiting the Northern Dales.

Facilities	Directions
Two toilet blocks built of local stone and blending in with the local surroundings, have been refurbished recently, are well tiled, kept immaculately clean and can be heated. Facilities for disabled visitors. Baby room. The former deer barn has been adapted for use as a laundry room and extra washrooms with basins for both men and women. Information leaflets and a few books for visitors can also be found here. Gas supplies. Gates closed 22.00-08.00. Off site: Irregular bus service from site gate. Fishing and golf within 5 miles.	Park is by the A684 between Bedale and Leyburn, 0.5 miles from the village of Constable Burton on the Leyburn side. O.S.GR: SE152907. GPS: 54.3125, -1.754167
Open: Late March - 31 October.	

Charges guide

Per unit incl. 2 persons	
and electricity	£ 16.00 - £ 20.00
extra person	£ 5.00 - £ 7.00
child (5-16 yrs)	£ 3.00
awning	£ 3.00
dog	free
No commercial vehicles.	

Malton

Wolds Way Caravan Park

West Farm, West Knapton, Malton YO17 8JE (North Yorkshire) T: **01944 728463**. E: info@ryedalesbest.co.uk
alanrogers.com/UK4545

Opened in 2004, this park is located along the top of the Yorkshire Wolds with super panoramic views across the Vale of Pickering to the North Yorkshire Moors. The one and a half mile tarmac and gravel track from the road to the park is well worth while to reach this peaceful location set amongst glorious countryside. There are 80 level pitches (50 for touring units), most with 16A electricity and some with water points. There are 34 pitches with hardstanding. Seating areas, picnic benches and barbecues are provided on the park. There are many footpaths and cycle ways in the area. As well as the obvious attractions of walking the Wolds Way national trail, the park is well placed for visiting all the local attractions which include Scarborough, Bridlington, Sledmere House and Scampston Hall.

Facilities	Directions
A brand new toilet block is very well appointed and heated. Family bathrooms. Laundry facilities. Very large heated room with sinks, microwave, fridge/freezers, hot drinks machine, TV and tourist information. Room for disabled visitors. Reception also provides a small shop selling basic supplies. Play area and football field for children and many places to walk dogs. Caravan storage. A well equipped chalet for up to five people is available to rent. Off site: Bus stop 1 mile. Fishing 3 miles. Golf and riding 5 miles. Beach 15 miles. **Open:** 1 March - 31 October.	Park entrance is on the south side of the A64 York - Scarborough road, just past the B1258 turn off and it is well signed. O.S.GR: SE896744. GPS: 54.16615, -0.654033

Charges guide

Per unit incl. 2 persons and electricity	£ 13.00 - £ 18.00
extra person (over 15 yrs)	£ 4.00
child (8-15 yrs)	£ 1.50
awning	£ 1.50
dog	free

The park is peacefully located adjacent to Wolds farmland and large areas of woodland providing peace and tranquillity, meaning visitors are able to relax amidst wildlife, flora and fauna.

Yorkshire
WOLDS WAY
CARAVAN & CAMPING
West Farm, West Knapton, Malton, North Yorkshire, YO17 8JE
Telephone/Fax 01944 728 463
www.ryedalesbest.co.uk

Landscaped site situated on a working farm with outstanding views over the Vale of Ryedale and North Yorkshire Moors.
Full Facilities including:-
Fantastic Shower/Toilet block with Family Bathroom
Miles of scenic walks and cycle tracks over adjoining farm and woodland
Electric Hook-Ups and Water to all pitches
Laundry Facilities
Shop

Northallerton

Cote Ghyll Caravan & Camping Park

Osmotherley, Northallerton DL6 3AH (North Yorkshire) T: **01609 883425**. E: hills@coteghyll.com
alanrogers.com/UK4775

Jon and Helen Hill are working hard to maintain the good standard and make improvements to their park, and their efforts are evident. The site is set on a secluded hillside with the higher pitches terraced and the lower ones on a level grassy area, bordered by the small Cod Beck stream. Of the 80 pitches, 50 are for tourers. There are also 18 pitches used for caravan holiday homes and 30 are seasonal. All pitches have 10A electricity hook-ups, 12 are fully serviced. A simple site, Cote Ghyll is highly suited for lovers of peace and quiet, for bird watching or for more energetic hobbies such as cycling and walking. On the western edge of the North York Moors, cycle paths and footpaths lead almost from the site entrance and the three main long distance footpaths, the Lyke Wake walk, the Cleveland Way and the Coast to Coast, all pass close by. A 10-minute stroll takes you to the pretty and popular Osmotherley village, where there is a post office and general store, tea rooms and two pubs and a bistro selling reasonably priced meals.

Facilities	Directions
Two heated toilet blocks, one new, provide free power showers, vanity style washbasins and hairdryers. Bathroom and facilities for babies and disabled visitors. Laundry room with washing machine, dryer, iron and board. Drying room. Motorcaravan service point. New reception and larger shop. Gas supplies. Play area. Caravan storage. Off site: Shop and pubs 10 minutes walk. Fishing 1 mile. Bicycle hire 6 miles. Golf and riding 8 miles. Mount Grace Priory 4 miles. Swimming pool and leisure centre 6 miles. Beach 18 miles. **Open:** 1 March - 31 October.	Osmotherley is east of the A19. Leave the A19 at A684 exit signed Northallerton and Osmotherely. Go to Osmotherley and site is at the northern end of the village, well signed. O.S.GR: SE460983. GPS: 54.37643, -1.29166

Charges guide

Per unit incl. 2 persons	£ 14.00 - £ 17.50
incl. electricity	£ 16.00 - £ 19.50
incl. full services plus	£ 4.50
extra person	£ 2.50
child (5-12 yrs, max. 4)	£ 1.00

193

Northallerton
Otterington Park

Station Farm, South Otterington, Northallerton DL7 9JB (North Yorkshire) T: 01609 780656
E: info@otteringtonpark.com alanrogers.com/UK4765

This family owned, five acre park is located near a farm and the entrance to the park is via stables, paddocks and the farm itself. Between Thirsk and Northallerton, in the Vale of York, it is ideally placed to visit the moors and dales of Yorkshire along with local market towns, theme parks and stately homes. Predominantly it is a flat grass site with pebble hardstanding providing 40 touring pitches, each with 16A electricity. There is a separate paddock for tents or visitors not needing electricity. The park is shared with seasonal caravans and some privately owned luxury chalets. At present, landscaping offers limited shade. A family oriented park, there is a playground and grassy play areas for children. The owners have supplied good tourist information and local nature walks for visitors. There is course fishing in a well stocked, spring fed, one acre lake located 200 m. from the site. The main London - Edinburgh railway line runs to the rear of the park, so some train noise may be experienced.

Facilities

One purpose built, clean block in a heated building. Unisex en-suite style shower rooms with free showers. Laundry. Facilities for disabled visitors incorporating a baby area. Small shop in reception. Play areas. Fishing. Off site: Large supermarket 3 miles. Local bus service to Thirsk and Northallerton run every 2 hours from park entrance (not Sunday) Several local country pubs serving meals within 1 mile. Riding 1 mile. Golf 3 miles.

Open: 1 March - 31 October.

Directions

From A1M join A684 for Leeming Bar and Morton-on-Swale. At roundabout bear right on A167 signed South Otterington and Topcliffe. At South Otterington crossroads (pub) turn left signed Thornton-le-Dale to park in 500 yards. O.S.GR: SE378881. GPS: 54.28771, -1.42046

Charges guide

Per unit incl. 4 persons and electricity	£ 15.00 - £ 19.00

Otterington Park Northallerton (01609) 780656 www.otteringtonpark.com
South Otterington, Northallerton, North Yorkshire DL7 9JB

A quality, purpose built, 11 acre park for up to 40 touring units and 40 mobile homes/lodges, with water and 16/32 amp electricity, heated amenity block with five individual bath and shower rooms & disabled shower room with toilet and hand basin. Static caravans and holiday lodges for sale. Situated in the Vale of York, Otterington is an ideal base for visiting the moors and dales of Yorkshire including TV locations e.g. Emmerdale, Brideshead Revisited – historic cities, market towns, leisure centres, theme parks, golf courses, equestrian facilities and stately homes. Coarse fishing also available on our own lake.

Pickering
Overbrook Caravan Park

Maltongate, Thornton-le-Dale, Pickering YO18 7SE (North Yorkshire) T: 01751 474417
E: enquiry@overbrookcaravanpark.co.uk alanrogers.com/UK4534

Situated in the very pretty village of Thornton-le-Dale, Overbrook has been developed on the site of the old railway station. With the line dismantled, the station building now provides holiday cottages and the caravan park toilet facilities. This is a level site with 50 pitches (20 for tourers, the remainder used for seasonal units) arranged either side of a tarmac access road and backed by trees. All are on hardstanding and all have electricity connections (16A). Neither children nor tents are accepted at this 'adult only' park. The owners will do all they can to assist you during your stay. A half mile, level walk brings you to the village. This is very convenient for shops, pubs, tearooms and even a chocolate factory. There is a good bus service to Pickering, Malton, Whitby, York and Scarborough. The beck which runs through the village and down under the railway property is home to kingfishers, herons, ducks and trout. There are plenty of footpaths for walking in this lovely area. Many local attractions are within half an hour's drive from the park. Dalby Forest is nearby with a visitor centre, walks and mountain bike trails.

Facilities

The toilet and shower facilities are situated in the old station house. Laundry facilities. Gas supplies. No tents accepted. Children are not admitted. Off site: Village with bus stop, shops, pubs, fish and chips 800 yds. Bicycle hire 800 yds. Fishing 3 miles. Golf 5 miles.

Open: 1 March - 31 October.

Directions

Thornton-le-Dale is on the A170 Pickering - Scarborough road. In the village follow sign for Malton and park is 800 yds. on the left (follow the stream on the left). O.S.GR: SE833821. GPS: 54.228533, -0.7229

Charges guide

Per unit incl. 2 persons and electricity	£ 14.50 - £ 16.00
incl. awning	£ 16.00 - £ 17.00
extra person	£ 2.50
dog (max. 2)	free

No credit cards.

Pickering
Forest Holidays Spiers House
Cropton Forest, Cropton, Pickering YO18 8ES (North Yorkshire) T: **01751 417591**
E: **info@forestholidays.co.uk** **alanrogers.com/UK4570**

Forest Holidays is a partnership between the Forestry Commission and The Camping and Caravanning Club. The Spiers House site is set in a sunny clearing in the middle of Cropton Forest. It is an ideal location for a cycling or walking holiday without having to move your car. The site buildings, built in local stone, are set around a central courtyard with a pedestrian archway leading to the pitches. Sloping fields provide for 150 pitches, which include 74 with 10A electricity and 19 with hardstanding (there are plans for more hardstanding pitches).

Facilities	Directions
The tiled toilet block is spacious, if a little Spartan, with open plan washbasins and roomy, preset showers (refurbishment is planned). Unit for disabled campers. Dishwashing sinks under cover with free hot water, laundry room with washing machine, dryer and sinks (hot water charged). Well stocked shop. Large adventure playground and games field set under tall pines. Raised barbecues are permitted. Off site: Pub with home-brewed beer 1 mile. Riding 5 miles. Fishing 7 miles. Golf 12 miles. **Open:** All year.	From the A170 Pickering head westwards towards Helmsley. Turn right signed Cropton and Rosedale (do not go into Cropton village). Forest and park signed after 4 miles. Entrance is via a 500 m. single track with passing places). O.S.GR: SE758918. GPS: 54.30765, -0.846267

Charges guide

Per unit incl. 2 persons	£ 11.00 - £ 21.50
extra person	£ 4.75 - £ 6.25

Pickering
Upper Carr Chalet & Touring Park
Upper Carr Lane, Malton Road, Pickering YO18 7JP (North Yorkshire) T: **01751 473115**
E: **info@uppercarrchaletandtouringpark.co.uk** **alanrogers.com/UK4620**

With a central location in the Vale of Pickering, Upper Carr is well placed for the many attractions the area has to offer. Now under new ownership, the enthusiastic manager is keen to develop it into a family-friendly park, introducing themed weekends and nature trails. The park is surrounded by a high, well trimmed hedge which protects it from the wind and deadens the road noise. Upper Carr's six acres provide 80 level pitches, 75 with 10A electricity and some with hardstanding. Seasonal units use 25 pitches. The picturesque village can be reached along the Upper Carr nature trail.

Facilities	Directions
The heated toilet blocks are dated (in 'chalet' style building) but clean. There are plans for these to be updated. Showers are charged for. Baby changing facilities. Separate room with WC and washbasin for disabled visitors. Laundry room. Motorcaravan service point. Small shop in reception for basics. Play area. Bicycle hire. Nature trail. Off site: Pub 100 yards. Golf (9-hole) or tennis adjacent. Swimming pool 1.5 miles. Pickering 2 miles. Fishing 5 miles. Riding 6 miles. **Open:** 1 March - 31 October.	Travelling on the Pickering - Malton A169 road, park is on the left about 1.5 miles south of Pickering. O.S.GR: SE804815. GPS: 54.222967, -0.769

Charges guide

Per unit incl. 2 adults, 2 children and electricity	£ 13.00 - £ 18.90
extra adult	£ 2.50
extra child	£ 1.50

Pickering
Rosedale Caravan & Camping Park
Rosedale Abbey, Pickering YO18 8SA (North Yorkshire) T: **01751 417272**. E: **info@flowerofmay.com**
alanrogers.com/UK4770

In a beautiful location below Rosedale Moor and on the edge of a popular village, this is a campsite that is highly suitable for walkers. The surrounding hillsides are a maze of public footpaths. The site is reasonably level, with 200 pitches, a few with hardstanding and with 28 electricity connections (10A). There are some caravan holiday homes (private) and seasonal touring pitches in their own areas, with the remainder for touring units. The majority have superb views of the surrounding hills. One field is set aside for tents only and many are sited near the river which runs along the edge of the park.

Facilities	Directions
Fully refurbished sanitary facilities with underfloor heating include free showers and hairdressing units. Facilities for disabled visitors and baby changing. Dishwashing and laundry facilities. Reception provides maps and a small selection of camping accessories, plus gas supplies. Games room with pool and video games. Large play area with space for ball games. Entrance barrier controlled by card (£10 deposit). Off site: The village has a general store with daily papers, a post office, bakery, pubs and a restaurant. 9-hole golf course (set on a picturesque hillside) 200 yards. **Open:** Easter - 28 October.	Rosedale is signed from the A170, 2 miles west of Pickering. Site is in the village of Rosedale Abbey, 8 miles north of the A170. O.S.GR: SE725958. GPS: 54.35366, -0.88795

Charges guide

Per unit incl. electricity and up to 4 persons	£ 14.00 - £ 19.00
tent incl. up to 4 persons	£ 11.50 - £ 15.50
10% discount on pitch fee for weekly bookings.	

195

Ripon

Woodhouse Farm Caravan & Camping Park

Winksley, Ripon HG4 3PG (North Yorkshire) T: 01765 658309. E: woodhouse.farm@talk21.com

alanrogers.com/UK4660

This secluded family park on a former working farm, is only six miles from Ripon and about four from the World Heritage site of Fountains Abbey. It is a very rural park with a spacious feel and various pitching areas are tucked away in woodland areas or around the edges of hedged fields with the centre left clear for children. There are hard roads and most of the 160 pitches have 16A electricity. There are 56 acres in total, 17.5 devoted to the site and 20 acres of woodland for walking. The 2.5-acre fishing lake is a big attraction and provides a pleasant area for picnics or walks. The tastefully developed bar (daily) and restaurant (weekends only) offers reasonably priced menus. Woodhouse Farm has a quiet, secluded location from which many excursions can be made – the Yorkshire Dales of Nidderdale, Wharfedale, Wensleydale and Swaledale are all within easy reach. As in most parts of the Dales, the peace is occasionally disturbed by passing jets, but happily not very often.

Facilities

The clean toilet block near the touring pitches has been upgraded and includes heating, roomy showers (20p) and some washbasins in cabins. Two bathrooms. Facilities for disabled visitors. Extra facilities are in the farm buildings along with a well equipped laundry, reception and shop. Gas supplies. Motorcaravan services. Bar (daily) and restaurant (weekends). Takeaway on request. Games room with TV. Play equipment. Fishing (day tickets from reception). Mountain bike hire. Caravan storage. Deposit for amenity block key £10. Off site: Twice daily bus service passes site gate. Many attractive villages with inns supplying food and drinks. The small historic city of Ripon has a beautiful cathedral. Riding 3 miles. Golf 6 miles.

Open: 1 March - 31 October.

Directions

From Ripon take Fountains Abbey - Pateley Bridge road (B6265). After about 3.5 miles turn right to Grantley and then follow campsite signs for further 1-2 miles. O.S.GR: SE241715.
GPS: 54.137417, -1.634667

Charges guide

Per unit incl. 2 persons	£ 11.00 - £ 14.00
incl. electricity	£ 12.50 - £ 15.50
extra person	£ 2.50
child (5-16 yrs)	£ 0.75
small tent incl. 2 persons	£ 9.50 - £ 12.50

Ripon

Riverside Meadows Country Caravan Park

Ure Bank Top, Ripon HG4 1JD (North Yorkshire) T: 01765 602964. E: info@flowerofmay.com

alanrogers.com/UK4760

Riverside Meadows is a rural park, although the approach to it belies that fact. The short approach from the main road passes a row of houses and a factory, but once they are passed, the park opens up before you and you are once again back in the countryside. There are plenty of caravan holiday homes here but they are, on the whole, quite separate from the 64 touring pitches. These pitches, practically all with electrical hook-ups, are mainly on gently sloping grass with just a few hardstandings. A meadow separates the park from the River Ure, a favourite place for strolling and fishing (licences available). Close to Ripon is the Lightwater Valley theme park, and a little further are Fountains Abbey, Harrogate, Knaresborough, the Yorkshire Dales and Thirsk with its market and the James Herriot centre. There is lots to see and do on and off the park for both families and couples.

Facilities

The tiled toilet block is quite new and includes a baby room, dishwashing room, a fully fitted shower room for disabled visitors. Laundry facilities. Shop. Bar with snacks. Games room. Well equipped play area. An indoor pool is planned. Off site: Fishing, bicycle hire and riding 800 yds. Golf 1.25 miles. The delightful market town (city) of Ripon with its ancient cathedral is only 20 minutes walk.

Open: Easter - 31 October.

Directions

At the most northern roundabout on the Ripon bypass (A61), turn onto the A6108 signed Ripon, Masham and Leyburn. Go straight on at mini-roundabout and park is signed on right. O.S.GR: SE317727.
GPS: 54.15045, -1.515

Charges guide

Per unit incl. up to 4 persons and electricity	£ 14.00 - £ 19.00
tent incl. up to 4 persons	£ 11.50 - £ 15.50
extra person (over 3 yrs)	£ 3.00
dog (max. 2)	£ 1.00

10% discount on pitch fee for weekly bookings.

Scarborough
Saint Helens in the Park

Wykeham, Scarborough YO13 9QD (North Yorkshire) T: 01723 862771. E: caravans@wykeham.co.uk
alanrogers.com/UK4540

St Helens is a high quality touring park with pleasant views, set within 30 acres of parkland. The site is divided into terraces with trees screening each area (one of which is set aside for adults only) and the 250 mainly level pitches have a spacious feel. Electrical hook-ups (16A) are available on 240 pitches, also in the late arrivals area. Set on a hillside, the park's buildings are built in local stone and all is maintained to a high standard. The Downe Arms, a short stroll away, is known for its good food and family-friendly atmosphere. Scarborough is only five miles away with its beaches and summer shows.

Facilities

Four heated toilet blocks are well equipped and maintained to a high standard. Some washbasins in cabins, free showers and baby baths. Unit for disabled visitors. Good central laundry room. Well stocked shop. Café and takeaway. Internet café. WiFi. Bicycle hire. Small games room. Tourist information cabin. Caravan storage. Off site: Nearby Wykeham Lakes offer fishing (trout and coarse), scuba diving, windsurfing and sailing (in your own boat), 1 mile. Golf or riding 2 miles.

Open: All year excl. 15 January - 13 February.

Directions

Park access road leads off the A170 (Pickering - Scarborough) road in Wykeham village 2 miles west of the junction with B1262. O.S.GR: SE963835. GPS: 54.238033, -0.500467

Charges guide

Per unit incl. 2 persons and electricity	£ 14.90 - £ 19.90
extra person (over 3 yrs)	£ 1.50
dog	£ 1.50

St Helens in the Park
250 Spacious pitches set in 30 acres of parkland.
Adventure playground, excellent shop,
games room & amusements
Nearby there is excellent fishing, diving,
windsurfing & sailing
Tel: 01723 862771

Scarborough
Cayton Village Caravan Park

Mill Lane, Cayton Bay, Scarborough YO11 3NN (North Yorkshire) T: 01723 583171
E: info@caytontouring.co.uk alanrogers.com/UK4550

Cayton Village Caravan Park can only be described as a gem. Just three miles from the hustle and bustle of Scarborough, it is a peaceful, attractive haven. Originally just a flat field with caravans around the perimeter, years of hard work have produced a park which is very pleasing to the eye and of which the owner, Carol, can be justly proud. The entrance is a mass of flowers. The 200 pitches are numbered and everyone is taken to their pitch. All of the 190 for touring units have electricity (many with hardstanding) and there are 91 fully serviced pitches. The late arrivals area here also has electrical hook-ups. This is useful as the gates are locked at night and anyone leaving early is also expected to use it, so as not to disturb others. A short walk across a field takes you to Cayton Village which has a popular pub providing excellent meals, a post office stores and a church, and Cayton Bay is half a mile. The North York Moors are a short distance away, as is the Forestry Commission's Dalby Forest with its scenic drive, mountain bike trails and way-marked walks.

Facilities

Three toilet blocks (key code locks) can be heated and have high quality tiling and fittings. Some showers are preset, others controllable. Two family shower rooms, family bathroom and baby facilities. Reception and shop with comprehensive range including gas and caravan spares. Adventure playground. Nature walk. Caravan storage. Off site: Fishing and bicycle hire 0.5 miles. Riding 4 miles. Golf 3 miles. Regular bus service from the village to Scarborough or Filey.

Open: 1 March - 31 October.

Directions

From A64 Malton - Scarborough road turn right at the roundabout (with MacDonald's and pub) signed B1261 Filey. Follow signs for Cayton, in Cayton Village take second left after Blacksmiths Arms down Mill Lane (at brown tourism sign) and park is 200 yds. on left. From roundabout to park is 2.25 miles. From A165 turn inland at Cayton Bay roundabout and park is 0.5 miles on right. O.S.GR: TA057837. GPS: 54.235733, -0.376117

Charges guide

Per unit incl. 2 persons, electricity and awning	£ 13.00 - £ 26.00
incl. services and hardstanding	£ 18.00 - £ 29.00
tent pitch without electricity	£ 10.00 - £ 20.00
extra person	£ 1.00
dog	£ 1.00

(197)

Scarborough
Flower of May Holiday Park

Lebberston Cliff, Scarborough YO11 3NU (North Yorkshire) T: **01723 584311**. E: **info@flowerofmay.com**
alanrogers.com/UK4520

Situated on the cliff tops, 4.5 miles from Scarborough and 2.5 miles from Filey, Flower of May is a large, family owned park for both touring caravans and caravan holiday homes. The entrance to the park is very colourful and the reception office is light and airy. The park is licensed for 300 touring units and 184 caravan holiday homes (45 to hire, the remainder privately owned). The touring pitches are pretty level, arranged in wide avenues, mainly on grass and divided by shrubs. There are 223 with electricity (10A), including 200 'star pitches' with water and drainage also. The range of leisure facilities grouped around reception. It includes an indoor pool with areas for both adults and children, a water flume and a jacuzzi. In the same building are two squash courts, ten-pin bowling, table tennis and amusement machines. The leisure centre is also open to the public (concessionary rates for campers) but during high season is only available to local regulars and the caravanners and campers on the park. There is a cliff walk to the beach but it is only suitable for the reasonably active – there is an easier walk down from a car park a mile away. Riverside Meadows at Ripon and Rosedale Country Caravan Park near Pickering are under the same ownership.

Facilities

Three toilet blocks, all refurbished in a light and colourful style, are fully tiled with washbasins in both cabins and vanity style. Baby rooms. Facilities for disabled visitors. Well stocked and licensed shop near the leisure centre, as is the laundry room. Two modern bar lounges, one for families and one for adults only, with discos in season. Café and takeaway fish and chips. Games room with TV. Large adventure playground. Pay and play golf course (£5 a round). Indoor swimming pool. Skateboard ramps. Basketball. Dog exercise area, but numbers and breeds are limited (one per pitch) and not allowed at all at B.Hs and the six week summer holiday. Off site: The Plough Inn near the park entrance offers good bar meals. Fishing, boat slipway or riding 2 miles. Bicycle hire 4 miles.

Open: Easter - 28 October.

Directions

Park is signed from roundabout at the junction of the A165 and B1261 roads from where it is 600 yds. O.S.GR: TA088836. GPS: 54.2292, -0.3425

Charges guide

Per unit incl. up to 4 persons	£ 18.00 - £ 25.00
tent (no electricity)	£ 14.00 - £ 20.00
child (under 3 yrs)	free

10% discount on pitch fee for weekly advance bookings.

Scarborough
Jacobs Mount Caravan Park

Stepney Road, Scarborough YO12 5NL (North Yorkshire) T: **01723 361178**. E: **jacobsmount@yahoo.co.uk**
alanrogers.com/UK4590

Situated just two miles from the centre of Scarborough, on the edge of the Forge Valley National Park, Jacobs Mount is well placed to meet many holiday needs. The sea and the sand are the main attractions, but this is also on the doorstep of the North York moors and the Dalby Forest Drive. In addition to caravan holiday homes in separate areas of the park, there are 142 touring pitches, all with electricity. Of these 131 are fully serviced (water, drainage) on well spaced gravel hardstandings. In sunny locations, some pitches have good views. There is a bar with a pleasant lounge (no children). Bar meals and a quite extensive range of takeaways can be purchased. For those with children, a family room is provided and a room for games with a TV. Amenities also include an activity centre and a play area.

Facilities

The heated toilet block is new and of a high standard. Washbasins in cubicles with WCs, large shower cubicles (free) and a family bathroom (metered hot water) and baby changing facilities. Separate unisex cubicles contain WC, washbasin and shower. Motorcaravan service point. Small shop in reception for basic needs. Bar with bar meals and takeaway. Two play areas (CCTV monitored) for different ages. Caravan storage. No gazebo style tents allowed. Up to two dogs per pitch are accepted. Off site: Scarborough centre and beach 2 miles. Golf, fishing and bicycle hire 2 miles. Riding 5 miles.

Open: 1 March - 6 November.

Directions

Site entrance is on the A170 Pickering - Scarborough road, about 2 miles west of Scarborough (on the right as you start to drop down into the town). O.S.GR: TA021877. GPS: 54.267283, -0.43455

Charges guide

Per unit incl. 4 persons and electricity	£ 11.00 - £ 19.50
extra person (3 yrs and over)	£ 2.00
awning	£ 2.50
dog (max. 2)	£ 2.50

No single sex parties.

Scarborough
Jasmine Park

Cross Lane, Snainton, Scarborough YO13 9BE (North Yorkshire) T: 01723 859240
E: enquiries@jasminepark.co.uk alanrogers.com/UK4740

Jasmine is a very attractive, quiet and well-manicured park with owners who go to much trouble to produce many plants to decorate a very colourful entrance. Set in the Vale of Pickering, the park is level, well drained and protected by a coniferous hedge. The 126 pitches (78 for touring units) are on grass, with electricity connections (10/16A) for all caravans and some tents. There is no play equipment for children, although a field is provided for games. Much tourist information is provided in a log cabin and the owners are only too happy to advise. This is an award-winning, peaceful park for a restful holiday. A member of the Countryside Discovery group. The market town of Pickering and the seaside town of Scarborough are both eight miles. Many local attractions are within easy reach, including Castle Howard, Dalby Forest, Sledmere House, Nunington Hall, Goathland (the setting for ITV's 'Heartbeat') and the North York Moors Railway. Some privately owned log cabins and seasonal tourers are also on the site.

Facilities

The heated toilet block has been refurbished to a high standard and is kept very clean. It includes a large room for families or disabled visitors containing a bath, shower, WC and washbasin (access by code). Laundry room with dishwashing sinks, washing machine, dryer and iron (hot water metered). Motorcaravan service point. Licensed shop selling essentials and gas. Dogs are welcome but there is no dog walk. Caravan storage. Off site: Bus service in village 0.5 miles. Riding 2 miles. Golf driving range and 9-hole course 2 miles. Fishing and bicycle hire 5 miles.

Open: 1 March - 31 October.

Directions

Snainton is on the A170 Pickering - Scarborough road and park is signed at eastern end of the village. Turn down Barker's Lane and at the small crossroads turn left and the Park is 230 yards on the left.
O.S.GR: SE928813. GPS: 54.218583, -0.575567

Charges guide

Per unit incl. 4 persons, electricity	£ 17.00 - £ 25.00
extra person	£ 2.00
child (under 14 yrs)	£ 1.00
awning	£ 2.00

Min. stay at Easter 4 nights, other B.Hs 3 nights.

Scarborough
Lebberston Touring Park

Filey Road, Lebberston, Scarborough YO11 3PE (North Yorkshire) T: 01723 585723
E: info@lebberstontouring.co.uk alanrogers.com/UK4780

Lebberston Touring Park is a quiet, spacious touring site and is highly suitable for anyone seeking a quiet relaxing break, such as mature couples or young families (although tents are not accepted). There is no play area or games room, the only concession to children being a large central area with goal posts, so teenagers may get bored. The park itself has a very spacious feel – it is gently sloping and south facing and the views are superb. There are 125 numbered pitches with 75 for touring units. All have 10A electricity and 25 are on hardstanding. The circular access road is tarmac, the grass is well manicured and the entrance a mass of flowers. Reception is part of a farmhouse style new build, also the home of the owners and their young family. The resorts of Filey, Bridlington, Scarborough and Hornsea provide something for everyone, the moors and the Dalby forest are also within a short distance. This being such a popular area, we feel justified in adding another site to this guide, especially one of such quality.

Facilities

Recently upgraded toilet blocks are of high quality and kept very clean. Large shower cubicles and washbasins in cubicles with curtains. Both blocks have dishwashing sinks and one has a family bathroom (20p). Good room for disabled visitors. Laundry with washing machine, dryer, spin dryer, iron and board. A key is supplied for the laundry and bathroom, with radar key access to the disabled shower room. Reception sells a few supplies, plus papers, ice cream and gas. Only 'breathable' groundsheets are permitted. WiFi (charged). Off site: Hourly bus 5 minutes walk. Local pub within 5 minutes walking distance. Each new arrival is given details of parking in Scarborough including a parking disc.

Open: 1 March - 31 October.

Directions

From A64 Malton - Scarborough road turn right at roundabout (MacDonald's, pub and superstore) signed B1261 Filey. Go through Cayton, Killerby and in 4.5 miles site is signed on the left (not easy to see). If you missing the turning to the Park, continue to roundabout and turn around. O.S.GR: TA082823. GPS: 54.22650, -0.34709

Charges guide

Per unit incl. 2 persons and electricity	£ 14.50 - £ 22.00
extra person	£ 1.50
child (5-14 yrs)	£ 1.00
trailer tent over 8 sq.m.	£ 2.00
full awning	£ 2.00

Selby

The Ranch Caravan Park

Cliffe Common, Cliffe, Selby YO8 6EF (North Yorkshire) T: 01757 638984
E: contact@theranchcaravanpark.co.uk alanrogers.com/UK4645

The Ranch is a small, family run caravan park set in six acres of woodland. There are 55 pitches in total, with 39 for touring units on well draining land with some hardstandings available. All have electricity (10/16A) and four also have water and drainage. Several pitches are most suitable for American style motorhomes and these are welcomed. The reception has a tiny shop that sometimes stocks UHT milk. This is a well maintained park with two areas of open grass, one surrounded by a gravel road. Most of the site is surrounded by trees. There is a security gate at the entrance. There is a slightly overgrown wooded area with some adventure playground equipment amongst it. A large function hall is attached to the toilet block with a small bar, lounge area, tables and a dance floor. Light meals and takeaways are offered on Friday and Saturday evenings only during the season and at the owner's discretion at other times.

Facilities

Heated toilet block has free showers (with dividing curtains). Facilities for disabled visitors that doubles as a family bathroom and baby room. Motorcaravan service point. Small laundry. Function hall with bar and lounge area. Light meals and takeaway (Friday and Saturday evenings). Off site: Selby 4 miles. York 12 miles. Fishing 2 miles. Golf and riding 15 miles.

Open: All year excluding 5 January - 5 February.

Directions

Leave M62 at exit 37 (Goole) and take A63 towards Selby. At Cliffe turn right and after 1 mile, turn left at crossroads. Park is 80 yards on the right. O.S.GR: SE663338. GPS: 53.79821, -0.99064

Charges guide

Per unit incl. 2 persons and electricity	£ 14.50
extra person	£ 1.50
child (5-16 yrs)	£ 1.00

Settle

Knight Stainforth Hall Caravan & Camping Park

Little Stainforth, Settle BD24 0DP (North Yorkshire) T: 01729 822200. E: info@knightstainforth.co.uk
alanrogers.com/UK4720

In a very attractive setting, this park is located in the heart of the Yorkshire Dales, the whole area a paradise for hill walking, fishing and pot-holing and with outstanding scenery. The camping area is on slightly sloping grass, sheltered by mature woodland. There are 100 touring pitches, 50 with electricity (16A) and ten with hardstanding, and a separate area contains 66 privately-owned caravan holiday homes. A gate leads from the bottom of the camping field giving access to the river bank where the Ribble bubbles over small waterfalls and rocks and whirls around deep pools where campers swim in warm weather. This area is not fenced and children should be supervised, although it is a super location for a family picnic. Settle is only two miles away and train buffs will want to travel on the Settle - Carlisle railway over the famous Ribblehead Viaduct.

Facilities

A modern, heated amenity block provides toilets and showers and includes some washbasins in cubicles. Facilities for disabled visitors and baby changing. Laundry facilities. Motorcaravan service point. Small shop. Games/TV room. Play area with safety base. Fishing (permit from reception). Security barrier. Deposit for key to toilet block and barrier £10. WiFi. Off site: Bicycle hire and golf 3 miles. Riding 6 miles. The Dales Falconry and Conservation Centre at Feizor.

Open: 1 March - 31 October.

Directions

From Settle town centre, drive west towards Giggleswick. Ignore turning marked Stainforth and Horton, and after 200 yards turn right into Stackhouse Lane (signed Knight Stainforth). After 2 miles turn right at crossroads. O.S.GR: SD815671. GPS: 54.10025, -2.284833

Charges guide

Per unit incl. 2 persons	£ 12.00 - £ 15.00
incl. electricity	£ 14.00 - £ 17.00
extra person	£ 2.50
child (5-16 yrs)	£ 1.50
backpacker	£ 4.50
Min. stay at B.Hs 3 nights. Special offers.	

Skipsea

Skipsea Sands Holiday Park

Mill Lane, Skipsea YO25 8TZ (East Yorkshire) T: 0871 664 9812. E: skipsea.sands@parkresorts.com

alanrogers.com/UK4496

This well established holiday park is now owned by Park Resorts and is primarily dedicated to caravan holiday homes, of which there are 600 privately owned and 61 to rent. There is however a pleasantly laid out touring park occupying its own corner of the site and bordered by an attractive duck pond and a large playing area (both well fenced). The 91 marked, level pitches are separated by hedges and all have electricity (16A), water and waste water points; 18 also have sewage connections. The park's leisure facilities are outstanding and a full daily programme of activities and entertainment is offered for children and adults. Situated on the cliffs on the Yorkshire coast south of Bridlington, beaches are either a good walk or a short drive away. There is a wide choice of possible days out: Beverley with its Minster or its horse racing; Spurn Point or Bempton Cliffs (RSPB); Cruckley Animal Farm or Bondville Miniature Village; Bridlington's beaches and its Harbour Heritage Museum; even Pickering and the North York Moors are within easy reach.

Facilities

Two heated toilet blocks are fairly basic, with pushbutton showers and open washbasins. En-suite facilities for disabled visitors are rather stark. Basic chemical disposal and motorhome service point. Washing machines and dryers. Well stocked shop. Bar, coffee shop and restaurant with takeaway. Leisure centre with sports hall, ten-pin bowling, heated indoor swimming pool, jacuzzi, sauna and steam room. Fitness centre with gym and sun bed. Games 'Kingdom' with electronic games and 'Kids Zone'. Off site: Beach 0.25 m (on foot) or 4 miles (by car). Fishing 2 miles. Golf 3 miles. Boat launching 6 miles. Riding and sailing 9 miles. Buses from park gates. Village with shops, pub, restaurant 1 mile.

Open: Easter - 31 October.

Directions

Skipsea is 20 miles northeast of Hull and 10 miles south of Bridlington. From the Humber Bridge or from the M62/A63 west of Hull, head north on the A164 to Beverley. Then take the A165 towards Bridlington and turn east on B1249 to Skipsea. In village, turn right then left to site (signed). O.S.GR: TA175565. GPS: 53.98957, -0.20716

Charges guide

Per unit incl. all services	£ 14.00 - £ 33.00
tent pitch	£ 3.00 - £ 24.00
dog	£ 1.00 - £ 3.00

Skipton

Wood Nook Caravan Park

Skirethorns, Threshfield, Skipton BD23 5NU (North Yorkshire) T: 01756 752412

E: enquiries@woodnook.net alanrogers.com/UK4670

Wood Nook is a family-run park in the heart of Wharfedale, part of the Yorkshire Dales National Park. The access road is narrow for a short distance, so care should be taken. The site includes six acres of woodland with quite rare flora and wildlife. Reception is in the farmhouse, as is the small shop. The gently sloping fields have gravel roads and provide 48 touring pitches with gravel hardstanding. All have electricity (10A) and nearby water and chemical disposal points. There is also room for 24 tents and there are some caravan holiday homes to let. The Thompson family are very friendly, always willing to have a chat, although Wood Nook is still a working farm producing beef cattle. The park itself adjoins the fells, with direct access from the top of the site. Nearby is the village of Grassington, with its cobbled main street and quaint gift shops. This is a delightful and peaceful base from which to explore the Yorkshire Dales.

Facilities

Converted farm buildings provide dated but clean sanitary facilities which can be heated. Washbasins in cubicles for ladies. Roomy showers (in another building – coin operated). Laundry facilities. Motorcaravan service points. Licensed shop for basics and gifts (from Easter). Gas. Small play area. American motorhomes are taken by prior arrangement. Internet access. WiFi (charged). Off site: Fishing and bicycle hire 2 miles. Riding 3 miles. Golf 9 miles. Leisure centre.

Open: 1 March - 31 October.

Directions

Threshfield is 9 miles north of Skipton on the B6265. Continue through village onto B6160 and after garage turn left into Skirethorns Lane. Follow signs for 600 yds, keeping left up narrow lane, then turn right up track for 300 yds. The last 900 yds. is single track – on arrival you could phone ahead to make sure it is clear. O.S.GR: SD974641. GPS: 54.07267, -2.04199

Charges guide

Per person	£ 3.00
child (5-16 yrs)	£ 1.50
serviced pitch incl. electricity	£ 9.00
hiker or cyclist incl. tent	£ 5.00
Payment also accepted in euros.	

Skipton

Howgill Lodge Caravan & Camping Park

Barden, Skipton BD23 6DJ (North Yorkshire) T: 01756 720655. E: info@howgill-lodge.co.uk

alanrogers.com/UK4750

Howgill Lodge is a traditional family park set in the heart of the Yorkshire Dales. Arranged on a sloping hillside, the terraced pitches have fantastic views. It is a small park catering for the needs of walkers, tourers and the people who like to just relax. The whole area is a haven for both experienced walkers or the casual rambler, without having to move your car. All the pitches at the upper part of the park are on hardstanding and have electricity connections (10A), the lower ones are mainly on grass (40 in total). Picnic tables and chairs are provided. There are four mobile homes available to rent. Reception also houses a small shop which sells most of the basics including fresh foods. Pretty villages abound in the area, all with attractive inns and nearby Embsay has the Dales Railway with steam trains.

Facilities

Heated toilet facilities are at the entrance, close to reception, with dishwashing sinks outside, under cover. Showers are large and adjustable (on payment). Fully equipped laundry room with four unisex showers also here. Outdoor washing lines are provided. Two small blocks housing WCs are lower down the site for the convenience of tent campers. Shop. No play area. Fishing licences are available from reception. Off site: Bus service within walking distance (3 per day). Skipton, an agricultural market town, is 8 miles and the well known Bolton Abbey, with its beautiful riverside walks is 3 miles. Fishing 1 mile. Golf, riding and bicycle hire 7 miles.

Open: 1 April - 31 October.

Directions

Turn off A59 Skipton - Harrogate road at roundabout onto B6160 Bolton Abbey, Burnsall road. Three miles past Bolton Abbey at Barden Towers, bear right signed Appletreewick and Pateley Bridge. This road is fairly narrow for 1.25 miles (with passing places). Park is signed on right at phone box. O.S.GR: SE065593. GPS: 54.025767, -1.909833

Charges guide

Per unit, 2 persons and electricity	£ 16.00 - £ 20.00
family unit incl. electricity	£ 22.00 - £ 26.00
tent incl. car and 2 persons	£ 16.00 - £ 20.00
hiker	£ 6.00
awning	£ 2.50

Wakefield

Nostell Priory Holiday Park

Nostell, Wakefield WF4 1QE (West Yorkshire) T: 01924 863938. E: park@nostellprioryholidaypark.co.uk

alanrogers.com/UK4700

This tranquil, secluded woodland park is within the Nostell Priory estate and provides 40 touring pitches, in addition to 84 caravan holiday homes in a separate area. In a grassy, flat and sheltered area edged with mature trees and with a gravel access road, all the touring pitches have electricity (5A) and hardstanding. The park's amenities are designed to blend into the environment and are built in rustic wood, including the sanitary block. The park is well cared for and the natural environment is encouraged so there is an abundance of birds and wildlife. Nostell Priory itself, with its collection of Chippendale furniture and attractive gardens, is well worth a visit. Fishing, golf and watersports are possible locally (details in reception). The Dales, York and the Peak District are all an easy drive away. Buses pass the end of the drive (a mile long).

Facilities

The toilet block, although older in style, has been refurbished and includes some washbasins in cubicles (coded entry). Separate room for dishwashing. Laundry with two washing machines and a dryer (opening times on the door). Gas supplies. Play area (no ball games on site). Fishing. Up to two dogs are accepted. 'Cocoon' luxury tent for hire. Off site: Nearest shops 2 miles. Golf 5 miles. Boat launching 8 miles.

Open: 1 March - 31 October.

Directions

Park entrance is off A638 Wakefield - Doncaster road, 5 miles southeast of Wakefield. Follow the drive for 0.5 miles (rose nursery on left). Approaching from the south on A638, the site entrance is almost a mile past the entry to the Priory, on the right. O.S.GR: SE394181. GPS: 53.65495, -1.3985

Charges guide

Per unit incl. 2 persons and electricity	£ 11.00 - £ 19.50

Less 10% for 7 night bookings.
Less 10% for senior citizens.

Wetherby
Maustin Caravan Park

Kearby with Netherby, Wetherby LS22 4DA (North Yorkshire) T: 01132 886234. E: judith@maustin.co.uk
alanrogers.com/UK4755

A tranquil site for couples only, this well manicured park is set within the North Yorkshire National Park. It offers 25 well spaced pitches sited on grass, all with peaceful, scenic views of the surrounding area. Caravan holiday homes are in a separate area. A bowling club on the site offers membership to all visitors and competitions are held throughout the season. Relax in the comfortable lounge or in the tasteful bar and restaurant area. A covered terrace overlooks the bowling green. There is a information building providing a books, DVDs, videos and games which you may borrow free of charge. Local wildlife and tourist information is also available, along with internet services. Close to Harewood House and Harrogate, you can enjoy country walks or scenic drives throughout 'Emmerdale country' and the surrounding villages. The attentive park managers ensure that the luxury facilities are spotlessly clean so that you have a pleasant stay.

Facilities

One heated, purpose built toilet block has luxury showers, free hairdryers and roomy toilet and washing cubicles, all with non-slip flooring. Designated facility for disabled visitors. Laundry room. Kitchen area with freezer. Milk, newspapers, etc. to order. Internet facilities. Off site: Riding 2 miles. Golf 4 miles.

Open: All year excl. February.

Directions

From A1 North take exit 47 for Harrogate (A59), then after three roundabouts (9 miles) turn left on A61 (Leeds). In 2 miles turn left (Kirkby Overblow) then right to Kearby and park. From A1 South follow Harewood House signs through Collingham (A61). At lights turn right over River Wharfe, right for Kirkby Overblow, then as above. O.S.GR: SE331468. GPS: 53.91818, -1.49518

Charges guide

Per unit incl. 2 persons	£ 15.50
incl. services	£ 17.50
extra person	£ 2.00
dog	free

Whitby
Sandfield House Farm Caravan Park

Sandsend Road, Whitby YO21 3SR (North Yorkshire) T: 01947 602660. E: info@sandfieldhousefarm.co.uk
alanrogers.com/UK4528

Although it is set on a hill in undulating countryside on the low cliffs near Whitby, this park provides 200 level pitches, all with electricity. There are 60 pitches for touring caravans, all on hardstanding, and these are mainly set to the front of the park giving wonderful views over the golf course and the sea. Tents are not accepted here. Whitby is only a mile away and a quarter of a mile walk down a gently sloping track from the park brings you to a two-mile-long sandy beach. From here it is a gentle stroll along the new promenade to Whitby harbour. Whitby offers a variety of attractions to interest all the family, from fishing trips and amusement arcades, to the Spa theatre, plus all the famous fish and chips.

Facilities

Two toilet blocks (one older, one new and very good) have free hot showers. Laundry room with washing machines, dryers and iron. No facilities for disabled visitors. Tents are not accepted. Off site: Shops 800 yards. Hourly bus service to town centre. Fishing 400 yds. Golf 200 yds. Boat launching 800 yds. Railway station 1 mile.

Open: 1 March - 31 October.

Directions

From Whitby follow signs for Sandsend on the A174. The park is on the landward side of the road, opposite the golf course and well signed. O.S.GR: NZ872117. GPS: 54.491717, -0.642767

Charges guide

Per unit incl. up to 4 persons and electricity	£ 14.50 - £ 17.50
extra person	£ 2.00
awning	£ 2.00
dog (max.2)	£ 1.00

No credit cards.

Robin Hood's Bay

Middlewood Farm Holiday Park

Middlewood Lane, Fylingthorpe, Robin Hood's Bay YO22 4UF (North Yorkshire) T: 01947 880414
E: info@middlewoodfarm.com alanrogers.com/UK4532

Middlewood Farm is a level park, surrounded by hills and with views of the sea from some of the pitches. A short walk through the farm fields and wild flower conservation areas leads to the picturesque old fishing village of Robin Hood's Bay and the sea. The park has 22 touring pitches for caravans and motorcaravans with 10A electricity, 17 with hardstanding and the remainder on grass. There is space for around 130 tents in two areas with 12 electricity connections (10A) available and 30 caravan holiday homes to rent. A good beach is only ten minutes walk through the fields. The nearby village of Fylingthorpe with a post office, stores and a pub is a level walk. This is a very tidy farm park.

Facilities

The central toilet block has clean facilities and is modern, heated and tiled with free showers. Another new block is planned. Fully equipped laundry room including iron and board. Facilities for babies and disabled persons. One private family shower/toilet room to rent. Play area with bark base set amongst the tents. Off site: Sandy beach with fishing 0.5 miles. Boat launching 2 miles. Golf 7 miles. Shop and public transport in village 5 minutes walk.

Open: Easter - early November.

Directions

From the A171 Scarborough - Whitby road turn right signed Robin Hood's Bay and Fylingthorpe (site signed). Just past the 30 mph sign bear right and after 100 yds. turn right into Middlewood Lane (site signed). From Whitby on the A171 turn left on the B1447 signed Robin Hood's Bay and Fylingthorpe. After 1.5 miles turn right signed Fylingthorpe and brown site sign. Follow for 1 mile to crossroads and shops and straight on to Middlewood Lane (site is signed). O.S.GR: NZ945045. GPS: 54.43012, -0.54670

Charges guide

Per unit incl. 2 persons, electricity	£ 13.00 - £ 22.00
extra person	£ 3.00
awning	£ 7.00
dog	£ 2.00

York

Golden Square Caravan & Camping Park

Oswaldkirk, Helmsley, York YO62 5YQ (North Yorkshire) T: 01439 788269
E: reception@goldensquarecaravanpark.com alanrogers.com/UK4560

Golden Square is a popular, high quality, family owned touring park. Mr and Mrs Armstrong are local farmers who have worked hard to turn an old quarry into a very attractive caravan park with a number of level bays that have superb views over the North York Moors. The 130 pitches are not separated but they do have markers set into the ground and mainly back on to grass banks. In very dry weather the ground can be hard, steel pegs would be needed (even in wet weather the park is well drained). All pitches have electricity (10A), 24 have drainage and six are 'deluxe' pitches (with waste water, sewage, electricity, water and TV aerial connection). The licensed shop is very well stocked, selling home-made fresh bread and cakes, dairy produce, fresh vegetables and groceries, newspapers, gas and gifts. Visitors may use the Ampleforth College sports centre (charged), with its indoor pool, tennis and gym, etc. The area abounds with footpaths and three well known long distance footpaths are near.

Facilities

Two heated toilet blocks have been refurbished and are of excellent quality, one with underfloor heating, with some washbasins in private cabins. Showers are free. Bathroom (£1) also houses baby facilities. Both ladies and men have full facilities for disabled visitors. Laundry with washing machines, dryers, spin dryer and iron and board. Motorcaravan service point. Tourist information room also houses a microwave and an extra iron and board. Shop. Two excellent play areas. Games field and a barn with games. Bicycle hire. All year caravan storage. Off site: Riding 2 miles. Golf 3 miles. Fishing 5 miles. Outdoor pool at Helmsley, sports centre at Ampleforth with indoor pool, both have shops and pubs with food.

Open: 1 March - 31 October.

Directions

From York take B1363 to Helmsley. At Oswaldkirk Bank Top turn left on B1257 to Helmsley. Take second left turn signed Ampleforth to site. O.S.GR: SE605797. GPS: 54.209333, -1.073783

Charges guide

Per unit incl. 2 persons and electricity	£ 14.00 - £ 20.00
extra person	£ 2.00
extra child (5-14 yrs)	£ 1.00
dog	£ 1.00

No credit cards.

York
Moorside Caravan Park
Lords Moor Lane, Strensall, York YO32 5XJ (North Yorkshire) T: **01904 491208**
alanrogers.com/UK4610

Strensall is only a few miles from York, one of England's most attractive cities and Moorside Adult Touring Park will provide a peaceful haven after a day's sightseeing. It will impress you with its pretty fishing lake, masses of flowers and the tranquillity (except for the odd passing daytime train). There are 57 marked pitches on neat well trimmed grass, most with electricity (5/10A) and 18 with paved hardstanding. The whole park is very well maintained. York golf course is almost opposite the site entrance. Children (under 16 years) are not accepted at this park.

Facilities
The purpose built toilet block can be heated and houses immaculately kept facilities with washbasins in cubicles for ladies. One WC is suitable for use by disabled visitors. Fully equipped laundry room. Tourist information and books to borrow. Coarse fishing (£3 per day). Caravan storage. Off site: Strensall village with shops and places to eat is less than a mile. Golf 0.5 miles. Riding 3 miles.

Open: March - end October.

Directions
From A1237 York outer ring road follow signs for Earswick and Strensall. At Strensall follow Flaxton road. The park entrance is on the left past signs to Strensall village and York Golf Club. O.S.GR: SE647614. GPS: 54.042733, -1.011683

Charges guide
Per unit incl. 2 persons, electricity	£ 12.00 - £ 15.00
extra person	£ 2.00

No credit cards.

York
Alders Caravan Park
Home Farm, Alne, York YO61 1RY (North Yorkshire) T: **01347 838722**. E: enquiries@homefarmalne.co.uk
alanrogers.com/UK4638

The Alders is located in the village of Alne, only nine miles from the centre of the ancient city of York. Carefully developed on a working farm in historic parkland, the drive to reach the pitches gives a real feeling of space. On reaching the 87 level pitches (25 for tourers, the rest for seasonal units), you will find an area of well trimmed grass and a pitch layout designed to give as much privacy and space as possible. Arranged in small bays, each group is named after a Yorkshire Abbey or Dale. Newly planted woodland and a water meadow with wild flowers enhance the wonderful peace and tranquillity.

Facilities
The central toilet block is heated with family sized shower rooms, one also has a bath (£1 charge). A new block includes en-suite bathrooms with bath or shower, laundry and dishwashing facilities. Provision for disabled visitors. Gas is sold at reception (shop in the village). Off site: Floodlit tennis courts in the village. Fishing 2 miles. Golf 3 miles. Riding 4 miles.

Open: 1 March - 31 October.

Directions
From the north on the A19: after leaving Easingwold bypass take next right turn signed Alne. From the south (A19), 5 miles north of Shipton turn left at sign for Alne. In 1.5 miles at T-junction turn left and in about 0.5 miles, site is signed in the centre of the village. O.S.GR: SE496651. GPS: 54.08185, -1.24105

Charges guide
Per unit incl. 2 persons and electricity	£ 14.00
extra person	£ 2.50

York
Goose Wood Caravan Park
Sutton-on-the-Forest, York YO61 1ET (North Yorkshire) T: **01347 810829**. E: edward@goosewood.co.uk
alanrogers.com/UK4640

A family owned park in a natural woodland setting, Goose Wood provides a quiet, relaxed atmosphere from which to explore York itself or the surrounding Yorkshire Dales, Wolds or Moors. The park has a well kept air and a rural atmosphere, with 100 well spaced and marked pitches, all with electricity (16A) on hardstanding (four also have water and drainage). Tents are not accepted. For children, there is a 'super plus' adventure playground in the trees at one side of the park and for adults, a small coarse fishing lake and woodland for walking. A member of the Best of British group.

Facilities
Tiled and heated, the modern toilet block is well maintained. Bathroom (£1). An additional unit provides shower rooms, WC and washbasins in cubicles and extra dishwashing sinks. Full facilities for disabled visitors. Laundry room. Motorcaravan service point. Small shop. Health Suite (can be hired for 45 minutes, max. 8 people at a time). Fishing lake. Large adventure playground. Games room with TV. Dogs (max. two per pitch), to be exercised in nearby woodland. No tents are accepted. Off site: Riding or golf 1 mile. Bicycle hire 6 miles. York 6 miles.

Open: All year excl. 15 - 31 January.

Directions
Park is 6 miles north of York; from the A1237 York outer ring-road take the B1363 for Sutton-on-the-Forest and Stillington, taking the first right after the Haxby and Wigginton junction and follow park signs. O.S.GR: SE595636. GPS: 54.05929, -1.09406

Charges guide
Per unit incl. 1 or 2 persons, and electricity	£ 17.50 - £ 20.50
extra person	£ 2.50
fully serviced pitch plus	£ 5.00

The northwest region boasts a wealth of industrial heritage with undiscovered countryside, the vibrant cities of Manchester and Liverpool, the seaside resorts of Blackpool and Morecambe Bay, plus miles of glorious coastline, home to a wide variety of bird species.

Alan Rogers

THIS REGION INCLUDES: CHESHIRE, LANCASHIRE, MERSEYSIDE, GREATER MANCHESTER AND THE HIGH PEAKS OF DERBYSHIRE

The miles of beautiful, North West countryside offers endless opportunities for recreation. For the more active, the peaceful plains of Cheshire are a walker's haven with endless trails to choose from. Lancashire is also good walking country, with way-marked paths passing through the outstanding forest of Bowland, which affords marvellous views over the Lake District in Cumbria and the Yorkshire Dales. Birdwatchers are catered for too, with the coast offering some of the best bird spotting activitiy in the country, most notably along the Sefton coast and around the Wirral Peninsula. The region's cities have their own charm. Manchester, with its fabulous shopping centres and vibrant nightlife, boasts a rich Victorian heritage; the maritime city of Liverpool has more museums and galleries than any other UK city outside London; Lancaster features fine Georgian buildings and an imposing Norman castle; while Chester is renowned for its medieval architecture and shopping galleries. And offering good, old-fashioned seaside fun is Blackpool. England's most popular seaside resort is packed full of lively entertainment and attractions, such as the white knuckle rides at the pleasure beach, amusement games on the pier and the observation decks in the famous Tower.

Places of interest

Cheshire: Tatton Park in Knutsford; Chester Cathedral and Zoo; Cheshire Military Museum; Lyme Park stately home in Macclesfield; Beeston Castle; Boat Museum at Ellesmere Port.

Lancashire: Williamson Park, Castle and Leisure Park in Lancaster; Camelot Theme Park; Museum of Football in Preston; Morecambe Bay; Hoghton Tower and National Museum of Football in Preston.

Merseyside: Liverpool Football Club Museum and Tour Centre; The Beatles Story Museum; Speke Hall Garden and Estate; The Wirral Country Park; Williamson Tunnels Heritage Centre.

Greater Manchester: Imperial War Museum North; Manchester United Football Club Museum; The Lowry; Corgi Heritage Centre in Rochdale; Stockport Air Raid Shelter.

Did you know?

The first public gallery to open in England was in Liverpool in 1877.

Lancaster Castle is infamous as host to the Pendle Witch trials in 1612.

The first passenger railway station was built in Manchester.

Hoghton Tower is where King James I knighted a loin of beef in 1617 – hence the name Sirloin.

To date 300 bird species have been recorded within the boundaries of Sefton.

Chester has the most complete set of city walls in Britain.

Opened in 1894, the Blackpool Tower was copied from the Eiffel Tower; the height to the top of the flagpole is 518 feet 9 inches.

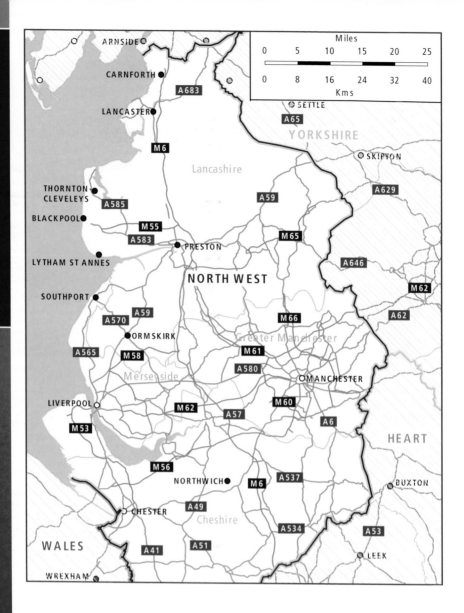

Maps and campsite listings

For this 2010 guide we have changed the way in which we list our parks and also the way in which we help you locate the parks within each region.

We now include a map immediately after our Introduction to that region. These maps show the towns near which one (or more) of our featured parks is located. Within each regional section of the guide, we list these towns and the park(s) in that vicinity in alphabetical order.

You will certainly need more detailed maps for navigation, for example the Ordnance Survey road atlas. We provide O.S. references and G.P.S. coordinates for each park to assist you. Our three indexes will also help you to find a park by its reference number and name, by region and park name, or by the town where the park is situated.

Blackpool
Marton Mere Holiday Village
Mythop Road, Blackpool FY4 4NX (Lancashire) T: **01253 767544**. E: sarah.corlett@bourne-leisure.co.uk
alanrogers.com/UK5330

If Blackpool is your holiday destination and your family are looking for lots to do then this Haven Holidays park may well be a suitable choice. Although mainly used for static caravan holiday homes, there are 148 touring pitches with hardstanding, of which 60 are fully serviced. All have electricity hook-ups (10/16A). A few trees give a small amount of shade, but as with a lot of coastal sites, it can be a little windy. During the day buses depart every 30 minutes from the main reception area to Blackpool. On site there is plenty of entertainment including three licensed bars.

Facilities

Two heated toilet blocks (key pad entry system) have piped music playing and although of older design are clean and well kept with large preset showers and hairdryers. Each block has a suite for disabled people, baby room, family bathroom and launderette. Well stocked supermarket with all day bakery, bars, fast food outlets and restaurants. New outdoor splash pool and heated indoor pool with flume, jacuzzi and sauna. Amusement arcades, multisport court, crazy golf and bowling. Two children's clubs with full entertainment schedule. Off site: Martin Mere nature reserve. Blackpool beach, entertainment, etc.

Open: 24 March - 30 October.

Directions

From M55 exit 4, turn right at roundabout taking A583 towards Blackpool. Pass the windmill, then right at the traffic lights by the Clifton Arms into Mythop Road. Park is on the left O.S.GR: SD344351. GPS: 53.80285, -2.991467

Charges guide

Per unit incl. up to 4 persons and electricity	£ 11.00 - £ 57.00
serviced pitch	£ 13.00 - £ 66.00
extra person	£ 2.00 - £ 3.00

Variety of special offers available.

Carnforth
Bay View Holiday Park
A6, Main Road, Bolton Le Sands, Carnforth LA5 8ES (Lancashire) T: **01524 732854**
E: info@holgatesleisureparks.co.uk **alanrogers.com/UK5270**

Previously two adjacent parks, Bolton Holmes and Detrongate are being developed by the Holgate family into an excellent addition to their group. Situated on the coast north of Lancaster, the park is an ideal base for exploring the Lake District, North Yorkshire and the Forest of Bowland. The park is divided into several grassy, sloping fields and many of the pitches have stunning views over Morecambe Bay, others look towards the Lakeland Fells. It is a very open park with little shade. Of the 240 touring pitches, 192 have 6-15A electricity and 15 are fully serviced. There are also 100 pitches for caravan holiday homes.

Facilities

Three toilet blocks, one refurbished the others to follow. Facilities for disabled visitors. Good laundry. Motorcaravan service point. Small shop. Playground for younger children, large field for ball games. Games room. Future plans include a bar/restaurant. Off site: Fishing 200 yds. Golf and riding 3 miles. Canal cruises on Lancaster Canal. Leighton Moss RSPB nature reserve. Good shopping in nearby Lancaster and Kendal 15 miles.

Open: 1 March - 31 October.

Directions

From M6 exit 35 take the A601M to roundabout and follow signs to Morecambe. Continue through Carnforth and after mini-roundabout look for site sign in 500 yds on the right. O.S.GR: SD480692. GPS: 54.11602, -2.78791

Charges guide

Per unit incl. 2 persons, car and electricity	£ 12.00 - £ 16.00
extra person	£ 2.00 - £ 3.00

Carnforth
Old Hall Caravan Park
Capernwray, Carnforth LA6 1AD (Lancashire) T: **01524 733276**. E: info@oldhallcaravanpark.co.uk
alanrogers.com/UK5271

In a woodland clearing, just five minutes' drive from junction 35 of the M6, Old Hall Caravan Park is a gem. Approached along a tree-lined road, this secluded park offers peace and tranquillity. There are 38 touring pitches which are accessed from a circular roadway, all on marked and level hardstandings and with 16A electricity, water and drainage (shared between two pitches). TV hook-ups are available for hire. Tents are not accepted. There are 220 privately owned holiday homes which are quite separate from the touring pitches.

Facilities

The central sanitary block (combination lock) is very clean and is heated during cooler months. Vanity style washbasins and large controllable showers. Separate unit for disabled visitors doubles as a family room. Laundry facilities. Gas supplies. Off site: Canal fishing 300 yds. Over Kellet 2 miles. Carnforth 3 miles. Historic Lancaster and the seaside town of Morecambe (15 minutes drive). Trough of Bowland, Yorkshire Dales and Grange-over-Sands (30 minutes drive).

Open: 1 March - 10 January.

Directions

From M6 exit 35 take link road signed Over Kellet. Turn left on B6254. At Over Kellet village green turn left signed Capernwray and follow for 1.5 miles. Park is on the right at the end of a 0.5 mile drive. O.S.GR: SD538718. GPS: 54.13958, -2.71357

Charges guide

Per unit incl. electricity	£ 16.50 - £ 18.50
awning	£ 1.00 - £ 2.00

209

Carnforth

Holgates Caravan Park

Middlebarrow Plain, Cove Road, Silverdale, Carnforth LA5 0SH (Lancashire) T: 01524 701508
E: caravan@holgates.co.uk **alanrogers.com/UK5350**

This attractive, very high quality park is in an outstanding craggy, part-wooded, hillside location with fine views over Morecambe Bay. It takes 80 touring units, with 339 privately owned caravan holiday homes and 14 to rent located in woodland away from the touring pitches. With just five grassy pitches for tents, the remaining 65 large touring pitches are on gravel hardstandings, all with electricity (16A), free TV connection, individual drainage and water points. The main complex with reception and the entrance barrier, provides a well stocked supermarket, lounge bar, restaurant with good value meals and a terrace with views over the bay. There is also an indoor leisure centre. Children have a choice of two adventure playgrounds and plenty of space for ball games. Also on site is a small but challenging 'pitch and putt' course. Everything is completed to the highest standards.

Facilities

Two modern, heated toilet buildings are fully equipped with top quality fittings and including some private cubicles with WC and washbasin. Excellent provision for disabled visitors with a reserved pitch and parking bay adjacent. Launderette. Shop. Gas supplies. Bar and restaurant. Indoor pool (17 x 17 m; with lifeguard) with spa pool, steam room and sauna. Playgrounds. Games room. Pitch and putt course (£2 per person). Facilities are limited mid week in January and early February. Off site: Riding, cycling, walking and fishing all within 9 miles. Morecambe or Lancaster 12 miles. Kendal 15 miles.

Open: All year excl. 6 November - 21 December.

Directions

From traffic lights in centre of Carnforth take road to Silverdale under low bridge. After 1 mile turn left signed Silverdale and after 2.5 miles over level crossing, carry on and turn right at T-junction. Follow Holgates sign from here watching for left then right forks (narrow roads). O.S.GR: SD460755. GPS: 54.17615, -2.8359

Charges guide

Per unit incl. 2 adults and 2 children	£ 32.50 - £ 33.50
extra person	£ 7.00
extra child (5-17 yrs)	£ 4.00
awning or pup tent	£ 3.00

Lancaster

Moss Wood Caravan Park

Crimbles Lane, Cockerham, Lancaster LA2 0ES (Lancashire) T: 01524 791041. E: info@mosswood.co.uk
alanrogers.com/UK5272

Moss Wood is a well established park set in a secluded rural location near the village of Cockerham. A sheltered field has 25 touring pitches on level hardstandings (steel pegs required) with 16A electricity. Most also have water and drainage. Screened from the touring area by a high fence so not visually intrusive are 175 privately owned holiday homes. There is a large adventure playground on site and, although well screened by mature trees, it could be lively and noisy at busy times. Although there are passing places, the approach road to the park is narrow so care should be taken.

Facilities

New centrally located sanitary block (key entry) is kept spotlessly clean and provides vanity style washbasins and roomy, preset showers. Fully equipped facilities for disabled visitors. Undercover food preparation area and laundry facilities. Play area. Large sports field and woodland dog walking. Off site: Pubs at Cockerham 1 mile. Garstang, Lancaster and Morecambe all within easy reach. Fishing nearby. Riding 3 miles. Golf 4 miles. Beach 5 miles.

Open: 1 March - 31 October.

Directions

Park is 1 mile west of Cockerham on the A588. Leave M6 at junction 33 and follow signs for Cockerham. A588 is about 4 miles. Site is signed on the left. O.S.GR: SD456498. GPS: 53.93788, -2.82087

Charges guide

Per unit incl. 2 adults, 2 children and electricity	£ 16.00 - £ 20.00
extra person	£ 3.00
awning	£ 3.00

210

Lytham Saint Annes

Eastham Hall Caravan Park

Saltcotes Road, Lytham Saint Annes FY8 4LS (Lancashire) T: 01253 737907. E: info@easthamhall.co.uk

alanrogers.com/UK5295

Eastham Hall is a well established, family run park set in rural Lancashire between the Victorian town of Lytham and the pretty village of Wrea Green. Entering by an electronic barrier system, one sees an area of 150 caravan holiday homes. Quite separate are around 150 pitches for touring units and seasonal rental on open plan, mostly level grass, with 10A electricity throughout. Tents are not accepted. Recent additions include 11 large 'super' pitches on hardstanding and grass with full services including 16A electricity. A further five extra large pitches are on grass (units up to 28 feet can be taken). Mature trees border the park and shrubs and bushes separate the various areas. The reception is spacious with lots of tourist information and, at one end, is a large well stocked shop. The park has no bar or clubhouse, but Lytham is just five minutes by car or a pleasant twenty minute walk. The flat terrain is also ideal for cycling.

Facilities

Four toilet blocks are old and fairly basic, but are kept clean. New laundry. New facilities for disabled visitors. Gas supplies. Well stocked shop. Adventure play area and large sports field. Barrier (£10 deposit). Off site: Excellent pub in Wrea Green. Shops and restaurants in Lytham 2.5 miles. Blackpool 6 miles. Golf and riding 1 mile. Fishing 2.5 miles. Boat launching 2 miles. Local bus stops at entrance to park.

Open: 1 March - 31 October.

Directions

From M55 take exit 3 and turn left for Kirkham. At roundabouts follow signs for Wrea Green and Lytham. Continue on B5259 passing Grapes pub and village green. After 1.5 miles cross level crossing (Moss Side) and park is 1 mile on left. O.S.GR: SD377290. GPS: 53.75375, -2.94225

Charges guide

Per unit incl. 1-4 persons	£ 10.00 - £ 15.00
incl. electricity	£ 15.00 - £ 22.00
serviced pitch	£ 18.00 - £ 25.00
dog	£ 1.00

Eastham Hall Caravan Park - a secluded tranquil Holiday Park

This family run park is a lovely oasis of calm in beautiful rural surroundings. Only 1½ miles from the stylish Victorian town of Lytham, 2 miles from the pretty village of Wrea Green and 6 miles from Blackpool.

01253 737907 • info@easthamhall.co.uk • www.easthamhall.co.uk

Eastham Hall Caravan Park, Saltcotes Road, Lytham St Annes, Lancashire, FY8 4LS

Eastham Hall

Northwich

Lamb Cottage Caravan Park

Dalefords Lane, Whitegate, Northwich CW8 2BN (Cheshire) T: 01606 882302. E: lynn@lccp.fsworld.co.uk

alanrogers.com/UK5240

This quiet, family run 'adult only' park is set in the midst of the lovely Vale Royal area of Cheshire. 15 landscaped seasonal caravan pitches are followed by the touring area which has 25 large pitches, all with 16A electric hook-ups, gravel hardstandings, water and drainage. There are an additional four motorcaravan pitches with hardstanding and electricity. Only 'breathable' groundsheets are permitted and tents are not accepted. Nearby are Delamere Forest with its walking and mountain biking trails, Whitegate Way walking trail, Oulton Park Motor Racing Circuit, castles at Peckforton and Beeston, and the city of Chester, which is 12 miles.

Facilities

Toilet and shower facilities are housed in a custom-built 'park home' style unit which includes washbasins in cubicles and facilities for disabled guests. Laundry room. Recycling of glass and paper. Calor gas stocked. Fenced dog walk (max. 2 dogs per unit permitted). Off site: Pub serving food under 1 mile. Riding 1.5 miles. Golf 2 miles. Supermarket 3 miles. Fishing 3 miles. Bicycle hire 4 miles.

Open: 1 March - 31 October.

Directions

From M6 exit 19 take the A556 towards Chester. After about 12 miles turn left at traffic lights (signed Winsford and Whitegate) into Dalefords Lane. Continue for about 1 mile and site entrance is on the right between white house and bungalow. O.S.GR: SJ614693. GPS: 53.218244, -2.578655

Charges guide

Per unit incl. 2 persons and electricity	£ 18.00 - £ 24.00

Preston

Royal Umpire Caravan Park

Southport Road, Croston, Preston PR26 9JB (Lancashire) T: **01772 600257**. E: reception@royalumpire.co.uk
alanrogers.com/**UK5290**

Royal Umpire is a spacious park near the coast and the beaches, and also the M6 for overnight or longer stays. The entrance to the park is past a large grass area leading to the security barrier with the shop and reception immediately to the left, and slightly ahead, an unusual sunken garden area that is a pleasing feature. Comprising 58 acres, the park has 200 pitches, almost all with 10A electricity, but a few with 16A. About 75 per cent of the pitches now have gravel hardstanding, some with TV and water connections. Tarmac and gravel roads connect the various pitch areas. A good choice of pubs serving bar or restaurant meals is nearby. The gates are closed 23.00 - 07.00.

Facilities

The two tiled toilet blocks, one beside reception, the other centrally situated. Fully equipped laundry. Very good facilities for disabled visitors that are shared with baby facilities (entrance with key, £5 deposit). Motorcaravan services. Adventure playground. Field area for ball games. Rally field. Off site: A short walk takes you to the nearby river for fishing. Riding 2 miles.

Open: All year.

Directions

From north use M6 exit 28 joining A49 going south (parallel to M6) for 2 miles. Then right across M6 on A581 to Croston (about 4 miles). From the south use M6 exit 27 onto A5209 but immediately right on B5250 and follow towards Eccleston, joining A581 at Newtown (about 5 miles). Site is clearly signed with wide entrance east of Croston. O.S.GR: SD505189. GPS: 53.66669, -2.74827

Charges -guide

Per grass pitch incl. 2 persons, electricity and awning	£ 8.50 - £ 13.00
hardstanding pitch	£ 9.50 - £ 14.00
'Royal' pitch	£ 11.50 - £ 16.20
'Super Royal' pitch	£ 12.50 - £ 17.40
extra adult	£ 2.50

Less 10% for 7 nights pre-booked.

Southport

Riverside Touring & Holiday Home Park

You might also like to consider...

Ormskirk

Abbey Farm Caravan Park

Dark Lane, Ormskirk L40 5TX (Lancashire) T: **01695 572686**. E: **abbeyfarm@yahoo.com**

alanrogers.com/UK5280

This quiet, well equipped, family park beside the Abbey ruins has views over open farmland. It is an ideal base for a longer stay with plenty of interest in the local area, including Ormskirk parish church, unusual for having both a tower and a spire. The park is divided into small paddocks, one of which is for privately owned seasonal units, one for tents, the others for touring units, plus a rally field for special events. The 60 touring pitches, all with electricity (16A), and 12 of which have water and waste water, are on neatly mown level grass, separated by small shrubs and colourful flower borders. Mature trees provide shade in parts. A member of the Countryside Discovery group.

Facilities

The main toilet block is modern, heated and spotless, providing controllable hot showers. Dual purpose family bathroom that includes facilities for disabled people. A second smaller unit has individual shower/WC/washbasin cubicles. Laundry room. Small well stocked shop at reception, with a butcher calling twice weekly. Indoor games room. Small adventure playground and large field for ball games. Fishing lake (£2 per rod, per day). Off site: Local market on Thursday and Saturday. Southport beach and Pleasureland 10 miles. Wigan Pier, Aintree for the Grand National, Southport Flower Show and Martin Mere Nature reserve are some of the attractions within easy reach.

Open: All year.

Directions

From M6 junction 27 take A5209 (Parbold) road. After 5 miles turn left (just before garage) onto B5240, and then first right into Hob Cross Lane, following signs to site. O.S.GR: SD433099. GPS: 53.5698, -2.85665

Charges guide

Per unit incl. 2 persons	£ 7.00 - £ 16.60
serviced pitch	£ 15.60 - £ 15.90
extra person	£ 2.50
child (5-15 yrs)	£ 1.50

Less 10% for 7 nights booked on or before arrival.

Southport

Willowbank Touring Park

Coastal Road, Ainsdale, Southport PR8 3ST (Mersey) T: **01704 571566**. E: **info@willowbankcp.co.uk**

alanrogers.com/UK5360

Willowbank Park is well situated for the Sefton coast and Southport, set on the edge of sand dunes amongst mature, wind swept trees. Entrance to the park is controlled by a barrier, with a pass-key issued at the excellent reception building which doubles as a sales office for the substantial, high quality caravan holiday home development. There are now 87 touring pitches, 30 on gravel hardstandings, 24 on grass (these all with 10A electricity) and a further 33 new pitches with 16A electricity. These are on grass hardstanding using an environmentally friendly reinforcement system. Tents, large units (longer than 8 m.) and caravans of foreign manufacture are not accepted. The owners are very well supported on the touring side by the reception team which has considerable experience in managing the touring park. There could be some noise from the nearby main road. This is a good area for cycling and walking with the Trans Pennine Way being adjacent. The attractions of Southport with its parks, gardens, funfair and shopping are four miles away. The area is famous for its golf courses including the Royal Birkdale championship links.

Facilities

The purpose built, heated toilet block is of a high standard including an excellent bathroom for disabled visitors, although the showers are rather compact. Baby room. Laundry. Motorcaravan service point. Play area. Field for ball games. Off site: Beach 1.5 miles. Golf and riding 0.5 miles. Fishing 4 miles. Bicycle hire 4.5 miles. Martin Mere nature reserve nearby.

Open: All year excl. 11 January - 28 February.

Directions

Park is 4 miles south of Southport. From Ainsdale on A565 travel south for 1.5 miles to second traffic lights (Woodvale) and turn right into Coastal Road to site on left in 150 yds. From south pass RAF Woodvale and turn left at second set of lights. O.S.GR: SD308108. GPS: 53.5888, -3.044

Charges guide

Per unit incl. 2 persons and electricity	£ 12.35 - £ 15.30
hardstanding	£ 1.60
extra person	£ 3.00
child (5-16 yrs)	£ 2.30
dog (max. 2)	£ 1.20

Latest arrival time 21.00.

Thornton-Cleveleys

Kneps Farm Holiday Park

River Road, Stanah, Thornton-Cleveleys FY5 5LR (Lancashire) T: **01253 823632**
E: **enquiries@knepsfarm.co.uk alanrogers.com/UK5300**

A well established park with top class modern facilities, Kneps Farm is still operated by the family who opened it in 1967. Next to Wyre Country Park, it makes an excellent base from which to explore the area. A VNPR operated barrier system flanks the reception building which also houses a well stocked shop. The 60 marked and numbered touring pitches are generally on hardstandings with electricity (16A) available to most, and all are accessed from tarmac roads. There are also some grassy pitches and a separate area with 60 caravan holiday homes (most privately owned). A path leads through a gate at the back of the site into the country park. Just down the lane is a public slipway and the Wyreside Ecology Centre. A list and map are provided of local services and amenities, including pubs, restaurants, takeaway, etc. Other local attractions include Marsh Mill Village with a restored windmill, the Freeport Shopping and Leisure village at nearby Fleetwood (discount shopping), and several bird-watching sites around the estuary and country park.

Facilities

The excellent, large, centrally heated sanitary building is warm and inviting with ten individual family bathrooms, each providing a WC, basin and bath/shower. Separate toilet facilities with electric hand-wash units for men and women. Well equipped room for disabled visitors. Combined baby care/first aid room. Laundry room. Shop. Small, fenced playground. Up to two dogs are accepted per unit. Off site: Sailing 300 yds. Fishing 3.5 miles. Golf and beach 2.5 miles.

Open: 1 March - 15 November.

Directions

From M55 junction 3, take A585 towards Fleetwood. Turn left at traffic lights, then turn right at traffic lights by Shell station (for Thornton-Cleveleys), straight across next traffic lights, then right at the next roundabout by River Wyre Hotel. After one mile (past school) turn right at mini-roundabout into Stanah Road, continue across second mini-roundabout and eventually into River Road with site entrance ahead of you. O.S.GR: SD350430. GPS: 53.87903, -2.98506

Charges guide

Per unit incl. 2 adults, 2 children and electricity	£ 22.50 - £ 25.00
tent incl. 2 adults and 2 children	£ 19.50 - £ 22.00
adult couple	£ 14.50 - £ 19.00
extra person	£ 3.25 - £ 3.75
extra child	£ 2.50 - £ 3.00

Special Senior Citizen rates.

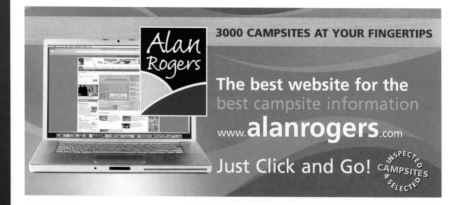

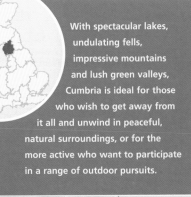

With spectacular lakes, undulating fells, impressive mountains and lush green valleys, Cumbria is ideal for those who wish to get away from it all and unwind in peaceful, natural surroundings, or for the more active who want to participate in a range of outdoor pursuits.

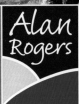

Cumbria is best known for the beautiful Lake District National Park, with the picturesque valleys and lakes of Windermere, Ullswater and Derwentwater, each with its own distinctive character. Windermere offers no shortage of watersports, whereas Ullswater mainly attracts peaceful sailing boats. While the Lake District is well known, there are also many quiet, undiscovered areas in the region including the wild, rugged moors of the north Pennines and the beautiful Eden Valley, an ideal place for a casual stroll along the riverside footpaths. The Western Lakes and Fells offer more tranquillity. Here the fells drop down to a long and spectacular coastline, with many undiscovered, quiet corners from Ennerdale and Esdale to the sandstone cliffs of St Bees Head, now part of a designated Heritage Coast. The Lake District Peninsulas along the southern coast of Cumbria also display beautiful scenery and are home to a cluster of ancient ruins such as Furness Abbey and the medieval castle, built by monks, on Piel Island. Rich in heritage, the historic city of Carlisle, which was sited on the Roman-built Hadrian's wall, boasts an impressive castle, Cumbria's only cathedral, a superb Victorian covered market and an array of speciality shops.

Places of interest

Barrow-in-Furness: South Lakes Wild Animal Park; Dalton Castle; Furness Abbey; Piel Island.

Carlisle: 11th-century castle; Birdoswald Roman fort; Lanercost Priory.

Ravenglass: Muncaster Castle, an historic haunted castle and Headquarters of the World Owl Trust.

Ulverston: the world's only Laurel and Hardy museum.

Kendal: historic riverside town situated between the Lakes and Dales, famous for its mint cake and castle ruins.

Lake Derwentwater: lakeside theatre open all year hosting plays, music, dance, comedy and film.

Windermere: Steamboat Centre, a collection of Windermere's nautical heritage with boats on display; World of Beatrix Potter.

Grasmere: Dove Cottage and Wordsworth Museum.

Did you know?

Cumbria has the steepest road in England, called the Hardknott Pass.

The Lake District was the inspiration for many poets, writers and artists, including William Wordsworth, Beatrix Potter and John Ruskin.

Ulverston is the birthplace of Quakerism and pole vaulting.

Bassenthwaite is the only real lake in the Lake District! All the others are either meres, (Windermere) or waters (Derwentwater, Coniston Water and Ullswater).

Stretching 73 miles, Hadrian's Wall was built by Romans in the second century.

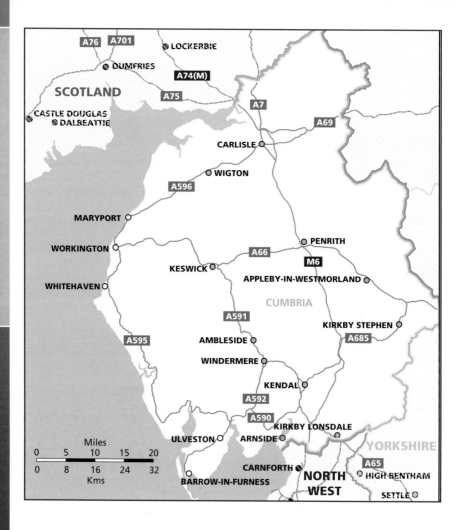

Ambleside

Skelwith Fold Caravan Park

Ambleside LA22 0HX (Cumbria) T: 01539 432277. E: info@skelwith.com

alanrogers.com/UK5520

Skelwith Fold has been developed in the extensive grounds of a country estate taking advantage of the wealth of mature trees and shrubs. The 300 privately owned caravan holiday homes and 150 touring pitches are absorbed into this unspoilt natural environment, sharing it with red squirrels and other wildlife in several discrete areas branching off the central, mile long main driveway. Touring pitches (no tents) are on gravel hardstanding and metal pegs will be necessary for awnings. Electricity hook-ups (10A) and basic amenities are available in all areas.

Facilities

Eight toilet blocks, well situated to serve all areas, have the usual facilities including laundry, drying and ironing rooms. Some blocks have facilities for disabled visitors. Well stocked, licensed shop. Motorcaravan service point. Battery charging, gas and caravan spares and accessories. Adventure play area. Family recreation area with picnic tables and goal posts in the Lower Glade.
Off site: Ambleside village 2.5 miles. Pubs within walking distance. Fishing 200 m. Riding and sailing 3 miles.

Open: 1 March - 15 November.

Directions

From Ambleside take the A593 towards Coniston. Pass through Clappergate and on the far outskirts watch for the B5286 to Hawkshead on the left. Park is clearly signed 1 mile down this road on the right. Do not use sat nav to find this park - this will bring you to a locked gate! O.S.GR: NY358028.
GPS: 54.41715, -2.995283

Charges guide

Per pitch	£ 18.50 - £ 23.00
incl. electricity	£ 21.50 - £ 26.00
awning	£ 3.00

Discounts for weekly or monthly stays.

Appleby-in-Westmorland
Wild Rose Park
Ormside, Appleby-in-Westmorland CA16 6EJ (Cumbria) T: **01768 351077**. E: reception@wildrose.co.uk
alanrogers.com/UK5570

Set in the Eden Valley within easy reach of the Lake District and the Yorkshire Dales, Wild Rose is a well known park. The entrance is inviting with its well mown grass, trim borders and colourful flower displays. It is immediately apparent that this is a much loved park, and this is reflected throughout the site in the care and attention to detail. There are 226 touring pitches with on-site wardens to ensure that everything is always neat and tidy. Wild Rose deserves its excellent reputation, which the owners strive to maintain and improve. There are five distinct areas on the park providing a variety of pitches and services. Hazel Heights and Egglestone Tiers provide fully serviced 'super' pitches with hardstanding, Braithwaite Fold and the Chesters have pitches with electricity and shared water points. The grass area of Donkey's Nest provides pitches with shared electricity and water. There are also 274 privately owned caravan holiday homes and lodges and four wooden 'wigwams' to rent for all year luxurious camping. Nothing is overlooked here, from recycling bins, electric buggies to keep the noise down, 'sac-o-mat' bags and bins in the dog walk to cycle racks around the park. A member of the Best of British group.

Facilities

Three toilet blocks (two heated) of excellent quality and kept spotlessly clean. Most washbasins are in cubicles. Facilities for babies and for disabled visitors. Fully equipped laundry with washing lines and drying rooms. Motorcaravan service point. Well stocked shop incl. gas (1/4-1/11. Licensed restaurant with takeaway and conservatory/coffee lounge (weekends only in low seasons). Outdoor pool (late May - Sept, 10.00 -18.00). Indoor playroom for under 5s. Games room (new machines). TV room. Cinema room. Tennis. Off site: Fishing 2 miles. Golf and riding 3 miles.

Open: All year.

Directions

Park is signed south off the B6260 road 1.5 miles southwest of Appleby. Follow signs to the park, in the direction of Ormside. O.S.GR: NY697165. GPS: 54.54893, -2.46422

Charges guide

Per unit incl. 2 persons and electricity	£ 17.00 - £ 31.50
extra person (over 4 yrs)	£ 3.00 - £ 4.00
dog	£ 1.50

Less 10% for 7 nights or more and for over 60s.

Eden's caravanning paradise
Nestling in magnificent Eden - very close to the Lake District and the Pennines, Wild Rose Park is a multi-award winning park set in beautiful tranquil surroundings. This superb park includes over 220 designated camping and touring pitches, mini market, restaurant, laundrette, adventure playgrounds, outdoor pools, TV and Games Rooms... paradise!

Call or write for a FREE brochure:
Ormside, Appleby, Cumbria, CA16 6EJ.
017683 51077 reception@wildrose.co.uk
www.wildrose.co.uk

Arnside
Hollins Farm Caravan & Camp Site
Far Arnside, Arnside LA5 0SL (Cumbria) T: **01524 701767**. E: info@hollinsfarm.co.uk
alanrogers.com/UK5595

Hollins Farm has been considerably improved since being taken over by the Holgate family just a year ago, without losing its appeal as a simple farm site. In a superb location overlooking Morecambe Bay, the park consists of several fields divided by trees. Of the 120 pitches, there are 50 for touring all with electricity (16A), water and TV connections, although large units may have difficulty negotiating the narrow country lanes. This is very popular walking country and leaflets may be obtained from reception. Visitors here are able to use the excellent facilities at the nearby Holgate Leisure Centre (charged). These include an indoor pool, gym, and very nice restaurant. There is also entertainment in high season.

Facilities

Smart new portacabins house the toilets and showers, including facilities for disabled visitors. Off site: Leighton Moss RSPB Nature reserve. Cross Bay walks. Golf 2 miles. Fishing 9 miles. Market town of Kendal 12 miles.

Open: 14 March - 31 October.

Directions

From M6 exit 35 take A601(M). At first roundabout take second exit A6 North. In 2.5 miles turn left signed Yealand Redmayne, then signs for Holgates through Silverdale. Hollins Farm is 0.5 miles beyond Holgates. O.S.GR: SD450764. GPS: 54.18077, -2.84352

Charges guide

Per unit incl. 2 adults, 2 children and services	£ 15.00 - £ 25.00

217

Carlisle

Green Acres Caravan Park

High Knells, Houghton, Carlisle CA6 4JW (Cumbria) T: 01228 675418. E: info@caravanpark-cumbria.com
alanrogers.com/UK5640

Green Acres is a small, family-run park, accepting adults only since 2009. Situated in beautiful, rural surroundings, yet only two miles from the M6/A74 it is perfect for an overnight stop or a longer stay to enjoy Cumbria, Hadrian's Wall and the delights of Carlisle city. The Browns have developed Green Acres into an attractive, well maintained and level touring park. There are 30 numbered pitches, all on large hardstandings with electricity connections and four serviced pitches. Divided by a long beech hedge is a large camping field including on one side 12 new hardstanding 'super' pitches for seasonal letting.

Facilities

Small, very clean toilet block with open style washbasins and coin operated showers (50p for 10 minutes). No facilities for disabled people. Laundry room in farm building. Car wash area. Caravan storage. Off site: Golf 3 miles. Fishing 8 miles. Riding and bicycle hire 10 miles.

Open: 1 April - end October.

Directions

Leave M6/A74 at junction 44 and take the A689 for 1 mile. Turn left towards Scaleby (site signed) and site is 1 mile on left. O.S.GR: NY419615. GPS: 54.94505, -2.90728

Charges 2010

Per unit incl. 2 persons and electricity (10/16A)	£ 13.00 - £ 16.00

Kendal

Waters Edge Caravan Park

Crooklands, Kendal LA7 7NN (Cumbria) T: 015395 67708. E: info@watersedgecaravanpark.co.uk
alanrogers.com/UK5645

Close to the M6 motorway, Waters Edge makes an ideal stopover. However it is also well worth a longer stay, being centrally situated for visiting the Lake District and the Yorkshire Dales. Surrounded by farmland the park is long and narrow, with pitches on either side of a central road. There are 26 level touring pitches, all with hardstanding and a little on the small side. At each end of the park there are six privately owned caravan holiday homes. There are no play areas for children, and parents of young children would need to be vigilant here, as there is a well-signed but unfenced, fast-flowing stream.

Facilities

Centrally located toilet block, although a little dated, is spotlessly clean with showers and washbasins in cubicles. Facilities for disabled visitors. Laundry. No motorcaravan service point. Shop. Bar with TV. Off site: Hotel serving food. Canal and boat trips. Kendal 15 minutes drive.

Open: March - November.

Directions

From M6 exit 36 take the A65 (east) signed Kirkby Lonsdale for 300 yds. At next roundabout take first exit signed Crooklands and Endmoor. Park entrance is about 1 mile on the right at Crooklands Motor Co. O.S.GR: SD536836. GPS: 54.24697, -2.7162

Charges guide

Per unit incl. electricity	£ 13.50 - £ 19.50
tent	£ 10.00

Kendal

Ashes 'Exclusively Adult' Caravan Park

New Hutton, Kendal LA8 0AS (Cumbria) T: 01539 731833. E: info@ashescaravanpark.co.uk
alanrogers.com/UK5650

The Ashes is a friendly, small, adult only park in an extremely peaceful setting in the rolling Cumbrian countryside, yet less than three miles from the M6, and only slightly further from Kendal. A very tidy park, the central grass area is attractively planted with shrubs and bushes and there is an open vista (with little shade). There are 25 hardstanding gravel pitches, all with 10A electrical connections. These are neatly placed around the perimeter, with an oval access road. The whole area slopes gently down from the entrance, with some pitches fairly level and others with a little more slope (levelling system for caravans on all pitches). No tents are accepted other than trailer tents.

Facilities

A small, purpose built stone building with a slate roof houses two unisex, heated shower rooms and the washing and toilet facilities. New facilities for disabled visitors. Laundry service. No shop. New electronic barrier. TV signal booster. WiFi. Off site: Mr and Mrs Mason have prepared a full information sheet with details of shopping, eating and many other local venues. Fishing 2 miles. Golf and riding 3 miles. Bicycle hire 4 miles. Kendal 4 miles.

Open: 1 March - 7 November.

Directions

From M6 junction 37 follow the A684 towards Kendal for 2 miles. Just past a white cottage turn sharp left at crossroads signed New Hutton. Site is on the right in 0.75 miles at a left bend. Only approach and depart using this road. O.S.GR: SD560908. GPS: 54.313133, -2.675

Charges 2010

Per unit incl. 2 persons and electricity	£ 14.50 - £ 17.00

Keswick
Castlerigg Hall Caravan & Camping Park
Keswick CA12 4TE (Cumbria) T: **01768 774499**. E: **info@castlerigg.co.uk**
alanrogers.com/**UK5660**

This well laid out park was started in the late 1950s by the Jackson family, who over the years have developed and improved the site whilst maintaining its character. Traditional stone buildings house the combined reception and shop. Tarmac roads wind their way around the site to the separate area for 110 tent pitches. Gently sloping with some shelter, these pitches have fine views across Keswick, Derwentwater and the western Fells. The 45 caravan pitches tend to be on terraces overlooking the lake.

Facilities

The main heated toilet block is beautifully fitted out with showers, vanity style washbasins (2 in cabins) and hair care areas. Unit for disabled visitors (key). Baby area. Fully equipped laundry. Games room and campers' kitchen. Two other toilet blocks are older in style but newly decorated and clean. Reception houses tourist information, internet point and a well stocked shop (with gas). Off site: Hotel/pub for meals adjacent to site. Fishing, golf, riding. bicycle hire and boat launching, all 1.5 miles.

Open: Mid March - November.

Directions

From Penrith take A66 towards Keswick and Cockermouth. Leave at first sign for Keswick (A591) and follow to junction (A5271). Turn left on A591 signed Windermere and after 1 mile, take small road on right signed Castlerigg and Rakefoot. Park entrance is on right after 400 yards. O.S.GR: NY282227. GPS: 54.5931, -3.112583

Charges guide

Per unit incl. 2 persons £ 12.00 - £ 15.95

Kirkby Lonsdale
Woodclose Caravan Park
Kirkby Lonsdale LA6 2SE (Cumbria) T: **01524 271597**. E: **info@woodclosepark.com**
alanrogers.com/**UK5605**

Woodclose is an established, nine acre park with new owners. Situated in the Lune Valley and just one mile from the market town of Kirkby Lonsdale, this park offers a peaceful and secluded setting catering for walkers, tourers and people who just want to relax. Access to the park is narrow, so care should be taken. The whole park has a very well cared for appearance with well mown grass, flowering tubs and neat hedges. The upper part contains many privately owned holiday homes with neat terraces built from local stone. Screened by a hedge and placed around the perimeter are several seasonal pitches with touring units being placed in the centre. These pitches are numbered and mostly level, some on hardstanding, some on grass, with 16A electricity and digital TV hook-ups. More seasonal pitches and holiday homes on the lower part of the park, again most attractively terraced with stone walling and paths. Reception is part of the well stocked shop which includes local produce and freshly-baked bread; an information room is adjoining with tables and chairs and internet access (£1 per half an hour).

Facilities

Two toilet blocks, the main one central to the touring area. These facilities are all unisex in large, heated, individual rooms with toilets, washbasin and toilet or washbasin and shower, all well equipped and very clean. Well equipped laundry. The second block is in the lower part, again all unisex in cubicles. Facilities for disabled visitors. No motorcaravan service point. Shop. Small adventure play area. Bicycle hire. Internet access. American style motorhomes accepted (limited space). Gates locked 24.00-07.30, warden and telephone on site for emergencies. Off site: Golf 1 mile. Fishing 7 miles. Beach 20 miles.

Open: 1 March - 1 November.

Directions

From M6 exit 36 take A65 to Kirkby Lonsdale. Site is off the A65 in 6 miles. O.S.GR: SD620781. GPS: 54.19835, -2.585017

Charges guide

Per unit incl. 2 persons
and electricity £ 10.00 - £ 20.00
tent incl. 2 persons £ 12.00 - £ 14.00
extra person £ 3.75
child (5-16 yrs) £ 2.00
awning £ 2.00
Book for 7 nights and receive 1 night free (high season only).

www.alanrogers.com for latest campsite news

Kirkby Stephen
Pennine View Caravan & Camping Park
Station Road, Kirkby Stephen CA17 4SZ (Cumbria) T: **01768 371717**
alanrogers.com/UK5600

Suitable for night halts or longer breaks to visit the Lake District or the Yorkshire Dales, Pennine View is a super small park, well managed and well maintained. With a very attractive rockery at the entrance, the whole site is very neat and tidy. Level, numbered pitches with gravel hardstanding are arranged around the perimeter with grass pitches in the centre. The pitches are of a good size (some being especially large) and are all are supplied with electricity hook-ups (16A). Pennine View is built on reclaimed land from a former railway goods yard. One end of the park adjoins the River Eden.

Facilities	Directions
Built of local stone, the modern toilet block is accessed by a digital keypad and includes individual wash cubicles and deep sink for a baby bath. Both ladies and men have large en-suite units for disabled visitors. Well equipped laundry room. Gas available. Play area. Off site: Nearby hotel offers bar meals. Kirkby Stephen 1 mile. Bicycle hire 300 m. Golf 4 miles.	Park is on the A685 on the southerly outskirts of Kirkby Stephen (just under a mile from the town centre). Turn left at small site sign opposite the Croglin Castle hotel. Site is 50 yds. on right. O.S.GR: NY772075. GPS: 54.461667, -2.353367

Open: 1 March - 31 October.

Charges guide

Per person	£ 5.10 - £ 5.50
child (4-15 yrs)	£ 2.00 - £ 2.50
pitch	£ 5.00 - £ 6.00

Penrith
Sykeside Camping Park
Brotherswater, Patterdale, Penrith CA11 0NZ (Cumbria) T: **01768 482239**. E: **info@sykeside.co.uk**
alanrogers.com/UK5560

This small touring park is located in a really beautiful, quiet spot in the northern Lakes area (it is just 400 yards from Brotherswater). With views up the Dovedale valley, the park has 100 pitches in the valley floor, mainly for tents. There are 19 for motorcaravans on hardstanding, 16 of which have electricity (10A). Pitches are not marked and campers arrange themselves to best enjoy the superb views. The stone-built building, an original barn, near the entrance houses all the facilities. These include the recently extended and refurbished Barn End bar where meals are served.

Facilities	Directions
The toilet block includes hot showers and has been refurbished, with a chemical disposal point added. Small launderette and dishwashing room. Self-service shop with camping equipment, gas and an ice pack service, doubles as reception. Cosy, licensed bar and restaurant (daily in summer, weekends only in winter). Bunkhouse accommodation for 30 persons in various groupings. Fishing nearby. Off site: Bicycle hire 3 miles. Good sailing on Ullswater 4 miles. Riding 8 miles. Golf 10 miles. The Brotherswater Inn is adjacent (open all year).	From junction 40 of the M6 take the A66 towards Keswick. At first roundabout take the A592 (for Ullswater and Glenridding), continue to Brotherswater and Sykeside is on the right of the A592. The entrance is just behind the Brotherswater Inn. O.S.GR: NY396005. GPS: 54.4985, -2.9255

Open: All year.

Charges guide

Per tent incl. 2 persons and car	£ 10.00 - £ 23.00
motorcaravan incl. 2 persons and electricity	£ 17.00 - £ 24.50
child (5-15 yrs)	£ 2.00 - £ 2.50

Penrith
Westmorland Caravan Park
Tebay, Orton, Penrith CA10 3SB (Cumbria) T: **01539 711322**. E: **caravans@westmorland.com**
alanrogers.com/UK5590

For caravans, motorhomes and trailer tents only, this is the ideal stopover for anyone heading either north or south, near the M6 motorway, but far enough away for the traffic noise not to be too disturbing. There are 83 level pitches on gravel, divided into bays of about six or seven units (30 are for touring units). All touring pitches have electricity (16A). The bays are backed by grassy banks alive with rabbits and birds – a long list in the office describes the large variety of birds to be seen on the site. There is good site lighting and a late arrivals area.

Facilities	Directions
The heated toilet block is kept very clean. Showers. Facilities for disabled visitors. Family room. Sinks for laundry and dishwashing. Laundry. Reception sells gas. Off site: Shops and restaurants five minutes walk away at the motorway service area.	From the M6, just north of junction 38, exit for Tebay Services (site signed). Site is accessible from the services travelling north or south. O.S.GR: NY607060. GPS: 54.4477, -2.606467

Open: 5 March - 2 November.

Charges guide

Per unit incl. 4 persons and electricity	£ 16.00 - £ 19.00
Special rates for 3, 5 or 7 days.	

Penrith
Cove Camping Park

Ullswater, Watermillock, Penrith CA11 0LS (Cumbria) T: 01768 486549. E: info@cove-park.co.uk

alanrogers.com/UK5620

Cove Camping is a delightful small site, some of the 50 pitches having great views over Lake Ullswater. A separate area behind the camping field holds 39 privately owned caravan holiday homes. The grass is well trimmed, there are ramps to keep speeds down to 5 mph. and the site is well lit. At the top of the park are 17 level pitches with electric hook-ups and hardstanding suitable for touring caravans and motorcaravans; the rest of the park is quite sloping. Rubbish bins are hidden behind wooden fencing, as are recycling bins. The park is well situated for walking, boating, fishing and pony trekking activities. The road up from the A592 is narrow, but a self imposed one way system is generally adhered to and the warden will advise on a different way to leave the site.

Facilities

The tiled toilet block is immaculate and heated in cooler months, providing adjustable showers, some washbasins in cabins and, for ladies, a hairdressing area with stool and a baby changing unit. Foyer containing a freezer (free), and tourist information. Laundry with washing machine, dryer and an iron. Gas supplies. Small, grass based play area. Off site: Shop nearby. Fishing 1.5 miles. Riding 3 miles. Golf 6 mile. Bicycle hire 7 miles (will deliver).

Open: March - 31 October.

Directions

We advise using the following directions rather than GPS. From A66 Penrith - Keswick road, take A592 south, signed Ullswater. Turn right at Brackenrigg Inn (site signed) and follow road uphill for about 1.5 miles to park on left. This road is narrow so if you have a larger unit, telephone the park for advice about an alternative route. O.S.GR: NY431236.
GPS: 54.604283, -2.881883

Charges guide

Per unit incl. 2 persons and electricity	£ 15.00 - £ 25.00
tent incl. 2 persons	£ 10.00 - £ 22.00
extra person (5 yrs and over)	£ 3.00
dog	£ 1.00

No credit cards.

Penrith
Waterfoot Caravan Park

Pooley Bridge, Penrith CA11 0JF (Cumbria) T: 01768 486302. E: enquiries@waterfootpark.co.uk

alanrogers.com/UK5610

Waterfoot is a quiet family park for caravans and motorcaravans only. It is set in 22 acres of partially wooded land, developed in the fifties from a private estate. The 146 private caravan holiday homes are quite separate from the 34 touring pitches. Lake Ullswater is only about 400 yards away and a half mile stroll through bluebell woods brings you to the village of Pooley Bridge. Waterfoot's touring pitches are arranged very informally in a large clearing. Most are level, there are some hardstandings and all have 10A electricity. The park no longer accepts American RVs. There is a bar in a large, imposing mansion, in the past a family home then a golf hotel. Public footpaths lead straight from the park. The regular lake steamer service calls at Pooley Bridge, and the Ullswater yacht club is only ten minutes' drive and the market town of Penrith is five miles away. The historic house and gardens of Dalemain are a short walk.

Facilities

The heated toilet block includes washbasins and preset showers in cubicles. New facilities for disabled visitors. Large, light and airy dishwashing room and fully equipped laundry. Small shop selling basics, gas and newspapers. Bar with strictly enforced, separate family room open weekend evenings in low season and every evening in high season. Large fenced field with play equipment to suit all ages and goal posts for football and a new play park. Off site: Fishing 0.5 miles. Riding 1.5 miles. Golf 5 miles. Pooley Bridge has a post office/general store, hotels and restaurants.

Open: 1 March - 14 November.

Directions

Do not use GPS here - it directs outfits the wrong way, finishing up on farm tracks. Please use the following directions. From M6 junction 40, take A66 signed Keswick. After 0.5 miles at roundabout take A592 signed Ullswater and site is on right after 4 miles. O.S.GR: NY460245.
GPS: 54.614017, -2.83115

Charges 2010

Per unit incl. all persons and electricity	£ 18.00 - £ 26.00

Pay for 7 nights in one payment and receive 1 night free.

221

Penrith

Lowther Holiday Park

Eamont Bridge, Penrith CA10 2JB (Cumbria) T: **01768 863631**. E: alan@lowther-holidaypark.co.uk

alanrogers.com/UK5625

Sitting on the banks of the River Lowther this holiday park occupies 50 acres of rural, wooded parkland, home to the rare red squirrel. There are 400 caravan holiday homes and lodges around the park, together with 200 touring pitches. A proportion of these are taken by seasonal lets. The pitches are marked and numbered, on mostly level ground between mature trees, they have 10A electricity and hardstanding. A separate elevated grass area is available for tents. There is a small touring office with 24-hour security adjacent to the holiday home sales office. Here too is a well-stocked, licensed shop also selling some caravan accessories. The Squirrel Inn is open all season and serves restaurant meals and takeaways. Outside is a large paved seating area with a play area to one side. A lovely riverside walk has been created with many benches to rest and enjoy the birds and other wildlife.

Facilities

Two toilet blocks are central to the touring areas (key entry). Very clean, they provide large, preset showers. Fully equipped bathroom with baby changing. Drive through motorcaravan service. Well equipped laundry. Full facilities for disabled visitors (Radar key). Licensed shop. Squirrel Inn with restaurant, terrace and games room. Play areas. Fly fishing on river (permit from office). Activity weekends. Live entertainment and children's parties. Max. two dogs per unit. Off site: Market town of Penrith 3 miles. Golf, riding and bicycle hire 2 miles. Boat launching 4 miles.

Open: March - November.

Directions

From M6 exit 40 take A66 towards Scotch Corner for 1 mile. At roundabout take A6 south for 1 mile towards Shap. Lowther is on the right as you pass through village of Eamont Bridge. O.S.GR: NY527264. GPS: 54.647667, -2.737017

Charges guide

Per unit incl. 1-6 persons
and electricity   £ 18.00 - £ 22.00

Penrith

The Quiet Site Caravan & Camping Park

Watermillock, Penrith CA11 0LS (Cumbria) T: **07768 727016**. E: info@thequietsite.co.uk

alanrogers.com/UK5630

The Quiet Site is a secluded, family run park, operating as a carbon neutral company. It is situated on a hillside in the National Park with views over the fells and just 1.5 miles from Lake Ullswater. There are 100 unmarked touring pitches, most with hardstanding and 50 with electricity. Most have been terraced to provide level surfaces, but a few are very sloping. The camping area is very undulating. In a separate part of the park, screened by mature trees, are 23 privately owned caravan holiday homes. There are two cottages to rent and recent additions are timber built 'camping pods' as an alternative to bringing your own tent. In converted old farm buildings, the amenities are centred around the reception and shop and include a comfortable first floor bar with oak beams and barrel seats. Many beautiful walks start from right outside the park and the numerous activities and attractions of the Lake District are within a short drive. The owners, the Holder family, are continuing to develop this attractive, well maintained park with an emphasis on green principles. A member of the Best of British group.

Facilities

The toilet block provides preset showers and open style washbasins. Three bathrooms and two private shower rooms. Bathroom with facilities for disabled visitors. Baby area. Laundry facilities. Motorcaravan services. Well stocked shop at reception. Gas supplies. Bar (weekends only in low season). TV and games room. Excellent adventure play area. Caravan storage. American motorhomes would find access very difficult. Off site: Fishing 1.5 miles. Riding and bicycle hire 3 miles. Golf 8 miles.

Open: All year excl. 17 January -28 February.

Directions

We advise using the following directions, rather than GPS. From M6, exit 40, take A66 (Keswick) for 1 mile, then A592 signed Ullswater for 4 miles. Turn right at Lake junction, still on A592 signed Windermere. After 1 miles turn right (at Brackenrigg Inn) and follow for 1.5 miles to site on right (large units should phone for an alternative route). O.S.GR: NY431236. GPS: 54.604683, -2.882783

Charges guide

Per unit incl. 2 persons, awning and electricity	£ 17.00 - £ 27.00
tent incl. 2 persons	£ 12.00 - £ 27.00
extra person	free - £ 4.00
dog	£ 1.00

Camping Cheques accepted.

Penrith
Ullswater Caravan, Camping & Marine Park
Watermillock, Penrith CA11 0LR (Cumbria) T: 017684 86666. E: info@uccmp.co.uk
alanrogers.com/UK5635

Located within the Lake District National Park, Ullswater Caravan Park is centrally situated for touring the many attractions of this glorious area. It has 220 pitches, 58 for touring units, the rest used for holiday homes. All have 10A electricity, 50 also have water and drains. Some are situated very close to the bar and are also overlooked by mobile homes with little privacy. At the far end of the park other pitches are in a more wooded area. In between is a large grassy space for tents.

Facilities	Directions
Two toilet blocks, one refurbished the other a little dated and unheated. Facilities for babies and disabled visitors. Laundry. Shop with off-licence. Bar and games room open 8pm at busy times. Well equipped playground for younger children. Off site: Walks in the hills above the park. Steamer rides on the lake from Pooley Bridge 2 miles.	From M6 exit 40 take the A66 west signed Keswick. At first roundabout (Rheged) take second exit signed Ullswater on the A592. At T-junction turn right still on the A592 and after Breckenrigg Inn on the right, carry on downhill to telephone box on right, and sign for church. Turn right here and up to entrance on right in 800 yds. O.S.GR: NY436229. GPS: 54.5978, -2.87482
Open: 1 March - 14 November.	

Charges guide

Per unit incl. 2 persons	£ 16.50 - £ 18.50
serviced pitch	£ 19.00 - £ 22.00
extra person	£ 2.50 - £ 3.50

Penrith
Flusco Wood Touring Caravan Park
Flusco, Penrith CA11 0JB (Cumbria) T: 01768 480020. E: admin@fluscowood.co.uk
alanrogers.com/UK5670

Flusco Wood Caravan Park is still being developed but everything is to a very high standard. Set amongst woodland with the 12 touring pitches in bays, this park will meet the needs of those requiring a quiet holiday (with plenty of walks from the site) and also those travelling up or down the M6 looking for a quiet night's rest. All pitches are on hardstandings. The area abounds with wildlife including deer and red squirrels. Member of the Countryside Discovery group.

Facilities	Directions
A log cabin style building houses very clean, heated facilities including preset showers and vanity style washbasins (1 cubicle). Large en-suite shower rooms for families or disabled visitors, one in the ladies' and one in the men's. Dishwashing sinks under cover. Laundry, drying room and boot washing sink. Second log cabin serves as reception/shop with basic supplies, gas and daily newspapers. Play equipment on bark. Grass area for ball games. Off site: Pub and P.O. stores 2 miles. Fishing, bicycle hire and golf 4 miles. Riding 5 miles.	From M6 take A66 towards Keswick. Go straight on at first roundabout, then third right at top of hill (signed Flusco, Recycling Centre, Pottery and caravan sign). After 0.5 miles road turns right up hill (narrow, so take care in large units), site is on left at the top. Site is 4 miles from M6. O.S.GR: NY457293. GPS: 54.655408, -2.841346
Open: Easter or 1 April - 29 October.	

Charges guide

Per unit incl. 2 persons and electricity	£ 17.50 - £ 20.50
extra person (over 3 yrs)	£ 3.00

Wigton
The Larches Caravan Park
Mealsgate, Wigton CA7 1LQ (Cumbria) T: 01697 371379. E: thelarches@hotmail.co.uk
alanrogers.com/UK5510

Mealsgate and The Larches lie on the Carlisle - Cockermouth road, a little removed from the hectic centre of the Lake District, yet with easy access to it (and good views towards it) and to other attractions nearby. This family run, adult only park takes 73 touring units of any type, 42 of which have electricity (10A), water and drainage. Touring pitches are in different grassy areas with tall, mature trees, shrubs and accompanying wildlife. Some are sloping and irregular, others on marked hardstandings. There are currently a few privately owned holiday homes and there are plans to extend this area of the park.

Facilities	Directions
Toilet facilities are clean but a little dated and provide en-suite facilities for both sexes. Washbasins for ladies are in cubicles, those for men set in flat surfaces. Separate unit for disabled visitors can be heated. Campers' kitchen with cooker and microwave (metered). Laundry room. Small shop selling mainly camping accessories, gas and off-licence. Small indoor heated pool. Wildlife pond. Caravan storage. Off site: Riding 1.5 miles. Golf 3.5 miles. Bicycle hire 7 miles. Fishing 8 miles.	Park entrance is south off A595 (Carlisle - Cockermouth road) just southwest of Mealsgate. O.S.GR: NY206415. GPS: 54.763267, -3.2358

Charges guide

Per unit incl. 2 persons	£ 12.50 - £ 14.90
incl. electricity	£ 14.50 - £ 16.90
extra person	£ 2.00 - £ 2.50
awning or extra car	£ 1.50 - £ 2.00
backpacker	£ 6.90 - £ 7.90
No credit cards.	

Open: 1 March - 31 October.

(223)

Wigton

Stanwix Park Holiday Centre

Greenrow, Silloth, Wigton CA7 4HH (Cumbria) T: 01697 332666. E: enquiries@stanwix.com

alanrogers.com/UK5505

Stanwix Park is a family run holiday park with absolutely everything anyone could want for a memorable holiday all year round. The park has 111 caravan holiday homes and chalets for rent, together with 212 which are privately owned. These are mostly located around the central complex. In addition at either end of the park, there are 121 fully serviced (10A electricity) pitches for touring units and tents, some on grass, some with hardstanding. A warm welcome awaits in the main reception, with lots of local and tourist information. Motorhomes over 8 m. accepted by prior arrangement. The indoor tropical leisure centre contains a 29 m. fun pool with slides, a steam room, sauna, spa, fitness gym and vertical sun shower (charge). The upper floor has the Sky Bar and Dunes Cabaret Bar (adults only) and the Sunset Inn licensed family club, all enjoying nightly entertainment and special themed weekends from November to March. A giant TV and snooker room are in the Gallery observation area with a state-of-the-art Astro Bowling Centre and amusement arcade, with a soft play area to one side. Outside a large, terraced swimming pool, an adventure play area and minigolf are all screened by plants and shrubs.

Facilities

The two heated sanitary blocks have been refurbished to a high standard, kept spotlessly clean and opened by combination lock. Large en-suite bathrooms, showers, vanity style washbasins, a unit in each for disabled visitors. Campers kitchen. Fully equipped laundry. Gas sales. Well stocked shop (6/3-15/11). Restaurant with takeaway (all year). Bars (adults only and family) with evening entertainment (6/3-15/11). TV and snooker room. Indoor leisure centre. Outdoor pool (31/5-1/9). Ten-pin bowling centre. Amusement arcade. Soft play area. Minigolf. Tennis. Bicycle hire. Dogs max. 2. Off site: Bus service 1 mile in Silloth. Silloth golf club, bowling club and sports ground only a short walk. Beach 1 mile.

Open: All year.

Directions

From the south, take exit 41 from the M6 and follow B5305 through Wigton to Silloth. From north on A74/M6 take exit 44 and the A595 and A596 to Wigton. On entering Silloth, turn left following signs for park. Entrance is on the right. O.S.GR: NY108525. GPS: 54.8614, -3.388333

Charges guide

Per person	£ 3.80 - £ 4.55
child (under 5 yrs)	£ 2.45 - £ 2.90
pitch	£ 11.70 - £ 14.50
dog (max. 2)	£ 3.00

Many special offers and short break prices.

Wigton

Hylton Caravan Park

Eden Street, Silloth, Wigton CA7 4AY (Cumbria) T: 01697 332666. E: ericstanwix@stanwix.com

alanrogers.com/UK5506

Hylton Caravan Park is owned and managed by the Stanwix family and although it is only a short walk away from the livelier Stanwix Leisure Park, it is a peaceful haven for people who prefer the 'quiet life'. The only activity is an adventure park for children which is not visible from the touring area. Divided by a circular road, the 170 privately owned caravan holiday homes are visible but not intrusive. There are 90 open plan, mostly level touring and tent pitches, all fully serviced and with 10A electricity.

Facilities

A high quality toilet block is superbly fitted out and includes toilets, showers, vanity style washbasins, extra large bathrooms and a separate cubicle for disabled people. Laundry. Max. 2 dogs per pitch. Off site: Bus stop 1 mile. Entertainment and amenities at Stanwix Park. Silloth golf course. Bowling. Fishing 1 mile. Riding 7 miles.

Open: 1 March - 15 November.

Directions

On entering Silloth, turn left following signs to Hylton Caravan Park. O.S.GR: NY114534. GPS: 54.868333, -3.39835

Charges guide

Per person	£ 3.80 - £ 4.55
child (under 5 yrs)	£ 2.45 - £ 2.90
pitch	£ 9.35 - £ 11.60

Windermere

Park Cliffe Camping & Caravan Estate

Birks Road, Windermere LA23 3PG (Cumbria) T: **01539 531344**. E: **info@parkcliffe.co.uk**

alanrogers.com/UK5545

This beautiful Park is situated in the heart of the Lake District National Park. Owned by the Holgate family, it is well managed and maintained, with welcoming staff. The 70 touring pitches are open and unshaded, on gravel hardstanding, with electricity (10A), water and drainage. There are some seasonal units and three mobile homes available for hire. Tucked away in a valley are privately owned mobile homes. Two areas have been set aside for tents, one of which has electric hook-ups (steel pegs required). There is no automatic barrier, but the gates are closed to both campers and caravanners 11.00-07.30 with a warden on site for emergencies.

Facilities

Two blocks of toilets and showers are heated and very clean. Full facilities for disabled visitors and excellent baby room. Four private bathrooms are available for hire (min 3 days), and one by the hour (with refundable deposit). Laundry. Motorcaravan service point. Bar, restaurant and takeaway. Small well stocked shop. Games room. Large outdoor adventure play area is set secluded to one side of the tourers, not fenced as a public footpath runs through to Moor How. Off site: Fellfoot Country Park with boat launching (sail), walking, climbing, cycling and many other activities possible. Cruises on the lake. Many visitor attractions.

Open: 1 March - 14 November.

Directions

From M6 exit 36 take A590 to Newby Bridge. Turn right on A592 for 3.6 miles and turn right. Site is signed shortly on the right. Caravans and trailers must approach Park Cliffe from the direction of Newby Bridge on the A592. The park does not advise the use of sat nav to reach it. O.S.GR: SD391911. GPS: 54.312517, -2.9375

Charges guide

Per unit incl. 2 persons and electricity	£ 23.50 - £ 26.50
extra person	£ 5.00
child (5-17 yrs)	£ 2.00
dog	£ 2.00

Park Cliffe Camping and Caravan Estate
AA Northwest campsite of the year 2009
ESCAPE RELAX UNWIND
Windermere, the Lake District
Birks Road, Windermere, Cumbria LA23 3PG
www.parkcliffe.co.uk   015395 31344   info@parkcliffe.co.uk

Windermere

Hill of Oaks Caravan Park

Tower Wood, Windermere LA12 8NR (Cumbria) T: **01539 531578**. E: **enquiries@hillofoaks.co.uk**

alanrogers.com/UK5615

This park on the banks of Lake Windermere lives up to its name 'Hill of Oaks'. Set on a hillside in mature woodland, the park offers families a safe natural environment with nature walks through the managed ancient woodlands, as well as six jetties for boat launching and access to watersport activities (jet skis are not allowed). The road into the park passing the farmhouse is long, winding and narrow, so care should be taken especially with long outfits, reception being about half a mile from the entrance. Although the park is situated on Lake Windermere the touring pitches nestle within the trees, not actually by the lake. All 43 have electricity (16A), digital TV hook-up and hardstanding.

Facilities

The central tiled toilet block, recently refurbished, is very clean and heated. Vanity style washbasins, controllable showers and free hairdryers. Baby changing areas. Laundry. Unit for disabled visitors (combination lock). Motorcaravan service point. Shop for basics. Fenced play areas, one for toddlers and adventure type for over 5s. Picnic areas and nature trails. Fishing (licence required). Off site: Fell Foot Park and Gardens 1 mile, with rowing boat hire or ferry rides to Lakeside or Ambleside. Aquarium of the Lakes 3.5 miles. Golf 4 miles. Riding and bicycle hire 6 miles.

Open: 1 March - 14 November.

Directions

From M6 exit 36 head west on A590 towards Barrow and Newby Bridge. Follow A590 to roundabout signed Bowness and turn right on A592 for about 3 miles. Site is signed on left. O.S.GR: SD384903. GPS: 54.30755, -2.9454

Charges guide

Per pitch	£ 10.00 - £ 24.00
car	£ 1.00
awning	£ 3.00
boat	£ 5.00 - £ 10.50

225

The most northerly reg
of England, Northumb
is steeped in history,
full of ancient forts an
fairytale castles. The gre
outdoors offers limitless
walking with plenty of trails
stretching across moorlands and
beaches, encompassing views of
the beautiful scenery.

THE REGION COMPRISES: NORTHUMBERLAND, DURHAM, TYNE AND WEAR, AND TEESIDE

The 400 square mile Northumberland National Park is one of the most peaceful, remote places in England. With endless walks across moorlands and hills, it stretches south from the Cheviot Hills, through the Simonside Hills, to the crags of Whin Sill, where it engulfs a section of the historic Hadrian's Wall, built by the Romans to mark the northern limit of their empire. The Pennine Way was the country's first official long-distance path and is still the longest. At 268 miles, it stretches from the Peak National Park to the border. The coastline is not to be forgotten, with mile upon mile of deserted, sandy beaches, with resorts that still have an old fashioned feel to them, such as Whitley Bay, South Shields and Seaton Carew. The majestic castles of Bamburgh, and Dunstanburgh can be seen for miles along the Northumberland coast. Surrounded on three sides by the river Wear, the small, historic city of Durham is dominated by England's greatest Norman Cathedral. With cobbled medieval streets and restricted car access it is a popular place with visitors. Further north is the bustling city of Newcastle. Home to an array of cosmopolitan restaurants and bars, music venues, and fabulous architecture, it also boasts a lively nightlife.

Places of interest

Northumberland: Bamburgh Castle; Alnwic Castle and gardens; Berwick-upon-Tweed; bird reserve on Farne Islands, home to larg colony of grey seals; Hauxley Nature Reserv Dunstanburgh Castle; Corbridge Roman sites at Hadrian's Wall.

Durham: Durham Castle and Cathedral; Barnard Castle, a ruined castle overlooking the River Tees; Diggerland at Langley Park; Harperley POW Camp.

Tyne and Wear: New Metroland, Europe's only indoor theme park within a large shopping complex; Newcastle with Life Science Centre, Discovery Museum and Castle Keep; Whitley Bay.

Teeside: Kirkleatham Owl Centre; Darlingtc Railway Centre and Museum; Guisborough Hall; Hartlepool Historic Quay and HMS Trinacomalee; Butterfly World in Stockton-on-Tees.

Did you know?

Alnwick Castle is used as the setting of Hogwarts in the Harry Potter films.

Stretching from Wallsend to Bowness-on-Solway, Hadrian's Wall is 81 miles long; it i possible to walk the entire length.

Born in Northumbria in 1825, George Stephenson was the first person to design the steam engine that ran on wheels.

In the past 300 years Berwick has changed hands between the Scottish and the Englis no less than 13 times.

The Angel of The North is made up of 200 tonnes of steel and rises 20 metres. from the ground.

Built in 1817, HMS Trinacomalee is the oldest ship afloat in the UK.

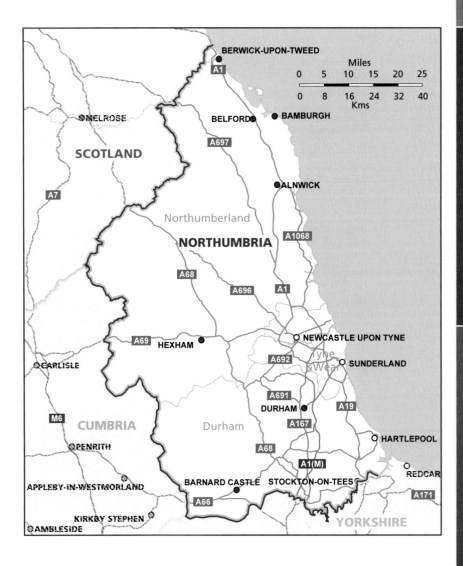

Maps and campsite listings

For this 2010 guide we have changed the way in which we list our parks and also the way in which we help you locate the parks within each region.

We now include a map immediately after our Introduction to that region. These maps show the towns near which one (or more) of our featured parks is located. Within each regional section of the guide, we list these towns and the park(s) in that vicinity in alphabetical order.

You will certainly need more detailed maps for navigation, for example the Ordnance Survey road atlas. We provide O.S. references and G.P.S. coordinates for each park to assist you. Our three indexes will also help you to find a park by its reference number and name, by region and park name, or by the town where the park is situated.

Alnwick

Dunstan Hill Camping & Caravanning Club Site

Dunstan Hill, Dunstan, Alnwick NE66 3TQ (Northumberland) T: 01665 576310

alanrogers.com/UK5770

Off a quiet lane between Embleton and Craster this is a rural site with a tree belt to shelter it from the north wind and access to the beach by a level footpath through the fields, across the golf course and past the ruins of Dunstanburgh Castle. This is just over a mile by car. With gravel access roads, the peaceful site has 150 level, well spaced pitches, 80 with 16A electricity. Reception is manned by very helpful managers and there is an area for outside parking and late arrivals at the entrance. This is a wonderful area to visit, with its unspoilt beaches and the whole area is steeped in history. Nearby are Holy Island, the Farne Islands, Bamburgh, Dunstanburgh, Walkworth and Alnwick castles (featured in many films including Macbeth and Harry Potter). The multimillion pound gardens project at Alnwick is well worth a visit. This site is not suitable for large American motorhomes.

Facilities	Directions
Two very clean and well maintained toilet blocks have some washbasins in cubicles, hairdryers (20p) and a washroom for children with deep sinks. Fully equipped facility for disabled visitors in one block, a laundry in the other. Small shop for gas and basic provisions. Bread and milk can be ordered and a mobile shop and the paper man visit. Well stocked tourist information room. Small play area. Torches are useful. Off site: Buses pass the entrance (request stop) and there are good eating places near including Craster (world famous fish restaurant). Fishing 1.5 miles. Golf 1.5 miles. Beach 1.5 miles. Riding 8 miles. Bicycle hire 10 miles.	From A1 just north of Alnwick take the B1340 or B6347 (further north) for Embleton. Site is signed in Embleton village. Avoid signs to Dunstanburgh Castle and follow those for Craster. Site is (south) on the left after about 0.5 miles. O.S.GR: NU236214. GPS: 55.4855, -1.6291

Open: March - October.

Charges guide

Per person	£ 4.90 - £ 7.25
child (6-18 yrs)	£ 2.15 - £ 2.25
non-member pitch fee	£ 5.65

Bamburgh

Waren Caravan & Camping Park

Waren Mill, Bamburgh NE70 7EE (Northumberland) T: 01668 214366. E: waren@meadowhead.co.uk

alanrogers.com/UK5750

Developed from 100 acres of undulating privately owned heath and woodland, Waren Park is a large, spacious family site with marvellous views over Northumberland's golden beaches and the sea. A large section of caravan holiday homes is separate from a self contained four acre touring area. Enclosed by sheltering banks, this provides 170 reasonably level pitches, 100 with 10A electrical connections. Wooden wigwams are also available to rent for a self-catered option. As well as the spacious grounds to wander in, there is much to see nearby from historic castles and the Farne Islands to the Cheviot Hills and miles and miles of sandy beaches.

Facilities	Directions
The older toilet facilities are poor and in need of refurbishment, whilst a newer block situated in a separate static holiday home section provides good facilities. Laundry room. Dishwashing sinks. Motorcaravan service point. Licensed shop. Bar with terrace serving bar meals (all season). Gaming machine room with pool table. Patio area. Children's play park and playing fields. Splash pool (June - Sept). WiFi internet access. Off site: Beach 500 yds. excellent for birdwatching, unsuitable for bathing. Safe bathing beach 4 miles (Bamburgh). Golf or bicycle hire 2 miles. Riding 5 miles. Birdwatching opportunities nearby.	Follow B1342 from the A1 to Waren Mill towards Bamburgh. After Budle Bay turn right and follow signs. O.S.GR: NU154342. GPS: 55.60045, -1.75487

Open: 14 March - 31 October.

Charges guide

Per unit incl. 2 persons	£ 13.00 - £ 23.00
extra person (over 5 yrs)	£ 3.00
1-man tent (no car)	£ 9.50 - £ 12.00
dog	£ 2.50
Less 10% for bookings of 7 days or over.	

Barnard Castle
Doe Park Touring Caravan Park
Cotherstone, Barnard Castle DL12 9UQ (Co. Durham) T: 01833 650302

alanrogers.com/UK5710

The Lamb family will make you very welcome and personally take you to your pitch at Doe Park. The camping fields have a lovely open aspect with wonderful views and the 70 pitches are spacious with well mown grass, all with 10A electricity, over 40 with hardstanding (no tents are taken). This is Hannah Hauxwell country and the Dales, less frequented than other upland areas, provide wonderful walking country; indeed part of the Pennine Way runs near this peaceful site. The park's reception is in a log cabin at the entrance to the pitch area and is well stocked with tourist information guides. The farm and park are close to where the River Balder joins the Tees at Cotherstone and the ancient oak wood beside the river is an SSSI (Site of Special Scientific Interest) for its insects and flowers, but is also a haven for birdwatchers. The farmhouse, formerly Leadgard Hall, is a mellow three storey, Grade II listed building with a history of its own. A bus service passes the park from Barnard Castle to Middleton and the village of Cotherstone is only half a mile with post office and a restaurant with bar meals, a pleasant walk by road or river bank.

Facilities
With toilet facilities at the farmhouse, two well kept blocks are closer to the pitches. Built in local stone, these are fully tiled with the newest one heated. Washbasins in cabins and adjustable showers. Well appointed unisex unit for disabled visitors. Small laundry. Eggs and milk are available from the farmhouse, plus gas supplies and battery charging. No play area but a large grass area in front of some of the pitches can be used for ball games. River fishing on site. Dogs and pets are accepted by arrangement only. Off site: Reservoirs (sailing, water skiing and fishing) 3 miles. Bicycle hire and golf 4 miles. Riding 2 miles. Local leisure centre with pool 4 miles.

Open: 1 March - 31 October.

Directions
Follow B6277 from Barnard Castle in direction of Middleton in Teesdale. The farm is signed on the left just after Cotherstone village (there is no need to go into Barnard Castle). O.S.GR: NZ005204.
GPS: 54.578217, -1.99235

Charges guide
Per unit incl. 2 persons and electricity	£ 12.50 - £ 15.00
family rate (2 adults, 2 children and awning)	£ 15.50 - £ 18.00
extra person (over 6 yrs)	£ 1.50
full awning	£ 1.00

No credit cards.

Barnard Castle
Barnard Castle Camping & Caravanning Club Site
Dockenflatts Lane, Lartington, Barnard Castle DL12 9DG (Co. Durham) T: 01833 630228

alanrogers.com/UK5720

Welcoming non-members and tents, the Camping and Caravanning Club site at Barnard Castle was opened in 1996. One side of the site is bordered by mature trees and further planting now gives privacy to individual pitches. There are 90 flat pitches, most on grass but including 12 hardstanding pitches (gravel base with room for both car and caravan and space for an awning on grass). There are 56 electrical hook-ups (16A). There is an attractive woodland dog walking area leading to a riverside footpath which takes you into Barnard Castle. There are many footpaths and walks in the area and numerous local attractions. These include the market town itself, Bowes Museum, Egglestone Abbey and Raby Castle, all within a 10 mile radius of the site.

Facilities
The centrally located toilet facilities are of good quality and kept spotlessly clean. Washbasins in cubicles and free, controllable showers are roomy. Baby room. Fully equipped unisex unit for visitors with disabilities. Large laundry with washing machine, dryer, iron and sink, with outside lines. Well stocked shop. Motorcaravan service point. Gas supplies. Central play area with rubber safety base. Caravan storage. Off site: Riding 200 m. Fishing 4 miles. Golf 2.5 miles. Bus service from end of lane.

Open: 30 March - 30 October.

Directions
Follow B6277 from Barnard Castle (towards Middleton in Teesdale) for 1 mile to Lartington. Turn left at club sign into narrow lane with passing places to site entrance on left (there is no need to go into Barnard Castle). O.S.GR: NZ025168.
GPS: 54.546883, -1.962583

Charges guide
Per person	£ 4.90 - £ 7.25
child (6-18 yrs)	£ 2.15 - £ 2.25
non-member pitch fee	£ 5.65

Belford

South Meadows Caravan Park

South Meadows, Belford NE70 7DP (Northumberland) T: **01668 213326**. E: **g.mcl@btinternet.com**
alanrogers.com/UK5755

South Meadows is set in the north Northumberland countryside, within walking distance of the village of Belford with its market cross and old coaching inn. Covering 6 acres of level grass, there are 100 hardstanding pitches, most with electricity (13A), water and TV aerial point. At present 20 pitches are available for touring units. A further area can accommodate 50 tents. The manager is environmentally aware and encourages recycling. Determined that visitors have a relaxing holiday, he will site your caravan using his own towing equipment. There is an area especially for disabled visitors with wider paths and safety features including a 24-hour telephone directly to the manager's home on site. The park is pleasantly landscaped and two short walks lead into the adjacent Blue Bell woods with streams, wildlife and spring flowers. Just off the A1 road, this would be a convenient stopover but Northumberland is an undiscovered county with castles and stately homes, the Farne Islands, Holy Island and long golden beaches, and you would be made most welcome here for a longer stay. This attractive, well maintained park is already popular with couples and young families and booking is advised.

Facilities

The fully tiled toilet block is excellent, heated in cool weather, with washbasins in cabins and roomy showers (free). Hairdryers. Full facilities for disabled visitors. Laundry facilities. Baby unit. Food preparation and cooking area. Coffee shop (weekends, incl. Sunday roast) and takeaway (daily until 16.00). Play area. Caravan storage and servicing. Off site: Village with pub and shops 0.5 miles. Golf 0.5 miles. Riding 3 miles. Beach 3 miles. Alnwick Castle of Harry Potter fame.

Open: All year.

Directions

Turn off A1 about 15 miles from Alnwick to Belford village and park is signed at the southern end. O.S.GR: NU115331. GPS: 55.590967, -1.822583

Charges guide

Per unit incl. 2 persons and electricity	£ 15.00 - £ 30.00
tent per adult	£ 6.00 - £ 12.00
extra person	£ 5.00 - £ 11.00
child (2-10 yrs)	£ 2.00

Berwick-upon-Tweed

Ord House Country Park

East Ord, Berwick-upon-Tweed TD15 2NS (Northumberland) T: **01289 305288**. E: **enquiries@ordhouse.co.uk**
alanrogers.com/UK5800

Ord House is 40-acre park for 260 privately owned holiday homes and 74 touring caravan and tent pitches. The park has a very well cared for appearance throughout with well mown grass and colourful arrays of flowering bushes. Ord House itself, an 18th-century mansion, has been tastefully converted to provide a bar, lounge bar and family room. The touring pitches, 67 with electricity (16A), are in small sections, from the secluded, walled orchard to the more open areas nearer the toilet blocks. There are 39 hardstanding pitches, each with electricity, water and drainage, 12 in the walled garden separated by shrubs and camomile lawns. At the entrance to the park an area with a few pitches is suitable for wheelchair users and close by is a small sanitary unit with WCs and showers plus a large, unisex, well appointed unit (Radar key). The whole site is 'wheelchair friendly' with good access to the airy reception. Although there are many caravan holiday homes, they are not overwhelming and their presence does mean that other amenities can remain open all season. A member of the Best of British group.

Facilities

The main, modern toilet building is of excellent quality and cleanliness, very well maintained and can be heated. Two good large family bathrooms (with two showers, a bath, WC and washbasin). Two rooms for disabled visitors. Large well equipped laundry. Motorcaravan service point. Gas supplies. Bar, bar food and family room (1/3-10/1). Crazy golf. Draughts. Play area. Commercial vehicles are not accepted. Dogs are only accepted by prior arrangement. Off site: Post office stores 50 yards from the entrance. Leisure centre with a pool 15 minutes walk. Fishing 1.5 miles. Riding 8 miles. Golf 2 miles. Sea fishing can be booked in Berwick. Beach 1.5 miles.

Open: All year.

Directions

From A1 Berwick bypass take East Ord exit and follow signs. O.S.GR: NT982515. GPS: 55.75416, -2.03348

Charges guide

Per unit incl. up to 4 persons and electricity	£ 16.50 - £ 26.50
extra person over 5 yrs	£ 2.50
tent pitch	£ 11.50 - £ 26.50
dog	free - £ 1.50

Discounts for 1- and 2-man tents and for longer stays.

Durham
Strawberry Hill Caravan Park

Running Waters, Old Cassop, Durham DH6 4QA (Co. Durham) T: **01913 723457**. E: **info@strawberryhf.co.uk**
alanrogers.com/UK5700

This park is owned and managed by Howard and Elizabeth who are experienced caravanners. They have terraced their site to offer panoramic views over the fields and woodland from all the pitches. The park is licensed to accommodate more units but the owners prefer to offer space to visitors by providing generous pitches on either grass or hardstanding. There are 44 touring pitches (with 16A electric hook-ups), including ten on hardstanding, plus a separate terrace for tents. At present the new landscaping on the park offers limited shade. Nature corridors and the surrounding countryside make this a haven for nature lovers and visitors are encouraged to enjoy the tranquillity of the area. The owners supply good tourist information and details of local nature walks. The easy access to the A1M and the proximity of the historic cathedral city of Durham (3 miles) make this an ideal location for visiting local attractions. These include Beamish museum, Gateshead metro centre and the historic Hartlepool Quays.

Facilities

The single toilet block can be heated and is kept immaculately clean. Free showers. Laundry. Facilities for disabled visitors incorporating a baby care area. Small but well stocked shop in reception. Gas. Off site: Country pub with meals 1 mile. Large hypermarket 3 miles. Riding 5 miles. Park and ride (07.00 - 19.00) into Durham city centre operates nearby. Buses (Durham - Hartlepool) from entrance.

Open: 1 March - 30 December.

Directions

From A1M exit 61 follow signs for the A177 towards Bowburn. At second set of traffic lights turn right and park is about 3.5 miles on the left. Do not use site postcode for satnav systems. O.S.GR: NZ338399. GPS: 54.75326, -1.47809

Charges 2010

Per unit incl. 2 persons and electricity	£ 15.50 - £ 17.50

Durham
Grange Caravan Club Site

Meadow Lane, Durham DH1 1TL (Co. Durham) T: **01913 844778**
alanrogers.com/UK5705

Fully refurbished and landscaped, this park offers 77 flat spacious pitches suitable for all units. Easy access to the A1M and the A690 make it an ideal stop-over for those travelling north or south or for visiting the historic cathedral city of Durham, Beamish museum or Gateshead Metro centre. A coppice of mature trees and newly planted shrubs mask road noise and make an attractive dog walking area. The park has been redesigned with attention to detail in all areas offering pockets of privacy or a central area with picnic tables and benches. A purpose built central block offers spacious, heated, modern and clean facilities. There are ample free showers and hairdryers, private washing cubicles and a larger cubicle for families or less able bodied visitors.

Facilities

The single toilet block is a heated building with free showers, hairdryers, and private cubicles. Laundry and food preparation area. Separate baby area and facilities for disabled visitors are via a key entry system. Shop in reception with limited supplies; bread, milk and newspapers to order. Gas. Secure caravan storage. Off site: Large supermarket 2 miles. Park and ride (07.00-19.00) into Durham city centre 800 yds. Local service buses run from Belmont and Carville.

Open: All year.

Directions

From A1M exit 62 follow signs for Durham city (A690). At roundabout take first exit left and after 20 yds. turn right (across dual carriageway A690); large units should continue along the A690 to next roundabout about 2 miles and return on A690 left hand turn (signed just before A1M).
O.S.GR: NZ302446. GPS: 54.79513, -1.52935

Charges guide

Per person	£ 4.50 - £ 6.00
child (5-16 yrs)	£ 1.50 - £ 2.45
pitch incl. electricity (non-member)	£ 11.70 - £ 14.55

Hexham

Fallowfield Dene Caravan & Camping Park

Acomb, Hexham NE46 4RP (Northumberland) T: **01434 603553**. E: **info@fallowfielddene.co.uk**

alanrogers.com/UK5810

Although only 2.5 miles from Hexham, Fallowfield Dene Caravan Park is very secluded, situated in mature woodland at the end of a no-through road. Set in woodland glades (formerly a Victorian lead mine), each with a Roman name (Hadrian's Wall is close), are 118 seasonal pitches and 32 touring pitches, all with 16A electricity. A further 10 tent pitches have been added, suitable for smaller tents, and a barbecue area with views of woodland and fields. The park entrance, with a new reception and shop, is neat, tidy and very colourful. There is no play area or games field, but the surrounding woods are a paradise for children. Fallowfield Dene itself is a network of tracks and there are footpaths from the site entrance. The site is a haven for wildlife with red squirrels, foxes and badgers to be seen. Hadrian's Wall is only a mile away, with Roman forts such as Housteads Fort and Chesters, being great attractions. The whole area abounds with well preserved Roman remains. Nearby, Hexham market town has its Border History museum, housed in the oldest purpose-built gaol in England, where one can learn about the Border Reivers. This site has a very friendly atmosphere.

Facilities

Brick built toilet blocks (one for each sex) are central and heated in cool weather. Well tiled and kept very clean, there are washbasins in cabins and free hairdryers. Separate, fully equipped room for disabled people. Laundry room with dishwashing sinks. Baby bath. Motorcaravan service point. Small shop for necessities, including gas. Barrier card £5 deposit. Off site: Supermarkets and other shops at Hexham or Corbridge. Good restaurant five minutes walk. Fishing or riding 3 miles. Golf 5 miles.

Open: 14 March - 1 November.

Directions

From A69 Newcastle - Carlisle road, take A6079 north signed Bellingham and Rothbury. At village of Acomb, site is signed to right. Follow site signs for about 1.5 miles. The last 0.5 mile is single track with passing places. O.S.GR: NY938676.
GPS: 55.00166, -2.09470

Charges guide

Per unit incl. 2 persons and electricity	£ 16.00 - £ 17.00
extra person	£ 3.00
child (5-15 yrs)	£ 1.50
dog	£ 0.50

Stockton-on-Tees

White Water Caravan Club Park

Tees Barrage, Stockton-on-Tees TS18 2QW (Teeside) T: **01642 634880**

alanrogers.com/UK5740

Being part of the multimillion pound development at the Tees Barrage, this pleasantly landscaped club site caters for all tastes, especially watersports enthusiasts. The Tees Barrage has transformed eleven miles of the Tees, providing clean, non-tidal water for many activities. The site itself provides 115 pitches, hedged with bushes, all with 16A electricity connections, and includes 21 fully serviced pitches set within bays and hedges (fresh water and waste disposal). The site is well lit, with a security barrier. The adjoining White Water Course (Britain's largest purpose-built canoe course) provides facilities for both advanced and beginner canoeists, and hosts major national and international events. Also close to the site are wetlands that provide a home for a variety of birds.

Facilities

The central, heated toilet block of high quality includes washbasins in cubicles, baby changing facilities and a well appointed unit for disabled visitors. Laundry room. Motorcaravan service point. Play area on fine gravel. Heated family room with TV and pool table for wet weather. Off site: Supermarket 6 minutes. Hotel near the entrance. Retail and leisure park, just across barrage bridge, with 14-screen cinema, 10-pin bowling, shops and fast food outlets. North Yorkshire Moors and the Hartlepool Historic Quay within 40 minutes drive.

Open: All year.

Directions

From A1(M1) take A66 for Darlington and follow until you pick up signs for Teeside Retail Park and the Tees Barrage. Cross railway bridge and the Barrage bridge, then first right to site on left in 400 yards.
O.S.GR: NZ463194. GPS: 54.567733, -1.286567

Charges guide

Per person	£ 3.35 - £ 4.90
child (5-16 yrs)	£ 1.30 - £ 1.95
pitch incl. electricity (non-member)	£ 10.75 - £ 13.10

Tent campers apply to site.

Land of ancient myths and Celtic legends, Wales is a small and compact country boasting a diverse landscape, from lakes and mountains, rivers and valleys to beautiful coastlines and rolling wooded countryside. It offers superb opportunities for an active holiday.

Wales' biggest asset is undoubtedly its countryside, home to three National Parks that make up almost a quarter of the country's total area. Snowdonia National Park in the north combines dramatic mountain scenery with glacial valleys, lakes and streams, while in the south the Brecon Beacons boast mountains, moorlands, forests and wooded gorges with deep caves. The surrounding area of the Wye Valley on the borders with England is a designated Area of Outstanding Beauty; as is the Gower Peninsula, the Lleyn Peninsula, the Anglesey Coast and the Clwydian Range. The endless miles of largely unspoilt and beautiful Pembrokeshire coastline in the west has some of the finest long beaches in Europe, with pretty little bays plus the lively traditional seaside resorts of Tenby and Whitesand. Further inland is the secluded and pretty Gwaun Valley. The capital of Wales, Cardiff, has many attractions, including its newly developed waterfront, the Millennium Stadium. Castles can be seen all over Wales, ranging from tiny stone keeps to huge medieval fortresses; some of the best preserved are Caernarfon, Conwy and Harlech, all built by Edward I.

Places of interest

North: Isle of Anglesey; Victorian School of 3Rs and Motor Museum at Llangollen; Victorian seaside resort of Llandudno; Colwyn Bay; Caernarfon Castle; Snowdon Mountain Railway at Llanberis.

West: Oakwood Park, Wales' only theme park; the National Botanic Gardens at Aberglasney; Dolaucothi Goldmines; historic, stone-walled Aberaeron.

Mid: Brecon Beacons National Park; the lakes of the Elan Valley; entertaining events all summer at Llanwrtyd Wells; the Centre for Alternative Technology near Machynllleth.

South: Merthyr Tydfil, the Iron Capital of the World; Caerphilly's truly massive medieval castle; Cardiff, capital of Wales; the Wye Valley and the Vale of Usk of the Welsh borderlands with Tintern Abbey.

Did you know?

The origins of the Red Dragon flag may date back to the Roman period, when the dragon was used by military cohorts.

St David's in Pembrokeshire is Britain's smallest city by virtue of its Cathedral to the patron saint of Wales.

There are many sites in Wales linked to the legend of King Arthur: Castell Dinas Brân, near Llangollen, is reputed to be the resting-place of the Holy Grail.

Towering at 1085 metres Mount Snowdon is the highest mountain in England and Wales.

'The Dam Busters' was filmed on location in the Elan Valley.

The Welsh language is one of Europe's oldest languages and shares its roots with Breton, Gaelic and Cornish.

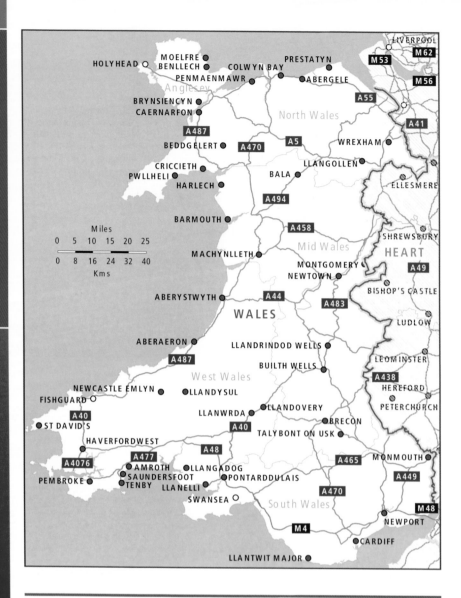

Maps and campsite listings

For this 2010 guide we have changed the way in which we list our parks and also the way in which we help you to locate the parks within each region.

We now include a map immediately after our Introduction to that region. These maps show the towns near which one (or more) of our featured parks is located. Within each regional section of the guide, we list these towns and the park(s) in that vicinity in alphabetical order.

You will certainly need more detailed maps for navigation, for example the Ordnance Survey road atlas. We provide O.S. references and G.P.S. coordinates for each park to assist you. Our three indexes will also help you to find a park by its reference number and name, by region and park name, or by the town where the park is situated.

234

www.alanrogers.com for latest campsite news

Aberaeron

Aeron Coast Caravan Park

North Road, Aberaeron SA46 0JF (Ceredigion) T: 01545 570349. E: enquiries@aeroncoast.co.uk

alanrogers.com/UK6280

Aeron Coast is a family holiday park with a wide range of recreational facilities, on the west coast of Wales. Although it has a high proportion of caravan holiday homes (200 privately owned), touring units of all types are provided for in two fields separated from the beach and sea by a high bank (although the best beach is on the south side of this traditional fishing village). Pitches are on level grass with all units regularly and well spaced in lines in traditional style. The main attraction of the park is its excellent provision for families, both in and out of doors. This includes two outdoor pools (one new) and a toddlers' pool (unsupervised) in a paved, walled area good for sunbathing, a tennis court and small half-court for youngsters, football and a sand pit with pirate ship. The indoor leisure area provides an under-5s room with slide, etc, teenagers-only room with juke box, table tennis, pool and games machines and TV room. In high season activities are organised nightly free of charge in the large entertainment and disco room. In low season reception is open 10.00-14.00 – choose a pitch from the numbers on the board and return to the office in the morning.

Facilities

Two modern toilet blocks offer excellent facilities including large family showers. Facilities for disabled people and babies are in one block. Basic motorcaravan service point. Swimming pools (heated 24/5-15/9). Club house and bar (from Easter, 12.00-14.00 and from 19.00) with family room serving bar meals and takeaway in school holiday periods. New entertainments room. Shop at the petrol station at the entrance. Only one dog per unit is accepted. Off site: Beach, fishing and boat launching 0.5 miles. A steam railway, craft centre, woollen mills and potteries can be visited locally.

Open: 1 March - 31 October.

Directions

Park is on northern outskirts of Aberaeron village with entrance on the right beside a petrol station. Brown sigpost. O.S.GR: SN461631.
GPS: 52.2445, -4.254917

Charges guide

Per unit incl. 4 persons and electricity	£ 15.00 - £ 24.00
extra person (over 2 yrs)	£ 3.00

Abergele

Hunters Hamlet Caravan Park

Sirior Goch Farm, Betws-yn-Rhos, Abergele LL22 8PL (Conwy) T: 01745 832237. E: huntershamlet@aol.com

alanrogers.com/UK6650

This small, family owned park is licensed for all units except tents (trailer tents allowed). On a gently sloping hillside providing beautiful panoramic views, one area provides 15 well spaced pitches with hardstanding and 10A electricity hook-ups, with access from a circular, hardcore road. A more recent area has been developed next to this of a similar design but with eight fully serviced 'super pitches' (water, waste water, sewerage, TV and electricity connections). Shrubs and bushes at various stages of growth enhance both areas. A natural play area incorporating rustic adventure equipment set amongst mature beech trees with a small bubbling stream is a children's paradise. Milk and papers can be ordered and the Hunters will do their best to meet your needs, even to survival rations! The park is well situated to tour Snowdonia and Anglesey and is within easy reach of Llandudno and Rhyl.

Facilities

The heated toilet block has fully tiled facilities including showers en-suite with toilets for both sexes. A sunroom to the rear houses laundry and dishwashing (hot and cold), washing machine and dryer, iron and board, freezer and fridge. Family bathroom (metered) and basic toilet and shower facilities for disabled visitors. Play area. All year caravan storage. Max. 2 dogs per pitch. WiFi. Off site: Fishing and golf 2 miles. Riding 10 miles.

Open: 21 March - 31 October.

Directions

From Abergele take A548 south for almost 3 miles; turn onto B5381 in direction of Betws-yn-Rhos and park is on left after 0.5 miles. O.S.GR: SH929736.
GPS: 53.248833, -3.6068

Charges 2010

Per unit incl. 2 persons incl. electricity	£ 16.00 - £ 21.00
super pitch (fully incl.)	£ 21.00 - £ 27.00
extra person	£ 4.00
child (at school)	£ 1.00

Less £5 on weekly bookings.

235

Abergele

Ty Mawr Holiday Park

Towyn Road, Towyn, Abergele LL22 9HG (Conwy) T: **01745 832079**. E: **nikkie.lawrence@park-resorts.com**
alanrogers.com/UK6655

Ty Mawr Holiday Park is located close to the many attractions of the North Wales Coast and the Snowdonia National Park. There are two areas for touring units, one on open meadows with facilities provided in excellent Portacabin-style units, the other in a more well established area with older, more traditional amenities near the playgrounds and entertainment complex. Both areas are flat with views of open countryside. There is some traffic noise from the road adjacent to the meadow. A large number of privately owned and rental caravan holiday homes are neatly sited on well manicured grass pitches. It is an easy walk into the town of Towyn with its seaside facilities and Rhyl, some three miles along the coast, is a busy resort. Ty Mawr is ideal for families seeking plenty of holiday park type activities.

Facilities

Two well maintained, functional blocks which can be heated with Portacabin-style units on the open meadows. Washbasins are open style, preset showers have curtains and hooks, but no seats. Baby rooms. Facilities for disabled visitors (key). Launderette. Ice pack service. Shop. Bar with meals, cafeteria and takeaway. Indoor pool. Multisport courts. Excellent play areas and children's clubs. Evening family entertainment. Off site: Beach 0.25 miles. Bicycle hire 0.5 miles. Golf and riding 3 miles. Fishing 6 miles.

Open: Easter - 30 October.

Directions

Take the A55 in a westerly direction into North Wales and take exit for Abergele. Follow signs for A548 Rhyl towards Towyn. Shortly after Towyn turn right into site. O.S.GR: SH965791 GPS: 53.29867, -3.55442

Charges guide

Per pitch	£ 5.00 - £ 33.00
incl. electricity	£ 8.00 - £ 36.00
dog	£ 1.00 - £ 3.00

Units over 6 m. are charged for 2 pitches.

Aberystwyth

Glan-y-Mor Leisure Park

Clarach Bay, Aberystwyth SY23 3DT (Ceredigion) T: **01970 828900**. E: **glanymor@sunbourne.co.uk**
alanrogers.com/UK6290

Follow the road to Clarach Bay and on the sea-front is Glan-y-Mor, a busy, holiday-style park with an enviable situation. On a wet day you may not wish to go far with the comprehensive leisure centre on site – it is open eight months of the year with reduced entry fee for campers. Although the balance of pitches is very much in favour of caravan holiday homes (3:1) which dominate the open park and bay, there are 50 touring pitches, 45 with electricity (10A) and four new 'super' pitches. They are rather small and are pressed together in two small sections on the lower part of the park. In high season, tents, tourers or motorcaravans can opt for space and fine views (but maybe winds) on a ridge of higher ground above the park. There is a well equipped leisure centre.

Facilities

The heated toilet block is on the lower touring area with dishwashing facilities and laundry room, plus a toilet for disabled people. A 'portacabin' type block (high season only) is on the ridge ground. A suite including shower for disabled people is in a block in the upper static site, with further facilities at the leisure centre (RADAR key). Motorcaravan service point. Freezer pack service. Gas supplies. Supermarket. Play area. Sports field. Swimming pool. Licensed restaurant and takeaway (from Easter). WiFi (charge). Off site: Reduced rates at local golf courses.

Open: 1 March - 31 October.

Directions

Clarach is signed west from the A487 (Aberystwyth - Machynlleth) in village of Bow Street (take care at narrow bridge). Follow signs to beach and park. Access for caravans from Aberystwyth on B4572 is difficult. O.S.GR: SN587841. GPS: 52.43625, -4.08025

Charges guide

Per unit incl. up to 6 persons and electricity	£ 15.00 - £ 26.50
dog (max 2)	free - £ 2.00

Top camping area max. charge £10 plus £2 electricity. Club membership (but not Leisure complex) included.

Amroth
Little Kings Park

Amroth Road, Ludchurch SA67 8PG (Pembrokeshire) T: **01834 831330**. E: **littlekingspark@btconnect.com**
alanrogers.com/UK5975

This superb family run park has a number of attributes to make your stay both comfortable and memorable. There are stunning views over Carmarthen Bay to the Gower and on beyond to the coast of Somerset and North Devon. At night no fewer than seven lighthouses can be seen blinking out their warnings. A touring field provides 56 well spaced, large touring pitches all with 10A electricity, 21 with gravel hardstanding and fully serviced. An attractive playground is in the central open grass area. A further seven pitches are in a different area. There are 40 pitches for tents in an adjoining paddock with 31 electricity hook-ups. A separate well hedged and screened paddock contains 20 caravan holiday homes (13 for hire) and a holiday bubgalow. The excellent amenities include a restaurant and bar, which has a conservatory overlooking a well presented, covered, heated swimming pool. The restaurant serves a good range of evening meals and has a children's menu. Last, but by no means least, is the comprehensively stocked shop which has just about everything you might need, including reception, tourist information and a bakery offering fresh bread daily and hot snacks (pasties, sausage rolls, etc.) cooked to order. This is an ideal site for a family holiday or for touring the area.

Facilities	Directions
The two toilet blocks are modern and well equipped, including controllable hot showers (20p for 6 minutes 30p for 9), open style washbasins, a family shower room and a full suite for disabled campers. Laundry rooms. Shop with bakery, Takeaway, bar and restaurant with conservatory (evenings only; low season at B.Hs and weekends only). Covered swimming pool. Games rooms. Playground. Ball games area. Gas supplies. Off site: Nearest supermarket and ATM at Kilgetty 2.5 miles. Tenby and Pendine Sands both 7 miles. Oakwood Adventure and Leisure Park 6 miles. Fishing 1 mile. Riding 4 miles. Golf 8 miles.	Site is 5 miles southeast of Narberth. From A477 Carmarthen to Pembroke road, 2 miles after Llanteg at petrol station, turn left towards Amroth, Wiseman's Bridge, Ludchurch. After 1 mile, at crossroads, turn right (signed Ludchurch, Narberth) and park is 800 m. O.S.GR: SN146093. GPS: 51.751517, -4.6879

Open: 1 March - 31 October.

Charges guide

Per unit incl. 2 persons and electricity	£ 14.00 - £ 23.00
extra person (over 3 yrs)	£ 2.00
awning	£ 2.00
dog (max. 2)	£ 2.00 - £ 3.00

Amroth
Pantglas Farm Caravan Park

Tavernspite, Amroth SA34 0NS (Pembrokeshire) T: **01834 831618**. E: **pantglasfarm@btinternet.com**
alanrogers.com/UK5974

A secluded, rural, family run park with a nice atmosphere, Pantglas Farm is four miles from the coast with extensive views over rolling countryside and down to the sea. Set in three gently sloping paddocks spread over 14 acres, there are 86 generously sized, fairly level pitches most with 10A hook-ups, 70 on gravel hardstanding. Around 86 are available for touring units. This is a popular and attractive site close to the main resorts but enjoying a more tranquil atmosphere. Some simple entertainment activities are arranged at Bank Holidays, weekends and in high season.

Facilities	Directions
Two toilet blocks (one can be heated) are of a good standard including large controllable showers and some washbasins in cubicles. Facilities for disabled campers. Wet room. Laundry facilities and a baby deck. Gas. Licensed clubhouse (evenings only every day for B.Hs and peak season, weekends only low season). Updated play area. Games field. Games room. TV lounge. Caravan and boat storage. Off site: Supermarket at Whitland 3 miles. Beaches at Amroth or Pendine 4 miles. Also nearby are Whitland Abbey, Oakwood Adventure and Leisure Park and Colby Woodland Gardens. Fishing 1 mile. Golf 10 miles.	Site is 3 miles southwest of Whitland. From A477 Tenby - Pembroke road turn right at Red Roses crossroads to Tavernspite for 1.25 miles. At the village pump take the middle road and site is about 0.5 miles on left. O.S.GR: SN 176122. GPS: 51.778317, -4.645417

Open: March - 3rd weekend in October.

Charges guide

Per unit incl. 2 persons, electricity	£ 16.00 - £ 18.00
tent incl. 2 persons	£ 12.00 - £ 14.00
extra person	£ 1.50 - £ 3.00

Credit cards accepted with surcharge.

Bala
Pen-y-Bont Touring & Camping Park

Llangynog Road, Bala LL23 7PH (Gwynedd) T: **01678 520549**. E: **penybont-bala@btconnect.co.uk**

alanrogers.com/UK6340

This is a pretty little park with 59 touring pitches, 42 of which have hardstanding. Connected by circular gravel roads, they are intermingled with trees and tall trees edge the site. Electricity connections (16A) are available, including 11 for tents, and there are 24 serviced pitches with hardstanding, electricity, water and drainage. There are also pitches for 25 seasonal units. The park entrance and the stone building that houses reception and the well stocked shop provide quite a smart image. With views of the Berwyn mountains, Pen-y-bont has a peaceful, attractive and useful location being the closest park to Bala town. Bala Lake is 100 yards and the park is 3 miles from the Welsh National White Water Centre, with Snowdonia on hand.

Facilities

The toilet block includes washbasins in cubicles and spacious hot showers. Two new cubicles with washbasin and WC. Separate laundry room and an en-suite unit for disabled visitors, that doubles as a baby room, operated by key (£2 deposit). Outside covered area with fencing and concrete floor for dishwashing sinks and bins. Motorcaravan service point. Shop. Bicycle hire. Caravan storage. WiFi. Off site: Fishing 200 yds. Boat launching, golf and riding 2 miles. Bala market on Mondays.

Open: 1 April - 31 October.

Directions

Park is 0.5 miles southeast of Bala village on the B4391. Bala is between Dolgellau and Conwen on the A494. O.S.GR: SH932350. GPS: 52.901717, -3.590117

Charges guide

Per unit incl. 2 persons and electricity	£ 17.00 - £ 21.00
tent pitch incl. 2 persons	£ 12.00 - £ 19.00
extra person	£ 6.00
child (4-16 yrs)	£ 4.00
dog	£ 1.00

Bala
Glanllyn Lakeside Caravan & Camping Park

Llanuwchllyn, Bala LL23 7ST (Gwynedd) T: **01678 540227**. E: **info@glanllyn.com**

alanrogers.com/UK6345

This 16-acre site lying alongside the southern end of Bala lake has 204 pitches. With around 40 seasonal units, this leaves 164 tourist pitches, 94 of which have electric hook-ups. In this location, virtually all the pitches have wonderful views of the lake or the surrounding mountain sides. The terrain is grassy, fairly open and level, but with natural terraces. There are around 19 individual hardstandings and a further hardstanding area by the beach is a favourite with motorcaravanners. The site is served by main tarmac access roads with speed bumps. Lake swimming is possible and the private beach allows easy access for windsurfing. Boats can be launched from the site (a day ticket must be purchased from the National Park wardens to use the lake). The park is also an ideal base for some serious walking.

Facilities

A complex of three modern buildings (one can be heated and is used in low season) is located centrally at the rear of the site. Pre-set hot showers, hairdressing and shaver stations. Facilities for babies and suite for disabled people (key code access). Laundry room. Motorcaravan service point. Well stocked shop at reception (Easter - Oct). Freezer pack service. Gas supplies. Splendid, well fenced adventure style playground on bark surface. Only 2 dogs per unit permitted (fenced dog walk area). Breathable groundsheets only and only for min. 3 day stay. Off site: Bus stops outside site gate. Bicycle hire, indoor swimming pool and golf in Bala 3 miles. Bala market on Mondays. Riding 18 miles.

Open: Mid March (Easter) - mid October.

Directions

From Bala take A494 southwest towards Dolgellau for about 3 miles, entrance is on left, on a right hand bend. O.S.GR: SH893324. GPS: 52.877667, -3.64665

Charges guide

Per unit incl. 2 persons and electricity	£ 16.00 - £ 20.00
tent pitch incl. 2 persons	£ 12.00 - £ 16.00
extra person	£ 5.00
child (3-16 yrs)	£ 3.00
dog (max .2)	£ 2.00

Barmouth

Hendre Mynach Touring Caravan & Camping Park

Llanaber, Barmouth LL42 1YR (Gwynedd) T: **01341 280262**. E: **mynach@lineone.net**

alanrogers.com/UK6370

A neat and tidy family park, colourful flowers and top rate facilities make an instant impression on arrival down the steep entrance to this park (help is available to get out if you are worried). The 240 pitches are allocated in various areas, with substantial tenting areas identified. 40 gravel hardstandings are available and around the park there are 110 electricity hook-ups (10A), 20 fully serviced pitches and ample water taps. The beach is only 100 yards away but a railway line runs between this and the park. It can be crossed by pedestrian operated gates, which could be a worry for those with young children. The quaint old seaside and fishing town of Barmouth is about a 30-minute walk along the prom. Here you will find 'everything'. Reception will provide leaflets with maps of local walks. Snowdonia National Park and mountain railway, the famous Ffestiniog railway, castles and lakes everywhere provide plenty to see and do – this is a classic park in a classic area.

Facilities

Two toilet blocks, one modern and one traditional, both offer excellent facilities including spacious showers (free) and washbasins in cubicles. An extension to the traditional block has added a good unit for disabled visitors with ramp access. Motorcaravan service point. Well stocked shop incorporating a snack bar and takeaway (Easter-1/11). WiFi. Off site: Beach 100 m. Fishing, boat launching and bicycle hire within 0.5 miles. Riding 5 miles. Golf 9 miles.

Open: All year excl. 10 January - 28 February.

Directions

Park is off the A496 road north of Barmouth in village of Llanaber with entrance down a steep drive. O.S.GR: SH606171. GPS: 52.73300, -4.06618

Charges guide

Per unit incl. 2 persons	
and electricity	£ 16.00 - £ 29.00
extra person	£ 4.00
child (2-14 yrs)	£ 2.00
first dog free, extra dog	£ 1.00

Plus £2 per night for certain weekends.
Mid-season and Christmas/New Year offers.

Beddgelert

Forest Holidays Beddgelert

Caernarfon Road, Beddgelert LL55 4UU (Gwynedd) T: **01766 890288**. E: **info@forestholidays.co.uk**

alanrogers.com/UK6590

Forest Holidays is a partnership between the Forestry Commission and The Camping & Caravanning Club. This well equipped site is in the heart of Snowdonia, set in a marvellous, natural, wooded environment on the slopes of Snowdon. Well equipped and well managed, the site provides 240 pitches – tents in a semi-wooded field area and caravans amongst the trees with numbered hardstandings, and 105 places with 10/16A electricity. Tents may pitch where they like in their areas leaving 6 m. between units or there are six new grass pitches with electrical hook-ups for tents. Metal tent pegs may be best (available from the shop). There is abundant fauna and flora, tumbling streams and always something to watch from the cheeky squirrels to the smallest bird in Britain. Free maps of the forest walks are provided in reception and orienteering and fishing are possible. A bus service stops at the top of the entrance lane (two hourly for Caernarfon and Porthmadog).

Facilities

Two fully equipped modern sanitary toilet blocks clad in natural wood provide large, free hot showers (with good dry areas). Laundry equipment is in one block. A small unit provides extra washbasins and toilets in peak season and there is a toilet and washbasin for disabled visitors. Excellent drive-through motorcaravan service point. Well provisioned shop (Easter - end Sept). Well equipped adventure playground. Log cabin common room. Off site: Pub within walking distance (under 1 mile) and other eating places nearby. Bicycle hire within 500 yds. in forest.

Open: All year.

Directions

Site is clearly signed to the left 1 mile north of Beddgelert on the A4085 Caernarfon road. O.S.GR: SH579492. GPS: 53.02075, -4.119767

Charges guide

Per unit incl. 2 persons	£ 8.00 - £ 20.50
extra person	£ 4.25 - £ 6.25
child (5-14 yrs)	£ 1.75 - £ 3.25

Discounts for families, disabled guests and senior citizens.

239

Benllech

Plas Uchaf Caravan & Camping Park

Benllech Bay, Benllech LL74 8NU (Isle of Anglesey) T: **01407 763012**

alanrogers.com/UK6636

This spacious, family run, campsite is set in 16 acres of flat, well mown grass with some hardstandings. Within the park there are woodland walks and a play route for children to explore. All in an open, rural setting this park offers a safe haven for young families to enjoy. The pitches are set around the perimeter of six individual areas, each with picnic tables for communal use and all 110 touring pitches offer electricity. Motorcaravans over 26 ft and motorbikes are not accepted. With five privately-owned mobile homes in a separate field, this popular campsite is ideally located with a safe sandy beach a mile away.

Facilities

Three clean, traditional style sanitary blocks have separate facilities for men and women, with hot showers (charge), open style washbasins, hairdryers and small baths. Baby areas. No facilities for disabled visitors. Limited laundry. Large playing field, play equipment and dog walk. Freezer facilities. Off site: Shops, bars, restaurants, fishing, golf, sandy beach, horse riding and sailing all within 1 mile.

Open: 14 March - 14 October.

Directions

From the Britannia Bridge take the A5025. In Benllech turn left onto the B5108. After the fire station on left, turn first right and the park is signed. O.S.GR: SH509832. GPS: 53.32676, -4.23956

Charges guide

Per unit incl. 2 persons	£ 9.00 - £ 14.00
extra person (over 3 yrs)	£ 2.00
electricity (10/16A)	£ 3.00

No credit cards.

Pencelli Castle Caravan & Camping Park

Peacefully set at the foothills of the Brecon Beacons and within walking distance of the highest peaks. Adjoining Brecon Canal and the Taff Cycle Trail. Village pub 150 metres. Shop, hardstandings, serviced pitches and luxurious shower block. Red deer, pigmy goats, vintage farm machinery, and children's play area. On bus route. Free WiFi. Closed 1st to 30th December. **Assistance Dogs Only**

Wales Cymru
Touring & Camping Park
Parc Teithio a Gwersylla
★★★★★

2009 - Wales In Bloom Winner
2009 - Gold - David Bellamy Conservation Award
2008 - Loo of the Year - National Winner Wales
2006 - AA Best Campsite in Wales
2005 - Wales Tourism Awards - Winner Best Place to Stay
2005 - Practical Caravan Top 100 Family Park - Winner Wales
2001 - Calor Gas - Best Park in Wales

Pencelli • Brecon • Powys • Wales • UK • LD3 7LX • Tel: 01874 665451
pencelli@tiscali.co.uk • www.pencelli-castle.com

Brecon

Pencelli Castle Caravan & Camping Park

Pencelli, Brecon LD3 7LX (Powys) T: **01874 665451**. E: pencelli@tiscali.co.uk

alanrogers.com/UK6040

Open all year round, this is a quality park with atmosphere and character which continues to improve. Set amidst the Brecon scenery, it offers excellent facilities in peaceful, rural tranquillity. The owners, Liz and Gerwyn Rees, have retained the country charm but have added an all-embracing range of spacious, heated, luxury facilities. There are three touring fields. The 'Orchard' provides 15 fully serviced pitches with hardstanding, amongst shrubs, fruit trees and a stone cider mill. The 'Oaks' taking 20 caravans and tents and the 'Meadow' for 40 tents are bordered by majestic trees and the Monmouthshire and Brecon Canal. All the fields are level with neatly mown grass and tarmac access roads. The historic manor house, that dates back to 1583, is adjacent to arched barns that house an increasing collection of vintage farm machinery including carts and rare tractors. For mountain bikers and walkers, a path leaves the village to reach the top of the Brecon Beacons or there is an easy towpath ramble to Tal-y-Bont where there are pubs, tea rooms and a post office.

Facilities

The toilet block is very well designed and includes some private cubicles, two large fully equipped rooms for families or disabled visitors incorporating double showers, baby changing and bath facilities, all humorously decorated. Laundry. Drying room with lockers. Information and planning room. WiFi (free). Food preparation room. Motorcaravan service point. Small shop at reception (basics). Playground and nature trail for children. Bicycle hire. Only 'assistance dogs' are accepted. Off site: The Royal Oak Inn with meals 100 m. Regular bus service for Brecon, Abergavenny. Riding 2 miles. Golf and bicycle hire 5 miles.

Open: All year excl. 1 - 30 December.

Directions

From A40 south after Brecon bypass take B4558 at signs for Llanfrynach and later Pencelli (narrow bridge). If travelling north on A40, approach via Tal-y-Bont. Site at south end of Pencelli. O.S.GR: SO095249. GPS: 51.914783, -3.317867

Charges guide

Per unit incl. 2 persons and electricity	£ 19.25 - £ 23.25
extra person	£ 6.00 - £ 6.50
child (5-15 yrs)	£ 4.50 - £ 6.00

Brynsiencyn
Fron Caravan & Camping Park
Brynsiencyn, Anglesey LL61 6TX (Isle of Anglesey) T: 01248 430310. E: mail@froncaravanpark.co.uk
alanrogers.com/UK6635

A traditional, all touring campsite in a peaceful rural location, Fron has panoramic views over the surrounding countryside. From the entrance gate a tarmac drive passes through a two acre level grass paddock, which is reserved for 35 large sized tent and trailer tent pitches. The drive leads up to the old farmhouse which houses reception, a well stocked shop, and plenty of tourist information. Behind the farmhouse is another two acre sloping paddock with 40 caravan and motorcaravan pitches, five with hardstandings, and 57 electricity hook-ups (10A). By the farmhouse a heated pool is well controlled by the owners and has a retractable roof. An adventure-style playground is located in the tent paddock.

Facilities
Toilet facilities are in three units of varying ages and designs located at both sides of the farmhouse. These include a unit for ladies with some basins in cubicles, good hot showers with dividers (20p), hairdryers, a baby area and a suite for disabled campers. Laundry with washing machine and dryer. Motorcaravan service point. Heated swimming pool (30 x 14 ft; May - Sept). Gas stocked. Max. 2 dogs per pitch. Torches useful. Off site: Nearby are Anglesey Sea Zoo, Plas Newydd House, Foel Farm Park, Anglesey Transport and Agriculture Museum and the Menai Bridges. Brynsiencyn Village (0.5 mile) has a hotel and Spar shop (with ATM). Fishing 1.5 miles. Riding 3 miles. Golf 4 miles.

Open: Easter - end September.

Directions
Cross the Britannia Bridge and take first slip road signed Llanfairpwll A4080, then next left signed Newborough and Brynsiencyn. Continue on A4080 for 5 miles, turning right in village at the Groeslon Hotel. Continue through Brynsiencyn for 1 mile to site at western end of village. O.S.GR: SH472668. GPS: 53.176217, -4.28785

Charges guide
Per unit incl. 2 persons and 2 children	£ 16.00
extra person	£ 2.50 - £ 5.00
electricity	£ 3.00

No credit cards.

Builth Wells
Fforest Fields Caravan & Camping Park
Hundred House, Builth Wells LD1 5RT (Powys) T: 01982 570406. E: office@fforestfields.co.uk
alanrogers.com/UK6320

This secluded 'different' park is set on a family hill farm in the heart of Radnorshire. Truly rural, there are glorious views and a distinctly family atmosphere. This is simple country camping and caravanning at its best, without man-made distractions or intrusions. The facilities include 80 large pitches on level grass on a spacious and peaceful, carefully landscaped field by a stream. Electrical connections (mostly 16A) are available and there are 17 hardstanding pitches, also with electricity. Several additional areas without electricity are provided for tents. There are two new lakes, one for boating and fly fishing, the other for coarse fishing. A new reception and toilet block are planned. George and Kate, the enthusiastic owners, have opened up much of the farm for moderate or ample woodland and moorland trails which can be enjoyed with much wildlife to see.

Facilities
The toilet facilities are acceptable with baby bath, dishwashing and laundry facilities including washing machines and a dryer. Milk, eggs and orange juice are sold in reception and gas, otherwise there are few other on-site facilities. The village of Hundred House, one mile away, has a pub. Fishing. Torches are useful. Off site: Bicycle hire and golf 5 miles. Riding 10 miles.

Open: Easter - 17 November.

Directions
Park is 4 miles east of Builth Wells near the village of Hundred House on A481. Follow brown signs. O.S.GR: SO098535. GPS: 52.17121, -3.31621

Charges guide
Per person	£ 3.50
child	£ 2.50
pitch	£ 4.50
electricity	£ 2.50

No credit cards.

241

Caernarfon

Tafarn Snowdonia Parc Brewpub & Campsite

Waunfawr, Caernarfon LL55 4AQ (Gwynedd) T: 01286 650409. E: info@snowdonia-park.co.uk

alanrogers.com/UK6605

Set on the banks of the River Gwyrfai and amongst spectacular scenery, this no frills campsite is adjacent to the station for the Welsh Highland Railway. There are 32 grass pitches, (20 with 16A electricity) of variable size. They are set in an open field and serviced by two small, basic, clean shower and toilet blocks. Enjoy riverside walks and free fishing (licence required) before calling in at the adjoining pub with its own microbrewery (listed in the CAMRA Good Beer guide) and home cooked food. Children are well catered for with a family room in the pub, two gardens (one safe for toddlers) and a playground. The campsite is located between Beddgelert and Caernarfon and four miles from the foot of Snowdon.

Facilities	Directions
One small toilet block in main camping field. A second block with separate showers and toilets for men and ladies, together with laundry facilities, is reach via a footbridge over the railway track. These may become stretched when the site is full. Full bar, restaurant and takeaway facilities. TV. Games room. Playground. Free fishing (licence required). Off site: Riding 800 yds. Golf 3 miles. Beach 5 miles. **Open:** All year.	From Caernarfon take the A4085 for around 4 miles and campsite is on the left. The entrance is at the far end of pub/railway station car park. O.S.GR: SH526587. GPS: 53.10611, -4.20176

Charges guide

Per unit incl. 2 persons	£ 12.00 - £ 16.00
electricity	£ 2.00
children and dogs	free

Caernarfon

Bryn Gloch Caravan & Camping Park

Betws Garmon, Caernarfon LL54 7YY (Gwynedd) T: 01286 650216. E: eurig@bryngloch.co.uk

alanrogers.com/UK6600

Bryn Gloch is a well kept, family owned touring park in the impressive Snowdonia area – an unusual feature is the mountain railway which passes through the park. Neat and quiet, it takes some 160 units on five flat, wide meadows with some breathtaking views. With tarmac access roads and free areas allowed in the centre for play, of the 152 touring pitches, 80 have hardstanding, electricity (10A), water and drainage. In addition, there are 15 caravan holiday homes. Fishing is possible on the river bordering the park with a barbecue and picnic area, adventure play area and field for ball games. Tourist information is provided in the complex by the reception/shop and the park is very popular with walkers and cyclists. Caernarfon with its famous castle is five miles.

Facilities	Directions
The two very clean and modern main toilet blocks include washbasins in cabins, large showers, a family bathroom (hot water £1), baby room and complete facilities for visitors with disabilities (coded access). The far field has a 'portacabin' style unit with all facilities, for use in peak season. Well equipped laundry and separate drying room. Motorcaravan service point and car wash. Shop (1/3-30/10). TV and games rooms with pool tables and amusement machines. Minigolf. Entrance barrier with coded access. Off site: Pub 1 mile. ATM at garage in Ceathro 3 miles. Riding 2.5 miles, bicycle hire or golf 5 miles. **Open:** All year, limited facilities 1 November - 1 March.	From Caernarfon take A4085 signed Beddgelert. Park is just beyond Waunfawr, 5.6 miles southeast of Caernarfon. After crossing river bridge, the entrance is immediately on the right, opposite St Garmon church. O.S.GR: SH536576. GPS: 53.095183, -4.1884

Charges guide

Per unit incl. 2 persons and electricity	£ 18.00 - £ 28.00
extra person	£ 4.00
child (3-16 yrs)	£ 2.00
dog	£ 1.00

Caernarfon
Plas Gwyn Caravan & Camping Park
Llanrug, Caernarfon LL55 2AQ (Gwynedd) T: 01286 672619. E: info@plasgwyn.co.uk
alanrogers.com/UK6620

In a beautiful location, this traditional, family run touring site is within the grounds of a house that was built in 1785 in the Georgian style with a colonial-style veranda. The 30 touring caravan pitches are set around the perimeter of a slightly sloping grass field, and there are eight hardstandings for motorcaravans. The separate tent field has 10 pitches. There are 36 electric hook-ups (16A), and with Large motorhomes and American RVs are accepted except on Bank Holidays, but it is essential to telephone ahead to check availability. A member of the Countryside Discovery Group.

Facilities

An older style building houses the toilet facilities – although the fittings and tiling inside are modern and are kept neat and tidy. Controllable free hot showers, dishwashing sinks, a good laundry room (by reception), but no dedicated facilities for babies or disabled campers. Drive-over motorcaravan service point. Gas stocked. Reception stocks basic food items, etc. Breakfast 'butties' made to order and delivered. Internet access. Off site: Llanberis and Snowdon Mountain Railway 2.5 miles. Golf 1 mile. Riding 2.5 miles.

Open: 1 March - 31 October.

Directions

Site is on A4086, 3 miles from Caernarfon, and 2.5 miles from Llanberis, well signed with easy access. O.S.GR: SH522634. GPS: 53.146733, -4.212233

Charges guide

Per person	£ 2.50
child (0-15 yrs)	£ 1.50 - £ 2.00
pitch incl. awning and electricity	£ 7.50 - £ 12.50
tent pitch	£ 2.50 - £ 10.50

Cardiff
Cardiff Caravan Park
Pontcanna Fields, via Sophia Close, Cardiff CF11 9LB (Cardiff) T: 02920 398362
alanrogers.com/UK5925

Run by the city council, this popular site is set within acres of parkland, one mile from the city centre, ideal for visiting the many attractions of the City of Cardiff. The campsite has 73 pitches which are on a fairly open area, with 43 on a grassed grid surface with electric hook-ups (16A), the remainder are on grass. There is a public right of way through the site. Security is good with an on-site warden 24 hours a day, and security cameras (infra red) constantly scanning the whole area. Remember though that you are in a city centre environment, so lock up your valuables.

Facilities

Two heated buildings each with key code entry systems, the one by reception has a laundry with washer and dryer, and facilities for disabled campers. Both have controllable hot showers. Baby facilities. Bicycle hire (the site specialises in cycles adapted for disabled people). Riding can be arranged. Off site: The Millennium Stadium, Glamorgan County Cricket Ground, Cardiff Bay. Local shops and services within easy walking distance. Fishing 0.25 mile, golf 4 miles.

Open: All year.

Directions

From the A48 turn south on A4119 (Cardiff Road). Pass church on left following signs for Institute of Sport and at next lights turn into Sophia Close and Gardens. Turn left at Institute of Sport and pass Cricket Ground on right. Continue along avenue to site on left. For satnavs use postcode CF11 9XR. O.S.GR: ST171772. GPS: 51.49155, -3.20313

Charges guide

Per person	£ 3.00 - £ 5.50
vehicle	£ 4.00
electricity	£ 3.50

Colwyn Bay
Bron-Y-Wendon Touring Caravan Park
Wern Road, Llanddulas, Colwyn Bay LL22 8HG (Conwy) T: 01492 512903
E: stay@northwales-holidays.co.uk alanrogers.com/UK6690

Bron-Y-Wendon is right by the sea between Abergele and Colwyn Bay on the beautiful North Wales coast road. This is a quiet park which, by its own admission, is not really geared up for the family unit – there is no playground here, although there is a games room with table tennis and a TV room. The park is manicured to the highest standards and caters for a large number of seasonal caravans on tidy pitches with gravel bases. There are a further 65 grass based, and 20 hardstanding touring pitches, all with electrical hook ups and tarmac access roads. All pitches have coastal views and the sea and beach are just a short walk away. Trailer tents are accepted, but not other tents.

Facilities

Two toilet blocks, both with heating, provide excellent facilities including men's and women's shower rooms separate from the toilets and washbasins. Good facilities for disabled visitors. Laundry with washing machines and dryers. Mobile shop visits daily. Gas supplies. WiFi. Off site: Llanddulas village with shops and good pubs is very near. Fishing 1 mile. Golf 4 miles. Riding 6 miles.

Open: All year.

Directions

From A55 Chester - Conwy road turn at Llanddulas interchange (A547), junction 23. Turn right opposite garage and park is 400 yards, signed on coast side. O.S.GR: SH903785. GPS: 53.29185, -3.6445

Charges guide

Per unit incl. 2 persons and electricity (16A)	£ 19.00 - £ 22.00
extra person	£ 1.00 - £ 4.00

243

Criccieth
Llanystumdwy Camping & Caravanning Club Site

Tyddyn Sianel, Llanystumdwy, Criccieth LL52 0LS (Gwynedd) T: **01766 522855**

alanrogers.com/UK6580

Overlooking mountains and sea, Llanystumdwy is one of the earliest Camping & Caravanning Club sites. Well maintained with good facilities, it is on sloping grass. However, the wardens are very helpful and know their site and can advise on the most suitable pitch and even have a supply of chocks. There are 70 pitches in total (20 ft. spacing), 45 with 10A electricity connections, spaced over two hedged fields with mainly caravans in the top field with four hardstandings for motorcaravans, and with tents lower down. A little library with a supply of tourist information is next to the small reception.

Facilities

A purpose-built toilet block to one side includes excellent, full facilities for disabled visitors including access ramp, one washbasin each in a cubicle for male and female and extra large sinks. Facilities for babies. Laundry (taps with fitting for disabled people). Gas supplies. Off site: Riding or fishing 0.5 miles. Golf 2.5 miles. Beach 3 miles.

Open: March - October.

Directions

Follow A497 from Criccieth west and take second right to Llanystumdwy. Site is on the right. O.S.GR: SH469384. GPS: 52.920867, -4.27885

Charges guide

Per person	£ 5.53 - £ 8.17
child (6-18 yrs)	£ 2.45 - £ 2.54
non-member pitch fee	£ 6.46

Harlech
Woodlands Caravan Park

Harlech LL46 2UE (Gwynedd) T: **01766 780419**. E: **grace@woodlandscp.fsnet.co.uk**

alanrogers.com/UK6355

This delightful little site is lovingly tended by its owners and has just 18 pitches for tourists, all with gravel hardstanding and electric hook-up (10A) for caravans and motorcaravans only. Tents are not accepted. There are also 21 privately owned holiday homes, one for rent and a holiday cottage. However, the location of this site certainly makes up for its diminutive size, nestling under the massive rock topped by Harlech Castle, now a designated World Heritage Site. The narrow lane running alongside the site up to the old town above, is the steepest hill in Britain – no wonder the town is considering installing a funicular railway in the future. The coastal railway runs close to the site and the station is just 100 yards away. Railway noise should not be a problem (the small 'Sprinter' trains do not run at night). The 'Blue Flag' beach is only 500 yards, and the Leisure Centre with its indoor pool is 250 yards.

Facilities

The modern stone built toilet facilities are heated, clean and tidy with controllable showers (50p), vanity style washbasins, a small laundry with a baby changing area, but with no dedicated facilities for disabled visitors (£5 deposit for the key to the facilities). Chemical disposal point but no motorcaravan service point. Off site: Harlech Castle. The town also has a theatre and cinema. Nearby is Portmeirion, location of the cult TV series 'The Prisoner', 8 miles. Barmouth (market Thursday and Sunday) 10 miles. Golf 0.25 mile. Fishing 3 miles. Riding 3 miles.

Open: 1 March - 31 October.

Directions

From Barmouth take A496 to Harlech and continue downhill past Royal St David's Golf Course. Fork right immediately before railway crossing, and site is 200 yards on right. DO NOT turn towards town centre which lies on B4573, it is very narrow and congested. O.S.GR: SH582314. GPS: 52.86155, -4.107633

Charges guide

Per unit incl. 2 persons and electricity	£ 15.00 - £ 17.00
extra person	£ 2.50
awning	£ 2.50
No credit cards.	

Harlech
Min-y-Don Holiday Home & Touring Park
Beach Road, Harlech LL46 2UG (Gwynedd) T: **01766 780286**. E: **manager@minydonholidayhomepark.co.uk**
alanrogers.com/UK6365

Set within the Snowdonia National Park, this super park was totally rebuilt for the 2009 season to a standard that others will strive to achieve. It is a level site with first class facilities and providing 82 well drained grass touring pitches. These include 21 pitches with full services, including waste water and sewerage connections (7 with hardstanding for large motorhomes). Tents are not accepted. In a separate area there are 112 caravan holiday homes. With 3 miles of golden sand beaches and the Snowdon mountain range as a backdrop, Min-y-Don overlooks the famous Royal St David's Golf Course. Harlech town, dominated by its 13th-century castle, is within walking distance. A great deal of thought has made this site ideal for disabled visitors, with each pitch fronting onto smooth, level, tarmac roads which continue to the toilet and shower facilities where there are wide reserved parking bays. Key cards are required for all the facilities. Children enjoy a secure play area, a bike track and a games field on site.

Facilities
New toilet facilities are excellent with private cabins and underfloor heating. Large separate unit for disabled visitors. Baby room. Two private bathrooms for rent. Motorcaravan services. Laundry facilities. Play area. Football pitch. Bike track. Wildlife area. Putting green. WiFi (free). Off site: Supermarket and leisure centre 800 yds. Harlech with shops, pubs and restaurants within walking distance. Beach nearby. Coastal train. Bus service. Ffestiniog steam railway. Portmeirion. Snowdon.

Open: March - November.

Directions
From Barmouth go north on the A496 to Harlech. Go over level crossing and turn left into Beach Road. From the north on the A496 in Harlech, right into Beach Road before level crossing. Park is on the right in 400 yards. O.S.GR: SH577314.
GPS: 52.862366, -4.11526

Charges guide
Per person	£ 5.00 - £ 6.50
child (5-15 yrs)	£ 1.50 - £ 2.20
pitch	£ 5.50 - £ 12.50
dog (max. 2)	£ 1.00

Haverfordwest
Creampots Touring Caravan & Camping Park
Broadway, Broad Haven, Haverfordwest SA62 3TU (Pembrokeshire) T: **01437 781776**
alanrogers.com/UK5992

This peacefully located and beautifully manicured, garden-like park is ideal for couples and families with very young children, and is a convenient base within easy reach of beaches or for touring the local area. Creampots has 72 spacious, level pitches all with 10A electric hook-ups, including 12 with gravel hardstanding, and ten pitches for tents. These are in two neat well hedged and sheltered paddocks. Around 40 seasonal units and one caravan holiday home for rent are also accommodated, and there is a separate rally field and an overflow area taking 30 touring units for the August peak holiday time. American RVs are accepted (maximum 36 ft – book in advance). There is a grassy games area for children. Nearby there are bird sanctuaries and the Pembrokeshire Coastal Path.

Facilities
The single small white-washed sanitary unit is a modern building which can be heated. Two free hot showers per sex, open style washbasins. Washbasin and WC for disabled campers. These facilities were clean and tidy but may come under pressure at peak times. Tiny laundry room with just about space for one person at a time but with washing machine, dryer and sink. Gas. Bread, milk, newspapers to order. Off site: Summer bus service (May-Sept) 500 m. from site entrance. Shop, post office, pub with hot food in Broad Haven 1 mile. Fishing and boat launching 1 mile. Beach 1.5 miles. Riding 4 miles. Sailing 6 miles. Golf 7 miles.

Open: March - October.

Directions
Site is 5 miles west of Haverfordwest. From the town take the B4341 to Broad Haven, at Broadway turn left (signed Milford Haven) and park is second entrance on right in under half a mile. O.S.GR: SM882132.
GPS: 51.777333, -5.072283

Charges guide
Per unit incl. 2 persons	£ 14.57 - £ 18.75
up to 4 persons	£ 17.00 - £ 20.00
electricity (10A)	£ 3.75
dog	free

245

Haverfordwest

Redlands Touring Caravan & Camping Park

Hasguard Cross, nr. Little Haven, Haverfordwest SA62 3SJ (Pembrokeshire) T: 01437 781300
E: info@redlandscamping.co.uk alanrogers.com/UK5994

This peaceful, family run site is located in the heart of the Pembrokeshire countryside, close to many lovely sandy beaches. Redlands takes around 80 touring units in three areas divided by banks topped with pine trees, 69 with 10A electricity. The first two areas take 60 caravans or motorcaravans and include 20 hardstandings, the third takes 19 tents on a level grassy meadow. There are fine views across rolling countryside to St Brides Bay. Reception has a small shop which is open only in peak periods. Breathable groundsheets must be used. American RVs – advance booking only. A sandy beach and the Pembrokeshire Coastal Path are 1.5 miles away.

Facilities

The traditional style toilet block is well kept and heated early and late season. It has all the usual requirements including two extra shower, basin and WC suites. Large utility room with washing machine, dryer and spin dryer. Ironing is free, and there are sinks for laundry and dishes. Shop. Freezers. Wet suit washing area. Off site: Shops and ATM in Broadhaven 2 miles. Summer bus service. Fishing and boat launching 1.5 miles. Riding and sailing 5 miles. Golf 6 miles.

Open: 1 March - mid December.

Directions

Site 6.5 miles southwest of Haverfordwest. From Haverfordwest take the B4327 road towards Dale and site is on the right at Hasguard Cross. N.B. Do not approach via Broad Haven. O.S.GR: SM853109. GPS: 51.755567, -5.112383

Charges guide

Per unit incl. 2 persons and electricity	£ 16.25 - £ 21.50
extra person	£ 4.50
dog	£ 1.00

No credit cards.

Llandovery

Erwlon Caravan & Camping Park

Brecon Road, Llandovery SA20 0RD (Carmarthenshire) T: 01550 721021. E: peter@erwlon.co.uk
alanrogers.com/UK5955

Just outside Llandovery and on the edge of the Brecon Beacons National Park, Erwlon is an attractive and welcoming campsite. Of the 110 pitches, 7 are used for privately owned caravan holiday homes, 33 have seasonal caravans and 70 are for touring units. Most are on hardstanding with electricity and 12 have water and a drain as well. There is a flat field for tents at the bottom of the park with some electrical outlets, an open-sided, covered area for eating, food preparation and bicycle storage. The site has a relaxed atmosphere where consideration for others minimises the need for formal rules.

Facilities

New heated toilet block with washbasins in cabins, 4 family rooms (basin, shower, toilet) and a room for families and disabled visitors which includes a baby unit. Combined, well equipped laundry and dishwashing room. Motorcaravan service point. Fridge freezer. Fishing. Bicycle hire. WiFi (charge). Off site: Supermarket 500 m. Town amenities (shops, pubs, restaurants and indoor pool) within 1 mile. Golf 1 mile. Riding 8 miles. Beaches about 25 miles.

Open: All year.

Directions

Park is about half a mile outside the town boundary of Llandovery on the A40 to Brecon. O.S.GR: SN778344. GPS: 51.99491, -3.78076

Charges guide

Per unit incl. 2 persons	£ 12.00 - £ 13.00
incl. services	£ 15.00 - £ 16.00
extra person	£ 1.00

No credit cards.

Llandovery

Rhandirmwyn Camping & Caravanning Club Site

Rhandirmwyn, Llandovery SA20 0NT (Carmarthenshire) T: 01550 760257
alanrogers.com/UK6070

This is a popular site with those who like a peaceful life with no on-site entertainment, just fresh air and beautiful countryside. The site is only a short drive from the magnificent Llyn Brianne reservoir and close to the Dinas RSPB nature reserve, where a two mile trail runs through oak and alder woodland alongside the River Tywi and the wildlife includes many species of birds including red kites. The site is in a sheltered valley with 90 pitches on level grass, 51 electric hook-ups (16A) and 17 hardstandings.

Facilities

The single heated sanitary block is kept very clean and tidy. Some washbasins in cubicles, dishwashing sinks and fully equipped laundry. Drive-over motorcaravan service point. Small playground with rubber base. Off site: The village has a Post Office and general store and the Royal Oak Inn serves good value meals. Farmers' market in Llandovery twice a month. Fishing 6 miles. Golf and bicycle hire 7 miles. Riding 11 miles.

Open: March - October.

Directions

From centre of Llandovery take A483 towards Builth Wells, after a short distance turn left by the fire station, signed Rhandirmwyn, continue for about 7 miles along country lanes. O.S.GR: SN779436. GPS: 52.077017, -3.783833

Charges guide

Per person	£ 5.53 - £ 8.17
child (6-18 yrs)	£ 2.45 - £ 2.54
non-member pitch fee	£ 6.46

Llandrindod Wells

Dolswydd Caravan Park

Dolswydd, Pen-y-Bont, Llandrindod Wells LD1 5UB (Powys) T: **01597 851267**
E: **Hughes@dolswydd.freeserve.co.uk alanrogers.com/UK6250**

Dolswydd is on the edge of a pretty, traditional working farm. Peaceful and tranquil, with fine views of the Welsh hills and surrounding area, it has modern facilities and 25 good spacious pitches mainly on hardstandings, all with electrical connections (16A). The Hughes family extends a warm and friendly welcome to their little park, surrounded by hills and wandering sheep, which is ideal as a touring base or for a one night stop, but booking is recommended, especially at peak times, Bank Holidays and during the Victorian Festival (last week in August). The park is within walking distance of the local pub which offers good, home cooked food.

Facilities

Modern facilities include lots of hot water, dishwashing, laundry, and a WC/washroom for disabled people. Fishing in the river alongside the site (free, but licence required). Off site: Within walking distance are the local pub and garage. Riding 1 mile. Golf and bicycle hire 5 miles.

Open: Easter - end October.

Directions

Pen-y-Bont is 2 miles east of the junction of the A44 and A483 roads at Crossgates. Take A44 (Kington). Go through Pen-y-Bont and immediately after crossing cattle grid, site is on right. O.S.GR: SO117639. GPS: 52.26321, -3.28087

Charges guide

Per unit incl. 2 persons,	
2 children and electricity	£ 10.00
extra person	£ 1.00
child	£ 0.50

Llandysul

Brynawelon Touring & Camping Park

Sarnau, Llandysul SA44 6RE (Ceredigion) T: **01239 654584**. E: **info@brynawlon.co.uk**
alanrogers.com/UK6005

Paul and Liz Cowton have turned Brynawelon into a friendly, attractive and well appointed campsite. It is in a stunning rural location within two miles of the Ceredigion coast with its beaches, and close to the River Teifi with plenty of water based activities. All the 40 pitches have electricity hook-ups and of these 26 are serviced pitches (water and waste) on hardstanding. The remainder are on level grass. The park has ample room for children to play, an enclosed play area, an indoor games room with TV and a sauna next to reception. Buzzards, red kites, owls and the occasional eagle can be seen from the park. There is also a wide variety of small birds. A wide choice of beaches can be found along the coast, there are dolphin trips from Newquay ten miles away and white water rafting on the Teifi at Llandysul. The Teifi is also a well known canoeing and fishing river.

Facilities

New modern toilet block with toilets, showers, washbasins in cabins, two full suites in each side and a separate room for families and disabled visitors. Laundry/kitchen with washing machine, tumble dryer, ironing board and iron, fridge/freezer, microwave, kettle and toaster. Small shop in reception selling basics (July-Sept). Enclosed play area. Games room with pool, electronic games, TV and library. Sauna. Dog walking area. Off site: Shops and pub 1 mile. Beaches, fishing, sailing and riding 3 miles. Dolphin trips at Newquay 10 miles. White water rafting and canoeing at Llandysul 10 miles.

Open: 15 March - 31 October.

Directions

Travelling north on the A487 from Cardigan turn right (southeast) at the crossroads in Sarnau village, signed Rhydlewis. Site is on the left after 650 yds. Note: the country roads from the south are not suitable for caravans and motorcaravans. O.S.GR: SN322508. GPS: 52.13001, -4.45401

Charges guide

Per unit incl 2 persons and electricity	£ 22.50
incl. 4 persons, hardstanding and services	£ 12.50
No credit cards.	

Llanelli

Pembrey Country Park Caravan Club Site

Pembrey, Llanelli SA16 0EJ (Carmarthenshire) T: 01554 834369

alanrogers.com/UK5940

This very popular Caravan Club site has a wonderful location on the edge of a 520 acre Country Park with a vast range of outdoor activities, including the use of an eight mile stretch of safe, sandy beach a mile away. This well sheltered site is set in 12-acre grounds and provides 50 large hardstanding pitches and 80 level, grass pitches for caravans and motorcaravans, all with 16A electricity. Tents are not accepted. Thoughtful landscaping includes the planting of many species of tree and a circular, one-way tarmac road provides easy access. Sensibly placed service points provide fresh water and waste disposal of all types. RAF jets do practise in this area (although becoming less frequent and generally not flying at the weekend). There may be occasional noise from the nearby motor racing circuit. However, the real plus for this site is its proximity to the Country Park – access to this is free on foot or cycle direct from the site, or the site can organise a special weekly car pass for around £12.

Facilities

The toilet block is of an excellent standard including washbasins in cubicles, facilities for disabled visitors and a baby room. Fully equipped laundry room. Dishwashing room and further sinks under cover. Motorcaravan service point. Gas available. Local tradesmen visit each morning selling milk, bread and newspapers. Play area. Late arrivals area (with electricity). Off site: Dogs are restricted on the beach May - Sept (follow signs).

Open: March - January.

Directions

Leave M4 at junction 48 onto A4138 (signed Llanelli). After 4 miles turn right onto A484 at roundabout signed Carmarthen. Continue for 7 miles to Pembrey. The Country Park is signed off the A484 in Pembrey village; site entrance is on right 100 yds before gates. O.S.GR: SN413006. GPS: 51.681817, -4.297417

Charges guide

Per person	£ 4.50 - £ 6.00
child (5-16 yrs)	£ 1.50 - £ 2.45
pitch incl. electricity (non-member)	£ 11.70 - £ 14.55

Llangadog

Abermarlais Caravan Park

Llangadog SA19 9NG (Carmarthenshire) T: 01550 777868. E: aberma@tiscali.co.uk

alanrogers.com/UK5960

Apart from the attractions of south or mid Wales for a stay, this sheltered, family run park could also double as a useful transit stop close to the main holiday route for those travelling to Pembrokeshire. In a natural setting, up to 88 touring units are accommodated in one fairly flat, tapering five acre grass field edged by mature trees and a stream. Pitches are numbered, and generously spaced around the perimeter or on either side of a central, hedged spine at the wider end, with 48 electrical hook-ups (10A) and some hardstanding. Backpackers have a small, separate area. The park is set in a sheltered valley with a range of wildlife and nine acres of woodland walks. There is also an old walled garden, with some pitches and lawns for softball games, that screens the park, both audibly and visibly, from the A40 road. However, the most sought after pitches are beside the stream, loved by children and a haven for wildlife. A torch would be useful.

Facilities

The one small toilet block is older in style, but is clean, bright, cheerful and adequate with controllable showers. Two external, covered dishwashing sinks but no laundry facilities (nearest about 5 miles). Motorcaravan service point. Shop doubling as reception. Gas supplies. Play area with tennis and volleyball nets and play equipment. Winter caravan storage. Off site: Restaurants nearby. Pubs, shops, etc. at Llangadog. Fishing 2 miles.

Open: 14 March - 14 November.

Directions

Park is on the A40, between the junctions with the A4069 and A482, between Llandovery and Llandeilo. O.S.GR: SN695298. GPS: 51.951583, -3.9003

Charges guide

Per person	£ 1.50
child (5-16 yrs)	£ 1.00
pitch	£ 7.00
awning	£ 1.00
electricity	£ 2.00

Llangollen

Ty-Ucha Farm Caravan Park

Maesmawr Road, Llangollen LL20 7PP (Denbighshire) T: **01978 860677**

alanrogers.com/UK6700

Only a mile from Llangollen, Ty-Ucha has a rather dramatic setting, nestling under its own mountain and with views across the valley to craggy Dinas Bran castle. It is a neat, ordered park, carefully managed by the owners and providing 40 pitches (30 with 10A electrical hook-up) for caravans and motorcaravans only (tents are not accepted). They are well spaced round a large, grassy field with an open centre for play. One side slopes gently and is bounded by a stream and wood in which a Nature Trail has been made. Because of overhead cables, kite flying is forbidden; no bike riding either. A path leads to various mountain walks, depending on your energy and ability. The world famous Eisteddfod is an international festival of music and dance held for six days starting on the first Tuesday of the first full week in July every year – it is a very busy time for the area.

Facilities	Directions
The single toilet block, although of 'portacabin' style, is clean and well maintained and can be heated. It includes two metered showers for each sex (a little cramped). Dishwashing sink with cold water outside. No laundry facilities but there is a launderette in Llangollen. Gas supplies. Games room with table tennis. Late arrivals area. Note: tents are not accepted. Off site: Hotel 0.5 miles with reasonably priced meals. Fishing 1 mile, golf 0.5 miles.	Park is signed off A5 road, 1 mile east of Llangollen (250 yds). O.S.GR: SJ228411. GPS: 52.96546, -3.14569

Open: Easter - October.

Charges guide

Per unit incl. 2 persons and electricity	£ 14.00 - £ 15.00
extra person	£ 2.00

Reductions for OAPs for weekly stays.
No credit cards.

Llantwit Major

Acorn Camping & Caravanning

Ham Lane South, Llantwit Major CF61 1RP (Vale of Glamorgan) T: **01446 794024**

E: **info@acorncamping.co.uk alanrogers.com/UK5927**

A peaceful, family owned, rural site, Acorn is situated on the Heritage Coast, one mile from the beach and the historic town of Llantwit Major. The 105 pitches are mostly on grass, with a few private and rental mobile homes at the far end, leaving around 90 pitches for tourers. These include ten serviced pitches and 4 gravel hardstandings with 74 electric hook-ups (10A), and a separate area for tents. Reception houses a very well stocked shop which includes groceries and essentials, souvenirs, children's toys, camping gear, a delicatessen, and takeaway meals cooked to order. There is occasional aircraft noise. Site lighting is kept to a minimum to allow guests to enjoy the night sky – a torch might be useful. The Glamorgan Heritage Coastal footpath is a short walk from the site and Llantwit Major is also worth a visit, particularly St Illtud's Church for its wall paintings, medieval altar, and collection of Celtic stones.

Facilities	Directions
A warm, modern building houses spacious shower cubicles with washbasins, ample WCs, a family/baby room, and a suite for disabled campers. Laundry facilities. Drinks machine. Shop. Gas. Snooker room. Games room (charged). Play area with free trampoline. Off site: Glamorgan Heritage Coastal footpath. Llanerch Vineyard. Cosmeston Lakes Country Park at Penarth. Sea fishing 1 mile. Riding 2 miles. Lake 4 miles. Golf, boat launching 9 miles.	From east from M4 exit 33 follow signs to Cardiff airport, take B4265 for Llantwit Major. Turn left at traffic lights, through Broverton and left into Ham Lane East, finally turning left into Ham Manor Park and follow signs to campsite. From west: M4 exit 35, turn south on A473 for 3 miles, then left on A48, turning right at Pentre Meyrick towards Llantwit Major on B4268/70. Left at roundabout on B4265, over mini-roundabout, right at traffic lights into Llanmaes Road, left at mini-roundabout, continue around back of the town, left at mini-roundabout, and right into Ham Lane East and continue as above. O.S.GR: SS974678. GPS: 51.40409, -3.48181

Open: 1 February - 8 December.

Charges guide

Per unit incl. 2 persons and electricity	£ 13.80 - £ 14.95
extra person	£ 4.50
dog	£ 0.65

Llanwrda

Springwater Lakes

Harford, Llanwrda SA19 8DT (Carmarthenshire) T: 01558 650788. E: bookings@springwaterlakes.com
alanrogers.com/UK5880

Set in 20 acres of Welsh countryside, Springwater offers a selection of fishing lakes to keep even the keenest of anglers occupied. However, it is not just anglers who will enjoy this site – it is a lovely base to enjoy the peace and tranquillity of this part of Wales. Springwater offers 30 spacious, flat pitches either on grass or gravel hardstanding, all with 16A electricity. Future plans include fully serviced pitches. Malcolm and Shirley Bexon are very proud of their site and welcome all visitors with a smile. This is not a site for children unless they enjoy fishing (no play areas). If you want to learn about fishing Malcolm will be happy to help.

Facilities

The modern toilet block is very clean and includes facilities for disabled visitors (there is also wheelchair access to the lakes for fishing). Fishing. Tackle/bait shop. Off site: Spar shop and garage 500 yards, other shops 5 miles. Bicycle hire and riding 2 miles. Golf 4 miles.

Open: 1 March - 31 October.

Directions

From A40 at Llanwrda take A482 to Lampeter. After 6 miles go through village of Pumsaint and site is 2 miles further on the left, just before garage shop. O.S.GR: SN642429. GPS: 52.067417, -3.98225

Charges guide

Per unit incl. 2 persons and electricity	£ 15.00 - £ 19.00
extra person (over 2 yrs)	£ 5.00
dog	free - £ 2.00

No credit cards.

Morben Isaf Caravan Park

Morben Isaf Caravan Park, Machynlleth, Powys. SY20 8SR

Set in a peaceful location, we are ideally located near the historic town of Machynlleth. Fishing is available in the park which is adjacent to the Dyfi Osprey Project at Cors Dyfi, part of the Montgomeryshire Wildlife Trust. It is also possible to play golf nearby. Our facilities include a fully serviced laundry room and a first class toilet/shower block. A selection of holiday homes are also available for purchase.

For more details please contact us on **01654 781473**

Machynlleth

Morben Isaf Touring & Holiday Home Park

Derwenlas, Machynlleth SY20 8SR (Powys) T: 01654 781473. E: manager@morbenisaf.co.uk
alanrogers.com/UK6245

Morben Isaf provides 13 touring pitches with multi-services, all with electricity (16A), water tap, waste water drain and a satellite TV hook-up. There is further grassy space below the touring pitches beyond the fishing lake which is normally used as a play field and football pitch but can accommodate around 30 tents who do not need any services. On a lower level, behind the site manager's bungalow, and barely visible from the touring site, are 87 privately owned caravan holiday homes. Also on the site is an unfenced coarse fishing lake which campers are free to use. Machynlleth is a market town, home of Owain Glyndwr's 15th-century Welsh Parliament building and the Celtica Centre, and is also close to the Tal-y-Llyn Steam Railway, the Centre for Alternative Technology, Corris Craft Centre and King Arthur's Labyrinth. Adjacent to the site is the Dyfi Osprey Project visitor centre – for the first time in 2007, a nest platform was erected and was occupied by a pair of ospreys. This park is in a convenient location for an overnight halt, or a short stay whilst visiting all these attractions.

Facilities

Small but well equipped, heated modern toilet block includes spacious controllable showers, baby changing and child seats in both ladies' and men's. Facilities for disabled campers. Well equipped laundry. Powered motorcaravan service point. Internet access (free). Off site: Pub serving hot food 1.5 miles. Leisure Centre, shops and services in Machynlleth 3 miles (market on Wednesday). Dyfi Osprey Project visitor centre adjacent. Centre for Alternative Technology 6 miles.

Open: Mid March - 31 October.

Directions

Site is 2.5 miles southwest of Machynlleth beside A487. O.S.GR: SN706986. GPS: 52.570067, -3.91145

Charges guide

Per unit incl. 2 persons and electricity	£ 15.00 - £ 17.50
tent (2 persons)	£ 10.50 - £ 12.50
extra person	£ 2.00
dog	free - £ 1.00

Moelfre

Home Farm Caravan Park

Marianglas, Anglesey LL73 8PH (Isle of Anglesey) T: **01248 410614**. E: enq@homefarm-anglesey.co.uk
alanrogers.com/UK6640

A tarmac drive through an open field leads to this neatly laid out quality park, with caravan holiday homes to one side. Nestling below what was once a Celtic hill fort, later decimated as a quarry, the park is edged with mature trees and farmland. A circular, tarmac access road leads to the 102 well spaced and numbered touring pitches. With five types available, there are pitches for everyone; ranging from grass with no electricity, to oversized, deluxe hardstandings with electricity, water tanks/taps, waste water drain and TV hook-ups. All electricity is 16A and there are separate well maintained grass fields/areas for tents. Some areas are slightly sloping. The 'pièce de résistance' must be the children's indoor play area, large super adventure play equipment, complete with tunnels and bridges on safe rubber matting, not to mention an outside fenced play area and fields available for sports, football, etc. and walking. Various beaches, sandy or rocky, are within a mile. A member of the Best of British group.

Facilities	Directions
Two purpose built toilet blocks, one part of the reception building, are of similar design, can be heated and are maintained to a high standard. En-suite provision for people with disabilities (with key). Excellent small bathroom for children with baby bath and curtain for privacy. Family room (with key). Laundry room. Motorcaravan service point. Ice pack service. Reception provides basic essentials, gas and some caravan accessories. Indoor and outdoor play areas. TV and pool table. Small library. Hard tennis (extra charge) with racquet hire. Off site: Restaurants, shops and ATM at Benllech 2 miles. Beach 1 mile. Fishing and golf 2 miles. Riding 8 miles.	From the Britannia Bridge take second exit left signed Benllech and Amlwch on the A5025. Two miles after Benllech keep left at roundabout and park entrance is 300 yards on the left beyond the church. O.S.GR: SH499850. GPS: 53.34055, -4.256367

Charges guide

Per unit incl. 2 persons and electricity	£ 16.50 - £ 29.50
extra person	£ 3.50 - £ 6.00
child (5-16 yrs)	£ 2.00 - £ 4.00
dog (max. 2)	£ 1.00 - £ 2.00

Open: April - October.

Monmouth

Glen Trothy Caravan & Camping Park

Mitchel Troy, Monmouth NP25 4BD (Monmouthshire) T: **01600 712295**. E: enquiries@glentrothy.co.uk
alanrogers.com/UK5890

Glen Trothy is a pretty park on the banks of the river Trothy and visitors are greeted by an array of colourful flowerbeds and tubs around the entrance and reception area. Three fields provide 40 level touring pitches. The first and largest field has a circular gravel road with seasonal pitches arranged on the outer side of the road and touring pitches on the inner side. These have slabs for vehicle wheels and electricity hook-ups. The second field, just past the toilet block, has pitches for trailer tents and tents only, whilst the camping field is for tents only (no cars allowed on this area). The owners, Horace and Merle Price, are working hard on their site bringing its facilities up-to-date, recently adding a security gate to the new reception office.

Facilities	Directions
The sanitary block is old and a little tired (possibly stretched at peak times). Facilities for disabled visitors. Laundry and dishwashing. Tourist information in hut opposite reception. Dogs are not accepted. Only purpose built barbecues are allowed. Small children' play area. Off site: Golf 2 miles. Shopping and supermarkets at the historic town of Monmouth. The Wye Valley and the Forest of Dean are nearby for outings.	At Monmouth, take A40 east to Abergavenny. Exit at first junction and at T-junction, where site is signed, turn left onto B4284. Follow signs for Mitchel Troy. Site is on right just past village sign. O.S.GR: SO495105. GPS: 51.790967, -2.7341

Charges guide

Per unit incl. 2 persons and electricity	£ 13.00
extra person (5 yrs and over)	£ 2.50

Open: 1 March - 31 October.

Montgomery
Smithy Park

Abermule, Montgomery SY15 6ND (Powys) T: **01584 711280**. E: **info@bestparks.co.uk**
alanrogers.com/UK6305

Smithy Caravan Park is set in four acres of landscaped ground bordered by the River Severn and the Shropshire Union Canal in the tranquil rolling countryside of central Wales. It does have 60 privately owned caravan holiday homes, but the touring area is separate and also has the benefit of being closest to the river with the best views and a small picnic and seating area on the bank. This area has 26 fully serviced hardstanding pitches (16A electricity, water, waste water and satellite TV hook-ups). A timber chalet provides all the sanitary facilities, and is located in one corner of the touring area. This is a well run site, which is under the same ownership as Westbrook Park, with a resident manager on-site here. The village has two pubs, a shop and Post Office, and a bus service – all within easy walking distance. American RVs are accepted with prior notice. Kite flying and cycling on the park are not permitted.

Facilities

The new timber clad chalet building provides two good sized showers per sex, washbasins in cubicles, a family room suitable for the less able (there is a step up to the building). Utility room housing a laundry with washing machine, dryer and dishwashing sink. Fishing in the river Severn. Fenced playground. Gas stocked. Off site: Bus stop in village opposite end of site access road. Supermarkets and all other services in Newtown 3 miles. Golf 3 miles. Riding 5 miles.

Open: 1 March - 30 October.

Directions

Site is 3 miles north of Newtown in the village of Abermule. Turn off the A483 into village, and turn down the lane beside the Waterloo Arms, opposite the village shop and Post Office. Site is at end of lane. O.S.GR: SO161948. GPS: 52.544217, -3.238717

Charges 2010

Per unit incl. 2 persons and electricity	£ 14.00 - £ 20.00
extra person	£ 4.00
child (4-10 yrs)	£ 4.00
dog	£ 1.00

Montgomery
Bacheldre Watermill Caravan Park

Churchstoke, Montgomery SY15 6TE (Powys) T: **01588 620489**. E: **info@bacheldremill.co.uk**
alanrogers.com/UK6310

A delightful little site, Bacheldre has just 25 pitches arranged around the perimeter of a grass meadow, with no site road. There is just one lamp on the outside of the toilet block and three small lights on the perimeter so torches are useful. However, there are 18 electric hook-ups (10A) and ten hardstandings. Ideal for tenters and small units, it is not really suitable for larger units (20 ft. plus) and American RVs. The watermill is fully operational, producing high quality organic wheat flour, which can be purchased from reception, together with eggs and bread. The mill is not normally accessible, although guided tours can be arranged. Note: there are obvious hazards for small children – a deep, partially-fenced millpond, moving waterwheel and the stream.

Facilities

A portacabin provides the usual facilities including one controllable hot shower per sex with dishwashing sinks in a separate room. Calor gas stocked. Off site: Walking and cycling along Offa's Dyke 800 yards from site. Clun Castle ruins are worth a visit. Steam enthusiasts are well catered for with the Welshpool and Llanfair light railway. Supermarket at Churchstoke 2 miles.

Open: All year.

Directions

Bacheldre is just off the A489 between Newtown and Churchstoke, about 9 miles east of Newtown and 2 miles west of Churchstoke. Turn into narrow lane (signed Bacheldre Mill), over the bridge and site entrance is almost immediately on your right. O.S.GR: SO243929. GPS: 52.52749, -3.11879

Charges guide

Per unit incl. 2 persons	£ 10.00 - £ 13.00
extra person	£ 2.00
awning	£ 2.50

Montgomery

Daisy Bank Touring Caravan Park

Snead, Montgomery SY15 6EB (Powys) T: **01588 620471**. E: **enquiries@daisy-bank.co.uk**

alanrogers.com/UK6330

For adults only, this pretty, tranquil park in the Camlad Valley has panoramic views, and is an ideal base for walkers. Attractively landscaped with 'old English' flower beds and many different trees and shrubs, this small park has been carefully developed. The Welsh hills to the north and the Shropshire hills to the south overlook the three fields which provide a total of 83 pitches . The field nearer to the road (perhaps a little noisy) is slightly sloping but there are hardstandings for motorcaravans, while the second field is more level. All pitches have 16A electricity, water and waste water drainage and TV hook up. With many walks in the area, including Offa's Dyke, a series of walk leaflets is available centred on Bishop's Castle three miles away. The owners will site your caravan for you and there is a late arrivals area with hook-up. The code for the security gate at the entrance is obtained at registration. Although technically in Wales, the park is 500 yards from the Shropshire border, an area rich in history.

Facilities

The well equipped, heated toilet block now incorporates modern, en-suite units (6 with shower, WC and washbasin, 2 with WC and washbasin and facilities for disabled visitors). Dishwashing sinks at the rear of the block are covered. Laundry facilities. Shop in reception (operates an honesty policy at certain times). Gas supplies. Brick built barbecues. Small putting green (free loan of clubs and balls). Bicycle hire. Tourist information. Small library. WiFi (charged). Off site: Supermarket 2 miles. Many eating places near. Fishing 3 miles. Golf and riding 10 miles.

Open: All year.

Directions

Site is by the A489 road 2 miles east of Churchstoke in the direction of Craven Arms. O.S.GR: SO302930. GPS: 52.529917, -3.0297

Charges guide

Per unit incl. 2 persons and all services	£ 17.00 - £ 22.00
extra person	£ 5.00
tent (per person	£ 7.00 - £ 8.00
dog	£ 1.00

Newcastle Emlyn

Cenarth Falls Holiday Park

Cenarth, Newcastle Emlyn SA38 9JS (Ceredigion) T: **01239 710345**. E: **enquiries@cenarth-holipark.co.uk**

alanrogers.com/UK6010

The Davies family has developed an attractively landscaped, part wooded holiday home park with 86 privately owned units and 3 for hire. However, a neat well cared for, sheltered grassy area at the top of the park provides 30 touring pitches, accessed via a semicircular tarmac road, and all with shingle hardstanding and electricity (16A). A sunken, kidney shaped outdoor pool with landscaped surrounds and sun beds is a focal point. The Coracles Health and Country Club provides an indoor pool, spa, sauna and steam rooms and fitness suite (reduced rates for campers). It also provides a bar, restaurant area, adult-only lounge and a large function room where live entertainment is organised weekly all season. Everything is of a high quality. A footpath leads to the village and the famous Cenarth Falls. The National Coracle Centre is well worth a visit. A member of the Best of British group.

Facilities

The excellent, heated sanitary block has easy ramped access, even to the chemical disposal unit. Etc. Accessed by key, it uses a 'P.I.R.' system that controls heating, lighting, water and air freshener on entry – very efficient. Tiled with non-slip floors, both men and ladies have an en-suite provision for disabled visitors (doubling as a family room), spacious well equipped showers and one of the washbasins in a roomy private cabin. Laundry room (used by the whole park). No laundry sinks, but two dishwashing sinks are under cover. Gas supplies. Outdoor pool (mid May - mid Sept). Coracles Health and Country Club (see above). Play area. Games room. No dogs on touring field (16/7-3/9). Off site: Shop within 0.5 miles. Fishing 0.25 miles. Riding 7 miles. Bicycle hire 8 miles. Golf 10 miles.

Open: 1 March - 16 December.

Directions

Follow A484 Cardigan - Newcastle Emlyn road and park is signed before Cenarth village. O.S.GR: SN265421. GPS: 52.0499, -4.531717

Charges guide

Per unit incl. up to 4 people and electricity	£ 14.00 - £ 25.00
extra person	£ 2.00
dog	£ 2.00

Newport

Cwmcarn Forest Drive Campsite

Cwmcarn, Crosskeys, Newport NP11 7FA (Newport) T: **01495 272001**. E: **cwmcarn-vc@caerphilly.gov.uk**

alanrogers.com/UK5930

This forest site, run by Caerphilly Council, is set in a narrow, sheltered valley with magnificent wooded slopes. The park is not only central for the many attractions of this part of Wales, but there is also much of the natural environment to enjoy including a small fishing lake and the seven-mile forest drive. The site has a slightly wild feel, but is well located and has 27 well spaced, flat pitches, most with 15A electricity (three with concrete hardstanding), spread over three small fields between the new Visitor Centre and the small lake. Wardens are on hand daily. The Visitor Centre and campsite reception are open 09.00 - 17.00 (18.00 at weekends, Oct - Easter Fridays 09.00 - 16.30). The forest drive (open daily in season) has several car parks en-route where visitors can stop to enjoy the great views, many picnic and barbecue areas, wood carvings and a play area. The climb up to the Twmbarlwm ancient hill fort is well worth making with its magnificent views across the Severn to Somerset, Devon and Gloucestershire.

Facilities

The single, heated toilet block includes toilet facilities for disabled visitors, laundry facilities, small cooker and fridge. Visitor Centre has a coffee shop selling refreshments and snacks. Guided walks and the popular Twrch (9 miles) mountain bike trail. Rallies accommodated. Dogs accepted by prior arrangement. Off site: Shops, leisure centre and takeaway food in village less than 1 mile. Riding 2 miles. Golf 3 miles.

Open: All year excl. 23 December - 2 January.

Directions

Cwmcarn Forest Drive is well signed from junction 28 on the M4. From the Midlands and the 'Heads of the Valleys' road (A465), take A467 south to Cwmcarn. O.S.GR: ST230935.
GPS: 51.63771, -3.11877

Charges guide

Per pitch	£ 7.00 - £ 13.00
electricity	£ 2.50

Newport

Tredegar House Country Park Caravan Club Site

Coedkernen, Newport NP10 8TW (Newport) T: **01633 815600**

alanrogers.com/UK6060

This immaculate Caravan Club site is ideally situated for breaking a journey or for longer stays. It can accommodate 80 caravans, all with 16A electricity hook-up and 47 with gravel hardstanding. A further grass area is allocated for 20 tents, with its use limited to families and couples – no single sex groups are accepted. The site itself is set within the gardens and park of Tredegar House, a 17th-century house and country park which is open to the public to discover what life was like 'above and below stairs'. The park entrance gates are locked at dusk so contact the site reception for details of latest arrival times. Some road noise may be expected at times, but otherwise this is an excellent site.

Facilities

The sanitary block is of an excellent standard with a digital lock system. It includes washbasins in cubicles. Facilities for disabled visitors. Baby and toddler bathroom. Laundry. Good motorcaravan service point. Calor gas available. Tredegar House visitor centre with tea rooms, gift shop and craft workshops (open Easter - Sept). Adventure play area in the park. Off site: Large supermarket 0.5 miles. Newport 3 miles. Cardiff 9 miles. Bus service 10 minutes walk.

Open: All year.

Directions

From M4 take exit 28 or from A48 junction with the M4 follow brown signs for Tredegar House. The caravan park is indicated to the left at the house entrance. O.S.GR: ST299855.
GPS: 51.55080, -3.02783

Charges guide

Per person	£ 3.90 - £ 5.40
child (5-16 yrs)	£ 1.30 - £ 2.10
pitch incl. electricity (non-member)	£ 11.20 - £ 13.95

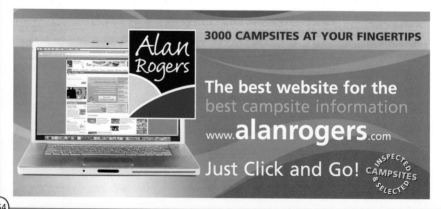

Newtown

Cringoed Caravan Park

Cringoed, Llanbrynmair, Newtown SY19 7DR (Powys) T: **01650 521237**

alanrogers.com/UK6240

Cringoed is a pleasant, peaceful, small park with a river to one side, hills on the other and trees at either end. There are 30 spacious pitches available for touring and these are in a level open field, each with hardstanding and 16A electricity. About 36 caravan holiday homes are placed at either end of the site, some amongst trees and some in a newer, more open area. There are also ten tent pitches, some with electricity. This is a relaxing base where you can sit and listen to the river and watch the wildlife, but it is also within easy reach of some of mid-Wales' best scenery and not far from the coast. Paul and Sue Mathers will make you very welcome.

Facilities

The single toilet block is neat, modern and quite adequate. Laundry and dishwashing. Adventure play area. Small tourist information room. Off site: Shops 1 mile. ATM at Spar in Carno 6 miles. Bicycle hire 1 mile. Fishing 5 miles. Golf 8 miles. Riding 12 miles.

Open: 7 March - 30 November.

Directions

From the A470 between Newton and Machynlleth in the village of Llanbrynmair take the B4518 signed Staylittle (caravan signs). After 1 mile just before bridge turn right, go over site bridge and turn right into site. O.S.GR: SH887013.
GPS: 52.598333, -3.644383

Charges guide

Per unit incl. 2 persons and electricity	£ 13.00 - £ 15.50
extra person	£ 5.00
child (3-14 yrs)	£ 2.50
No credit cards.	

Pembroke

Freshwater East Caravan Club Site

Trewent Hill, Freshwater East, Pembroke SA71 5LJ (Pembrokeshire) T: **01646 672341**

alanrogers.com/UK5990

This Caravan Club site in the Pembrokeshire Coast National Park is open to non-members (for all units). At the bottom of a hill, it has 130 mainly level pitches bounded by trees, all with 16A electrical hook-ups and half on hardstanding. There are a further 12 pitches for tents. The beach and the Pembroke Coastal Path are about a five minute walk. This is an excellent area for walking with magnificent cliff views and bird watching. You will find St David's, the smallest cathedral city, well worth a visit. Note: TV aerial connections are available, but you will need your own extension cable.

Facilities

The two heated toilet blocks are modern and clean with washbasins in cubicles, and free hairdryers or sockets for your own. Facilities for disabled visitors. Fully equipped laundry rooms. Waste point for motorcaravans. Gas supplies. Reception keeps basic food items. Information kiosk. Small play area. Off site: Public transport 1 mile. Shop 0.5 miles. Beach 400 yards. Fishing 5 miles.

Open: 27 March - 26 October.

Directions

From the east on A477, fork left 1.25 miles past Milton onto A4075 Pembroke road. After 2 miles in Pembroke immediately (after railway bridge) turn sharp left at roundabout on A4139 Tenby road. In 1.75 miles in Lamphey turn right onto B4584 signed Freshwater East. In 1.75 miles turn right signed Stackpole and Trewent and after 400 yds at foot of hill, right into lane at Club sign. Do not tow to the beach area. O.S.GR: SS014980.
GPS: 51.64791, -4.86894

Charges guide

Per person	£ 3.90 - £ 5.50
child (5-16 yrs)	£ 1.30 - £ 2.10
pitch incl. electricity (non-member)	£ 11.00 - £ 15.00

Penmaenmawr

Tyddyn Du Touring Park

Conwy Old Road, Penmaenmawr LL34 6RE (Conwy) T: 01492 622300. E: stay@tyddyndutouringpark.co.uk
alanrogers.com/UK6695

This attractively landscaped campsite for adults only is conveniently situated close to the A55 and positioned on a hillside with panoramic views across Conwy Bay to The Great Orme at Llandudno and Puffin Island. Offering peace and quiet in a superb location between mountains and the sea and being within easy reach of Conwy, Snowdonia National Park and many historic regions of North Wales, this is an ideal base for exploring the area. Tarmac roads connect the three levels which are tiered to maximise the views for everyone. There are 92 touring pitches on either grass or hardstanding and all have 16A electricity. One modern, roomy and well equipped utility building houses separate facilities for men and women, whilst an additional, older, more traditional sanitary block is located at the top of the site. Some traffic noise from the A55 can be heard but this should not spoil the enjoyment of this pretty campsite. Units over 26 ft. in length are not accepted No arrivals before 14.00 please and visitors under the age of 18 are not allowed on site.

Facilities	Directions
Two well maintained sanitary blocks provide showers, open style washbasins and hairdryers. En-suite facilities for disabled visitors (Radar key). Motorcaravan service point (care needed to access). Well equipped laundry room. Small library. £5 (cash only) refundable deposit for entry card. Off site: Shops and restaurants within 1 mile. Pub at entrance to park. Sandy beach 10-15 minutes walk. Fishing and sailing 1 mile. Golf 0.5 miles. Conwy 4 miles. Llandudno 9 miles.	From the A55 take exit 16 and at roundabout signed Penmaenmawr turn immediately sharp left into Ysguborwen Road. Entrance to park is about 300 yards on the right. O.S.GR: SH728768. GPS: 53.27425, -3.90632

Open: 22 March - 31 October.

Charges guide

Per unit incl. 2 persons and electricity	£ 16.00 - £ 18.00
extra person (over 16 yrs)	£ 2.00
awning	£ 1.00 - £ 2.00

Pontarddulais

River View Touring Park

The Dingle, Llanedi, Pontarddulais SA4 0FH (Carmarthenshire) T: 01269 844876
E: info@riverviewtouringpark.com alanrogers.com/UK5945

Keith and Kath Brasnett with their warm welcome and helpful efficiency ensure that this park remains attractive, quiet and friendly. Nestling in the valley of the River Gwili, it is made up of three fields: one by the river which is kept mainly for adults and two on a plateau up a steep slope on the opposite side of the lane. Particular care has been taken to protect the natural environment. There are 60 level, generously sized pitches of which 45 are touring pitches, the remainder seasonal. All have electricity (16A), 20 have hardstandings and five are fully serviced. This is a popular rural retreat for young families and older couples. The park is close to the end of the M4, allowing easy access and there is plenty to do or see in the near vicinity, castles, gardens, beaches, wildfowl reserves and a water park, and there is an SSSI immediately at the back of the site. The bird life visible from the site is varied and includes buzzards and red kites, and dippers on the river. The toilet block, including an en-suite family room with baby changing facilities and one for the disabled, is modern and equipped to a very high standard, including underfloor heating and automatic lighting.

Facilities	Directions
The modern, heated, toilet block is spotless with spacious showers, family room and suite for disabled visitors. New laundry with sinks, washing machine, tumble dryer, iron and ironing board. Small shop for basics and local fresh produce. Large grassy recreation area on main field. Fishing. Off site: Shop, bar and restaurant 1 mile. Bicycle hire and golf 5 miles. Beach 12 miles.	From the M4 exit 49 take A483 signed Llandeilo. Take the first turn left (after layby) and park is on left after 300 yds. O.S.GR: SN578086. GPS: 51.75817, -4.06288

Open: 1 March - 6 December.

Charges guide

Per unit incl. 2 persons and electricity	£ 13.00 - £ 17.00
incl. services	£ 15.50 - £ 19.50
extra person	£ 2.50 - £ 3.00
infant (under 4 yrs)	£ 1.00
dog	free - £ 1.00

No credit cards.

Prestatyn

Nant Mill Family Touring Caravan & Tenting Park

Gronant Road, Prestatyn LL19 9LY (Denbighshire) T: 01745 852360. E: nantmilltouring@aol.com
alanrogers.com/UK6660

This traditional style, family owned and run park of around five acres, takes some 150 units arranged over four fields. There are some distant sea views to be had from many pitches. These are carefully allocated to ensure that the largest, central, sloping field is reserved for families. A smaller more intimate field for tents only is to one side of this and two small paddocks on the other side are for couples who might prefer a quieter, more level location. There are 96 electrical connections (10/16A) but tents are not permitted on pitches with hook-ups. The immaculate sanitary buildings are located in the central field and reception is at the farmhouse. Fresh milk and eggs can be purchased. Lighting is fairly minimal, being located at the service points and around the toilet block, therefore a torch is useful. Children have a designated ball games area and a very good, enclosed adventure playground on a bark surface. Small children might like to visit the duck pond at the rear of the farmhouse. The best beach is the Blue Flag Prestatyn central beach which is about half a mile from the site. Note: The main site gate is locked at night generally around dusk until 08.00 each morning. An alternative entry point is available during these hours. There is a length restriction of 26 ft for touring vehicles.

Facilities

The main toilet block is older in style but very well kept, with showers, an ample number of open style washbasins and baby changing in both ladies' and men's rooms. Extra showers are in a small modern 'portacabin' style unit alongside. Showers are charged (50p), with a £1 deposit for the cubicle key (return after each shower). A separate 'portacabin' unit with ramp provides a full suite of services for disabled visitors. Large utility room with washing machines, dryers, spin dryer, ironing facilities, together with sinks for hand washing and dishes plus a hairdressing station. Playground and play field. Off site: Beach 0.5 mile. Town with supermarkets, shops, services and gas supplies 0.5 mile. Sea fishing 0.5 mile. Golf 0.5 miles. Bicycle hire 4 miles.

Open: Easter - mid October.

Directions

Site entrance is 0.5 mile east of Prestatyn on the A548 coast road. O.S.GR: SJ073832. GPS: 53.33765, -3.3932

Charges guide

Per unit incl. 2 persons and electricity	£ 116.50 - £ 19.50
extra person (over 3 yrs)	£ 1.50

No credit/debit cards.

Pwllheli

Bolmynydd Camping Park

Llanbedrog, Pwllheli LL53 7UP (Gwynedd) T: 01758 740224. E: bolmynydd@btinternet.com
alanrogers.com/UK6585

The drive to Bolymynydd is not for the faint hearted. The roads are extremely narrow with plenty of bends, and are not recommended for large units. However, those who do make the drive are rewarded with spectacular views and a campsite which is ideal for tents and those who wish for peace and quiet in a wonderful rural setting. Two fields are available for tents, and other fields offer safe play areas for young children. With ten seasonal caravan pitches and only eight touring pitches (all with 10/16A electricity), the owners request that you telephone ahead to discuss access and availability. The one modern, well-maintained utility block, serves both the camping fields and caravan pitches. There is no games room or swimming pool, just beautiful Welsh scenery and nature.

Facilities

One clean sanitary block, maintained to a high standard (may be under pressure in peak season). Separate modern showers, toilets and open style washbasins. Baby bath in well equipped laundry room. No motorcaravan service point. Off site: Five minute walk to small supermarket and pub. Riding, beach and sailing 400 yds. Fishing 1 mile. Golf 3 miles.

Open: Easter - 31 October.

Directions

From Pwllheli take the A499 toward Abersoch. After 4 miles pass through Llanbedrog and at the campsite sign turn sharp left. Continue for about half a mile, site is on the left. O.S.GR: SH325530. GPS: 52.85231, -4.48844

Charges guide

Per unit incl. 2 persons	£ 15.00 - £ 16.00
incl. electricity	£ 18.50 - £ 19.50
extra person	£ 5.00
child (3-16 yrs)	£ 2.50

No credit cards.
Must phone prior to arrival to discuss access and availability.

Pwllheli

Hafan y Môr Holiday Park

Pwllheli LL53 6HJ (Gwynedd) T: **07949 642 534**

alanrogers.com/UK6575

One of Haven's flagship parks, Hafan y Mor has a substantially redeveloped leisure and activity area, The park is set on the coast with direct access to the beach. A full range of clubs is provided for toddlers to teens and there is a popular splash zone and adventure playground. This is a large park with 700 caravan holiday homes for rent or privately owned. The site is has been well designed and with hedges, trees, planting, green spaces and lakes. The 74 touring pitches are in a separate area, all with 16A electricity and with a choice of hardstanding or grass. Tents are not accepted on this site. Sports activities (with coaching available) include swimming (heated indoor pool with flumes and slides), football, archery and fencing. There is an all-weather multisport court, tennis, basketball, rollerblading, 'Ropeworks', gokarts and much more. Entertainment is staged every evening for all ages in one of three 'Show Bars' and there are several choices for good food and drink.

Facilities

Sanitary facilities are in new 'portacabin' style units. Two children's units, two family shower units, three baby changing units. Facilities for disabled visitors. Washing machines and dryers. Two well stocked supermarkets with bakery, off licence. Gift shop. Sweet shop. Hire shop. Bars. 'Starbucks' coffee bar. Afon Gardens restaurant, Lakeside Inn with Grill menu, Fish and Chips, 'Burger King'. Fast food takeaway. WiFi. Indoor pool with flumes and slides. Sporting facilities and coaching. Entertainment and activity programmes including clubs for children. WiFi (charge). Off site: Llyn peninsula beaches.

Open: March - 2 November.

Directions

From Caernarfon take the A499 to Pwllheli, then the A497 to Pothmadog. Park is on the right, about 3 miles out of Pwllheli. From the Midlands and the South M54 to Telford, A5 past Oswestry and Llangollen. Take A494 to Bala. In Bala turn right for Porthmadog. Turn left at roundabout in Porthmadog, signed Criccieth and Pwllheli. Park is on the left, 3 miles out of Criccieth. O.S.GR: SH427367. GPS: 52.906137, -4.334579

Charges 2010

Contact the park.

Saint Davids

Caerfai Bay Caravan & Tent Park

Caerfai Road, Saint Davids SA62 6QT (Pembrokeshire) T: **01437 720274**. E: info@caerfaibay.co.uk

alanrogers.com/UK5995

About as far west as one can get in Wales, St David's is Britain's smallest city, noted for its Cathedral and Bishops Palace. This cliff-top park in West Wales has direct access to the Pembrokeshire Coastal Path and a magnificent sandy beach is just a few minutes away, down the path from the car park by the site entrance. Altogether there are 105 touring pitches and 45 electric hook-ups (10A). Main access roads are tarmac. The camping area is spread over three open and sloping fields (chocks are often necessary). All have magnificent views over St Brides Bay. The caravan field also has a small number of holiday homes and is closest to reception. The second and third fields are for tents and motorcaravans, almost all on grass with a few hardstandings available.Caerfai Farm Shop is just across the lane (opens end of May), and other shops and services are just a mile. Site lighting is deliberately minimal, so a torch is useful.

Facilities

Three main buildings house the sanitary facilities, one by reception which is heated, contains facilities for disabled visitors and families and a room with sinks, microwave and hot drinks machine. Adjacent a small new block offers 3 unisex cubicles (WC and basin). The third in the tent field (extensively refurbished) includes 4 family rooms. Motorcaravan services. Bicycle storage. Wet suit washing facility and enclosed drying area. Gas. Takeaway (July/Aug). Barbecue stands for hire. Off site: Walk the Pembrokeshire coastal path, visit Ramsey Island Bird and Grey Seal Reserve. Sea fishing 400 yds. Indoor pool and bicycle hire 1 mile. Golf 2 miles. Riding 10 miles. Boat launching 1.5 or 3 miles.

Open: 1 March - 14 November.

Directions

From Haverfordwest take the A487 to St Davids. On passing the city boundary, turn left into lane immediately before the National Park Visitor Centre (site signed), and continue on for 0.75 mile to site entrance on right. O.S.GR: SM759244. GPS: 51.872983, -5.2569

Charges guide

Per unit incl. 2 persons	£ 12.00 - £ 16.00
tent incl. 2 persons	£ 10.00 - £ 14.00
extra person	£ 4.50
child (3-12 yrs)	£ 3.00
electricity	£ 4.00

Discounts for early payment, and for senior citizens in low season.

Saundersfoot

Moreton Farm Leisure Park

Moreton, Saundersfoot SA69 9EA (Pembrokeshire) T: 01834 812016. E: moretonfarm@btconnect.com

alanrogers.com/UK5980

Moreton Farm has been developed in a secluded valley, a 10-20 minutes' walk from Saundersfoot and four miles from Tenby. It provides 30 caravan pitches with 16A electricity (17 with hardstanding) and 30 tent pitches on two sloping, neatly cut grass fields, with 12 pine holiday lodges and four cottages for letting occupying another field. The site is approached under a railway bridge (height 10 ft 9 ins, width across the top 6 ft 6 ins, but with alternative access over the railway line for slightly larger vehicles just possible). There are a few trains during the day, none at night. This is a quiet family site. An attractive lake at the bottom of the valley is home to ducks, geese and chickens (no fishing). Pembroke and Carew castles and a variety of visitor attractions are close.

Facilities

The toilet blocks (which can be heated) are light and airy, providing pre-set hot showers (on payment). Unit for disabled visitors with ramp (shower, toilet and washbasin). Baby bath. Laundry facilities. Fenced, outside clothes drying area. Small shop for basics and gas. Playground. Bicycle hire can be arranged. No dogs or other pets are accepted. Off site: Fishing and riding 1 mile. Golf 4 miles.

Open: 1 March - 31 October.

Directions

From A477 Carmarthen - Pembroke road take A478 for Tenby at Kilgelly. Park is signed on left after 1.5 miles. Watch carefully for sign and park is 0.5 miles up poorly made-up road and under bridge. O.S.GR: SN116050. GPS: 51.711983, -4.727683

Charges guide

Per unit incl. 2 persons	£ 12.00 - £ 15.00
extra person	£ 2.00
electricity	£ 3.00

Talybont-on-Usk

Gilestone Camping & Caravan Park

On A40, Talybont-on-Usk LD3 7JE (Powys) T: 01874 676236. E: gilestonefarm@aol.com

alanrogers.com/UK6045

Only opened in 2006, Gilestone is situated in the Usk valley within a 300-acre arable and beef farm in the Brecon Beacons National Park. It has 100 pitches, 50 for caravans and 50 for tents, all with electricity, plus 22 fully serviced pitches suitable for large units. Unusually the park can provide horse B&B facilities for those who wish to take their horses and ponies on holiday and has direct access to large areas of trekking country. There is a dedicated area for those with tents which has its own toilet facilities. This rural park caters for all ages and has a four acre play area for children, a well stocked Farm Shop selling local fresh produce and hot tubs to relax in after all those strenuous activities. The owners Chris and Geraint Thomas are extremely knowledgeable about the area and can arrange most requests (with a little advance warning). Ready erected tents can be rented on the site, as can bicycles. Llangorse Lake is only three miles away where windsurfing, sailing and scuba lessons are all on offer. Alternatively, you can just enjoy the peace and tranquility of the 300 acres where red kite, herons, buzzards, swans and lapwings are readily seen from the lanes.

Facilities

Toilet and shower facilities in the single new main block also housing reception, the Farm Shop and café, should now be available. Hot tubs to rent. Facilities for disabled visitors. Laundry room. Motorcaravan service area. Shop with local produce (all year). Play area. Fishing. Bicycle hire. Horse B&B. Teepee hire for woodland camping. Nature trail. Rallies welcome. Off site: Four pubs with meals within 5 minutes walk. Lake for watersports 3 miles. Riding 2 miles. Golf 5 miles. Two local Play Barns for children.

Open: All year.

Directions

From Brecon on the A40 follow brown tourism signs along the 40 to new junction. Site is on right after bridge over the river. O.S.GR: SO120231. GPS: 51.901733, -3.286617

Charges guide

Per unit incl. 2 persons and electricity	£ 16.00 - £ 18.00
incl. services	£ 21.00 - £ 25.00
extra person	£ 6.00 - £ 7.00
child (0-8 yrs)	free

Tenby
Trefalun Park

Devonshire Drive, St Florence, Tenby SA70 8RD (Pembrokeshire) T: **01646 657514**. E: **trefalun@aol.com**
alanrogers.com/UK5982

Only four miles from Tenby and the beaches of Carmarthen Bay, Trefalun Park is an open, well laid out campsite with a friendly atmosphere engendered by the owners. The 100 pitches, including ten occupied by caravan holiday homes in their own enclave and 22 seasonal units, are mainly level, although the park has gentle slopes. There are 34 hardstandings, of which 12 are serviced pitches. Except for the tent area, pitches are generously sized and have electricity (10/16A). This park will suit those, particularly families, looking for a quiet holiday and also the more active who favour walking, cycling or watersports. A large fenced recreational area has a variety of adventure type play equipment and a football pitch. A wildlife park is about 600 yards away opposite the turning to Trefalun Park. Pembroke, with its castle is only four miles away and there are many other historic monuments close by.

Facilities

Modern heated toilet block, with some washbasins in cabins. Water to showers and laundry and dishwashing sinks is metered (20p). Separate, fully equipped suite for disabled visitors and families. Separate baby room. Laundry. Play area. Gas sold. Off site: Shop, pub (with food) and outdoor pool 1.5 miles. Fishing, riding and wildlife park 600 yds. Golf 3 miles. Tenby with all town facilities, beach, boat launching and sailing 4 miles.

Open: 16 March - 31 October.

Directions

From the A477 at Sageston (about 4 miles east of Pembroke) turn southeast just to the east of the village on B4318 signed for the Wildlife Park. Trefalun Park is signed to the left after 2.5 miles, opposite the entrance to the Wildlife Park.
GPS: 51.69326, -4.75340

Charges guide

Per pitch	£ 9.50 - £ 15.00
incl. services	£ 11.00 - £ 17.00
'super' pitch	£ 13.00 - £ 19.50

Tenby
Manorbier Country Park

Station Road, Manorbier, Tenby SA70 7SN (Pembrokeshire) T: **01834 871952**
E: **enquiries@countrypark.co.uk alanrogers.com/UK5985**

This area of southwest Wales is quite attractive, with a variety of historic buildings, sandy beaches and an extensive coastal footpath. This park has 103 caravan holiday homes and 28 seasonal units, which leaves only around 22 pitches for tourists. There are seven orderly rows of concrete and gravel hardstanding pitches set into a level grass field; 32 pitches have electric hook-ups (16A), cable TV and a shared water tap, and four are multi-service pitches (electricity, water, waste water, sewerage, TV). Additionally, ten grass pitches are on the opposite side of the car park with electric hook-ups, and four grass pitches at the front of the main field with no services. Cars park away from the caravans on a wide tarmac parking area. A small grassy recreation area is at one end of the touring site, with an adventure playground. The complex offers a bar with family entertainment each evening, a good value restaurant, wellness centre and an indoor pool. Larger units should book in advance and motorhomes over 25 ft. are not accepted.

Facilities

A single building at one end of the car parking area provides all toilet facilities, it can be heated, and has controllable hot showers (on payment), a multi-purpose room suitable for families, babies and disabled campers. Small laundry room and dishwashing sinks outside under cover. Shop. Bar and restaurant. Indoor heated swimming and paddling pools. Jacuzzi. Sauna and steam room, vertical solarium, gym and tennis (all charged). Adventure play area and playground. Dogs are not accepted. Off site: Bicycle hire, boat launching, sailing and beach 1.5 miles. Golf and riding 3 miles. Adjacent garden centre restaurant serves cream teas and Sunday lunches. Fish and chip bar opposite. Manorbier Castle overlooks the sandy beach. Tenby 6 miles.

Open: 1 March - 31 October.

Directions

From Tenby take A4139 towards Pembroke, passing through Penally and Lydstep. At crossroads (Manorbier signed to left) continue straight on following signs to the station. Turn right by Baptist Chapel into Station Road, and continue to site entrance (do not go into Manorbier village). O.S.GR: SS068991.
GPS: 51.657917, -4.794283

Charges guide

Per unit incl. up to 4 persons	£ 16.50 - £ 23.50
extra person	£ 2.00
awning	£ 2.00

Wrexham

The Plassey Leisure Park

Eyton, Wrexham LL13 0SP (Wrexham) T: 01978 780277. E: enquiries@theplassey.co.uk

alanrogers.com/UK6670

The Plassey has been carefully developed over the past 45 years. Originally a dairy farm, the park is set in 247 acres of the Dee Valley and offers an extensive range of activities. It has been divided into discreet areas with pitches around the edges. There are 120 touring pitches with electrical connections (16A), including 30 new fully serviced pitches with hardstanding. Five further areas accommodate 120 seasonal caravans. There is much to do and to look at in the rural setting at the Plassey but it is probably best enjoyed midweek, avoiding the busy Bank Holidays. The Edwardian farm buildings have been tastefully converted to provide a restaurant, coffee shop, health, beauty and hair studio, a small garden centre and 16 different craft and retail units, open all year. Unusually there is also a small brewery on site, producing its own unique Plassey Bitter! In addition to recent landscaping to the park, the pool and the golf clubhouse have been refurbished to provide improved facilities. A member of the Best of British group.

Facilities

Some refurbished toilet facilities are supplemented by a new heated block with individual washbasin cubicles, a room for disabled visitors or families. Laundry. Motorcaravan services. Shop (with gas). Club room with games room for children. Heated indoor pool with sun bed, sauna and new viewing area (charged). Adventure play area. Nine hole golf course. Fishing lakes. Wildlife meadow and countryside footpaths. No bicycles, skateboards or footballs permitted. Winter caravan storage. Off site: Riding 2 miles. Bicycle hire 5 miles.

Open: January - November.

Directions

Follow brown and cream signs for The Plassey from the A483 Chester - Oswestry bypass onto the B5426 and park is 2.5 miles. Also signed from the A528 Marchwiel - Overton road. O.S.GR: SJ349452. GPS: 53.00257, -2.96208

Charges guide

Per unit incl. 2 persons	
and electricity	£ 12.50 - £ 21.50
incl. services	£ 16.00 - £ 28.50
extra person (over 5 yrs)	£ 3.75
dog	£ 2.00

Includes club membership, coarse fishing, badminton and table tennis (own racquets and bats required).

Wrexham

James' Caravan Park

Ruabon, Wrexham LL14 6DW (Wrexham) T: 01978 820148. E: ray@carastay.demon.co.uk

alanrogers.com/UK6680

Open all year, this park has attractive, park-like surroundings with mature trees and neat, short grass. However, edged by two main roads it is subject to some road noise. The old farm buildings and owner's collection of original farm machinery, carefully restored and maintained, add interest. The park has over 40 pitches, some level and some on a slope, with informal siting giving either a view or shade. Electricity (6/10A) is available all over, although a long lead may be useful. Tourist information and a free freezer for ice packs are in the foyer of the toilet block. This is a useful park with easy access from the A483 Wrexham - Oswestry road.

Facilities

The heated toilet block offers roomy showers with a useful rail to help those of advancing age with feet washing. En-suite facilities for visitors with disabilities complete with special 'clos-o-mat' toilet! Motorcaravan service point. Gas available. Off site: The village is a 10 minute walk with a Spar shop, fish and chips, a restaurant, launderette and four pubs. Golf 3 miles.

Open: All year.

Directions

Park is at junction of A483/A539 Llangollen road and is accessible from the west-bound A539. O.S.GR: SJ302434. GPS: 52.98286, -3.04093

Charges guide

Per unit incl. 2 persons	
and electricity	£ 12.00
extra person	£ 2.00
awning	£ 2.00
gazebo	£ 5.00
dog	£ 1.00

No credit cards.

From gentle rolling hil
and rugged coastlines,
to dramatic peaks,
punctuated with beauti
lochs, Scotland is a land
steeped in history that provide
superb opportunities to enjoy wil
untamed and spectacular scenery.

Alan Rogers

Probably the most striking thing about Scotland is the vast areas of uninhabited landscape. Southern Scotland boasts beautiful fertile plains, woodlands and wild sea coasts. It also has a rich heritage with ancient castles, abbeys and grand houses. Further north are the Trossachs with their heather-clad hills, home of Rob Roy, the folk hero. The Highlands and Islands, including Skye, Mull and Islay, have some of the most dramatic landscapes in Europe, dominated by breathtaking mountain ranges, such as Ben Nevis and the Grampians, plus deep glistening lochs: the largest being Loch Ness, where the monster reputedly lives. And lying at the very edge of Europe, the islands of the Inner and Outer Hebrides share a rugged natural beauty, with unspoilt beaches and an abundance of wildlife. The two largest cities, Edinburgh and Glasgow, have their own unique attractions. The capital, Edinburgh, with magnificent architecture, comprises the medieval Old Town and the Georgian New Town, with the ancient castle standing proud in the middle. A short distance to the west, Glasgow has more parks and over 20 museums and galleries, with works by Charles Rennie Mackintosh scattered around the city.

Places of interest

Lowlands: Floors Castle near Kelso; Museum of Scotland and Balmoral Castle in Edinburgh; People's Palace, Burrell Collectic in Pollock Park, Glasgow; Sweetheart Abbe near Dumfries; New Lanark World Heritage Site; Melrose Abbey.

Heart of Scotland: fishing town of Oban; Stirling Castle and Wallace Monument; Loch Lomond; Pitlochry; university town of St Andrews; Aberdeen; Dunfermline Abbey fishing villages of Crail and Anstruther; Famous Grouse Experience in Crieff.

Highlands and Islands: Fort William; Eilean Donan Castle near Dornie; the Cairngorms, Highland Wildlife Part at Kingussie; Inverness; Aviemore; Urquhart Castle near Drumnadrochit; Jacobite Steam Train, operates between Fort William and Mallaig Dunvegan Castle on the Isle of Skye.

Did you know?

Dunfermline Abbey is the final resting place of 22 kings, queens, princes and princesses of Scotland, including Robert the Bruce.

Whales can be seen off the west coast of the Highlands, and the Moray Firth is home to bottle-nosed dolphins.

Arbroath Abbey is the site where Scotland's nobles swore independence from England in 1320.

Since 1861, every day (except on Sundays), the one o'clock gun has boomed out from Edinburgh castle.

Charles Rennie Mackintosh, famous archite and designer, was born in Glasgow in 1868

Eas Coul Aulin near Kylesku in Sutherland Britain's highest waterfall at 200 metres – four times the height of Niagara.

Ben Nevis is the highest mountain in the U

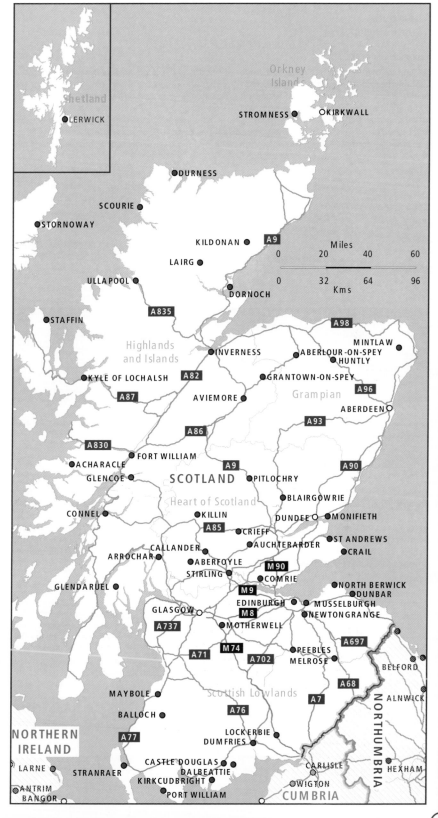

Aberfoyle

Trossachs Holiday Park

Aberfoyle FK8 3SA (Stirling) T: **01877 382614**. E: info@trossachsholidays.co.uk

alanrogers.com/UK7230

Nestling on the side of a hill, three miles south of Aberfoyle, this is an excellent base for touring this famously beautiful area. Lochs Lomond, Ard, Venachar and others are within easy reach, as are the Queen Elizabeth Forest Park and, of course, the Trossachs. Very neat and tidy, there are 45 well laid out and marked pitches arranged on terraces with hardstanding. All have electricity and most also have water, drainage and TV connections. There is also a large area for tents. There are trees between the terraces and lovely views across the valley. The adjoining oak and bluebell woods are a haven for wildlife, with wonderful walks. You will receive a warm welcome from the friendly staff at this well run, family park. A member of the Best of British group.

Facilities

A timber building houses sanitary facilities providing a satisfactory supply of toilets, showers and washbasins, the ladies' area being rather larger, with two private cabins. Laundry room. Well stocked shop (all season). Games room with TV. Play equipment (on gravel). Off site: Golf, boat launching and fishing 3 miles. Sailing 6 miles. Discount scheme arranged with a local leisure centre provides facilities for swimming, sauna, solarium, badminton, tennis, windsurfing, etc.

Open: 1 March - 31 October.

Directions

Park is 3 miles south of Aberfoyle on the A81 road, well signed. O.S.GR: NS544976.
GPS: 56.140133, -4.3555

Charges guide

Per unit incl. 2 persons and electricity	£ 14.00 - £ 20.00
incl. all services	£ 16.00 - £ 22.00
tent pitch incl. 2 persons	£ 14.00 - £ 18.00
extra person	£ 2.00

TROSSACHS HOLIDAY PARK - ABERFOYLE STIRLING FK8 3SA
www.trossachsholidays.co.uk   Tel: 01877 382614 (anytime)

One of the finest Environmental parks on the edge of the National Park
40 Exclusive landscaped Touring Pitches - mostly fully serviced
Holiday Caravans and Lodges For Sale and Hire
• Practical Caravan Top 100 Parks Winner 2006 - 2008 Inclusive • Visit Scotland 5 Star Holiday Park
• 2004 Thistle Awards Customer Care • Park of the Year • Green Tourism Business Scheme Gold Award
• David Bellamy 10 Year Gold Award

Acharacle

Resipole Farm Caravan & Camping Park

Loch Sunart, Acharacle PH36 4HX (Highland) T: **01967 431235**. E: info@resipole.co.uk

alanrogers.com/UK7800

This quiet, open park is marvellously set on the banks of Loch Sunart, eight miles from Strontian, on the Ardnamurchan peninsula. It is a must for anyone seeking peace and tranquillity and really worth the journey. With views across the water and regularly visited by wild deer, Resipole Farm offers a good base for exploring the whole of this scenic area or, more locally, for fishing, boating (launching from the site's own slipway) and walking in the unspoilt countryside. There are 48 level and well drained touring pitches here, 40 with electric hook-ups (10/16A). Tents are sited by the hedges. This is a good location for day trips to Mull via the Lochaline ferry.

Facilities

The central, modern sanitary block can be heated and is kept very clean. Good dishwashing facilities. Excellent provision for visitors with disabilities. Laundry facilities. Motorcaravan service point. Caravan storage. Art gallery and studios. Off site: Riding 5 miles.

Open: Easter or 1 April - 31 October.

Directions

From A82 Fort William road, take Corran ferry located 5 miles north of Ballachulish and 8 miles south of Fort William. Leaving ferry, turn south along the A861. Park is on the north bank of Loch Sunart, 8 miles west of Strontian. Single track road for 8 miles approaching Resipole - care needed. O.S.GR: NM676740.
GPS: 56.710933, -5.720217

Charges guide

Per unit incl. 2 persons	£ 11.00 - £ 13.00
extra person	£ 3.00
child (5-16 yrs)	£ 1.00
serviced pitch incl. electricity	£ 13.00 - £ 15.00
backpackers or cyclists (2 persons)	£ 8.00 - £ 8.50

Aberlour-on-Spey

Aberlour Gardens Caravan & Camping Park

Aberlour-on-Spey AB38 9LD (Moray) T: **01340 871586**. E: Aberlourgardens@aol.com

alanrogers.com/UK7540

This pleasant park is within the large walled garden of the Aberlour Estate on Speyside. The owners have made many improvements to the sheltered, five acre, family run park which provides a very natural setting amidst spruce and Scots pine. Of the 73 level pitches, 35 are for touring units leaving the remainder for holiday homes (two for rent) and seasonal units. All pitches have electrical connections (10A) and nine are 'all-weather' pitches. This is an ideal area for walking, bird watching, salmon fishing and pony trekking or for following the only 'Malt Whisky Trail' in the world, while Aberlour has a fascinating old village shop – a time capsule.

Facilities	Directions
The ladies toilet block has been refurbished. The men's is traditional in style (there are plans for refurbishment) with four large showers. Facilities for visitors with disabilities can also be used as family or baby changing room. Laundry facilities. Motorcaravan service point. Small licensed shop stocking basics and with an information area. Play area. Caravan storage. Off site: Riding 0.5 miles. Swimming and bicycle hire 1 mile. Fishing 1 or 5 miles. Golf 4 miles.

Open: 1 March - 28 December. | Turn off A95 midway between Aberlour and Craigellachie onto unclassified road. Site signed in 500 yds. Vehicles over 10'6" high should use the A941 Dufftown road (site signed). O.S.GR: NJ282432. GPS: 57.47485, -3.1986 |

Charges guide

Per unit incl. 2 persons	£ 14.70 - £ 18.40
tent	£ 11.65 - £ 18.40
extra person (over 5 yrs)	£ 2.00
dog	free
backpacker (per person)	£ 6.70 - £ 7.80

Tel/Fax: 01340 871586
Open: 1st March - 28th December
Tourers, Motorhomes & Campers Always Welcome. Holiday Homes For Sale.
info@aberlourgardens.co.uk

Aberlour Gardens enjoys a beautiful setting within an historic walled garden in the magnificent valley of the river Spey, and is ideally situated in the heart of the Malt Whiskey Trail & for exploring the coast of the Moray Firth to the Mountains of the Cairngorms. So if you are looking just to relax with a stroll by the river or take your bike up a mountain, all is within easy reach.

See website for special offers: www.aberlourgardens.co.uk

Arrochar

Forest Holidays Ardgartan

Ardgartan, Arrochar G83 7AR (Dunbartonshire) T: **01301 702293**. E: fe.holidays@forestry.gsi.gov.uk

alanrogers.com/UK7260

Forest Holidays is a partnership between the Forestry Commission and The Camping & Caravanning Club. Ardgartan is a rugged site in the Argyll Forest Park. Splendidly situated with mountains all around and lovely views of Loch Long, there are lots of sightseeing and activity opportunities. The 175 pitches are in sections which are well divided by grass giving an uncrowded air. Most with hardstanding and marked by numbered posts, they are accessed from hard surfaced roads and 54 have electrical hook-ups. There are additional grass areas for tents. Midges can be a problem in this area of Scotland – go prepared. At the northern end of the Cowal Peninsula, the site is on a promontory on the shores of Loch Long, with good sea fishing and facilities for launching small boats. Walking and climbing, as well as sea and river fishing (permits obtainable locally), are all possible nearby. The site gate is locked 22.00 - 07.30.

Facilities	Directions
The main toilet block is opposite the reception and shop. Refurbished for 2009 it includes facilities for disabled visitors and babies. Launderette. Play equipment (bark surfaces). Raised barbecues are allowed. Bicycle hire. Fishing. Boat launching. Off site: Arrochar village (2 miles) has fuel, general stores and a restaurant.

Open: All year. | From A82 Glasgow - Crianlarich road take A83 at Tarbet signed Arrochar and Cambletown. Site is 2 miles past Arrochar, the entrance on a bend. O.S.GR: NN275030. GPS: 56.188783, -4.781667 |

Charges guide

Per unit incl. 2 persons	£ 10.00 - £ 20.50

Discounts for families, disabled guests and senior citizens.

265

Auchterarder

Auchterarder Caravan Park

Nether Coul, Auchterarder PH3 1ET (Perth and Kinross) T: 01764 663119. E: info@prestonpark.co.uk

alanrogers.com/UK7270

This is a charming small park, purpose designed and landscaped by the owners Stuart and Susie Robertson. In a sheltered position, it is conveniently situated for exploring central Scotland and the Highlands with many leisure activities close at hand (particularly golf) and within walking distance of the village (one mile). The 21 original pitches, all with electricity (6A) and hardstanding, 12 with drainage, are well spaced around the edge of the elongated, level grass park. Marked pitches with grass frontage back on to raised banks which are planted with trees. Further pitches have been developed to one side of the site. There is a trout fishing pond (exclusively for campers) and a woodland walk. A tarmac area at the entrance for late arrivals (with electricity) ensures that no one is disturbed. Also at the entrance, a modern pine chalet blending with the environment houses reception and a small library. There is easy access from the nearby A9 road which does create some background road noise, although it is peaceful at night.

Facilities

Toilet facilities (with key system) include controllable, well equipped hot showers. A toilet for disabled people is provided in both the male and female units. Laundry room with sink and washing machine; an iron can be provided. Fishing. Caravan storage. Off site: Village 1 mile. Golf 1 mile. Bicycle hire and riding 4 miles. The historic cities of Perth and Stirling are less than half an hour's drive away.

Open: All year.

Directions

Park is between the A9 and A824 roads east of Auchterarder village, 2 miles from the main road. Turn on to the B8062 (Dunning) road from the A824. O.S.GR: NN964138. GPS: 56.304333, -3.676167

Charges guide

Per unit incl. up to 4 persons and electricity	£ 14.50
extra person (over 5 yrs)	£ 1.00
awning	£ 1.00

No credit cards.

Aviemore

Forest Holidays Glenmore

Aviemore PH22 1QU (Highland) T: 01479 861271. E: info@forestholidays.co.uk

alanrogers.com/UK7680

Forest Holidays is a partnership between the Forestry Commission and The Camping & Caravanning Club. This site is attractively laid out in a fairly informal style in several adjoining areas connected by narrow part gravel, part tarmac roads, with access to the lochside. One of these areas, the Pinewood Area, is very popular and has 32 hardstandings (some distance from the toilet block). Of the 260 marked pitches on fairly level, firm grass, 122 have electricity (16A). This site with something for everyone would be great for family holidays. The Glenmore Forest Park lies close to the sandy shore of Loch Morlich amidst conifer woods and surrounded on three sides by the impressive Cairngorm mountains. It is conveniently situated for a range of activities, including skiing (extensive lift system), orienteering, hill and mountain walking (way-marked walks), fishing (trout and pike) and non-motorized watersports on the Loch.

Facilities

New toilet and shower blocks. Next to the site is a range of amenities including a well stocked shop (open all year), a café serving a variety of meals and snacks, and a Forestry Commission visitor centre and souvenir shop. Barbecues are not permitted in dry weather. Sandy beach. Off site: The Aviemore centre with a wide range of indoor and outdoor recreation activities including skiing 7 miles. Golf within 15 miles. Fishing and boat trips.

Open: All year.

Directions

Immediately south of Aviemore on the B9152 (not the A9 bypass) take B970 then follow sign for Cairngorm and Loch Morlich. Site entrance is on right past the loch. O.S.GR: NH976097. GPS: 57.167033, -3.694717

Charges guide

Per unit incl. 2 persons	£ 11.00 - £ 25.50
extra person	£ 5.25 - £ 8.25
child	£ 2.75 - £ 4.25

Discounts for families, disabled guests and senior citizens.

www.alanrogers.com for latest campsite news

Balloch

Lomond Woods Holiday Park

Tullichewan, Old Luss Road, Balloch G83 8QP (West Dunbartonshire) T: 01389 755000
E: lomondwoods@holiday-parks.co.uk alanrogers.com/UK7240

A series of improvements over the last few years has made this one of the top parks in Scotland. Almost, but not quite, on the banks of Loch Lomond, this landscaped, well planned park is suitable for both transit or longer stays. Formerly known as Tullichewan Holiday Park, it takes 110 touring units on well spaced, numbered pitches on flat or gently sloping grass. Most have hardstanding, all have electrical connections (10A) and 27 have water and waste water too. Watersport activities and boat trips are possible on Loch Lomond, with a visitor attraction, 'Lomond Shores' opened nearby. This is a well run park, open all year, with very helpful wardens and reception staff.

Facilities

The single large heated, well kept toilet block includes some showers with WCs, baths for ladies, a shower room for disabled visitors and two baby baths. Covered dishwashing sinks. Launderette. Motorcaravan service points. Games room with TV, table tennis and pool table. Playground. Caravan storage. American motorhomes accepted with prior notice. WiFi (charged). Off site: Fishing and boat launching 400 yards. Riding 4 miles. Golf 5 miles. Rail and road connections to Glasgow. Restaurants, bar meals and buses in Balloch (5 minutes).

Open: All year.

Directions

Turn off A82 road 17 miles northwest of Glasgow on A811 Stirling road. Site is in Balloch at southern end of Loch Lomond and is well signed. O.S.GR: NS389816. GPS: 56.00155, -4.592233

Charges guide

Per unit incl. up to 2 persons and electricity	£ 18.00 - £ 22.00
incl. mains services and awning	£ 22.00 - £ 26.00
extra person	£ 2.00
dog	£ 0.50

Blairgowrie

Nether Craig Caravan Park

By Alyth, Blairgowrie PH11 8HN (Perth and Kinross) T: 01575 560204. E: nethercraig@lineone.net
alanrogers.com/UK7280

Nether Craig is a family run touring park, attractively designed and beautifully landscaped, with views across the Strathmore valley to the long range of the Sidlaw hills. The 40 large pitches are accessed from a circular, gravel road; 26 have hardstanding (for awnings too) and 10A electrical connections. The majority are level and there are nine large tent pitches on flat grass. There is a personal welcome for all visitors at the attractive wooden chalet beside the entrance (with a slope for wheelchairs) which doubles as reception and shop providing the necessary essentials, gas and tourist information. A one mile circular woodland walk from the park has picnic benches and a leaflet guide is provided. Otherwise you can just enjoy the peace of the Angus Glens by hill walking, bird watching, fishing or pony trekking. Alyth with its Arthurian connections is only four miles away and Glamis Castle, the childhood home of the Queen Mother, is nearby, as is the beautiful Glenshee and Braemar with its castle.

Facilities

The central, purpose built toilet block is modern, well equipped and maintained, and can be heated. Unit for disabled visitors (entry by key). Separate sinks for dishwashing and clothes are in the laundry room (metered hot water), plus a washing machine, dryer and iron, and clothes line. Shop. Play area. Small football field. Bicycle hire. Caravan storage. Off site: Fishing 2 miles. Riding 4 miles. Golf within 4 miles. Boat launching 6 miles.

Open: 15 March - 31 October.

Directions

From the A926 Blairgowrie - Kirriemuir road, at roundabout south of Alyth join B954 (Glenisla). Follow caravan signs for 4 miles and turn right onto unclassified road (Nether Craig). Park is on left after 0.5 miles. O.S.GR: NO265528. GPS: 56.6614, -3.1998

Charges guide

Per unit incl. 2 persons and electricity	£ 14.00 - £ 16.00
tent per person	£ 7.00
extra person	£ 1.50 - £ 5.00

Callander
The Gart Caravan Park
Stirling Road, Callander FK17 8LE (Perth and Kinross) T: 01877 330002. E: enquiries@theholidaypark.co.uk
alanrogers.com/UK7220

Gart Caravan Park is situated within the Loch Lomond and Trossachs National Park, just a mile from the centre of Callander. Surrounded by mature trees, this attractive, family run park is peaceful and spacious. All is kept in a pristine condition and a very warm welcome awaits on arrival with a superb information pack given to all. The 128 all grass touring pitches are reasonably level, open plan and marked, with electricity (16A), water and drain. Tents or pup tents are not accepted, groundsheets are not permitted. Privately owned caravan holiday homes are located away from the touring section near the river which runs for 200 m. along the park boundary.

Facilities
Modern heated central facilities are immaculate, kept spotlessly clean with toilets and showers, plus extra areas with showers, baby changing and hair washing basins. Separate facilities for disabled visitors. Drive-over motorcaravan service point. Gas sales. No shop on site but a breakfast car arrives at 09.00 with papers and basic provisions. Large adventure play area. Free fishing (not Sundays). Max. two dogs permitted. Off site: Golf and bicycle hire 1 mile. Riding 6 miles. Bus 1 mile.

Open: 1 April - 15 October.

Directions
From the south take M9. Near Stirling, leave at exit 10 and follow A84 through Doune. Park is on the left, 1 mile before Callander town centre. O.S.GR: NN643070. GPS: 56.2365, -4.1891

Charges guide
Per unit incl. services	£ 19.50
awning	£ 2.00
Reduced rates for the over 50s.	

Castle Douglas
Mossyard Caravan Park
Gatehouse of Fleet, Castle Douglas DG7 2ET (Dumfries & Galloway) T: 01557 840226
E: enquiry@mossyard.co.uk alanrogers.com/UK6890

Mossyard is a family run park set within a working farm right beside the sea in a sheltered bay. The park and farmhouse appear together suddenly over the horizon and in the distance as you approach, with some breathtaking views across the Solway where the Galloway Hills and the waters of Fleet Bay meet. There are 37 grass pitches, 12 for caravans and motorcaravans on an elevated area that slopes in parts. The remaining 25 pitches for any unit are on a level field which adjoins the beach but is a little way from the sanitary facilities. Electrical connections (16A) are available to all.

Facilities
Some of the farm buildings around the main farmhouse have been utilised for the toilet facilities, which are of traditional design. Showers are coin-operated (20p). Roomy facilities for disabled visitors can also be used as a family bathroom. Purpose built building with laundry, dishwashing area and information room with freezer and fridge for visitors' use. No shop. Off site: Gatehouse of Fleet with shops, pubs and restaurants 4 miles.

Open: 26 March - 31 October.

Directions
Take A75 road from Dumfries towards Stranraer and park is signed to the left, 4 miles west of Gatehouse of Fleet, about 1 mile down a single track farm road. O.S.GR: NX547518. GPS: 54.840183, -4.26015

Charges guide
Per pitch	£ 12.00 - £ 15.00
electricity	£ 2.00
awning	£ 1.00 - £ 2.00

Castle Douglas
Loch Ken Holiday Park
Parton, Castle Douglas DG7 3NE (Dumfries & Galloway) T: 01644 470282
E: penny@lochkenholidaypark.co.uk alanrogers.com/UK6940

Loch Ken Holiday Park sits right on the shore of the loch, adjacent to the RSPB bird reserve and the Galloway Forest Park – it is a peaceful haven in an area of outstanding beauty. This is a family owned park with 52 touring pitches and 33 caravan holiday homes, ten of which are for rent. The touring pitches, all with 10A electricity, are quite separate and are arranged in a mostly open-plan way on a large, neatly mown grass area beside the water. Some of this area is gently undulating. Mature trees border the park and provide an area for walking dogs.

Facilities
The toilet block is old and fairly basic, butclean. Showers 50p. Facilities for disabled visitors, laundry and dishwashing are also old and in need of refurbishment (planned). Gas supplies. Well stocked shop. Small play area. Bicycles, canoes and dinghies for hire. Boat launching (permit from reception). Fishing (permit). Off site: Bars and restaurants in Castle Douglas, 9 miles. Kirkcudbright 15 miles. Golf and riding 7 miles. Skiing 0.5 miles. Buses stop at the entrance, but are limited.

Open: 1 March - 31 October.

Directions
From Castle Douglas take the A713 north for 7 miles. Site entrance is on left in Parton. O.S.GR: NX688701. GPS: 55.0104, -4.05568

Charges guide
Per unit incl. 2 persons, 2 children under 10 yrs and electricity	£ 14.00 - £ 18.00
tent, no electricity	£ 11.00 - £ 13.00
extra person over 10 yrs	£ 2.00
dog	£ 2.00

Castle Douglas
Barlochan Caravan Park
Palnackie, Castle Douglas DG7 1PF (Dumfries & Galloway) T: 01557 870267. E: info@barlochan.co.uk
alanrogers.com/UK6945

Barlochan Caravan Park is situated on a hillside overlooking the Urr Estuary on the Solway Coast close to Dalbeattie and Castle Douglas, with the small village of Palnackie being a short walk away. Set on terraces, level, marked and numbered, most of the touring and tent pitches are on grass with a limited number of hardstandings available. There are 12 with electrical connections (16A). In addition, 55 mobile homes (five for rent) are positioned on terraces high above the touring areas and screened by mature shrubs and trees. Just to the left of the entrance there is a minigolf course and an adventure play area screened from the park with mature trees.

Facilities

The refurbished sanitary facilities are kept spotlessly clean. Shower cubicles have recently been made larger suitable for wheelchair entry, but if required there is also a separate unit with WC and basin. Fully equipped laundry with outside drying area. Dishwashing under cover. Reception and well stocked shop. Large games/TV room. Off site: Fishing 400 yds. Bicycle hire 6 miles. Golf 7 miles. Riding 10 miles. Beach 10 miles.

Open: Easter - end October.

Directions

From Dumfries take A711 west to Dalbeattie. Go through Dalbeattie for 0.5 miles then bear left at T-junction (Auchencairn). Site is 2 miles on right. O.S.GR: NX819571 GPS: 54.895023, -3.842564

Charges guide

Per unit incl. 2 persons	
and electricity	£ 15.89 - £ 20.95
extra person	£ 1.25 - £ 1.85
dog	£ 2.35

Comrie
Twenty Shilling Wood Caravan Park
Comrie PH6 2JY (Perth and Kinross) T: 01764 670411. E: alowe20@aol.com
alanrogers.com/UK7310

Everyone gets a warm welcome from the Lowe family on arrival at Twenty Shilling Wood. Set amongst 10.5 acres of wooded hillside, this park has a few touring pitches for caravans and motorcaravans (no tents), plus a number of owner-occupied caravan holiday homes. However, with terracing and landscaping, few are visible and flowering trees and shrubs help to hide them. The lowest level is the entrance where there is a late arrivals area and visitor car park. You will be escorted to your pitch. There are just ten level touring pitches on gravel with grass bays between, all with electricity hook-ups (10A).

Facilities

The clean and spacious toilet blocks have some washbasins in cubicles for sexes. No shop but rolls, milk and papers can be ordered at reception. Games room with pool table, table tennis (both free) and lounge area with comfortable seating and well-stocked library. Fenced adventure playground. Entrance barrier (£10 deposit for card). Only two dogs per pitch. Off site: Buses pass the gate. Comrie 1 mile. Golf or fishing within 1 mile, riding or bicycle hire 6 miles. Auchingarrich Wildlife centre 2.5 miles, Loch Earn, 11 miles.

Open: 1 April - 17 October.

Directions

Park is on north side of A85 Crieff - Lochearnmead road, about 0.75 miles west of B827 junction, 0.5 miles west of Comrie. O.S.GR: NN762222. GPS: 56.375217, -4.0065

Charges guide

Per unit incl. 2 persons, electricity	£ 16.00
extra person (over 2 yrs)	£ 1.75
dog (max. 2)	free
awning (rock pegs required)	£ 1.50

Connel
Oban Camping & Caravanning Club Site
Barcaldine, By Connel PA37 1SG (Argyll and Bute) T: 01631 720348
alanrogers.com/UK7810

Owned by the Camping and Caravanning Club, this site at Barcaldine, 12 miles north of Oban, is a small, intimate site taking 75 units. Arranged within the old walled garden of Barcaldine House, the walls give it some protection from the wind and make it quite a sun trap. There are 23 level, fairly small pitches with hardstanding and 52 electrical hook-ups (16A). (It can be wet underfoot in bad weather). Being a small site, it has a very cosy feel to it, due no doubt to the friendly welcome new arrivals receive. Unusually for a club site there is a lounge bar selling very reasonably priced meals most evenings.

Facilities

The central toilet block can be heated and is kept very clean with free hot showers, hair dryers and plenty of washbasins and WCs. Excellent unit for disabled visitors. Motorcaravan service point. Small shop open a few hours each day for basic provisions and gas. Small play area with safety base. WiFi. Off site: Sea Life Centre 2 miles. Bus hourly at gate.

Open: 2 April - 2 November.

Directions

Entrance is off A828 road on south side of Loch Creran, 6 miles north of Connel Bridge. From the south, go past Barcaldine House' site is 300 yards on right. O.S.GR: NM966420. GPS: 56.5265, -5.309933

Charges guide

Per person	£ 5.65 - £ 8.35
child (6-18 yrs)	£ 2.50 - £ 2.60
non-member pitch fee	£ 6.60

269

Crail
Sauchope Links Park
Crail KY10 3XJ (Fife) T: 01333 450 460. E: info@sauchope.co.uk
alanrogers.com/UK7285

Sauchope Links Park is a member of the Largo Leisure Parks group and has a good range of facilities on offer, notably a heated swimming pool, an indoor recreation room and a play area for children. The site's location is very attractive with miles of rocky shore to be explored. Pitches here are grassy and of a good size. A number of fully serviced pitches are available and also hardstandings. Alternatively, a number of mobile homes and micro lodges (small wooden chalets) are available for rent. The village of Crail, a short walk from Sauchope Links Park, is the most easterly of Fife's fishing ports. It has an impressive history and one of the finest harbours in the area. Fresh fish and shellfish, including lobster and crab, is on sale at the harbour for you to prepare yourself, or should you wish to dine out, the local restaurants and hotels all offer seafood dishes from local produce. It is a well kept, unspoilt village with steep, narrow streets leading down to the quaint old harbour. Crail also boasts a small stretch of sandy beach, popular with sunbathers, swimmers and canoeists alike.

Facilities

Small shop. Games room. Play areas. Tourist information. Mobile homes and other accommodation for rent. Off site: Top class golf (Crail golf club is the seventh oldest in the world and the Royal and Ancient club at St Andrews needs little introduction). Walking and cycle tracks. Fishing. Riding. Scone Palace. Craigtoun Country Park.

Open: 21 March - 31 October.

Directions

Approaching from St Andrews on the A918, on entering Crail at a sharp right hand corner, turn left down an unclassified road. Site is signed 400 yards on right. Follow signs to the site which is down by the sea. O.S.GR: NO620078. GPS: 56.261606, -2.612724

Charges guide

Per unit	£ 14.00 - £ 25.00

Largo Leisure Parks

Largo Leisure Ltd is a group of four Holiday Parks situated in the Fife and Perthshire areas of Scotland. We can offer you a variety of holidays, utilising the diverse and original facilities and stunning natural surroundings our parks offer

So whether you are looking for a base for your own touring caravan, campervan or tent, or if you wish to enjoy the unique experience that our Micro Lodges, Wigwams, Yurts and our Five Star static holiday homes have to provide, you will be sure to find it at one of Largo Leisures' Holiday Parks

Please contact any of the parks directly or for further information please see our website at www.largoleisure.co.uk

Braidhaugh Park, Crieff, Perthshire. 01764 652951 info@braidhaugh.co.uk
Letham Feus Park, Largo, Fife. 01333 351900 info@lethamfeus.co.uk
Sauchope Links Park, Crail, Fife 01333 450460 info@sauchope.co.uk
Loch Tay Highland Lodges, Killin Perthshire. 01567 820323 info@lochtay-vacations.co.uk

Crieff
Braidhaugh Holiday Park
South Bridgend, Crieff PH7 4DH (Perth and Kinross) T: 01764 652951. E: info@braidhaugh.co.uk
alanrogers.com/UK7275

Braidhaugh is a member of the Largo Leisure Parks group and is situated on the banks of the River Earn among the scenic surroundings of Perthshire. There are 25 touring pitches, all with electricity. The site is well located for exploring Central Scotland, as well as being within walking distance of restaurants, shops, places of interest and many sporting facilities. The Earn is renowned for its salmon and trout fishing and permits can be purchased from the reception. Other on-site amenities include a games room with TV. For younger children, there is an outdoor play area and the public play ground next to the park provides a larger play area and space for ball games. The small shop is well stocked and provides all the essentials (including morning papers and fresh bread rolls).The beautiful countryside surrounding the park offers many country walks in all directions and this is also excellent mountain biking terrain. A range of accommodation is for rent here including attractive camping cabins, micro lodges and yurts.

Facilities

Small shop. Games room. Play areas. Fishing. Tourist information. Mobile homes and other accommodation for rent. Off site: Top class golf (courses at Muthill, Crieff and Comrie). Walking and cycle tracks. Fishing. Riding. Leisure centre.

Open: All year.

Directions

Approaching from Perth, drive through Crieff and turn left onto the A822 (Stirling). At the bottom of the hill cross a bridge over the River Earn. Turn right straight after the bridge and take the first right to enter park. O.S.GR: NN855209. GPS: 56.366771, -3.853455

Charges guide

Per unit	£ 19.50 - £ 23.00

Dalbeattie

Glenearly Caravan Park

Dalbeattie DG5 4NE (Dumfries & Galloway) T: **01556 611393**. E: **enquiries@glenearlycaravanpark.co.uk**
alanrogers.com/**UK6870**

Glenearly is owned and managed by Mr and Mrs Jardine. Rurally located, it has been tastefully developed from farmland into a touring and mobile home, all year park. There are 39 marked, open pitches, all with 16A electrical connections (and TV), most on hardstandings. Seasonal units use some pitches. Walls and shrubs divide the touring section from the caravan holiday homes (two for rent), with mature trees around the perimeter. There are attractive views over the hills and forest of Barhill and buzzards, yellow wagtails, woodpeckers and goldfinch are some of the birds that can be seen, along with the park's own donkeys and ponies.

Facilities

Situated in the centre of the touring area, the toilets and showers are fitted out to a high standard. Unit for disabled visitors or families. Laundry room with washing machines and dryer and an outside drying area. Large games room. Play area. Off site: Shops, pubs, restaurants, etc. at Dalbeattie. Bicycle hire at Mabie Forest just 3 miles from Dumfries on the A710.

Open: All year.

Directions

From Dumfries take A711 towards Dalbeattie. Six miles beyond Beeswing, after Edingham Farm sign, park is signed with entrance on right (by bungalow). O.S.GR: NX834626. GPS: 54.944867, -3.822283

Charges guide

Per unit incl. 2 persons and electricity	£ 15.75 - £ 17.75
extra person (over 5 yrs)	£ 2.00
animal	free

Dalbeattie

Sandyhills Bay Leisure Park

Sandyhills, Dalbeattie DG5 4NY (Dumfries & Galloway) T: **01387 780257**. E: **info@sandyhills-bay.co.uk**
alanrogers.com/**UK6880**

Sandyhills Bay is a small, quiet park beside a sheltered, sandy beach. Reception is on the left through a car park used by visitors either walking the hills or enjoying the beach. Beyond is a large flat camping area, above which, divided by a tree lined hedge, are 60 pitches, half taken by mobile homes situated around the perimeter. The 30 touring pitches, 28 with electrical connection (16A) are in the centre of the all grassed flat area and wigwams are available to hire. This is an excellent family park, with the beach and a children's play area at the site, whilst up the hill next to the park is an 18-hole golf course where you can enjoy a bar meal in the clubhouse.

Facilities

The sanitary facilities are of traditional design, in one central block to the side of the touring area. Laundry room (tokens from reception). Shop and small takeaway. New adventure play area by the beach. Visitors can also use the facilities at Brighouse Bay, the largest park in the Gillespie Group. Barrier at entrance and beach car park (returnable deposit). Off site: Clifftop walk from Sandyhills to Rockcliffe 10 miles. Pleasant drive to Rockcliffe and Kippford (sailing centre).

Open: Easter - 31 October.

Directions

From Dumfries take A710 Solway coast road (about 16 miles). Site is on left just after signs for Sandyhills. O.S.GR: NX890549. GPS: 54.879017, -3.731033

Charges guide

Per unit incl. 2 persons and electricity	£ 16.40 - £ 21.70
extra person	£ 1.95
child (4-15 yrs)	£ 1.15

Dornoch

Pitgrudy Caravan Park

Poles Road, Dornoch IV25 3HY (Highland) T: **01862 821253**
alanrogers.com/**UK7700**

In a rural situation, Pitgrudy has superb views over the Dornoch Firth and the Ross-shire hills. There are 40 touring pitches for caravans, motorcaravans or tents, mostly on slightly sloping grass and with electrical connections (10A). A few have hardstanding (still on a slope) and six are fully serviced (drinking water, waste water disposal point and electricity). At the top of the park are 35 caravan holiday homes, of which 25 are privately owned. The whole park is on immaculately tended grass with tarmac roads. The pleasant little town of Dornoch is less than a mile away with shops, restaurants, plus the cathedral.

Facilities

Sanitary facilities are in a modern, superior Portacabin-style unit which is very clean and well equipped. Laundry with washing machine, dryer and iron. Dishwashing sinks. Gas supplies. Off site: Safe sandy beach 1 mile. The area is good for walking and golf (there are 7 courses within 15 miles of the park). Fishing 1 mile, bicycle hire or boat launching 3 miles, riding 5 miles.

Open: 25 April - 30 September.

Directions

At the war memorial in Dornoch, turn north (park signed) on the B9168. Park is 0.5 miles on the right (45 miles north of Inverness). O.S.GR: NH795911. GPS: 57.88408, -4.03965

Charges guide

Per unit incl. 2 persons	£ 7.50 - £ 12.00
extra person	£ 0.75 - £ 1.50
awning	£ 1.50
No credit cards.	

271

Dumfries
Park of Brandedleys

Crocketford, Dumfries DG2 8RG (Dumfries & Galloway) T: 01387 266700. E: brandedleys@holgates.com
alanrogers.com/UK6930

Brandedleys is a first-class park providing pitches for some 75 caravans and a limited number of tents, plus 55 self-contained caravan holiday homes in three or four flat and variably sloping fields with tarmac access roads, 15 for rent. It has excellent facilities and amenities. Caravan pitches are on lawns or terraced hardstandings, many with a pleasant outlook across a loch. All have electrical connections (10A) and 21 pitches also have water and drainage. Improvements continue with more serviced pitches. The heated indoor pool adjacent to the bar/restaurant is open all season with changing room and a sauna. The bar and licensed restaurant are open for dinner with full menus at reasonable prices and a patio area overlooking Auchenreoch Loch. Walks on the open moors or forest and beautiful sandy beaches 12 miles away from this popular, quality park.

Facilities

The main heated toilet block has been extensively modernised with clean, well-appointed shower cubicles with toilet and washbasin (just one for men), in addition to the normal provision. Bathroom for disabled visitors. Baby room. Covered dishwashing sinks. A second block is in the lower field, also with laundry and dishwashing facilities. Bar and restaurant. Takeaway food to order (18.00-21.30). Swimming pool. All-weather tennis courts, outdoor badminton court. Play area. Games room, pool table and air-hockey table. Off site: Riding, fishing 1.5 miles. Golf 6 miles. Bicycle hire 9 miles. Beach 12 miles.

Open: All year.

Directions

Park is 9 miles from Dumfries on the south side of the A75 Dumfries - Stranraer road, just west of the village of Crocketford. O.S.GR: NX830725. GPS: 55.032767, -3.831633

Charges guide

Per unit incl. 2 persons and electricity	£ 16.25 - £ 21.55

No single sex groups.

Explore the surrounding countryside, the Solway Coast or just take time out to relax and unwind.

Restaurant, bar, indoor pool and sauna.

Touring and camping pitches, holiday homes available to hire or buy.

The Park of Brandedleys
Crocketford DG2 8RG.
Tel. 01387 266 700 **AA**

visit us online at
www.brandedleys.co.uk

Dumfries
Southerness Holiday Village

Southerness, Dumfries DG2 8AZ (Dumfries & Galloway) T: 01387 880256
E: enquiries@parkdeanholidays.co.uk alanrogers.com/UK6875

Set beside a two-mile stretch of sandy beach, at the foot of the beautiful Galloway Hills, is Southerness Holiday Village. Part of the Parkdean Group, it is a large park with the main emphasis on caravan holiday homes. However, there are also 100 open-plan pitches for caravans, motorcaravans and tents. Set away from the static units, these are divided into two areas, some on level hardstanding with water connection, others on grass and all with 16A electrical connections. The light and airy reception office displays local information including a weekly 'What's On' programme as the main leisure complex is located a short walk from the touring area.

Facilities

A modern toilet block provides en-suite facilities throughout (key entry). Well maintained, it is kept very clean by on-site wardens. Excellent unit for disabled visitors. Well equipped laundry. Shop. Bar with large TV. Bistro, takeaway and coffee shop. Indoor swimming pool. Indoor soft play area. Amusement arcade. Bowling (charge). Comprehensive evening entertainment programme in the Sunset Showbar. Note: All venues are non-.smoking. Outdoor adventure play area. Crazy golf. Nature trails. Off site: Golf course adjacent. Fishing 2 miles. Bus from outside gate.

Open: Before Easter - 31 October.

Directions

From Dumfries take A710 Solway Coast road for about 10 miles. Sign for Holiday Village is on the left. O.S.GR: NX974545. GPS: 54.87613, -3.60037

Charges guide

Per unit incl. up to 8 persons	£ 8.00 - £ 22.00
incl. services	£ 10.00 - £ 26.00
dog	£ 2.00

Dunbar

Belhaven Bay Caravan & Camping Park

Belhaven Bay, West Barns, Dunbar EH42 1TU (East Lothian) T: **01368 865956**
E: **belhaven@meadowhead.co.uk alanrogers.com/UK7065**

Located in the John Muir Country Park, Belhaven Bay Caravan Park is just one mile from the historic town of Dunbar, where the ancient castle ruin stands guard over the town's twin harbours. This is an excellent family park with easy access to the beach and to the clifftop trail which has spectacular views capturing the beauty of the countryside and seascapes. The park's 67 caravan holiday homes (seven for rent) are located quite separately from the touring and tent areas. These are surrounded by mature trees and are arranged in large open bays. There are 27 reasonably level, mostly grass touring pitches with electricity connections (10A). Two separate areas accommodate 25 pitches for tents. There is much to see nearby with Dunbar's Lifeboat and underground museums, golf courses, a local smokery and the Belhaven Brewery. Attractions for children include the John Muir Country Park, Lauderdale Park and a tropical leisure pool. During the daytime some train noise may be heard on the park.

Facilities

Facilities are central and include a unit for disabled visitors. Laundry room. Motorcaravan service point. Reception also has a small shop and tourist information. Cyber Café and WiFi internet access. Play area and ball game area. Off site: Golf 1 mile. Riding and boat launching 2 miles. Bus stop at entrance.

Open: 13 March - 31 October.

Directions

From the A1 (north or south) exit at the Thistley Cross roundabout west of Dunbar. Park is about 1 mile down the A1087 towards Dunbar. O.S.GR: NT655784. GPS: 55.996767, -2.545117

Charges guide

Per unit incl. 2 persons	£ 13.75 - £ 23.50
extra person (over 5 yrs)	£ 2.00
tent, 2 persons with car	£ 7.00 - £ 9.00
dog	£ 2.50

Durness

Sango Sands Oasis Caravan & Camping Site

Durness via Lairg IV27 4PZ (Highland) T: **01971 511726**. E: **keith.durness@btinternet.com**
alanrogers.com/UK7735

Sango Sands Oasis is a quiet, ten acre site overlooking the beautiful Sango Bay, a Blue Flag beach. The site was established by the family in 1978 and they have worked hard improving the facilities over the years. There are 82 pitches for tents and touring caravans, 48 with electricity hook-ups (16A). The land is well drained and fairly level. It is possible to see whales, porpoise, dolphins and seals from the site plus a variety of sea birds which nest nearby. An ideal area for walkers, including the less adventurous, there are numerous marked paths and there is an excellent variety of angling, from rivers to the sea. The nearby Durness golf course with its superb views welcomes visitors. Smoo Cave with the waterfall down into the dramatic tidal gorge is close by and worth seeing also it is possible to visit Cape Wrath. A good value café, bar and licensed restaurant serves home cooked meals and malt whiskies and Scottish beers. There are occasional dances or discos in the bar and a TV.

Facilities

Traditional toilet and shower blocks are lit at night but a torch may be useful. Free showers with curtains. Showers and toilets are separate. With the beach so close don't be surprised to find sand in the showers. En-suite facilities for disabled visitors. Laundry with sinks, washing machines, dryers, irons and boards. Campers kitchen with cooking rings. Café, bar and licensed restaurant. TV. Games room with pool and darts. Off site: Two grocery stores, post office, ATM, petrol, diesel and gas supplies in the village. Nearby Visitor Centre with extensive information on the area. Golf 2 km. Boat launching 3 km.

Open: All year.

Directions

From Thurso take the North Coast road (A836 as far as Tongue, where it continues on as the A838 to Durness). Site is on the right as you go through the village. From Ullapool follow A835 north to Ledmore Junction and turn left on the A837. After 8 miles turn right onto the A894 and continue to Laxford Bridge. Turn left on A838. Durness is 19 miles further on this road. Site is on the left going through the village. O.S.GR: NC420668. GPS: 58.56449, -4.74221

Charges guide

Per person	£ 5.50
child (5-15 yrs)	£ 1.50 - £ 3.00
electricity	£ 3.00

Edinburgh

Linwater Caravan Park

West Clifton, East Calder, Edinburgh EH53 0HT (West Lothian) T: 0131 333 3326. E: linwater@supanet.com

alanrogers.com/UK7045

This delightful small family run park is set in the countryside but is still close to the city of Edinburgh. The park is level and the 60 large touring pitches are a mixture of grass and hardstanding; 49 have 16A electricity connections. Parts of the park are screened off by trees and fences. Two sides are sheltered by trees and shrubs and one side is open with views over fields. With just the occasional sound of aircraft from the airport, it is difficult to believe that you are so close to a major city. Linwater is a useful park for visiting Edinburgh and areas outside the city. The reception area has a wealth of information on places to visit. Just four miles down the road is a 'park and ride' scheme and the purchase of a Day Saver ticket is a cheap way to get into Edinburgh and to explore the area. The Falkirk Wheel, houses, castles and gardens are all within easy reach.

Facilities	Directions
The modern and well maintained heated sanitary block has private cabins. Facilities for disabled visitors. Laundry. Gas supplies. Milk, bread and newspapers to order (by 21.00 for the next morning). Home produced free range eggs and bacon from reception (and strawberries in season). Sand pit. Three timbertents for hire. Off site: Fishing 1 mile.	From the A720 Edinburgh bypass, leave at sign for Wilkieston on the A7. In Wilkieston turn right at traffic lights (park signed). Continue to next sign indicating left and site 1 mile further on the right. O.S.GR: NT102697. GPS: 55.91104, -3.43588

Open: 13 March - 1 November.

Charges guide

Per unit incl. 2 persons	£ 12.00 - £ 15.00
tent incl. 2 persons	£ 10.00 - £ 13.00
extra person	£ 3.00
child (5-18 yrs)	£ 1.50

Edinburgh

Edinburgh Caravan Club Site

35-37 Marine Drive, Edinburgh EH4 5EN (Edinburgh) T: 01313 126874

alanrogers.com/UK7050

Situated as it is on the northern outskirts and within easy reach of the city of Edinburgh, this large, busy Caravan Club site (open to non-members) provides an ideal base for touring. Enter the site through rather grand gates to find the visitors' car park and reception to the left. There are 147 large flat pitches (103 hardstandings, 12 with water tap and waste water disposal) with 16A electricity hook-ups and TV aerial and provision for 50 tents in a separate field (hook-ups available) with a covered cooking shelter and bicycle stands close by. As the bushes planted around the site mature, there will be shade. The nearest hotel/restaurant is under a mile away, Royal Yacht Britannia and many other attractions in the city, Firth of Forth bridge about two miles.

Facilities	Directions
Two heated, well kept toilet blocks provide washbasins in cubicles, hair and hand dryers, an en-suite room for campers with disabilities, plus a baby and toddler room with child-size facilities. Each block houses a dishwashing and vegetable preparation area, and a laundry. Drying room. No shop, but milk, bread, and newspapers can be ordered, with ice creams and gas from reception. Fenced play area. Boules. Dog walk in the only natural wood in Edinburgh (part of the site). WiFi internet access. Off site: Bicycle hire nearby. Health club (with internet access) 400 yds – ask at site for introduction card.	Turn right off A720 at Gogar roundabout at end of bypass signed City Centre, A8). Shortly turn left on to A902 (Forth Road Bridge), then right onto A90. At Blackhall junction traffic lights fork left into Telford Road (A902). At Crewe Toll roundabout turn left (B9085) and at T-junction (after bridge) turn right at traffic lights towards Leith, A901. Turn left at traffic lights (Silverknowes, Davidson's Mains). In half a mile at roundabout turn right into Marine Drive. Site is half a mile on the left. O.S.GR: NT212768. GPS: 55.97755, -3.2645

Open: All year.

Charges guide

Per person	£ 4.50 - £ 6.00
child (5-16 yrs)	£ 1.50 - £ 2.45
pitch incl. electricity (non-member)	£ 11.70 - £ 14.55

Tent campers apply to site.

Edinburgh
Mortonhall Caravan & Camping Park
38 Mortonhall Gate, Frogston Road East, Edinburgh EH16 6TJ (Edinburgh) T: 0131 664 1533
E: mortonhall@meadowhead.co.uk alanrogers.com/UK6990

Mortonhall Park makes a good base to see the historic city of Edinburgh and buses to the City leave from the park entrance every ten minutes (parking in Edinburgh is not easy). Although only four miles from the city centre, Mortonhall is in quiet mature parkland, in the grounds of the Mortonhall estate, and easy to find with access off the bypass. There is room for 250 units mostly on numbered pitches on a slight slope with nothing to separate them, but marked by jockey wheel points. Over 180 places have electricity (10/16A), several with hardstanding, water and drainage as well, and there are many places for tents. The park is very popular but only part is reserved and tourists arriving early may find space. An attractive courtyard development houses a lounge bar and restaurant, open all year and to all, with good value meals in pleasant surroundings. There are mobile homes (20) and wooden family camping cabins (wigwams) for rent.

Facilities
Two modern toilet blocks with outside, but covered dishwashing sinks, but the only cabins are in the third excellent facility at the top of the park, which has eight unisex units incorporating shower, washbasin and WC. The courtyard area provides further basic facilities and Portacabin-type units are added for the high season to serve the large number of tents. Facilities for disabled visitors. Laundry room with washing machines and dryer. Motorcaravan services. Bar/restaurant. Self-service shop (all season). Games and TV rooms. Play area. Internet access. Late arrivals area with hook-ups. Torches useful in early and late season. Security lockers. Internet access at reception (£1 per half an hour). WiFi internet access (£5 per day). Off site: Bus from site gate. Golf courses and driving range 2 miles. Riding 2 miles. Bicycle hire 4 miles.

Open: 20 March - 4 January.

Directions
Park is well signed south of the city, 5 minutes from A720 city bypass. Take the Mortonhall exit from the Straiton junction and follow camping signs. Entrance road is alongside the Klondyke Garden Centre. O.S.GR: NT262686. GPS: 55.902889, -3.181705

Charges guide
Per unit incl. 2 persons and electricity	£ 13.75 - £ 28.50
tent pitch (4 persons)	£ 11.75 - £ 22.00
extra person (5 yrs and over)	£ 2.50
dog	£ 3.00

Fort William

Glen Nevis Caravan & Camping Park

Glen Nevis, Fort William PH33 6SX (Highland) T: **01397 702191**. E: camping@glen-nevis.co.uk

alanrogers.com/UK7830

Just outside Fort William in a most attractive and quiet situation with views of Ben Nevis, this spacious park is used by those on active pursuits as well as sightseeing tourists. It comprises eight quite spacious fields, divided between caravans, motorcaravans and tents (steel pegs required). It is licensed for 250 touring caravans but with no specific tent limits. The large touring pitches, many with hardstanding, are marked with wooden fence dividers, 174 with 13A electricity and 100 also have water and drainage. The park becomes full in the peak months but there are vacancies each day. If reception is closed (possible in low season) you site yourself. There are regular security patrols at night in busy periods. The park's own modern restaurant and bar with good value bar meals is a short stroll from the park, open to all. A well managed park with bustling, but pleasing ambience, watched over by Ben Nevis. Around 1,000 acres of the Glen Nevis estate are open to campers to see the wildlife and explore this lovely area.

Facilities

The four modern toilet blocks with showers (extra showers in two blocks); and units for visitors with disabilities. An excellent block in Nevis Park (one of the eight camping fields) has some washbasins in cubicles, showers, further facilities for disabled visitors, a second large laundry room and dishwashing sinks. Motorcaravan service point. Shop (Easter - mid Oct), barbecue area and snack bar (May - mid Sept). Play area on bark. Off site: Pony trekking, golf and fishing near.

Open: 15 March - 31 October.

Directions

Turn off A82 to east at roundabout just north of Fort William following camp sign. O.S.GR: NN124723. GPS: 56.804517, -5.073917

Charges guide

Per person	£ 1.60 - £ 2.50
child (5-15 yrs)	£ 0.80 - £ 1.30
pitch incl. awning	£ 4.40 - £ 12.00
serviced pitch plus	£ 2.00 - £ 3.00

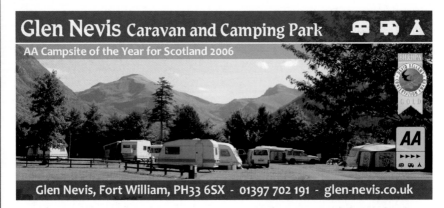

Glen Nevis Caravan and Camping Park

AA Campsite of the Year for Scotland 2006

Glen Nevis, Fort William, PH33 6SX - 01397 702 191 - glen-nevis.co.uk

Fort William

Linnhe Lochside Holidays

Corpach, Fort William PH33 7NL (Highland) T: **01397 772376**. E: relax@linnhe-lochside-holidays.co.uk

alanrogers.com/UK7850

This quiet well run park has a very peaceful situation overlooking Loch Eil, and it is beautifully landscaped with wonderful views. There are individual pitches with hardstanding for 65 touring units (12 seasonal) on terraces leading down to the water's edge. They include 32 with electricity connection (16A), water and drainage, plus 30 with electricity only (10A). A separate area on the lochside takes 15 small tents (no reservation). There are also 60 caravan holiday homes and 14 centrally heated pine chalets for hire. Fishing is free on Loch Eil and you are welcome to fish from the park's private beach or bring your own boat and use the slipway and dinghy park.

Facilities

Toilet facilities are excellent, heated in the cooler months and include baths (£1). Dishwashing room. First class laundry and separate outdoor clothing drying room (charged per night). Self-service, licensed shop (end May - end Sept). Gas supplies. Barbecue area. Toddlers' play room and two well equipped play areas on safe standing. Large motorhomes are accepted but it is best to book first. Caravan storage. Up to two dogs per pitch are accepted. Off site: Bicycle hire 2.5 miles. Riding and golf 5 miles.

Open: 20 March - 31 October.

Directions

Park entrance is off A830 Fort William - Mallaig road, 1 mile west of Corpach. O.S.GR: NN072772. GPS: 56.847817, -5.16025

Charges guide

Per person	£ 2.00
pitch	£ 11.00 - £ 14.50
tent	£ 7.50 - £ 10.50
dog (max. 2, not on tent pitches)	£ 1.00
Seasonal rates available.	

Glencoe

Invercoe Caravan & Camping Park

Invercoe, Glencoe PH49 4HP (Argyll and Bute) T: **01855 811210**. E: **holidays@invercoe.co.uk**

alanrogers.com/UK7790

On the edge of Loch Leven, surrounded by mountains and forest, Iain and Lynn Brown are continually developing this attractively located park in its magnificent historical setting. It provides 63 pitches for caravans, motorcaravans or tents on level grass (can be a bit wet in bad weather) with gravel access roads (some hardstandings). You choose your own numbered pitch, those at the loch side being very popular. The only rules imposed are necessary for safety because the owners prefer their guests to feel free and enjoy themselves. This is a park you will want to return to again and again. There is much to do for the active visitor with hill walking, climbing, boating, pony riding and sea loch or fresh water fishing in this area of outstanding natural beauty.

Facilities

The well refurbished toilet block can be heated. Excellent laundry facilities with drying room. New large under-cover eating area. Motorcaravan service point comprising multi-drainage point, fresh water, dustbins, and chemical disposal point. Shop (Easter - end Oct). Play area with swings. Fishing. New foreshore hardstanding with slipway. WiFi. Off site: The village with pub and restaurant is within walking distance. Visitors' Centre at Glencoe 2 miles. Bicycle hire 2 miles. Golf 3 miles.

Open: All year.

Directions

Follow A82 Crianlarich - Fort William road to Glencoe village and turn onto the B863; park is 0.5 miles along, well signed. O.S.GR: NN098594.
GPS: 56.686567, -5.105983

Charges guide

Per unit incl. 2 persons and electricity	£ 19.00 - £ 22.00
extra person	£ 3.00
child (3-15 yrs)	£ 1.00

Senior citizens less £1 per person outside July/Aug.

INVERCOE CARAVAN and CAMPING PARK
GLENCOE

A family owned park set amidst spectacular scenery on the shores of Loch Leven. An ideal base for exploring the West Highlands. The park has excellent toilets and wash-up facilities & fully serviced laundrette. Level grassy and hard standing pitches with ample hook-ups available. The park is a short 5 minute stroll from the village of Glencoe. Open all year. Won Best Park in Scotland 2002.

Telephone: 01855 811 210 Email: holidays@invercoe.co.uk www.invercoe.co.uk

Glendaruel

Glendaruel Caravan Park

Glendaruel PA22 3AB (Argyll and Bute) T: **01369 820267**. E: **mail@glendaruelcaravanpark.co.uk**

alanrogers.com/UK7860

Glendaruel is in South Argyll, in the area of Scotland bounded by the Kyles of Bute and Loch Fyne, yet is less than two hours by road from Glasgow and serviced by ferries from Gourock and the Isle of Bute. There is also a service between Tarbert and Portavadie. Set in the peaceful wooded gardens of the former Glendaruel House in a secluded glen surrounded by the Cowal hills, it makes an ideal centre for touring this beautiful area. The park takes 35 units on numbered hardstandings with electricity connections (10A), plus 15 tents, on flat oval meadows bordered by over 50 different varieties of mature trees. In a separate area are 28 privately owned holiday homes and two for rent.

Facilities

The toilet block is ageing but it is kept very neat and tidy and can be heated. Washing machine and dryer. A covered area has picnic tables for use in bad weather and dishwashing sinks. Shop (hours may be limited in low season). Gas available. Games room with pool table, table tennis and video games. Behind the laundry is a children's play centre for under 12s and additional play field. Fishing. Torches advised. Off site: Sea fishing and boat slipway 5 miles, adventure centre (assault courses, abseiling and rafting) and sailing school close. Golf 12 miles.

Open: 28 March - 26 October.

Directions

Entrance is off A886 road 13 miles south of Strachur. Alternatively take ferry service from Gourock to Dunoon, then B836 which joins A886 about 4 miles south of the park - not recommended for touring caravans. Do not use Sat Nav as this takes you along a very narrow back road and there is no entrance from here. Note: the park has discount arrangements with Western Ferries so contact the park before making arrangements (allow 7 days for postage of tickets). O.S.GR: NS001865. GPS: 56.033967, -5.212833

Charges guide

Per person	£1.50 - £ 3.00
pitch incl. electricity	£ 10.00

Special weekly rates and senior citizens' discount outside July/Aug.

Grantown-on-Spey

Grantown-on-Spey Caravan Park

Seafield Avenue, Grantown-on-Spey PH26 3JQ (Highland) T: **01479 872474**
E: warden@caravanscotland.com **alanrogers.com/UK7670**

John Fleming takes care of this excellent park. Peacefully situated on the outskirts of the town, with views of the mountains in the distance, the park consists of well-tended gravel (raked so that it is perfect for each occupant) and grass pitches. There are 136 pitches for caravans or motorcaravans, of which 14 offer fresh and waste water facilities and 16 have individual fresh water taps. A further 12 pitches are used for seasonal occupation, and there is space for 50 or more tents. More than 71 pitches have 10A electrical hook-ups, WiFi internet for a small charge on every pitch. There are a further 53 super pitches with individual water and waste hook up, 16A electricity and individual Sky TV box. Trees and flowers are a feature of this landscaped location. The wardens escort visitors to their pitch and will help to site caravans if necessary. Caravan holiday homes are located in a separate area of the park.

Facilities

New toilet and shower block complete with laundry and drying room. A further block provides good, clean toilet facilities, with new wash cabins for ladies. Facilities for disabled visitors. Dishwashing sinks. Laundry room. Motorcaravan service point. Gas cylinders, ice creams, cold drinks and camping accessories available at reception. Games room. Touring and motorcaravan secure storage. Off site: Fishing, golf and mountain bike hire within 1 mile. Riding 3 miles.

Open: 15 December - 31 October.

Directions

Go into the town. Turn north at Bank of Scotland. Park straight ahead half a mile. O.S.GR: NJ028283. GPS: 57.3348, -3.618617

Charges guide

Per unit incl. 2 persons and 10A electricity	£ 14.50 - £ 18.50
small 2-man tent	£ 9.50 - £ 14.00
extra person	£ 1.50 - £ 3.00

Huntly

Huntly Castle Caravan Park

The Meadow, Huntly AB54 4UJ (Aberdeenshire) T: **01466 794999**. E: enquiries@huntlycastle.co.uk
alanrogers.com/UK7550

Huntly Caravan Park was opened in '95 and its hard-working owners, the Ballantynes, are justly proud of their neat, well landscaped 15-acre site. Managed under contract for the Caravan Club (non-members welcome), the 11 level grass and 41 hardstanding touring pitches are separated and numbered, with everyone shown to their pitch. Arranged in three bays with banks of heathers and flowering shrubs separating them, most pitches have electric hook-ups (16A) and 15 are fully serviced with water and waste water. Two bays have central play areas and all three have easy access to a toilet block, as has the camping area. Campers are provided with a covered cooking shelter (with work tops) should the weather turn inclement. The park also has 33 privately owned caravan holiday homes (three to hire). An Activity Centre near the entrance contains two indoor safe play areas (one for up to two years old, the other up to height 1.37 metres). There are snooker and pool tables, table tennis, badminton and short tennis. The area abounds with things to do, from forest trails to walk or cycle, a falconry centre, malt whisky distilleries and an all year Nordic ski track. A member of the Best of British group.

Facilities

The three heated toilet blocks are well designed and maintained, with washbasins (in cubicles for ladies) and large showers. Each block also has a family shower room, dishwashing sinks and a room for disabled visitors. Laundry room. Milk and papers may be ordered at reception. Activity centre (charged and facilities are also open to the public; open weekends and all local school holidays). Off site: Huntly is 10 minutes walk. Fishing, golf or bicycle hire within 1 mile. Riding 5 miles.

Open: 1 April - 1 November.

Directions

Site is well signed from A96 Keith - Aberdeen road. O.S.GR: NJ526402. GPS: 57.45205, -2.7916

Charges guide

Per unit incl. 2 persons and electricity	£ 15.25 - £ 18.90
extra person	£ 4.50
child (5-16 yrs)	£ 1.30 - £ 2.15
awning/pup tent	£ 1.95

Inverness

Torvean Caravan Park

Glenurquhart Road, Inverness IV3 6JL (Highland) T: **01463 220582**
alanrogers.com/**UK7690**

Torvean is a small and neat, select touring park for caravans and motorhomes only. It is situated on the outskirts of Inverness beside the Caledonian Canal and is within easy reach of the town's amenities which include an ice rink, theatre and leisure sports centre. Excursions to the coast and Highlands, including Loch Ness, are possible in several directions. The pitches on level grass are clearly marked with a tarmac access road and street lighting giving a very neat appearance. There are 47 touring pitches (27 with 10A electricity connections, 18 fully serviced with fresh water tap, waste water disposal and electricity).

Facilities

Two heated toilet blocks are of good quality – ladies have two cubicles with washbasin and toilet and a hair washing cubicle. Controllable hot showers on payment. Suite for disabled people with toilet and shower over a bath. Launderette. Motorcaravan service point. Gas supplies. Play area. Only one dog per unit is accepted. Off site: Golf adjacent, bicycle hire or fishing 3 miles.

Open: Easter - end October.

Directions

Park is off the main A82 road on the southwest outskirts of the town on the west side of the Tomnahurich Canal Bridge (looks like a railway crossing rather than a bridge). O.S.GR: NH638438. GPS: 57.4654, -4.245517

Charges guide

Per unit incl. 2 persons	£ 9.00 - £ 9.50
de-luxe pitch incl. electricity	£ 12.50 - £ 13.00
extra person	£ 1.00 - £ 2.00

No credit cards.

Kildonan

Seal Shore Camping & Touring Site

Kildonan, Isle of Arran KA27 8SE (North Ayrshire) T: **01770 820320**. E: enquiries@campingarran.com
alanrogers.com/**UK7025**

A warm welcome awaits here on the Island of Arran from the resident owner, Maurice Deighton. Located on the southernmost point of the island, this is a quiet and peaceful park situated along its own private beach with wonderful sea views. The open, grassy area, sloping in parts, takes caravans, motorcaravans and tents with 8 electrical connections (16A). The reception doubles as a shop selling basics with a TV room adjacent. There are communal picnic and barbecue areas. The Kildonan Hotel is next door serving restaurant and bar meals. Permits are available for loch fishing and charters available from the owner, a registered fisherman. Golfers can choose from seven golf courses.

Facilities

The good toilet block is clean and tidy and includes full facilities for disabled visitors that double as a baby room. No laundry but you may use the owner's washing machine, dryers and iron. Indoor dishwashing with fridge and freezer for campers use. Shop. Camping gas. Fishing. Sailing. Covered barbecue area. Off site: Nearest golf course at Whiting 4 miles. Heritage Museum in Brodick and to the North of the Island Lochranza castle and distillery.

Open: March - October.

Directions

From Brodick take A841 south for 12 miles to sign for Kildonan. Site is downhill, on the seashore, next to the Kildonan Hotel. O.S.GR: NS022209. GPS: 55.44100, -5.11397

Charges guide

Per unit incl. 2 persons and electricity	£ 16.50
extra person	£ 6.00
child (6-15 yrs)	£ 3.00
tent pitch	£ 1.00 - £ 4.00

www.**alanrogers**.com for latest campsite news

Killin

Loch Tay Highland Lodges

Milton Morenish Estate, by Killin, Loch Tay FK21 8TY (Perth and Kinross) T: **01567 820323**
E: info@lochtay-vacations.co.uk **alanrogers.com/UK7315**

Loch Tay Highland Lodges Leisure Park is situated in the central highlands on the shores of Loch Tay. Arguably one of the most beautiful areas of Scotland surrounded by mountains, rivers and lochs and still within easy driving distance of Edinburgh, Stirling or Glasgow. Loch Tay Highland Lodges are just a short drive from the scenic village of Killin and the picturesque Falls of Dochart. Highland Perthshire is renowned for its wealth of historical sites, natural beauty and wildlife. Tent pitches are grassy and of a good size. Additionally, a good selection of chalets and lodges is available for rent. Motorcaravans are not accepted. Fishing is understandably popular and the site offers salmon fishing packages, to include boat hire and self catering accommodation in a pine lodge. Alternatively, a chauffeur driven tour visits some of the local area's best known distilleries including Scotland's smallest distillery, the 'Erdradour'. The Boathouse Restaurant has become a focal point of the Loch Tay Park and combines fine food with warm hospitality in an undeniably beautiful location with uninterrupted views over Loch Tay.

Facilities

Restaurant. Small shop. Games room. Play area. Equestrian centre. Marina. Sailing. Archery. Canoeing. Quad biking. Chalets, yurts, teepees and other accommodation for rent. Camp fires not permitted. Off site: Deer stalking. White water rafting. Wildlife safaris. Golf (Pitlochry, Aberfeldy and Taymouth Castle). Fishing. Whisky tours. Nature reserve.

Open: All year.

Directions

Loch Tay Highland Lodges Leisure Park is situated between Aberfeldy and Killin on the A827. O.S.GR: NN612359. GPS: 56.494024, -4.250357

Charges guide

Per tent	£ 15.00 - £ 18.00

See advertisement on page 270

Kyle of Lochalsh

Reraig Caravan Site

Balmacara, Kyle of Lochalsh IV40 8DH (Highland) T: **01599 566215**. E: warden@reraig.com
alanrogers.com/UK7760

This is a small, level park close to Loch Alsh with a wooded hillside behind (criss-crossed with woodland walks). Set mainly on well cut grass, it is sheltered from the prevailing winds by the hill and provides just 45 numbered pitches. There are electrical connections (10A) and 35 hardstandings (2 without electricity). Large tents and trailer tents are not accepted at all. Small tents are permitted at the discretion of the owner, so it would be advisable to telephone first if this affects you. Reservations are not taken so it may be best to arrive before late afternoon in July and August. Awnings are not permitted during July and August in order to protect the grass. The ground can be stony so there could be problems with tent pegs. Reraig makes a good base from which to explore the area, the Isle of Skye and the pretty village of Plockton with its palm trees (remember Hamish Macbeth on TV?)

Facilities

The single sanitary block has been extensively refurbished and is kept immaculately clean. Children have their own low basins. Controllable hot showers are on payment (10p for 2 minutes). Sinks for laundry and dishwashing. Use of a spin dryer is free. A slope replaces the small step into the ladies and sink rooms. Motorcaravan drainage point. Off site: Adjacent to the park is the Balmacara Hotel (with bar), shop (selling gas), sub-post office and off licence.

Open: 1 May - 30 September.

Directions

On the A87, park is 2 miles west of the junction with the A890, beside the Balmacara hotel. O.S.GR: NG815272. GPS: 57.283133, -5.626517

Charges guide

Per unit incl. 2 persons	£ 12.50
extra person (13 yrs or over)	£ 2.00
awning (May, June, Sept only)	£ 3.00
electricity (10A)	£ 1.30

Kirkcudbright

Brighouse Bay Holiday Park

Brighouse Bay, Borgue, Kirkcudbright DG6 4TS (Dumfries & Galloway) T: 01557 870267
E: info@gillespie-leisure.co.uk **alanrogers.com/UK6950**

Hidden away within 1,200 exclusive acres, on a quiet, unspoilt peninsula, this spacious family park is only some 200 yards through bluebell woods from a lovely sheltered bay. It has exceptional all weather facilities, as well as golf and pony trekking. Over 90% of the 210 touring caravan pitches have electricity (10/16A), some with hardstanding and some with water, drainage and TV aerial. The three tent areas are on fairly flat, undulating ground and some pitches have electricity. There are 120 self-contained holiday caravans and lodges of which about 30 are let, the rest privately owned. On site leisure facilities include a golf and leisure club with 16.5 m. pool, water features, jacuzzi, steam room, fitness room, games room (all on payment), golf driving range, bowling green and clubhouse bar and bistro. The 18-hole golf course extends onto the headland with superb views over the Irish Sea to the Isle of Man and Cumbria. A 9-hole family golf course is a popular attraction. Like the park, these facilities are open all year. The TRSS Approved Pony Trekking Centre, also open all year, offers treks for complete beginners and a range of hacks for the more experienced. Also available are 'weenie rides' for under 5s, riding lessons and stable management sessions for adults and children. Brighouse Bay is a well run park of high standards and a member of the Best of British group.

Facilities

The large, well maintained main toilet block includes 10 unisex cabins with shower, basin and WC, and 12 with washbasin and WC. A second, excellent block next to the tent areas has en-suite shower rooms (one for disabled people) and bathroom, separate washing cubicles, showers and baby room. One section is heated in winter. Laundry facilities. Motorcaravan service point. Gas supplies. Licensed supermarket. Bar, restaurant and takeaway (all year). Golf (new practise area) and Leisure Club with indoor pool (all year). Play area (incl. new one for under 5s). Riding centre. Mountain bike hire. Quad bikes, boating pond, 10 pin bowling, playgrounds, putting. Nature trails. Coarse fishing ponds plus sea angling and an all-tide slipway for boating enthusiasts. Caravan storage. New purpose built chalet for tourist information and leisure facility bookings.

Open: All year.

Directions

In Kirkcudbright turn onto A755 and cross the river bridge. In 400 yards turn left onto B727 at the international camping sign. Or follow Brighouse Bay signs off A75 just east of Gatehouse of Fleet. O.S.GR: NX630455. GPS: 54.7875, -4.1291

Charges guide

Per unit incl. 2 persons and electricity	£ 18.40 - £ 24.25
extra person	£ 2.45
child (4-15 yrs)	£ 1.65

Contact site for full charges.
Golf packages in low season.
Camping Cheques accepted.

Kirkcudbright

Seaward Caravan Park

Dhoon Bay, Kirkcudbright DG6 4TJ (Dumfries & Galloway) T: 01557 870267. E: info@seaward-park.co.uk
alanrogers.com/UK6900

Seaward Caravan Park is little sister to the much larger Brighouse Bay Holiday Park, 3.5 miles away. Set in an idyllic location overlooking the bay, this park is suitable for all units. The terrain is slightly undulating, but most of the numbered pitches are flat and of a good size. There are 35 pitches (21 hardstandings) designated for caravans and motorcaravans, a further 14 for tents, plus 43 caravan holiday homes (six for hire). Electric hook-ups (16A) are on 32 of the touring pitches and 12 are also serviced with water and drain. This is a quiet park with excellent views ideally suited for that relaxing holiday or for touring the region.

Facilities

The principal, fully-equipped toilet block is to the rear of the park. Four rooms with en-suite facilities are also suitable for disabled campers. Well-equipped baby room. Laundry facilities. No motorcaravan service point but waste water tanks can be emptied. The reception/shop stocks basic provisions, books, gifts, gas, and tourist information. Unsupervised heated outdoor swimming pool with sunbathing area (15/5-15/9). Central play area, rocking horse, table tennis and picnic tables. Excellent games room. Pitch and putt. Off site: Beach and sea angling nearby. Riding or bicycle hire 3.5 miles. Kirkcudbright 2.5 miles.

Open: 1 March - 31 October.

Directions

In Kirkcudbright turn onto A755 signed Borgue. Go over river bridge and after 400 yards turn left onto B727 at international camping sign. Take care when turning right into site entrance as the turn is tight. O.S.GR: NX680510. GPS: 54.819767, -4.082117

Charges guide

Per unit incl. 2 persons and electricity	£ 16.40 - £ 21.70
extra person	£1.50 - £ 1.95

Less 5-10% for bookings (not valid with some other discount schemes).

Lairg

Woodend Camping & Caravan Park

Achnairn, Lairg IV27 4DN (Highland) T: 01549 402248
alanrogers.com/UK7720

Woodend is a delightful, small park overlooking Loch Shin and perfect for hill walkers and backpackers. Peaceful and simple, it is owned and run single-handedly by Mrs Cathie Ross, who provides a wonderfully warm Scottish welcome to visitors. On a hill with open, panoramic views across the Loch to the hills beyond and all around, the large camping field is undulating and gently sloping with some reasonably flat areas. The park is licensed to take 55 units and most of the 30 electrical hook-ups (16A) are in a line near the top of the field, close to the large, fenced play area which has several items of equipment on grass. There are opportunities for fishing and hill walking. The famous Falls of Shin with a Visitor Centre is an ideal place to see the salmon leap (about 10 miles).

Facilities	Directions
The sanitary facilities are of old design but kept very clean and are quite satisfactory. Laundry with two machines and a dryer. Kitchen with dishwashing sinks and eating room for tent campers. Reception is at the house, Sunday papers, daily milk and bread may be ordered. Fishing licences for the Loch (your catch will be frozen for you). Off site: Mountain bikes can be hired in Lairg, 5 miles. Several scenic golf courses within 20-30 miles.	Achnairn is near the southern end of Loch Shin. Turn off the A838 single track road at signs for Woodend. From the A9 coming north take the A836 at Bonar Bridge, 11 miles northwest of Tain. O.S.GR: NC558127. GPS: 58.080267, -4.44705

Open: 1 April - 30 September.

Charges guide

Per unit incl. electricity	£ 10.00
tent	£ 8.00

No credit cards.

Lerwick

Clickimin Caravan & Camp Site

Clickimin Leisure Complex, Lochside, Lerwick ZE1 0PJ (Shetlands) T: 01595 741000
E: clickimin.centre@srt.org.uk alanrogers.com/UK7980

The caravan and camping site is in the grounds of the Clickimin leisure complex, but it is not dominated by the building with its swimming pool, restaurant and other amenities. The site is arranged in two tiers which are well laid out with a tarmac road in the centre of each tier. The lower grass tier is separated into areas by shrubs and provides a camping area for 30 tents. The upper tier has 50 touring pitches, each with a large gravel area and divided from its neighbour by a wide impressed concrete section for sitting out. A small lamppost with electricity, water and waste disposal points is provided at each pitch. From the pitches there is a view across a lake with its ruined 'broche' that is floodlit at night. The site is on the edge of Lerwick (ferry terminal), but with easy access to the town and its facilities. Lerwick is ideal as a base to explore Shetland. Travel between the islands is exceptionally easy with drive on and off ferries running regularly between the islands and booking not essential. Daily ferries go to Shetland from Orkney and Aberdeen.

Facilities	Directions
The modern toilet block is clean and includes a toilet and shower cubicle for disabled visitors. Large, warm and well equipped laundry and drying room with an area for food preparation. Bar (evenings). Café and takeaway. Heated indoor and outdoor swimming pools. Off site: Shop and bicycle hire within 1 mile. Golf 3 miles. Riding 12 miles.	Site is on the west side of Lerwick and is signed as you start to leave Lerwick. Take the A969 north or south. Just before leaving the town is the road North Lochside (turn south) or South Lochside (turn north). Clickimin Leisure Centre is on this road. O.S.GR: HU464413. GPS: 60.15348, -1.15934

Open: May - September.

Charges guide

Per unit incl. electricity	£ 11.10
tent	£ 5.30 - £ 9.90

Lockerbie
Hoddom Castle Caravan Park

Hoddom, Lockerbie DG11 1AS (Dumfries & Galloway) T: 01576 300251. E: hoddomcastle@aol.com

alanrogers.com/UK6910

The park around Hoddom Castle is landscaped, spacious and well laid out on mainly sloping ground with many mature and beautiful trees, originally part of an arboretum. The drive to the site is just under a mile long with a one way system. Many of the 120 numbered pitches have good views of the castle and have gravel hardstanding with grass for awnings. Most have electrical connections (16A). In front of the castle are flat fields used for tents and caravans with a limited number of electricity hook-ups. The oldest part of Hoddom Castle itself is a 16th-century Borders Pele Tower, or fortified Keep. This was extended to form a residence for a Lancashire cotton magnate, became a youth hostel and was then taken over by the army during WW2. Since then parts have been demolished but the original 'Border Keep' still survives, unfortunately in a semi-derelict state. The site's bar and restaurant have been developed in the courtyard area from the coach houses, and the main ladies' toilet block was the stables. Amenities include a comfortable bar lounge with a TV. The park's nine-hole golf course is in an attractive setting alongside the Annan river, where fishing is possible for salmon and trout (tickets available). Coarse fishing is also possible elsewhere on the estate. This is a peaceful base from which to explore historic southwest Scotland.

Facilities

The main toilet block can be heated and is very well appointed. Washbasins in cubicles, 3 en-suite cubicles with WC and basin (one with baby facilities) and an en-suite shower unit for disabled visitors. Two further tiled blocks, with washbasins and WCs only. Laundry room at the castle. Motorcaravan service point. Licensed shop at reception (gas available). Bar, restaurant and takeaway (restricted opening outside high season). Games room. Large, grass play area. Crazy golf. Mountain bike trail. Fishing. Golf. Guided walks (high season). Caravan storage. Off site: Tennis nearby.

Open: 1 April - 30 October.

Directions

Leave A74M at junction 19 (Ecclefechan) and follow signs to park. Leave A75 at Annan junction (west end of Annan by-pass) and follow signs.
O.S.GR: NY155725. GPS: 55.041367, -3.311

Charges guide

Per unit incl. 2 persons	£ 9.00 - £ 16.00
incl. electricity	£ 12.00 - £ 19.00
extra person	£ 3.00
child (7-16 yrs)	£ 1.00

Maybole
Culzean Castle Camping & Caravanning Club Site

Maybole KA19 8JJ (South Ayrshire) T: 01655 760627

alanrogers.com/UK7010

With wonderful views of the Firth of Clyde and over to the Isle of Arran, this quiet Camping and Caravanning Club site is next door to Culzean Castle (pronounced Kullayne). Visitors are given a pass to walk in the grounds (when open) with their 17 miles of footpaths as many times as they wish. The campsite has 90 pitches, some level others slightly sloping, and 60 have electrical hook-ups (10A). A few level pitches are suitable for motorcaravans and 20 pitches have hardstanding. American style motorhomes (more than 25 ft) must contact the site prior to arrival as large pitches are limited.

Facilities

The toilet blocks, kept very clean, can be heated and include some washbasins in cubicles. Unit for disabled visitors has a WC, washbasin and shower – an excellent facility. Dishwashing sinks. Well equipped laundry. Small shop for basics opens for short periods morning and evening. Adventure playground. Units over 25 ft. long only accepted by prior arrangement. Off site: Golf or bicycle hire 4 miles. Fishing 8 miles. Buses pass the gate.

Open: 30 March - 30 October.

Directions

From Maybole follow signs for Culzean Castle and Country Park, turning in the town on B7023 which runs into the A719. Country Park entrance is clearly signed on right after 3.75 miles; entrance to caravan park is on the right in Country Park drive.
O.S.GR: NS247103. GPS: 55.35345, -4.76945

Charges guide

Per person	£ 4.90 - £ 7.25
child (6-18 yrs)	£ 2.15 - £ 2.25
non-member pitch fee	£ 5.65

283

Maybole

The Ranch Holiday Park

Culzean Road, Maybole KA19 8DU (South Ayrshire) T: **01655 882446**

alanrogers.com/UK7015

This holiday park is situated in the Ayrshire countryside, four miles from the small town of Maybole. The Ranch, a Caravan Club affiliated site, is managed by the McAuley family. Barrier controlled, the park is beautifully set out with 60 spacious touring pitches, all with 16A electricity connections and including eight super pitches. Most are on level hardstanding with a few level, all grass pitches arranged open plan facing a huge playing field. There are also 65 caravan holiday homes, one for rent. There are plans to extend the number of touring pitches and holiday homes. The superb facilities include a private Leisure Centre with an indoor heated pool, sauna, solarium and well equipped gym, complete with changing room, toilets, shower and free hair dryers. To the rear is a small unfenced play park adjacent to the small camping area which has undercover seating for those rainy days. A 'Wee Honesty Shop' offers exchange books and magazines and a kiddies corner for the under fives. This is an excellent park for relaxing and enjoying the amenities or for touring the area with nearby sandy beaches at Maybole Shore and Croy Bay plus the wonderful freak of nature, where the laws of gravity are turned upside down at the Electric Brae, where you can see water run uphill.

Facilities

The older-style sanitary facilities are away from the touring area but kept spotlessly clean, (a new block is planned). Washbasins in vanity units, four in cubicles with WCs for ladies. Large preset showers. Individual unit with WC and basin for disabled visitors. Wooden building housing well equipped laundry with dishwashing. No shop on site but reception has a good information area. Off site: Golf courses at Turnberry and fishing at Mochram Loch.

Open: March - October (and weekends).

Directions

From Maybole turn onto B7023 (signed Culzean Maidens) for 1 mile and site is signed on left. O.S.GR: NS286102. GPS: 55.3559, -4.7061

Charges guide

Per unit incl. 2 persons	£ 10.60 - £ 16.60
extra person	£ 3.30 - £ 4.80
child	£ 1.10 - £ 1.60

Melrose

Gibson Park Caravan Club Site

High Street, Melrose TD6 9RY (Borders) T: **01896 822969**

alanrogers.com/UK7030

This is an ideal transit park, being so close to the A68, but is also a perfect base for exploring this Southern Scotland area or indeed a trip to Edinburgh, as this is only 35 miles away by car or one of the regular buses which run from the park entrance. This small, three acre park has only 60 touring pitches plus, unusually, an extra 12 tent pitches (summer only) next to the adjacent rugby pitch. All touring pitches have electricity (16A) and TV connections (otherwise it is a bad signal here), 57 have hardstanding and ten are serviced with water and drainage. A one-way system on the tarmac roads is in operation. This is Sir Walter Scott country – visit Abbotsford House, his romantic mansion on the banks of the River Tweed. Melrose's Abbey ruins are believed to be the final resting place of Robert The Bruce and the starting place of St Cuthbert's Way. A 62 mile, cross border trail leads to Northumberland's Lindisfarne.

Facilities

First rate toilet facilities are in a new building with spacious showers, washbasins in cabins, centrally heated and all fitted out with purpose made faced boarding giving a very pleasing finish. Laundry facilities. Separate room with shower and WC for disabled visitors. Motorcaravan service point. Gas is available. Security barrier (operated by card). Off site: Situated on the edge of the little town of Melrose, a five minute walk, shops, pubs and restaurants are all in easy reach. Play area next to site.

Open: All year.

Directions

Turn left off A68 Jedburgh - Lauder road at roundabout about 2.5 miles past Newton St Boswell onto A6091 Galashiels road. In about 3.25 miles at roundabout turn right onto B6374 to Melrose (not at first turning into town). Site is on right at filling station opposite Melrose Rugby Club, just before town centre. O.S.GR: NT545340. GPS: 55.598017, -2.724233

Charges guide

Per person	£ 4.90 - £ 6.10
child (5-16 yrs)	£ 1.50 - £ 2.50
pitch incl. electricity (non-members)	£ 11.80 - £ 14.70
For tent pitches apply to site.	

Mintlaw

Aden Country Park Caravan Park

Station Road, Mintlaw AB42 8FQ (Aberdeenshire) T: **01771 623460**
alanrogers.com/UK7530

Aden Country Park is owned by the local authority and is open to the public. The caravan and camping site is on one side of the park. Beautifully landscaped and well laid out with trees, bushes and hedges, it is kept very neat and tidy. It provides 48 numbered pitches for touring units, with varying degrees of slope (some level) and all with electrical hook-ups (16A), plus an area for tents. There are also 12 caravan holiday homes. The park is in a most attractive area with plenty to offer.

Facilities

The modern toilet block is clean, with good facilities for disabled visitors. It can be heated and provides free, preset hot showers, hairdryer for ladies, and a baby bath, but no private cabins. Dishwashing and laundry facilities (metered). Motorcaravan service point. Gas supplies. Small shop in reception area. Restaurant in the Heritage Centre. Games areas. Play equipment. Dog exercise area. Off site: Shops in Mintlaw 0.5 miles. Fishing 1 mile. Riding 2 miles.

Open: Easter - 25 October.

Directions

Approaching Mintlaw from west on A950 road, park is shortly after sign for Mintlaw station. From east, go to the western outskirts of village and entrance is on left – Aden Country Park and Farm Heritage Centre. O.S.GR: NJ985484. GPS: 57.52475, -2.026117

Charges guide

Per unit incl. electricity	£ 13.40 - £ 15.00
tent (2 persons)	£ 6.40 - £ 7.10
awning	£ 2.00

Monifieth

Riverview Holiday Park

Marine Drive, Monifieth DD5 4NN (Angus) T: **01382 535471**. E: **info@riverview.co.uk**
alanrogers.com/UK7410

A quiet, family park, Riverview overlooks a long sandy beach and has magnificent views over the River Tay towards the Kingdom of Fife and yet is within walking distance of Monifieth town. The park is neatly set out with flowering shrubs and bushes dividing 40 numbered touring pitches. Some enjoying river views, they are grassy and level, each with 16A electricity and two also with water and drainage. Bordering the park are 46 privately owned caravan holiday homes and four to rent. At the entrance to the park is a small reception office and separate tourist information room and a leisure suite with sauna, steam baths and gym (charge). A member of the Best of British group.

Facilities

The spotlessly clean amenity block (key entry) has open washbasins, one in a cabin with WC, and preset showers. Baby bath. Full facility for disabled visitors. Well equipped laundry. Leisure suite. Games room and play area. Adventure play area. Off site: Picnic areas and small boat slipway adjacent. Opposite the Riverview recreation park offers football pitches, putting, crazy golf, tennis, bowling and adventure play park. Golf 800 yds. Fishing 2 miles. Riding 3 miles. Dundee city 5 miles. Bus service nearby.

Open: 1 April - 31 October.

Directions

From Dundee follow signs for Monifieth on A930, after passing Tesco. Turn right at sign for golf course and right again under railway bridge. Park is signed on the left. O.S.GR: NO501322. GPS: 56.47995, -2.811533

Charges guide

Per unit incl. 2 adults, 2 children	£ 13.00 - £ 15.00
extra person	£ 2.00
awning	£ 2.00

Motherwell

Strathclyde Country Park Caravan Site

Strathclyde Country Park, 366 Hamilton Road, Motherwell ML1 3ED (North Lanarkshire) T: **01698 266155**
E: **strathclydepark@northlan.gov.uk** alanrogers.com/UK7000

The 1,200-acre Country Park is a large green area less than 15 miles from the centre of Glasgow. Well kept and open to all, it provides many amenities and sports facilities. The touring site, part of the park, is suitable for both overnight or longer stays (max. 14 days) and has 80 numbered pitches for caravans or tents, 70 with electrical connections (10A). Arranged in semicircular groups on flat grass they are served by made-up access roads and the site is well lit. As it is close to the motorway, there may be some traffic noise. The Country Park provides many leisure activities for all ages.

Facilities

Four solidly built toilet blocks make a good provision. Enclosed sinks for dishwashing or food preparation. Laundry in two blocks (irons from reception). Block 4 has facilities for visitors with disabilities, block 3 has a baby room. Motorcaravan services. Shop within reception sells basic provisions. Play equipment. Bicycle hire. American motorhomes accepted up to 22 ft. Barrier card and toilet block key £10 deposit. Off site: Bar and restaurant facilities (100 yds) in the Country Park. Fishing 400 yards. Bus 1 mile.

Open: Easter - 18 October.

Directions

Take exit 5 from the M74 and follow sign for Strathclyde Country Park. Turn first left for site. O.S.GR: NS720584. GPS: 55.803917, -4.046733

Charges guide

Per caravan pitch incl. 2 persons and electricity	£ 13.65
tent pitch (4 persons)	£ 9.05
extra person	£ 1.30
child	£ 1.15

No credit cards.

Musselburgh

Drum Mohr Caravan Park

Levenhall, Musselburgh EH21 8JS (East Lothian) T: 01316 656867. E: bookings@drummohr.org

alanrogers.com/UK6980

This family owned, attractively laid out touring park is on the east side of Edinburgh. It is a secluded, well kept modern park, conveniently situated for visits to Edinburgh, the Lothian and Borders regions. It has been carefully landscaped and there are many attractive plants, flowers and hedging. There are 120 individual pitches, 40 with hardstanding, for touring units of any type, well spaced out on gently sloping grass in groups of 12 or more, marked with white posts. All have electricity and 13 are fully serviced. Free space is left for play and recreation. A member of the Best of British group.

Facilities

The two sizeable toilet blocks are clean, attractive, and can be heated. Free hot water to washbasins (one cabin for men, two for ladies) and to four external dishwashing sinks, but hot water is on payment for the showers (outside the cubicle) and laundry sinks. Baby changing facilities. Laundry facilities in each block. Motorcaravan service point. Well stocked shop (gas available, bread and papers to order). Playground. Excellent dog walk. Caravan storage. Security barrier with code access. No late night arrivals area. WiFi (on payment). 'Bothy' for hire. Off site: Golf course adjacent.

Open: 1 March - 31 October.

Directions

From Edinburgh follow A1 signs for Berwick-on-Tweed for 6-7 miles. Turn off for Wallyford and follow camp and Mining Museum signs. From south follow A1 turning after Tranent village (A199 Musselburgh) and follow signs. O.S.GR: NT371732. GPS: 55.950033, -3.011667

Charges 2010

Per unit incl. 2 persons and electricity	£ 17.00 - £ 20.00
extra person (over 5 yrs)	£ 2.00
dog	£ 1.00

Newtongrange

Lothianbridge Caravan Park

Craigesk, Newtongrange EH22 4TP (Mid Lothian) T: 0131 663 6120. E: lothianbridge@tiscali.co.uk

alanrogers.com/UK7035

You will receive a warm welcome at this small, family run park. It is situated beside the A7, a major road into Edinburgh, and the entrance is through a disused but very grand railway viaduct which crosses one side. The park is level with hardstanding and grass pitches, 45 of which are for touring. The central area is grassed with some electrical points (long leads useful for some) and newly planted trees. A key controls access to the park and the sanitary facilities. There are several picnic tables for visitors to use and tall trees and shrubs provide a green perimeter.

Facilities

A modern toilet block also housing a well equipped en-suite for disabled visitors. Laundry facilities, iron (from reception) and microwave. No shop but a few items are available in peak season. Motorcaravan service point. Play area. Free WiFi internet access. Two bungalows available to rent. Off site: Supermarket (24 hour) 2 miles with ATM. Golf, riding and fishing all within 5 miles. Beach 8 miles.

Open: 1 April - 6 January.

Directions

Travelling on the A7, just southeast of Edinburgh and due west of Newtongrange, the site is clearly marked by brown camping signs. A viaduct at the entrance. O.S.GR: NT326648. GPS: 55.87131, -3.07633

Charges guide

Per unit incl. 2 persons	£ 14.00 - £ 16.00
electricity	£ 2.00
extra person (over 5 yrs)	£ 1.00 – £ 2.00

North Berwick

Tantallon Caravan & Camping Park

Tantallon Road, North Berwick EH39 5NJ (East Lothian) T: 01620 893348. E: tantallon@meadowhead.co.uk

alanrogers.com/UK7060

Tantallon is a large park with views over the Firth of Forth and the Bass Rock. The park has 147 quite large, grass touring pitches in two lower, more sheltered areas (Law Park), with the rest having good views at the top (Bass Park). Many have some degree of slope. There are 75 electrical connections (10A) and ten pitches also with water and waste water. Each area has its own sanitary facilities, the top block a little way from the end pitches. About 55 caravan holiday homes for sale or hire are in their own areas. Wooden wigwams are also available. This a mature, well managed park with good facilities.

Facilities

Bass Park has 8 unisex units with shower, washbasin and toilet. The other areas have open washbasins. Two heated units for disabled visitors. Good launderette. Motorcaravan service point. Reception sells basic provisions at weekends. Games room with TV. Internet access in reception and WiFi. Good playground and putting green. Dogs only by prior arrangement. Off site: Tesco supermarket nearby. Golf next door, sea fishing, safe sandy beaches in walking distance. Town 1 mile. Riding 5 miles. Bicycle hire 1 mile.

Open: 13 March - 31 October.

Directions

Park is beside the A198 just to the east of North Berwick, which lies between Edinburgh and Dunbar. It is easily accessible from the A1. O.S.GR: NT567850. GPS: 56.05575, -2.690833

Charges guide

Per unit incl. 2 persons	£ 13.50 - £ 26.00
extra person (over 5 yrs)	£ 2.50
dog	£ 3.00

Peebles

Crossburn Caravan Park

Edinburgh Road, Peebles EH45 8ED (Borders) T: **01721 720501**. E: enquiries@crossburncaravans.co.uk
alanrogers.com/UK6960

A peaceful, friendly small park, suitable as a night stop, Crossburn is on the south side of the A703 road, half a mile north of the town centre. The entrance has a fairly steep slope down to reception and the shop which also sells a very large selection of caravan and camping accessories. Passing the caravans for sale and the holiday homes you might think that this is not the site for you, but persevere as the touring area is very pleasant, with attractive trees and bushes. Of the 40 pitches, all have electricity (16A), 20 have hardstanding and eight are fully serviced. There is also a sheltered area for tents. If you decide to stay longer, the area has many places to visit and things to do. From historic homes, abbeys, woodland walks, fishing, horse riding, golf and canoeing – it's all there. Edinburgh is only 40 minutes drive. Perhaps the night halt may turn into a longer visit.

Facilities

There are two toilet blocks, the smaller one (which can be heated) with fairly basic facilities, the other more modern with washbasins in cubicles, free hairdryers and spacious, controllable free showers. Campers' kitchen (key access) with free use of an electric hot plate, kettle and fridge. Shop. Large games room with snooker table and games machines. Good play area on bark chippings. Riverside dog walk. Card-operated barrier (£10 deposit). Off site: Buses from site gate or in Peebles (a short walk).

Open: Easter/1 April - end October.

Directions

Park is by the A703 road, about 0.5 miles north of Peebles. O.S.GR: NT248417.
GPS: 55.662167, -3.193333

Charges guide

Per unit incl. 2 persons and awning	£ 16.00 - £ 18.00
incl. services	£ 20.00

Pitlochry

The River Tilt Park

Golf Course Road, Blair Atholl, Pitlochry PH18 5TB (Perth and Kinross) T: **01796 481467**
E: **stuart@rivertilt.co.uk** **alanrogers.com/UK7295**

This good quality, family-owned park is set on the banks of the River Tilt, a short walk from the village of Blair Atholl, where the 16th-Century Blair Castle stands proud. There are 51 caravan holiday homes including 3 for rent. Two central areas have been set aside for touring caravans, motorcaravans and tents, with 31 pitches mostly with hardstanding. Divided by mature shrubs and hedges, all have 10A electricity connections, 18 have water and a drain. One of the areas is reserved for dog owners and their pets. The Steadings Spa provides an indoor pool, solarium, steam room, spa pool and multigym, plus Waves hair salon. Also open to the public, there are charges for these facilities. The park also has an award winning restaurant. Adjacent are a riverside walk and a golf course. There may be some noise from the railway line that runs alongside the park.

Facilities

The purpose built toilet block is centrally situated (with key entry) and provides en-suite toilet and washbasin cabins and individual large pre-set showers, one suitable for disabled visitors. Baby facilities. Well equipped laundry. Motorcaravan service point. Bar and restaurant. Leisure spa complex with indoor pool, etc. Hair salon. Tennis. Max. 2 dogs per pitch. No ball games. Off site: Private fishing and golf adjacent. Bicycle hire and riding 1 mile. Pitlochry with its famous salmon leap 6 miles. Bus or train from Blair Atholl.

Open: 17 March - 13 November.

Directions

From the A9 just north of Pitlochry, take B8079 into Blair Atholl and follow signs for River Tilt.
O.S.GR: NN874655. GPS: 56.76538, -3.83962

Charges guide

Per unit incl. 2 persons	£ 10.00 - £ 16.00
incl. electricity	£ 12.00 - £ 18.00
extra person	£ 1.00
dog	£ 2.00

Pitlochry
Blair Castle Caravan Park

Blair Atholl, Pitlochry PH18 5SR (Perth and Kinross) T: **01796 481263**. E: mail@blaircastlecaravanpark.co.uk
alanrogers.com/**UK7300**

This attractive, well kept park is set in the grounds of Blair Castle, the traditional home of the Dukes of Atholl. It has a wonderful feeling of spaciousness with a large central area left free for play or for general use. There is space for 277 touring units, 190 with electricity (10/16A), 144 hardstandings and 44 fully serviced pitches with water and waste water facilities also. Caravan holiday homes, 83 privately owned and 27 for hire, are in separate areas. A quality park, quiet at night and well managed. The castle is open to the public, its 32 fully-furnished rooms showing a picture of Scottish life from the 16th-century to the present day, while the beautiful grounds and gardens are free to those staying on site. The castle grounds provide many walking trails and the village is within walking distance with hotels, shops, a water mill craft centre and folk museum.

Facilities

The five toilet blocks can be heated and are of excellent quality and very clean. Large hot showers, some with WC and washbasin, and further cubicles with WC and washbasin. Facilities for disabled visitors with bath or shower, WCs and washbasins. Baby changing mats. Motorcaravan service point. Reception, shop, games room, laundry and internet gallery. Gas supplies. American motorhomes are accepted (max. 30 ft or 5 tons). Off site: Mountain bike hire, riding, golf and fishing nearby.

Open: 1 March - 27 November.

Directions

From A9 just north of Pitlochry take B8079 into Blair Atholl. Park is in grounds of Blair Castle, well signed. O.S.GR: NN868659. GPS: 56.767039, -3.845791

Charges guide

Per unit incl. 2 persons	£ 13.50 - £ 16.00
tent (no car)	£ 13.50 - £ 16.00
child (6-14 yrs)	£ 1.20 - £ 1.50
electricity	£ 3.00
dog (max. 2)	£ 1.00

Pitlochry
Tummel Valley Holiday Park

Tummel Bridge, Pitlochry PH16 5SA (Perth and Kinross) T: **01882 634221**
E: enquiries@parkdeanholidays.co.uk alanrogers.com/**UK7305**

Set in the Tay Forest Park on the banks of the River Tummel, this large family holiday park is part of the Parkdean Group. Divided into two areas by the roadway, the main emphasis is on chalets to let on the side that overlooks the river. Privately owned caravan holiday homes and touring pitches are on the other, quieter side. The 36 touring pitches, open plan with hardstanding, electricity hook-up and a shared water point, overlook a small fishing lake which is an added attraction for all the family. On arrival, you should turn right and park, then cross back to book in. The leisure complex with indoor and outdoor activities is on the river side, as is the reception office.

Facilities

The very clean toilet block has vanity style washbasins, preset showers and a bathroom in each section. Good facilities for disabled visitors. Well equipped laundry. Chemical disposal but no motorcaravan service point. Shop. Riverside entertainment complex with bar with terrace, restaurant and takeaway. Indoor heated pool and toddlers' splash pool. Solarium and sauna. Amusements. Separate area with pool tables. All weather sports court. Adventure play area. Crazy golf. Nature trails. Bicycle hire. Fishing. Note: all venues are non-smoking. Max. 2 dogs per unit. Off site: Golf and riding 10 miles. Buses leave near park entrance.

Open: 24 March - 1 November.

Directions

Travel through Pitlochry. After 2 miles turn left on B8019 to Tummel Bridge (10 miles). Park is on both the left and right. Tourers should turn right and park, then return to reception on the left. O.S.GR: NN764590. GPS: 56.70742, -4.02002

Charges guide

Per pitch	£ 12.50 - £ 29.50

Port William
Kings Green Caravan Park
South Street, Port William DG8 9SG (Dumfries & Galloway) T: 07988 700880. E: enquiries@portwilliam.com
alanrogers.com/UK6885

Kings Green Caravan Park is now owned and run by the Port William Community Association. Kept very natural and situated beside the sea overlooking Luce Bay and the Mull of Galloway, it is within walking distance of Port William, well known for its harbour and fishing community. The all grass, open site provides 30 marked and numbered pitches for caravans, motorcaravans and tents (21 with 10A electricity). On arrival visitors are given a welcome pack which includes a guide on the history of the area and local information. Second Sands at the northern end of the village is perfect for the launching and recovery of boats at any stage of the tide and provides wheelchair and pushchair access to the beach. When we inspected the park, volunteers were in charge. Reception may not therefore always be open. You are invited to park and details of reserved pitches are placed on the notice board.

Facilities
The small toilet block (key entry) is kept very clean and has vanity-style washbasins, free electric showers and hair dryers. Facilities for disabled visitors include WC and washbasin (Radar key). Basic outdoor dishwashing. No laundry, motorcaravan point or gas sales. Large play and ball game area adjacent. Off site: Shops, restaurants and bars in Port William. Fishing 50 yds. Golf 2 miles. Sailing and boat launching 600 yds. Riding 3 miles. Bladnoch distillery and the Isle of Whithorn just a short drive away or further to Stranraer with boats to Ireland.

Open: 30 March - 31 October.

Directions
From Dumfries, take A75 to Newton Stewart. Follow A714 to Wigtown, then B7085 to Port William. O.S.GR: NX337433. GPS: 54.755967, -4.581533

Charges guide
Per pitch	£ 8.00 - £ 9.00
incl. electricity	£ 10.00 - £ 11.00

Saint Andrews
Craigtoun Meadows Holiday Park
Mount Melville, Saint Andrews KY16 8PQ (Fife) T: 01334 475959. E: craigtoun@aol.com
alanrogers.com/UK7290

This attractively laid out, quality park has individual pitches and good facilities and although outnumbered by caravan holiday homes, the touring section is an important subsidiary. Its facilities are both well designed and comprehensive. With 67 units taken on gently sloping land, caravans go on individual hardstandings with grass alongside for awnings on most pitches. All caravan pitches are large (130 sq.m) and are equipped with electricity (16A), water and drainage. There are 15 larger 'patio pitches' with summer house, barbecue patio, picnic table and chairs, partially screened. Tents are taken on a grassy meadow at one end, also with electricity available. The 157 caravan holiday homes stand round the outer parts of the site; 27 are owned and let by the park. Buses pass the entrance and Craigtoun park with boating pond and miniature railway, etc. is within walking distance. This is a well run park, two miles from St Andrews with its golf courses and long, sandy beaches, from where there is a picturesque view of St Andrews and its ruined Abbey and Castle.

Facilities
An excellent, de-luxe, centrally heated sanitary building serves the touring area. All washbasins are in cabins and each toilet has its own basin. Showers are unisex, as are two bathrooms, with hand and hair dryers. Facilities for disabled people and babies. Launderette. Shop and licensed restaurant (both restricted hours in low seasons), also providing takeaway. Games room. Well equipped playground, play field and 8 acres of woodland. Barbecue area. Tennis. Information room. Dogs and other pets are not accepted. Off site: Golf or bicycle hire 1.5 miles. Fishing 5 miles. Riding 6 miles.

Open: 15 March - 15 November.

Directions
From M90 junction 8 take A91 to St Andrews. Just after sign for Guardbridge (to left, A919), turn right at site sign and sign for Strathkinness. Go through village, over crossroads at end of village, left at next crossroads, then 0.75 miles to park. O.S.GR: NO482151. GPS: 56.324617, -2.83745

Charges guide
Per unit	£ 18.00 - £ 24.50
tent	£ 18.00

Only 'breathable' type groundsheets maybe used in awnings.

Scourie

Scourie Caravan & Camping Park

Harbour Road, Scourie IV27 4TG (Highland) T: **01971 502060**

alanrogers.com/UK7730

Mr Mackenzie has carefully nurtured this park over many years, developing a number of firm terraces with 60 pitches which gives it an attractive layout – there is nothing regimented here. Perched on the edge of the bay in an elevated position, practically everyone has a view of the sea and a short walk along the shore footpath leads to a small sandy beach. The park has tarmac and gravel access roads, with well drained grass and hardstanding pitches, some with 10A electric hook-ups. A few are on an area which is unfenced from the rocks (young children would need to be supervised here). Reception, alongside the modern toilet block, contains a wealth of tourist information and maps. There are very good facilities for disabled visitors on the park and at the restaurant, although the ramps leading to them are a little steep. Mr Mackenzie claims that this is the only caravan park in the world from where, depending on the season, you can see palm trees, Highland cattle and Great Northern divers from your pitch. Red throated divers have also been seen. Trips to Handa Island (a special protection area for seabird colonies) are available from here and Tarbet. The clear water makes this area ideal for diving.

Facilities

The toilet facilities can be heated. Showers have no divider or seat. Laundry. Motorcaravan service point. The 'Anchorage' restaurant at the entrance to the park (used as reception at quiet times) serves meals at reasonable prices, cooked to order (l/4-30/9). Boat launching. Fishing permits can be arranged. Off site: Village with shop and post office, gas is available from the petrol station and mobile banks visit regularly.

Open: Easter (or April if Easter is in March) - 30 September, but phone first to check.

Directions

Park is by Scourie village on A894 road in northwest Sutherland. O.S.GR: NC153446. GPS: 58.351417, -5.156767

Charges guide

Per unit incl. 2 persons	£ 12.00 - £ 16.00
extra person	£ 2.50
child (3-16 yrs)	£ 1.50
electricity	£ 2.00

No credit cards.

Staffin

Staffin Caravan & Camping Site

Staffin IV51 9JX (Isle of Skye) T: **01470 562213**. E: **staffincampsite@btinternet.com**

alanrogers.com/UK7750

This simple camping site is on the side of a hill just outside Staffin, where the broad sweep of the bay is dotted with working crofts running down to the sea. With 50 pitches, the site is quite sloping but there are some reasonably level pitches with improved hardstanding for caravans and motorcaravans, 26 with electrical hook-ups (16A). The first section of road from Portree should be treated with caution by those with caravans and large motorhomes. The entrance to the site from the main road is by a single track road. A marked walk from the site leads to the seashore and slipway (good for walking dogs but too far to be taking a boat). Skye has many activities to offer and for the truly dedicated walker the Cuillins are the big attraction but the hills above Staffin look demanding!

Facilities

The sanitary block includes large, controllable showers. There are some dishwashing sinks outside but these have cold water only. Large hardstanding area has a motorcaravan service point. Gas available. Off site: Fishing or boat launching 1 mile. Bicycle hire 5 miles. Riding 9 miles. Staffin village is 400 yards and has a large shop (open six days a week), a restaurant and a launderette (useful as the site has no laundry). The Columbia centre in the village provides internet access.

Open: 1 April - 30 September.

Directions

Site is 15 miles north of Portree on A855 (2 miles of single track at the start), just before 40 mph signs on the right. O.S.GR: NG496668. GPS: 57.622017, -6.196

Charges guide

Per unit incl. 2 persons	£ 12.00
tent incl. 2 persons	£ 10.00
extra person	£ 1.50
electricity	£ 1.50

No credit cards.

Stirling

Witches Craig Caravan Park

Blairlogie, Stirling FK9 5PX (Stirling) T: 01786 474947. E: info@witchescraig.co.uk

alanrogers.com/UK7320

Witches Craig is a neat and tidy park, nestling under the Ochil Hills and the friendly Stephen family take each visitor to their pitch to make sure that they are happy. All 60 pitches have electrical hook-ups (10A) and 26 have hardstanding, seven of these being large (taking American style motorhomes easily). Reasonably level, the park covers five well maintained acres with the grass beautifully manicured. Being by the A91, there is some day-time road noise. Trees have been planted to try to minimise this but the further back onto the park you go, the less the traffic is heard, although the main touring section with the sanitary facilities is at the front. Seven residential park homes are well kept and surrounded by flowering shrubs. The area has a wealth of historic attractions, starting with the Wallace Monument which practically overlooks the park. Its 220 ft. tower dominates the surrounding area and the climb up its 246 steps gives spectacular views. Stirling is known as the 'Gateway to the Highlands' and its magnificent castle is world renowned.

Facilities

The modern, heated toilet block is well maintained, and includes one cubicle with washbasin and WC each for ladies and men. Free controllable showers. Baby bath and mat. Good unit for disabled campers. Laundry, with free fridge/freezer facilities. New reception. Bread, milk, drinks and papers are available daily (supermarket 2.5 miles). Large fenced play area. Field for team games. Off site: Riding or bicycle hire 2 miles, fishing 3 miles, golf 1 mile. Buses stop at the park entrance. Within 10 miles there are castles, museums, cathedrals and parks. There are many walks from the site into the Ochil Hills.

Open: 1 April - 31 October.

Directions

Park is on the A91, 3 miles northeast of Stirling. O.S.GR: NS822968. GPS: 56.148033, -3.898667

Charges guide

Per unit incl. 2 persons and electricity	£ 16.00 - £ 18.00
extra person	£ 2.00
child (2-13 yrs)	£ 1.00
awning (no groundsheet)	£ 2.00
£5 deposit for key to facilities.	

Stornoway

Laxdale Holiday Park

6 Laxdale Lane, Stornoway HS2 0DR (Isle of Lewis) T: 01851 706966. E: info@laxdaleholidaypark.com

alanrogers.com/UK7920

Whilst not in the most scenic of locations, this good park is well placed for touring. Surrounded by trees, it is on the edge of Stornaway (ferry port) and is well laid out with a tarmac road running through the centre. A level hardstanding area for touring caravans has 14 electricity hook-ups plus two for tents and a grassy area for the tents gently slopes away to the trees and boundary. There are five holiday caravans and a self catering holiday bungalow available for rent on the site, plus a bunkhouse. The site is centrally situated in an ideal spot for touring the Isle of Lewis with easy access to all parts of the island. The Butt of Lewis, the Callanish standing stones and the Black House Village are all within easy reach as well as many other attractions. Some parts have rocky coastal scenery but there are some lovely beaches around the island. The main road south leads to Harris passing through the mountainous area to the south of the Isle of Lewis. Ferries come into Stornoway from Ullapool and also Uig (Skye) to Tarbert (north Harris). Ferries to Berneray/North Uist go from Leverburgh in the south of Harris.

Facilities

The well maintained and modern toilet block is heated and raised above the hardstanding area. Access is via steps or a gravel path to the ramp. Good (but narrow) showers with dividing curtain (50p). Well equipped laundry with washing machine, dryer, iron and board, sink and clothes line. Telephone. WiFi in reception. Off site: Bus stop 200 m. The busy fishing port of Stornoway has a comprehensive range of shops and restaurants. New sports centre with swimming pool. Library with free internet access.

Open: 1 April - 31 October.

Directions

From Stornoway take the A857 for 1 mile then take the second turning on the left past the hospital. O.S.GR: NB420348. GPS: 58.22738, -6.39254

Charges guide

Per person	£ 2.00 - £ 3.00
child (5-15 yrs)	£ 2.00
pitch	£ 5.00 - £ 8.00
electricity	£ 2.00
Credit cards accepted (over £50).	

291

Stranraer

Aird Donald Caravan Park

London Road, Stranraer DG9 8RN (Dumfries & Galloway) T: 01776 702025. E: enquiries@aird-donald.co.uk

alanrogers.com/UK7020

Aird Donald is a good stopping off place when travelling to and from the Irish ferries, but it is also useful for seeing the sights around Stranraer. This tidy park comprises 12 acres surrounded by conifers, flowering trees and shrubs and the 300 yard drive is lit and lined with well trimmed conifers. There are grass areas for caravans or tents and hardstandings with electricity hook-up (these are very handy for hardy winter tourers). A small play area caters for young children, but the local leisure centre is only a walk away and provides swimming, table tennis, gym, etc, and a theatre that hosts everything from country and western to opera.

Facilities	Directions
Two toilet blocks, the new block modern and heated. Very clean with excellent, tiled facilities, and kept locked with a key deposit of £5. Two types of shower, an electric one (20p meter) and two others which are free but still excellent. Washbasins are in vanity units, ladies having one in a cubicle. Unit for visitors with disabilities has a washbasin and WC. The original block is being renovated but is more basic with free showers and open all the time. Dishwashing sinks and a small laundry with sinks, dryer, washing machine. Motorcaravan services. Play area.	Enter Stranraer on A75 road. Watch for narrow site entrance on left entering town, opposite school. O.S.GR: NX075605. GPS: 54.90185, -5.006217

Charges 2010

Per unit incl. 2 persons and electricity	£ 17.00
tent	£ 13.00
No credit cards.	

Open: All year.

Stromness

Point of Ness Caravan & Camping Site

Well Park, Ness Road, Stromness KW16 3DN (Orkney) T: 01856 873535. E: recreation@orkney.gov.uk

alanrogers.com/UK7950

This quiet site is in an idyllic position bounded by the sea one side (an entrance to the harbour). It is sheltered by the land from the open sea and has views to the mountains and the island of Hoy. There is a rocky beach close by and walks from the site. It is a level, firm grassy site, protected from the small drop to the sea by a low fence. Access to the steps to the sea is gained by a gate in the fence. Whilst being located at one end of Orkney, it is still easy to visit the Churchill Barriers and the Italian Chapel as well as the closer Maes Howe and Skara Brae sites.

Facilities	Directions
The well maintained traditional style toilet block has good-sized showers (20p) with curtains separating the changing area. Well equipped laundry. Telephone and tourist information. Lounge for campers is at one end of the block. Off site: Fishing, golf and bicycle hire all nearby.	Site is just west of Stromness and signed from town. Access along the narrow high street to the site for campers. Caravans and motorcaravans should take the marked road at the back of the town (about 2 miles). O.S.GR: HY256079. GPS: 58.95443, -3.30041

Open: 28 April - 30 September.

Charges guide

Per pitch	£ 8.30
tent	£ 4.40 - £ 7.95
No credit cards.	

Ullapool

Ardmair Point Caravan Park

Ardmair Point, Ullapool IV26 2TN (Highland) T: 01854 612054. E: sales@ardmair.com

alanrogers.com/UK7710

This spectacularly situated park, overlooking the little Loch Kanaird, just round the corner from Loch Broom, has splendid views all round. The 68 touring pitches are arranged mainly on grass around the edge of the bay, in front of the shingle beach. Electrical hook-ups (10A) are available and some gravel hardstandings are on the other side of the access road, just past the second toilet block. Tent pitches, together with cheaper pitches for some tourers are in a large field behind the other sanitary facilities. Scuba diving is popular at Loch Kanaird because the water is so clear.

Facilities	Directions
Two toilet blocks, both with good facilities. One block has wonderful views from the large windows in the launderette and dishwashing rooms. Large en-suite rooms for disabled people. Motorcaravan service point. Shop. Play area. Fishing. Sailing and boating (with your own boat). Off site: Ullapool for shopping 3 miles. Golf and bicycle hire 3 miles.	Park is off the A835 road, 3 miles north of Ullapool. O.S.GR: NH109983. GPS: 57.933967, -5.197017

Charges guide

Per unit incl. 2 persons	£ 13.00 - £ 19.00
backpacker tent (1 person)	£ 7.00

Open: 1 April - late September, depending on the weather.

With a diversity of unspoilt landscapes, ranging from wild coastlines to green valleys, rugged mount and shimmering lakes, t the natural phenomenon o the Giant's Causeway, Northern Ireland, though small, is cramme full of sights offering something for everyone.

NORTHERN IRELAND COMPRISES THE FOLLOWING COUNTIES: ANTRIM, ARMAGH, DOWN, FERMANAGH, LONDONDERRY AND TYRONE

The rugged coastline of the Causeway Coast and the nine Glens of Antrim, in the north, is an area of outstanding natural beauty, with white sandy shores and little bays, tranquil forests and romantic ruins and castles, full of tales of the ancient Irish Giants and other myths and legends. At over 60 million years old, with a mass of 4,000 tightly packed basalt columns, each a polygon shape, the Giant's Causeway is a popular attraction. One of the most beautiful regions is in the west around Londonderry, a delightful walled city set on a hill on the banks of the Foyle estuary. Further south is the beautiful region of Fermanagh, with glistening lakes and little islands all surrounded by lush green fields, hillsides and forests. The large lake of Lough Erne is to be found here: made up of two channels, the lower and upper Loughs, the meeting point of these channels is Enniskillen, a town steeped in history, boasting numerous preserved buildings including a castle. Across to the eastern shores lies the ancient Kingdom of Down, with its endless miles of spectacular coastline, little fishing villages, country parks and the Mountains of Mourne. And ringed by hills, sea lough and river valley is Belfast, a bustling city full of theatres, concert halls, art galleries and restaurants.

Places of interest

Antrim: Antrim Lough Shore Park; Rathlin Island; Giant's Causeway; Dunluce Castle near Portrush.

Belfast & environs: Belfast zoo and castle; Irish Linen Centre in Lisburn; Carrickfergus Castle.

Armagh: Gosford Forest Park near Markethill; Lough Neagh Discovery Centre on Oxford Island.

Down: County Museum and Downpatrick Cathedral; Mourne Mountains; Castlewell forest park; Ballycopeland Windmill near Millisle.

Fermanagh: Enniskillen Castle and Castle Coole; village of Belleek; Marble Arch Cav near Lough Macnean; Devenish Island on Lough Erne.

Londonderry: St Columb's Cathedral, Harbour Museum, Foyle Valley Railway Centre in Derry.

Tyrone: Omagh; Beaghmore stone circles near Cookstown; Dungannon; Sperrin Mountains.

Did you know?

Northern Ireland measures 85 miles from north to south and is about 110 miles wi

The world's most famous ship the Titanic, was built in Belfast.

Legend has it that the rugged Giant's Causeway was built by Finn McCool, the legendary Irish Giant, when he travelled t Scotland to bring back his sweetheart.

At 2,240 yards an Irish Mile is 480 yards longer than a standard English mile.

Mountsandel near Coleraine is where Ireland's first known house was built 9,000 years ago.

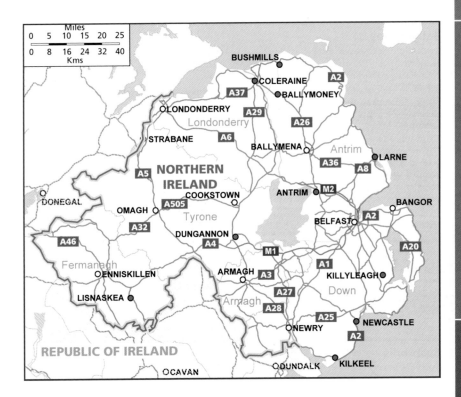

Antrim

Six Mile Water Caravan & Camping Park

Lough Road, Antrim BT41 4DG (Co. Antrim) T: **028 9446 4963**. E: **sixmilewater@antrim.gov.uk**

alanrogers.com/UK8330

Six Mile Water is located at the Lough Shore Park and is adjacent to the Antrim Forum leisure complex, a major amenity area that includes swimming pools, a bowling green, an adventure playground for children, fitness and health gyms and sports fields. Managed by Antrim Borough Council, the park is easily accessible when travelling to and from the ports of Belfast and Larne making it perfect for stop overs. There are 20 pitches with 13A electricity, arranged in a herringbone layout of hardstandings with grass for awnings, and 24 pitches for tents to one side, plus picnic and barbecue areas. Advance booking is advisable. Six Mile Water is central for sightseeing in the area including the Antrim Castle Gardens and Clotworthy Arts Centre or for shopping in Antrim town. The Lough Shore Park offers visitors boating and water activities and boat launching on the beautiful Lough Neagh, as well as walking and cycling the Lough Shore Trail which takes in 25 places of interest along its 128-mile cycle route. The nearby golf club also offers a 20-bay driving range.

Facilities

The small, modern toilet block provides bright facilities including toilets, washbasins and showers. Facilities for disabled campers. Baby changing unit. Laundry room. TV lounge and games room. Fishing and boat launching. Off site: The facilities of Lough Shore Park including a café open all year round. Antrim Forum leisure centre. Bus service 1 mile. Shops, pubs and restaurants within 1.5 miles. Golf 1.5 miles. Riding 6 miles.

Open: 27 February - 2 November.

Directions

Site is 1 mile south of the city centre. Follow signs for Antrim Forum and Lough Shore Park. On the Dublin road, turn off into Lough Road. Pass Antrim Forum and park is at the end of the road.
GPS: 54.71533, -6.23375

Charges guide

Per unit incl. electricity	£ 17.00
tent	£ 11.00 - £ 17.00

Ballymoney
Drumaheglis Caravan Park
36 Glenstall Road, Ballymoney BT53 7QN (Co. Antrim) T: 028 2766 0280
E: drumaheglis@ballymoney.gov.uk **alanrogers.com/UK8340**

A caravan park which continually maintains high standards, Drumaheglis is popular throughout the season. Situated on the banks of the lower River Bann, approximately four miles from the town of Ballymoney, it appeals to watersports enthusiasts or makes an ideal base for exploring this scenic corner of Northern Ireland. This attractive site is well laid out with trees, shrubs, flower beds and tarmac roads. There are 35 serviced pitches for touring units with hardstanding, electricity (5/16A) and water points. The marina offers superb facilities for boat launching, waterskiing, cruising, canoeing or fishing. Getting out and about can take you to the Giant's Causeway, seaside resorts such as Portrush or Portstewart, the sands of Whitepark Bay, the Glens of Antrim or the picturesque villages of the Antrim coast road. Ballymoney is a popular shopping town and the Joey Dunlop Leisure Centre provides a high-tech fitness studio, sports hall, etc. There is much to see and do within this Borough and of interest is the Ballymoney museum in Townhead Street.

Facilities

Modern toilet blocks were very clean when we visited. Individual wash cubicles. Facilities for disabled visitors. Baby room and four family shower rooms. Washing machine and dryer. Play area. Barbecue and picnic areas. Barrier with key system. Off site: Marina. Bus service from park entrance. Bicycle hire and golf 4 miles. Riding 6 miles. Beach 10 miles.

Open: 19 March - end October.

Directions

From A26/B62 Portrush - Ballymoney roundabout continue for about 2 miles on the A26 towards Coleraine. Site is clearly signed - follow International camping signs. GPS: 55.07212, -6.59082

Charges 2010

Per unit incl. electricity	£ 19.00 - £ 20.00
tent pitch	£ 14.00

Bushmills
Bush Caravan Park
97 Priestland Road, Bushmills BT57 8UJ (Co. Antrim) T: 028 2073 1678
alanrogers.com/UK8350

An ideal base for touring the North Antrim Coast, this family run, recently extended park is only minutes away from two renowned attractions, the Giant's Causeway and the Old Bushmills Distillery. This fact alone makes Bush popular, but its fast growing reputation for friendliness and top class facilities makes it equally appealing. Located just off the main Ballymoney - Portrush Road (B62), it is approached by a short drive. The site is partly surrounded by mature trees and hedging, but views across the countryside can still be appreciated. Tarmac roads lead to 47 well laid out and spacious pitches with hardstanding and 16A electricity or to a grass area for tents. Unique features on site are murals depicting the famed scenery, sights and legends of the Causeway Coast. The enthusiastic owners organise tours to the Distillery and coastal trips – a musical evening cannot be ruled out.

Facilities

The toilet block (opened by key-pad) is modern, clean and equipped to a high standard. Facilities include controllable showers with excellent provision for people with disabilities (can also be used by families). Washing machine and dryer. Central play area. Recreation room for all ages. Off site: Riding 2 miles. Golf and fishing 3 miles. Bicycle hire and boat launching 4 miles. Beach 3 miles.

Open: Easter - 31 October.

Directions

From the A26 turn onto the B62 for 7 miles. Turn onto the B17 Priestlands Road and site is immediately on the left. GPS: 55.17103, -6.57114

Charges guide

Per unit incl. 2 persons and electricity	£ 18.00 - £ 20.00

Bushmills

Ballyness Caravan Park

40 Castlecatt Road, Bushmills BT57 8TN (Co. Antrim) T: **028 2073 2393**. E: **info@ballynesscaravanpark.com**

alanrogers.com/UK8360

Ballyness is immaculately cared for and is designed with conservation in mind. In keeping with the surrounding countryside, it is extensively planted with native trees and shrubs which attract local wildlife and birds and there are ponds with ducks and swans. The overall appearance of this site, with its entrance gate, white stone pillars and broad tarmac drive is attractive. The drive leads to 48 hardstanding pitches with electricity hook-ups, water and drainage. There are several caravan holiday homes, but these are placed away from the touring pitches. From the site you can enjoy a relaxing walk by way of the meadow ponds and winding pathway alongside the stream known as St Columb's Rill. The village of Bushmills, with its famous Whiskey Distillery, is within walking distance and the Causeway Coast a short drive.

Facilities	Directions
One spotlessly clean and well decorated, cottage style heated sanitary block (key coded). Facilities for disabled visitors (toilet and shower). Family room with bath. Laundry room. Play are and play park. Wifi and internet. Wildlife area and ponds. Off site: Bus service 0.5 miles. Bicycle hire 1 mile. Beach and fishing 1 mile. Golf and boat launching 1.5 miles. Riding 5 miles.	From M2 follow A26. At Ballymoney turn right on B66 towards Dervock and turn left. Stay on B66 and site is 5.5 miles on right. GPS: 55.20121, -6.52096

Open: 17 March - 31 October.

Charges guide

Per unit incl. 2 persons, electricity,
water and drainage   £ 20.00

Coleraine

Tullans Farm Holiday Park

46 Newmills Road, Coleraine BT52 2JB (Co. Londonderry) T: **028 7034 2309**. E: **tullansfarm@hotmail.com**

alanrogers.com/UK8590

A high quality, well run family park convenient for the Causeway coast, Tullans Farm is one of the most popular in the area. It has a quiet, heart of the country feel, yet the University town of Coleraine is within a mile, the seaside resort Portrush and Portstewart five miles and a shopping centre a five minute drive. Tullans Farm has earned a reputation for its spotlessly clean toilet block, attractive flower displays and its well cared for appearance. Around the park roads are gravel and the 32 pitches are on hardstanding; all with electric hook-ups (10A), water and drainage. In season the owners organise barbecues, barn dances and line dancing (raising funds for charity). In a central position, fronted by a parking space, stands a long white building housing the sanitary facilities and reception.

Facilities	Directions
The toilet and shower rooms, including a family shower unit, are spacious, modern and include facilities for people with disabilities. Laundry and washing up room with sinks, washing machine, dryers and a large fridge. Play areas. TV lounge. Games room. Barn used for indoor recreation. Caravan storage. Off site: Public transport in Coleraine 1 mile. Fishing and riding 1.5 miles. Golf and bicycle hire 5 miles. Beach 5 miles.	From the Lodge Road roundabout (south end of Coleraine) turn east onto A29 Portrush ring road and proceed for 0.5 miles. Turn right at sign for park and Windy Hall. Park is clearly signed on left. GPS: 55.12557, -6.63923

Open: March - 30 September.

Charges guide

Per unit incl. all persons, electricity and awning	£ 17.00
tent	£ 8.00 - £ 12.00

No credit cards.

Coleraine

Bellemont Caravan Park

10 Islandtasserty Road, Coleraine BT52 2PN (Co. Londonderry) T: **028 7082 3872**

alanrogers.com/UK8600

Close to Coleraine and Portstewart, this well kept park makes an immediately favourable impression with its white concrete roads, its perfect grass areas and well laid out appearance. The gently sloping ground rises at the far right of the park to give views over Portstewart and towards the sea. To the left of the entrance and security gate are five privately owned caravan holiday homes. There are 30 touring pitches, all with hardstanding, electric hook-up and water. These are spacious and well distributed around this open, parkland style setting. In a central position stands a gleaming white building, with flower tubs decorating the forecourt, which houses reception and heated sanitary facilities. Bellemont makes a good base for visiting the university town of Coleraine, the resorts and beaches of Portstewart and Portrush, or famous sights such as Dunluce Castle, Carrick-a-Rede rope bridge and the Giant's Causeway.

Facilities

Toilet facilities with good sized showers (token operated). En-suite unit for disabled visitors. Laundry room with two washing machines, two dryers and iron (token operated), plus dishwashing sink and drainer to the outside. Play area with swings and slide on a bark surface. Dogs are not accepted. Off site: Bus service 0.5 miles. Fishing, bicycle hire, riding and golf 2 miles. Beach 2.5 miles.

Open: Easter - 30 September.

Directions

From Lodge Road roundabout on eastern outskirts of Coleraine follow A29 north to fourth roundabout. Continue towards Portrush and site is clearly signed on left after 400 yards. GPS: 55.17196, -6.67547

Charges guide

Per unit incl. all persons and electricity	£ 18.00
awning	£ 2.00

No credit cards.

Dungannon

Dungannon Park

Moy Road, Dungannon BT71 6DY (Co. Tyrone) T: **028 8772 8690**. E: dpreception@dungannon.gov.uk

alanrogers.com/UK8550

This small touring park nestles in the midst of a 70-acre park with a multitude of tree varieties, brightly coloured flower beds and a 12-acre fishing lake. The 12 pitches, which are discreetly sited, some with lake views, are on hardstanding with water, waste and 16A electricity connections. There is also an unmarked grass area for tents. Run by Dungannon Council the park, which also incorporates tennis courts, football and cricket pitches lies about one mile south of Dungannon town. Walkers can enjoy three miles of parkland walks which command from the high ground, views of the surrounding countryside and Lough Neagh. A modern Visitor Amenity Centre houses reception, sanitary facilities, a TV area and vending machines.

Facilities

Sanitary facilities which include showers (by token), washbasins, baby changing mat and spacious unit for disabled visitors are to the rear of the Amenity Centre. Laundry room with washing machine and dryer, dishwashing area and chemical disposal unit. Night watchman (until 06.00). Excellent play area. Tennis, fishing and walking, orienteering. Off site: Bus stop and shop at main entrance to park. Restaurants, shops, leisure facilities in Dungannon. Tyrone Crystal (guided tours), walking and cycling in Clogher Valley, local markets.

Open: 1 March - 31 October.

Directions

Leave M1 motorway at junction 15 to join A29 towards Dungannon. Turn left at second traffic lights signed Dungannon Park. GPS: 54.390217, -6.757967

Charges 2010

Per unit incl. electricity	£ 12.00
tent	£ 8.00

Kilkeel

Cranfield Caravan Park

123 Cranfield Road, Cranfield West, Kilkeel BT34 4LJ (Co. Down) T: **028 417 62572**
E: **jimchestnut@btconnect.com** **alanrogers.com/UK8405**

On the shores of Carlingford Lough with direct access to a blue flag beach, this friendly family run park immediately impresses with its well cared for flower beds, neat hedging, cordyline trees and the elegant building which incorporates the family home and reception. Despite the many privately owned caravan holiday homes on site, touring pitches are kept separate and situated towards the park entrance. Each pitch has a sea view, has hardstanding and all have tower units providing an electricity hook up (16A), water, waste water point and TV outlet; 19 have a mains sewerage connection. Situated at Northern Ireland's most southerly point, the surrounding scenery of the Mourne Mountains, the Lough and distant vistas is stunning. A focal point is the Haulbowline lighthouse, built in the 1800s, which sits in the middle of the sea.

Facilities

A modern, heated toilet block (entrance by key) is well maintained with tiled walls/floors, preset showers (50p token) and open style washbasins. Excellent suite for disabled visitors doubles as a family room, also a night WC (by key). Dishwashing sinks and well equipped laundry in a separate building. Play area (outside park). Sea fishing, boat launching and beach (with lifeguard). Off site: Kilkeel town (3.5 miles). Golf, hill walking in the Mournes, Anglo Norman castle.

Open: 17 March - 31 October.

Directions

Travelling southeast on A2 Newry - Kilkeel Road turn right about 5.5 miles after passing through Rostrevor onto local road, signed Cranfield/Greencastle. Site signed at end of road. GPS: 54.029933, -6.0683

Charges guide

Per unit incl. all persons and electricity   £ 15.00

Killyleagh

Delamont Country Park Camping & Caravanning Club Site

Delamont Country Park, Downpatrick Road, Killyleagh BT30 9TZ (Co. Down) T: **028 4482 1833**
alanrogers.com/UK8460

This is Northern Ireland's first Camping and Caravanning Club site and although not long in existence, it is proving to be one of the country's most popular sites. Facilities on the campsite itself are excellent and it has an orderly, neat and tidy appearance. Reception stands to the fore of the site and the sanitary block towards the rear. The 64 all weather pitches on level terrain all have electricity, plus water and waste hook-ups. Although the site is surrounded by trees and the rich vegetation of the country park, the young shrubs and trees around the pitches will take time to mature. Within the boundaries of Delamont Country Park, it is an idyllic location for those seeking an away from it all feel, yet wanting to be within easy reach of major attractions. The country park is a designated area of outstanding natural beauty and commands from its highest point, breathtaking vistas of Strangford Lough and surrounding countryside.

Facilities

The single modern toilet block, with heating, has wash cubicles and a baby bath. En-suite facilities for disabled visitors. Laundry sinks, washing machine and dryer; dishwashing inside. Small shop area selling basics. Adventure playground and miniature railway in country park. Free admittance to country park for campers. Off site: Tyrella beach 7 miles. Fishing and riding 1 mile. Golf 4 miles.

Open: March - October.

Directions

From Belfast follow A22 southeast to village of Killyleagh. Pass through village and site entrance is on left after 1 mile. GPS: 54.38656, -5.67657

Charges guide

Per person	£ 4.90 - £ 7.25
child	£ 2.15 - £ 2.25
non-member pitch fee	£ 5.65

(299)

Larne

Carnfunnock Country Park Caravan Park & Campsite

Coast Road, Drain's Bay, Larne BT40 2QG (Co. Antrim) T: 028 2827 0541. E: carnfunnock@larne-gov.uk

alanrogers.com/UK8310

In a magnificent parkland setting overlooking the sea, what makes this touring site popular is its scenic surroundings and convenient location. It is 3.5 miles north of the market town of Larne on the famed Antrim Coast Road and offers 28 level 'super' pitches, all with hardstanding, water, electricity (15A), drainage, individual pitch lighting and ample space for an awning. The site has a neat appearance with a tarmac road following through to the rear where a number of pitches are placed in a circular position with allocated space for tents. Run by the Borough Council and supervised by a manager, the surrounding Country Park is immaculately kept. The Visitor Centre includes a gift shop and information about local attractions and the restaurant/coffee shop is pleasant and looks towards the sea. Spending time around the parkland, you find a walled time garden with historic sundials, a maze, forest walk, children's adventure playground, putting green, nine-hole golf course, wildlife garden and miniature railway. There is also a summer events programme.

Facilities	Directions
A small building beside the entrance gates houses toilet facilities (entry by key) which are kept clean, but are now starting to show signs of wear. There are shower units, facilities for disabled people and dishwashing. Motorcaravan service point. Off site: Larne with bus services 3.5 miles. Fishing and boat launching 400 yds.	From ferry terminal in Larne, follow signs for Coast Road and Carnfunnock Country Park; well signed 3.5 miles on A2 coast road. GPS: 54.88330, -5.8333

Charges guide	
Per caravan or motorcaravan	£ 12.50 - £ 14.00
serviced hardstanding	£ 14.00 - £ 16.00
tent	£ 8.00 - £ 14.00

Open: Easter - 31 October.

Larne

Curran Court Caravan Park

131 Curran Road, Larne BT40 1XB (Co. Antrim) T: 028 2827 3797. E: curran.court-hotel@virgin.net

alanrogers.com/UK8320

Formerly run by the local Borough Council, this park is now managed by the Curran Court Hotel (opposite the park). Attractive garden areas add to the charm of this small, neat site which is very conveniently situated for the ferry terminal and only a few minutes walk from the sea. The 29 pitches, all with hardstanding and electricity connections (14A), give reasonable space off the tarmac road and there is a separate tent area of 1.5 acres. Larne market is on Wednesdays. You may consider using this site as a short term base for discovering the area as well as an ideal overnight stop. The warden can usually find room for tourists so reservations are not normally necessary.

Facilities	Directions
The toilet block is clean and adequate without being luxurious. Laundry room with dishwashing facilities. Play area with good equipment and safety surfaces. Bowls and putting on site. Late arrivals can call at the hotel. Off site: Train station and bus stop within a few minutes walk. Bicycle hire 0.5 miles. Golf 2 miles. Boat launching 500 yds. Many other amenities are very close including a shop (100 yds), the hotel for food and drink, tennis and a leisure centre with swimming pool (300 yds).	Immediately after leaving the ferry terminal, turn right and follow camp signs. Site is 400 yards on the left. GPS: 54.84995, -5.80818

Charges guide	
Per caravan, motorcaravan or large tent	£ 11.00
tent	£ 5.00 - £ 10.00
electricity	£ 1.00

Open: Easter - 30 September.

Lisnaskea

Mullynascarthy Caravan Park

Lisnaskea BT92 0NZ (Co. Fermanagh) T: 028 6772 1040

alanrogers.com/UK8510

This is a well kept touring site situated on the banks of the Colebrooke River. It has instant appeal, for the setting at Mullynascarthy is more like a mature garden. The pitches to the right of reception, which are grass on hardstanding, are mostly angled between the many tree varieties, also separated by low hedging and flowering shrubs. To the left of the facility block additional pitches are spread over meadow-like terrain and all have electric hook-ups. Sanitary facilities, although not ultra modern, are kept very clean and housed alongside reception, which doubles up as a sub-post office. The attention and care this site obviously receives is due to the warden who also extends a friendly warm welcome to her guests. Lisnaskea makes an ideal base for exploring this lakeland county which abounds in historic treasures, stately homes, and is excellent for watersports enthusiasts. The county town of Enniskillen is within a short drive and the Marble Arch caves are an experience not to be missed.

Facilities

The toilet block (key operated) has showers, open-style washbasins, facilities for people with disabilities (washbasin/WC), laundry room and dishwashing sinks. Games and sports area. Play area. River fishing (licences and permits available). Off site: Bus service 1.5 miles. Golf and bicycle hire 10 miles.

Open: 17 March - 31 October.

Directions

From Enniskillen take A4 towards Dungannon for 8 miles, then turn right on A34 signed Lisnaskea. Continue on A34 for 2.5 miles and turn right onto B514 where site is signed Mullynascarthy. GPS: 54.26842, -7.48343

Charges guide

Per unit incl. 2 persons and electricity	£ 15.00
tent	£ 8.00 - £ 14.00

Newcastle

Tollymore Forest Caravan Park

178 Tullybrannigan Road, Newcastle BT33 6PW (Co. Down) T: 028 4372 2428

alanrogers.com/UK8420

This popular park, for touring units only, is located within the parkland of Tollymore Forest. It is situated away from the public footpaths and is noted for its scenic surroundings. The forest park, which is approached by way of an ornate gateway and majestic avenue of Himalayan cedars, covers an area of almost 500 hectares. It is backed by the Mourne mountains and situated two miles from the beaches and resort of Newcastle. The site is attractively laid out with hardstanding pitches, 72 of which have electricity (6A). The Head Ranger at Tollymore is helpful and ensures that the caravan site is efficiently run and quiet, even when full. Exploring the forest park is part of the pleasure of staying here, and of note are the stone follies, bridges and entrance gates. The Shimna and Spinkwee rivers flow through the park adding a refreshing touch and tree lovers appreciate the arboretum with its many rare species.

Facilities

Toilet blocks, timbered in keeping with the setting, are clean and modern with wash cubicles, facilities for disabled people, dishwashing and laundry area. Off site: Confectionery shop and tea room nearby. Small grocery shop a few yards from the exit gate of the park with gas available.

Open: All year.

Directions

Approach Newcastle on the A24. Before entering the town, at roundabout, turn right on to A50 signed Castlewellan and follow signs for Tollymore Forest Park. GPS: 54.22630, -5.93449

Charges guide

Per unit incl. car and occupants	£ 9.00 - £ 13.00
electricity	£ 1.50
Low season mid-week special rates.	

Famed for its folklore traditional music, and friendly, hospitable people, the Republic Ireland offers spectacu scenery contained withi a relatively compact area. With plenty of beautiful areas to discover, and a decidedly relaxed pace of life, it is an idea place to unwind.

Alan Rogers

IRELAND IS MADE UP OF FOUR PROVINCES: CONNAUGHT, LEINSTER, MUNSTER AND ULSTER, COMPRISING 32 COUNTIES, 26 OF WHICH FALL IN THE REPUBLIC OF IRELAND

Ireland is the perfect place to indulge in a variety of outdoor pursuits while taking in the glorious scenery. There are plenty of way-marked footpaths, which lead through woodlands, across cliffs, past historical monuments and over rolling hills. The dramatic coastline, with its headlands, secluded coves and sandy beaches, is fantastic for watersports: from sailing to windsurfing, scuba diving and swimming; or for just simply relaxing and watching the variety of seabirds that nest on the shores. The Cliffs of Moher, in particular, is a prime location for birdwatching and Goat Island, just offshore, is where puffins make their nesting burrows. Fishing is another popular activity; the country is full of pretty streams, rivers, hidden lakes and canals, which can all be explored by hiring a boat. In the south the beautiful Ring of Kerry is one of the most visited regions. This 110-mile route encircles the Inveragh Peninsula, and is surrounded by mountains and lakes. Other sights include: the Aran Islands, home to some of the most ancient Christian and pre-Christian remains in Ireland, and the Rock of Cashel, with its spectacular group of medieval buildings; not to mention the bustling cities of Dublin, Galway and Cork.

Places of interest

Connaught: Boyle Abbey; Connemara National Park; Céide Fields at Ballycastle; Kylemore Abbey; Aran Islands; Galway cit Westport; Sligo Abbey; megalithic tombs Carrowmore.

Leinster: Wicklow Mountains National Pa Rock of Cashel; Killkenny Castle; Guinnes brewery, Trinity College and National Museum in Dublin; Dunmore Cave at Ballyfoyle; Wexford Wildfowl Reserve.

Munster: harbour towns of Kinsale and Clonakilty; Blarney Castle in Cork; histori city of Limerick with 13th century castle fortress and old town; Ring of Kerry; Bunratty Castle; Cliffs of Moher; Killarney National Park.

Ulster: Glenveagh National Park; Slieve League, the highest sea cliffs in Europe; Donegal Castle; Newmills Corn and Flax Mills in Letterkenny.

Did you know?

The official currency of the Republic of Ireland is the Euro.

The international dialling code for the Republic of Ireland is 00 353 (then drop the first '0' of the number).

The Blarney Stone, reputedly cast with a spell by a witch to reward a king who saved her from drowning, is said to besto the gift of eloquence on all those who kis

The harp is a symbol of the Irish people's love of music: since mediaeval times it ha been the official emblem for Ireland.

Hurling is the oldest native sport.

On display in Trinity College, the Book of Kells is one of the oldest books in the we written around the year 800 AD.

Maps and campsite listings

For this 2010 guide we have changed the way in which we list our parks and the way in which we help you locate the parks within each section of the guide.

We now include a map immediately after our Introduction to the country or region. These maps show the towns near which one (or more) of our featured parks is located. Within each section of the guide, we list these towns and the park(s) in that vicinity in alphabetical order.

You will certainly need more detailed maps for navigation in Ireland, for example the Michelin road atlas. We provide G.P.S. coordinates for each park to assist you. Our three indexes will also help you to find a park by its reference number and name, by region and park name, or by the town where the park is situated.

303

www.alanrogers.com for latest campsite news

Athlone
Lough Ree (East) Caravan & Camping Park
Ballykeeran, Athlone (Co. Westmeath) T: **090 647 8561**. E: **athlonecamping@eircom.net**

alanrogers.com/IR8960

This touring park is alongside the river, screened by trees but reaching the water's edge. Drive into the small village of Ballykeeran and the park is discreetly located behind the main street. The top half of the site is in a woodland situation and after the reception and sanitary block, Lough Ree comes into view and the remaining pitches run down to the shoreline. There are 60 pitches, 20 with hardstanding and 52 with 6A electricity. With fishing right on the doorstep there are boats for hire locally and the site has its own private mooring buoys, plus a dinghy slip and harbour. A restaurant and 'singing' pub are close.

Facilities

The toilet block is clean without being luxurious. Hot showers (€ 1). Dishwashing sinks outside. Laundry room (wash and dry € 8). A wooden chalet houses a pool room with open fire and campers' kitchen (no cooking facilities). Off site: Riding 4 km. Golf 8 km.

Open: 1 April - 30 September.

Directions

From Athlone take N55 towards Longford for 4.8 km. Park is in the village of Ballykeeran, clearly signed. GPS: 53.44815, -7.88992

Charges 2010

Per unit incl. 2 persons and electricity	€ 23,00

No credit cards.

Athy
Forest Farm Caravan & Camping Park
Dublin Road, Athy (Co. Kildare) T: **059 863 1231**. E: **forestfarm@eircom.net**

alanrogers.com/IR9080

This site makes an excellent stopover if travelling from Dublin to the southeast counties. It is also ideally placed to visit local places of interest including the Shackleton exhibition, the Japanese Gardens and the Irish National Stud. Part of a working farm, the campsite spreads to the right of the modern farmhouse, which also provides B&B and holiday apartments. The owners have cleverly utilised their land to create a site which offers 64 unmarked touring pitches on level ground. Of these, 32 are for caravans, all with electricity and ten with hardstanding, and 32 places are available for tents. Full Irish breakfasts are served at the farmhouse and farm tours are arranged on request. The park is signed on the N78 and approached by a 500 m. avenue of tall pines.

Facilities

The centrally located, red brick toilet block is heated and double glazed, providing quality amenities. Spacious shower unit for disabled visitors. Family room with shower and WC. Laundry room. Campers' kitchen with fridge/freezer, cooker, table and chairs. Comfortable, large lounge/games room (a TV can be provided). Sand pit and picnic tables. Off site: Shop, bar and restaurant 3 km. Golf courses nearby. Course and game fishing 4 km.

Open: All year.

Directions

Site is 4.8 km. northeast of Athy town off the main N78 Athy - Kilcullen road. GPS: 53.0139, -6.9256

Charges guide

Per person	€ 4,00
child	€ 2,00
pitch incl. electricity	€ 2,00
hiker, cyclist or motorcyclist incl. tent	€ 6,00

Ballaghaderreen

Willowbrook Camping & Caravan Park

Kiltybranks, Ballaghaderreen (Co. Roscommon) T: **094 986 1307**. E: info@willowbrookpark.com

alanrogers.com/IR8815

This is a campsite with a difference. Willowbrook is a small family run caravan and camping park, which offers a unique holiday in an unspoiled part of Ireland. It has eight hardstanding pitches with electricity and a central level grass area without power, all with ample water points. An additional tent area is in the adjoining field. The main difference is that meditation, Tai Chi and other relaxation techniques, all adding to the tranquillity of the setting, are organised by Dave and Lin Whitefield whose aim is to ensure their guests relax and unwind in this idyllic hideaway. Archery, guided walks on the Suck Valley Way and in the Ox and Curlieu mountains, and coarse fishing for more active relaxation are also provided. A bunkhouse (for up to twelve), a library and reading room with a TV in a renovated 100-year-old cottage add to the ambiance of the park. The camper's kitchen is spotless and homely. This clean and well cared for park is in an area rich with archaeology and heritage, about 20 minutes from Knock airport. It is ideal as a holiday base or as a stop-over on the Dublin - Mayo route to the west of Ireland.

Facilities	Directions
The toilet block is immaculate and lit at night, with separate shower cubicles and facilities for disabled campers. Laundry room. Campers' kitchen with microwave, kettle and toaster. Library and reading room with TV. Fishing. Torches useful. Off site: Local sporting activities available include tennis, golf and fishing.	Park is 6 km. from Ballaghaderreen. Take the R293 from Ballaghaderreen towards Castlerea and Ballyhaunis, then the R325 over the bridge. Bear left, still towards Castlerea and Ballyhaunis for 1.5 km. Turn right at sign to site in 500 m. GPS: 53.86672, -8.60214
Open: All year.	**Charges guide**

Per unit incl. 2 persons and electricity	€ 23,00
family tent incl. 2 adults and 2 children	€ 24,00
No credit cards.	

Bantry

Eagle Point Caravan & Camping Park

Ballylickey, Bantry (Co. Cork) T: **027 506 30**. E: eaglepointcamping@eircom.net

alanrogers.com/IR9510

Midway between the towns of Bantry and Glengarriff, the spectacular peninsula of Eagle Point juts into Bantry Bay. The first impression is of a spacious country park rather than a campsite. As far as the eye can see this 20-acre, landscaped, part-terraced park, with its vast manicured grass areas separated by mature trees, shrubs and hedges, runs parallel with the shoreline providing lovely views. Suitable for all ages, this is a well run park devoted to touring units, with campers pitched mostly towards the shore. It provides 125 pitches (60 caravans, 65 tents), and electric hook-ups, thus avoiding overcrowding during peak periods. For wet weather, a timbered building towards the water's edge houses three lounges, two for children and all with TV – the brightly decorated interior is guaranteed to brighten the dullest of days. Eagle Point makes an excellent base for sightseeing throughout West Cork and Kerry, and for watersports enthusiasts – swimming is safe and there is a slipway for small craft.

Facilities	Directions
Three well maintained, well designed toilet blocks are above expected standards. Laundry. Motorcaravan services. Play area. Tennis. Football field to the far right, well away from the pitches. Fishing. Supermarket at park entrance. Dogs are not accepted. Off site: Bicycle hire 6 km. Riding 10 km. Golf 2 km.	Take N71 to Bandon, then R586 Bandon to Bantry. From Bantry take N71 to Glengarriif. 6.4 km. from Bantry; park entrance is opposite EMO petrol station. GPS: 51.72008, -9.44949
Open: 24 April - 27 September.	**Charges guide**

Per unit incl. 2 persons	€ 26,00 - € 28,00
child	€ 3,00
motorcyclist, hiker or cyclist (per person)	€ 12,00
electricity (6A)	€ 4,00

305

Belleek

Belleek Caravan & Camping Park

Belleek, Ballina (Co. Mayo) T: **096 715 33**. E: **lenahan@belleekpark.com**

alanrogers.com/IR8750

Belleek has a quiet woodland setting, only minutes from Ballina, a famed salmon fishing centre. With excellent pitches and toilet block, the family owners are committed to ensuring that it is immaculate at all times. From the entrance gate, the park is approached by a drive that passes reception and leads to 58 well spaced pitches. With a very neat overall appearance, 32 pitches have hardstanding, 45 have electricity hook-ups, and you may choose your pitch. Sports facilities within a short distance of the park include a swimming pool, tennis and bicycle hire. There is a Blue Flag beach at Ross. Other local attractions are Ceide Fields (a Neolithic farm), Down Patrick Head, Mayo North Heritage Centre or a seaweed bath at Kilcullen's Bath House, Enniscrone.

Facilities

Spotlessly clean, tastefully decorated toilet block providing showers (€ 1.00 token). Baby bath. Facilities for disabled people. Laundry facilities. Reception includes a shop (June - Sept) and a tea room also serving breakfast. Campers' kitchen and emergency accommodation with beds provided. TV room. Games room. Play area. Ball game area. Tennis. Barbecue area. Off site: Fishing 1 km. Bicycle hire 2 km. Golf 3.5 km. Beach 10 km.

Open: 15 March - 1 November, by arrangement all year.

Directions

Take R314 Ballina - Killala road. Park is signed on right after about 3 km. GPS: 54.1345, -9.1585

Charges guide

Per unit incl. 2 persons	€ 19,00
extra person	€ 5,00
child	€ 2,50
electricity (10A)	€ 4,00
hiker/cyclist and tent	€ 9,00

Bennettsbridge

Nore Valley Park

Annamult, Bennettsbridge (Co. Kilkenny) T: **056 772 7229**. E: **norevalleypark@eircom.net**

alanrogers.com/IR9230

This lovely site is set on a grassy hillock overlooking the valley and the river Nore, with a woodland setting behind. Situated on a working farm, it offers 70 touring pitches, 50 of which have 6A electricity. There is an additional area for tents and four mobile homes for rent. The owners, Samuel and Isabel, are proud of their park and Isabel's baking and jams must be sampled. An attractive courtyard houses several unusual facilities including a sand pit and a straw loft play area for wet weather. There are outdoor chess and tractor rides and go-karts in the fields. This is an ideal park for families, especially in school holidays, offering children and adults alike the opportunity to feed the animals (goats, lambs, ducks, chickens and donkey). It is a peaceful holiday base from which to explore the sunny southeast, including the historic city of Kilkenny, renowned for its history and craftwork, Kells Abbey and Dunmore Caves.

Facilities

The modern toilet block is kept very clean and can be heated. Two units suitable for disabled visitors. Laundry room. Motorcaravan services. The original block in the courtyard is used mainly in the low season. Shop (basic items such as milk, bread and camping gaz) and café (June - Aug). Comfortable lounge. Games room. Play area. Minigolf. Off site: Bennettsbridge 3 km with shops and eating places. Outdoor pursuits such as canoeing, walking or fishing 4 km. Riding 6 km. Golf 10 km.

Open: 1 March - 31 October.

Directions

From Kilkenny take R700 to Bennettsbridge. Just before the bridge turn right at sign for Stoneyford and after about 3 km. site is signed Nore Valley Park. GPS: 52.56307, -7.19506

Charges guide

Per person (over 2 yrs)	€ 4,00
pitch	€ 8,00 - € 12,00
electricity (6A)	€ 3,00

Blarney

Blarney Caravan & Camping Park

Stone View, Blarney (Co. Cork) T: 021 451 6519. E: con.quill@camping-ireland.ie
alanrogers.com/IR9480

There is a heart of the country feel about this 'on the farm' site, yet the city of Cork is only an 8 km. drive. What makes this friendly, family run park so appealing is its secluded location and neatly laid out, open appearance. The terrain on the three acre park is elevated and gently sloping, commanding views towards Blarney Castle and the surrounding mountainous countryside. The 80 pitches, 39 of which have hardstanding and 10A electrical connections, are with caravans sited to the centre and left and tents pitched to the right. There are gravel roads, well tended young shrubs and a screen of mature trees and hedging marks the park's perimeter. In the Blarney area, apart from Blarney Castle, house and gardens, there are shops, restaurants, pubs with traditional music and an abundance of outdoor pursuits such as walking, riding and fishing, and easy access to sightseeing in Cork city.

Facilities

Excellent toilet areas, one new, are housed in converted farm buildings with reception and small shop. Facilities for disabled visitors. Laundry room. Campers' kitchen. Motorcaravan service point. Shop (1/6-31/8). TV lounge. 18-hole golf and pitch and putt course. Off site: Bar and restaurant 100 m. serving food all day. Within easy reach of the ports of Cork and Rosslare.

Open: 1 April - 25 October.

Directions

Site is 8 km. northwest of Cork, just off the N20. Take N20 from Cork for about 6 km. and then left on R617 to Blarney. Site clearly signed at Top Filling station in village, in 2 km. GPS: 51.94787, -8.54622

Charges guide

Per person	€ 6,50
child	€ 3,00
pitch	€ 8,00 - € 10,00
electricity (10A)	€ 4,00

Boyle

Lough Key Caravan & Camping Park

Lough Key Forest Park, Boyle (Co. Roscommon) T: 071 966 2212. E: info@loughkey.ie
alanrogers.com/IR8825

This caravan and camping park is set deep in the 320 hectares of the Lough Key Forest Park. Comprising mixed woodland including giant red cedar, beech, ash and oak trees, the forest is bounded by Lough Key and incorporates several of its islands. The rustic design of the main building on the park (which houses reception, a camper's kitchen, a TV room, and the sanitary and laundry facilities) blends well with the wooded environment. The well landscaped, five-hectare site provides space for 52 touring units with electricity connections and ample water points. There is a separate area for tents. The history of the parkland goes back to 1184. A visit to the Lough offers views of islands inhabited by monks and hermits in days gone by, ring forts and tunnels, and natural and historical features including the Temple, the Wishing Chair, the Bog Gardens and Rockingham House and harbour. The location in Lough Key Forest Park offers a base for visiting Strokestown House, Boyle Abbey, Famine Museum and Garden, and the Elphin 18th century windmill. A fisherman's dream, there are pike, bream, roach and perch in Lough Key and brown trout at nearby Lough Arrow. Walks combine the historical and the legend with wildlife, flora and fauna. Boat tours of the lake and boat hire are also available. Coillte, the Irish Forestry Board, who manage the amenity, strictly enforces the forest code.

Facilities

The main toilet block includes metered hot showers (€2). Facilities for disabled campers (key required). Campers' kitchen and sheltered eating area. Laundry. TV room. Play area in the centre of the park with adventure type play equipment in a hedged area, plus seating for parents. Forest walks and trails. Boat tours and boat hire. Security barrier closed at night. Off site: Restaurant at Rockingham harbour. Nearby town of Boyle for bars, restaurants and entertainment 3 km. Bicycle hire and golf 5 km.

Open: Easter - mid September.

Directions

Park is 4 km. east of Boyle on the N4 Dublin - Sligo Road. GPS: 53.98125, -8.235167

Charges guide

Per pitch	€ 10,00 - € 20,00
electricity	€ 2,00

No credit cards.

Caherdaniel

Wave Crest Caravan & Camping Park

Caherdaniel (Co. Kerry) T: 066 947 5188. E: wavecrest@eircom.net

alanrogers.com/IR9560

It would be difficult to imagine a more dramatic location than Wave Crest's on the Ring of Kerry coast. Huge boulders and rocky outcrops tumble from the park entrance on the N70 down to the seashore which forms the most southern promontory on the Ring of Kerry. There are spectacular southward views from the park across Kenmare Bay to the Beara peninsula. Sheltering on grass patches in small coves that nestle between the rocks and shrubbery, are 65 hardstanding pitches and 20 on grass offering seclusion. Electricity connections are available (13A). This park would suit older people looking for a quiet, relaxed atmosphere. A unique feature is the TV room, an old stone farm building with a thatched roof. Its comfortable interior includes a stone fireplace heated by a converted cast iron marker buoy. Caherdaniel is known for its cheerful little pubs and distinguished restaurant. The Derrynane National Park Nature Reserve is only a few kilometres away, as is Derrynane Cove and Bay.

Facilities

Two blocks house the sanitary facilities and include hot showers on payment (€ 1). Toilet for disabled people. Laundry service. Small shop and takeaway service (May - Sept). Play area. Fishing and boat launching. Off site: Riding 1 km. Bicycle hire and golf 10 km. Small beach near and Derrynane Hotel with bar and restaurant.

Open: 27 April - 30 September.

Directions

On the N70 (Ring of Kerry), 1.5 km. east of Caherdaniel. GPS: 51.75826, -10.08875

Charges guide

Per person	€ 2,00
child	€ 1,00
pitch	€ 12,00 - € 13,00
electricity (13A)	€ 2,00

Cahir

The Apple Camping & Caravan Park

Moorstown, Cahir (Co. Tipperary) T: 052 74 414 59. E: con@theapplefarm.com

alanrogers.com/IR9410

This fruit farm and campsite combination offers an idyllic country holiday venue in one of the most delightful situations imaginable. For tourers only, it is located off the N24, midway between Clonmel and Cahir. The park has 32 pitches in a secluded situation behind the barns and are mostly grass with a few hardstandings, with electricity connections to 25. Entrance is by way of a 300 m. drive which follows straight through the heart of the farm. Apple trees guard the route, as do various non-fruit tree species, which are named and of interest to guests who are free to spend time walking the paths around the farm. When we visited, strawberries were being gathered – the best we had tasted all season – and award-winning apple juice, cordials, jams, etc. are also sold by Con and Noreen in the farm shop. Reception is housed with the other site facilities in a large farmyard barn. Although a rather unusual arrangement, it is central and effective. The towns of Cahir and Clonmel are of historic interest and the countryside around boasts rivers, mountains, Celtic culture and scenic drives.

Facilities

Toilet facilities, kept very clean, quite modern in design and with heating, comprise showers, washbasins with mirrors, electric points, etc. in functional units occupying two corners of the large floor space. Facilities for disabled visitors. Also in the barn are dishwashing sinks, washing machine and a fridge/freezer for campers to use. Motorcaravan service point. Tennis. Play area. Dogs are not accepted. Off site: Fishing, golf, bicycle hire and riding within 6 km.

Open: 1 May - 30 September.

Directions

Park is 300 m. off main N24, 9.6 km. west of Clonmel, 6.4 km. east of Cahir. GPS: 52.37663, -7.84262

Charges guide

Per person	€ 6,50
child (0-12 yrs)	€ 4,50
electricity (13A)	€ 2,50
No charge per unit.	
Less 20% for groups of 4 or more.	

Cahirciveen

Mannix Point Camping & Caravan Park

Cahirciveen (Co. Kerry) T: 066 947 2806. E: mortimer@campinginkerry.com

alanrogers.com/IR9610

A tranquil, beautifully located seashore park, it is no exaggeration to describe Mannix Point as a nature lovers' paradise. Situated in one of the most spectacular parts of the Ring of Kerry, overlooking the bay and Valentia Island, the seven acre park commands splendid views in all directions. The park road meanders through the level site and offers 42 pitches of various sizes and shape, many with shelter and seclusion. There are 36 electrical connections (13A) available. A charming, flower bedecked old fisherman's cottage has been converted to provide facilities including reception, a cosy sitting room with turf fire, and an 'emergency' dormitory for campers is a feature. There is no television, but compensation comes in the form of a knowledgeable, hospitable owner who is a Bord Fáilte registered local tour guide. A keen gardener, Mortimer Moriarty laid out the site over 20 years ago and his intention to cause as little disruption to nature as possible has succeeded. The site opens directly onto marshland which teems with wildlife (a two acre nature reserve) with direct access to the beach and seashore. This park retains a wonderful air of Irish charm aided by occasional impromptu musical evenings. A viewing platform allows observation of seals and birdlife and to consider the secrets of the park sculpture, 'the pinicle'. This is also an ideal resting place for people walking the Kerry Way.

Facilities

Toilet and shower facilities were immaculate when we visited. Modern and well equipped campers' kitchen and dining area. Laundry facilities with washing machines and dryer. Motorcaravan service point. Picnic and barbecue facilities. Off site: Bicycle hire 800 m. Riding 3 km. Golf 14 km. Pubs, restaurants and shops 15 minutes walk. Watersports, bird watching, walking and photography. Local cruises to Skelligs Rock with free transport to and from the port for walkers and cyclists.

Open: 15 March - 1 October.

Directions

Park is 300 m. off the N70 Ring of Kerry road, 800 m. southwest of Cahirciveen (or Cahersiveen) on the road towards Waterville. GPS: 51.94281, -10.2434

Charges guide

Per person	€ 6,00
child (1 or 2)	€ 2,00

Reductions for groups and rallies if pre-paid. No credit cards.

Castlebar

Carra Caravan & Camping Park

Belcarra, Castlebar (Co. Mayo) T: 094 903 2054. E: post@mayoholidays.com

alanrogers.com/IR8790

This is an ideal location for those seeking a real Irish village experience in a 'value for money' park. Small, unpretentious and family run, it is located in Belcarra, a regular winner of the 'Tidiest Mayo Village' award. Nestling at the foot of a wooded drumlin, it is surrounded by rolling hills and quiet roads which offer an away from it all feeling, yet Castlebar the county's largest town is only an 8 km. drive. On the pleasant 1.5-acre park, the 20 unmarked touring pitches, seven with electric hook-up (13A), are on flat ground enclosed by ranch fencing and shaded in parts by trees. An additional novel idea at Carra are eight horse-drawn caravans for hire. Also of interest are the talks that the owner Sean and daughter Deirdre give on the area. There are recommended walks and maps provided. New to the area is the National Museum of Country Life at Turlough (8 km) which is now a super attraction.

Facilities

The basic toilet block has adequate, well equipped showers (€ 0.50). Combined kitchen with dishwashing, laundry area with fridge/freezer, sink, table, chairs, washing machine and dryer. Comfortable lounge with TV, books and magazines located at reception. Off site: Village shops, a post office and 'Flukies' cosy bar which serves Irish breakfast and where Irish stew is a speciality. Leisure centre and tennis courts. Free fishing area and special walkway to the river. Golf 8 km.

Open: 2 May - 22 September.

Directions

From Castlebar take N60 Claremorris road for 8.5 km. southeast and turn right at sign for Belcarra. Continue for 4.5 km. to village and site on left at end of village. GPS: 53.80205, -9.21622

Charges guide

Per unit incl. all persons	€ 12,00
electricity	€ 2,00

No credit cards.

Castlebar

Lough Lannagh Caravan Park

Old Westport Road, Castlebar (Co. Mayo) T: **094 902 7111**. E: info@loughlannagh.ie

alanrogers.com/IR8810

Lough Lannagh is an attractive holiday village on the lake shore which comprises quality accommodation, self catering cottages and a caravan park. It is within walking distance of Castlebar with its many restaurants, pubs theatres and shops. County Mayo's main attractions are also within a short drive. The caravan park has 20 touring pitches, well laid out in a separate dedicated corner of the village, all on hardstanding with electric connections. One reception area serves all and is situated to the right of the security barrier. When not out and about, there are many on site activities for all the family. The main attraction is the fitness suite, sauna and steam room, plus reflexology and therapies available (over 18s only admitted to the gym). Popular with the young is the three times weekly club held in July/August. Anglers need only travel 500 metres, or if you prefer cycling, bicycles can be hired.

Facilities

One modern heated sanitary block provides washbasins and well equipped, pre-set showers. En-suite unit for disabled visitors. Laundry room with sink, washing machines and dryers. Café (serving breakfast). Fitness suite. Tennis. Bicycle hire.

Open: 10 April - 31 October.

Directions

To get to Castlebar take the N5, N60 or N84. At Castlebar ring road follow directions for Westport. Site is signed on all approach roads to the Westport roundabout. GPS: 53.8491, -9.3119

Charges guide

Per unit incl. 2 persons, electricity and hardstanding	€ 21,00 - € 28,00
tent incl. 2 persons	€ 16,00 - € 18,00
child	€ 1,50

Castlegregory

Anchor Caravan Park

Castlegregory (Co. Kerry) T: **066 713 9157**. E: anchorcaravanpark@eircom.net

alanrogers.com/IR9550

Of County Kerry's three long, finger-like peninsulas which jut into the sea, Dingle is the most northerly. Tralee is the main town and Anchor Caravan Park is 20 km. west of this famed town and under 4 km. south of Castlegregory on Tralee Bay. A secluded and mature, five-acre park, it is enclosed by shrubs and trees that give excellent shelter. A gateway leads to a beautiful, sandy beach which is safe for bathing, boating and shore fishing. There are 30 pitches, all with electric hook-ups and some also with drainage and water points. Although there are holiday homes for hire, these are well apart from the touring pitches. In this area of great beauty, miles of sand abound and taking in the panorama of mountain scenery from the top of the Conor Pass is a wonderful experience.

Facilities

Toilet facilities (entry by key) are kept very clean and provide showers on payment (€ 0,50), two private cabins, some low level basins and a toilet with handrail. No facilities for disabled campers. Laundry facilities (incl. drying room, clothes lines and ironing). Campers' kitchen with fridges, freezers and seating. Motorcaravan services. Two play areas. Games and TV rooms. Off site: Beautiful sandy beach 2 minutes. Fishing 2 km. Riding or bicycle hire 3 km. Golf 4 km.

Open: Easter - 30 September.

Directions

From Tralee follow the Dingle coast road for 19 km. Park is signed from Camp junction. GPS: 52.24393, -9.98579

Charges guide

Per unit incl. 2 persons and electricity	€ 20,00 - € 22,00
extra person	€ 5,00
child	€ 2,00
No credit cards.	

Clondalkin

Camac Valley Tourist Caravan & Camping Park

Green Isle Road, Clondalkin Dublin 22 (Co. Dublin) T: 014 640 644. E: reservations@camacvalley.com
alanrogers.com/IR9100

Opened in 1996, this campsite is not only well placed for Dublin, but also offers a welcome stopover if travelling to the more southern counties from the north of the country, or vice versa. Despite its close proximity to the city, being located in the 300 acre Corkagh Park gives it a 'heart of the country' atmosphere. There are 163 pitches, 48 for tents placed to the fore and hardstandings for caravans laid out in bays and avenues with electrical connections, drainage and water points. Maturing trees and shrubs separate pitches and roads are of tarmac. Beyond the entrance gate and forecourt stands an attractive timber fronted building housing the site amenities. Its design includes various roof levels and spacious interior layout, with large windows offering a view of the site. Housed here are reception, information, reading, TV and locker rooms plus a shop and the sanitary facilities. After a day of sightseeing in Dublin, which can be reached by bus from the site, Camac Valley offers an evening of relaxation with woodland and river walks in the park or a number of first class restaurants and pubs nearby. The site entrance and sign are distinctive and can be spotted in adequate time when approaching on the busy N7 road.

Facilities

Heated sanitary facilities include good sized showers (token). Facilities for disabled people. Baby room. Laundry. Shop and coffee bar. Playground with wooden play frames and safety base. Fishing. Electronic gate controlled from reception and 24 hour security. Off site: Bicycle hire 1.5 km. Golf 6 km. Riding 9 km.

Open: All year.

See advertisement opposite

Directions

From north follow signs for West Link and the M50 motorway. Exit M50 at junction 9 onto N7 Cork road. Site is on right of dual-carriageway (beside Green Isle Hotel) after 2 km. and is clearly signed. At City West business park, cross over bridge and return on dual-carriageway following site signs – site is on the left after 800 m. GPS: 53.30445, -6.41533

Charges guide

Per unit incl. 2 persons	€ 22,00 - € 24,00
incl. up to 4 children	€ 26,00
tent, car and 2 persons	€ 19,00 - € 22,00
extra person	€ 5,00
electricity (10A)	€ 5,00

Cong

Cong Caravan & Camping Park

Lisloughrey, Quay Road, Cong (Co. Mayo) T: 094 954 6089. E: info@quietman-cong.com
alanrogers.com/IR8740

It would be difficult to find a more idyllic and famous spot for a caravan park than Cong. Situated close to the shores of Lough Corrib, Cong's scenic beauty was immortalised in the film 'The Quiet Man'. This well kept park is 1.6 km. from the village of Cong, near the grounds of the magnificent and renowned Ashford Castle. The owner's house that incorporates reception, shop and the hostel, stands to the fore of the site. The 40 grass pitches, 36 with electricity, are placed at a higher level to the rear, with the sheltered tent areas below and to the side. The park can be crowded and busy in high season.

Facilities

Toilet facilities are tastefully decorated, kept clean and are heated when necessary. Hot showers with curtains (€ 1 charge). Campers' kitchen. Launderette service. Shop. Full Irish or continental breakfast, dinner or packed lunch may be ordered, or home baked bread and scones purchased in the shop. Barbecue, games room and play area. TV lounge. Bicycle hire. Off site: Riding and golf within 2 km. Fishing and boat slipway 500 m.

Open: All year.

Directions

Leave N84 road at Ballinrobe to join R334/345 signed Cong. Turn left at end of the R345 (opposite entrance to Ashford Castle), slow down take next road on right (about 300 m) and the park is on right (200 m). GPS: 53.53945, -9.27263

Charges guide

Per unit incl. 2 persons, electricity	€ 26,00
extra person	€ 2,50 - € 3,00

Corofin
Corofin Village Camping & Caravan Park
Main Street, Corofin (Co. Clare) T: 065 683 7683. E: corohost@iol.ie
alanrogers.com/IR9460

This compact green oasis in the centre of the village of Corofin occupies one acre and adjoins the family's hostel. The owners, Jude and Marie Neylon live on the site and have a policy of always having a family member on hand at all times. They are very environmentally aware and have excellent recycling facilities. The 20 pitches all have electricity and there are ample water points. A campers' kitchen, laundry room and the TV and games room are separate to the hostel facilities. This little site is neat and well maintained and makes an ideal base for sightseeing throughout Clare. Attractions include the world famous Burren and the Aillwee Caves, Quinn Abbey, Craggaunown and Knappogue Castles, as well as places of interest in Galway and Limerick. Public transport is available to the famous Lahinch beach and to the large town of Ennis. It is a peaceful location, yet central for the restaurants, takeaway, shops and pubs in the village. This area is renowned for its traditional music. There are several lakes in the immediate locality for boating and fishing enthusiasts.

Facilities
The sanitary block is bright and clean with free hot showers. Separate facilities for disabled campers. Laundry room with washing machine and dryer. CCTV security. Torches useful. Site is not suitable for large units. Off site: Fishing and boat launching 2 km. Riding 8 km. Bicycle hire 10 km. Golf 20 km. Beach 20 km.

Open: 1 April - 30 September.

Directions
Corofin village is 12 km. from Ennis, from where you take the N85 towards Ennistymon and after 2 km. (well signed) turn right onto R476. Site is in the centre of the village. GPS: 52.9407, -9.058933

Charges guide

Per unit with 2 persons and electricity	€ 30,00
plus 2 children	€ 35,00

Donard
Moat Farm Caravan & Camping Park
Donard (Co. Wicklow) T: 045 404 727. E: moatfarm@ireland.com
alanrogers.com/IR9160

Providing a true feel of the countryside, this park is part of a working sheep farm. It offers incredible vistas across a scenic landscape, yet is within driving distance of Dublin and Rosslare. Driving into the village of Donard you little suspect that alongside the main street lies a pleasant, well cared for and tranquil five-acre campsite. The entrance is approached by way of a short road where the ruins of a Medieval church sit high overlooking the forecourt and reception. There are 40 pitches for caravans and tents. Spacious pitches with hardstanding line both sides of a broad avenue, incorporating ample space for awnings and all with electricity and drainage. A large field takes tents and further caravans. The site makes a good base for touring or going on foot, for this area is a walker's paradise with a 30 minute circular walk around the perimeter of the site. Those with larger units are advised to contact the site to check accessibility.

Facilities
The toilet block is kept very clean and includes spacious showers. Facilities for visitors with disabilities. Well equipped laundry room. Good quality campers' kitchen. Large recreation/entertainment room with open fire. Three large barbecues and patio area. Caravan storage. Off site: Mountain climbing or sites of archaeological interest nearby. Fishing 3 km. Bicycle hire 15 km. Golf 13 km.

Open: 15 March - 30 September.

Directions
Park is 16.5 km. south of Blessington. Leave M50 Dublin ring motorway at exit 10 to join N81 southwest for 19 km. to Blessington. Continue on N81 for a further 16.5 km. and turn left at Old Toll House pub onto local road and follow signs to park in Donard village (3.5 km). GPS: 53.0212, -6.61562

Charges guide

Per unit incl. 2 persons and electricity	€ 23,00
extra person	€ 5,00
child	€ 3,00
motorcyclist, cyclist or hiker incl. tent	€ 10,00
No credit cards.	

Dungarvan

Casey's Caravan & Camping Park

Clonea, Dungarvan (Co. Waterford) T: **058 419 19**

alanrogers.com/**IR9330**

Set on 20 acres of flat grass, edged by mature trees, this family run park is well managed and offers 284 pitches which include 110 touring pitches all with electrical hook-ups and 39 with hardstanding. The remainder are occupied by caravan holiday homes. There is direct access from the park to a sandy, 'Blue Flag' beach with a resident lifeguard during July and August. A highly recommended leisure centre is adjacent should the weather be inclement. The park is 5.5 km. from Dungarvan, a popular town for deep sea angling, from where charter boats can be hired and three 18 hole golf courses are within easy driving distance. Suggested drives include the scenic Vee, the Comeragh Drive and the coast road to Tramore.

Facilities

The central toilet block (key system), has good facilities kept spotlessly clean. Showers on payment (€1). Small laundry with washing machine and dryer. A further modern block provides an excellent campers' kitchen, laundry room and toilet for disabled visitors. Large adventure play area. Games room. TV lounge. Minigolf. Gas supplies. Full time security staff in high season. Tiny tots play area for those under 4 yrs. Off site: Two village stores near the beach. Golf 5 km. Fishing 4 km. Riding 20 km.

Open: 1 April - 12 September.

Directions

From Dungarvan centre follow R675 east for 3.5 km. Look for signs on the right to Clonea Bay and site. Site is about 1.5 km. GPS: 52.094767, -7.546167

Charges guide

Per unit incl. 2 persons	
and electricity	€ 27,00 - € 31,00
extra person	€ 7,00 - € 8,00
child	€ 3,00
hiker, biker, cyclist	€ 10,00 - € 10,50

No credit cards.

Grade Category 4★ • Bord Failte Registered • Bord Failte / ICC Park Awards
Best 4★ 2004 • 2000 & 2002 Overall Winner Best Park
2001 & 2002 Personal Choice Awards • Merit Award 4★ 2003

Top class facilities including; playground, electric sites for tents & tourers (10A), crazy golf, games & TV rooms and also laundry & kitchen facilities. The park is situated next to EU Blue Flag beach. 2 shops with takeaway are also nearby.

Dungarvan town is 5.5km away and there's a choice of scenic views to visit. Adjacent hotel with 19 metre pool and leisure centre with bowling alley. Other activities can include deep sea and river angling and an 18 hole golf course which are all within easy reach.

Best Coastal park 2008
Best Seaside Park Award 2007
Ambience Award 2006

Clonea, Dungarvan, Co Waterford   Tel: +353 (0)58 41919

Fermoy

Blackwater Valley Caravan & Camping Park

Mallow-Killarney Road, Fermoy (Co. Cork) T: **025 321 47**

alanrogers.com/**IR9470**

The location of this park provides the best of both worlds, as it backs onto green fields adjacent to the Blackwater river, yet is within 200 metres of Fermoy town. Pat and Nora Ryan live overlooking the park which ensures supervision and attention to detail. Ideal for touring, there are 25 pitches with hardstanding and electricity connections (13A) and water supply nearby, and considerable additional space for tents towards the rear of the park. There are five caravan holiday homes to rent. Fermoy provides local amenities, such as a cinema and the town park with a leisure centre with pool and a play area. There are restaurants and pubs, many providing traditional music. The Mitchelstown Caves, Mount Mellary, Lismore Castle and many other attractions are within easy reach of the park.

Facilities

Modern, tiled toilet block provides the usual facilities including for disabled visitors. Laundry room with ironing facilities. Campers' kitchen with cooking facilities and dining area. TV and games room. Motorcaravan service point. Off site: Fishing adjacent to park. Bicycle hire 500 m. Golf 3.5 km. Beach 35 km. Internet access 100 m. Petrol station with gas across the road.

Open: 15 March - 31 October.

Directions

In Fermoy town take the N72 for Mallow. Park is 200 m. from the junction. GPS: 52.1398, -8.3126

Charges guide

Per unit incl. 2 persons	€ 17,00
extra person	€ 5,00
child	€ 2,00
electricity	€ 3,50

No credit cards.

Glandore
The Meadow Camping Park
Glandore (Co. Cork) T: 028 332 80. E: meadowcamping@eircom.net
alanrogers.com/IR9500

The stretch of coast from Cork to Skibbereen reminds British visitors of Devon before the era of mass tourism. This is rich dairy country, the green of the meadows matching the emerald colours of the travel posters. Thanks to the warm and wet Gulf Stream climate, it is also a county of gardens and keen gardeners. The Meadows is best described not as a site, but as a one acre garden surrounded, appropriately, by lush meadows. The owners, who live on the park, have cunningly arranged accommodation for 19 pitches among the flower beds and shrubberies of their extended garden. There are ten hardstandings for motorcaravans with 6A electric hook-ups.

Facilities

Facilities are limited but well designed and immaculately maintained. Showers on payment. Washing machine and dryer. Larger units may be accepted depending on length and available space; contact park before arrival. Football and cycling are not permitted on the park. Off site: Riding 5 km. Fishing, swimming, boat launching and sailing at Glandore 2 km. Bicycle hire 10 km. Golf 19 km.

Open: 30 April - 15 September.

Directions

Park is 1.5 km. east of Glandore, off N71 road, on the R597 midway between Leap and Rosscarbery (coast road). GPS: 51.56693, -9.09702

Charges 2010

Per unit incl. 2 persons and electricity	€ 23,00
extra person	€ 6,00
child (under 16 yrs)	€ 3,00

No credit cards.

Glenbeigh
Glenross Caravan & Camping Park
Glenbeigh (Co. Kerry) T: 066 976 8451. E: glenross@eircom.net
alanrogers.com/IR9600

Its situation on the spectacular Ring of Kerry and the Kerry Way gives Glenross an immediate advantage, and scenic grandeur around every bend of the road is guaranteed as Glenbeigh is approached. Quietly located before entering the village, the park commands a stunning view of Rossbeigh Strand, which is within walking distance. On arrival, a good impression is created with the park well screened from the road and with new stone entrance and gates. With 30 touring pitches, all with hardstanding and electricity, and six caravan holiday homes, the park is attractively laid out.

Facilities

Well maintained modern toilet block includes facilities for laundry and dishwashing. Motorcaravan service point. Games room. Bicycle hire. Shelter for campers and new dining area. Off site: Playground at Rossbeigh beach (5 minutes). Watersports and tennis near. Riding and fishing 200 m. Golf 500 m.

Open: 1 May - 23 September.

Directions

Park is on the N70 Killorglin - Glenbeigh road, on the right just before entering the village. GPS: 52.05887, -9.93198

Charges guide

Per person	€ 8,00
child (under 14 yrs)	€ 3,00
pitch incl. electricity	€ 13,00 - € 14,00

No credit cards.

Keel
Keel Sandybanks Caravan & Camping Park
Keel, Achill Island (Co. Mayo) T: 098 432 11. E: info@achillcamping.com
alanrogers.com/IR8730

This is a park offering a taste of island life and the opportunity to relax in dramatic, scenic surroundings. Achill, Ireland's largest island, is 24 km. long and 19 km. wide and is connected to the mainland by a bridge. The site is situated beside Keel village and approached by the R319 from the swivel bridge at Achill Sound. Although there are static holiday mobile homes on this site, the 42 pitches for caravans and 42 for tents are kept separate. Some with hardstanding are located at the perimeter fence overlooking the beach. Although sand based, the ground is firm and level. Roads are tarmac and there is direct access to the beach which is supervised by lifeguards.

Facilities

Two modern toilet blocks serve the site, one at the entrance gate beside reception and the other in a central position. Heated facilities include WCs (one for disabled visitors), washbasins and hot showers (on payment). Hair and hand dryers. Play area. TV room. Surfing, canoeing and board sailing on Keel Strand and Lough. Fishing trips can be arranged. Off site: Bicycle hire and golf 200 m. Riding 6 km. In the village there is a food shop, takeaway, restaurants and music at night in the pubs.

Open: 27 May - 4 September.

Directions

From Achill Sound follow the R319 for 16 km. Site is on the left before Keel village. GPS: 53.97535, -10.0779

Charges guide

Per pitch	€ 16,00 - € 18,00
electricity (6A)	€ 3,00
cyclist/hiker incl. tent	€ 10,00 - € 12,00

Kilkenny

Tree Grove Caravan & Camping Park

Danville House, Kilkenny (Co. Kilkenny) T: **056 777 0302**. E: treecc@iol.ie
alanrogers.com/IR9240

The entrance gate to this small family run site is easily spotted off the R700 road. An orderly, neat park, it appeals because its young owners are friendly and have designed a logical layout to suit both the terrain and campers needs. It is terraced with the lower terrace to the right of the wide sweeping driveway laid out with 11 hardstanding pitches for caravans. All 30 pitches have electrical hook-ups (10A) and plenty of water points are to be found. On a higher level, is a grass area for hikers and cyclists with further caravan and tent pitches sited near the elevated sanitary block.

Facilities

House plants add decoration inside the toilet block giving a cared for look to this modern building. Family room with shower, WC and washbasin which can be used by disabled people. Laundry room. Open, covered kitchen for campers with fridge, worktop, sink and electric kettle adjoins a comfortable games/TV room with pool table, and easy chairs. Bicycle hire. Tents to rent. Off site: Fishing 500 m. Riding 1 km. Golf 2 or 15 km.

Open: 1 March - 15 November.

Directions

Travelling north on the N10 Waterford - Kilkenny Road turn right at roundabout on ring road. Continue to 2nd roundabout and turn right onto R700. Site is 150 m. on right. GPS: 52.63998, -7.22955

Charges guide

Per unit incl. 2 persons, electricity	€ 17,00 - € 22,00
incl. 2 children	€ 22,00 - € 27,00
tent (per person)	€ 6,50 - € 7,50
extra person	€ 6,50

No credit cards.

Killarney

Fleming's White Bridge

Ballycasheen Road, Killarney (Co. Kerry) T: **064 663 1590**. E: info@killarneycamping.com
alanrogers.com/IR9620

Once past the county border, the main road from Cork to Killarney (N22) runs down the valley of the Flesk river. On the final approach to Killarney off the N22 Cork road, the river veers away from the road to enter the Lower Lake. On this prime rural position, between the road and the river, and within comfortable walking distance of the town, is Fleming's White Bridge, a nine-acre woodland park. The ground is flat, landscaped and generously adorned with flowers, shrubs and trees. There are now 92 pitches (46 caravans and 46 tents) that extend beyond a wooden bridge to an area surrounded by mature trees. A new toilet block, one of three, is sited in this area. This is obviously a park of which the owners are very proud, and the family personally supervise the reception and grounds, maintaining high standards of hygiene, cleanliness and tidiness. The park's location so close to Ireland's premier tourism centre makes this park an ideal base to explore Killarney and the southwest.

Facilities

Three toilet blocks are maintained to high standards. Motorcaravan service point. Campers' drying room and two laundries. Shop (1/6-1/9). Two TV rooms and a games room. Fishing (advice and permits provided). Canoeing (own canoes). Bicycle hire. Woodland walks. Off site: Riding 3 km. Golf 2 km.

Open: 9 April - 5 October, 23-26 October (2009).

Directions

From Cork and Mallow: at N72/N22 junction continue towards Killarney and take first turn left (signed Ballycasheen Road). Proceed for 300 m. to archway entrance on left. From Limerick: follow N22 Cork road. Pass Super Valu and The Heights Hotel take first right (signed Ballycasheen Road) and continue as above. From Kenmare: On N71, pass Gleneagles Hotel and Flesk Bridge. Turn right at traffic lights into Woodlawn Road and Ballycasheen Road and continue 2 km. to archway. GPS: 52.05595, -9.47458

Charges guide

Per unit incl. 2 persons	€ 27,00 - € 28,00
child (under 14 yrs)	€ 3,00
hiker, cyclist and tent	€ 10,00 - € 11,00
electricity (10A)	€ 5,00

No credit cards.

Killarney
Killarney Flesk Caravan & Camping Park

Muckross Road, Killarney (Co. Kerry) T: 064 317 04. E: killarneylakes@eircom.net

alanrogers.com/IR9640

At the gateway to the National Park and Lakes, near Killarney town, this family run, seven-acre park has undergone extensive development and offers high quality standards. Pitches are well spaced and have electricity (10A), water, and drainage connections; 21 also have hardstanding with a grass area for awnings. The grounds have been well cultivated with further shrubs, plants and an attractive barbecue and patio area. This is to the left of the sanitary block and is paved and sunk beneath the level road. Surrounded by a garden border, it has tables and chairs, making a pleasant communal meeting place commanding excellent views of Killarney's mountains.

Facilities

Modern, clean toilet blocks are well designed and equipped. Baby room. Laundry room. Campers' kitchen. Comfortable games room. Night time security checks. Winter caravan storage. Off site: Adjacent hotel (same ownership) with bar and restaurant. Fishing 300 m. Boat launching 2 km.

Open: 17 April - 30 September.

Directions

From Killarney town centre follow the N71 and signs for Killarney National Park. Site is 1.5 km. on the left beside the Gleneagle Hotel. GPS: 52.04304, -9.49954

Charges guide

Per person	€ 8,00
child (under 14 yrs)	€ 3,00
pitch incl. electricity (10A)	€ 13,00 - € 14,00

Killarney
Fossa Caravan & Camping Park

Fossa, Killarney (Co. Kerry) T: 064 663 1497. E: fossaholidays@eircom.net

alanrogers.com/IR9590

This mature, well equipped park is in a scenic location, ten minutes' drive from the town centre. Fossa Caravan Park is recognisable by its forecourt on which stands a distinctive building with reception area and shop. The well laid out park is divided in two – the touring area lies to the right, tucked behind the main building and to the left is an open grass area mainly for campers. Touring pitches, with electricity (10/15A) and drainage, have hardstanding and are angled between shrubs and trees in a tranquil, well cared for garden setting. To the rear at a higher level and discreetly placed are 30 caravan holiday homes. Sheltered by the thick foliage of the wooded slopes which climb high behind the park, these are unobtrusive. Not only is Fossa convenient for Killarney (5.5 km), it is also en-route for the famed Ring of Kerry, and makes an ideal base for walkers and golfers.

Facilities

Modern toilet facilities kept spotlessly clean include showers on payment. Laundry room. Campers' kitchen. Shop. Takeaway (8/7-25/8). TV lounge. Tennis. Play area. Picnic area. Games room. Security patrol. Off site: Fishing and golf 2 km. Riding 3 km. Bicycle hire 5 km.

Open: 1 April - 30 September.

Directions

Approaching Killarney from all directions, follow signs for N72 Ring of Kerry/Killorglin. At last roundabout join R562/N72. Continue for 5.5 km. and Fossa is the second park to the right. GPS: 52.07071, -9.58573

Charges 2010

Per unit incl. 2 persons, electricity	€ 24,00 - € 26,00
extra person	€ 6,00
child (under 14 yrs)	€ 2,50

Killarney
Donoghues White Villa Farm Caravan & Camping Park

Killarney - Cork Road N22, Lissivigeen, Killarney (Co. Kerry) T: 064 662 0671

E: killarneycamping@eircom.net **alanrogers.com/IR9630**

This is a very pleasing small touring park in scenic surroundings on the N22 Killarney-Cork road. Set in the countryside surrounded by green fields, yet is only five minutes away from Killarney town. Trees and shrubs surround the park but dominant is a magnificent view of the MacGillicuddy's Reeks. There are 30 pitches for caravans and tents, 20 with hardstanding and a grass area for awnings, electricity (10A), water points and night lighting. One is designated for disabled campers. An unusual novelty is old school desks placed around the site, plus an antique green telephone box. One can also enjoy walking through the oak wood, fishing on the Flesk or visiting the site's own National Farm Museum.

Facilities

The toilet block, a sandstone coloured building, is kept spotlessly clean and houses showers on payment, a good toilet/shower room for disabled visitors, laundry room and dishwashing sinks. Motorcaravan service area. Campers' kitchen with TV. Play area. Max. 2 dogs per pitch (not certain breeds). Daily coach tours from park. Off site: Riding, golf and bicycle hire 3 km. Pub/restaurant 1 km. Killarney town 5 minutes, the National Park is 10 minutes away.

Open: 1-15 April and 26 April - 4 October.

Directions

From Killarney follow N22 Cork road signs and White Villa Farm finger signs from Park Road roundabout. From Kenmare take R569 via Kilgarvan to the N22, or N71 to Killarney, then the N22 Cork road. GPS: 52.04724, -9.45358

Charges 2010

Per unit incl. 2 persons, electricity	€ 22,00 - € 23,00

No credit cards.

Kilmacanogue

Valley Stopover & Caravan Park

Killough, Kilmacanogue (Co. Wicklow) T: 012 829 565. E: rowanbb@eircom.net

alanrogers.com/IR9140

In a quiet, idyllic setting in the picturesque Rocky Valley, this small, neat, family run park is convenient for the Dublin ferries. Situated in the grounds of the family home, covering under an acre, it can be used either as a transit site or for a longer stay. It will appeal to those who prefer the more basic 'CL' type site. There are four grassy pitches with electric hook-ups, nine hardstandings, a separate area for three tents, two water points, night lighting and a security gate. Staying put here you are only minutes from Enniskerry which lies in the glen of the Glencullen river. Here you can enjoy a delight of forest walks, or visit Powerscourt, one of the loveliest gardens in Ireland. To be at the sea, travel 6 km. to Bray and you are in one of the oldest seaside resorts in the country.

Facilities

Toilet facilities, clean when we visited, are housed in one unit and consist of two WCs with washbasins, mirrors, etc. and a shower. Laundry sink, spin dryer. Campers' kitchen. Full cooked Irish breakfast in the family guest house. Off site: Riding 3 km. Golf 7 km. Fishing 16 km.

Open: Easter - 31 October.

Directions

Turn off N11 Dublin - Wexford road at Kilmacanogue, following signs for Glendalough. Continue for 1.6 km. and take right fork signed 'Waterfall'. Park is second opening on the left in about 200 m. GPS: 53.1671, -6.1634

Charges guide

Per unit incl. 2 persons and electricity	€ 20,00
extra person	€ 1,25

Knock

Knock Caravan & Camping Park

Claremorris Road, Knock (Co. Mayo) T: 094 938 8100. E: caravanpark@knock-shrine.ie

alanrogers.com/IR8780

This park is immediately south of the world famous shrine that receives many visitors. Comfortable and clean, the square shaped campsite is kept very neat with tarmac roads and surrounded by clipped trees. The pitches are of a decent size accommodating 50 caravans or motorcaravans, 20 tents and 18 caravan holiday homes (for rent). All pitches have hardstanding (five doubles) and there are 52 electrical connections (13A), with an adequate number of water points. There is also an overflow field. Because of the religious connections of the area, the site is very busy in August and indeed there are unlikely to be any vacancies at all for 14-16 August. Besides visiting the shrine and Knock Museum, it is also a good centre for exploring scenic Co. Mayo.

Facilities

Two heated toilet blocks have good facilities for disabled visitors and a nice sized rest room attached, hot showers (on payment) and adequate washing and toilet facilities. Laundry room. Gas supplies. Playground. Off site: Fishing 4.5 km. Golf and riding 11 km.

Open: 1 March - 31 October.

Directions

Exit from the N17 at the Knock bypass and from the roundabout follow signs to the site which is just south of the village. GPS: 53.7877, -8.9194

Charges guide

Per person	€ 2,00 - € 2,50
child	€ 1,00
pitch	€ 16,00 - € 17,00
electricity (13A)	€ 3,50
hiker or cyclist incl. tent	€ 10,50 - € 11,50
No credit cards.	

Lauragh

Creveen Lodge Caravan & Camping Park

Healy Pass, Lauragh (Co. Kerry) T: 064 831 31. E: info@creveenlodge.com

alanrogers.com/IR9570

The address of this park is rather confusing, but Healy Pass is the well known scenic summit of the road (R574) crossing the Beara Peninsula, which lies between Kenmare Bay to the north and Bantry Bay to the south. Several kilometres inland from the north coast road (R571), the R574 starts to climb steeply southward towards the Healy Pass. Here, on the mountain foothills, is Creveen Lodge, a working hill farm with a quiet, homely atmosphere. There are 20 pitches, 16 for tents, four for caravans, with an area of hardstanding for motorcaravans, and electrical connections are available. To allow easy access, the steep farm track is divided into a simple one-way system. Creveen Lodge, commanding views across Kenmare Bay, is divided among three gently sloping fields separated by trees. The park is carefully tended with neat rubbish bins and rustic picnic tables informally placed. Although not so famed as the Iveragh Peninsula, around which runs the Ring of Kerry, the northern Beara is a scenically striking area of County Kerry. This is walking and climbing countryside or, of interest close by, is Derreen Gardens.

Facilities

Well appointed and immaculately maintained, the small toilet block provides showers on payment (€ 0.65). Communal room with very good cooking facilities, a fridge, freezer, TV, ironing board, fireplace, tables and chairs. Reception is in the farmhouse. Play area. Off site: Water sports, riding, 'Seafare' cruises, shops and a restaurant nearby. Fishing 2 km. Bicycle hire and boat launching 9 km.

Open: Easter - 31 October.

Directions

Park is on the Healy Pass road (R574) 1.5 km. southeast of Lauragh. GPS: 51.75562, -9.76193

Charges guide

Per unit incl. 2 persons	€ 16,00
extra person	€ 3,00
child	€ 1,00
electricity (5A)	€ 4,00

No credit cards.

Mullingar

Lough Ennell Camping & Caravan Park

Tudenham Shore, Mullingar (Co. Westmeath) T: **044 934 8101**. E: eamon@caravanparksireland.com

alanrogers.com/IR8965

Nature and rustic charm is the visitor's first reaction on arrival at Lough Ennell Caravan Park. Set in 18 acres of mature woodland beside a Blue Flag lake, Eamon and Geraldine O'Malley run this sheltered and tranquil park with their family who live on the site. They receive a blend of visitors – seasonal residents in camping holiday homes (private and to rent), caravanners and motorcaravanners and there are ample areas for tents. Pitches are varied, sheltered with trees and natural shrubbery, and spacious with gravel or gravel and grass combinations. Electricity is available on 44 hardstanding and grass pitches and there are water points on or near all the pitches. Just an hour from Dublin, it provides a good holiday base or a useful stop over en-route to the West of Ireland. The watersports permitted on the lake include canoeing, sailing, windsurfing, boating, fishing and safe swimming. The woodlands offer ample opportunities for walking and cycling. Numerous other lakes in the area provide fishing for all varieties especially wild trout. Other activities might include tennis, horse riding, golf, dog racing and of course forest walks. Belvedere House and Tullynally Castle are nearby and the large town of Mullingar is just 6 km.

Facilities

The toilet block provides toilets, washbasins and hot showers (€1 coin). Additional dishwashing areas are around the park. Laundry. Small shop. Café and coffee shop with takeaway. TV and games room. Play areas and area for ball games. Small lakeside beach. Fishing. Late arrivals area outside. Security including CCTV. Some breeds of dog are not accepted. Off site: Bus service 8 km. Golf 1.5 km. Riding 4 km. Bicycle hire 6 km.

Open: Easter/1 April - 30 September.

Directions

From N4 take the N52. Follow signs for Belvedere House and take turn 300 m. south of Belvedere House (signed for site). Continue to the shores of Lough Ennell and turn left. GPS: 53.4857, -7.36299

Charges guide

Per unit incl. 2 persons and electricity	€ 23,00 - € 25,00
extra person	€ 5,00
child	€ 3,00

No credit cards.

Redcross Village

River Valley Caravan & Camping Park

Redcross Village (Co. Wicklow) T: **040 441 647**. E: info@rivervalleypark.com

alanrogers.com/IR9150

In the small country village of Redcross, in the heart of County Wicklow, you will find this popular, family run park. Based here you are within easy reach of beauty spots such as the Vale of Avoca (Ballykissangel), Glendalough and Powerscourt, plus the safe beach of Brittas Bay. The 145 touring pitches at River Valley are mostly together in a dedicated area, all have 6A electricity and a choice of hardstanding or grass – you select your pitch. There is a new, hardstanding area for adults only, with its own amenity block and where dogs are allowed. A late arrivals area has electricity hook-ups, water and night lighting. There is Fort Apache, the adventure playground, a play area for small children or a mountain stream where it is safe to paddle. There is also a pets corner. An attractive wine and coffee bar with a conservatory is inviting, or an alternative may be the restaurant where home made, traditional dishes are on the menu.

Facilities

A luxurious new sanitary block is modern and well designed. Excellent facilities for disabled visitors. Showers are on payment (€ 1). Laundry area. Campers' kitchen. Motorcaravan service points. Gas supplies. Wine/coffee bar and restaurant (1/6-31/8). TV and games room. Three tennis courts. Par 3 golf course. Bowling green. Sports complex. Adventure and toddlers' playgrounds. Caravan storage. Dogs are not accepted in July/Aug. in the family area. Off site: Riding 2 km.

Open: 12 March - 1 November.

Directions

From Dublin follow the N11 Wexford road south, bypassing Ashford and Rathnew. After passing The Beehive pub look out for Doyle's pub on the right. Turn right at the pub and continue for 5 km. to the park at the top of Redcross village. GPS: 52.8884, -6.14528

Charges guide

Per unit incl. 2 persons, electricity	€ 23,00 - € 25,00
extra person	€ 6,00
child (2-15 yrs)	€ 4,00
hiker or cyclist incl. tent	€ 11,00 - € 12,00

Roscrea

Streamstown Caravan & Camping Park

Streamstown, Roscrea (Co. Tipperary) T: 050 521 519. E: streamstowncaravanpark@eircom.net

alanrogers.com/IR9420

This family run site, set on a dairy farm in the centre of Ireland, has been open for over 30 years. It is conveniently situated off the N7 Dublin - Limerick road and makes a good overnight halt or for a longer stay if you are seeking a quiet, restful location with little to disturb the peace. There are 27 touring pitches, ten with hardstanding and separated by low hedges. The remainder are on grass and more suitable for units with awnings. This is a working farm and the owners, who are friendly and welcoming, are in the process of improving and developing their site.

Facilities

The sanitary facilities, very clean when we visited, are housed in a modern block. Showers (free), toilets and washbasins (two washbasins are in cubicles. Facilities for disabled visitors in family shower room. Good laundry room. Good campers' kitchen with fridge/freezer, electric cooker and TV. Play area. TV and games room. Caravan storage. Off site: Fishing 1.8 km. Golf 5 km. Riding 8 km.

Open: 12 April - 8 October.

Directions

From Roscrea centre follow signs for R491 Shirone. Continue towards Shirone following site signs for about 2.5 km. and site entrance is on left. GPS: 52.95720, -7.83937

Charges guide

Per unit incl. 2 persons and electricity	€ 23,00
extra person	€ 4,50
child (under 14 yrs)	€ 2,00
hiker or cyclist	€ 12,00

Rosses Point

Greenlands Caravan & Camping Park

Rosses Point (Co. Sligo) T: 071 917 7113. E: noelineha@eircom.net

alanrogers.com/IR8690

Just off the N15 road and 8 km. from Sligo town, this is a well run park at Rosses Point, in the sand hills adjoining a championship golf course. It is thoughtfully laid out with small tents placed to the front of reception and the hardstanding touring pitches separated from the trailer tent pitches which occupy the rear. The ground is undulating and adds interest to the overall appearance. Your view depends on where you are pitched – look towards Coney Island and the lighthouse which guards the bay, take in the sight of Benbulben Mountain or appreciate the seascape and the water lapping the resort's two beaches.

Facilities

Modern toilet facilities, recently extended and refitted, are kept exceptionally clean, with hot showers (€ 1 token). Washing machine, dryer and iron. Motorcaravan service point. Campers' kitchen. Information point and TV room beside reception. Play area. Outdoor chess and draughts sets. Night security. Off site: Shop and restaurant in the village. Fishing and boat launching 100 m. Golf 50 m. Bicycle hire 8 km. Riding 14 km.

Open: 30 April - 14 September.

Directions

From Sligo city travel about 800 m. north on the N15 road, turn left onto R291 signed Rosses Point. Continue for 6.5 km. and park is on right after village. GPS: 54.30628, -8.56889

Charges guide

Per unit incl. 2 persons	€ 19,00 - € 21,00
extra person	€ 3,00 - € 5,00
electricity (10A)	€ 4,00
hiker/cyclist incl. small tent	€ 11,00 - € 16,00

Rosslare

Saint Margaret's Beach Caravan & Camping Park

Lady's Island, Rosslare Harbour, Rosslare (Co. Wexford) T: 053 913 1169. E: stmarg@eircom.net

alanrogers.com/IR9170

'This park is loved' was how a Swedish visitor described this family run, environmentally friendly caravan and camping park, the first the visitor meets near the Rosslare ferry port. Landscaping with flowering containers and maze-like sheltered camping areas and a pretty sanitary block all demonstrate the Traynor family's attention to detail. Most pitches give shelter from the fresh sea breeze and ferries can be seen crossing the Irish sea. Just metres away, the safe, sandy beach (part of the Wexford coastal path) curves around in a horseshoe shape ending in a small pier and slipway. Tourist information on the area is provided in the well stocked shop.

Facilities

The toilet block is spotless. Laundry room. Campers' kitchen including toaster, microwave and TV. Shop (June - Aug). Fresh milk and bread daily. Mobile homes for rent. Off site: Walking, beach and fishing. Boat slipway 2.5 km. Pitch and putt 2 km. Riding 6 km. Pubs and restaurants. The JFK Arboretum, Johnstown Castle and Gardens, the Irish National Heritage Park, Kilmore Quay and Marina, and Curracloe beach (featured in the film 'Saving Private Ryan').

Open: Mid March - 30 September.

Directions

From the N25 south of Wexford town, outside village of Tagoat, follow signs for Lady's Island and Carne. After 3 km. pass Butlers Bar and take next left and continue for 2.5 km. Site is well signed. GPS: 52.20655, -6.35591

Charges guide

Per unit incl. 2 persons and electricity	€ 15,00 - € 25,00
extra person	€ 2,50
child (2-16 yrs)	€ 1,50

Roundwood

Roundwood Caravan & Camping Park

Roundwood (Co. Wicklow) T: **012 818 163**. E: **info@dublinwicklowcamping.com**
alanrogers.com/IR9130

In the heart of the Wicklow mountains, the hospitable owner of this park maintains high standards. It is neatly laid out with rows of trees dividing the different areas and giving an attractive appearance. There are 46 hardstanding pitches for caravans and motorcaravans, all with electricity (6A), plus 33 pitches for tents, arranged off tarmac access roads. There are excellent walks around the Varty Lakes and a daily bus service to Dublin city. Close by are the Wicklow Mountains and the Sally Gap, Glendalough, Powerscourt Gardens, plus many other places of natural beauty. Apart from its scenic location, this site is well placed for the ferry ports.

Facilities

The renovated sanitary block is kept clean, with adequate washing and toilet facilities, plus spacious showers on payment (€ 1). Good laundry facilities, but ask at reception as machines are not self-service. Motorcaravan service point. Campers' kitchen and dining room. TV room. Adventure playground. Off site: Roundwood village has shops, pubs, restaurants, takeaway food, and a Sunday market. Fishing within 1 km. Riding, golf 3 km. Bicycle hire 3 km.

Open: 30 April - 31 August.

Directions

Turn off N11 Dublin - Wexford road at Kilmacanogue towards Glendalough and then 15 km. to Roundwood. Park is on the north side of the village. GPS: 53.06924, -6.22269

Charges guide

Per unit incl. 2 persons and electricity	€ 28,00 - € 30,00
extra person	€ 8,00
child (under 14 yrs)	€ 4,00
dog	€ 2,00

No credit cards.

Skibbereen

The Hideaway Camping & Caravan Park

Skibbereen (Co. Cork) T: **028 222 54**. E: **skibbereencamping@eircom.net**
alanrogers.com/IR9505

A sister park to The Meadow at Glandore, the Hideaway is ideally situated as a touring base for the southwest of Ireland. It is a well run site under the constant supervision of the owners and although it enjoys tranquil surroundings, including preserved marshland, it is only ten minutes walk from the busy market town of Skibbereen. The Hideaway is a touring only park with 60 pitches, including 50 with hardstanding and 6A electricity. The remainder are for tents. Shrubs and low hedges divide the park giving an open feel overall and commanding views across the fields and hills. One long building houses reception, the toilet facilities and a games room. This is an ideal base from which to tour West Cork, including Lissaard Gardens and not forgetting the only inland sea lake in northern Europe, Lough Ine.

Facilities

The modern toilet block has non slip floors, well equipped showers (on payment). Baby room with bath. En-suite unit for disabled visitors. Laundry. Campers' dining room. Motorcaravan service point. Adventure play area. Football and cycling not permitted on the park. Off site: Fishing 1.6 km. Golf 2 km. Riding 4 km. Bicycle hire 1 km.

Open: 2 - 8 April, then 30 April - 15 September.

Directions

From Skibbereen town centre take R596 (signed Casteltownsend). Site is on the left after 1 km. GPS: 51.54167, -9.26008

Charges 2010

Per unit incl. 2 persons and electricity	€ 23,00
extra person	€ 6,00
child (under 16 yrs)	€ 3,00

No credit cards.

Strandhill

Strandhill Caravan & Camping Park

Strandhill (Co. Sligo) T: 071 916 8111. E: strandhillcvp@eircom.net

alanrogers.com/IR8695

This seaside park is located on 20 acres of undulating grass with a sandy base with natural protection from the onshore breezes of the famous Strandhill beach. There are 55 hardstanding pitches for caravans and motorcaravans, with electricity and ample water points, and two camping areas for tents, one with views of the sea and the second more sheltered. Throughout the site many hollows provide ideal pitches for tents. Strandhill, world recognised as a surfing Mecca, also provides activities for all the family. There are miles of sandy beach and dunes and the Knocknarea Mountain provides walkers with choice.

Facilities

The toilet block (keys provided on deposit) is clean and fresh with hot showers (token € 1), electric hand dryers and hairdryer. Laundry including ironing facilities. TV and games room. Book swapping. Security on site all season. Off site: Public transport from village. Shops, restaurants, takeaway, pubs and ATM in the village. Strandhill golf course 500 m. Riding 2 km. Sports centre in Sligo 8 km.

Open: Easter - 30 September.

Directions

Strandhill is 8 km. west of Sligo city on the R292. Site is on the airport road. GPS: 54.27242, -8.60448

Charges guide

Per unit incl. 2 persons	€ 20,00
plus 2 children	€ 22,00
electricity (10A)	€ 5,00
extra person	€ 3,00 - € 5,00

Tipperary

The Glen of Aherlow Caravan & Camping Park

Newtown, Glen of Aherlow, Tipperary (Co. Tipperary) T: 062 565 55. E: rdrew@eircom.net

alanrogers.com/IR9400

The owners of one of Ireland's newest parks, George and Rosalind Drew, are campers themselves and have set about creating an idyllic park in an idyllic location. This five-acre park is set in one of Ireland's most picturesque valleys and is open all year. There are beautiful views of the wooded and hilly areas of Slievenamuck and the Galtee Mountains. There are 42 large and level pitches, with both hardstanding and grass places, each with a 10A electricity connection and water point. The Drew family is happy to welcome large groups and rallies and large units can be accommodated. The excellent facilities are located in a purpose built building.

Facilities

The modern toilet block includes free showers and facilities for disabled visitors. Motorcaravan service point. Laundry room with ironing. Campers' kitchen. Recreation and TV rooms. Off site: Holiday homes to rent 300 m. Restaurant 300 m. Outdoor activities. Fishing. Golf and riding 7 km.

Open: All year.

Directions

From Tipperary town take N24 via Bansha, then the R663 to Newtown. Continue through village and pass Coach Road Inn to park in 300 m. GPS: 52.4161, -8.2105

Charges guide

Per unit incl. 2 persons and electricity	€ 24,00
extra person	€ 4,00
child (2-14 yrs)	€ 2,00

Tipperary

Ballinacourty House Caravan & Camping Park

Glen of Aherlow, Tipperary (Co. Tipperary) T: 062 565 59. E: info@camping.ie

alanrogers.com/IR9370

Ballinacourty House and its cobble-stoned courtyard form the centrepiece of this south-facing park with views of the Galtee Mountains. Accessed by a tree-lined lane, the reception area is in part of the renovated 18th century building, as is the adjoining restaurant. The park is level with 26 touring pitches with 6A electricity and 25 grassy pitches for tents. Some areas are shaded areas and there are open spaces to accommodate rallies and larger groups. Self-catering cottages and B&B are also available. This tranquil site is an ideal base from which to tour the Rock of Cashel, the Mitchelstown Caves, Swiss Cottage and the towns of Tipperary, Cahir and Cashel. Activities in the area include horse riding and trekking, fishing for perch and brown trout, cycling, forest walks, three 18-hole golf courses, leisure centre with swimming pool,cinema theatre and pottery shop.

Facilities

Sanitary facilities provide free hot water and showers. Baby room. Facilities for disabled visitors are planned. Laundry with ironing facilities. Campers' kitchen. Ice pack freezing. Licensed restaurant (early booking advised). Motorcaravan services. Gas supplies. Minigolf. TV and games rooms. Picnic benches. Tennis. Play area. Off site: Riding, fishing, golf.

Open: 1 May - 21 September.

Directions

From the N24 Tipperary - Cahir road, take Glen of Aherlow scenic route 6.5 km. from Cahir and follow signs. GPS: 52.41614, -8.21047

Charges guide

Per unit incl. 2 persons	€ 8,00 - € 10,00
extra person	€ 5,00
child	€ 2,00
electricity	€ 3,00

Tralee

Woodlands Park Touring Caravan & Camping Park

Dan Spring Road, Tralee (Co. Kerry) T: 066 712 1235. E: wdlands@eircom.net

alanrogers.com/IR9650

This family run park is located in the heart of Kerry, on the gateway to the Dingle peninsula and just north of the Ring of Kerry and Killarney. Woodlands is an ideal base, only ten minutes walk from Tralee town centre via the town park and famous rose garden. Located on a 16 acre elevated site approached by a short road and bridge that straddles the River Lee, once on site the town seems far removed with a countryside environment taking over. Hedging, trees, grazing fields and the distant Slieve Mish Mountain create the setting. There are 135 pitches including 85 'super' pitches with hardstanding, electricity, water and drainage to the left and centre behind the main building. A grass area for 50 tents is to the right. The park has a landscaped entrance using tropical shrubs and cordyline trees and flower beds have been planted around the park. The owners of Woodlands have designed and equipped their park to a high standard including a clubhouse. The town park is home to the Kerry County Museum and 'Siamsa Tire', the National folk theatre of Ireland with nightly performances. In addition to the river, there is a canal bank walk to Blennerville Windmill.

Facilities	Directions
Excellent, heated sanitary facilities include sizeable showers (€1 token) and provision for disabled guests. Campers' kitchen. Laundry room with washing machines and dryer. Motorcaravan service point. Club house with café/snack bar. Shop. Games room. TV and adult only room. Internet access. Fenced adventure play area. Off site: The nearby Aqua Dome offers half price admission after 18.00. Golf 6 km. Riding 2 km. Blue Flag beaches on the Dingle Peninsula. Sailing 10 km.	Site is 1 km. southwest of Tralee town centre. From N21/N69/N86 junction south of Tralee follow site signs for 2.4 km. to park, 200 m. off the N86 Tralee - Dingle road. Site is 300 m. east of the Aqua Dome GPS: 52.26157, -9.70338

Open: Easter - 30 September.

Charges guide

Per unit incl. 2 persons	€ 15,50 - € 23,00
extra person	€ 6,00
child (under 16 yrs)	€ 2,00 - € 3,00
electricity (10A)	€ 4,00

Tramore

Newtown Cove Camping & Caravan Park

Newtown Road, Tramore (Co. Waterford) T: 051 381 979. E: info@newtowncove.com

alanrogers.com/IR9340

Well run and friendly, this very attractive small park is only five minutes walk from the beautiful Newton Cove. It offers views of the famous and historic Metal Man and is 2.5 km. from Tramore beach and 11 km. from Waterford. Neatly set out on gently sloping grass are 40 pitches, with the abundance of shrubs and bushes reflecting the efforts of the owners. All pitches have electrical connections (10A), some with hardstanding also, and access is by well lit, tarmac roads. There are around 50 privately owned caravan holiday homes. A modern building at the entrance houses reception, the amenities and additional sanitary facilities. The village of Tramore, with a wide range of shops and eating houses, is close and there is a choice of many delightful cliff walks in the immediate vicinity.

Facilities	Directions
The main sanitary block at the bottom end of the site is not very modern but provides good, clean facilities including a bathroom. Showers on payment (token from reception). Facilities for disabled visitors. Motorcaravan services. Campers' kitchen with cooking facilities, sheltered eating area, lounge and small laundry. Small shop (1/7-30/8). TV room. Games room. Small play area. Off site: Beach 400 m. Fishing 400 m. Golf 800 m. Riding 3 km.	From Tramore on R675 coast road to Dungarvan. Turn left 2 km. from town centre, following signs. GPS: 52.14763, -7.17274

Open: 1 April - 26 September.

Charges guide

Per unit incl. 2 persons and electricity	€ 24,00 - € 31,00
extra person	€ 6,00
child (3-15 yrs)	€ 3,00
hiker, cyclist or motorcyclist	€ 8,00 - € 11,00

No single sex groups.

Tuosist
Beara Camping The Peacock
Coornagillagh, Tuosist, Post Killarney (Co. Kerry) T: 064 66842 87. E: bearacamping@eircom.net
alanrogers.com/IR9580

Five minutes from Kenmare Bay, The Peacock is a unique location for campers who would appreciate the natural surroundings of a campsite where disturbance to nature is kept to a minimum. This five-acre site offers simple, clean and imaginative camping facilities. Located on the Ring of Beara, bordering the counties of Cork and Kerry, visitors will be treated with hospitality by a Dutch couple, almost more Irish than the Irish, who have made Ireland their home and run the site with their family and Kleintje, the pot-bellied Vietnamese pig. The variety of accommodation at Beara Camping includes the hostel, caravan holiday homes, secluded hardstanding pitches with electricity and level grass areas for tenting. In addition, there are cabins sleeping two or four people and hiker huts sleeping two, ideal to avoid a damp night or to dry out. Bert and Klaske are only too anxious to share with visitors the unspoiled natural terrain, the local wildlife, the opportunity of a cosy sheltered campfire and advice on the walking and hiking routes in the area aided by maps provided on loan. The homely restaurant provides Bert an opportunity to exhibit his artistic talents, not only with his paintings on display, but with simple and wholesome salmon or fillet of steak and salads that are meals in themselves. Breakfast, lunch and dinner plus 'good' coffee are available, plus fresh bread each morning. All of this and the possibility of travelling the Ring of Beara to see stone circles, the Healy Pass, Ardea Castle, Derreen Gardens and the fishing town of Castletownbere and much more. The well known towns of Kenmare and Killarney are both havens for tourists.

Facilities
Three small blocks, plus facilities at the restaurant provide toilets, washbasins and free hot showers. Laundry service for a small fee. Campers' kitchens and sheltered eating area. Restaurant and takeaway (May - Oct). Bicycle hire. Pets are not permitted in rental accommodation or tents. Off site: Public transport from the gate during the summer months. Pub and shop 900 m. Riding 6 km. Golf 12 km. Boating, fishing and sea angling 200 m. Beach (pebble) 500 m.

Open: 1 April - 31 December.

Directions
From the A22, 17 km. east of Killarney, take the R569 south to Kenmare. In Kenmare take R571, Castletownbere road and site is 12 km. GPS: 51.8279, -9.7356

Charges guide
Per unit incl. 2 persons	€ 17,50
extra person	€ 3,50
child (0-10 yrs)	€ 2,00
electricity	€ 2,50

Westport
Parkland Caravan & Camping Park
Westport House Country Park, Westport (Co. Mayo) T: 098 277 66. E: camping@westporthouse.ie
alanrogers.com/IR8770

Located in the grounds of an elegant country estate, this is a popular park. From Westport Quay, you enter the grounds of the estate by way of a tree lined road that crosses the river and leads to the site. In an attractive, sheltered area of the parkland, set in the trees, are 155 pitches. There are 65 with hardstanding and 76 electric hook-ups. Early in the season the site may not be fully prepared, and only minimal facilities may be available. There is the choice of a 'pitch only' booking, or a 'special deal' (min. stay three nights). This includes free admission to Westport House and many of the activities of the adjoining leisure park. There is a children's animal and bird park, boating and fishing on the lake and river, pitch and putt, 'slippery dip', ball pond and 'supabounce', a play adventure world, hillside train rides and a flume ride. Stay one week or more and all the above are free, plus tennis, a par 3 golf course and 20% discount on bar food in the Horse and Wagon bar on the site. Westport is an attractive town with splendid Georgian houses and traditional shop fronts. There are many good restaurants and pubs.

Facilities
Toilet facilities are provided at various points on the site, plus a 'super-loo' located in the farmyard buildings. Facilities for disabled people. Laundry facilities. Fifties style function room and bar with food and musical entertainment (all 1/6-31/8). Westport House and Country Park. Off site: Within 5 km. of the estate are an 18-hole golf course and deep sea angling on Clew Bay.

Open: 14 May - 5 September.

Directions
Take R335 Westport - Louisburgh road and follow signs for Westport Quay, then turn in through gates of Westport House and continue through estate following signs for camping. GPS: 53.8053, -9.5395

Charges guide
Per unit incl. 2 persons and electricity	€ 28,00 - € 33,00
hiker or cyclist	€ 25,00 - € 27,50

Family weekend rates in June.

A visit to the Channel Islands offers a holiday in part of the British Isles, yet in an area which has a definite continental flavour. All the islands have beautiful beaches and coves, pretty scenery and fascinating histories.

THE CHANNEL ISLANDS ARE MADE UP OF THE ISLANDS OF: JERSEY, GUERNSEY, SARK, HERM AND ALDERNEY

The largest of the Channel Islands is Jersey, which is also the most commercial with more entertainment on offer. It has long stretches of safe beaches for swimming and water-based activities such as windsurfing and banana rides. Caravans and motor caravans are allowed on Jersey, but with a number of limitations (for example, length of stay, width and length of the unit). A permit is required which is obtained as part of the booking procedure with the campsite of your choice. You must book in advance but the campsite owner will advise you on all aspects of your visit.

Guernsey will suit those who prefer a quieter, more peaceful holiday. Caravans and motorcaravans are not allowed here. Guernsey too has wide, sandy beaches plus sheltered coves. The historic, harbour town of St Peter Port has steep and winding cobbled streets, with plenty of shops, cafes and restaurants.

For those who want total relaxation, one of the smaller islands – Sark or Herm, would be ideal. No cars are permitted on either of these islands. Explore on foot, by cycle or horse-drawn carriage.

Shopping on all the islands has the advantage of no VAT – particularly useful when buying cameras, watches or alcohol.

Places of interest

Jersey: St Helier; Jersey Zoo; Jersey War tunnels; Elizabeth Castle;German Underground Hospital in St Lawrence; Samarès Manor in St Clement; Shell Garden at St Aubin; Battle of Flowers Museum in St Ouen.

Guernsey: Castle Cornet at St Peter Port Harbour; Victor Hugo's House; Guernsey Folk Museum; German Occupation Museum; Fort Grey Shipwreck Museum; Saumarez Park.

Sark: La Coupée; La Seigneurie, with old dovecote and gardens; Gouliet and Boutique Caves; Le Pot on Little Sark; Venus Pool; Little Sark Village.

Herm: This tiny island has beautiful, quiet, golden beaches and a little harbour village and hotel. Arrive by ferry from Guernsey for a wonderful day out.

Did you know?

Jersey has been associated with knitting for nearly 400 years.

The Channel Islands were the only part of the British Isles to be occupied by the Germans during the Second World War.

Herm island is just one and a half miles long and only half a mile wide.

Le Jerriais is the native language of Jersey, a blend of Norse and Norman French.

Note: The reciprocal health services agreement between the British Government and the Channel Islands ended in April 2009. The EHIC card does not cover emergency health care as the Channel Islands are not part of the EU. Travel insurance is now essential.

Castel

Fauxquets Valley Campsite

Castel, Guernsey GY5 7QA T: **01481 255460**. E: info@fauxquets.co.uk

alanrogers.com/UK9780

Situated in the rural centre of the island, Fauxquets is in a pretty sheltered valley, hidden down narrow lanes away from busy roads and is run by the Guille family. It was once a dairy farm, but the valley side has now been developed into an attractive campsite, with the old farm buildings as its centre. Plenty of trees, bushes and flowers have been planted to separate pitches and to provide shelter around the various fields which are well terraced. The 86 touring pitches are of a good size, most marked, numbered and with electricity, and there is lots of open space. There are also 15 smaller places for backpackers. The site has 23 fully equipped tents for hire, but there are no tour operators. The Haybarn licensed restaurant and bar provides breakfast, morning coffee and cake and evening meals. There is plenty of room to sit around the heated swimming pool, including a large grassy terrace with sun beds provided. A car would be useful here to reach the beaches, St Peter Port and other attractions, although there is a bus service each day (20 minutes' walk).

Facilities

Good toilet facilities have controllable showers, some washbasins in private cabins with a shower, baby bath and changing unit. Dishwashing facilities under cover and a tap for free hot water. Laundry room with free irons, boards and hairdryers. Heated swimming pool (20 x 45 ft) with paddling pool. Restaurant and bar (25/6-7/9). Small shop with ice-pack hire and gas. TV room. Table football and table tennis. Small play area and play field. Bicycle hire. Torches useful. Off site: Riding and golf 2 miles. Fishing, sailing and boat launching 3 miles.

Open: April - 15 September.

Directions

From harbour take second exit from roundabout. At top of hill, turn left at 'filter in turn' into Queens Road, then right at next filter. Follow straight through traffic lights and down hill past hospital, through pedestrian lights and straight on at next lights at top of hill. Continue for 0.75 miles, then turn right opposite sign for German Hospital. Fourth left is pedestrian entrance, cars carry on for 400 yds to gravel entrance on left. GPS: 49.46812, -2.58843

Charges guide

Per person	£ 7.90 - £ 9.00
child (at school)	£ 3.50 - £ 7.70
electricity (6A)	£ 3.00

Fully equipped tents with fridge for hire.

Herm Island

Seagull Campsite

The Administration Office, Herm Island GY1 3HR T: **01481 722377**. E: camping@herm-island.com

alanrogers.com/UK9830

This tiny site, and indeed the island of Herm, will appeal to those who are looking for complete tranquillity and calm. Reached by boat (20 minutes and approx. £8.50 return fare for adults, £4.25 for children) from Guernsey, the 300-acre island allows no cars only tractors on its narrow roads and paths (no bicycles either). The campsite is a 20 minute uphill walk from the harbour, but your luggage will be transported for you by tractor. It consists of several terraced areas offering a total of 90 pitches, and 26 fully equipped tents for hire on flat grass areas. There are no electricity hook-ups. One may bring one's own tent and equipment or hire both (but not bedding, crockery and lighting) from the site. One is free to stroll around the many paths, through farmland, heath and around the coast, where there are beautiful beaches. Herm is definitely not for those who like entertainment and plenty of facilities, but for total relaxation, with the absence of any bustle and noise it takes some beating! Due to the stony footpaths on Herm, sensible walking shoes are advised.

Facilities

Small, modern, but open, toilet block. Hot showers (£1 payment – there is a shortage of water on Herm). Laundry facility and small kitchen. Freezer for ice-packs. No dogs or pets are allowed. Torches useful. Off site: The harbour village is about ten minutes walk for small shop, gas, a post office, pub, restaurants and café. Fishing on the island.

Open: May - first weekend in September.

Directions

Reached by boat from St Peter Port - report to Administration Office on arrival. Do not take your car as it is unlikely you will be able to park long term in St Peter Port. GPS: 49.47665, -2.45665

Charges guide

Per person	£ 6.30
child (under 14 yrs)	£ 3.15
transportation of luggage	£ 7.50

Equipped tents for hire.
Groups of single people not accepted.

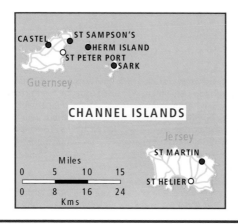

Sark
Pomme de Chien Campsite
Sark GY9 0SB T: **01481 832316**. E: rangjill@hotmail.com
alanrogers.com/**UK9870**

The island where 'time stands still' is an apt description of Sark, one of the smallest inhabited Channel Islands, some 45 minutes from Guernsey by boat. Situated five minutes from the shops and ten from the beach, the Pomme de Chien campsite is small with only 50 pitches, of which eight are occupied by fully equipped tents for rent. The remainder are for campers with their own tents (no caravans, motorcaravans or trailer tents of course). The pitches are large, on fairly level ground, but none have electricity hook-ups. There is a warm welcome from the owners Chris and Jill Rang with the famous charm of Sark.

Facilities
Modern sanitary block with free hot showers (large, with bench and hook), toilets and washbasins. Dishwashing sinks are outside. Outside washing line. Dogs are not accepted. Torches are necessary. Baggage can be transferred from the harbour to the site by tractor trailer, at a cost of £1 per item. Off site: Bicycle hire 5 minutes. Beach and fishing 10 minutes walk.

Open: All year.

Directions
Take the tractor drawn 'train' up Harbour Hill (cost is 90p; you can walk but it is a ten minute hike). Once at the top take road leading off left, then second right, and follow the lane to the site entrance. Reception is at house with white gates.
GPS: 49.43665, -2.36331

Charges guide
Per person	£ 7.50
child	£ 5.00
No credit cards.	

Saint Martin
Rozel Camping Park
Rozel, Saint Martin, Jersey JE3 6AX T: **01534 855200**. E: rozelcampingpark@jerseymail.co.uk
alanrogers.com/**UK9710**

This family owned park is within walking distance of the famous Jersey Zoo and the pretty harbour and fishing village of Rozel, where the north coast cliff path commences. There are two main camping areas providing 130 pitches of which 120 have electric hook ups (10/16A) and 16 are used for fully-equipped tents to hire. Some pitches, mainly for smaller tents are arranged on terraced areas. The remainder are on a higher, flat field where pitches are arranged in bays with hedges growing to separate them into groups. The site has provided easy access for caravans and motorcaravans, plus chemical and grey waste disposal facilities. In addition to package deals for tent hire and travel, the site offers a good range of camping equipment for daily hire. Boats are accepted by prior arrangement.

Facilities
Two first rate, heated sanitary buildings include a bathroom for disabled people with a shower, toilet and washbasin. Family shower room with small heater for cooler weather. Fully equipped laundry. Shop. Takeaway (peak season). Swimming pool (June-Sept) with children's pool and sunbathing areas. Play area. Crazy golf. Games room, reading and TV room. Torches useful. Bicycles for hire can be delivered to the site. Off site: Fishing 1 mile. Beach 2 miles. Riding 3 miles. Golf 4 miles.

Open: 21 May - 9 September.

Directions
Leave harbour by Route du Port Elizabeth, take A1 east through the tunnel and the A17. At fourth set of lights turn left on A6. Keep in the middle lane. Continue to Five Oaks and on to St Martin's church. Turn right, then immediately left at the 'Royal' pub on B38 to Rozel, continue to end of road, turn right and park is on the right. GPS: 49.23841, -2.05058

Charges guide
Per person	£ 7.60 - £ 9.00
child (4-11 yrs)	£ 3.80 - £ 4.50
electricity	£ 1.80
Tent hire and travel packages.	

Saint Martin

Beuvelande Camp Site

Beuvelande, Saint Martin, Jersey JE3 6EZ T: **01534 853575**. E: **info@campingjersey.com**
alanrogers.com/UK9720

What a pleasant surprise we had when we called here – the outstanding sanitary building gives campers facilities often associated with top class hotels. A licensed restaurant with covered terrace area is also situated in this building, open mornings and evenings all season, but perhaps a few less hours at quiet times. There are 150 pitches, 60 with fully equipped tents for hire, but with plenty of space for those with their own. Cars may be parked next to your tent. 100 pitches have electric hook ups (5/10A). Torches would be useful. Car and bicycle hire can be arranged. This family run park prides itself on quality, cleanliness and hospitality.

Facilities

The toilet block is tiled top to bottom and spotlessly clean, with controllable showers, two fully equipped bathrooms for disabled people, and a baby room. Plenty of dishwashing facilities and a laundry. Games room with arcade games and pool. TV room. Well stocked shop open 08.00-19.00 during peak times and stocks gas. Licensed restaurant. Ice pack and battery charging services for a small charge. Outdoor heated swimming pool (41 x 17 ft) with a sun terrace and small waterslide. Play area and large playing field. Evening entertainment. Off site: Beach and sailing 1.5 miles. Fishing, golf or riding within 2 miles.

Open: 1 April - 30 September.

Directions

On leaving the harbour by Route du Port Elizabeth, take A1 east through the tunnel and the A17. At the fourth set of traffic lights turn left on A6. Continue to Five Oaks and on to St Martin's RC church, then right into La Longue Rue, right again Rue de L'Orme then left to site. GPS: 49.21294, -2.05615

Charges guide

Per person	£ 6.00 - £ 9.00
child (2-14 yrs)	£ 6.00
Single sex groups not accepted.	

Saint Sampson's

Vaugrat Camping

Route de Vaugrat, Saint Sampson's, Guernsey GY2 4TA T: **01481 257468** E: **enquiries@vaugratcampsite.com**
alanrogers.com/UK9770

Vaugrat Camping is a neat, well tended site, close to the beach in the northwest of the island. Owned and well run by the Laine family, it is centred around attractive and interesting old granite farm buildings dating back to the 15th century, with a gravel courtyard and attractive flower beds. It provides 150 pitches (six with electricity) on flat grassy meadows, that are mostly surrounded by trees, banks and hedges to provide shelter. Tents are arranged around the edges of the fields, giving open space in the centre, and while pitches are not marked, there is sufficient room and cars may be parked next to tents. Only couples and families are accepted. It also offers 30 fully-equipped tents for hire. Housed in the old farmhouse, now a listed building, are the reception area, and shop where fresh croissants are baked every morning. Upstairs is the Coffee Barn/TV room, with views to the sea, where breakfast is served; one can also sit here in the evenings. There are plans to include caravans and motorhomes subject to permission.

Facilities

Well kept sanitary facilities are in two buildings. The first block is in the courtyard, with hot showers on payment. Unit for disabled visitors with shower, basin and toilet (although there is a 6-inch step into the building). Laundry facilities. Second block near the camping fields provides toilets, washbasins and dishwashing facilities. Shop with ice pack hire and gas (open at certain times by arrangement). Café serving breakfast only. Dogs are not accepted. Torches may be useful. Off site: Bus service within easy reach. Car or bicycle hire can be arranged. Fishing, riding and golf within 1.5 miles. Hotel and bar nearby.

Open: May - September.

Directions

On leaving St Peter Port, turn right onto coast road for 1.5 miles. At filter turn left into Vale Road. Straight over at two sets of lights then first left turn by church. Follow to crossroads (garage opposite) turn right. Carry on past Peninsula Hotel, then second left, signed for site. Site on left after high stone wall (400 yds) with concealed entrance. GPS: 49.49584, -2.55433

Charges guide

Per person	£ 7.95
child (under 14 yrs)	£ 6.30
car	£ 1.50
electricity	£ 3.00
Families and couples only.	
Fully equipped tents to hire (details from site).	

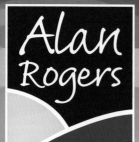

Holiday Caravans and Chalets

Over recent years many of the campsites featured in this guide have added large numbers of high quality caravan holiday homes, chalets and lodges. Many park owners believe that some former caravanners and motorcaravanners have been enticed by the extra comfort this type of accommodation can now provide, and that maybe this is the ideal solution to combine the freedom of camping with all the comforts of home.

Quality is consistently high and, although the exact size and inventory will vary from park to park, if you choose any of the parks detailed here, you can be sure that you're staying in some of the best quality and best value caravan holiday homes or chalets available.

Home comforts are provided and typically these include a fridge with freezer compartment, gas hob, proper shower – often a microwave and CD player too, but do check for details. All caravan holiday homes and chalets come fully equipped with a good range of kitchen utensils, pots and pans, crockery, cutlery and outdoor furniture. Many even have an attractive wooden sundeck or paved terrace – a perfect spot for outdoors eating or relaxing with a book and watching the world go by. An efficient heating system is invariably included and some models may also incorporate air conditioning.

Regardless of model, colourful soft furnishings are the norm and a generally breezy décor helps to provide a real holiday feel.

Although some parks may have a large number of different accommodation types, we have restricted our choice to one or two of the most popular accommodation units (either caravan holiday homes or chalets) for each of the parks listed.

The caravan holiday homes here will be of modern design, and recent innovations such as pitched roofs undeniably improve their appearance.

Design will invariably include clever use of space and fittings/furniture to provide for comfortable holidays – usually light and airy, with big windows and patio-style doors, fully equipped kitchen areas, a shower room with shower, washbasin and WC, cleverly designed bedrooms and a comfortable lounge/dining area (often incorporating a sofa bed).

In general, modern campsite chalets incorporate all the best features of caravan holiday homes in a more traditional, wood-clad structure, sometimes with the advantage of an upper mezzanine floor for an additional bedroom.

Our selected parks offer a massive range of different types of caravan holiday home and chalet, and it would be impractical to inspect every single accommodation unit. Our selection criteria, therefore, primarily takes account of the quality standards of the campsite itself.

However, there are a couple of important ground rules:

- FEATURED CARAVAN HOLIDAY HOMES MUST BE NO MORE THAN 5 YEARS OLD

- CHALETS NO MORE THAN 10 YEARS OLD

- ALL LISTED ACCOMMODATION MUST, OF COURSE, FULLY CONFORM WITH ALL APPLICABLE LOCAL, NATIONAL AND EUROPEAN SAFETY LEGISLATION

For each park we given details of the type, or types, of accommodation available to rent, but these details are necessarily quite brief. Sometimes internal layouts can differ quite substantially, particularly with regard to sleeping arrangements, where these include the flexible provision for 'extra persons' on sofa beds located in the living area. These arrangements may vary from accommodation to accommodation, and if you're planning a holiday which includes more people than are catered for by the main bedrooms you should check exactly how the extra sleeping arrangements are to be provided!

Charges

An indication of the tariff for each type of accommodation featured is also included, indicating the variance between the low and high season tariffs. However, given that many parks have a large and often complex range of pricing options, incorporating special deals and various discounts, the charges we mention should be taken to be just an indication. We strongly recommend therefore that you confirm the actual cost when making a booking.

We also strongly recommend that you check with the park, when booking, what (if anything) will be provided by way of bed linen, blankets, pillows etc. Again, in our experience, this can vary widely from park to park.

On every park a fully refundable deposit (usually between £100 and £250) is payable on arrival. There may also be an optional cleaning service for which a further charge is made. Other options may include sheet hire (typically £20 per unit) or baby pack hire (cot and high chair).

UK0380 Wooda Farm Holiday Park
see report page 16

Poughill, Bude EX23 9HJ

AR1 – CEDAR – Mobile Home

Sleeping: 3 bedrooms, sleeps 6: 1 double, 4 singles, pillows and blankets provided

Living: living/kitchen area, heating, TV, shower, seperate WC

Eating: fitted kitchen with hobs, oven, microwave, grill, fridge, freezer

Outside: table & chairs

Pets: not accepted

AR2 – BRAMBLES – Bungalow

Sleeping: 4 bedrooms, sleeps 7: 2 doubles, 3 singles, pillows and blankets provided

Living: living/kitchen area, heating, TV, shower, seperate WC

Eating: fitted kitchen with hobs, oven, microwave, grill, dishwasher, fridge, freezer

Outside: table & chairs

Pets: not accepted

Other (AR1 and AR2): cot, highchair to hire

Open: 1 April - 31 October.

Weekly Charge	AR1	AR2
Low Season (from)	£ 300	£ 350
High Season (from)	£ 735	£ 1100

UK0016 Lanyon Holiday Park
see report page 32

Loscombe Lane, Four Lanes, Redruth TR16 6LP

AR1 – LAVENDER – Mobile Home

Sleeping: 3 bedrooms, sleeps 6: 1 double, 2 singles, pillows and blankets provided

Living: living/kitchen area, heating, TV, shower, seperate WC

Eating: fitted kitchen with hobs, oven, microwave, grill, coffee maker, fridge, freezer

Outside: table & chairs, parasol

Pets: accepted (with supplement)

AR2 – CHALET – Chalet

Sleeping: 3 bedrooms, sleeps 6: 1 double, 2 singles, pillows and blankets provided

Living: living/kitchen area, heating, TV, shower, seperate WC

Eating: fitted kitchen with hobs, oven, microwave, grill, coffee maker, fridge, freezer

Outside: table & chairs, parasol

Pets: accepted (with supplement)

Other (AR1 and AR2): bed linen, cot to hire

Open: Easter - 31 October.

Weekly Charge	AR1	AR2
Low Season (from)	£ 290	£ 320
High Season (from)	£ 620	£ 890

UK0505 The Laurels Holiday Park
see report page 45

Padstow Road, Whitecross, Wadebridge PL27 7JQ

AR1 – HEDGEROW COTTAGE – Cottage

Sleeping: 3 bedrooms, sleeps 6: 1 double, 2 singles, bunk bed, pillows and blankets provided

Living: living/kitchen area, heating, TV, shower, WC, seperate WC

Eating: fitted kitchen with hobs, oven, microwave, grill, coffee maker, fridge, freezer

Outside: table & chairs

Pets: accepted (with supplement)

AR2 – LOVE COTTAGE – Cottage

Sleeping: 1 bedroom, sleeps 2: 1 double, pillows and blankets provided

Living: living/kitchen area, heating, TV, shower, WC

Eating: fitted kitchen with hobs, oven, microwave, grill, dishwasher, coffee maker, fridge, freezer

Outside: table & chairs

Pets: accepted (with supplement)

Other (AR1 and AR2): bed linen to hire

Open: Easter - 31 October.

Weekly Charge	AR1	AR2
Low Season (from)	£ 306	£ 195
High Season (from)	£ 742	£ 453

UK0847 Landscove Holiday Park
Berryhead, Brixham TQ5 9EP

▶ see report page 50

AR1 – BRONZE 2 BEDROOM – Chalet

Sleeping: 2 bedrooms, sleeps 6: 1 double, 2 singles, sofa bed, pillows and blankets provided

Living: living/kitchen area, heating, TV, shower, WC

Eating: fitted kitchen with hobs, oven, microwave, grill, fridge

Pets: not accepted

AR2 – SILVER 2 BEDROOMS COTTAGE – Mobile Home

Sleeping: 2 bedrooms, sleeps 6: 1 double, 2 singles, sofa bed, pillows and blankets provided

Living: living/kitchen area, heating, TV, shower, seperate WC

Eating: fitted kitchen with hobs, oven, microwave, grill, fridge

Pets: not accepted

Other (AR1 and AR2): bed linen, cot, highchair to hire

Images for guideline purposes only, accommodation may vary by park

Open: 1 March - 31 October.

Weekly Charge	AR1	AR2
Low Season (from)	£ 179	£ 215
High Season (from)	£ 623	£ 745

UK1085 Golden Sands Holiday Park
Week Lane, Dawlish Warren EX7 0LZ

▶ see report page 54

AR1 – BRONZE 2 BEDROOM – Mobile Home

Sleeping: 2 bedrooms, sleeps 6: 1 double, 2 singles, sofa bed

Living: living/kitchen area, heating, TV, shower, WC

Eating: fitted kitchen with hobs, oven, microwave, grill, fridge

Pets: not accepted

AR2 – GOLD 3 BEDROOM – Mobile Home

Sleeping: 3 bedrooms, sleeps 8: 1 double, 4 singles, sofa bed

Living: living/kitchen area, heating, TV, shower, WC

Eating: fitted kitchen with hobs, oven, microwave, grill, fridge

Pets: not accepted

Other (AR1 and AR2): bed linen, cot, highchair to hire

Images for guideline purposes only, accommodation may vary by park

Open: 1 March - 31 October.

Weekly Charge	AR1	AR2
Low Season (from)	£ 182	£ 241
High Season (from)	£ 641	£ 846

UK0970 Cofton Country Holidays
Starcross, Dawlish EX6 8RP

▶ see report page 55

AR1 – EASTDON – Cottage

Sleeping: 3 bedrooms, sleeps 6: 2 doubles, 2 singles

Living: living/kitchen area, heating, TV, shower, WC, seperate WC

Eating: fitted kitchen with hobs, oven, microwave, grill, dishwasher, fridge

Outside: table & chairs

Pets: not accepted

AR2 – TEIGN – Cottage

Sleeping: 3 bedrooms, sleeps 8: 1 double, 4 singles, pillows and blankets provided

Living: living/kitchen area, heating, TV, shower

Eating: fitted kitchen with hobs, oven, microwave, grill, fridge

Pets: not accepted

Other (AR1 and AR2): bed linen, cot, highchair to hire

Open: All year.

Weekly Charge	AR1	AR2
Low Season (from)	£ 315	£ 265
High Season (from)	£ 799	£ 705

UK0800 Higher Longford Caravan Park

▶ see report page 70

Moorshop, Tavistock PL19 9LQ

AR1 – OAK – Bungalow

Sleeping: 2 bedrooms, sleeps 4: 1 double, 2 singles, pillows and blankets provided

Living: living/kitchen area, heating, TV, shower, WC

Eating: fitted kitchen with hobs, oven, microwave, grill, coffee maker, fridge

Outside: table & chairs, parasol

Pets: accepted

AR2 – SYCAMORE – Bungalow

Sleeping: 1 bedroom, sleeps 2: 1 double, sofa bed, pillows and blankets provided

Living: living/kitchen area, heating, TV, shower, WC

Eating: fitted kitchen with hobs, oven, microwave, grill, coffee maker, fridge

Outside: table & chairs, parasol

Pets: accepted

Other (AR1 and AR2): bed linen, cot, highchair to hire

Open: All year.		
Weekly Charge	AR1	AR2
Low Season (from)	£ 250	£ 230
High Season (from)	£ 440	£ 420

UK1545 Cheddar Bridge Touring Park

▶ see report page 88

Draycott Road, Cheddar BS27 3RJ

AR1 – THE MENDIP – Bungalow

Sleeping: 1 bedroom, sleeps 2: 1 double, pillows and blankets provided

Living: living/kitchen area, heating, TV, shower, WC

Eating: fitted kitchen with hobs, oven, microwave, grill, fridge

Outside: table & chairs, parasol

Pets: accepted (with supplement)

AR2 – RIVERSIDE – Mobile Home

Sleeping: 2 bedrooms, sleeps 4: 1 double, 1 single, pillows and blankets provided

Living: living/kitchen area, heating, TV, shower, WC

Eating: fitted kitchen with hobs, oven, microwave, grill, fridge

Outside: table & chairs, parasol

Pets: accepted (with supplement)

Open: 1 March - end October.		
Weekly Charge	AR1	AR2
Low Season (from)	£ 200	£ 200
High Season (from)	£ 400	£ 450

UK1780 Freshwater Beach Holiday Park

▶ see report page 81

Burton Bradstock, Bridport DT6 4PT

AR1 – BUDGET – Mobile Home

Sleeping: 3 bedrooms, sleeps 6: 1 double, 4 singles, pillows and blankets provided

Living: living/kitchen area, heating, TV, shower, seperate WC

Eating: fitted kitchen with hobs, oven, microwave, grill, fridge, freezer

Outside: table & chairs

Pets: not accepted

AR2 – SUPER DELUXE – Mobile Home

Sleeping: 3 bedrooms, sleeps 6: 1 double, 4 singles, pillows and blankets provided

Living: living/kitchen area, heating, TV, shower, seperate WC

Eating: fitted kitchen with hobs, oven, microwave, grill, fridge, freezer

Outside: table & chairs

Pets: not accepted

Open: 17 March - 12 November.		
Weekly Charge	AR1	AR2
Low Season (from)	£ 210	£ 290
High Season (from)	£ 580	£ 820

UK1575 Holiday Resort Unity

 see report page 84

Coast Road, Brean Sands, Burnham-on-Sea TA8 2RB

AR1 – VILLA DELUXE – Mobile Home	AR2 – LUXURY LODGE – Mobile Home
Sleeping: 3 bedrooms, sleeps 6: 1 double, 4 singles, pillows and blankets provided	**Sleeping:** 3 bedrooms, sleeps 6: 1 double, 4 singles, pillows and blankets provided
Living: living/kitchen area, heating, TV, shower, seperate WC	**Living:** living/kitchen area, heating, TV, shower, seperate WC
Eating: fitted kitchen with hobs, oven, microwave, grill, fridge, freezer	**Eating:** fitted kitchen with hobs, oven, microwave, grill, dishwasher, fridge, freezer
Pets: not accepted	**Outside:** table & chairs
	Pets: not accepted

Other (AR1 and AR2): bed linen, cot, highchair to hire

Open: 10 February - 20 November.		
Weekly Charge	**AR1**	**AR2**
Low Season *(from)*	£ 345	£ 500
High Season *(from)*	£ 593	£ 644

UK2290 Sandy Balls Holiday Centre

 see report page 111

Godshill, Fordingbridge SP6 2JZ

AR1 – PINE LODGE ENSUITE – Chalet	AR2 – READY TENT – Tent
Sleeping: 3 bedrooms, sleeps 6: 1 double, 4 singles, pillows and blankets provided	**Sleeping:** 2 bedrooms, sleeps 6: 6 singles, pillows and blankets provided
Living: living/kitchen area, heating, TV, shower, WC	**Living:** living/kitchen area
Eating: fitted kitchen with hobs, oven, microwave, grill, fridge, freezer	**Eating:** fitted kitchen with hobs, fridge
	Outside: table & chairs
Outside: barbecue	**Pets:** not accepted
Pets: not accepted	

Other (AR1 and AR2): bed linen, cot, highchair to hire

Open: All year.		
Weekly Charge	**AR1**	**AR2**
Low Season *(from)*	£ 250	£ 240
High Season *(from)*	£ 895	£ 425

UK2920 Bay View Park

see report page 134

Old Martello Road, Pevensey Bay, Eastbourne BN24 6DX

AR1 – FESTIVAL SUPER – Mobile Home	AR2 – RICHMOND DELUXE – Mobile Home
Sleeping: 2 bedrooms, sleeps 6: 1 double, 2 singles, sofa bed, pillows and blankets provided	**Sleeping:** 2 bedrooms, sleeps 6: 1 double, 2 singles, sofa bed, pillows and blankets provided
Living: living/kitchen area, heating, TV, shower, seperate WC	**Living:** living/kitchen area, heating, TV, shower, WC
Eating: fitted kitchen with grill, fridge	**Eating:** fitted kitchen with grill, fridge
Outside: table & chairs	**Outside:** table & chairs
Pets: not accepted	**Pets:** not accepted

Other (AR1 and AR2): bed linen, cot, highchair to hire

Open: 1 March - 31 October.		
Weekly Charge	**AR1**	**AR2**
Low Season *(from)*	£ 218	£ 255
High Season *(from)*	£ 525	£ 595

UK3085 New Beach Holiday Park
see report page 139

Hythe Road, Dymchurch TN29 0JX

AR1 – BRONZE 2 BEDROOM – Chalet

Sleeping: 2 bedrooms, sleeps 6: 1 double, 2 singles, sofa bed, pillows and blankets provided

Living: living/kitchen area, heating, TV, air conditioning, shower, WC

Eating: fitted kitchen with hobs, oven, microwave, grill, fridge

Pets: not accepted

AR2 – SILVER PLUS 3 BEDROOM – Mobile Home

Sleeping: 3 bedrooms, sleeps 8: 1 double, 4 singles, sofa bed, pillows and blankets provided

Living: living/kitchen area, heating, TV, shower, WC

Eating: fitted kitchen with hobs, oven, microwave, grill, fridge

Pets: not accepted

Other (AR1 and AR2): bed linen, cot, highchair to hire

Images for guideline purposes only, accommodation may vary by park

Open: 1 March - 31 October.

Weekly Charge	AR1	AR2
Low Season (from)	£ 134	£ 166
High Season (from)	£ 445	£ 578

UK3287 Seawick Holiday Park
see report page 148

Beach Road, St Osyth, Clacton-on-Sea CO16 8SG

AR1 – BRONZE 2 BEDROOM – Chalet

Sleeping: 2 bedrooms, sleeps 6: 1 double, 2 singles, sofa bed, pillows and blankets provided

Living: living/kitchen area, heating, TV, shower, WC

Eating: fitted kitchen with hobs, oven, microwave, grill, fridge

Pets: not accepted

AR2 – GOLD PLUS 3 BEDROOM – Mobile Home

Sleeping: 3 bedrooms, sleeps 8: 1 double, 4 singles, sofa bed, pillows and blankets provided

Living: living/kitchen area, heating, TV, shower, WC

Eating: fitted kitchen with hobs, oven, microwave, grill, fridge

Pets: not accepted

Other (AR1 and AR2): bed linen, cot, highchair to hire

Images for guideline purposes only, accommodation may vary by park

Open: 1 March - 31 October.

Weekly Charge	AR1	AR2
Low Season (from)	£ 171	£ 231
High Season (from)	£ 445	£ 589

UK3850 Rivendale Caravan & Leisure Park
see report page 165

Buxton Road, Alsop-en-le-Dale, Ashbourne DE6 1QU

AR1 – SENATOR – Mobile Home

Sleeping: 2 bedrooms, sleeps 6: 2 doubles, 1 single, pillows and blankets provided

Living: living/kitchen area, heating, TV, shower, WC

Eating: fitted kitchen with hobs, oven, microwave, grill, fridge, freezer

Outside: table & chairs, barbecue

Pets: not accepted

AR2 – ALSOP VIEW – Appartment

Sleeping: 1 bedroom, sleeps 3: 1 double, 1 single, pillows and blankets provided

Living: living/kitchen area, heating, TV, shower, WC

Eating: fitted kitchen with coffee machine

Outside: table & chairs

Pets: not accepted

Open: All year excl. 9/1-2/2.

Weekly Charge	AR1	AR2
Low Season (from)	£ 330	£ 538
High Season (from)	£ 540	£ 655

UK4532 Middlewood Farm Holiday Park

▶ see report page 205

Middlewood Lane, Fylingthorpe, Robin Hood's Bay YO22 4UF

AR1 – HOLIDAY CARAVAN 4 BERTH – Mobile Home	**AR2** – HOLIDAY CARAVAN 6 BERTH – Mobile Home
Sleeping: 2 bedrooms, sleeps 4: 1 double, 2 singles, pillows and blankets provided	**Sleeping:** 3 bedrooms, sleeps 6: 1 double, 4 singles, pillows and blankets provided
Living: living/kitchen area, heating, TV, shower, WC	**Living:** living/kitchen area, heating, TV, shower, WC
Eating: fitted kitchen with hobs, oven, microwave, grill, fridge	**Eating:** fitted kitchen with hobs, oven, microwave, grill, fridge
Pets: accepted (with supplement)	**Pets:** accepted (with supplement)

Other (AR1 and AR2): cot, highchair to hire

Open: Easter - early November.

Weekly Charge	AR1	AR2
Low Season *(from)*	£ 165	£ 185
High Season *(from)*	£ 460	£ 555

UK5300 Kneps Farm Holiday Park

▶ see report page 214

River Road, Stanah, Thornton-Cleveleys FY5 5LR

AR1 – SUPER DELUXE – Mobile Home	**AR2** – DE LUXE – Mobile Home
Sleeping: 2 bedrooms, sleeps 6: 1 double, 2 singles, sofa bed, pillows and blankets provided	**Sleeping:** 2 bedrooms, sleeps 6: 1 double, 3 singles, sofa bed, pillows and blankets provided
Living: living/kitchen area, heating, TV, shower, seperate WC	**Living:** living/kitchen area, heating, TV, shower, WC
Eating: fitted kitchen with hobs, oven, microwave, grill, fridge	**Eating:** fitted kitchen with hobs, oven, microwave, grill, fridge
Pets: not accepted	**Pets:** not accepted

Other (AR1 and AR2): cot, highchair to hire

Open: 1 March - 15 November.

Weekly Charge	AR1	AR2
Low Season *(from)*	£ 290	£ 260
High Season *(from)*	£ 425	£ 395

UK5975 Little Kings Park

▶ see report page 237

Amroth Road, Ludchurch SA67 8PG

AR1 – KING OAK DELUXE – Mobile Home	**AR2** – LITTLE KINGS PARK BUNGALOW – Bungalow
Sleeping: 3 bedrooms, sleeps 6: 1 double, 4 singles, pillows and blankets provided	**Sleeping:** 3 bedrooms, sleeps 5: 1 double, 3 singles, pillows and blankets provided
Living: living/kitchen area, heating, TV, shower, seperate WC	**Living:** living/kitchen area, heating, TV, shower, WC
Eating: fitted kitchen with hobs, oven, microwave, grill, fridge, freezer	**Eating:** fitted kitchen with hobs, oven, microwave, grill, dishwasher, coffee maker, fridge, freezer
Outside: table & chairs	**Outside:** table & chairs
Pets: accepted	**Pets:** accepted

Other (AR1 and AR2): cot, highchair to hire

Open: 1 March - 31 October.

Weekly Charge	AR1	AR2
Low Season *(from)*	£ 325	£ 420
High Season *(from)*	£ 784	£ 876

UK6950 Brighouse Bay Holiday Park

▶ see report page 281

Brighouse Bay, Borgue, Kirkcudbright DG6 4TS

AR1 – LODGE – Chalet	AR2 – THISTLE CARAVAN – Mobile Home
Sleeping: 4 bedrooms, sleeps 8: 2 doubles, 6 singles, pillows and blankets provided	**Sleeping:** 2 bedrooms, sleeps 6: 1 double, 4 singles, pillows and blankets provided
Living: living/kitchen area, heating, TV, shower, WC	**Living:** living/kitchen area, heating, TV, shower, WC
Eating: fitted kitchen with hobs, oven, microwave, grill, fridge, freezer	**Eating:** fitted kitchen with hobs, oven, microwave, grill, fridge, freezer
Outside: table & chairs	**Outside:** table & chairs
Pets: accepted (with supplement)	**Pets:** accepted (with supplement)

Other (AR1 and AR2): bed linen, cot, highchair to hire

Open: All year.

Weekly Charge	AR1	AR2
Low Season *(from)*	£ 425	£ 345
High Season *(from)*	£ 780	£ 625

Low Cost Flights
An Inexpensive Way To Arrive At Your Campsite

Many campsites are conveniently served by a wide choice of low cost airlines. Cheap flights can be very easy to find and travellers increasingly find the regional airports often used to be smaller, quieter and generally a calmer, more pleasurable experience.

Low cost flights can make campsites in more distant regions a much more attractive option: quicker to reach, inexpensive flights, and simply more convenient.

Campsites are seeing increased numbers of visitors using the low cost flights and are adapting their services to suit this clientele. An airport shuttle service is not uncommon, meaning you can take advantage of that cheap flight knowing you will be met at the other end and whisked to your campsite. No taxi queues or multiple drop-offs.

Obviously, these low cost flights are impractical when taking all your own camping gear but they do make a holiday in campsite owned accommodation much more straightforward. The low cost airline option makes caravan holiday home holidays especially attractive: pack a suitcase and use bed linen and towels provided (which you will generally need to pre-book).

The following parks are understood to accept caravanners and campers all year round. It is always wise to phone the park to check as the facilities available, for example, may be reduced.

England

UK0018	Bone Valley
UK0030	Ayr
UK0165	Monkey Tree
UK0180	Carnon Downs
UK0185	Cosawes
UK0270	Mena
UK0300	Colliford Tavern
UK0310	Trekenning
UK0320	Polborder House
UK0430	Padstow
UK0440	Dolbeare
UK0690	Stowford Farm
UK0710	Hidden Valley
UK0745	Riverside (S. Molton)
UK0790	Harford Bridge
UK0800	Higher Longford
UK0810	Riverside (Plymouth)
UK0820	Moor View
UK0870	Beverley
UK0970	Cofton
UK0980	Lemonford
UK1250	Woodland Springs
UK1340	Cornish Farm
UK1350	Quantock Orchard
UK1390	Old Oaks
UK1420	Southfork
UK1440	Baltic Wharf
UK1460	Newton Mill
UK1500	Long Hazel
UK1510	Chew Valley
UK1520	Waterrow
UK1630	Brokerswood
UK1640	Greenhill Farm
UK1655	Church Farm
UK1700	Devizes
UK1820	Bagwell Farm
UK2030	Wareham Forest
UK2050	Rowlands Wait
UK2290	Sandy Balls
UK2530	Waverley
UK2590	Greenhill Farm
UK2600	Barnstones
UK2800	Alderstead Heath
UK2810	Chertsey
UK2930	Sheepcote
UK2940	Honeybridge
UK2950	Washington
UK2955	Kloofs
UK3030	Tanner Farm
UK3040	Broadhembury
UK3070	Canterbury
UK3090	Black Horse
UK3260	Abbey Wood
UK3270	Crystal Palace
UK3310	Low House
UK3322	Run Cottage
UK3345	The Dell
UK3382	Rose Farm
UK3455	Deer's Glade
UK3470	Breckland
UK3520	Searles
UK3575	Stroud Hill
UK3580	Ferry Meadows
UK3690	Bainland
UK3730	Skegness Sands
UK3765	Woodland Waters
UK3815	Lickpenny
UK3845	Clover Fields
UK3865	Golden Valley
UK3890	Stanford Hall
UK3910	Teversal
UK3920	Riverside (Worksop)
UK3940	Smeaton's Lakes
UK3945	Milestone
UK4075	Hollyfast
UK4130	Moreton-in-Marsh
UK4160	Christchurch
UK4170	Tudor
UK4210	Lickhill Manor
UK4300	Poston Mill
UK4400	Stanmore Hall
UK4410	Beaconsfield
UK4430	Oxon Hall
UK4570	Spiers House
UK5280	Abbey Farm
UK5290	Royal Umpire
UK5505	Stanwix Park
UK5560	Sykeside
UK5570	Wild Rose
UK5705	The Grange
UK5740	White Water
UK5755	South Meadows
UK5800	Ord House

Wales

UK5925	Cardiff
UK5955	Erwlon
UK6045	Gilestone
UK6060	Tredegar House
UK6310	Bacheldre
UK6330	Daisy Bank
UK6590	Beddgelert
UK6600	Bryn Gloch
UK6605	Tafarn Snowdonia
UK6680	James'
UK6690	Bron-Y-Wendon

Scotland

UK6870	Glenearly
UK6930	Brandedleys
UK6950	Brighouse Bay
UK7020	Aird Donald
UK7030	Gibson Park
UK7050	Edinburgh
UK7240	Lomond Woods
UK7260	Ardgartan
UK7270	Auchterarder
UK7275	Braidhaugh
UK7315	Loch Tay Lodges
UK7680	Glenmore
UK7735	Sango Sands
UK7790	Invercoe

Northern Ireland

UK8420	Tollymore

Republic of Ireland

IR8740	Cong
IR8815	Willowbrook
IR9080	Forest Farm
IR9100	Camac Valley
IR9400	Glen of Aherlow

Channel Islands

UK9870	Pomme de Chien

Dogs

For the benefit of those who want to take their dogs with them or for people who do not like dogs at the parks they visit, we list here the parks that have indicated to us that they do not accept dogs. If you are planning to take your dog we do advise you to phone the park first to check – there may be limits on numbers, breeds, etc. or times of the year when they are excluded.

Never – these parks do not accept dogs at any time:

UK0065	Wayfarers	UK1490	Greenacres	UK5980	Moreton Farm
UK0250	Pentewan Sands	UK2130	Grove Farm	UK6040	Pencelli Castle
UK0302	South Penquite	UK2300	Ashurst	UK7290	Craigtoun Meadows
UK0860	Whitehill	UK2590	Greenhill Farm	UK8600	Bellemont
UK0870	Beverley	UK3060	Yew Tree	UK9770	Vaugrat
UK0940	Holmans Wood	UK3120	Gate House Wood	UK9830	Seagull
UK1075	Golden Coast	UK4100	Hoburne Cotswold	UK9870	Pomme de Chien
UK1130	Hoburne Torbay	UK4160	Christchurch	IR9410	The Apple
UK1150	Ruda	UK4498	South Cliff	IR9510	Eagle Point
UK1380	Blue Anchor	UK5890	Glen Trothy		

Sometimes – these parks do not accept dogs at certain times of the year or have other restrictions:

UK0280	Eden Valley	UK5350	Holgates	UK6660	Nant Mill
UK0306	Ruthern Valley	UK5710	Doe Park	UK6990	Mortonhall
UK0720	Easewell Farm	UK5750	Waren	UK7060	Tantallon
UK0850	Galmpton	UK5800	Ord House	UK9710	Rozel
UK0865	Byslades	UK5930	Cwmcarn Forest	IR8810	Lough Lanagh
UK1550	Bucklegrove	UK5995	Caerfai Bay	IR9150	River Valley
UK2510	Whitecliff Bay	UK6010	Cenarth Falls	IR9580	Beara The Peacock
UK4180	Ranch	UK6290	Glan-y-Mor		

Fishing

We are pleased to include details of parks which provide facilities for fishing on site. Many other parks, particularly in Scotland and Ireland, are in popular fishing areas and have facilities within easy reach. Where we have been given details, we have included this information in the reports. It is always best to contact parks to check that they provide for your individual requirements.

England

UK0165	Monkey Tree
UK0170	Trevella
UK0185	Cosawes
UK0220	Trevornick
UK0250	Pentewan Sands
UK0270	Mena
UK0302	South Penquite
UK0380	Wooda Farm
UK0415	Trencreek
UK0530	Trethiggey
UK0725	Warcombe Farm
UK0745	Riverside Sth Molton
UK0750	Minnows
UK0790	Harford Bridge
UK0810	Riverside (Plymouth)
UK0950	River Dart
UK0970	Cofton
UK1060	Yeatheridge
UK1075	Golden Coast
UK1090	Peppermint Park
UK1150	Ruda
UK1390	Old Oaks
UK1460	Newton Mill
UK1480	Home Farm
UK1520	Waterrow
UK1540	Batcombe Vale
UK1545	Cheddar Bridge
UK1570	Northam Farm
UK1575	Unity
UK1580	Warren Farm
UK1590	Exe Valley
UK1630	Brokerswood
UK1640	Greenhill Farm
UK1740	Golden Cap
UK1760	Wood Farm
UK1780	Freshwater Beach
UK2150	Woolsbridge
UK2290	Sandy Balls
UK2360	Hill Cottage
UK2450	The Orchards
UK2510	Whitecliff Bay
UK2515	Nodes Point
UK2610	Bo Peep
UK2700	Hurley
UK2810	Chertsey
UK2820	Horsley
UK2900	Horam Manor
UK2915	Fairfields Farm
UK2965	Brakes Coppice
UK3030	Tanner Farm
UK3290	Fen Farm
UK3300	Homestead Lake
UK3400	Old Brick Kilns
UK3430	Kelling Heath
UK3455	Deer's Glade
UK3480	Little Lakeland
UK3520	Searles
UK3555	Wyton Lakes
UK3575	Stroud Hill
UK3655	Thorpe Park
UK3675	Willow Holt
UK3680	Ashby Park
UK3750	Foreman's Bridge
UK3760	Tallington Lakes
UK3765	Woodland Waters
UK3855	Callow Top
UK3865	Golden Valley
UK3940	Smeaton's Lakes
UK3945	Milestone
UK3970	Glencote
UK4080	Riverside Stratford
UK4090	Island Meadow
UK4100	Hoburne Cotswold
UK4140	Winchcombe
UK4150	Croft Farm
UK4170	Tudor
UK4185	Weir Meadow
UK4190	Kingsgreen
UK4210	Lickhill Manor
UK4300	Poston Mill
UK4310	Luck's All
UK4320	Broadmeadow
UK4345	Townsend
UK4380	Fernwood
UK4390	Westbrook
UK4410	Beaconsfield
UK4500	Burton Constable
UK4510	Thorpe Hall
UK4610	Moorside
UK4640	Goose Wood
UK4660	Woodhouse Farm
UK4715	Riverside Lancaster
UK4720	Knight Stainforth
UK5280	Abbey Farm
UK5600	Pennine View
UK5615	Hill of Oaks
UK5625	Lowther
UK5710	Doe Park

Wales

UK5880	Springwater
UK5945	River View
UK5955	Erwlon
UK6040	Pencelli Castle
UK6045	Gilestone
UK6245	Morben Isaf
UK6250	Dolswydd
UK6290	Glan-y-Mor
UK6305	Smithy Park
UK6320	Fforest Fields
UK6345	Glanlynn
UK6590	Beddgelert
UK6600	Bryn Gloch
UK6605	Tafarn Snowdonia
UK6670	The Plassey

Scotland

UK6890	Mossyard
UK6910	Hoddom Castle
UK6940	Loch Ken
UK6950	Brighouse Bay
UK7025	Seal Shore
UK7220	The Gart
UK7260	Ardgartan
UK7270	Auchterarder
UK7275	Braidhaugh
UK7285	Sauchope Links
UK7295	River Tilt
UK7305	Tummel Valley
UK7315	Loch Tay Lodges
UK7710	Ardmair Point
UK7790	Invercoe
UK7800	Resipole
UK7850	Linnhe Lochside
UK7860	Glendaruel

Northern Ireland

UK8330	Sixmilewater
UK8340	Drumaheglis
UK8405	Cranfield
UK8420	Tollymore
UK8510	Mullynascarthy
UK8550	Dungannon

Republic of Ireland

IR8815	Willowbrook
IR8960	Lough Ree
IR8965	Lough Ennell
IR9100	Camac Valley
IR9230	Nore Valley
IR9470	Blackwater Valley
IR9510	Eagle Point
IR9560	Wave Crest
IR9620	Flemings
IR9630	White Villa

Bicycle Hire

We understand that the following parks have bicycles to hire on site or can arrange for bicycles to be delivered. However, we would recommend that you contact the park to check as the situation can change.

England

UK0014	Porthtowan
UK0025	Roselands
UK0306	Ruthern Valley
UK0690	Stowford Farm
UK0750	Minnows
UK0950	River Dart
UK1075	Golden Coast
UK1150	Ruda
UK1250	Woodland Springs
UK1350	Quantock Orchard
UK1390	Old Oaks
UK1490	Greenacres
UK1575	Unity
UK1590	Exe Valley
UK1640	Greenhill Farm
UK1725	Hawkchurch
UK2050	Rowlands Wait
UK2100	Sandford
UK2120	South Lytchett
UK2290	Sandy Balls
UK2315	Riverside (Hamble)
UK2450	The Orchards
UK3325	The Oaks
UK3330	Moat Barn

UK3370	Kessingland
UK3390	Dower House
UK3430	Kelling Heath
UK3485	Clippesby
UK3520	Searles
UK3655	Thorpe Park
UK3660	Walesby Woodlands
UK3750	Foreman's Bridge
UK3855	Callow Top
UK3904	Greendale Farm
UK4540	Saint Helens
UK4560	Golden Square
UK4620	Upper Carr
UK5330	Marton Mere
UK5505	Stanwix Park
UK5605	Woodclose

Wales

UK5925	Cardiff
UK6040	Pencelli Castle
UK6045	Gilestone
UK6330	Daisy Bank
UK6340	Pen-y-Bont
UK6345	Glanlynn

Scotland

UK6940	Loch Ken
UK6950	Brighouse Bay
UK7000	Strathclyde
UK7230	Trossachs
UK7260	Ardgartan
UK7280	Nether Craig
UK7305	Tummel Valley
UK7315	Loch Tay Lodges

Channel Islands

UK9780	Fauxquets

Republic of Ireland

IR8740	Cong
IR8790	Carra
IR9400	Glen of Aherlow
IR9600	Glenross
IR9620	Flemings
IR9640	Killarney Flesk

Horse Riding

We understand that the following parks have horse riding stables on site. Where facilities are within easy reach and we have been given details, we have included this information in the individual reports. However, we recommend that you contact the park to check that they meet your requirements.

UK0360	Lakefield	UK1370	Burrowhayes	UK2515	Nodes Point
UK0690	Stowford Farm	UK1575	Unity	UK2900	Horam Manor
UK0735	Woolacombe Sands	UK1780	Freshwater Beach	UK6950	Brighouse Bay
UK1060	Yeatheridge	UK2290	Sandy Balls	UK8510	Mullynascarthy

Golf

We understand that the following parks have facilities for playing golf on site. Where facilities are within easy reach and we have been given details, we have included this information in the individual reports. However, we recommend that you contact the park to check that they meet your requirements.

UK0220	Trevornick	UK3230	Lee Valley	UK4710	Rudding
UK0380	Wooda Farm	UK3320	Moon & Sixpence	UK6670	The Plassey
UK0690	Stowford Farm	UK3520	Searles	UK6910	Hoddom Castle
UK0720	Easewell Farm	UK3655	Thorpe Park	UK6950	Brighouse Bay
UK1020	Oakdown	UK3690	Bainland	UK7060	Tantallon
UK1070	Woolacombe Bay	UK4070	Somers Wood	UK7690	Torvean
UK1575	Unity	UK4300	Poston Mill	UK8310	Carnfunnock
UK2920	Bay View	UK4520	Flower of May	IR9150	River Valley

Boat Launching

We understand that the following parks have boat slipways on site. Where facilities are within easy reach and we have been given details, we have included this information in the individual reports. However, we recommend that you contact the park to check that they meet your requirements.

UK0250	Pentewan Sands	UK4310	Luck's All	UK7710	Ardmair Point
UK0750	Minnows	UK4500	Burton Constable	UK7800	Resipole
UK1530	Slimeridge	UK5330	Marton Mere	UK7850	Linnhe Lochside
UK1540	Batcombe Vale	UK5615	Hill of Oaks	UK8330	Sixmilewater
UK2510	Whitecliff Bay	UK6345	Glanlynn	UK8340	Drumaheglis
UK2520	Thorness Bay	UK6890	Mossyard	UK8405	Cranfield
UK2700	Hurley	UK6940	Loch Ken	IR8960	Lough Ree
UK3290	Fen Farm	UK6950	Brighouse Bay	IR8965	Lough Ennell
UK3760	Tallington Lakes	UK7025	Seal Shore	IR9510	Eagle Point
UK4080	Riverside Stratford	UK7260	Ardgartan	IR9560	Wave Crest
UK4150	Croft Farm	UK7315	Loch Tay Lodges	IR9610	Mannix Point
UK4210	Lickhill Manor	UK7410	Riverview		

Adults Only

We list here the parks that have indicated to us that they do not accept children at any time during the year, at certain times, or in certain areas of their park.

The following parks have made the decision not to accept children or young adults:

UK0010	Chacewater	UK1640	Greenhill Farm	UK3904	Greendale Farm
UK0012	Killiwerris	UK1680	Plough Lane	UK3980	Longnor Woods
UK0820	Moor View	UK1770	Bingham Grange	UK4070	Somers Wood
UK0900	Widdicombe Farm	UK2620	Wysdom	UK4410	Beaconsfield
UK1250	Woodland Springs	UK3325	The Oaks	UK4534	Overbrook
UK1355	Lowtrow Cross	UK3410	Sandy Gulls	UK4580	Foxholme
UK1390	Old Oaks	UK3420	Two Mills	UK4610	Moorside
UK1500	Long Hazel	UK3450	Little Haven	UK5240	Lamb Cottage
UK1510	Chew Valley	UK3470	Breckland	UK5510	The Larches
UK1520	Waterrow	UK3575	Stroud Hill	UK5650	The Ashes
UK1545	Cheddar Bridge	UK3650	Cherry Tree	UK6330	Daisy Bank

The following parks also do not accept children at certain times or in certain areas of their park:

UK4400	Stanmore Hall
UK4430	Oxon Hall

TRY 3 ISSUES FOR JUST £3

GREAT SAVINGS!
Secure a 20% discount after your trial ends.

EXCLUSIVE OFFERS!
Get access to unique offers and discounts.

FREE DELIVERY!
Your copy direct to you door before it goes on sale in the shops.

OR

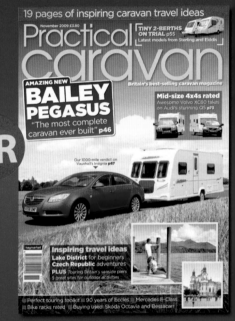

- Touring inspiration and motor caravanning tips
- Common sense advice on maintaining and improving your motorhome
- In-depth motorhome reviews of all the latest models
- The complete motorhome magazine

- Holiday inspiration and travel guides for the UK and abroad
- Expert hints and tips to help you holiday better
- Buying advice and in-depth tests for towcars and caravans
- Britain's favourite caravan magazine for over 40 years

> CALL **08456 777 812** now and quote AT10T or visit
> www.themagazineshop.com/PRCA/AR10T or
> www.themagazineshop.com/PRMO/AR10T

relax
& unwind

special offers & discounts online

Pet Friendly

...et away from it
...with a relaxing holiday or
...hort break at one of darwin's
...ward winning parks across
...e beautiful south west

...e range of facilities include*
- Fully Serviced Caravan Pitches
- Grass Camping Pitches
- Motor Home Facilities
- Timber Lodges
- Holiday Homes for Sale & Rent
- Seasonal Pitches

- » Children's Playgrounds
- » Shops, Bars & Restaurants
- » Swimming Pools
- » Olympic BMX Track
- » Dedicated Rally & Festival Areas
- » Modern Toilet & Wash Facilities
- » Transport Links

...make a booking or for more information
...ase visit our website or email us

www.darwinholidays.co.uk
enquiries@darwinholidays.co.uk

darwin holiday parks

...ebsite for individual park site facilities. Darwin Holiday Parks are managed by Darwin Contract Management Ltd. Terms & Conditions apply.

Enjoy your UK holidays more with The Caravan Club

Choose from 200 superb Club Sites in the finest locations

Troutbeck Head Caravan Club Site, one of The Club's eight sites in Cumbria

With the UK's increasing popularity as a holiday destination, there's no better way to discover Britain & Ireland's beauty and heritage than by staying at one of The Caravan Club's 200 quality Club Sites.

Caravan Club Sites are renowned for their excellence. With most of those graded achieving 4 or 5 stars from VisitBritain, you can be sure of consistently high standards.

And with over 40 Club Sites open all year, you can enjoy superb touring all year round.

You can be assured of excellent facilities and a friendly welcome from our Resident Wardens. Why not discover the best of Britain this year?

Why choose a Caravan Club Site?

- Choice of superb locations throughout Britain & Ireland
- Sites are immaculately maintained
- Most Club Sites are in peaceful settings, ideal for a relaxing holiday
- Care for the local environment and wildlife is paramount

Clumber Park Caravan Club Site, Nottinghamshire

Call today for your FREE Site Guide on 0800 521 161 quoting ARG 10

Trewethett Caravan Club Site, Cornwall

You don't have to be a member to stay on most Caravan Club Sites but members save £7 per night on pitch fees!

For Caravan Club Site details and locations visit www.caravanclub.co.uk

THE CARAVAN CLUB

FIND YOUR PERFECT PITCH

- ■ **Sites Finder – The UK's biggest online directory!**
- ■ **Easy-to-use with over 4700 sites**
- ■ **Search by region, type of pitch or site facilities**

More and more people are choosing UK holidays and *Caravan* magazine's new online directory, Sites Finder will make finding your ideal campsite easy! So if you're looking for a pet-friendly campsite or one that's open all year round, Sites Finder will help you to find that perfect pitch.

Check out Sites Finder at caravanmagazine.co.uk/sitesfinder

Caravan SITES FINDER

caravanmagazine.co.uk/sitesfinder

There's so much

Haven caravan
+camping

included

on a Haven Caravan & Camping Break!

With 22 Holiday Parks offering superb Touring pitches and amenities at great coastal locations throughout the UK and each one offering an exciting range of holiday facilities & activities, it's no wonder more and more people are making Haven their holiday choice!

Save up to 50%† off

Call or go online for a brochure & our latest offers!

CAREFREE TOURING...

✔ Superb Touring areas with well maintained pitches

✔ 5 pitch types from Basic to Premier pitches with electric hook up, water and drainage facility

✔ Convenient hot shower, toilet and dishwashing facilities

✔ 24-hour security

✔ Touring wardens*

✔ Pets welcome*

HOLIDAY FUN INCLUDED...

✔ Indoor & outdoor heated pool complexes

✔ Kids' clubs for all ages

✔ Sports facilities & activities

✔ Fantastic music, dance & stage entertainment - perfect for all the family!

Plus, there's a great range of 'pay as you go' activities including fencing*, archery*, golf* and more!

Haven caravan +camping

We Welcome

Tourers

Motorhomes

Tents

Trailer Tents

Call our UK Caravan & Camping Team on
0871 230 1933
Quote: TO_ART
Open 7 days a week, 9am-9pm
Calls to the number above will cost no more than 10p per minute from a BT landline - calls from other networks may vary.

For 24/7 booking & information visit
caravancamping.co.uk/art

THE CARAVAN & MOTORHOME SHOWS

The best start to your next adventure...

MANCHESTER CENTRAL

CARAVAN & MOTORHOME

SHOW 2010 MANCHESTER 21-24 JANUARY

Come and see the widest choice of caravans and a great selection of motorhomes from leading UK and overseas manufacturers. If it's a bargain you are looking for, many exhibitors are offering amazing deals that you won't find anywhere else!

INTERNATIONAL

CARAVAN & MOTORHOME

2010 NEC BIRMINGHAM 12-17 OCTOBER

The UK's biggest selection of caravans, motorhomes, holiday homes, awnings, folding campers and of course accessories! The NEC is the first place to see all the latest products, have a great day out and find exactly what you want for your next holiday.

For more information visit:
www.caravanshows.com or email:
info@caravanshows.com

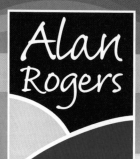

Alan Rogers Insurance Service
...we've got it covered

Personal travel insurance
European vehicle assistance insurance

Whatever form your camping or touring holiday may take, you'll need proper insurance for complete peace of mind. Our policies provide exactly the right cover for self-drive campsite-based holidays - at fantastic prices!

One call and you're covered

Visit www.**alanrogers.com/insurance**

or call us **NOW** for a no-obligation quote
0844 824 6314

Policies despatched within 24 hours

Scotland
page 262

Northern
Ireland
page 294

Northumbria
page 226

Cumbria
page 215

North West
England
page 207

Yorkshire
page 188

Republic of Ireland
page 302

Heart of England
page 162

Wales
page 233

East of England
page 144

Southern
England
page 102

South West England
page 12

South East
England
page 127

London
page 140

Channel Islands
page 325

Index - Town and Village

Index - Campsite Number

Wales

Scotland

England

South West England

Cornwall

Devon

Somerset

Index - Campsite Region, County and Name